Measuring
and
Monitoring
Biological
Diversity

Standard Methods
for

Amphibians

Biological Diversity Handbook Series

Series Editor: Mercedes S. Foster

This series has been established by the National Biological Survey (U.S. Department of the Interior) and the National Museum of Natural History (Smithsonian Institution) for the publication of manuals detailing standard field methods for qualitative and quantitative sampling of biological diversity. Volumes will focus on different groups of organisms, both plants and animals. The goal of the series is to identify or, where necessary, develop these methods and promote their adoption worldwide, so that biodiversity information will be comparable across study sites, geographic areas, and organisms, and at the same site, through time.

Measuring and Monitoring Biological Diversity

Standard Methods for Amphibians

Amphibians

Edited by
W. Ronald Heyer,
Maureen A. Donnelly,
Roy W. McDiarmid,
Lee-Ann C. Hayek,
and Mercedes S. Foster

SMITHSONIAN INSTITUTION PRESS
Washington and London

Editorial consultant and typesetter:
   Peter Strupp/Princeton Editorial Associates
Designer: Janice Wheeler

Library of Congress Cataloging-in-Publication Data

Measuring and monitoring biological diversity.
   Standard methods for amphibians / edited by
   W. Ronald Heyer . . . [et al.].
        p.   cm.
    Includes bibliographical references (p.   ) and
   index.
    ISBN 1-56098-270-5 (cloth)   1-56098-284-5
   (pbk.)
    1. Amphibians—Speciation—Research. 2.
   Biological diversity—Measurement. I. Heyer,
   W. Ronald.
   QL645.4.M43   1993
   597.6′045248′0723—dc20   92-44743

British Library Cataloging-in-Publication Data is
available.

Cover art by Randy Babb: *Ambystoma tigrinum
stebbinsi.*

Manufactured in the United States of America
00 99 98 97 96 95 94   5 4 3 2

Contents

Figures

Tables

Authors and Contributors

Ross A. Alford, James Cook University

Ronald G. Altig, Mississippi State University

Ray E. Ashton, Jr., Water and Air Research, Inc.

John E. Cadle, Harvard University

Reginald B. Cocroft, Cornell University

Daniel G. Cole, Smithsonian Institution

Paul Stephen Corn, National Biological
    Survey

Ronald I. Crombie, Smithsonian Institution

Martha L. Crump, Northern Arizona University

Ted M. Davis, University of Victoria

C. Kenneth Dodd, Jr., National Biological Survey

Maureen A. Donnelly, University of Miami

Michael E. Dorcas, Idaho State University

George E. Drewry, U.S. Fish and Wildlife Service

Charles A. Drost, University of California at
    Davis

Kevin M. Enge, Little River Ranch

Gary M. Fellers, Point Reyes National
    Seashore

Mercedes S. Foster, National Biological Survey

Richard Franz, Florida Museum of Natural
    History

Claude Gascon, Instituto Nacional de
    Pesquisas da Amazônia

Craig Guyer, Auburn University

Steve Hammack, Fort Worth Zoological Park

Lee-Ann C. Hayek, Smithsonian Institution

W. Ronald Heyer, Smithsonian Institution

Robert F. Inger, Field Museum of Natural History

Jeremy F. Jacobs, Smithsonian Institution

Robert G. Jaeger, University of Southwestern Louisiana

J. Eric Juterbock, Ohio State University at Lima

James F. Lynch, Smithsonian Environmental Research Center

Roy W. McDiarmid, National Biological Survey

Michael J. Oldham, Ontario Ministry of Natural Resources

Charles R. Peterson, Idaho State University

George R. Pisani, University of Kansas

A. Stanley Rand, Smithsonian Tropical Research Institute

Robert P. Reynolds, National Biological Survey

Stephen J. Richards, James Cook University

Lily O. Rodriguez, Universidad Nacional de San Marcos

Douglas E. Runde, Florida Game and Fresh Water Fish Commission

David E. Scott, Savannah River Ecology Laboratory

Norman J. Scott, Jr., National Biological Survey

H. Bradley Shaffer, University of California at Davis

Ulrich Sinsch, Universität Koblenz-Landau

Samuel S. Sweet, University of California at Santa Barbara

Richard C. Vogt, Universidad Nacional Autónoma de México

David B. Wake, University of California at Berkeley

Bruce D. Woodward, Reynolds Electrical and Engineering

Barbara L. Zimmerman, Consultant, Toronto, Canada

Foreword

For some years individual biologists in different parts of the world have known that species of frogs, and in some cases salamanders, that once were common or occurred in dense populations seemed to be in decline. By the time of the First World Congress of Herpetology, in the fall of 1989, these cases had grown in number so that there was general concern. In February 1990 the Board on Biology of the National Research Council (USA) held a two-day workshop to investigate whether there was in fact a general decline in amphibian populations and, if so, to inquire into the causes. The workshop found that species of amphibians in many parts of the world had indeed declined, some possibly to the point of extinction, but that other species showed no decline. Some regions and habitats were af-

fected, and others apparently were not. No single factor, or set of factors, could be advanced to explain the declines, although habitat destruction and general environmental degradation were clearly implicated in many instances. Especially disturbing was the disappearance of certain celebrated species, such as the gastric-brooding frog and the golden toad, from well-protected and large nature preserves.

One outcome of the workshop was public education concerning biodiversity and its loss, a result of widespread media attention to the workshop and the phenomena discussed there. Another was a series of recommendations by the participants, nearly all of which were undertaken in one form or another. An important outcome was the establishment of the Declining Amphibian Populations Task Force, as a part of the Species Survival Commission of the International Union for the Conservation of Nature and Natural Resources. The task force has been functioning since 1991.

Early in its activities, the task force realized that an important need was the establishment of methods and protocols for sampling natural populations of amphibians. One of the most difficult problems in conservation biology is the lack of baseline data against which to measure population changes. The result has been that much of the information concerning amphibian declines is anecdotal. In some instances, especially in the case of disappearances, the anecdotal information is useful, but all ecologists are aware that populations undergo fluctuations in size under ordinary circumstances. Accordingly, a decline over a period of two to three years might be more than offset by a single year of successful recruitment. Both professional amphibian biologists and amateur naturalists, as well as managers of nature reserves and many others, appealed for help in formulating procedures to be followed in establishing baselines and in undertaking monitoring efforts.

Those concerned with biodiversity, in general, have long realized the need to establish long-term studies, using standardized methods, for natural populations. There is a growing interest in species and groups that might serve as indicators of the state of health of the environment. Many different taxa will be useful as indicators, and amphibians have received considerable attention because of a combination of biological attributes: permeable skin that acts in respiration and osmoregulation, biphasic life cycle with aquatic and terrestrial phases, feeding shifts in many species from herbivorous diets as larvae to carnivorous diets as adults, and exposed developmental biology offering ease of investigation. For humans, it is also important that amphibians are vertebrates. In addition, much excellent biological work has been conducted on amphibians, including laboratory and field studies and both observational and experimental investigations. In sum, amphibians have promise as bioindicators. The decision to make the amphibian volume the first in the series on standardized methods for measuring biological diversity is, thus, biologically appropriate and timely.

The book before you represents the concentrated efforts of many individuals who have set aside their personal research and other duties in order to produce this badly needed manual. I greatly appreciate their efforts and accomplishments. This volume is the first in a series of taxon-based treatments, and judging from the quality and dimensions of this work, future books will be eagerly awaited.

The loss of biological diversity is the great tragedy of our age—I consider it to be the single most important and lasting impact of our species on this planet. We must define and study problems in biodiversity before other people will be convinced of a need for action. For many parts of the world we still have a very incomplete knowledge of the numbers of species present, let alone the status of their populations. Time is short, and we must move forward in an organized manner and with well-formulated guidelines and goals. This book is an important first step, but it is only a point of departure. Now we need action.

David B. Wake
Chair
Task Force on Declining Amphibian
  Populations
June 1992

Preface

Antecedents

This book is the first in a series that recommends standardized methods for measuring biological diversity. Three conditions led to its production. For some time, Mercedes Foster recognized the need for such books and was willing to invest the time needed to bring them to fruition. About the same time, the Biological Diversity in Latin America (BIOLAT) program in the National Museum of Natural History, Smithsonian Institution, was seeking new areas for program development. Foster presented her ideas to the BIOLAT steering committee (chaired by Ronald Heyer and consisting of Jonathan Coddington, Kristian Fauchald, Mercedes Foster, Vicki Funk, and Richard Vari), which enthusiastically provided the resources to initiate the series. At the same time, the scientific community was learning of an ostensible worldwide decline in some conspicuous amphibian populations in relatively undisturbed habitats. Scientists who study amphibian populations recognized the potentially critical nature of the situation, and, under the guidance of David B. Wake, some among them mobilized to address the issue.

Two disturbing problems were immediately encountered. First, much of the information on amphibian declines was anecdotal. Second, standardized methods critical for documenting population changes either did not exist or were not generally known. Because of the perceived need for and interest in standardized sampling methods for amphibians, this group was selected as the subject of the first book in the series.

Foster set up a core committee to plan the book and oversee the production of a manuscript on amphibians. The committee included Maureen A. Donnelly, W. Ronald Heyer, Robert F. Inger, and Roy W. McDiarmid. The committee and Foster met in April 1990 and decided to contact individuals with experience with the inventory and monitoring of amphibians, in order to request their input about the value of the proposed book and about the techniques and issues that should be covered. Overall the response from the 35 individuals throughout the world who were contacted was positive and enthusiastic. In December 1990 the core committee asked the respondents to form working groups and to draft manuscripts to be included. Copies of the draft manuscripts were circulated prior to a workshop that was held 29–31 March 1991 in Arlington, Virginia. The participants at the workshop were Stephen Corn, Martha Crump, Maureen Donnelly, Lee-Ann Hayek, Ronald Heyer, Robert Jaeger, Roy McDiarmid (Workshop Chair), Norman Scott, Jr., Bradley Shaffer, Bruce Woodward, and Barbara Zimmerman. Robert Inger was unable to attend. Crump, Donnelly, Hayek, Heyer, Jaeger, and McDiarmid continued working on 1 and 2 April 1991 to complete tasks identified during the workshop.

Just before the workshop, David Wake asked the group developing the book to serve as the Working Group on Protocols for the Declining Amphibian Populations Task Force (DAPTF) of the International Union for the Conservation of Nature and Natural Resources (IUCN) Species Survival Commission (SSC). The group agreed.

The workshop participants completed three large tasks in a brief time: (1) They identified and recommended a set of standard procedures for measuring amphibian biological diversity by monitoring populations and inventorying species. Partly as a result of that process, they also developed the essentials of the final outline of the book. (2) They wrote all or substantial parts of three chapters. (3) They outlined and assumed responsibility for the tasks needed to complete the book.

Maureen Donnelly, Lee-Ann Hayek, Ronald Heyer, and Roy McDiarmid took on the responsibilities of compiling and editing the publication. Contributions of a few additional experts were sought for the final manuscript. For publication purposes, the order of the editors was determined randomly. Mercedes Foster's editorial contribution to the book so exceeded that of a traditional series editor that the first four editors added her as a fifth editor to the volume.

A draft of the manuscript was completed in early December 1991. It was reviewed, revised, and sent for outside review in May 1992. The final draft was sent to press in September 1992.

Authorship

The text of this book was developed by many individuals. The editors asked the chairs of the working groups to identify as *authors* those who participated significantly in the writing of the manuscript and to identify as *contributors* those who provided information. All sections for which authorship is not assigned were written either by the core committee, the editors, or the workshop participants as a group.

Acknowledgments

During the preparation of this book the authors and editors were aided by many people. The editors especially want to thank Sarah Klontz, who provided assistance with the initial manuscript and integrated the chapter bibliographies into a single document, and Robert B. Hole, Jr., who tirelessly attended to hundreds of details for the editors, including verification of all biblio-graphic citations. Carolyn S. Hahn provided expert assistance in locating library reference materials. Cassandra Phillips, Linda Wolfe, and Fiona Wilkinson incorporated numerous manuscript corrections into computer files and provided other assistance. Rosemary Sheffield provided expert advice on editorial matters.

In addition Paul Ustach used his considerable talent to illustrate the amphibian life cycle in Figure 1; Jennifer Shoemaker and Dale Crawford prepared standardized versions of most of the figures; and Dale Crawford and Frances Irish provided artwork to enliven the text. Victor Krantz took the photograph for Figure 32. Charles R. Mann prepared the novel random numbers table.

Robert Inger critically read the entire manuscript in its penultimate version, and several anonymous reviewers commented on specific sections. Their comments helped us immeasurably in improving the final draft of the book.

John Carr (Conservation International), Peter Cannell (Smithsonian Institution Press), Robert Unash (The Nature Conservancy), Adele Conover (*Smithsonian* magazine), and Don Wilson (Biodiversity Programs, National Museum of Natural History) attended the workshop as observers and provided useful input.

Finally, the editors want to acknowledge the authors, contributors, and workshop participants for their substantial efforts. Without their cooperation and advice, this volume would not have been possible. To all of these persons, we express our sincerest thanks.

Institutional support and financial support were provided by the U.S. Fish and Wildlife Service, Department of the Interior; the American Museum of Natural History; and the Smithsonian Institution. This book is contribution number 55 from the Biological Diversity in Latin America (BIOLAT) program.

The Volume Editors

## Chapter 1

Introduction

Biological diversity is the term used to describe the variety of all living organisms on earth. It encompasses at least three levels of biological organization: genetic (individual), species, and ecosystem. This book focuses on biological diversity at the species level, which is basic to the study of organisms. Studies of the abundance and distribution of species have provided a wealth of basic knowledge, led to the development of a large body of ecological and evolutionary theory, and formed the underpinning of a considerable body of research in the areas of ecology, systematics, biogeography, and conservation biology.

The continuing loss of biological diversity through human activities will have a major impact on our ability to pursue science and to understand the scientific complexity of our surroundings; it also will affect the ways in which ecosystems continue to function. This impact increases the urgency for scientists to comprehend exactly what is being lost and to communicate their perspective on the consequences of that loss to society, before the general quality of life on this planet suffers irreversible deterioration.

Knowledge of which species occur in which areas is fundamental to an understanding of the intricacies of biological diversity. Species lists of some conspicuous organisms (e.g., butterflies, monkeys, birds, and trees) are available for many sites in the more developed countries and for a few sites in less developed regions, but comparable data for most of the world's biota are lacking. Even when specific data on the richness and relative abundances of species at a site are available, they often vary greatly in type and have been collected using a variety of procedures, hindering their comparability.

Because amphibians are abundant and functionally important in most freshwater and terrestrial habitats in tropical, subtropical, and temperate regions, they are significant components of the earth's biota. For example, species of North American woodland salamanders of the genus *Plethodon* may occur in densities of several thousand per hectare (Merchant 1972). Their total biomass in some areas equals that of all the resident species of small mammals combined and is more than twice that of all species of birds during the peak of avian breeding activity (Burton and Likens 1975). Many species of amphibians are wide ranging and potentially could serve as key species against which to evaluate broad geographic or global changes in the environment. Other species are habitat specialists or have restricted distributions and could signal local perturbation. Certain physiological traits (e.g., permeable skin) and ecological traits (e.g., complex, biphasic life cycle) make amphibians potentially excellent indicators of environmental health.

Because amphibian populations in certain areas are declining sharply (Barinaga 1990; Blaustein and Wake 1990; Borchelt 1990; Phillips 1990) or are exhibiting significant local fluctuations (Pechmann et al. 1991), we suggest that arbitrary use of procedures to assess the status of amphibian populations is a luxury with which we should dispense. Probable species declines provide an impetus for monitoring the status of amphibian populations in a variety of biomes in many parts of the world. In this book we provide recommendations and guidelines for the inventory and monitoring of amphibians. We present a set of standardized methods whose use will ensure comparability between sites, at least within biomes, and lead toward greater understanding of amphibian species diversity in particular and biological diversity in general.

We have assumed (1) that quantitative data about an assemblage of organisms are more useful than qualitative information, and (2) that qualitative information, such as a list of species, may be derived from quantitative data, but not the reverse. Although long-term population monitoring would often be desirable, we recognize that in many cases only single inventories will be possible. Even in those cases, sampling procedures should be quantitative, so that an initial inventory can be extended into a monitoring program should the need and opportunity arise. An inventory protocol with quantitative characteristics can also facilitate comparisons with initial stages of monitoring programs and inventories elsewhere.

Previous Work

Much of the scientific community has recognized that use of standardized methods is critical to comparisons of data gathered by different workers at different times and places (e.g., Davis 1982; Fellers et al. 1988; Corn and Bury 1990). Yet the technique-related sections of publications promoting this view are either brief or specific to species or habitats. For example, the *CRC Handbook of Census Methods for Terrestrial Vertebrates* (Davis 1982) devotes only six pages to methods for censusing amphibians. The absence of standard techniques is reflected in the work of many conservation, government, and scientific groups that are beginning to assess the status and health of amphibian populations. For example, we are aware of ongoing amphibian monitoring programs in Great Britain; the province of Ontario, Canada; and Illinois, Kansas, and Wisconsin in the United States. Unfortunately, the methodologies used in these monitoring studies differ. At present, no single reference describes techniques for the inventory or monitoring of amphibians and the circumstances in which each is appropriate. Our intent is to fill this void.

Intended Audience

We have designed this book to meet the needs of conservation organizations, environmental consultants, government agencies, wildlife managers, and scientists. We also believe that it will serve as a teaching and research aid in colleges and universities at both the undergraduate and the graduate levels. We have tried to make the book comprehensive so that individuals with an undergraduate degree in science, or equivalent training, can measure the biological diversity of amphibians using only this volume. We also provide references to pertinent literature to expedite data analyses and facilitate comparisons with information gathered in other studies. Many of the techniques require or recommend processing or marking live amphibians and preparing various types of vouchers. We have included instructions for these procedures as a series of appendices.

We have attempted to involve experts from throughout the world in the preparation of this book and to include examples from all geographic areas. Nevertheless, the volume retains a New World bias because most of the contributors work in that area. We are confident that this bias will not influence the general applicability of the methods discussed, which should be appropriate for amphibians in all parts of the world.

## Chapter 2

Amphibian Diversity and Natural History: An Overview

Roy W. McDiarmid

Introduction

Few vertebrates are as dependent on environmental moisture as amphibians, whose geographic ranges, ecologies, behaviors, and life histories are strongly influenced by the distribution and abundance of water, usually in the form of rain. In fact, the abrupt and often synchronized breeding of many species of frogs with the first rains is a well-known natural phenomenon, especially in areas where rainfall is distinctly seasonal. Likewise, the annual breeding migrations of certain north temperate salamander and frog species to traditionally used vernal ponds are closely linked to melting ice, rising temperatures, and warm spring rains. In contrast, how rainfall, humidity, phases of the moon, and a

multitude of other ecological factors interact to affect amphibian activity in tropical wet forests is not well understood. Just when a researcher thinks that he or she knows the "typical" situation, something unusual or unexpected happens. In fact, in some complex assemblages of tropical frogs, the normal pattern may best be described as chaotic or unpredictable. The complex and often poorly understood relation between the behavior and ecology of amphibians and local weather patterns makes designing a sampling protocol for amphibians difficult. This complicated interdependency is something that users of this book need to keep in mind. The three orders of living amphibians—caecilians (Gymnophiona), salamanders (Caudata), and frogs (Anura)—are found in a variety of freshwater aquatic and terrestrial environments throughout the world (Table 1). Whether in shallow seeps on steep slopes or buried in decaying organic material at the bottom of bogs, in deep leaf litter in tropical evergreen rain forest or in bromeliads high in the forest canopy, amphibians occur in nearly every kind of terrestrial and freshwater habitat.

Most species have a biphasic, complex life cycle (Fig. 1). In response to certain environmental cues (e.g., first rain of the season), terrestrial adults typically move to suitable aquatic habitats to breed. Following some form of courtship, adults of oviparous species deposit eggs in or near the water. These eggs hatch into free-swimming larvae that are major consumers in aquatic environments. After a period of growth, larvae undergo metamorphosis and move back into the terrestrial environment where they feed and continue to grow. When mature, they return to the aquatic environment to breed, thereby completing the life cycle.

Other species undergo direct development, that is, they lack an independent larval stage. Their eggs hatch into nonfeeding larvae or small copies of adults. A few forms are ovoviviparous or viviparous.

An understanding of the distributions and life histories of the species under study and knowledge of the habitats in which the organisms occur are essential to project design and to selection of suitable sampling methods. Such information also enhances the effectiveness of sampling and, thereby, the accuracy with which amphibian species richness and abundance can be estimated. In the following pages I briefly discuss pertinent aspects of the life histories of living amphibians and summarize the basic habitats used by different groups. I also provide an overview of the amphibian groups likely to be encountered on each continent and their respective habitats (Table 1). Once the goals of a biodiversity project have been defined (Chapter 3), data in the table should aid in the selection of suitable inventory techniques.

Consider, for example, a study of frog diversity at a lowland rain forest site in South America. Only 3 of approximately 10 families in the region have aquatic adults, and 2 of these families (Pipidae and Pseudidae) include very few species. Thus, aquatic sampling should have low priority if adults are the target stage. However, if an investigator were to inventory both adults and larvae, then aquatic sampling would be appropriate. Nearly all families have aquatic larvae, and sampling for larvae might turn up purely aquatic adults as well. On the other hand, adults of some species in 6 families potentially in the area are arboreal, and several of these families have high species diversity. A check of the literature would show that adults of nearly all species in 1 of the families (Centrolenidae) are arboreal, but only in streamside vegetation, and that adults of many species of 2 other families (Hylidae and Leptodactylidae, especially species in the large genus *Eleutherodactylus*) occur above ground, but only in forest. Thus, the study design should stress techniques for sampling arboreal habitats, but it would also have to specify transects across or along streams and transects in the forest.

In most instances, researchers will be better prepared to initiate studies if they first read about the general ecology and life history of amphibians likely to be found in the area and consult original literature on specific groups. Excellent summaries of pertinent information can be found in general references (e.g., Duellman and Trueb 1986; Tyler 1989) or in geographically oriented publications (e.g., Africa—Schiøtz 1975; Passmore and Carruthers 1979; Lambiris 1988, 1989; Madagascar—Blommers-Schlösser and Blanc 1991; Europe—Arnold and Burton 1978; Engelmann et al. 1986; Asia—Berry 1975; Inger and Stuebing 1989; Maeda and Matsui 1989; Australia—Cogger 1983; Tyler and Davies 1986; North America—Stebbins 1985; Pfingsten and Downs 1989; Conant and Collins 1991; Middle America—Duellman 1970; Villa

1972; South America—Duellman 1978; Cei 1980; Heyer et al. 1990).

Order Gymnophiona (caecilians)

Caecilians are elongate, limbless amphibians; they lack tails or have short ones. They are pantropical and occur in mesic, forested areas in all parts of the world except Madagascar and the Australopapuan region. Living caecilians are grouped into 6 families and 36 genera; about 165 species are recognized (Frost 1985, updated through 1992 by Frost and McDiarmid, unpubl. data).

Caecilians are difficult to sample because they are aquatic or fossorial and are rarely observed. Because of their secretive habits, we know little about their ecology or life history. Male caecilians have a median, protrusible copulatory organ, and fertilization presumably is internal in all species. Most caecilians are viviparous, although a few are oviparous; some have aquatic larvae, which live in ponds or streams.

There are no widely known techniques for sampling caecilians. However, methods for capturing aquatic frogs, salamanders, and their larvae may be useful (Chapter 6). Aquatic species may be removed with a dipnet from deeper parts of fast-flowing creeks at mid-elevations or found in leaf mats and shallows of meandering lowland streams. Fossorial species may be encountered in soil beneath piles of rotting plant materials, in loose soil and fine gravel along streams, and beneath logs. Individuals occasionally are captured in ditches or on roads, trails, or the forest floor after torrential rains.

Order Caudata (salamanders)

Adult salamanders are terrestrial, aquatic, fossorial, or arboreal amphibians with four legs (no hind limbs in sirenids) and a moderate to long tail. Most groups are prevalent in the Holarctic region, but a major radiation of plethodontid salamanders with direct development has evolved in the New World tropics. Living salamanders are assigned to 10 families, 61 genera, and about 390 species (Frost 1985, updated through 1992 by Frost and McDiarmid, unpubl. data). Salamanders have a variety of courtship patterns and an equally diverse array of reproductive modes. Visual and chemical signals seem to be more important for courtship in salamanders than in frogs. Most salamanders have internal fertilization without copulation, but a few large aquatic species have external fertilization. Eggs of aquatic species are laid singly, in strings, or in clumps in ponds or streams, sometimes beneath stones or attached to vegetation. These species have aquatic larvae that typically metamorphose and move to a terrestrial environment where they feed, grow, and mature. As adults, in response to pertinent environmental cues, they return to aquatic environments, often their natal sites, and reproduce. Some species are permanently aquatic, and larval metamorphosis is incomplete (obligate paedomorphs). Others are facultative paedomorphs and occasionally reproduce while retaining certain larval traits. Many species (most plethodontids) are terrestrial, deposit clumps of eggs in moist sites in burrows, in leaf litter, or beneath rocks and logs, and have direct development; in many of these species the female parent attends the clutch. A few species of salamandrids are ovoviviparous or viviparous, producing live aquatic larvae or fully developed (metamorphosed) young.

Salamanders are primarily nocturnal and have activity patterns that may vary ontogenetically. Individuals may be clumped or dispersed within a habitat, and spatial distributions often vary with sex and reproductive status. Some common temperate species have a synchronous migration from terrestrial habitats to aquatic sites for reproduction. Because of their abundance and position in the food web, in certain habitats salamanders may be the most important vertebrate organism. For ex-

Table 1. Habitat Utilization by Amphibians[a]

Taxon[b]	North America[c]					Middle America[d]					South America[e]				
	Aq	Se	Te	Fo	Ar[j]	Aq	Se	Te	Fo	Ar	Aq	Se	Te	Fo	Ar
CAECILIANS (Gymnophiona)															
Caeciliaidae			—						A[k]					A	
(24 genera, 89 sp.)									V					V	
Epicriidae			—					—					—		
(2 genera, 36 sp.)															
Rhinatremidae			—					—			A			A	
(2 genera, 9 sp.)											L	E			
Scolecomorphidae			—					—					—		
(2 genera, 5 sp.)															
Typhlonectidae			—					—			A				
(5 genera, 22 sp.)											V				
Uraeotyphlidae			—					—					—		
(1 genera, 4 sp.)															
SALAMANDERS (Caudata)															
Ambystomatidae	A		A			A		A					—		
(2 genera, 33 sp.)	L					L									
Amphiumidae	A							—					—		
(1 genus, 3 sp.)	L	E													
Cryptobranchidae	A							—					—		
(2 genera, 3 sp.)	L														
Dicamptodontidae	A	A						—					—		
(1 gen, 4 sp.)	L														
Hynobiidae			—					—					—		
(10 genera, 35 sp.)															
Plethodontidae	A	A	A	A				A	A	A			A	A	A
(27 genera, 244 sp.)	L	E	D	D				D	D	D			D		
Proteidae	A							—					—		
(2 genera, 6 sp.)	L														
Rhyacotritonidae		A						—					—		
(1 genus, 4 sp.)	L														
Salamandridae	A	A	A					A					—		
(13 genera, 55 sp.)	L					L									
Sirenidae	A							—					—		
(2 genera, 3 sp.)	L														
FROGS (Anura)															
Allophrynidae			—					—							A
(1 genus, 1 sp.)											L?				
Arthroleptidae			—					—					—		
(7 genera, 73 sp.)															
Ascaphidae		A						—					—		
(1 genus, 1 sp.)	L														

Europe[f]					Africa[g]					Asia[h]					Australia[i]				
Aq	*Se*	*Te*	*Fo*	*Ar*	*Aq*	*Se*	*Te*	*Fo*	*Ar*	*Aq*	*Se*	*Te*	*Fo*	*Ar*	*Aq*	*Se*	*Te*	*Fo*	*Ar*
		—					A	A					A D				—		
		—					—			L	A E		A				—		
		—					—					—					—		
		—						A D				—					—		
		—					—					—					—		
		—					—						A D?				—		
		—					—					—					—		
		—					—					—					—		
		—					—			A L		—					—		
		—					—					—					—		
		—					—			A L	A	A					—		
		A D					—					—					—		
A L		—					—					—					—		
		—					—					—					—		
A L	A	A V			A L		A V			A L	A	A V					—		
		—					—					—					—		
		—					—					—					—		
		—			A L	A	A D					—					—		
		—					—					—					—		

(*Continued*)

Table 1. (*Continued*)

Taxon[b]	North America[c]					Middle America[d]					South America[e]				
	Aq	*Se*	*Te*	*Fo*	*Ar*[j]	*Aq*	*Se*	*Te*	*Fo*	*Ar*	*Aq*	*Se*	*Te*	*Fo*	*Ar*
Brachycephalidae			—					—					A		
(2 genera, 3 sp.)													D?		
Bufonidae			A					A	A				A	A	A
(31 genera, 356 sp.)	L					L		D?			L		D		L
Centrolenidae			—							A					A
(3 genera, 88 sp.)						L				E	L				E
Dendrobatidae			—					A		A		A	A		A
(6 genera, 148 sp.)						L		E		L	L		ED		L
Discoglossidae			—					—					—		
(4 genera, 15 sp.)															
Heleophrynidae			—					—					—		
(1 genus, 5 sp.)															
Hemisotidae			—					—					—		
(1 genus, 8 sp.)															
Hylidae		A	A	A	A		A	A	A	A		A	A		A
(39 genera, 686 sp.)	L					L		B		BL	L		B		BL
Hyperoliidae			—					—							
(19 genera, 227 sp.)															
Leiopelmatidae			—					—					—		
(1 genus, 3 sp.)															
Leptodactylidae			A				A	A	A	A	A	A	A	A	A
(50 genera, 813 sp.)	L	E	D			L	E	D	D	DV	L	L	DLN	LN	DL
Microhylidae			A	A				A	A				A	A	
(66 genera, 308 sp.)	L					L					L	E	DN	N	
Myobatrachidae			—					—					—		
(20 genera, 114 sp.)															
Pelobatidae			A					A					—		
(11 genera, 89 sp.)	L					L									
Pelodytidae			—					—					—		
(1 genus, 2 sp.)															
Pipidae			—			A					A				
(5 genera, 27 sp.)						L					BL				
Pseudidae			—					—			A				
(2 genera, 4 sp.)											L				
Ranidae		A	A			A	A	A				A			
(48 genera, 669 sp.)	L					L					L				
Rhacophoridae			—					—					—		
(10 genera, 197 sp.)															
Rhinodermatidae			—					—					A		
(1 genus, 2 sp.)											L		NB		
Rhinophrynidae				A					A				—		
(1 genus, 1 sp.)	L					L									

Europe[f]					Africa[g]					Asia[h]					Australia[i]				
Aq	*Se*	*Te*	*Fo*	*Ar*	*Aq*	*Se*	*Te*	*Fo*	*Ar*	*Aq*	*Se*	*Te*	*Fo*	*Ar*	*Aq*	*Se*	*Te*	*Fo*	*Ar*
		—					—					—					—		
		A					A		A		A	A		A			—		
L					L	L	NV			L				N					
		—					—					—					—		
		—					—					—					—		
	A	A	A			A	A			A	A						—		
L		B	B		L		B			L?									
		—				A						—					—		
					L														
		—						A				—					—		
					L			E											
				A					A					A		A	A	A	A
L					L					L					L				
		—					A	A	A			—					—		
					L		E	E	E										
		—					—					—				A	A		
																N	N		
		—					—					—					—		
		—					A	A	A		A	A	A	A		A	A	A	A
					L			D	L	L	N?					D?	D	D	D
		—					—					—			A	A	A	A	
															BL		BLD	D	
		A					A				A	A					—		
L					L					L									
		A					—					—					—		
L																			
		—			A							—					—		
					L														
		—					—					—					—		
	A	A				A	A	A	A		A	A	A	A		A	A		A
L					L		DN		DE	L		DL		DL	L		D		
		—					A	A				A		A			—		
					L				E	L	E	E		DEL					
		—					—					—					—		
		—					—					—					—		

Table 1. (*Continued*)

Taxon[b]	North America[c]					Middle America[d]					South America[e]				
	Aq	*Se*	*Te*	*Fo*	*Ar*[j]	*Aq*	*Se*	*Te*	*Fo*	*Ar*	*Aq*	*Se*	*Te*	*Fo*	*Ar*
Sooglossidae			—					—					—		
(2 genera, 3 sp.)															

[a] Only naturally occurring species are scored. Generally a species is scored only once and is assigned to the habitat that most typifies the life history stage; exceptions are salamanders that have populations that are facultatively neotenic and populations that regularly undergo metamorphosis. A dash signifies that the taxon does not occur on the continent indicated.

[b] Family designations and the numbers of genera and species follow Frost (1985) as updated to 1992 (Frost and McDiarmid, unpubl. data).

[c] Includes the United States and Canada.

[d] Includes Mexico, Central America, and the Caribbean.

[e] Includes Trinidad.

[f] Includes the area west of 36° E (see Arnold and Burton 1978).

ample, in a northern hardwood forest in New Hampshire the eastern red-backed salamander (*Plethodon cinereus*) exists in densities approaching 2,500 per hectare and converts energy into new tissue at about 5,000/kcal/ha/yr. Its standing crop biomass of about 1,650 g/ha is about 2.6 times the biomass of birds in the area at the peak of their breeding season, and about equal to that of the shrews and mice (Burton and Likens 1975). In contrast, certain tropical arboreal salamanders are encountered only rarely, when bromeliads are removed from trees and systematically searched. Unfortunately, this sampling method also destroys their habitats.

The diversity of salamander life histories, behaviors, and habitat preferences necessitates a diversity of methods for sampling populations and estimating their sizes. Fortunately, salamanders are reasonably well known and, except for some tropical species, easily sampled.

Order Anura (frogs)

Frogs are jumping amphibians with elongate hind limbs and no tails (all larval anurans and male *Ascaphus truei* have tails). They are the most diverse and abundant group of living amphibians, are cosmopolitan in distribution, and occur in essentially all terrestrial and freshwater habitats. Their species diversity is highest in tropical wet forests. Taxonomically, living frogs are distributed among 25 families; currently about 333 genera and 3,843 species are recognized (Frost 1985, updated through 1992 by Frost and McDiarmid, unpubl. data). Frogs may be aquatic, terrestrial, fossorial, arboreal, or some combination thereof. Some are diurnal, but most are nocturnal. Adults of most species are widely dispersed in the environment except at specific times of the year when they congregate at aquatic sites to breed.

Vocalization is an important component of the reproductive behavior of most frogs. Among terrestrial vertebrates (perhaps all vertebrates), frogs have the highest diversity of reproductive behaviors and parental care known. Breeding may be explosive (synchronous over one or a few days at aquatic sites) or prolonged (spread over a few weeks or months at aquatic or terrestrial sites) [Wells 1977]. Most species breed only once each year, but certain tropical forms

Europe[f]					Africa[g]					Asia[h]					Australia[i]				
Aq	*Se*	*Te*	*Fo*	*Ar*	*Aq*	*Se*	*Te*	*Fo*	*Ar*	*Aq*	*Se*	*Te*	*Fo*	*Ar*	*Aq*	*Se*	*Te*	*Fo*	*Ar*
		—					A					—					—		
							BD												

[g] Includes Madagascar and the Seychelles.

[h] Includes the area east of Europe to Wallace's line.

[i] Includes all areas east of Wallace's line, including New Guinea, New Zealand, and certain Pacific Island groups.

[j] Habitats: *Aq* = aquatic; *Se* = semiaquatic; *Te* = terrestrial; *Fo* = fossorial; *Ar* = arboreal.

[k] Life history stages and developmental modes: A = adults; E = eggs; L = larvae; D = direct development; N = nidicolous larvae (nidicolous endotrophs of Altig and Johnston 1989); V = live birth, ovoviviparous or viviparous species; B = "brooded" eggs and/or larvae (attached to or in some modified structure [e.g., pouch] of adult), equal to paraviviparous and exoviviparous endotrophs of Altig and Johnston (1989). L in one habitat with no E in another habitat indicates a species that places eggs in the same habitat in which the larvae occur; an E in the arboreal habitat and L in the aquatic habitat, for example, indicate a species whose eggs are placed on leaves and whose tadpoles, on hatching, drop into water to feed. D? or L? indicates the habitat in which eggs with direct development or eggs and larvae presumably are placed, but data are lacking.

are reported to breed throughout the year whenever conditions are favorable. Most frogs have external fertilization, aquatic eggs, and feeding larvae called tadpoles; a major reorganization of the tadpole during metamorphosis distinguishes frogs from most other amphibians.

Females of a few species deposit eggs in leaf litter or wet moss; the eggs hatch into nonfeeding larvae that undergo metamorphosis at the nest site. Adults of other species carry strings of eggs wrapped around their hind legs or transport tadpoles from terrestrial sites to aquatic sites on their backs. In a few species, females place tadpoles in water held in bromeliads and then return to feed the larvae with nonfertile eggs that they deposit. Many species, especially in the Neotropics, have direct development (no free-swimming larval stage). These species deposit eggs in moist terrestrial or arboreal sites; after an appropriate period, the eggs hatch into small copies of the adult. Some frogs brood eggs on their backs; others brood eggs or tadpoles in pouches on their backs or sides, in vocal pouches, or even in their stomachs. Some of these brooding species have typical aquatic larvae, but most exhibit direct development. Almost every reproductive mode, including nonplacental viviparity and ovoviviparity, occurs in frogs.

The high species diversity of frogs, their variety of life history modes, and the wide assortment of habitats they use pose a substantial challenge to the researcher interested in sampling these organisms. Fortunately, the aquatic breeding behavior of most species, the pervasiveness of the aquatic larval stage, and the species specificity of reproductive vocalizations allow for effective sampling methods.

Amphibian larvae

Most amphibian larvae occur in aquatic habitats, including moving water (streams and rivers), still water (ponds and lakes), and phytotelmata (tree holes, plant axils and stems, bromeliads, and so forth). Terrestrial larvae develop in moist microhabitats such as moss, under and within

Figure 1. Representative life cycles of a salamander and of a frog. Adults move from the terrestrial to the aquatic environment to breed. In salamanders, mating follows a brief period of courtship; in frogs, a period of calling by the male is followed by amplexus. In both groups, eggs are laid in or near water and hatch into feeding, swimming larvae. Following a period of growth, the aquatic larvae undergo metamorphosis and move onto land, where they feed and mature, eventually repeating the cycle. Printed by permission of Paul C. Ustach.

decaying logs, and in hollows in stems of plants (e.g., bamboo). The relationships among developmental mode, larval morphology, and habitat of anuran tadpoles are summarized in Altig and Johnston (1989). No comparable publication exists for salamander larvae, although references to differences in gill structure, body form, and fin shape among stream, pond, and direct-developing forms are scattered through the literature. Little is known about caecilian larvae.

Amphibian larvae often are found in large concentrations at breeding sites over long periods. As a result, sampling larvae may be a more efficient and quicker method for inventorying species at a site than sampling adults (Gascon 1991), even though eggs and larvae of many species are poorly known. In fact, for many species these stages are reasonably well documented, and more are being described every year. In addition, collecting vouchers of amphibian larvae often is easier and probably has less impact on the population than collecting adults. Even though larval sampling may be somewhat destructive of certain aquatic habitats (e.g., ponds with dense, submerged aquatic vegetation, or bromeliads), it should form an integral part of any sampling program.

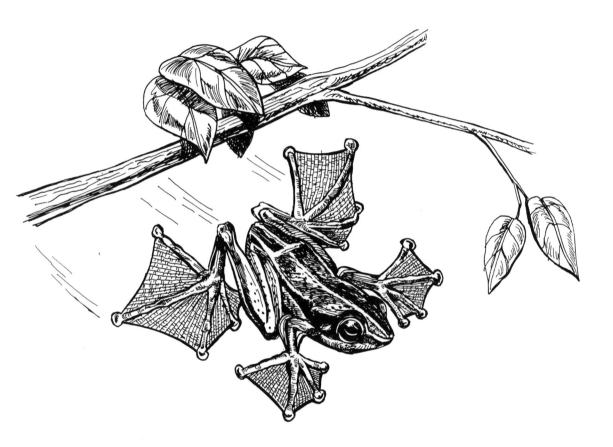

## Chapter 3

Essentials of Standardization and Quantification

Introduction

Throughout this book, we emphasize the need for standardization of techniques across and within studies. Our rationale reflects the rationale for the book in general; if a primary goal of field inventories and monitoring studies is to provide comparative data for analyses of biodiversity and examination of population trends, local extinctions, and the impact of human activities on amphibian populations, then studies must use standard techniques. The importance of standardization cannot be overemphasized, because studies using different techniques are often simply not comparable, even at the simplest levels. Thus, if one field researcher uses visual encounter techniques to derive a species richness list for an anuran breeding area, and another researcher later uses aural transects, it is impossible to determine whether any differences in the species listed reflect real changes in species composition, different sampling biases of the two techniques, or both. If both studies used the same technique, either visual surveys or aural transects, any changes in the list over time could be attributed to a real change in species composition. Even so, certain species certainly would be missed (semifossorial leaf-litter species by visual surveys and voiceless ones by the aural transects). Obviously, the best approach in this case would be for both techniques to be used in both studies; we always advocate using a combination of techniques to survey a habitat as completely as possible.

In preparation for this volume, we attempted to review all known techniques for the inventory and monitoring of amphibians. Here, we endorse and describe 10 techniques, and we encourage their use. These techniques may not be equally effective under all conditions, but it is our collective opinion that they represent the field sampling strategies that can best be standardized over the widest range of conditions.

A number of techniques are described and recommended for inventory and monitoring, because amphibians occupy a variety of habitats. The biphasic life cycle of most amphibians also means that different techniques are needed to sample larvae and adults. Several methods may be needed to sample an assemblage of amphibians, but methods must be consistent among study areas and across years.

Study questions

The approach used depends on the questions being asked. Thus, the purpose of a study should be clearly stated before the study begins. If the purpose is to compile a list of species for a poorly studied area, then an inventory is appropriate. If comparisons of species abundance among areas or across years are desired, then more-detailed monitoring methods must be used.

An *inventory* is a study of a specific area (for example, a national park or a defined geographic region) to determine the number of species of amphibians present (species richness). Inventories produce presence-absence data for species. Inventories are most often conducted (1) in areas in which little work has been done previously, and for which an enumeration of species richness will provide a baseline for biodiversity analyses, (2) across areas or habitats in which geographic or ecological distributions of single species need to be established or verified, and (3) in regions in which point comparisons over time can document changes in species distribution (presence or absence) and habitat use.

Monitoring is used to determine species composition and abundance (numbers of individuals per species) at one or more sites through time. Because all taxa in all habitats cannot be monitored with equal success, investigators most often target a specific type of habitat or an individual species or group of species for study.

Sampling considerations

Scale

Just as it is crucial to focus on the questions being asked, it also is important to define the sampling design and methods of analysis well before the field program begins. This maximizes the utility of the information gathered in the field, the comparability of that information with information from other studies, and the extent to which the data can be used to answer the questions being posed. Design considerations (discussed in Chapter 4) are as important for a one-day survey to produce a list of species for one locality as they are for a multiyear study of species abundances across a range of habitats.

Two extremely important points that should always be addressed are (1) the goal of the study (i.e., why the study is being done) and (2) the geographic scale over which the results will ultimately apply. These factors define the spatial scale of the sampling program that will follow. For example, if one were interested in a complete enumeration of the breeding population of the toad *Melanophryniscus moreirae* in one pond in Itatiaia National Park in Brazil, a sampling strategy that counts every individual from that pond should be used, not a randomized sampling design. However, if the goal were to compile species abundance information for all amphibians in Itatiaia Park, one might divide the park into ecologically relevant habitat types and randomly sample within them. Finally, if the goal were to compare species abundances throughout the Serra da Mantiqueira of Brazil, one might divide the mountain range into elevational zones and randomly sample one-hectare plots within each zone. All of these approaches, if properly used, would provide quantitative results comparable with other identically designed studies. Which approach is most appropriate, however, depends on the goal of the comparison. Thus, in the first case, the data could be used to track the absolute abundance of *M. moreirae* in that pond over time; they could not be used to track abundance among ponds (because there is no sampling among ponds). In the second example, inferences could be made about the amphibian fauna of Itatiaia over time or space, although information on any given species might be relatively poor. Similarly, in the final example, a point sample for comparisons of changes in amphibian diversity over one mountain range would have been established, although information on the amphibians of Itatiaia or on the species *M. moreirae* might not be available, if the randomized samples missed Itatiaia and the small area where *M. moreirae* occurs within the park.

Randomization and Bias

Studies of biodiversity can yield insights at three levels. At one level, species' presences are documented to produce a list for the study area. At another level, abundances and distributions of individual species in time and space are determined. At a third level, general patterns of diversity derived from the data, and processes that account for these patterns are deduced. Comparisons can be made at all three levels.

Whether two investigators estimate biodiversity of different areas or of the same area at different times, interpretations of the results hinge on a few fundamental elements of sampling procedure. The question or hypothesis to be pursued determines the general boundaries

for sampling, but the sampling protocol within those boundaries must be selected. Because environments are never truly homogeneous, different sampling protocols can give substantially different results. In particular, if sampling points are not distributed randomly through the area of interest, then analyses of the resulting samples are likely to underestimate or overestimate biodiversity. Environmental heterogeneity can effectively be removed (1) by recognizing the variation, subsampling within different types of habitat, and then comparing resulting estimates among the habitat types (this procedure is called blocking or stratified sampling in statistics) or (2) by ignoring the heterogeneity and sampling randomly without regard to habitat type. In either case, distributing samples randomly in the study area is an excellent way to minimize the problem of sampling bias, both for internal comparisons within a study and for comparisons across studies. Chapter 4 provides an in-depth discussion of random sampling.

Replication and Assumptions

Replication is another major component of study design. It is important for two reasons. First, replication provides a basis for confidence in the estimates obtained, because the bounds within which a population estimate falls can then be determined with appropriate statistical techniques. Second, replication minimizes the effects of localized factors that can obscure the study-site-wide variables of interest.

Sampling programs should be designed such that resulting data can be subjected to objective statistical testing. Thus, it is important to understand the assumptions of the sampling program and to attempt to satisfy the assumptions imposed by particular statistical tests. Two basic assumptions for most statistical procedures in this book are (1) that sampling is randomized and (2) that observations are independent. These assumptions present real problems for some of the techniques described in this book, but reliable statistical inferences can be expected only when the assumptions are reasonably approximated. If sample sizes are reasonably large and samples are obtained randomly, then statistical tests can be used to determine whether observed differences between sampled areas are due to chance alone (the null case) or reflect significant differences attributable to biological factors (see Chapter 4).

Reporting data

The primary data that emerge when most of the techniques discussed in this book are used are species richness and abundance information.

Frequently these basic results are summarized and reported as "simpler" summary statistics, such as a diversity index for a given habitat or species assemblage; such indices can make cross-study comparisons difficult or impossible. The proper use and interpretation of diversity indices are complex and controversial topics that are discussed in Chapter 9. However, all diversity indices must be derived from accurate, statistically sound species abundance information, and presentation of those data is the most important contribution a field survey can make to biodiversity issues. We strongly encourage authors to make such data available for cross-study comparisons by including them in journal articles or depositing them in an accessible repository.

## Chapter 4

Research Design for Quantitative Amphibian Studies

Lee-Ann C. Hayek

Introduction

Research on biological diversity includes description of phenomena observed in the field, as well as controlled and objective investigation of these phenomena and the relationships among them. Basic to such research is the generation of hypotheses and the formulation of plans for testing them. In this chapter I discuss procedures necessary to develop such plans.

It is impossible to carry out research or evaluate research literature in today's environment without understanding probabilistic and statistical aspects of research. Toward this end, I consider some general conditions basic to the proper application of statistical techniques. I do not list specific assumptions or tests appropriate for particular sampling techniques. Rather, I acquaint the reader with the circumstances under which certain probabilistic approaches can best be used. I also provide an overview of the connection between the biological reality being tested or examined and the conditions under which results meaningful for its evaluation can be obtained.

Project design

The Research Question

A scientific research question is one that asks about the relationship between two or more factors or variables (e.g., species, environmental conditions) within a defined context. The question should be precise and limited and asked in definitive, quantitative terms. It must contain the basis of and clear implications for testing. An example would be, "Does the number of amphibian species increase with an increase in rainfall in rain forest habitats in western Amazonia?" Generalized or metaphysical questions, such as, "Does good weather affect catchability of frogs?" will not suffice.

Generally, research questions are formulated in terms of concepts and constructs. A *concept* is an abstraction or idea of a universal term that is developed by generalization from many individual cases. For example, the concept of "frog" is not derived from the characteristics of one specimen of *Rana ingeri* but is a generalized idea of the collection of characteristics that make up the nature of all frogs. A *construct* is an abstraction of an unobservable, postulated phenomenon (e.g., aggressiveness, dominance behavior, territoriality, conformity), the idea for whose existence is synthesized from specialized cases of behavioral observations. It is an impression of the behavior of the object of study.

FOCUS OF THE RESEARCH QUESTION

The question, once defined, should be applied to a specific group. In this context, the *population* is the set of all possible observations of the same kind that can be obtained. The *sample,* in contrast, is all the observations actually made, or all the data obtained. One population, therefore, can give rise to many different samples. The core of statistics is to determine the extent to which generalizations pertaining to the population can be developed from the sample obtained during fieldwork. Often, observational or sampling studies can be improved by more clearly specifying the population and ensuring that the samples are representative of that population.

It is necessary to distinguish between two types of populations in a statistical sense. The *target population* includes those individuals to

which the researcher would like to generalize the results of her/his study. The *available population* is the actual group of individual amphibians that the investigator can reach for participation in the study; it is the group of potential subjects from which the sample is drawn. For example, the investigator may wish to generalize about all the species of *Ambystoma* in the United States (in terms of the concepts of richness or diversity); these species then would constitute the target population. The study plan, however, may call for sampling these salamanders only along a series of transects in the southeastern United States or in Virginia. The *Ambystoma* species occupying the area sampled constitute the available population. When the target and available populations are not the same, potential inferences are weakened. Whenever possible, these two populations should coincide.

DEFINITION

A *definition* is a set of terms or characteristics used to delimit the essential qualities or nature of a particular variable, procedure, or phenomenon. Definition plays a vital role in scientific inquiry—especially in formulating research questions—by setting out the specific conditions under which an observation constitutes a particular type of information and by identifying the actual and inferential targets of the research. The terms used in a scientific research question must be clear and precise. Imprecision is one reason that contradiction and confusion exist in studies of species associations and diversity. The following rules should be used in formulating definitions:

1. A definition should give the essence or nature of the thing defined and not its accidental properties. By means of a definition, one attempts to show how the object or individual belongs to a group or general classification. A definition also delimits how the

object or individual differs from all others in that group, which is, of course, the commonly accepted basis for biological systematic classification.

2. A definition should identify the specific category into which the thing falls and the differentia, as well. A frog is not defined as an animal that jumps, because many other animals also jump. An amphibian that jumps narrows the field but is not specific enough for study purposes. The importance of this rule cannot be overstated. Without a way to eliminate extraneous factors from a study design, one cannot construct valid inferences.
3. A definition should be concise but inclusive.
4. A definition should not be based on synonyms. The vagueness that characterizes spoken language has no place in science. Rather, the individualized concept or construct must be coupled with an objectively measurable phenomenon.
5. A definition should not be based on metaphor. A metaphorical definition—for example, "Calling activity at ponds sometimes is tumultuous, and the full chorus sounds like distant thunder"—has low information content and provides no objectively measurable character of the item being defined.
6. A definition should not be based on negative or correlative terms. Although such statements are acceptable and even authoritative in technical fields, they are frequently ambiguous and imprecise in nontechnical studies. For example, in mathematics, $f^{-1}(x)$ is unquestionably the inverse of the function $f(x)$. However, in ecological studies, cold weather cannot be defined as the opposite of hot or warm weather.

OPERATIONAL DEFINITION

The definition of the variable, object, state, or individual in a scientific study must be precise and reproducible; it is a rule of correspondence between a set of constructs and the observable data (Torgerson 1958). A definition thus constructed is termed an *operational definition* (Bridgeman 1927; Carnap 1936; Margenau 1950; Kerlinger 1973). The alternative to an operational definition is a *constitutive definition* in which the constructs or concepts are defined with other constructs (Margenau 1950; Kerlinger 1973)—for example, "The weight of this frog is its heaviness." Constitutive definitions are neither appropriate nor sufficiently informative for amphibian sampling.

An operational definition clarifies how the object of study functions as a result of its specialized nature, focusing on its observable characteristics (e.g., Bridgeman 1927; Kerlinger 1973). Basically, this type of definition assigns meaning to a construct or variable by specifying the activities or "operations" necessary to measure it. It connects the scientific concepts to experimental and quantitative procedures with terms that have empirical meaning. In fact, this type of definition is a manual of precise instructions to the investigator.

For example, let us say that we isolate a breeding pond with an enclosure. Operationally, we could define a breeding male as a male found within the enclosure during the relevant season. This statement could be correct, but the criterion of definition is not unique; nonbreeding males might also be found within the enclosure. To define breeding males, we would have to include as many singularly observable characteristics as possible (e.g., calling from the water, in amplexus) in order to eliminate all other males from consideration.

For amphibian research, it is useful to distinguish three types of operational definition: procedural, behavioral, and structural.

A *procedural definition* is an operational definition that sets forth the manipulations or procedures required to induce or to observe the phenomenon or state to be studied. For example, for an observational experiment to be performed on "an abundant species," *abundant* could be defined by a certain number of specimens observed per kilometer of transect. Within the context of the study, anyone can agree whether a selected species is abundant or not by noting the numbers found per kilometer; opinions open to interpretation are avoided. This type of definition is especially useful for describing independent variables subject to causal or correlative relationships.

A *behavioral definition* is an operational definition that focuses on dynamic aspects of the behavior of the object, state, or individual, linking observable antecedent behavior with an associated change, outcome, or dependent variable. The behavioral type of definition is most useful for defining the dependent variable in investigations involving behavior and is little used in studies of biodiversity.

A *structural definition* is an operational definition in which the demonstration of a specific behavior or other character constitutes the definition. This type of definition focuses on the characteristics of the individual or object, specifying static rather than dynamic qualities. It is useful for defining any variable, independent or dependent. For example, a breeding male frog could be defined as "a male frog found calling at the breeding pond."

Operational definitions set precise, concrete preconditions (e.g., operations, procedures, events, behaviors) that are observable and that lead invariably to the phenomenon under study. Such definitions satisfy the requisite of quantitative study, which is the specification and measurement of variables and their relationships. When the sex of an amphibian or the species is the variable, measurement is usually straightforward. When assemblage structure, calling activity, diversity, association, or dominance are being investigated, measurement is not so simple, and peak precision is mandatory for successful study. Although an entire theory or sampling plan cannot be laid out in operational terms, such terms must be used to define the

quantitative, measurable, and testable aspects of the study.

In an inventory or monitoring study, the investigator is concerned with nonmanipulated, or naturally occurring, variables rather than with the manipulated and carefully controlled variables that characterize a laboratory study. Classical statistical experimental designs must be modified to deal with this reduced control, with minimal loss to the quality of inference. For such observational or field studies, the aim is to describe the procedures used to identify the state of a variable already characterizing each individual, locality, or habitat in the target population. Operationalism in this context simply indicates how the variable states are to be identified and the situations in which they are to be observed and recorded.

Formulating the Research Hypothesis

Development of a research project requires the statement of the research question or problem and then its restatement in terms of a testable or working *hypothesis*. The research question may first be formulated in theoretical terms that link concepts, but then it must be translated into operational terms, which requires the researcher to consider measurement in precise terms. Unless the hypothesis is stated in a testable form, one cannot distinguish positive from negative evidence. For example, an investigator may believe that "*Plethodon cinereus* prefers deep litter in eastern United States deciduous forest" or that "*Phrynohyas resinifictrix* prefers tree holes in lowland rain forest," but these ideas are not testable as stated. Is "preference" to be defined in terms of correlation, association, or dependence? And what does it mean in operational terms, only that *P. cinereus* will be found in deep leaf litter, or, in addition, that it will not be found in other substrates? Definitions that are too vague may preclude generalization because conditions cannot be replicated. In contrast, extreme precision (e.g., patch sampling using logs only 25 cm by 1.5 m or less) may be too restrictive, limiting a study to just one log or one tree, and not allowing for any generalization.

A hypothesis should be the proposed answer to the research problem or one facet of the problem. The hypothesis must contain a statement of the relationship between two or more quantities, species, or measurable variables and must convey clear implications for testing that relationship. Legitimate hypotheses exist that do not provide criteria of relationship between variables (see below). These types of hypotheses are not appropriate for inventory and monitoring studies but may be useful for study of ancillary variables collected with the basic sampling data.

The actual purpose of the test of a hypothesis is to ascertain the probability that the hypothesis is supported by fact. Strictly speaking, empirical evidence can never be said to prove or disprove a hypothesis, but it can support or "confirm" the hypothesis under suitable conditions of repetition (e.g., Braithwaite 1955).

The object of a hypothesis test is the relationship among the variables. These relationships are identified by *propositions,* statements that can be either true or false. There are several types of propositions:

1. *Simple qualitative proposition.* **A has characteristic B.** Such a statement does not establish a relationship between the (two or more) factors or variables, and, therefore, is not testable. Nevertheless, it may contribute to the development of theory by (a) serving to specify antecedent conditions under which certain affinities among the variables may be expected; (b) suggesting other related propositions and providing a basal amount of knowledge; or (c) becoming a component of more-developed and testable propositions. An example of this type of proposition is "Bromeliads are the unique habitat of *Osteopilus brunneus* in Jamaica."

2. *Consequent proposition.* **If A, then B.** This type of statement establishes that B is always a consequence of A. Such statements can indicate a causal relationship. It is quite often possible to convert a simple qualitative proposition into a consequent proposition. For example, in order to provide testability, the statement from proposition 1 above becomes, "If *O. brunneus* is found, then the habitat is a bromeliad."

3. *Positive correlational proposition.* **The more A, the more B.** For example, "The greater the structural diversity of aquatic vegetation in ponds, the greater the species diversity of tadpoles." The obverse of this type of proposition may also be used: **The less A, the less B.**

4. *Negative correlational proposition.* **The more A, the less B.** For example, "As elevation increases from 1600 m to 2500 m in tropical Peru, the number of species of pond breeding frogs decreases."

5. *Null proposition.* **A and B are unrelated.** A null proposition indicates that no relationship between variables will be detected. For example, "There is no associative relationship or interaction (other than geographic association) between *Hyalinobatrachium valerioi* and *Smilisca sordida* along streams in lower Central America." The disconfirmation of the statement does not include a preferred direction, so this is a *nondirectional hypothesis.* In contrast, proposition types 1 through 4 are *directional hypotheses.* Directional hypotheses relay more information about the testable relationship and may form the basis for more powerful statistical tests.

Validity

TYPES AND DEFINITIONS

The most important consideration in problem formation, operational definition of variables with their attendant relationships, and formulation of testable hypotheses is the maintenance of balance between specificity and generality. In this regard, the investigator must be keenly aware of the validity of the research design.

Validity is conformation to declared purpose and is used with reference to propositions, including causal propositions (e.g., see Cook and Campbell 1979). For observational studies, it is a measure of the degree to which the research design will actually produce the results or measure the variables that it says it will. High validity implies close approximation to intended purpose, and low validity suggests poor approximation or larger "error." In ecological work, *error* is used to describe all departures from representativeness regardless of their cause. Alternatively, in statistical work, *error* is used only to refer to nonrepresentativeness caused by inappropriate sampling methods; all other problems are called *biases*. The source of any compromise to the validity of a study is called a *threat*.

In designing sampling studies for amphibians, the investigator must be concerned with two major categories of validity. *Internal validity* is the extent to which differences detected in a dependent variable can be ascribed directly to changes in an independent variable in a specific sampling instance. *External validity* is the extent to which results obtained and statements inferred from a specific sampling situation apply or can be generalized to individuals, populations, objects, or settings not directly participating in the study.

THREATS TO INTERNAL VALIDITY

To achieve internal validity in a research investigation, one must be able to rule out all extraneous causative variables as explanations for the observed result. When a rival variable is eliminated, it is said to be *controlled;* uncontrolled variables are threats to internal validity.

A controlled variable is not associated with or related to the independent variable, so its effects cannot be confused or confounded with those of the independent variable. Internal validity must be ascertained for each study by asking if a given (independent) variable really has a primary associative relationship with another (dependent) variable and, if so, if the independent variable actually produced a change in the dependent variable. Before validity can be evaluated, the investigator must be sure that no extraneous variables have affected the result or been mistaken for the variable of prime interest.

When a team has only a few days to obtain a species count and list of the target fauna at a remote site, the study usually is poorly controlled and has poor internal validity. Thus, when results of such a sampling study are used to evaluate faunal change or to design a management program, conclusions may be misleading or inappropriate. Sampling in this manner often involves "misplaced precision," in which excessive care is taken in the collection of data about which conclusions can be, at best, impressionistic and imprecise and, at worst, indefensible. Because this type of one-shot study design is frequently used (particularly to evaluate the potential impact of environmental modification), we have included it as a technique (see "Complete Species Inventories" in Chapter 6), but with as much standardization as possible. Data obtained in this way may be used at least as a comparative base for more-intensive studies or as a preliminary estimate of the composition of a species assemblage.

There are several potential threats (selectively adapted from Campbell and Stanley 1963) to internal validity for amphibian studies:

1. *Historical threat.* A historical threat is an extraneous or unexpected event occurring in the environment at the time the observations are made (especially between the first and subsequent observations) that may confound the data on the selected relationships between variables. *Confound* is used here in a statistical sense to indicate that an obtained

effect can be attributed to two or more variables, and the unique portion due to each cannot be disentangled. For example, consider a study design in which night driving along selected roads is used to sample amphibian presence and activity. The investigator carefully identifies the two samples to be compared and controls for time, date, weather conditions, seasonal factors, speed, and vehicle. On the first night several species are encountered, but the second night yields many fewer. Further checking shows that on the second night a herpetology class collected amphibians along the road 30 minutes before the investigator appeared. Comparison of sample results is impossible.

2. *Maturation threat.* Maturation threats are changes (e.g., in age, breeding status, fatigue level, seasonal activity) in the individuals in the population during the period of observation that may affect the final outcome of the study. Maturation can be a consequential threat when organisms are sampled at time intervals of considerable length relative to the length of their life cycles.

3. *Instrumentation and observer threats.* These threats result from differences in measurement calibration that may lead to differences in results. The problems encompass not only laboratory and field instruments (e.g., weak batteries can affect the quality and accuracy of frog recordings) but also differences among observers or observations, which may be even more of a threat. For example, a novice and an experienced person likely would record different values for the distance a frog call can be detected or for the number of frogs calling along a transect in a tropical forest. Likewise, a person who hears a species-specific call in two distinct microhabitats, or before and after observation of another variable of interest, may judge the calls differently because of increased experience and discrimination, increased fatigue, or plain carelessness. Such variation can be minimized with standardization of methods and checks of inter-observer uniformity prior to fieldwork.

4. *Statistical regression threat.* These threats result when amphibians or other organisms are selected for study on the basis of the extreme of any character. For example, it is inappropriate to draw a conclusion about abundance based only on visible frogs if their typical inclination is to remain hidden in leaf litter. If frogs are selected for strength of call (i.e., the louder the call, the higher the probability of selection) or other character, the effect of statistical regression can be mistaken for the effect of the variable under study. The more deviant or extreme (in either direction) the first measurement, the more the second set of measurements will vary. This phenomenon is especially pronounced with variables subject to unreliable measurement. If two large samples are drawn randomly from two different populations, or from the same population at different times, without any matching, then regression threats are not a consideration.

5. *Interaction with selection effects.* Selection effects occur when samples are selected nonrandomly and the resulting groups of amphibians differ in size, variability, or type. Such differences jeopardize group comparisons and may be a threat to internal validity. The extent to which randomization assures group equality is shown by tests on the sampling statistics (e.g., means and variances). The chance that the assumption of group equality is not tenable increases for small samples.

Interaction may occur between sample selection and any of threats 1 through 4, above. *Selection-maturation* interaction is possible when two groups (e.g., two species of anuran larvae in a pond) mature at different rates or in different proportions (e.g., more males than females). *Se-lection-historical threat* interaction can result when groups have distinct local histories. Such effects are especially likely when a known source of variability is ignored. For example, if males and females of a particular species have different behaviors or habitat distributions, then random sampling may be inappropriate. Blocking or stratifying the sampling on the basis of sex, prior to random selection within each sex, will increase sampling precision and decrease the interactive threat to internal validity.

THREATS TO EXTERNAL VALIDITY

Because investigators are almost always interested in the relevance of their work beyond the confines of the selected sample (i.e., generalizability), concern about external validity is important. External validity can be strengthened by describing the population, settings, and variables to which the results will apply, before the study is initiated. The representativeness of these factors will determine how extensively the results can be applied.

The following factors may threaten external validity if they are not evaluated prior to data gathering:

1. *Interactive effect of selection.* The characteristics of the sample selected from the available population determine how extensively the findings can be generalized. External factors (e.g., weather, environmental conditions) as well as internal characteristics (e.g., breeding status, age) of the particular group selected may contribute to an atypical finding. The diversity found in artificial pools, for example, may not be representative of diversity in natural ponds.
2. *Reactive or interactive effect of preselection methods.* A treatment or method used in a study influences subsequent results through its effect on the behavior of the subject. For example, an animal captured and marked

prior to a sampling effort may be more likely to avoid capture than a naive animal. Likewise, the presence of an observer in the immediate area may affect normal amphibian behavior in unregulated ways. This may not, in itself, limit generalizability, if standard preconditions are met, because all inventories and monitoring efforts to some extent are observational studies.
3. *Multiple effects interference.* Measurements taken from individuals subjected to more than one procedure may be representative only of measurements taken from other individuals that have experienced the same series of procedures.

SUMMARY

For any inventory or monitoring study, the internal and external validity of each stage of the study design must be evaluated in detail, and the presence and extent of any threat determined. The frequency and importance of each threat will vary within and among studies, and particular threats are not inevitably correlated with particular sampling designs. I have listed here only those threats that I consider to be plausible in field biodiversity studies. The list is not exhaustive (see e.g., Wright 1991), but it may help the investigator to recognize threats and to minimize or eliminate them from the study plan.

Field observation and statistical design

Data Accuracy

A fundamental assumption underlying any amphibian study is that the data have been accurately recorded and processed. As emphasized in Chapter 6, observations should be recorded in the field and later coded (if necessary) and entered into a computer (if available or desirable) for analysis, to reduce the likelihood of introducing errors. Confidence in the analytical results cannot exceed confidence in the accuracy of each observation.

If computers are used, the data should be checked as they are entered. Spreadsheet and database programs allow limits to be placed on each column of input in order to prevent errors of excess. For example, if season is coded as an integer between 1 and 4, the program can be set to prevent other digits from appearing in that column. Even with such precautions, it is wise to check the data a second time against a hard (paper) copy of the completed file.

Despite careful checking, input errors may remain undetected. One of the most common problems is that of extreme values, or *outliers*— that is, patently unrealistic observations. Both the computer data and the original field notes should be checked. Only when a source of error is clearly identified (e.g., a code of 4 for sex or a species count of 100 incorrectly copied as 1,000) should the extreme observation be corrected.

Other situations that may affect data accuracy are accidents (e.g., rain gauge tipped over) and mechanical or personnel problems (e.g., weak batteries on data recorder, investigator sick). Any decision to ignore observations because of possible data contamination must be made before the data are examined, so that the actual value of the observation cannot influence the decision. All contaminated data must be either discarded or retained. Quite frequently in field studies, values representing genuine biological effects cannot be reliably distinguished from accidental irregularities or input errors. If the investigator cannot be certain that an extreme value is the result of a problem, the value should be retained.

Even if there is an obvious reason to discard an observation, internal or external validity may be threatened. It is possible that extreme values or measurement errors are more likely to occur under one set of study conditions than another. If so, and if these values are discarded, then the remaining data may not be representative of the study population. For example, the set of quadrat observations from certain microhabitats in a study area may be faulty because of high observer error or patchiness of species occurrence. If these observations are edited or eliminated, the remaining quadrats may not be representative of the target area's true heterogeneity, and a statistical estimate then could be severely biased. Care must be taken to examine extreme observations within the frame of reference of the study before any value is discarded. This possible source of bias should be clearly mentioned in the final report or publication. It may be of value to compare the results of analyses made with and without the suspect values.

Measurement Scales and Statistical Analysis

Numbers that result from an inventory or monitoring effort may have one or more of three cardinal features: intrinsic meaningful ordering; ordered differences between number pairs; or a unique "zero" point, or natural origin, indicating absence or deficiency. Stevens (1946) named four numerical scales based upon the number of these features observed and the amount of information represented about the measured property:

1. *Nominal scale*. Numbers on this scale are used to name categories in a classification, but they do not measure any property and have no intrinsic order. In this case, numerals are actually unnecessary; word descriptions such as male and female, or letters such as m and f, can be used. When the classification is subjected to statistical analysis, numerals without an underlying order relationship may be used. For example, sex may be coded 1 or 0, and a male can be designated as either value with no sacrifice in meaning.

2. *Ordinal scale*. Ordinal numbers are those assigned to the amounts of a property, so that the order of the numbers corresponds to the order of magnitude of the amounts (Torgerson 1958). Ordinal scales may have a natural origin (Torgerson 1958) or not (Stevens 1946). On an ordinal scale, objects can be arranged in a meaningful serial order with respect to some property, showing that some individuals or objects have more of a particular attribute than do others. For analytical purposes, any order-preserving (i.e., monotonically increasing) transformation of the numbers will serve as well as the original set.

3. *Interval scale*. An interval scale denotes equal incremental amounts of a property of an individual with equally valued numerical increments. In addition to the order of the numbers corresponding to the order of magnitude of the various amounts of the property, the size of the difference between the pairs of numbers corresponds to the distance (in a generalized sense) between the corresponding pairs of amounts of the property. Any set of numbers satisfying the requirements of such a scale is not affected by a linear transformation (of the familiar form $y = ax + b$) of the set. An increase in one unit from any region of the scale is identical to a unit increase from any other region.

4. *Ratio scale*. A ratio scale is formed when the requirement for a unique natural origin is appended to the rules for forming the interval scale. Any set of numbers satisfying the requirements is insensitive to a linear transformation (of the form $y = ax$).

Baker et al. (1971) provided at least a partial answer to the question of how to relate the measurement scale for data to computational procedures and statistical tests. They showed that probabilities estimated from the sampling distributions of so-called strong statistics, such as the *t*-test, are almost unaffected by the type of measurement scale used. In general, therefore, an inferential statistical test can answer the research question it was designed to answer, regardless of the original scale of measurement.

Randomness

The basic statistical tests used with observational data from inventories or monitoring studies require that the initial selection of subjects or localities or the application of field techniques (e.g., quadrat placement) be random. The term *random* is used in a technical sense in research design; it does not describe the data in the observed sample but the process by which the data were obtained. Sampling is random if each possible sample or combination of *n* selections of individuals in the population has the identical chance of becoming the sample actually drawn. Random sampling does not mean, as is often stated, that each individual in the population has an equal chance of being in the sample. In practice, a sample is drawn individual by individual, and each has an equal chance of selection at the time of selection. This procedure is also called *simple random sampling* in the sense that it is sampling without further restriction (Kempthorne 1955; Cochran 1963). Implicit in this discussion of procedures for simple random sampling is selection from a finite population. If the population is of infinite size, random sampling procedures do not apply, and a sample is selected randomly only by assumption.

Many people believe that any sample drawn randomly from a population is highly representative of that population or equivalent to it in all essential characteristics. A second widely accepted notion is that chance events are self-correcting. Both of these assumptions are untrue and can affect the validity of a study.

REPRESENTATIVENESS OF SAMPLES

The law of large numbers predicts that very large samples will be representative of the populations from which they are drawn, but it does not speak to the medium and small samples obtained during the course of most fieldwork. Five tosses of a coin can yield 4 heads and 1 tail, or 80% heads, whereas the proportion of heads in 5,000 tosses is likely to be close to the theoretical value of 50%. In a similar manner, 5 quadrats randomly placed in a forest with 95% canopy cover might fall in the open over 4 small ponds and 1 trail; locations of 100 or 1,000 quadrats would likely be more representative of the area's true habitat profile.

The comparability of random assignments to groups is probabilistic, not deterministic. Individual samples can vary greatly, but the distribution of samples will depend upon the nature of the population from which they were selected. For a given sample size, one will obtain more heterogeneous samples from populations in which the individuals are more variable among themselves. Averages and proportions will vary less in large samples than in small samples from the same population. The value of random selection does not emanate from fairness or lack of bias with which any selected samples portray the population, but lack of bias is an important consideration in large samples. Among R. A. Fisher's greatest contributions was furtherance of the idea that random processes can be used to achieve group equivalence prior to an experiment or study. No test of significance requires de facto that all confounded, uncontrolled extraneous variables be removed, that is, that randomization be effected (McGinnis 1958). However, the process of randomization assures that conditions of equivalence of samples will be met within reasonable limits; failure to randomize does not guarantee, however, that such conditions will be violated.

SAMPLING METHODS

All methods of sampling have some attached pattern (distribution) of variability. Knowledge of this pattern is a basic tool of statistical inference and can be obtained only through the laws of mathematical probability, which are applicable only to samples obtained under random processes.

Other sampling methods are available. Some rely in part on random procedures, and some exploit certain features of random processes. *Convenience sampling* is a generic term for a type of sampling used for convenience rather than for formal representativeness. Sampling of a certain fauna by an expert herpetologist might well approximate the true proportion of species in the area. The numbers obtained, however, are still subject to sampling variability, but of an unspecified amount, and the possibility of scientific replication is diminished. There are three common types of convenience sampling: accidental, grab, and haphazard. *Accidental sampling* occurs when the data on a species or genus are obtained peripherally as part of a larger or unrelated study and are not randomly selected. Such sampling does not guarantee that the achieved observations are representative of the population, nor is it clear how to specify the target population.

Cochran et al. (1954) discussed *grab sampling,* in which an investigator, in effect, just "grabs a handful." Whether the sample units be individuals in the available population or cards with random numbers, the ones in the handful almost always resemble one another more, on average, than those from a simple random sample; variability is underestimated. These authors showed that even if the grabs are randomly spread such that each one has an equal chance of entering the sample, they do not share the characteristics of a randomly obtained sample.

Haphazard sampling heightens the implication of chance and, unfortunately, can pass for random sampling in some ecological applications (e.g., quadrat sampling). However, unless investigators employ a device, such as a random number table or generator, to select localities, microhabitats, or sites for the placement of quadrats or transects, they may create a *halo effect.* A halo effect occurs when an investigator selects the "best" or the "good" sites or individuals for sampling. For example, the frog just outside the actual study area boundary is selected because the frog displays the desired characteristic. Such a selection method certainly may allow for larger samples or species abundance limits. However, haphazard sampling threatens external validity and can influence the results of subsequent statistical testing.

In contrast to convenience sampling, *probability sampling* is a process wherein randomness is a requisite. Randomness can enter the sampling procedure at any stage. A few such sampling methods are of interest for inventory and monitoring studies. With *stratification (stratified random sampling)* a target population is divided into relatively homogeneous groups or strata prior to sampling, based on factors (e.g., sex, size, breeding condition, life history state) known to influence variability in that population. Subsequent selection within each stratum is random. Factors are selected on the advice of amphibian experts. Such expert judgment may be inappropriate as a basis for statistical sampling, but it is vital for controlling variables extraneous to the phenomenon being studied and, thereby, for increasing internal validity. Stratified random sampling is also a useful operational strategy for screening individual specimens, events, or microhabitats for possible exclusion from the study and for reducing study variability.

Randomization within stratified groups adds precision to a study by ensuring that the sample contains the same proportional distribution of amphibians, events, or microhabitats as in the target population. It increases the likelihood that the research will be representative of the population. Stratified random sampling is appropriate for populations that tend to be patchy (Seber 1986). In such a case, each sample of size *n* in each stratum has a known probability of being selected for the study. The actual probability of selection does not have to be known; only the relation of this probability to the proportion of such samples in the population is necessary.

In sampling, a major effort must be made to reduce any large or important threat and any random sampling error. After this reduction, the easiest way to increase sample accuracy is to increase sample size. Other things being equal (Yates 1981), the random sampling error is approximately inversely proportional to the square root of the number of units included in the sample. The accuracy attained will depend on the sample size as well as on the variability in the population of subjects that contributes to the sampling error.

Methods other than simple random sampling and stratification that do not introduce further bias but substantially reduce variability and, in turn, reduce the sample size required to attain the level of accuracy desired are of considerable benefit. One method is *systematic sampling* with a random start point in which a sample is obtained by a systematic, not random, method (e.g., sampling at equal intervals in space or time). For example, one might choose among localities on a list by selecting every fifth entry. Another method, *cluster sampling,* uses groups or clusters (e.g., ponds, tree holes), not individuals, as the basic (multistage) sampling unit; this approach may be preferred in ecological situations that require even area coverage (Scherba and Gallucci 1976; Seber 1986). Many authors (e.g., Seber 1986) have noted the need for more sample designs that use sampling approaches with higher *efficiency,* that is, that provide for reduced variability. Both Yates (1981) and Krebs (1989) provided readable discussions of this problem.

It is important to realize that random assignment of individuals or objects to groups only minimizes but does not eliminate all threats to validity. Random assignment does not guarantee a productive research design or a testable hypothesis. It provides a proper environment for inference but does not guarantee the infallibility of the inferences; assumptions of comparability are merely assumptions and must be examined for plausibility. Randomization is the best way to avoid accidental bias, but if group sizes are small, then large intrinsic differences that bias the estimated effects can still occur between groups by chance (Gilbert 1989). Alternatively, the judicious selection of control variables (McGinnis 1958) and the use of the more sophisticated sampling plans discussed above can reduce required sample sizes and add to both the internal and the external validity of the research.

USE OF A RANDOM NUMBER TABLE

We include in this book a table of edited random numbers (Appendix 7). Use of such a table in designing sampling studies is probably the most widely accepted method of obtaining random samples and is recommended in many of the techniques, but it must be properly used.

For purposes of inventory and monitoring studies, the first step is to list the objects, habitats, quadrats, or transects to be subjected to the random assignment process. Individuals, although the primary objects of concern, are not randomized in a field study; the sites at which they will be studied or trapped are. Each item on the list is assigned a unique numeral. The next step is the selection of the tabled numbers for use in selecting the sample. Let us assume we want to place 10 one-meter-square quadrats randomly throughout a specified habitat that is 25×25 m, or 625 m^2, in area. A map of the area could be subdivided into 25 equal-sized (5×5 m) plots, with each assigned a unique consecutive numeral, from 1 to 25. We then would need to select, at random, the 10 plots in which to place one each of the 10 quadrats. To do so, we would use the table of random numbers (Appendix 7) to select 10 numbers, each representing a specific plot in the set of 25. Use of this table, which was devised for this book, is explained in detail in Appendix 7.

At times a second application of the random sample procedure may be required to ensure that the selected sites are observed in random order. We also could select a "control" group in the same manner. The purpose would be to create two groups that are equivalent in a probabilistic sense. The two sets of quadrats would be located in areas representative of the total 625 m^2 of area selected for study. The use of such a control group does not necessarily mean that the target population under study has some unifying characteristic or forms a biological population of interest.

In some circumstances it may be desirable to employ an alternative form of probability sampling. For example, if the target population were stratified by microhabitat before sampling, plots within each of the strata would be selected separately using the random number table.

Stratifying, or blocking, prior to study is preferable to adjusting initial random assignment to groups (Cook and Campbell 1979). Nevertheless, if new information on the fauna indicates that microhabitat differences may be important in the study, the location of each randomly placed quadrat can be checked for noncomparability. The investigator might find, for instance, that 7 quadrats include parts of streams, 2 include small ponds, and 1 is covered with a deep layer of dry litter. If such a bias were noted prior to actual field observation, rerandomization (the selection of 10 new values) would be a possibility. However, in this case, stratification or blocking should be given serious consideration. To be maximally effective, the research design should determine the point at which randomization should enter.

Another common procedure for making random assignments of sampling units is to write numbers representing the sampling units available (e.g., 1, 2, ... 25) on slips of paper, put them into a container, shake it thoroughly, and select slips until the sample size is reached (e.g., 10). This method can involve unforeseen bias (e.g., the slips of paper stick to the container or each other). Computer-generated tables of random numbers can also be used, but each program must be checked because many authors have identified inaccuracies with particular generators.

Connor (1977) suggested the following procedures as aids to reliable randomization:

1. The individual or individuals who design the study and best understand the rationale for sampling make the random assignment.
2. The investigators control the assignment, not an agency's operating personnel.
3. One person makes the assignments, not a group.
4. Investigators do not use "loopholes," in which random assignment is circumvented for a small number of individuals or objects (e.g., the investigator includes a subject slightly outside the quadrat because of desirable characteristics).

Another point may be added to this list:

5. Randomization is carried out before entering the field. This practice eliminates unintentional as well as conscious bias in selection and prevents direct substitution of one unit, specimen, or plot for another that is less convenient or less apt to provide information.

A sample will be sufficiently representative of a population only if errors introduced by the sampling process in the field are adequately minimized. Even so, bias that affects wholly objective conclusions does not necessarily invalidate the total study. Many times, constant or small biases are inconsequential. For example, when limited bias is constant from species to species, inventories designed to look across species at one site are little affected. Investigators must avoid attaching exaggerated importance to minor sources of bias that, in fact, can only produce errors that are trivial relative to random sampling error (Yates 1981). Ascer-

taining the relative importance of bias and sampling error is a vital concern in statistical inference.

Independence

Statistical tests may lack validity if research events are not independent. Events are said to be *statistically independent* when the probability of occurrence of one event remains constant regardless of the occurrence of another. Successive samples from a population are independent if the probability of selecting any one sample is independent of the selection of the others (Marriott 1990). Samples of amphibians removed from a plot one by one (see "Quantitative Sampling of Amphibian Larvae" in Chapter 6 and "Removal Sampling," in Chapter 8) can be assumed to be independent if the population is large. Observations of amphibians along a transect are also independent as long as the individuals are not highly mobile and not likely to be recorded in more than one sample. In contrast, removal of males from a chorus probably affects the calling activity of other males and, thereby, makes their location and removal difficult. Likewise, samples from night driving at short time intervals may lack independence.

Transects at a study site must be placed far enough apart to make overlap of aural or visual encounters unlikely. When working with a small population, for example, larvae from a tree hole or a very small pond (e.g., one dip with a net), the initial sampling affects subsequent sampling by drastically reducing numbers. In this instance, the remaining larval population may take on a character different from those in the initial intact population. Another example in which dependence is possible involves sampling frogs from ponds within easy walking distance on successive days. Unless the frogs are marked, at least a few, and possibly many, individuals may be included in both samples.

Sample Size

In the design stage, it is common to raise questions about the sample size necessary for both testability and generalizability. Factors of time, money, and personnel act to keep the size small, whereas statistical and biological considerations call for larger samples. The prime concern is determining the minimal biological sample size needed to provide statistically credible findings.

Consideration of statistical tests, degree of sample comparability, and representativeness achieved by randomization persuades most investigators that bigger is always better. Explanations and apologies for small samples abound in the ecological literature. However, "the bigger the better" as a maxim is neither invariably true nor always a mandate for statistical analysis.

For inventory and monitoring projects we need to consider at least two aspects of sample size: (1) the numbers of quadrats, transects, or trips to the site and (2) the numbers of specimens collected and species sampled. Suggestions for the former are provided in the sections on sampling techniques, but with two caveats. First, for simple random sampling of quadrats, transects, or patches, suggested sample sizes are based on the number that experts have found necessary to achieve biological or ecological representativeness of the target area. Second, if stratification is involved, it is optimal to select judiciously one to three variables upon which to stratify and to achieve comparability of groups through random sampling within strata. This methodology will eliminate problems of missing or unattainable specimens in a large, multifaceted array.

Determining numbers of replicates in fieldwork is troublesome, especially because cost may dictate numbers of site visits. Although an investigator can specify a model, formulae to predetermine sample sizes usually are at best asymptotic rather than exact, and at worst impossible to achieve under study limitations. For our purposes, expert guidance should prove more reliable. In fact, revisiting a site according to a standard timetable is probably more vital to success than making a predetermined number of visits.

The number of specimens collected or species to be sampled presents a different problem. In field observation studies of the type we discuss in this book, predetermined numbers of specimens are not the norm; investigators find what they can. Likewise, in the realistic biological situation of inventories and monitoring, specimens and species are the topics of study but not the *sampling unit* and, unlike the transect or quadrat, they are not the direct object of the random selection. Nevertheless, it is possible to ascertain after sampling has been completed whether the sample size gives the null hypothesis a reasonable chance of being confirmed.

Investigators often are pleased to obtain a small sample and delighted with a moderate one. Field studies do not require the a priori use of formulae to determine sample sizes but rather the post hoc determination of the observed power of the fieldwork. Some authors (e.g., Rotenberry and Wiens 1985) have discussed the use of power and sample size formulae in the design of field studies. I focus on use of the concepts of power and sample size as they relate to interpretability.

Testing Errors

Both the *null hypothesis,* that the variable under investigation has no effect or the relationship has no meaning, and the *alternative hypothesis,* that the variable does have an effect or the relationship is meaningful, are under consideration when a statistical test is run. Statistical work in biology focuses on the null hypothesis. It also emphasizes the *type 1,* or *alpha, error.* The alpha error is usually called the *significance level* chosen for the study; it indicates how likely one is to reject a hypothesis when it is true and should not be rejected. This level, when allowed to range over the interval (0, 1), actually may be seen as a random variable or as a statistic that measures the consistency of the data under the null hypothesis. The *type 2*, or *beta, error* of a particular test refers to how likely one is not to reject a hypothesis when it is false and should be rejected (a null hypothesis cannot be "accepted"); this type of error cannot be controlled simply by selecting a significance level. It is usual to preset the level of type 1 errors and to minimize the probability of type 2 errors.

Either of the two errors can be costly; circumstances of testing determine which has the more deleterious effect. It is simple to conjure up examples involving life or death in which the cost of committing a type 1 error is decidedly more than the cost of making a type 2 error. In this case, the significance level (alpha) could be set at 0.01 or even 0.001 for decision making to offset the seriousness of the possible error. When there is no life-threatening aspect to the research, a type 1 error is usually less costly than a type 2. This is especially true in exploratory studies or studies involving innovative features or elusive species effects. Toft and Shea (1983), however, have pointed out circumstances in basic research in which the cost of a type 1 error could exceed that of a type 2 error.

THE 0.05 CONVENTION

In order to make a rational choice for the levels of error, there should be some specification of the loss involved. Such specification is practically impossible in a general inventory or in a monitoring effort, which is a problem when testing hypotheses with such amphibian data. Generally, biologists have resolved the problem by adopting the conventional but arbitrary level of 0.05 (or occasionally 0.01) for alpha for all research, thereby ignoring effectively the second type of error, *and* the *power* of the test. The 0.05 level of alpha, which is listed as if it were indisputable truth (and even may determine publishability), is but convention. Use of a constant value

(0.05) for alpha introduces an impartiality into the test procedure, but it can be a serious impediment to interpretation because it is a convenience that ignores other important aspects of the inference process. In addition, it addresses the question of error, not the utility or importance of the obtained result. A decision to use a fixed alpha error is not always the best strategy for observational work. The selection of paired values for alpha and beta errors, based upon the complexity of the sampling design, may well serve biodiversity purposes better. Alpha should equal beta to provide an equal chance of detection as a standard for observational fieldwork, unless circumstances make one error more costly or more difficult to detect than the other.

POWER, EFFECT SIZE, AND SAMPLE SIZE

The probability of making a type 2, or beta, error (failing to reject a false hypothesis) and the probability of correctly rejecting a hypothesis (power) are necessarily related (1 − beta error = power). Therefore, a *powerful test* is one that allows for a high probability of claiming there is a real difference when such a difference actually exists in the population. Summaries of research findings commonly report sample sizes as well as alpha error or observed probability (p) level but not type 2 error or power. In addition, the observed p value is often the only criterion used in making decisions about the correctness of a hypothesis, with no reference to sample size, research design, or the potential costs of the decision (Yoccoz 1991).

Interpretative remarks in amphibian literature reveal the attitude that significant results acquired with large samples are more compelling and meaningful than those based on small samples. In addition, when an investigator concludes that a statistically significant relationship exists, generally he or she is confident not only that a biological or ecological relationship exists in the target population, but also that the degree or size of that affinity or effect is worthy of further consideration. However, the size of the effect (relationship or difference) is not a product of the size of the sample.

It is certainly true that the smaller the values of alpha and the observed probability, *p,* the surer one can be that the obtained result is not attributable to sampling error. However, neither alpha nor *p* indicates how far apart the parameters (e.g., means) are or how large an effect actually is being discussed. The *effect size* (Cohen 1977) is a relative measure, in population standard deviation units, of the difference the investigator desires to detect. It is not possible in many observational studies, however, to specify the effect size a priori. This difference may be estimated after the data have been obtained; the *observed effect size* (i.e., a standardized difference between the two observed parameter estimates) estimates this separation for a given procedure or test (Cohen 1977; Lipsey 1990). If the null hypothesis is rejected, then some real differences may exist between the situations specified by the two hypotheses. The magnitude of this difference will have a considerable influence on the likelihood of attaining significance. For equivalent-sized heterogeneous samples, the larger the effect (relationship), the more likely it will be determined statistically significant, and the greater the statistical power of the test. Likewise, any variable, regardless of how inconsequential, will manifest a statistically significant difference in large enough samples. But would one really accept that a statistically significant difference between means of 0.343 frogs/km transect and 0.341 frogs/km indicates a real change in species abundance? This type of issue must be resolved. With large samples the difference being tested may be tiny and still be called statistically significant; with small samples this difference would have to be quite large (but, as we shall discuss, still not necessarily substantive) to be detectable. For a reported difference to be evaluated, not only its significance, but also its size must be known.

When sample sizes are about the same, the maximum observed difference (in terms of an appropriate measure of effect size) between the groups of results termed nonsignificant and the difference between those that have been called statistically significant should be evaluated. The observed effect size for the first group should never be larger than any effect size in the second group. A moment's reflection should reveal this standard to be the basic minimum for avoiding problems of illogical summary interpretation.

In experimental settings and even some survey studies it is possible to set a minimum effect size or smallest detectable difference before the work begins. This value, determined a priori either by expert opinion (Cohen 1977) or from previous research results (e.g., Ferrari and Hayek 1990), is used in formulae to make power and sample size determinations.

An opinion not often presented is that tests of null hypotheses are not actually the most appropriate for fieldwork. However, in many instances interpretative problems and ambiguities could well be relieved or eliminated by an alternative approach. If the size of the effect of interest were specified in the statement of the scientific hypothesis, simple statistical tests would become only one aspect of the total statistical inferential picture. For example, a researcher could test whether the population sizes of *Ambystoma tigrinum* dropped by at least 10% over time, or whether the SVL (snout-vent length) of *Rana limnocharis* differed by less than one standard unit across two localities. In this way, the accumulated knowledge of the expert is drawn into play, and the exact situation to be tested has biological significance. The level of statistical significance clearly would refer to the confidence a person has in the final decision, and confidence interval estimation would play a more integral role. More important, the result would no longer be confused with the size of the effect itself, and an unrealistic effect would not be tested.

In correlational studies, workers commonly report a measure of effect size called the coefficient of determination (square of the correlation coefficient). In this setting, researchers apparently recognize that the correlation coefficient, its significance, and the probability level do not provide a measure of the size of the relationship under study. The value of a measure of the size of a relationship goes unappreciated in observational (and experimental) studies when tests of null hypotheses are the sole method used for statistical inference.

When the question of how large a sample is necessary arises, it is commonly stated that 25 (or 30 or 50 or 100) is the correct number to use to provide for statistically reasonable results. Usually the number is chosen to provide for relatively narrow bounds on the error about the mean; it is not related to any power considerations. Choosing a number on that basis can be a serious problem.

Because inventory and monitoring efforts are concerned primarily with uncovering important changes (particularly declines) in biodiversity over time, the most powerful tests possible should be used. Recommendations for additional study of areas, faunas, or species will depend upon the reported power levels. Nonsignificant findings (possibly contrary to informed perceptions) from a well-designed study with large sample sizes that minimize threats to internal and external validity do not necessarily require that the study be terminated. The best recommendation would be to revisit and resample with a higher-powered study before the investigative avenue is abandoned. Borenstein and Cohen (1988) provided a program for calculating power and determining requisite sample size for increasing power.

If the observed effect size is large and the sample size is sufficient to detect it, then confidence in nonsignificant results (based on alpha level) may well be justified. If the observed effect size is small and/or the sample size is insufficient to detect such a value, then investigation

should be continued. If both power and observed effect size are calculated, the reader can make an informed decision about the population, and the investigator will know what limits to place on interpretations and recommendations.

Any statistical test procedure involves considerable subjectivity that usually is ignored by conventional methods of amphibian data analysis. Consideration and reporting of the values of observed power, observed effect size, and alpha level, as well as sample size, should lessen the tendency to accept the result of a statistical test of a hypothesis as a definitive research conclusion. The subjectivity inherent in statistical inferential procedures demands that the investigator consider whether the biological story that the statistics tell makes sense. Gilbert (1989) emphasized that the size of the biological effect must be worth bothering about or the story worth pursuing. A probability level indicating hypothesis rejection cannot provide that information. A statistical test answers the question asked; it is up to the investigator to be sure that this question bears a relationship to biological reality.

Statistical versus Substantive Significance

Strictly speaking, classical statistical inference provides valid answers in the context of long-term outcomes only, but individuals investigating amphibian biodiversity often need an answer as soon as the monitoring is complete. For example, when the findings, with 95% confidence, are that one habitat harbors significantly fewer species than another, statistical inference allows the researcher to say only that if the same habitats were randomly sampled over and over, in only 5 times out of 100, on the average, would differences as large or larger than those actually observed occur purely as a result of chance. Unfortunately, there is no way of knowing whether or not a particular set of results represents one of those cases.

Exclusive reliance on tests of significance without incorporation of other forms of inference (e.g., confidence interval estimation) obscures the relationship between the observations themselves and the magnitude of the effects to be examined. Null hypotheses of no difference are usually known to be false before the data are collected (see e.g., Savage 1957). No amphibian worker could actually believe in the possibility of a *sharp null hypothesis*—that is, that two means are absolutely equal. In field biology, systems are too noisy to allow for such absolute equality. Even though biologists know this intuitively, they still treat the test of such a null hypothesis as if it expressed a realistic and meaningful difference (zero), and many books present the null test as the only choice (see e.g., Siegel 1989).

A statistical test reflects only the size of the sample and the power of the test, not the biological question raised by the hypothesis. The existence of a specific effect must be demonstrated across settings or times to be biologically significant; it must be large enough to matter and therefore must be examined with a test powerful enough for detection. Mere graphical procedures often can show the proposed relationships to be less than meaningful. It is interesting that most people would accept that about 5 (the 0.05 level) of 100 coin-tossing experiments would show that the proportion of heads is significantly different from 0.50. Turn this situation into a test of the existence of an interesting ecological effect, and most would interpret those few of the 100 tested showing significance as affirmation of the original hypothesis and publication. Among the alternative hypotheses in any study is that of having discovered an improbable random event

through sheer diligence—that is, if you look hard enough for a difference, you will find it.

Consider the problem when four articles on the same frog species indicate a relationship between certain microhabitat conditions and frog abundance, and two articles report no relationship. How can the results be evaluated? This is an example of a situation in which statistical and biological significance must be distinguished. The statistical test questions whether the variability in the sample indicates that one can place confidence in the result. That is not the primary interest of the amphibian biologists conducting inventory or monitoring projects. Rather, they wish to know whether the relationship shown is of biological importance because of its size and its intrinsic nature. Investigators who use statistical tests must keep in mind that the test itself merely asks if the relationship is large enough to require explanation (because it is not chance fluctuation).

Simple tests of significance should be de-emphasized in favor of examination of the magnitudes of effects in all tests of hypotheses. Doing so would help eliminate noncomparability of results. The size of an effect can be measured as a function of the difference between means or the proportion of variance explained, or it can be measured by, for example, a biserial correlation (Cohen 1977; Lipsey 1990). For interpretation of the results, investigators should always publish the sample size, significance level, and power (see, e.g., Cohen 1977) of the specific statistical test used (and the observed probability level, if desired), and the size of the effect encountered in the variable studied. The types 1 and 2 error rates and calculated measures will serve as a basis for comparison of study outcomes across samples of different sizes.

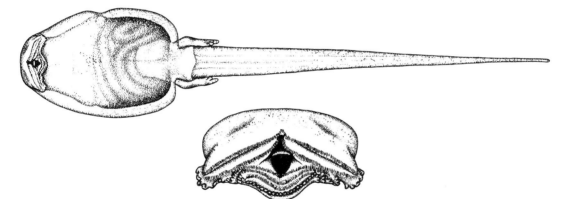

## Chapter 5

Keys to a Successful Project: Associated Data and Planning

Introduction

Once the research question, target species, and general regions for investigation have been determined, details relating to site selection, logistics, and sampling protocols must be refined. As part of this process, it is important to consider factors that are related to the inventory or monitoring study, but are not a primary focus of it, about which data should be taken. In this chapter, we review types of associated data that we believe merit special attention.

Because amphibian activity and reproductive biology are so closely tied to local weather patterns, we recommend that several kinds of weather data be collected, and we suggest appropriate instruments that can be used to obtain them.

We discuss the importance of well-documented collections and recommend minimum standards for associated data. We also provide guidelines for describing habitats, localities, and sampling sites and for recording observations during the fieldwork. We advocate the recording of microhabitat data for all specimens encountered and present lists of sample descriptors that may be used. Finally, we discuss the importance of voucher specimens to inventory projects and make recommendations concerning their identification and deposition.

Attention to these several points before beginning a project should facilitate the work, provide a better-documented and hence more complete sample, and increase the overall quality of the study. Because inventory and monitoring projects demand major commitments of time and personnel and frequently are significant logistical undertakings, well-conceived projects and amply prepared staff are keys to success. We encourage investigators contemplating a monitoring or inventory project to contact local residents near potential study sites. Such contact is particularly important on private land where access to ponds and streams used by amphibians often is possible only with the help of landowners. In addition, because amphibians are obvious components of wetlands and similar aquatic environments, they often are known to local residents. Persons living in the area can be extremely knowledgeable about the biota and can contribute immensely to a project. Likewise, local scientists and other persons may be familiar with the organisms and areas to be inventoried and can provide scientific expertise and guidance. Contacts made before beginning an inventory or monitoring study can be beneficial to the project and in certain instances may be essential to its success. Collaboration on inventory projects can result in rewarding friendships and better science.

Climate and environment

MARTHA L. CRUMP

Weather data are especially critical for interpretation of results in amphibian studies because amphibians are so dependent on moisture. Although different species have different ranges of tolerance, all amphibians exchange gases and lose water through the skin and are, therefore, vulnerable to drying conditions. Temperature, precipitation, and other climatic factors influence the geographic and ecological distributions of amphibians and the timing and intensity of feeding, reproduction, and migration. Climatic conditions also affect population densities and assemblage-wide interactions.

Another rationale for collecting weather data concerns the apparent decline of amphibian populations around the world, even in remote and protected areas (Barinaga 1990; Blaustein and Wake 1990). Possible explanations for the declines include air and water pollution, acidified precipitation, habitat destruction or modification, introduced predators, and changes in global climatic conditions, such as increased temperature and decreased rainfall. Thus, it is critical to document environmental conditions with the hope that the factors responsible for amphibian declines can be identified.

The following example underscores the importance of factoring weather conditions into a study of biological diversity. Imagine that the goal of a study is to compare amphibian species richness between two seasons (2 weeks in the warmer, wetter season and 2 weeks in the cooler, drier season) within 2 types of forest in a region. Ten persons spend 1 week in forest A and a second week in forest B. Heavy thunderstorms occur every day during the first sampling week of the wet season, but no rain falls during the second week. During the dry-season surveys, week 1 is warm whereas week 2 is approximately $10°$ C cooler than week 1. In the wet-season inventories, 18 species are recorded in forest A, and 5 species in forest B. During the dry season, 13 species are found in forest A, and 2 in forest B. Based on the number of species found, the investigator concludes that the amphibian assemblage in forest A is considerably larger than the assemblage in forest B during both seasons. Actually, they may be equal, or the assemblage in B may be larger. The data may not reflect the true species richness, because of uncontrolled weather variables. Most amphibians are more active during wet periods than during dry periods, and they are more active during warm periods than during cold periods. If the weather data are not recorded, the amphibian data obtained cannot be properly evaluated.

The effect of weather can be minimized in several ways, depending on time and personnel constraints. In the above example, a better design would have been to have 5 persons work in forest A at the same time that 5 persons surveyed forest B. If personnel were limited (e.g., a field crew of 3 persons), one option would be to carry out half-day inventories using all personnel, thus surveying both sites each day (alternating sampling times for each site) for 2 weeks. If the sites were too far apart to reach within one day and still have time to survey both areas, inventories in the two sites could be done on alternate days. (This design does not solve the problem entirely, but alternating days would be preferable to surveying for 7 days at one site followed by 7 days at the other.) If time were not a constraint (i.e., if the survey could be done over several months each season), investigators might do many replicate inventories in the two sites; the increased samples should minimize effects caused by differences in weather.

Basic Weather Data

In order to interpret inventory or monitoring data, baseline weather data are needed not only during the survey but also for some time prior to the survey. Whenever possible, weather data should be collected for several weeks preceding the survey because these data often provide insights for the interpretation of the inventory or monitoring results.

Maximum and minimum temperatures and precipitation are essential data for every inventory or monitoring project and should be recorded continuously or daily at the same time at each site. If a standard weather station is located near the study site (often available at airports or universities), it can provide information on general weather patterns and long-term climatic data. Often, however, the only way to obtain such information is to gather the data oneself.

TEMPERATURE

Temperature is critical to measure because it significantly influences amphibian development and growth, and it often controls reproductive cycles and behavior (particularly for temperate zone species). Temperature changes can affect predation, parasitism, and an amphibian's susceptibility to disease. Cooling or warming trends can initiate migrations and thus influence distribution and activity patterns. Changes in water temperature can affect oxygen concentration and primary production essential to larval stages, thus influencing growth, development, and survivorship. Depending on the goals of the study, any or all of the following temperatures may be relevant: animal body, air, water, soil, leaf litter, or substrate.

For a general inventory, one should record the maximum and minimum temperatures continuously or at regular times each day. Often, recording temperature at the beginning and end of a sampling period will provide information useful in evaluating amphibian activity. If time permits, additional information can be gained if air and substrate temperatures are recorded for each animal encountered during the inventory. However, if recording temperatures for each animal decreases the habitat area sampled, the data may not be worth the effort. Before any temperature data are recorded, the investigator must consider the exact questions to be answered, the statistical analyses to be done, and the cost-benefit ratio of recording various types of weather data.

Instruments for measuring temperature range from standard mercury thermometers to elaborate recording devices. Hand-held thermocouples are often preferable to standard thermometers for measuring air temperature because thermocouples are more durable. Maximum-minimum thermometers provide the high and low temperature for any time interval (usually 24 hr is used). Thermometers can be placed at any height above the ground and thus can yield information relevant to terrestrial or arboreal amphibians. Two meters above ground is a standard reference height for meteorological stations. Thermometers also can be attached to a stake underwater to record high and low water temperatures at any desired depth. Accurate temperatures for microhabitats such as soil and leaf litter can be obtained with resistance thermometers or with thermistors and microprobes buried in the substrate. Continuous recordings of temperature can be made with recording thermographs or with sensors interfaced to data loggers (see "Automated Data Acquisition," below).

PRECIPITATION

Precipitation, likewise, strongly influences amphibian activity, distribution and dispersion patterns, reproductive cycles, and rates of growth and development. Many species remain underground or in aboveground retreats except during wet periods. Therefore, the best time to survey an area is often during the wet season or following rain. Because the seasonal distribution of rainfall is more relevant than average annual precipitation, daily precipitation should be recorded.

The simplest way to measure rainfall is with a rain gauge. If the data desired are measures of the actual amounts of precipitation, the gauge should be set in an open area. On the other hand, if one wishes to know how much water falls through the canopy onto the forest floor or into a forest pond, the rain gauge should be installed so that through-fall precipitation is measured. Gauges range from simple plastic devices that must be manually emptied, to automatic electronic rain gauges that measure rainfall, forward the information to a remote recorder, and then empty themselves. Automatic gauges can accumulate the total amount of rainfall over any specified period of time and have the obvious advantage of never needing to be checked or emptied.

Additional Environmental Data

Depending on the goals of the study and on available resources and personnel, specific microhabitat data for each animal encountered may be desirable. Following are some relevant factors that are known to influence distribution and activity of amphibians.

RELATIVE HUMIDITY

The combination of temperature and humidity determines the rate of water loss from an amphibian's surface. For this reason, the amount of moisture in the air strongly affects distribution and activity patterns. The simplest method of obtaining humidity measurements in the field is with a sling psychrometer or battery-operated hand-held thermohygrometer (the latter is convenient because it provides a digital readout of both temperature and humidity). Air temperatures should always be recorded in conjunction with measurements of relative humidity. A hygrothermograph continuously records both temperature and humidity.

SUBSTRATE MOISTURE

Moisture levels of substrates such as soil, leaves, and leaf litter likewise can affect distribution and activity patterns. Soil moisture measurements can be taken with a tensiometer, and leaf wetness sensors are available that give both temperature and wetness readings for leaf surfaces. For continuous readings, moisture sensors can be interfaced to data loggers.

BAROMETRIC PRESSURE

The environmental factors that trigger calling behavior of male anurans and that stimulate changes in hormone levels preparatory for breeding activity are not clearly understood. Moisture and temperature are important, and they doubtlessly have synergistic effects. Another factor that may be important is change in barometric pressure. Whenever field conditions permit, barometric pressures should be recorded and analyzed in conjunction with patterns of amphibian activity. Barometric pressure can be measured with hand-held barometers or with automatic recording devices (see "Automated Data Acquisition," below).

WIND SPEED AND DIRECTION

Because amphibians are sensitive to water loss, they are strongly influenced by wind currents. Wind speed can be determined easily by hand-held anemometers. If data are recorded at the site of observation for each amphibian found, correlations between wind speed and occurrence of individuals and their activity patterns can be determined. If general trends are desired, daily mean wind velocity and direction can be obtained from a standard weather station if one is located nearby.

WATER LEVEL OF THE BREEDING SITE

For amphibians that oviposit in water, the amount of water present in the breeding site may determine distribution and activity patterns. Whether the study is a one-time inventory or a long-term monitoring program, water depth of the breeding site should be measured. In an inventory, perhaps the only points of interest are maximum and minimum depths. On the other hand, in a monitoring study, changing profiles of water depth in the lake, pond, or stream may be useful. The number of points at which water depth should be measured depends upon the size of the habitat. In a puddle, 5 points may be sufficient; in a large lake 50 or more points may be useful. In a monitoring study, water depth should be measured at these same points each time the habitat is sampled or read from previously located depth markers. Water depths are easy to obtain with a collapsible meter stick. For continuous readings, mechanical recorders are available, or sensors can be connected to data loggers.

pH

Because excessive acidification of water has detrimental effects on amphibian growth, development, and survivorship (Pierce 1985) and has been suggested as a cause of amphibian declines, I encourage investigators doing inventories and long-term monitoring around the world to document pH conditions at their study sites. Relevant sites to measure range from water-filled bromeliad tanks and tree cavities (developmental sites for arboreal tadpoles), and water-filled roadside ditches and shallow ponds, to larger bodies of water such as lakes and streams; measuring the pH of rainwater is also encouraged. Most experts agree that pH indicator paper gives unreliable and misleading results that often are worse than no data at all. Many types of portable pH meters appropriate for field use are available.

Measuring Weather Variables

Whenever possible, weather and microhabitat data should be collected automatically with recording instruments; such instruments increase accuracy of the data collected and provide daily or weekly records of changes. A record of the overall variation in an environmental factor is preferable to individual measurements taken at predetermined times. Another advantage is that recording instruments reduce the field time required to collect the data. If recording equipment cannot be used, manual instruments can be employed successfully, given sufficient time and personnel.

Data should always be recorded in the field with actual numbers rather than codes. The reasons for this are many and include minimization of confusion when multiple persons are involved in data collection, difficulty of remembering the codes used, and ease of making mistakes under adverse field conditions.

Digital recorders (data acquisition systems and data loggers) are generally more accurate and reliable than are mechanical, battery-powered, or electrical recording devices (see "Automated Data Acquisition," below). A drawback to use of data acquisition systems in the field is that typically they must interface directly with a computer. In contrast, field data loggers can operate in a stand-alone mode because they typically have internal memories; data loggers can collect the data as integrated, averaged, or point values over logging periods ranging from 1 minute to 24 hours. Data stored in the memory can then be transferred to a compatible computer or printer. In recent years, rapid advances have been made in the development of portable data acquisition systems and data loggers suitable for use in the field, with new models continually being introduced (Pearcy 1989). Investigators should consult with manufacturers (see Appendix 6) prior to purchase regarding suitability of a particular digital recorder for use in connection with environmental monitoring systems.

Weather recording equipment will not be an option for all field studies because of cost (recording equipment, especially an automated device, is expensive), security considerations (in many instances the risk of theft precludes the use of expensive instruments), and risk of equipment failure (a serious consideration if the study site is a long way from the nearest repair shop). Backup, manually operated instruments should always be available in case recording devices fail or are stolen during a study.

The following are merely examples of the sorts of instruments available from scientific suppliers. Anyone seriously contemplating purchase of equipment is advised to search through catalogues for the prices and specifications best suited to the study (see Appendix 6). The estimated prices (all in U.S. dollars = U.S.$) indicated below are from scientific equipment catalogues for 1991, from companies in the United States.

The most efficient field method of obtaining baseline weather data is to set up a portable weather station at each survey site. Machines that measure maximum-minimum temperature, precipitation, relative humidity, barometric pressure, wind speed, and wind direction can be purchased for U.S. $1,000–$1,300. These units run on size D batteries and thus are convenient for field use. More-restrictive recording units include spring-wound, 7-day recording thermometers (U.S. $220–$250), automatic electronic rain gauges (U.S. $70–$100), spring-wound and battery-run hygrothermographs for 1-, 7-, 31-, or 62-day continuous recording (U.S. $550–$1,500), electric-powered anemometers for continuous 30-day recording of wind velocity (U.S. $600), and 7-day electric-powered barometers for continuous recording of data (U.S. $310–$350). Data acquisition systems cost about U.S. $500 or more, and data loggers about U.S. $1,300 or more.

Numerous nonrecording instruments are available: maximum-minimum thermometers (U.S. $25–$40); digital thermocouple thermometers (U.S. $150–$200); standard rain gauges (U.S. $7–$25); sling psychrometers (U.S. $30–$65); battery-operated, hand-held thermohygrometers (U.S. $100–$400); anemometers (U.S. $12 for hand-held portable wind meters); tensiometers (U.S. $50–$250); soil moisture and leaf wetness sensors (U.S. $40–$80); barometers (U.S. $25 to $250 or more); and battery-powered pH meters (U.S. $200–$300).

Acknowledgments. I thank Maureen Donnelly, Frank Hensley, Ron Heyer, and Roy McDiarmid for helpful comments on the manuscript and Steven Oberbauer for information concerning weather instruments.

Automated data acquisition

CHARLES R. PETERSON AND MICHAEL E. DORCAS

In this section we describe methods for automatically measuring variation in the physical environment and in the behavior, particularly calling, of amphibians. Data quantifying the relationship between environmental variation and amphibian activity can be used as a basis for optimizing sampling procedures for inventory and monitoring programs and for interpreting population changes (Peterson and Dorcas 1992).

We have restricted the scope of this section to continuous, automated measurements rather than single, manual measurements. Because many factors vary through time, it is important to sample regularly over hours, days, and even seasons. For example, the pH of pond water may vary by more than one unit during the course of a day (James T. Brock, pers. comm.) and may change dramatically at certain times of the year (e.g., following the spring snowmelt; Pierce 1985). Automated sampling systems make it possible to measure a wide variety of variables continuously, accurately, and easily at one or more sites.

Data loggers, environmental sensors, automated recording of anuran calls, and automated radiotelemetry are discussed in this section. Most of the information concerning data loggers and environmental sensors was obtained from Pearcy et al. (1989), Campbell (1990), and Tanner (1990). We include the names of various manufacturers, especially for the equipment and materials that we use (Appendix 6). However, our experience with different brands is limited, and the listing of a particular vendor does not indicate our endorsement. Furthermore, technical aspects of instrumentation are advancing rapidly, and many of our specific comments will soon be out of date.

Data Loggers

Within the past 10 years, the task of gathering continuous data has been greatly facilitated by the development of microprocessor-based data loggers that receive, process, and store data from environmental sensors. They can be programmed to record the variables at stipulated time intervals for periods of varying duration.

Important characteristics of field data loggers include portability, battery power, programmability, and the ability to read input from several types of sensors at user-selected intervals (Campbell 1990). Data loggers have numerous advantages over devices such as mechanical recorders and strip chart recorders, including a wider range of operating temperatures, increased sensor compatibility, higher accuracy, greater data storage capacity, and easy transfer of data to computers (Pearcy et al. 1989).

Factors to consider when selecting a data logger include cost, reliability, the range of operating conditions (temperature and humidity), accuracy, resolution, number of channels, sensor compatibility, processing power, data storage and retrieval options, and power requirements (Tanner 1990). Costs range from approximately U.S. $500 to more than U.S. $5,000. Small, inexpensive, single-channel data loggers have recently been introduced (Hobo-Temp or Hobo-RH, Onset Computer Corp.). Although these data loggers are dedicated to a single sensor and have a limited storage capacity (1,800 values), they should be adequate for many studies. The ability to record data from several temperature sensors and to control a device such as a tape recorder automatically can be achieved now, even with relatively low-cost systems. Powerful, versatile systems, capable of reading most sensors and recording the data, are available for less than U.S. $1,700 (including the interface and software for downloading data). Features to look for in this price range include 12-bit or greater resolution, the ability to measure microvolts (e.g., thermocouples), switch or pulse counting capability (for cup anemometers and tipping-bucket rain gauges), the ability to provide excitation voltages (for thermistors and electrical resistance humidity sensors), and digital outputs for controlling devices such as tape recorders, radiotelemetry systems, and fans in ventilated psychrometers. A more expensive data logger, capable of resolving nanovolts, is required for measurements of some variables (e.g., soil water potentials using thermocouple psychrometers).

If funds are not available for purchase of a data logger, it may be possible to borrow one or simply to add sensors to one already in use at or near the study site. As costs decline, data loggers are becoming more common, and many universities, field stations, government agencies, parks, and other institutions make such equipment available to scientists.

For many users, learning to program data loggers is difficult. Becoming comfortable with the more powerful systems may take several days. To minimize learning time, we recommend working with someone already familiar with the equipment. Some manufacturers offer training sessions. Initially, modifying an existing program to suit a given situation may be easier than writing a new one. We have included sample programs for a Campbell Scientific CR10 data logger that direct it to record temperature, radiation, wind speed, and humidity and to operate a tape recorder to record frog calls (Tables 2 and 3). Data loggers need to be enclosed to protect them from weather conditions and vandals. Some manufacturers offer enclosures. A less expensive alternative is a small ice chest or cooler. For electrical equipment, we have also used metal boxes, which can be obtained locally from an electrical supply house. In areas exposed to direct sunlight, it may be necessary to paint the enclosure white or to shade it to prevent overheating. The use of a desiccant (e.g., silica gel) may be required in humid environments to keep conditions in the

Table 2. Sample Computer Program for Operating an Automated Weather Station with a Campbell Scientific CR10 Data Logger[a]

01: 1		Execution Interval (in seconds)
01: P11		Temp 107 Probe
	01: 1	Rep
	02: 1	IN Chan
	03: 3	Excite all reps w/EX Chan 3
	04: 28	Loc :
	05: 1	Mult
	06: 0.0000	Offset
02: P10		Battery Voltage
	01: 27	Loc :
03: P13		Thermocouple Temp (SE)
	01: 6	Reps
	02: 1	2.5 mV slow range
	03: 2	IN Chan
	04: 1	Type T (Copper-Constantan)
	05: 28	Ref Temp Loc
	06: 1	Loc :
	07: 1	Mult
	08: 0.0000	Offset
04: P2		Volt (DIFF)
	01: 1	Rep
	02: 3	2.5 mV slow range
	03: 5	IN Chan
	04: 7	Loc :
	05: 100	Mult
	06: 0	Offset
05: P3		Pulse
	01: 1	Rep
	02: 1	Pulse Input Chan
	03: 2	Switch closure
	04: 8	Loc :
	05: 0.6521	Mult
	06: 0.2303	Offset
06: P11		Temp 107 Probe
	01: 1	Rep
	02: 11	IN Chan
	03: 1	Excite all reps w/Exchan 1
	04: 26	Loc :
	05: 1	Mult
	06: 0.0000	Offset

Table 2. (*Continued*)

07:	P12	RH 207 Probe
	01: 1	Rep
	02: 12	IN Chan
	03: 1	Excite all reps w/Exchan 1
	04: 26	Temperature Loc
	05: 9	Loc :
	06: 1	Mult
	07:0.0000	Offset
08:	P92	If time is
	01: 0000	minutes into a
	02: 5	minute interval
	03: 10	Set high Flag 0 (output)
09:	P77	Real Time
	01: 0110	Day,Hour-Minute
10:	P71	Average
	01: 9	Reps
	02: 1	Loc:

[a] The execution interval of the data logger is set to 1 second. The first P11 command measures the temperature of the panel thermistor, which is then used as a reference temperature for thermocouple measurements. The next command (P10) reads the voltage of the battery used to power the data logger. This measurement is not output to final memory but is used to examine battery voltage in the field. The P13 command is used to make six single-ended readings of copper-constantan thermocouples (e.g., soil, water, and air temperatures). The P2 command reads the voltage of a pyranometer. A multiplier of 100 and an offset of 0 convert the measurements to watts/m^2. The P3 command reads the pulses of a cup anemometer. A multiplier of 0.6521 and an offset of 0.2303 convert the measurements to m/sec. The multiplier and offset used with cup anemometers vary with the execution intervals used. In general, the multiplier and offset values are used to convert the output from specific sensors into engineering units and often vary among individual instruments. The second P11 command reads the temperature of the thermistor in a relative humidity probe. This temperature is then used as a reference for the P12 command, which measures the relative humidity. The P92 command sets the output interval to 5 minutes. The P77 command outputs the Julian day, hour, and minute. The P71 command averages the measurements of all sensors and outputs that average to final memory. See the Campbell Scientific (1990) CR10 manual for detailed explanations of commands.

Table 3. Computer Program for Turning a Cassette Tape Recorder On and Off with a Campbell Scientific CR10 Data Logger[a]

	01: 1	Execution Interval (in seconds)
01:	P92	If time is
	01: 0000	minutes into a
	02: 5	minute interval
	03: 30	Then Do
02:	P20	Set Port(s)
	01: 0000	C8,C7,C6,C5 options
	02: 0001	C4..C1=low/low/low/high
03:	P22	Excitation with Delay
	01: 1	EX Chan
	02: 0000	Delay w/EX (units = 0.01 sec)
	03: 1000	Delay after EX (units = 0.01 sec)
	04: 0.0000	mV Excitation
04:	P20	Set Port(s)
	01: 0000	C8,C7,C6,C5 options
	02: 0000	C4..C1=low/low/low/low
05:	P95	End

[a] This program instructs the data logger to turn the tape recorder on for 10 seconds every 5 minutes. The execution interval is 1 second. The program begins with a P92 command, which sets the 5-minute recording interval. The first P20 command sets the control port at high, providing the 5-volt signal required to toggle the relay switch and turn the tape recorder on. The P22 command usually is used to control the excitation ports of the data logger. In this case, zero voltage is specified, and the command is used only to provide a 10-second delay until the port is set low with another P20 command, which turns the tape recorder off. The End command (P95) terminates the program.

enclosure within the operating range of the data logger. Sometimes, we have buried enclosures to hide them from vandals. Burial also reduces the range of temperatures to which the data logger is exposed.

Environmental Sensors

The following sections describe sensors that are most often used in conjunction with data loggers to measure important environmental variables. It also is possible to use a data logger to measure the signals from manual, stand-alone instruments with millivolt outputs that normally would go to strip chart recorders. Sensors usually are mounted on an instrument tripod, which can be purchased from a supplier or constructed. Data loggers receive input from sensors, which can be plotted against time (e.g., Fig. 2). We do not have firsthand experience with using sensors for some variables (e.g., ultraviolet radiation) and have had to rely on the literature or advice from engineers or other scientists to prepare some of the following material. Publications by Flowers (1978), Fritschen and Gay (1979), World Meteorological Organization (1983), Marshall and Woodward (1985), Finklestein et al. (1986), Bingham and Long (1988), Pearcy et al. (1989), Skaar et al. (1989), Campbell (1990), and Tanner (1990) provide additional information on instrumentation. Information on manufacturers and suppliers of sensors can be found in Appendix 6.

TEMPERATURE

Thermocouples are the preferred sensors for use in most field studies requiring automated temperature measurements. They are relatively accurate and inexpensive, come in a wide range of sizes, respond quickly, and can be used over long distances without a change in the signal (Pearcy et al. 1989). For temperature measurements in the range of biological interest (–70° to 100°C), Type T (copper-constantan) thermocouples are most appropriate. This combination of metals produces a relatively large voltage that changes linearly with temperature (approximately 40 μv/°C) within the range of interest. Thermocouples made from 24-gauge (0.5-mm diameter) wire are commonly used for measuring water, soil, and air temperatures. Thermocouple wire is relatively inexpensive (< U.S. $1 per m) depending on type, size, and quality. Thermocouples can be purchased or easily made

by stripping the ends of the wire and then twisting the exposed ends together and soldering them; the other wire ends are installed in the wiring panel of the data logger (Pearcy et al. 1989). The actual site of temperature measurement lies at the first junction of the twisted wires (i.e., the thermocouple). Thermocouples usually do not have to be calibrated individually. Potential problems with thermocouples include heat conduction via the thermocouple wire and inaccurate measurements of the reference temperature (usually taken where the thermocouple wire attaches to the data logger).

Thermistors (temperature sensitive resistors) are another device commonly used for measuring temperature. Advantages include high sensitivity, accuracy, and fast response time. However, thermistors are more expensive and less rugged, cannot be used easily over long distances, and require individual calibration. Some data loggers can read both thermocouples and thermistors easily, whereas other data loggers may be unable to read, or have difficulty reading, one or the other sensor accurately.

We usually measure air temperatures at animal height (e.g., 1 cm) and at 2 m (a standard reference height for meteorological stations), water temperatures on the bottom and 1 cm below the surface, and soil temperatures from at least two depths (e.g., 1 and 20 cm), if we are interested in burrow temperatures. Thermocouples used to measure air temperatures should be shaded unless they are small and highly reflective (e.g., painted white).

HUMIDITY

Electrical resistance humidity sensors (e.g., Physical Chemical Scientific Corporation) or capacitance humidity sensors (e.g., Vaisalia) provide a convenient way of measuring atmospheric water vapor automatically (Tanner 1990). Costs range from U.S. $200 to $800. Some of these sensors require an AC excitation voltage from the data logger. Some electrical

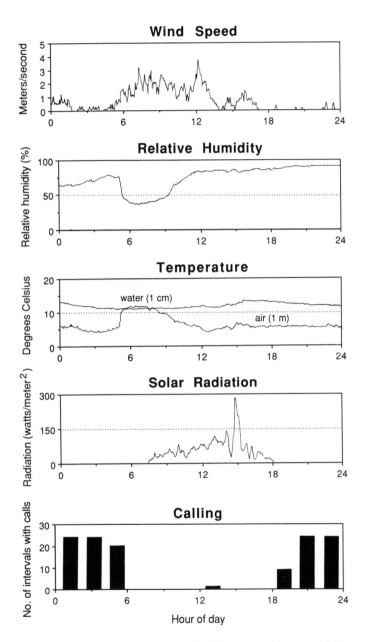

Figure 2. Measurements of the calling activity of southwestern toads (*Bufo microscaphus*), solar radiation, water and air temperatures, relative humidity, and wind speed at Lytle Ranch in southwestern Utah, 18 March 1991. Calling was recorded for 10 seconds every 5 minutes using a cassette tape recorder controlled by a Campbell Scientific CR10 data logger. The same data logger was used to sample environmental variables at 1-second intervals and to provide average values every 5 minutes.

humidity sensors may be damaged by condensation or air contaminants (Campbell 1990). Sensor elements need to be calibrated individually at least annually and may need to be replaced periodically. Skaar et al. (1989) compared commercial hygrometers. Ventilated wet-bulb, dry-bulb psychrometers are more accurate than electrical resistance humidity sensors but usually are more expensive, require power to run a fan, require attention to keep the water reservoir filled, and will not read accurately below 0° C (Tanner 1990).

PRECIPITATION

Precipitation can be measured automatically with a tipping-bucket rain gauge (e.g., Texas Electronics) connected to a pulse-counting channel on a data logger (Tanner 1990). When a specified depth of water has collected, the bucket tips and empties. The number of tips is counted with the data logger. Resolution in the range of 0.1 to 0.2 mm is possible (World Meteorological Organization 1983). To measure precipitation in the winter, tipping buckets can be heated so that snow will melt and the water will drain from the bucket. Weighing-bucket rain gauges are a more accurate, but more expensive, way to measure precipitation (Tanner 1990).

RADIATION

Solar radiation sensors (pyranometers) that are commonly used with data loggers are silicon photocells (e.g., LI-COR LI200SZ) and thermopile devices (e.g., Eppley model PSP, Kipp and Zonen model CM11). The silicon cells are considerably less expensive than the thermopile devices (about U.S. $200 vs. $1,300–$3,000). However, because their spectral response is limited to between 400 nm and 1,100 nm, silicon cells should not be placed under vegetation or used to measure reflected radiation (Tanner 1990).

Measurement of ultraviolet radiation is of particular interest to herpetologists because of pos-sible adverse effects on amphibians (especially in the 290–320 nm wavelength band known as ultraviolet B [UVB]). Ideally, an investigator would like to know the irradiance (watts/m^2) at specific wavelengths and the response of amphibians to UVB. Unfortunately, the spectral radiometer required to make these measurements is very expensive (> U.S. $60,000) and requires considerable expertise to use. Useful UVB data may be obtained from sensors with spectral responses that approximately parallel the sunburn response of human skin. These sensors are available from Solar Light Company and Yankee Environmental Systems (YES) at U.S. $3,500 and $4,000, respectively. The Solar Light sensor reads in units of minimum erythemal dose (MED), and the YES sensor reads in watts/m^2, which can be converted into MED units. These sensors can be easily connected to a data logger, but their output needs to be corrected for temperature variation. A program for reading a UVB meter with a data logger is available from Campbell Scientific. Approximately 18 stations in the United States use these sensors as part of the National Oceanic and Atmospheric Administration RB Meter UV Network (John De Luisi, pers. comm.); about 20 stations elsewhere in the world use them as well.

WIND SPEED

Wind speed can be measured automatically with a cup anemometer and the pulse-counting channel of a data logger. Cup anemometers are omnidirectional, have linear responses, and are reasonably precise (Campbell 1990). Factors to consider when selecting an anemometer include size, the range of wind speeds over which the sensor operates (especially the starting and stopping thresholds), cost, and durability. Propeller anemometers have lower thresholds and can be used to measure wind direction, but they are more expensive (Campbell 1990). We usually mount our anemometer at a height of 2 m. If more than one anemometer is available, wind profiles can be determined so that the 2-m wind speed can be used to calculate wind speeds at other heights.

pH AND CONDUCTIVITY

Continuous monitoring of pH with a data logger presents a variety of problems, including matching the input impedance from the pH electrode to the data logger, isolation of the electrode from the data logger to prevent ground loops, temperature compensation of the sensor output, and maintenance of the pH electrode in operating condition. An example of an equipment configuration (Omega Engineering) for measuring pH includes a submersible, industrial-grade, flat-sensing-surface pH probe (U.S. $95), a two-wire pH transmitter (U.S. $225), a 24-volt battery (or two 12-volt batteries wired in series), and a loop-powered isolator (U.S. $125). Alternatively, a pH probe can be read with a pH 220 Probe Amplifier (Campbell Scientific). The data logger can be used to measure sensor temperature and make the temperature compensation calculation. Electrodes need to be checked, cleaned, and recalibrated regularly to ensure proper operation. Freezing will damage electrodes. For short-term monitoring of pH (several days or less), we are experimenting with feeding the analog output of a manual pH meter to a data logger.

Water conductivity can be measured automatically with a similar system but with a conductivity sensor (U.S. $130) and conductivity transmitter (U.S. $230). If the conductivity transmitter does not have an isolator, one should be added. Conductivity sensors also need to be cleaned periodically.

Thermal Environment

Temperature is one of the most important factors influencing the activity of amphibians (especially in the temperate zone) and, thus, our ability to determine their presence and abundance (Peterson and Dorcas 1992). For this reason, it is important to describe accurately the thermal environments of amphibians. The thermal environment of submerged, aquatic amphibians (e.g., larval salamanders) can be characterized relatively easily by measuring the temperature of the surrounding water. Describing the thermal environments of terrestrial amphibians is more complex because a variety of factors interact to determine body temperatures. These factors include air temperature, substrate temperature, radiation, humidity, soil moisture, wind speed, and animal properties such as size, shape, reflectivity, and permeability of the skin to water (Tracy 1976).

A single-number representation of the thermal environment that incorporates these factors is the operative temperature (Bakken and Gates 1975; Bakken 1992). Operative temperatures can be calculated using computer models of heat transfer, but this approach may be difficult to apply at small spatial scales and requires considerable instrumentation and expertise. A simpler and less expensive approach for measuring operative temperatures involves the use of physical models that incorporate animal properties such as size, shape, and reflectivity (Bakken and Gates 1975). This approach has been applied with considerable success to dry-skinned ectothermic vertebrates, that is, reptiles (Crawford et al. 1983; Peterson 1987; Grant and Dunham 1988). It is more difficult to make models of most amphibians, because the models must be kept wet to incorporate the effect of evaporation. Consequently, most amphibian models have been used for short periods. Although the use of physical models has proven valuable in studies of temperature and water relationships of amphibians, the usefulness of such studies to inventory and monitoring studies remains to be demonstrated. Numerous articles provide information on the construction and use of different model types: agar (Spotila and Berman 1976; Wygoda 1984); plaster of Paris (Tracy 1976;

O'Connor 1989; Wygoda and Williams 1991); metal casts (Bakken and Gates 1975; Bradford 1984); copper tubing (C. R. Peterson and M. E. Dorcas, unpubl. data). All models require further validation through comparison of the temperatures they record with those of live amphibians.

Recording Frog Calls

The automated recording of anuran vocalizations is a relatively simple but effective way not only to determine the presence or absence of anuran species, but also to establish their temporal calling patterns (see "Acoustic Monitoring at Fixed Sites," in Chapter 7). Automated sampling has several advantages when compared with manual sampling procedures: (1) It allows continuous 24-hour sampling; (2) it can be used to monitor several sites simultaneously; and (3) it

frees the investigator for other tasks. We describe two types of systems that can be used to record anuran vocalizations automatically. The first type is data logger-based and allows the simultaneous measurement of environmental variables. The second type is timer-based and less expensive, but it cannot be used to monitor environmental variables.

Data logger-based systems periodically activate a tape recorder via a relay switch. For example, the control port on a Campbell Scientific CR10 data logger (Fig. 3) can be used to send a 5-volt impulse to a relay switch at regular intervals (e.g., 5 min). The relay switch turns the battery power to the tape recorder on and off. The relay switch design is described in the CR10 instruction manual (Campbell Scientific 1990: sect. 14.9; Fig. 3). Cost of construction is approximately U.S. $20. A comparable relay can

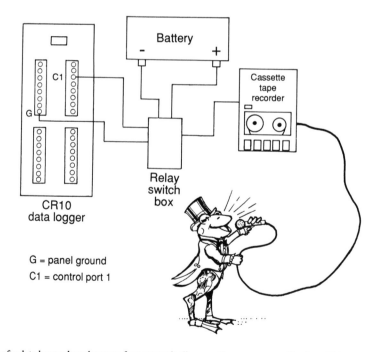

Figure 3. Diagram of a data logger-based system for automatically recording anuran vocalizations. This system consists of a Campbell Scientific CR10 data logger, a cassette tape recorder, a microphone, a relay switch box, and a battery. The data logger is programmed (Table 3) to turn the cassette tape player on and off (via the relay switch box) at designated intervals (e.g., 5 min). The data logger also can be programmed (Table 2) for simultaneous monitoring of various environmental sensors, such as thermocouples, pyranometers, anemometers, and relative humidity probes.

be purchased (e.g., Hexfet relay #44F7743, Newark Electronics, U.S. $38) and modified slightly by inserting a 1N4001 diode (#610, Campbell Scientific) into the circuit. When analyzing the tape recordings, the starting and ending times and the number of recorded intervals must be noted, so that the times of calling activity can be determined accurately.

Data logger-based systems have several advantages, including (1) accurate, precisely timed intervals; (2) capability to monitor environmental variables or to control an automated telemetry system (see "Recording Radiotelemetry Signals," below); and (3) efficient use of tape. For example, if anurans are calling only at night, the data logger can be programmed to record only at night, thus conserving both cassette tape and battery power. Disadvantages include the cost of the data logger (about U.S. $1,700) and the time involved in learning how to program it. A less expensive data logger (e.g., Tattletale Lite, Onset Computer Corp., about U.S. $500) can be used in place of a CR10, but measurement capabilities are more limited (e.g., 5 channels, thermistors only, without additional signal conditioning circuitry).

A data logger-based system was used to study the effects of environmental variation on calling activity of the southwestern toad (*Bufo microscaphus*) in southwestern Utah in March (Dorcas and Foltz 1991). Calling was sampled for 10 seconds every 5 minutes using a Tandy TRS-80, CCR-82 computer cassette tape recorder controlled by a Campbell Scientific CR10 data logger. A 2-liter plastic soda bottle, with the bottom removed, was placed over the microphone to protect it from precipitation. When tape recordings were played back, the authors were able to determine times of precipitation from the sound of the rain hitting the microphone cover. Solar radiation was measured with a LI-COR LI200SZ pyranometer; relative humidity was measured using a Campbell Scientific model 207 relative humidity probe; wind speed was measured using a Qualimetrics Micro Response Contact Anemometer; and temperatures were measured using 24-gauge copper-constantan thermocouples. All instruments were read every second, and 5-minute average values were calculated and recorded using the CR10 data logger. Results of this study (Fig. 2) indicate that sampling for southwestern toads would be most successful at night, at high humidities, and when water temperatures are 10–18°C.

An alternative system for periodically recording anuran vocalizations uses a solid state timer to control a cassette tape recorder. In this system, a timer is connected to a 12-volt battery and tape recorder (Fig. 4). Because the timer requires 12 volts and most tape recorders require only 6 volts, several inexpensive electrical parts are needed to reduce the voltage to the tape recorder and avoid damaging the timer. Figure 4 includes a circuit diagram, and part numbers are provided in the caption. All of these parts can be purchased at local electronics stores and cost less than a total of U.S. $10. The timer can be set to activate the tape recorder for a specified period (0.1–102.3 sec) at specified intervals (0.1–102.3 min). Timers with different ranges also can be purchased. The advantages of this system are low cost (U.S. $100) and simplicity. Little expertise is needed to assemble the system. Because of the low cost, several systems can be used simultaneously to monitor numerous sites. This system does not have the ability to make synchronous environmental measurements as does the data logger-based system. However, an inexpensive single-channel data logger can be used to monitor environmental temperatures.

Recording Radiotelemetry Signals

We have used automated telemetry systems to monitor the body temperatures and activity pat-

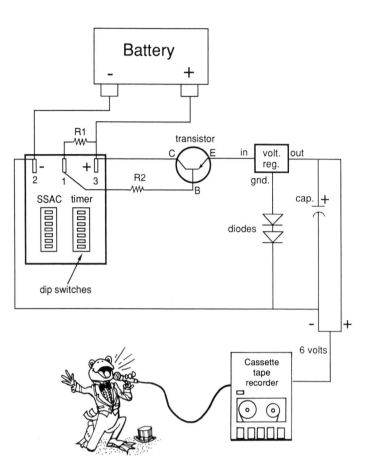

Figure 4. Diagram of a relatively inexpensive, timer-based system for automatically recording anuran vocalizations. This system consists of an SSAC timer (Radio Shack [RS] #1A12), a 6-volt cassette tape recorder, a microphone, a 12-volt battery, and several electronic parts that cost less than U.S. $10: one PNP plastic power transistor TIP42 (RS #276–29027), one 5-volt 7805 voltage regulator (RS #276–1770; *volt. reg.* in figure), two 1N4001 diodes (RS #276–1101), one 4.7 MFD electrolytic capacitor (RS #272–1012; *cap.* in figure), one 1,000-ohm resistor (RS #271–153; *R1* in figure), and one 100-ohm resistor (RS #271–152; *R2* in figure). The proper polarity must be observed when connecting the tape recorder to the external power source (many recorders have a negative center pin). In figure, *gnd.* = ground wire.

terns of snakes (Peterson 1987; Peterson and Cobb 1991), and we believe that this technique could be applied successfully to amphibians that are large enough to carry radio transmitters (see "Radio Tracking" under "Tracking," in Chapter 7). Tracking transmitters weighing less than 1.0 g and temperature-sensitive transmitters weighing less than 2.0 g are now commercially available (AVM Instrument Company; Holohil Systems). Multiple animals can be continuously sampled by interfacing a data logger with a scanner, a radio receiver, and a signal processor (Petron et al. 1987; C. R. Peterson and M. J. McDonald, unpubl. data). Such systems can be used in several ways; for example, the times of arrival and departure at a breeding site of amphibians with radio transmitters can be determined. If temperature-sensitive transmitters are used, considerable information about an ectotherm's behavior, such as emergence times, retreat times, and microhabitat selection, can often be inferred from body temperature patterns, especially if operative temperature measurements are recorded simultaneously (Peterson 1987; Huey et al. 1989). It also may be possible to use variation in signal strength to infer the activity patterns of animals (e.g., Chappell and Bartholomew 1981; Nams 1989; Stanner and Farhi 1989). Information derived from telemetry complements data from mark-recapture studies and also can aid in the location of animals without radio transmitters.

Two key problems associated with radiotelemetry are the need to replace batteries periodically and the minimum size of animals that can be studied. In the future, passive integrated transponders (PIT tags—small, glass-encapsulated diodes that, when activated by a detector, transmit a unique code back to a receiver) may offer a solution to this problem because they are small (e.g., 0.1 g) and do not require batteries (Camper and Dixon 1988). Unfortunately, transponder systems that allow identification of individual animals also have a very short range. Nevertheless, it should be possible to interface data loggers with transceiver units to monitor activity in certain situations (e.g., salamanders passing through a gate in a drift fence). This approach should become more effective as the range of these systems improves.

Acknowledgments. We thank the following persons and companies for providing information: George Bakken, Art Beaubian (YES), Dan Berger and Saul Berger (Solar Light), Andrew Blaustein, Dave Bradford, Jim Brock, Gaylon Campbell, John De Luisi, Jeff Foster, Joel Green (Campbell Scientific), Joanne Jerolman, Mark Kallgren (Solomat), Leslie Long, Dave Meek (Campbell Scientific), Michael O'Connor, Warren Porter, Bert Tanner (Campbell Scientific), and Dave Waitman. Dave Bradford lent us electroformed frog models. Scott Grothe helped with the illustrations. Jeff Foster reviewed the manuscript.

Data standards

ROY W. McDIARMID

The many individual salamanders, frogs, caecilians, and their larvae encountered during the course of an inventory or monitoring project will have to be identified to species. Depending on the goals and sampling method(s) used, some individuals will be identified from a distance by their calls; others will be handled. At the same time, some will be marked for recapture, and others will be sampled as vouchers. For each, certain minimum data should be recorded. In this section, data pertaining to locality and sampling methodology are considered; information on microhabitats and specimen vouchers is covered in sections that follow. I feel strongly that the data outlined here should be the minimum for any project. Investigators with specific goals may require additional types of data as well.

Standardized, printed sheets containing the required data categories provide a convenient, inexpensive, and effective way to ensure that all the desired information is recorded in a consistent format. Data sheets should be well organized, printed on good-quality paper (75%–100% cotton content) and include extra space (e.g., other side of sheet) for notes that do not fit preestablished categories.

Data should be recorded in the field with permanent (waterproof) ink as simply and directly as possible. I strongly recommend against the use of data codes in the field; it is too easy to forget codes or to enter the wrong code. Original data sheets can be photocopied for security, but they should not be copied by hand. If data are to be coded for computer analysis, the original or photocopied sheets should be used for data entry to minimize transcription errors. Some workers prefer recording information on small tape recorders; this also works well if a list of the standard data categories is checked during taping to ensure that all required information is recorded.

Information recorded on tapes should be transcribed to data sheets or into a computer within 24 hours of the sample.

Geographic Characterization

Specific information about the locality should include geographic and political characterizations of the study site and descriptions of the habitats sampled. The geographic and political descriptions of the locality minimally should include the following information:

1. *Country or island group.* The country name is normally equivalent to the political unit, but substituting island names for country may be of value in some instances.
2. *State or province.* A secondary political unit should be part of every locality record.
3. *County, district, or other tertiary division.* For specimens collected in the United States and certain other countries, a tertiary political unit should be included. In countries in which tertiary divisions exist but are infrequently used or rarely mapped, this category may not be useful.
4. *Drainage system and other geographic data.* Some reference to the closest river system is important, especially in remote areas for which detailed maps are not readily available. Inclusion of other geographic names may also be extremely helpful (e.g., mountain range, savannas, zoogeographic region), but the case for including them in these minimal data elements is less compelling than for drainage.
5. *Specific locality.* The locality should be as detailed and specific as possible. Distances and compass directions from easily located places (e.g., towns, mouths of rivers, mountain peaks) are essential. Whether the distances are by road or straight-line on a map should be specified. Inclusion of a map or gazetteer reference often is helpful.

6. *Latitude and longitude.* This geographic attribute is independent of political units. It is the only generally recognized locator that allows universal retrieval of data from any geographic area, and electronic mapping. Workers should include coordinates for each locality as specifically as possible. However, approximate coordinates, clearly identified as such, are also of value if specific coordinates cannot be obtained. Latitude and longitude are reported with the standard notation of degree, minute, and second, rather than with a decimal. Portable global positioning devices that provide accurate measures of latitude and longitude are available for field use (about U.S. $3,000, see Appendix 6).
7. *Elevation.* When available, elevation should be noted. Approximate elevation, clearly indicated as such, is better than none. Elevations and distances should be given in standard metric units.

Habitat

Amphibians occupy both terrestrial and freshwater aquatic habitats. Habitat descriptions should include the following information.

TERRESTRIAL HABITATS

1. Moderately detailed description of the kind(s) of vegetation (e.g., evergreen lowland tropical forest, temperate deciduous forest, thorn scrub, savanna-woodland) at each site. For forests, some mention of canopy cover, epiphyte load and type, nature of other water-holding structures (tree holes), etc. For savannah-woodland habitats, designation as natural, agricultural, or fire-maintained; indication of extent and regularity of seasonal flooding. For other terrestrial sites, some indication of plant type and cover. If plant species are known, a list of

some of the dominant forms is useful. Published references to vegetation at the site should be noted.

Descriptive lists of vegetation types exist for most regions of the world (e.g., Walter 1973) and can be used as a foundation for specific site descriptions. Representative vegetation types for tropical and subtropical forests in Southeast Asia might include the following: primary rain forest, hilly; primary rain forest, flat; evergreen oak/chestnut montane forest; mossy montane forest; coniferous forest; deciduous forest; gallery forest; selectively logged forest; rubber plantation; secondary growth; large clearing; camp.

2. Description of the climate at each site, including details of weather with distribution and abundance of rainfall and annual and diel variations in temperature.
3. Some indication of the degree of disturbance. For forests, designation as primary, secondary, or plantation may be adequate. For grasslands, some mention of the influence of grazing, agricultural use, or frequency of fire or flooding may be important. Sampling done near or through a forest edge should be indicated.
4. Brief mention of other habitat factors (e.g., soil type and water-holding capacity, frequency of flooding) potentially important to amphibians is helpful.

AQUATIC HABITATS

Details of surrounding vegetation (see item 1 under "Terrestrial Habitats," above) and climate (item 2 above), water temperature and water clarity, and information for the type of water body sampled.

LENTIC—PONDS AND LAKES
1. Habitat type (e.g., lake, pond, swamp, ditch, rain puddle), size (surface area in ha or length × width), and depth (minimum, maximum, and average); percentages of the water surface that are open or occupied by emergent or surface vegetation; notation of whether the site is open above or covered by forest canopy.
2. Some indication of the relative duration of the habitat (e.g., is permanent, has water most years, fills in a good rain, results from flooding, lasts 2–4 weeks).
3. Nature of any shoreline or emergent aquatic vegetation; species or types of vegetation (e.g., reeds, water lilies), if known.
4. Bottom type (e.g., silt, sand, leaf pack).

LOTIC—STREAMS AND RIVERS
1. Habitat type (e.g., river, stream, spring, creek, seep), width, and depth (e.g., pools and shallows, riffles); some indication of the flow rate (e.g., cascades and falls, white water-high gradient, moderate current, slow and meandering, meters per second).
2. Some indication of the relative duration (life) of the habitat (e.g., flows all year, only in the wet season, or only after a good rain).
3. Nature of any bordering vegetation (e.g., trees, small bushes, broad-leaf plants); plant types and species, if available.
4. Substrate types (e.g., rocks, boulders, gravel, sand, mud, leaf pack).

WATER IN PLANTS (PHYTOTELMATA) AND ARTIFICIAL STRUCTURES
1. Nature of the water-holding structure (e.g.,bromeliad, leaf axil, tree hole, bucket, bowl), size (surface area), depth, water volume, location (open forest, clearing, canopy), height above ground, and distance from natural (larger) bodies of water.
2. Relative age and duration of the habitat (is permanent, has water most years, is 2 weeks old).
3. Identification and description of the water-holding plant.
4. Substrate in the structure (e.g., bare, detritus, sand, leaf pack).

Sampling Methodology

Information pertinent to sampling procedures should be recorded, with reference to the specific method (or methods) used (see Chapter 6). In addition, the following information should be taken for each specimen encountered during an inventory or monitoring project (see also "Microhabitat Description" and "Voucher Specimens," below):

1. Date and time of encounter.
2. Identification of specimen (e.g., *Rana pipiens, Bufo* sp., brown salamander of type A).
3. Size of specimen. Total length probably is the most reliable indicator of size (snout–vent for frogs and snout–tail tip for salamanders, caecilians, and anuran larvae; broken tails are indicated with a + after the measurement). Normally one would not disturb individuals identified by their calls. Adult, juvenile, and metamorph may be convenient size categories for use in monitoring studies of well-known species, but the use of these terms can present problems (e.g., adult-size frogs are not necessarily mature nor are juvenile-size frogs necessarily immature, as the names imply). For larvae, only representatives of each (distinctive) size class are measured.
4. Sex. Recorded only if the determination is confirmed or the specimen is not collected. Presence of nuptial pads, vocal sacs, and coloration can be useful, but positive determinations may require dissection or observation of egg laying or of calling (usually males only). If in doubt, a voucher should be collected.
5. Position in environment, that is, the horizontal and vertical position of each individual, in as much detail as possible.
6. Activity of individual, that is, the behavior of the individual at the time it was encountered. Typical descriptors include calling, sitting, moving, swimming, hopping, coiled around eggs.

Microhabitat description

ROBERT F. INGER

Amphibians typically are irregularly, often patchily, distributed in a habitat, particularly in complex habitats. Individual species occur in microhabitats, that is, limited subsets of habitats at each site. Microhabitats, as used here, are the precise places where individual amphibians occur within the general environment. Although simple species richness at a site can be determined without knowing the microhabitats used by the amphibians living there, I advocate recording microhabitat data for each individual amphibian observed. The resulting data are scientifically richer by orders of magnitude. For example, differential microhabitat use by the same species at different sites can be determined, as can seasonal differences of microhabitat use at a given site. Knowing that certain amphibian species are restricted to given microhabitats can have profound conservation implications (Zimmermann and Bierregaard 1986).

Recording microhabitat data requires advance planning, especially in the design of an appropriate checklist for registering microhabitat features. Taking such data can be time-consuming and may result in a decrease in the number of specimens captured and preserved. However, the general utility of specimen records that include microhabitat data is so superior to those without them that the trade-off in reduced numbers of specimens preserved overwhelmingly favors collection of the data. Microhabitat information is essential for determining ecological distributions in a manner that is repeatable from site to site and that yields data easily subjected to statistical analysis. By combining all data from a microhabitat classification scheme, it should be possible to describe the ecological distribution of each species at a site and to compare distributions across sites.

Each major biome type has its unique environmental features and will, therefore, require a distinct descriptive checklist, with two important caveats. First, no paper scheme can duplicate the actual complexity of the real world; consequently, investigators must expect to amplify certain records with supplementary notes. Second, the use of a microhabitat checklist does not obviate the need to record gross aspects of the environment, such as vegetation type, elevation, general topography, weather, and so forth. Nevertheless, it should be possible to create a microhabitat classification scheme for every major environment in which amphibians occur. A microhabitat checklist will have both unique and general characteristics and will vary in complexity depending on the habitats sampled. For example, tropical wet forest sites presumably will require a more complex microhabitat classification scheme than temperate grassland sites. Such a scheme has been used successfully for tropical rain forest sites in several parts of the world.

Whatever checklist is assembled must balance detail and generality. The goal is to achieve generality without undue loss of information. Another important characteristic of a good microhabitat checklist is expandability; it should be possible to add elements as local situations demand. For example, an investigator should be able to add vegetation or habitat types as amphibians are encountered in them.

Characteristics of a Microhabitat Checklist

Analysis of the information recorded with each observation leads to an understanding of the ecological distribution and habitat use of amphibian species. Therefore, it is important that the data

with each specimen be complete and recorded in a standard way. Generally, six major elements of the microhabitat of each individual observed are described. For each element, there is a checklist of environmental features about which information should be noted, as well as a series of standard descriptions for each feature. The notion is that for every amphibian encountered a single notation for each feature of each element will describe that microhabitat. Use of the checklist of features and the standard descriptors facilitates complete and standard notation of data. Separate checklists are used for adults and larvae.

The six elements to be recorded for each observation are as follows:

1. Date and time of observation (24-hr clock).
2. General location, vegetation type, and elevation (refer to descriptions and standards in the section "Data Standards," above).
3. Horizontal position, with reference to bodies of water, shade-casting vegetation, and, in the case of some lacustrine environments, the shore. Each position needs to be qualified in detail (see checklist below).
4. Vertical position. In terrestrial environments, vertical position is defined as subsurface, at soil surface exposed, at soil surface under shelter, above ground, or in water. In lacustrine environments or in deep rivers, vertical position is defined as depth.
5. Substrate, usually mineral soil, dead leaves, log, rock, or vegetation. Each substrate often requires finer subdivision (see checklist below).
6. Special information that does not fit easily into the preceding categories—for example, limb projecting over water, under exfoliating rock, in termite mound.

A sample field catalogue sheet summarizing microhabitat data for adult amphibians is provided in Figure 5.

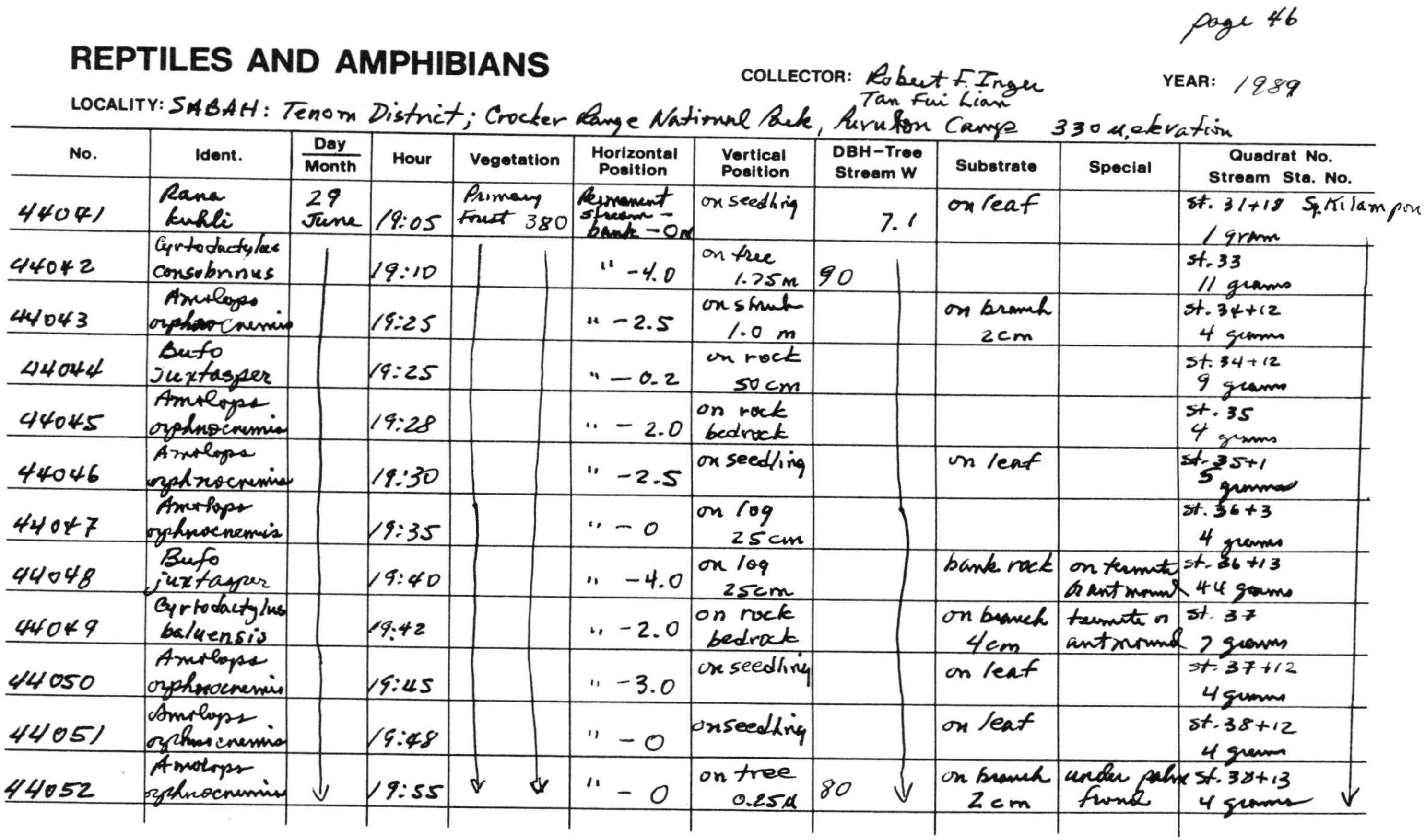

REPTILES AND AMPHIBIANS

COLLECTOR: Robert F. Inger, Tan Fui Lian, ...

LOCALITY: SABAH: Tenom District; Crocker Range National Park, Rerumbon Camp 330 m elevation

YEAR: 1989

page 46

No.	Ident.	Day/Month	Hour	Vegetation	Horizontal Position	Vertical Position	DBH–Tree Stream W	Substrate	Special	Quadrat No. Stream Sta. No.
44041	Rana kuhlii	29 June	19:05	Primary Forest 380	Permanent stream bank – 0m	on seedling	7.1	on leaf		St. 31+19 Sp. Kilam pon / gram
44042	Cyrtodactylus consobrinus		19:10		" – 4.0	on tree 1.75 m	90			St. 33 11 grams
44043	Amolops orphnocnemis		19:25		" – 2.5	on shrub 1.0 m		on branch 2 cm		St. 34+12 4 grams
44044	Bufo juxtasper		19:25		" – 0.2	on rock 50 cm				St. 34+12 9 grams
44045	Amolops orphnocnemis		19:28		" – 2.0	on rock bedrock				St. 35 4 grams
44046	Amolops orphnocnemis		19:30		" – 2.5	on seedling		on leaf		St. 35+1 5 grams
44047	Amolops orphnocnemis		19:35		" – 0	on log 25 cm				St. 36+3 4 grams
44048	Bufo juxtasper		19:40		" – 4.0	on log 25 cm		bank rock	on termite & ant nnns	St. 36+13 44 grams
44049	Cyrtodactylus baluensis		19:42		" – 2.0	on rock bedrock		on branch 4 cm	termite on ant nnns	St. 37 7 grams
44050	Amolops orphnocnemis		19:45		" – 3.0	on seedling		on leaf		St. 37+12 4 grams
44051	Amolops orphnocnemis		19:48		" – 0	on seedling		on leaf		St. 38+12 4 grams
44052	Amolops orphnocnemis		19:55		" – 0	on tree 0.25 m	80	on branch 2 cm	under palm frnnds	St. 38+13 4 grams

Figure 5. Field catalogue sheet summarizing microhabitat data for adult amphibians from a primary forest site in Sabah.

Some of the above information categories also are needed for larval microhabitat descriptions: date, hour, general location, and general habitat and vegetation types. In addition, information should be collected on the general type of the aquatic environment, microhabitat type, aspects of the physical environment (see checklist below), vertical and horizontal positions of the larva(e), and kinds of other organisms present. A sample data sheet used to describe the microhabitats of larval amphibians is presented in Figure 6.

Basic Descriptors for a Microhabitat Checklist

The following descriptive categories were devised for tropical and subtropical forests to illustrate the method. Investigators will need to develop similar descriptors for microhabitat checklists to be used in other biomes such as temperate forest, grassland, and desert.

ADULT AMPHIBIANS IN TROPICAL AND SUBTROPICAL FORESTS

DATE

HOUR (24-hr clock)

VEGETATION (Use separate descriptors for each major vegetation and habitat type at the site. See the section "Habitat" under "Data Standards," above).

MICROHABITAT DATA SHEET
LARVAL AMPHIBIANS

DATE _____   HOUR _____

LOCALITY _____
_____

    elevation_____latitude/longitude_____station#_____
    vegetation/habitat_____

COLLECTORS _____

TYPE OF AQUATIC ENVIRONMENT _____
   measurement _____
MICROHABITAT TYPE _____
   Description _____
   Substrate/Bottom Type_____
_____
Other Physical Attributes: current _____   pH _____
   oxygen _____   temperature _____   turbidity _____

VERTICAL POSITION _____
_____

BIOTA -- (Field number)
   Larvae
   _____
   _____
   _____
   _____

   Other
   _____
   _____
   _____

Figure 6. Sample data sheet for information on microhabitats of larval amphibians.

HORIZONTAL POSITION
  Permanent stream
    In water
    Midstream on bar or snag
    On bank; distance (m) to water
    On exposed dry bed; distance (m) to water
    On overhanging vegetation; height (m)
      above water
  Intermittent stream
    Actually in water
    Midstream on bar or snag
    On bank; distance (m) to water
    In dry bed
    On overhanging vegetation; height (m)
      above water
  Permanent pond
    In water
    On bank; distance (m) to water
    On overhanging vegetation; height (m)
      above water
  Temporary pond
    In water
    On bank; distance (m) to water
    On overhanging vegetation; height (m)
      above water
  Permanent marsh
  Distant from any body of water; approxi-
    mate distance to nearest water

VERTICAL POSITION
  Under surface of soil; depth (cm)
  In or under dead leaves
  Under rock; maximum dimensions (cm) of
    rock
  Under log; diameter (cm) of log
  In log; diameter (cm) of log
  On surface of bare mineral soil
  On surface of leaf litter
  On rock; maximum dimensions (cm) of
    rock
  On log; diameter (cm) of log
  On seedling or herbaceous plant (< 1 m tall)
  On shrub or sapling (1–7 m); height (m)
    above ground or water

On tree or large vine (> 7 m); height (m)
  above ground or water; diameter (cm)
  at breast height (DBH) for woody
  plants
On dead stump; height (m) above ground
In crown of fallen dead shrub or tree; height
  (m) above ground or water
On grass blade; height (m) above ground or
  water
In grass

SUBSTRATE
  Leaf of plant; maximum dimensions (cm) of
    leaf
  Stem or branch of herbaceous plant
  Twig or branch of woody plant; diameter
    (cm) of perch
  Stem of shrub or tree
  In epiphyte
  Under bark of log, stump, or tree
  Bank of mud, of sand, of small gravel, or of
    rock

SPECIAL ATTRIBUTES OF MICROHABITAT
  Isolated pool in stream floodplain
  Seepage area
  Tree hole
  Burrow
  Bank: flat (< 20°), moderately sloping (20–
    45°), or steep (> 45°)
  Between tree buttresses
  On or in floating vegetation
  Among roots of floating vegetation
  On termite or ant mound
  In or under termite or ant mound; distance
    (cm) to surface
  Under fallen palm fronds
  On fallen palm fronds
  In or on building
  In terrestrial bromeliads
  Other (describe on back of field sheet or
    elsewhere)
  Stream width or pond diameter (m)

Depending on the nature of the study, the following information also may be appropriate:

PLOT, STREAM STATION, OR LOCAL GRID NUMBER

TYPE OF ACTIVITY
  Quiescent or resting
  Disturbed by investigator
  Active and alert
  Calling
  Uncovered by investigator
  In amplexus
  In nest

DETECTION METHOD
  Observed
  Heard
  Uncovered
  Dug up
  Pitfall trap
  Funnel trap
  Trench
  Seine or other net

LARVAL AMPHIBIANS IN TROPICAL AND SUBTROPICAL FORESTS

DATE

HOUR (24-hr clock)

VEGETATION (Use separate descriptors for each major vegetation and habitat type at the site. See the section "Habitat" under "Data Standards," above.)

TYPE OF AQUATIC ENVIRONMENT
  Temporary pond; length × width × depth (m)
  Permanent pond; length × width × depth (m)
  Perennial stream; width (m)
  Intermittent stream; width (m)
  Phytotelmata (plant-held water)
  Marsh or swamp
  Spring; distance (m) from head
  Seep

Terrestrial (describe)
Artificial structure (e.g., barrel, pit)

MICROHABITAT TYPE
  Streams; width (m)
    Torrent
    Riffle
    Open pool, in main flow; length × width × depth (m) of pool
    Side pool, off main current; length × width × depth (m) of pool
    Leaf drift or mass of dead leaves and other debris held by eddy or back current; length × width (m) of mass
    Pothole in bank rock; height (m) above stream flow; dimensions (cm) of pothole
    Interstitial in gravel or sand; depth (cm)
  Ponds or lakes
    Open area; area (ha) or length × width × depth (m) of pool
    Among rotted vegetation
    Among floating vegetation or algae
  Plant-held water
    Buttress tank; height (m) above ground; approximate volume (cm^3)
    Epiphyte tank; height (m) above ground; approximate volume (cm^3); type of plant
    Log or tree hole; height (m) above ground; approximate volume (cm^3)
    "Cup" pool (fruit husk, palm spathe, or other natural cup in litter); approximate volume (cm^3)
  Artificial structure or container
    Describe structure; height (m) above ground; approximate volume (cm^3)
  Other
    On or in adult frog
  Substrate or bottom type
    Mud or silt
    Sand
    Gravel
    Large rock
    Bed rock
    Dead leaves

Wood
Other (describe)
Other physical attributes
Current (cm/sec)
Oxygen (ml/l; % saturation)
Temperature
pH
Turbidity

VERTICAL POSITION
On bottom; depth (cm) below surface
Midwater; depth (cm) below surface
At surface

BIOTA
Odonate naiads, present or absent; approximate sizes
Dytiscid larvae or adults, present or absent; approximate sizes
Belostomatid or other predaceous hemipterans, present or absent; approximate sizes
Fishes, present or absent; approximate sizes
Other vertebrate predators present

Field Methods

Recording microhabitat information in the field can be simplified greatly with temporary data sheets. Such sheets are ruled into columns corresponding to the major categories of information required by the microhabitat descriptor checklist being used. As animals are observed, appropriate information is entered. Upon return to camp the data are transferred into permanent field catalogues or notebooks. I strongly recommend that the data be transferred within a few hours of collection. A computer should be used in the field only if hard copy can be produced at the site, because total reliance on disk storage in the field can be risky. In either case, original data sheets should be maintained indefinitely.

If animals are collected, each should be placed in a separately numbered bag, and the bag number should be included as part of the temporary field record. A mixture of plastic (mostly) and cloth (for larger specimens) bags are required. Animals should be processed as soon as possible to avoid mixing of data and loss of specimens.

Voucher specimens

ROBERT P. REYNOLDS, RONALD I. CROMBIE, AND ROY W. McDIARMID

Specimens that permanently document data in an archival report are called *vouchers*. Voucher specimens serve to verify the identity of organisms encountered or used in a study and to ensure that the study, which can never be repeated exactly, can be reevaluated accurately. Voucher specimens are the only mechanism for validating the presence of a species in a study and for making historical comparisons. In addition to their importance in systematic studies and as documentation of floral and faunal surveys, vouchers provide irreplaceable data regarding biochemical properties, demographic trends, and geographic distributions for future investigation. Lee et al. (1982) provided a cogent review of voucher specimens and their importance to biological studies, and we have adopted many of their points in this presentation.

Voucher specimens are always needed to provide scientific credibility to an inventory or monitoring project and should be collected unless there is a compelling reason not to do so. Valid reasons for not collecting voucher specimens include protection of the species by law, endangered or threatened status of the species, and serious species survival risk from loss of an individual. If undisputed reasons exist not to collect the animal, a good-quality photograph together with a recording of the call (for anurans), a tissue sample for molecular analysis (even a clipped digit), or some other useful secondary representation of the organism may serve as a voucher. To fulfill its function, a voucher must illustrate the recognized diagnostic traits appropriate for the level of identification required (species), be preserved in good condition by the collector, be documented with appropriate field data, be deposited and maintained in a suitable institution, and be readily accessible (Lee et al. 1982).

Anuran calls should be recorded (Appendix 3) and tissue samples taken (Appendix 5) when possible, although such materials are not strictly required for all inventory and monitoring work. Frog calls provide important behavioral and evolutionary information, and tissues can be used to estimate genetic relatedness. Calls and tissues increase the information available with each voucher and may reduce the need to take additional specimens at a future time. However, recording calls and taking tissue samples require significant amounts of time. The investigator must plan for these activities before the study is initiated; otherwise, the goals of the inventory or monitoring study may be compromised.

Field Identifications

Accurate specific identification of amphibians in the field is rarely possible except in areas for which the fauna has been studied in detail. Even there, diagnostic characters are often subtle and difficult to see without magnification or, sometimes, dissection. Even herpetologists with considerable experience in an area usually provide only generic or tentative specific identifications of specimens in the field. These names serve for bookkeeping purposes rather than for identification, and they facilitate tracking of numbers of species and specimens sampled.

Accurate species identifications are such an integral part of all aspects of comparative biology that studies without voucher specimens violate a basic premise of scientific methodology, that is, the ability of subsequent workers to repeat the study. Correct identifications of organisms are essential to all biological investigation. Only voucher specimens provide a basis for verification of identifications and thereby duplication of a study. The literature is replete with examples of comparative studies in physiology, ecology, behavior, morphology, and systematics for which research results are questionable or even useless because of species misidentifications or failure to recognize that more than one species was involved. Most decisions relating to the management and conservation of species also depend on accurate species identifications. Voucher specimens are the only means to verify or, if necessary, correct specimen identifications and, therefore, are essential to scientific investigation in the above-mentioned disciplines.

All field identifications should be verified by a person with experience with the group, through the use of reliable and authoritative keys, or by comparison with specimens in museum collections. Vouchers should be deposited in appropriate repositories, usually a natural history museum. With erroneous field identifications, specimens of poorly known species may be overlooked, and important data may not be collected because the investigator assumes the species involved is well known. For purposes of sampling in little-studied regions, we recommend that all field identifications be treated as tentative and that all species be considered equally important.

Except for well-studied areas such as North America and Europe, few useful field guides or identification manuals for amphibians exist, and for many countries even lists of the recorded species are not available. Many of the older monographs on amphibian faunas (e.g., Cochran 1955; Taylor 1962; Laurent 1964; Cochran and Goin 1970) were based almost entirely on (often poorly) preserved museum specimens and are of limited utility for field identifications or as sources of general information on geographic and habitat distributions. We suggest, therefore, that investigators become familiar with available primary literature before commencing an inventory and, whenever possible, that they examine preserved specimens of species from the area of interest prior to beginning the fieldwork. Notes on the amphibian fauna of the region with a list of the species and their diagnostic features should allow the worker to identify the more common species, focus on those of specific interest, and recognize any taxa that may be protected (see the section "Permits," below).

Because vouchers serve as the sole means of verifying data collected during investigations of biological diversity and provide critical information for future investigations, the importance of voucher materials should be generally recognized and their preparation considered essential to good science. We acknowledge, however, that the removal and preservation of specimens for scientific purposes can be an emotional issue. Therefore, it is essential that field investigators carefully plan their studies in advance, clearly identify their objectives, and evaluate the need to collect voucher specimens.

Sample Size

What constitutes an adequate or optimal sample for the purposes of identification is not easily determined. For some species, identification is possible from a single specimen (although this is rare); for other species, 20 individuals would not adequately sample the variation in the population, and a larger sample would be necessary. Some species are amazingly polymorphic (see color plate of *Dendrobates pumilio* in Myers and Daly 1983), some have striking sexual, ontogenetic, geographic, and/or individual variation, and others are relatively uniform even across broad geographic areas. Modern systematics takes into account this potential for variation and the significance of ancillary biological data in attempting to determine species limits. Gone are the days of running a single specimen through a key and magically achieving a reliable specific

identification. This "cookbook" approach and the idea that a single specimen could be "typical" of a deme or a population, much less an entire species, are scientifically unsound. Keys, if properly constructed, can be useful tools in providing identifications, but these preliminary identifications must be tested by comparisons with descriptions in the literature and with preserved museum specimens.

We agree with Frith (1973:3) that the number of animals sampled "really has no [biological] significance unless it is related to the total number of animals in the population and their rate of replacement." Concerned readers will find a cogent discussion of what many consider an unwarranted preoccupation with survival of individuals, as well as quantitative data on the relative impacts of scientific collecting, natural mortality, habitat destruction, and commercial collecting on amphibian populations in Ehmann and Cogger (1985, esp. table 3). It is revealing that not a single species of animal is known to have been exterminated as a result of scientific collecting during the 250-year history of systematics (Hedges and Thomas 1991). In contrast, hundreds to thousands of species have likely gone extinct as a result of habitat destruction.

With few exceptions, amphibians are prolific, with reproductive potentials sufficient to accommodate increased levels of predation. As predators on amphibians, scientists usually are singularly inefficient compared to snakes, birds, and other organisms. Furthermore, preparing specimens and recording the data associated with them (Appendix 4) are time-consuming tasks and, when done correctly, discourage human collectors from random oversampling (see also Foster 1982:6–7; Ehmann and Cogger 1985:439).

It would be convenient if we could provide an absolute value for, or formula to calculate, the number of vouchers of a given species that should be collected, but science is rarely convenient. Providing a meaningful formula for the more than 4,000 species of amphibians is beyond our capability. For areas where the amphibian fauna is well known, a single representative adult specimen of each population at each site minimally will suffice as a voucher for an inventory or monitoring study. Normally, the first adult of every species encountered during a project is suitable. For monitoring studies, we recommend that a voucher be preserved at the initiation of the study. If additional vouchers are required, they can be taken at the end of the study or from an area adjacent to the study site. As an operational figure, we recommend that 10 to 20 specimens of adults and larvae would better represent the species at each site in well-studied areas.

Because we are in the early discovery phase and do not understand the taxonomic relationships of many tropical forms, and because many areas are poorly known and numerous species are undescribed or inadequately represented in systematic collections, we usually recommend collecting many more than one voucher specimen. Generally speaking (and with an awareness of the frailties of any generalization), we recommend a sample of 25 individuals (ideally 10 adult males, 10 adult females, and 5 immatures) for identification purposes. We strongly encourage additional sampling of polymorphic species and those known to be inadequately understood taxonomically or suspected to include several taxa; for such species, samples of up to 25 males, 25 females, and 25 juveniles may be adequate. A researcher who is interested in assessing genetic diversity within and among sites should prepare tissue samples for biochemical analysis (Appendix 5) and preserve voucher specimens of a minimum of 5 to 10 males and females from each site.

Larval amphibians also should be collected whenever they are encountered. After the adults have finished breeding, the larvae may represent the only accessible specimens of a species during the study period. Because larvae are poorly known and generally underrepresented in natural history collections, we recommend a minimum voucher sample of 20 to 30 larvae of each species from each site. Ideally, subsamples should be preserved at various stages to provide a developmental series. If conditions permit, samples of larvae should be raised through metamorphosis. This approach will ultimately yield larvae that can be positively associated with identifiable adults. This is especially important in areas where the fauna is poorly known.

Factors other than sample size can also affect the potential for accurate identification of specimens. Improperly or carelessly prepared specimens are often difficult or impossible to identify because diagnostic features are obscured or modified. Anyone collecting material for scientific purposes should be intimately familiar with proper techniques for specimen preparation and documentation. Ecological information, notes on color in life (dorsal and ventral color, other pattern elements, hidden portions of limbs and groin, iris color), recordings of calls (preferably with a definitely associated voucher specimen), and confidently associated juveniles and larvae often aid identification. Generally speaking, a small number of carefully prepared specimens with detailed data is preferable to a large, carelessly prepared sample with inadequate biological data. Instructions for preparing and preserving amphibian specimens as vouchers are provided in Appendix 4.

Specimen Data

To fulfill their function as vouchers of monitoring or inventory studies, all specimens must be thoroughly documented with locality and relevant specimen data. Data associated with voucher specimens enhance the value of the vouchers and potentially make identifications easier, but those data must be accurate. Even for critically important information, having no data is better than having inaccurate data.

In addition to full locality data in a standard format and information on sampling procedures and habitat (see the section "Data Standards," above), the minimum information required for each voucher specimen includes the following:

1. *Unique sample designation.* This unique field number is assigned by the collector to a specimen or lot obtained at one place and time during the inventory. The number is noted on a field tag that is tied to juveniles or adults or is associated in a single container with larvae.
2. *Date and time of collection.* The date and time (24-hr clock) that the specimen was collected and the date it was prepared (if different) are essential. The month should be written out (i.e., numeric designations or abbreviations are not used).
3. *Name of collector.* The collector is the person (or persons) making the collection. The collector's name is never abbreviated, and the middle initial is included when available.
4. *Taxonomic identification.* Ideally each specimen should be identified to genus and species. This level of identification often is impossible in the field, especially with larvae; a family or other taxon name (caecilian, tadpole, *Bufo*) can be substituted for the scientific name until the animal is identified.
5. *Number of specimens.* For specimens sampled in small lots (eggs and larvae), exact counts should be given. Counts of large lots ($\geq$ 50 specimens) can be designated as "more than 50," "about 90," or "$\geq$ 200."
6. *Other information.* The existence of an associated special preparation (e.g., tissue sample) or other specimen data (e.g., behavioral observation, color notes, recorded call, or photograph) should be entered in the field notes and associated with the unique field number of the voucher specimen. Maps of the study area and trip itineraries are always useful for identification, cataloguing, and historical or archival purposes.

Call Vouchers

When frog calls are used as part of the sampling methodology, tape recordings of the calls of all species are an integral part of the documentation. Recordings are particularly important in habitats with many poorly known species. To serve as a voucher, any tape-recorded frog call must be accompanied by a well-preserved voucher specimen. In this instance the voucher is the male giving the call and the tape recording. If the calling male eludes capture or escapes, that is noted in the field notes and on the tape. Ambient temperature recorded at the time and site of calling should accompany the tape. Appendix 3 provides additional information regarding call vouchers and tape recordings.

Most institutions require that the original or clear photocopies of a collector's field notes and catalogue accompany any incoming collection. The importance of good field notes to all subsequent use of the collection cannot be overemphasized. Poorly recorded field data can seriously mislead the specialist and reduce the usefulness of specimens. If the data accompanying the collection are a secondary compilation from the original field notes, they should be clearly labeled as such.

Selection of a Specimen Repository

Voucher specimens from faunal surveys that are accompanied by detailed field notes and associated documentation have almost incalculable scientific value. Given the inevitable widespread habitat destruction that may preclude collection of additional material from many areas, and the rapid technological advances that allow for previously unsuspected uses of specimens, we can only guess at the possible significance of such specimens in the future. Consequently, this often irreplaceable "time capsule" of information should be permanently stored in a secure institutional collection with a documented long-term commitment to conserving specimens and making them available for study by qualified researchers.

The amount of time, space, and money required to maintain a museum collection is enormous, and relatively few institutions are able to provide the long-term security necessary for large research collections. Therefore, selection of an appropriate institution for the deposition of field vouchers is of critical importance. Using field collections as an enhancement for employment or to ensure acceptance to graduate school is inappropriate; establishing a private collection unavailable for study by qualified researchers does a disservice to the scientific community and often imperils the long-term survival of the study specimens. Many important collections are lost or destroyed when the collector dies or retires and his or her home institution loses interest or realizes it no longer can provide the space or funds required for their maintenance.

When a researcher from one country collects specimens from another country, it is highly appropriate (and often a requirement of the collecting permit) for representative material to be returned, after identification, to designated institutions in the country of origin for the purpose of establishing functional reference collections. Excessive nationalism or misplaced possessiveness, however, should not obscure the economic realities of establishing and maintaining an extensive natural history collection. The primary concern of all responsible biologists should be the long-term maintenance of specimens and associated data and their availability to qualified scientists for study.

Several variables influence the choice of a deposition site for collections; they are discussed by Lee et al. (1982). If identifications are required, an institution that has a history of research in the geographic area, an appropriate specialist on the staff, and access to extensive library facilities is optimal. The prospective donor should, however, obtain a statement of the museum's policies regarding acquisition, preservation, maintenance, and deaccessioning of collections to determine if the policies meet his or her needs. Most institutions will honor reasonable requests from the donor, but policy is determined by many other factors as well.

The identification, distribution, and cataloguing of voucher collections is a service provided by museums to the scientific community. Many museums are currently suffering from budget cuts and staff shortages. The identification of a large collection often occupies hours of staff time. It may require a curator to borrow specimens or to visit other institutions so that pertinent materials may be compared directly, to lend specimens to specialists for identification, and to search the literature. Altruism, if it exists, has its limits. The donor must keep in mind that few museums can afford to invest the time and energy required to identify a major collection without the complete cooperation of the donor. If assistance with identifications is requested of an institution but the collection is to be deposited elsewhere, the requester should offer at least to deposit representative material in the institution that provides the service. Donors often expect institutions to maintain a voucher collection as a discrete unit, separate from the main collection. This desire is understandable, but most institutions will not be able to accommodate it, because of limited space and curatorial support. Whether a voucher collection should be maintained in a single institution or distributed among several is also debated. Each option has merit. The first obviously simplifies future study of the collection; the latter provides for greater access by researchers in many areas. Donors concerned about this issue should ask about an institution's exchange policy before depositing specimens there.

Permits

ROY W. McDIARMID, ROBERT P. REYNOLDS, AND RONALD I. CROMBIE

During the past few decades, the number of laws regulating the collection, acquisition, study, transport, and disposition of wildlife and wildlife products has increased significantly. These laws have been proposed and promulgated in an effort to control activities that are deemed harmful to animals and plants. Although habitat loss generally is acknowledged to be the primary factor affecting species' distributions, abundances, recruitment, and extinctions, commercial exploitation also has had a detrimental effect on certain species of wildlife. Some species considered to be endangered, threatened, or otherwise in need of protection have been protected by international treaty or various federal, state, and local laws. The laws and regulations contained in the U.S. Endangered Species Act and in the Convention on International Trade in Endangered Species of Wild Fauna and Flora (CITES) are those of primary concern, but many other foreign, federal, state, and local regulations may also apply to users of this manual. For example, many states require permits for the use of seines or traps in aquatic habitats; permission to use such devices to sample aquatic amphibians should be clarified with the local authority. Other regulations with which travelers should be familiar restrict the transport of liquid nitrogen (see Appendix 5), alcohol, and formalin or the possession and transport of syringes and certain killing agents, drugs, or chemicals used in specimen preparation.

Laws regulating scientific collecting vary widely among states and countries and change constantly. Furthermore, the government agencies responsible for issuing collecting permits sometimes change or are restructured. Current information on most international and federal regulations and responsible agencies can be obtained by writing to or calling the U.S. Fish and Wildlife Service, Office of Management Authority, 4401 N. Fairfax Drive, Arlington, VA 22203 USA (telephone: [703] 358-1708). Information on state and local regulations can be obtained from the appropriate conservation or management agency in the jurisdiction of interest. The variation in requirements often makes obtaining collecting and export permits a trying process. Nevertheless, it is the responsibility of the individual collector to learn about and comply with the appropriate regulations as they apply to amphibians. Although certain provisions of a collecting permit may appear to have little bearing on the conservation of species or protection of habitats and in some instances may even restrict the conduct of scientific research, all of us are obliged to abide by the regulations.

Because obtaining the necessary permits often is a crucial step in ensuring the success of a field study and often is the most difficult part of the preliminary work, it is essential that the investigator present a carefully planned proposal with clearly defined objectives to the permit-granting agency. We recommend that investigators be prepared for delays, which often are inevitable, by allowing a long lead time between the request for permits and the initiation of the field study.

Most institutions cannot or will not accept voucher material unless it is accompanied by documents verifying that the specimens were legally collected and, where appropriate, exported and imported. In many countries, permits for specimen collection and export are issued by different government agencies. In addition, some countries require an animal health permit, issued by a third agency, before specimens can be legally exported. In other countries collection and export are unregulated, at least for non-commercial purposes. In these cases, a letter on official stationery from the most appropriate government agency stating that such permits are not required may suffice for purposes of importation.

Endangered and protected species require special permits beyond the normal collecting and export permits. In addition, in CITES-member countries, export permits for any species covered by CITES must be issued by the designated CITES official. The U.S. Fish and Wildlife Service (see address above) maintains an international directory of CITES Management Authorities, that is, of offices authorized to issue permits or equivalent documentation in accordance with CITES regulations. It is the responsibility of the researcher to ensure that he or she has complied with all laws governing the collection and export of scientific specimens and that the appropriate permits are secured.

For import into the United States a completed U.S. Fish and Wildlife Service form 3-177 (available from a Fish and Wildlife Service agent at a designated port of entry or from the U.S. Fish and Wildlife Service, Division of Law Enforcement, P.O. Box 3247, Arlington, VA 22203-3247 USA) accompanied by the above documents (copies are sufficient) from the country of origin must be presented at the port of entry. It is prudent to notify the agent at the port of entry of your anticipated date and time of arrival. If it is not possible to meet with a Fish and Wildlife agent at the time of arrival, the completed 3-177 form should be left with the customs inspector and a copy sent to the address specified on the form within the specified time. For purposes of declaration, scientific specimens, by definition, have "no commercial value." Importation of specimens into countries other than the United States and shipments through other countries will require other permits. In these instances local agencies should be consulted for information regarding regulations and appropriate procedures.

## Chapter 6

Standard Techniques for
Inventory and Monitoring

Selection of techniques

In this book we recommend 10 standard techniques that can be used for inventory and monitoring projects. Here we provide basic guidelines for selection among them. We emphasize that the questions being asked by the investigator will determine which technique or techniques are selected. Therefore, the first step in any project is definition of the research question(s) and identification of the kind(s) of information required to answer it.

Questions concerning amphibian biodiversity basically fall into two broad categories: (1) those related to habitats, sites, or areas and (2) those concerned with species or assemblages. The primary goal of habitat- or area-based questions is

to inventory the species that occur in habitats or areas at a specific site. In some instances, a site will be visited only once. In most cases, however, if a complete species list is desired, a site must be visited several times because it is unlikely that all species occurring at the site will be encountered during a single sampling session (particularly in species-rich tropical assemblages).

Species-based studies may focus on one or more populations across space or over time. In the former instance, the goal is to determine the geographic distribution (e.g., counties in a state, states in a country, or countries) or the ecological distribution (e.g., habitat or microhabitat types) of a species. For such spatially oriented studies, an investigator may select an inventory method appropriate for use across several habitats in a region or between regions.

If the study focuses on a species or species assemblage over time, then the goal is to determine the status of each species at a site and to look for population changes. In this instance, the species or assemblage is sampled several times (monitored) over a suitable period (e.g., years). If the goal is to determine general trends in the status of species (e.g., worldwide), then it is necessary to monitor many sites.

Amphibian biologists are likely to concentrate on organisms, that is, a single species, several species, or an entire assemblage of amphibians. Others will use the techniques in this book to determine amphibian use of specific habitats. For example, resource managers (e.g., persons in charge of parks, wildlife refuges, or federal or state lands) may be interested in the impact of successional or other habitat changes on amphibian species or on total amphibian biodiversity. Based on what is discovered during the inventory process, the investigators could decide that particular species (e.g., those that are endangered or suspected to be in decline) should be monitored.

Once an investigator has identified the question(s) and the kind(s) of information required, several important points must be considered prior to selecting from the 10 techniques. Foremost among these points is the biology of the amphibians targeted for study (e.g., are they aquatic, fossorial, or arboreal; are they prolonged or explosive breeders; and do they have aquatic larvae?). Time, funds, and number of field personnel available for the work also are of major importance in selecting techniques, as are the complexity of the habitat, the diversity of the fauna (e.g., number of species), and the size of the area to be studied. We have evaluated each of the techniques (Table 4) according to the amount of information it supplies, the time and number of persons required for its implementation, and its relative cost. For example, if the goal of the

project is to determine the density of a species, then techniques 4, 5, 6, and 10 of Table 4 should be considered.

The values given in Table 4 change if the area being covered is large or if mark-recapture methods are used. For example, if an investigator uses a visual encounter survey (technique 2) and mark-recapture techniques to sample amphibians in a given area, then information gained will increase because density estimates as well as relative abundance and species richness will be provided. Time required also will increase because at least two visits to the site are necessary (initial marking sample and one recapture sample). Cost may also increase, depending on the marking system used and whether additional personnel are needed.

To summarize, selection of the appropriate technique or techniques depends on the question being asked, the information required, the nature of the organism(s) or habitat being studied, and the resources available for the project. For a successful project, all of these factors must be considered prior to initiation of the study. We also strongly recommend a careful reading (or rereading) of Chapter 4 prior to selection of techniques.

Standard techniques

We begin the description of each technique with a brief review of its purpose, followed by a discussion of the specific amphibians and habitats for which the technique is known to work and, if known, those for which it is inappropriate. A section on background information on the development of the technique and any inherent assumptions and limitations regarding its use is followed with an exploration of questions relative to the research design associated with the technique. Because executing a specific experimental design under field conditions is rarely a straightforward procedure, we also discuss the

Table 4. Factors to Consider in Selecting Standard Techniques

Technique	Information gained[a]	Time[b]	Cost[c]	Personnel[d]
1. Complete species inventories	Species richness	High	Low	Low
2. Visual encounter surveys	Relative abundance	Low	Low	Low
3. Audio strip transects	Relative abundance	Medium	Medium	Low
4. Quadrat sampling	Density	High	Low	Medium
5. Transect sampling	Density	High	Low	Medium
6. Patch sampling	Density	High	Low	Medium
7. Straight-line drift fences and pitfall traps	Relative abundance	High	High	High
8. Surveys at breeding sites	Relative abundance	Medium	Low	Medium
9. Drift fences at breeding sites	Relative abundance	High	High	High
10. Quantitative sampling of amphibian larvae	Density or relative abundance[e]	Medium	Medium	Medium

[a] Designations are hierarchical; techniques that provide a density estimate also give relative abundance and species richness. Those that estimate relative abundance also provide species richness. If a technique gives species richness only, then some other technique must be used to obtain relative abundance or density.

[b] Relative time investment.

[c] Relative financial cost: high = expensive; medium = moderately expensive; low = relatively inexpensive.

[d] Personnel requirements: high = more than one person required; medium = one or more persons recommended; low = can be done by one person.

[e] Some methods included in technique 10 give relative abundance only, and some yield density values.

reality of implementing the technique in the field, including personnel and materials needed. Guidelines on how to collect and organize data include sample data sheets where appropriate. We briefly discuss data interpretation and analysis and provide technique-specific information that supplements the general guidelines provided in Chapter 9. We also examine specific features of the technique, make recommendations about its use, and review other important technical points.

The 10 techniques are not mutually exclusive. For example, an audio strip transect could be treated as a special case of either the general transect or the quadrat sampling technique, and a drift fence encircling a breeding pond could be a special application of a straight-line drift fence and pitfall trap sampling array. Nevertheless, the focus of each technique is different, and each has sufficient importance unique to amphibians to justify separate treatment. Separate treatment also will better ensure standardization, repeatability, and quality results.

The first technique deals with how to assemble species lists. Such lists are critical for conservation-related decisions, among other applications. The approaches recommended sacrifice quantification in favor of maximizing numbers of species obtained. In this respect, technique 1 differs from the other nine recommended techniques. The field procedures recommended in the first section on assembling species lists should be used only when time is limited and specific site inventory data are more important than comparing the data gathered with data from other sites.

1. Complete Species Inventories

NORMAN J. SCOTT, Jr.

Several techniques are available for generating species lists or information on species richness for a site. For the most part, the field techniques are methods of general collecting, as historically practiced by herpetologists. Typically, they involve searching for and collecting amphibians in all possible (appropriate) microhabitats both during the day and at night and result in modest habitat modification, such as dismantling of rotten logs or removal of epiphytes. These general collecting techniques have been used for both long-term and short-term sampling projects, although long-term sampling often includes both data retrieval and fieldwork and thus is more eclectic.

I discuss three approaches to species inventories: (1) compilation of faunal lists; (2) short-term, time-constrained quantitative sampling; and (3) rigorous, short-term, number-constrained sampling, an approach that I call the Systematic Sampling Survey (SSS). The SSS has been used with birds (Terborgh 1989:75; see also Hurlbert 1971) and would appear appropriate for sampling amphibians. The three approaches provide an enumeration of the amphibian fauna at a site and, with some qualification, may be used to compare species richness among sites or to detect changes in faunal composition at one site through time. This type of information often serves to guide conservation efforts.

TARGET ORGANISMS AND HABITATS

The field techniques can be used for sampling any amphibian species in any habitat. Secretive,

fossorial, canopy-dwelling, and deep-water species, however, are more difficult to inventory and may require specialized searching methods.

BACKGROUND

Species lists may be developed through long-term, gradual accumulation of records or by intense general collecting over a relatively short period. Numerous published checklists and herpetofaunal descriptions of specific areas attest to the usefulness of the long-term accumulation of species records. If the understanding of the systematic relationships among species and sampling of the faunas are comparable, site-specific lists can be used to compare species richness and details of faunal composition among sites, as was done by Duellman (1990) for five Neotropical rain forests.

General, nonquantitative, short-term collecting efforts cannot be used to estimate total species richness in complex faunas of more than about 25 species. Even for faunas of fewer than 25 species, I recommend use of quantitative short-term sampling techniques.

COMPILATION OF FAUNAL LISTS

ASSUMPTIONS. Faunal lists can be accumulated by integrating the results of general collecting by a few to many investigators with many research objectives; usually these collections are made using different techniques. The major assumptions are that differences in results caused by variation in technique and effort are smoothed over time and that the area does not change during the sampling period. Because most areas undergo change during long periods of investigation, however, these habitat changes must be documented. Most commonly, a few amphibian species disappear when water conditions change, as vegetational succession proceeds, or when habitats become insular (Myers and Rand 1969; Heyer et al. 1990; Rand and Meyers 1990). For example, on Barro Colorado Island,

Panama, at least three amphibian species disappeared from, and two others invaded, an original fauna of about 34 species over the 70-year period of record (Rand and Myers 1990).

LIMITATIONS. Long periods (usually in the scale of years) are needed to sample complex faunas (e.g., faunas with many species), areas with a highly seasonal climate, and areas where individual amphibians are scarce. For example, in a wet lowland forest in Ecuador, 90% of the species in an exceptionally diverse herpetofauna (185 species, including amphibians and reptiles) were taken after 500 collecting-days, and 97% after 800 days; the total was based on 1,300 collecting-days (Duellman 1978). Two to five times such effort may be needed in Southeast Asian wet forests where the amphibian fauna is equally species rich but individuals are relatively scarce (Lloyd et al. 1968a).

Long-term data accumulation is appropriate when a site (such as a field station) is visited irregularly by many collectors over many years or decades, as at La Selva, Costa Rica (Guyer 1990); Barro Colorado Island, Panama (Rand and Meyers 1990); and Boracéia, Brazil (Heyer et al. 1990).

SHORT-TERM SAMPLING

Short collecting visits to a single site cannot give much insight into the total number of species present. However, using time-constrained collecting techniques, rates of species accumulation in different habitats or sites can be compared if animal population densities are similar. If densities are dissimilar, scanty data suggest that samples derived from the protocol of Systematic Sampling Surveys (SSS) may be used to rank habitats and sites according to relative species richness. Quantitative short-term sampling techniques also can be used with other methods to gather more-detailed data on microhabitat variables for niche and assemblage analyses (see Chapter 5 and Inger and Colwell 1977).

ASSUMPTIONS. The results from short-term sampling are highly dependent on collecting and environmental variables. Some of these variables include weather (both prior to and during sampling), collectors' experience, level of sampling effort in each habitat, diversity of collecting techniques used, and phenology of the amphibian species. Before results from similar habitats at different sites are compared, any effects of these variables must be recognized and controlled.

Time-constrained searches (yielding a number of species collected per person-hour) must standardize collecting effort within habitat types. For example, Campbell and Christman (1982a:198) carried out a study in which each habitat type was sampled for 6 person-hours in the spring, summer, and autumn. In general, time-constrained sampling is a less robust form of the visual encounter survey (technique 2), which should be used when possible.

The SSS (number-constrained) method depends on the validity of another assumption: that more species are present in a limited sample of a species-rich fauna than are present in a similarly sized sample from a less rich fauna. This assumption seems to be valid for tropical herpetofaunas inhabiting forest litter (Scott 1976) but must be tested further to determine its general applicability for amphibians. As few as 100 specimens from each habitat, taken by a variety of techniques, may be adequate to rank a series of diverse faunas according to species richness. Cumulative plots of the numbers of species against numbers of individuals for litter-inhabiting reptiles and amphibians are available for wet tropical forests in Costa Rica (two sites), Borneo, and Cameroon (Scott 1982). The probably correct rank order of sites based on species richness was established after sampling about 80 individuals, and the order was preserved even after almost 200 individuals had been taken at the three most extensively sampled sites.

LIMITATIONS. Data resulting from time-constrained, short-term, general collecting can be compared among habitats at a single site but, given the large number of variables that potentially may influence composition of the samples, comparisons among sites usually are inappropriate. The number-constrained SSS technique, when applied to amphibians, enables an investigator to rank areas and habitats according to their species richness, but the actual number of species present will not be estimated accurately unless species richness is already known for one of the areas being compared.

RESEARCH DESIGN

There usually is no research design for long-term accumulation of faunal lists. In most cases, research museums are the major repositories of historic information on species presence, but other sources of information include private collections, published works, field notes, and station lists. Inventory lists can be augmented at any time by fieldwork specifically directed at discovering additional species. Time-constrained, short-term sampling should be stratified by major habitat type. The SSS methodology usually can be combined with time-constrained general collecting to provide a firmer basis for comparisons among habitats and sites. The SSS requires that an effort be made to record every animal encountered in each habitat, up to some preselected number (e.g., 100). Then, if the habitat has not been adequately sampled in the judgment of the investigator, efforts can be concentrated on the collection of additional species, not specimens. However, only data from the number-constrained collections can be used to compare sites.

**FIELD METHODS FOR
SHORT-TERM SAMPLING**

The first step in time-constrained, short-term sampling is to identify and define the major habitat types at the study site. These habitats should be described in detail sufficient (see Chapter 5) to allow the identification of similar habitats at other sites or in other studies. All habitats should be sampled during the first few days of the sampling period. Information derived from this broad scale sampling can be used to plan how to distribute subsequent sampling among habitats.

Many factors influence the efficiency of short-term surveys, and they must be recognized and controlled if comparisons are to be made among different sites and habitats. Some of these variables are (1) total time spent on the survey and time spent using each type of collecting technique; (2) number and experience of fieldworkers; (3) topography; (4) area of the site; (5) local weather and climate; (6) season, date, and time of day; and (7) time required to sample each major habitat type.

Before each search, the exact locality, date, starting time, and observers should be noted along with vegetation, habitat, habitat disturbance, slope and aspect of the area, and temperature and weather at the time of searching and during the recent past.

The goal of the search is to collect as many species of amphibians as possible. Persons who live on or near the site often know where and when certain species may be found. A common method of organizing a search is to survey a habitat rapidly during the day, identifying possible amphibian breeding sites that can be investigated more thoroughly at night, and looking for tadpoles or egg masses. All accessible amphibian habitats should be searched, and as much area as possible should be covered. Ears are among the best tools for detecting amphibians. Some large breeding choruses can be heard up to 2 km away, whereas calls of males of some species are audible over a distance of only 1 to 2 m. Some frogs call underwater, and others from beneath the ground. Each distinct call should be traced to its source, and a voucher specimen captured. Many amphibians can be located visually, as one walks along trails, streams, and lake margins during the day and at night.

Certain microhabitats often are unusually productive, including those in epiphytes, under loose bark, at the bases of buttressed trees, under and inside logs, under rocks, in rock crevices, in puddles and springs, along streambeds, and inside tree and bamboo hollows. Depending on the moisture regime, amphibians living in forest leaf litter are often highly concentrated. Accumulations of leaf litter around tree buttresses and moist spots, such as seeps and springs or dry streambeds, often harbor many individuals.

Every animal seen should be identified. Breeding choruses should be worked until the source of each different call has been located and identified. The decision to quit searching in one habitat and move to another is made by the investigator; searches within habitats are stopped either when all of the available habitat has been thoroughly searched or when no new species has been found for a predetermined period of time. Undue concentration on calling males of one species, to the exclusion of males of other species, will always be counterproductive when trying to characterize the entire fauna over a short period. The searcher records the time when the search period ends. The efficiency and comparability of short-term sampling efforts are enhanced if sampling is carried out at a time of year and during weather conditions when amphibians are most active. In most areas, that time is early in the warm, rainy season.

The SSS follows the above procedures but focuses on gathering data on (and usually capturing) specimens, not species. With the exception of members of breeding aggregations, individual amphibians are tallied as they are encountered, up to the previously determined number. Species occurring in aggregations, such as breeding choruses, should be counted only once in the specimen count. The decision to leave one habitat and proceed to another is dictated by the number of specimens tallied. The suggested sample size per habitat for diverse tropical faunas is 100 specimens. For less diverse faunas, fewer observations may adequately represent any single habitat.

PERSONNEL AND MATERIALS

General collecting and SSS can be performed by any number of workers, but one person should be in charge of describing the habitats and keeping the time records and should be responsible for the data collected by other workers. All of the collectors for an SSS should be experienced.

A machete or potato rake can be used to tear up logs, to turn stones, to pull down epiphytes, to rake through leaf litter, and to probe in holes and crevices. One should never use bare hands, especially in areas where poisonous snakes may occur.

If the fauna is complex (many species) or poorly known, amphibian eggs and frog larvae often cannot be identified reliably, and sometimes cannot be identified at all, unless samples are reared through metamorphosis or large larvae are reared from eggs obtained from known parents. Investigators should carry containers for rearing larvae and food for tadpoles (commercial tropical fish food, rabbit or trout chow, or leafy vegetables to be boiled) into the field with them.

Preparing for the field trip is time well spent. Many collectors, from lack of forethought, do not carry the specialized tools, such as seines, nets, machetes, rakes, and traps, that can make the difference between superficial and adequate sampling of a site.

DATA TREATMENT AND INTERPRETATION

Data derived from long-term historical records vary in quality and reliability. As a general rule, museum catalogue identifications should be verified by examining the specimens, and any unusual locality data should be questioned. Records not supported by voucher specimens, photographs, or recordings of calls should be clearly listed as tentative.

SYSTEMATIC SAMPLING SURVEY

OBSERVER(S) *Norman J. Scott, Douglas C. Robinson*   DATE/TIME *12 October 1968 / 19:20*

GENERAL LOCALITY *Costa Rica: Heredia Province; La Selva*

SPECIFIC LOCALITY *Swamp, 100 m East of headquarters clearing*

HABITAT TYPE *Forest Swamp*   SEARCH TYPE *General Collecting*

HABITAT DESCRIPTION *1/4 ha. swamp with emergent aroids. Open water 20 x 20 m., 0.5 m. deep. Ringed by forest.*

SLOPE/ASPECT *± 20° / 180°*   CANOPY *Complete except over pond*

WEATHER *Overcast, still. Vegetation still wet from rain in P.M.*

TEMPERATURE
air *30.2*   water at surface *28.3*   water *50* cm deep *26.2*

SPECIES ACRONYM OR ID	INDIVIDUALS OBSERVED (C) = CALLING
OLEL – *Ololygon elaeochroa*	OLEL (c), HYEB (c)
HYEB – *Hyla ebraccata*	AGCA (c), GAPI (c)
AGCA – *Agalychnis callidryas*	SmBA (c), LEPE,
GAPI – *Gastrophryne pictiventris*	LEmE (c), BOCO,
SmBA – *Smilisca baudinii*	ELDI (c), CEPR
LEPE – *Leptodactylus pentadactylus*	LEPE, AGSA (c),
LEmE – *Leptodactylus melanonotus*	ELSP1, ELSP1,
BOCO – *Bolitoglossa colonnea*	ELTA, PHVE, ELRI
ELDI – *Eleutherodactylus diastema*	
CEPR – *Centrolenella prosoblepon*	
AGSA – *Agalychnis saltator*	
ELSP1 – *Eleutherodactylus sp.1*	
ELTA – *Eleutherodactylus talamancae*	
PHVE – *Phrynohyas venulosa*	
ELRI – *Eleutherodactylus ridens*	

TOTAL "SPECIMEN" RECORDS (Species/chorus count as one) ___*17*___
APPROXIMATE AREA SEARCHED *1 ha*   ENDING TIME *23:20*

Figure 7. Field data sheet used for adult amphibians in a systematic sampling survey (SSS) in a forest swamp in Costa Rica.

Observations made during an SSS should be recorded immediately in notebooks carried by each investigator. A sample data sheet for a hypothetical SSS in forest swamp habitat is illustrated in Figure 7. Different data sheets would be needed for other major habitat types. In the present example, a swamp and its surrounding vegetation were surveyed. Eight species of amphibians were congregated in breeding choruses; 7 species were not calling. For the purposes of SSS, a single entry was made for frogs (males and females) participating in each species' chorus. Otherwise, chorusing individuals would have overwhelmed the sample, and the data could not have been compared with those from other sites.

This sample contributes 17 "specimens" of 15 species to the target of 100 specimen records for this habitat type. Other forest swamps at the same site would have been sampled until data for 100 specimens had been gathered. The species richness of these 100 specimen records can be compared with that of forest swamps in other areas. In like fashion, samples of 100 specimens from other major habitat types (e.g., forest, forest stream, riverbank) can be compared with

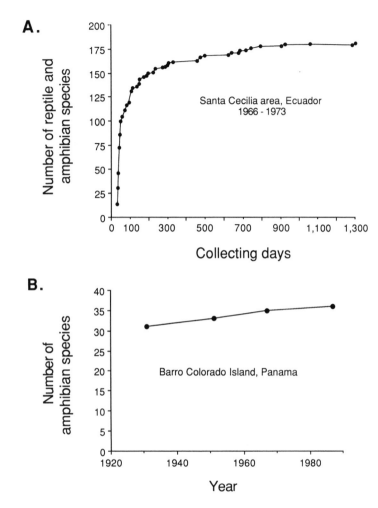

Figure 8. Species accumulation rates. A. Rate of accumulation of reptile and amphibian species in the vicinity of Santa Cecilia, Ecuador (redrawn from Duellman 1978). B. Rate of accumulation of amphibian species over a 56-year period for Barro Colorado Island, Panama (data from Myers and Rand 1969 and Rand and Myers 1990).

samples from other areas with similar habitats, and the characteristics of the entire site can be summarized in a species list derived from all of the samples. If the SSS procedure is valid, species lists and relative richness can be compared among all sites that have been summarized in the same way.

It is important to maintain up-to-date summaries during the actual fieldwork. They can be used to guide the remainder of the collecting effort.

The completeness of a species list derived from long-term records is evaluated by inspecting a graph of the cumulative number of species versus cumulative search time. Search time is usually expressed in days, months, or years. Curves plotting species versus search time rise sharply during the initial search periods but approach an asymptote as the species list nears completion. The asymptote approximates the total species richness of the site. Curves derived from the long-term studies in Panama (Rand and

Myers 1990) and Ecuador (Duellman 1978) are clearly asymptotic (Fig. 8).

The number of reptile species cannot be separated from amphibians in some published graphs (i.e., Duellman 1978). Typically, a greater proportion of the species collected late in the sampling period has been fossorial reptiles and snakes, with a greater proportion of amphibians sampled earlier. In the only study to compare long-term species accumulation rates among taxa, 95% of the amphibian species but only 90% of the lizards and snakes had been taken after 20 years of collecting (Myers and Rand 1969).

If the time-constrained technique is used in similar habitats and with similar faunas, then resulting species accumulation rates from general, short-term collecting can be compared. If the areas are dissimilar, the SSS may be appropriate. An SSS produces lists of the species present in the first x number of specimens collected in each habitat. The number of species then can be compared directly.

For comparisons among sites with nearly complete species lists, real data can be compared with randomly generated lists to determine whether among-site differences are greater, smaller, or the same as randomly expected differences (Guyer 1990).

SPECIAL CONSIDERATIONS

General collecting is the most efficient way for experienced collectors to take the largest number of species in the least amount of time. No other collecting method is as productive in amassing species for a list and in obtaining series of specimens.

The precision of indices derived from SSS depends on the sampling efficiency in different habitats and the accuracy of the species identifications. Even seasoned herpetologists are less efficient when sampling unfamiliar habitats. For this reason, data collected over time by the same collectors are more comparable than data taken by many collectors.

The SSS is most comparable among sites when a variety of collecting techniques is used and search times are well distributed among habitats and times of day and night. For example, searches based primarily on collections of calling males cannot be compared meaningfully with searches made only in forests during the day. The SSS collections used for data analysis should be the result of individual collecting efforts, not of some passive technique such as pitfall arrays. Collectors using an SSS can reduce bias in collecting effort. Species caught with passive systems depend on trap location and individual species susceptibility, so many species are missed.

The species richness index derived from SSS needs to be tested to determine its generality and usefulness. First, tests of the variation due to collectors and time period can be determined by a two-way analysis of variance of the data from independent collections made by different collectors working in the same habitat at different times. Second, data derived from SSS can be compared among sites with well-known herpetofaunas to determine whether SSS produces concordant results.

CONTRIBUTOR: BARBARA L. ZIMMERMAN

2. Visual Encounter Surveys

MARTHA L. CRUMP AND NORMAN J. SCOTT, Jr.

A visual encounter survey (VES) is one in which field personnel walk through an area or habitat for a prescribed time period systematically searching for animals. Time is expressed as the number of person-hours of searching in each area to be compared. The VES is an appropriate technique for both inventory and monitoring studies.

The VES is used to determine the species richness of an area, to compile a species list (species composition of an assemblage), and to estimate relative abundances of species within an assemblage. This technique by itself is not an appropriate method for determining densities (number of individuals per unit area) because not all individuals actually present in an area are likely to be visible during the survey. However, if repeated VESs are done in conjunction with a mark-recapture study, density can be estimated reasonably (Donnelly 1989).

Visual encounter surveys differ from transect sampling (technique 5). A VES can be done along a transect, in a plot, along a stream, around a pond, and so forth, and it samples all amphibians that are visible. Transect sampling uses lines of fixed length in fixed locations and focuses on surface-dwelling amphibians.

TARGET ORGANISMS AND HABITATS

The VES has been used most extensively for rapid evaluation of large forest areas, especially in uniform habitats where visibility is good. The VES works especially well for forest understory anurans that are active in the open (e.g., Toft et al. 1982) and for salamanders that live most or all of their lives in the forest litter but are on the surface after rains (e.g., Pough et al. 1987; Corn and Bury 1990).

Visual surveys also can be used effectively for target species that inhabit easily identified habitats, such as logs or riparian zones, or habitats that are widely spaced, such as talus slopes. They are also appropriate for target species that are highly clumped, such as frogs at temporary ponds; in these cases, the surveys are done in the restricted areas of interest. For example, a VES can be carried out at an aquatic breeding site by setting up multiple transects from the edge of the water into the center of the site.

The VES can be used to inventory aquatic assemblages under certain conditions (e.g., relatively shallow, clear pools with minimal vegetation), but generally such surveys are better for monitoring only certain target species, because not all species in an aquatic assemblage can be observed equally. Frazer (1978) and Griffiths (1984) surveyed aquatic newts at night by VES using flashlights. The VES can also be used effectively to monitor larval amphibians in small, shallow pools where the water is clear and the vegetation is sparse.

A VES is often the best way to survey species that are rare or unlikely to be caught with traps. The technique is not appropriate for surveying canopy or fossorial species.

BACKGROUND

Because the VES is simple it has been used for a long time. The technique has been formalized as the time-constrained technique by Campbell and Christman (1982a) and as the time-constrained searches by Corn and Bury (1990). The results of a VES search are measured against the time spent in the search.

ASSUMPTIONS. The VES is based on the following assumptions:

1. Every individual of every species has the same chance of being observed during a survey (i.e., each individual is equally conspicuous to an observer; there are no differential effects of coloration, size, behavior, activity, or microhabitat preference on the likelihood of being encountered).

2. Each species is equally likely to be observed during each sampling session (i.e., there are no seasonal effects of activity, weather, predators, or competitors on a species' likelihood of being encountered).

3. An individual is recorded only once during a survey (i.e., the observer can keep track of all movement so as not to record multiple encounters for the same individual).

4. Results from two or more observers surveying the same area simultaneously are identical (i.e., there are no observer-related effects).

Although these assumptions have never been rigorously tested and the validity of the results of a VES is unknown, we know intuitively that the assumptions will not hold in most instances. Species do differ in their conspicuousness, and people do differ in their abilities to see amphibians. The resulting potential biases should be recognized and minimized to the extent possible. For example, comparable training and expertise of the individuals involved in a VES are crucial. Some people can develop an excellent search image for amphibians; others never do. Most people improve with practice. If more than one person is required to carry out a VES, individuals should conduct independent surveys in the same test area simultaneously, and their results should be compared. Biases between individual observers may reflect differences in the amount of time spent looking up versus looking down or differences in walking speed. With effort, such biases can be controlled.

LIMITATIONS. Two obvious limitations are associated with a VES:

1. Not all strata or microhabitats within the habitat can be sampled with equal success.
2. Not all habitat types can be sampled with equal success. As a result, relative species abundances can be compared only among sites of the same habitat type.

Dissimilar habitats cannot be surveyed by VES with an equivalent degree of reliability because of differences in visibility; open habitats are surveyed more efficiently than are habitats with dense vegetation. Time of day can also affect a VES; most people find surveying the environment using natural light easier than surveying with a headlamp. Weather conditions can affect a VES; visibility generally decreases with rainy, misty, and cloudy conditions. Thus, surveys of areas to be compared directly should be done under comparable weather conditions, as much as possible, and at the same times of day or night.

RESEARCH DESIGN

The design for a VES will depend on the goals of the study (whether it is a one-time inventory or a long-term monitoring program and, if the latter, whether the intent is to determine phenology of species composition, phenology of species abundances, or both), the specific habitat and the size of the area to be surveyed, the desired periodicity of the sampling regime (diel and seasonal), and the species composition. For purposes of statistical analysis, censusing ten 100-m transects within a given habitat type is preferable to censusing one 1,000-m transect. Regardless of the experimental design, at some point early in the study the data and field methods should be evaluated and the methods modified as appropriate. Three basic sampling designs are used for the VES (Fig. 9): randomized walk, quadrat, and transect.

A *randomized-walk design* is appropriate when a large area is to be sampled. Prior to going into the field, the observer chooses at random a sequential series of compass directions (preferably at least 50); he or she also selects at random a number of meters (up to 50 m) to be walked in each selected direction. The start point can be determined by breaking the area into blocks, randomly selecting one, and starting from the middle of it. All amphibians observed within 1 m on either side of the path are recorded. This design (Fig. 9A) satisfies the assumption of randomized sampling, which allows statistical comparisons among replicated walks in different areas or habitats. Because the VES is a time-constrained field technique, the time spent per unit area must be specified for each investigator and for each area to be compared.

A *quadrat design* is appropriate for sampling a specific area thoroughly. A quadrat of given dimensions is established (we recommend 10 × 10 m or 25 × 25 m, depending on amphibian

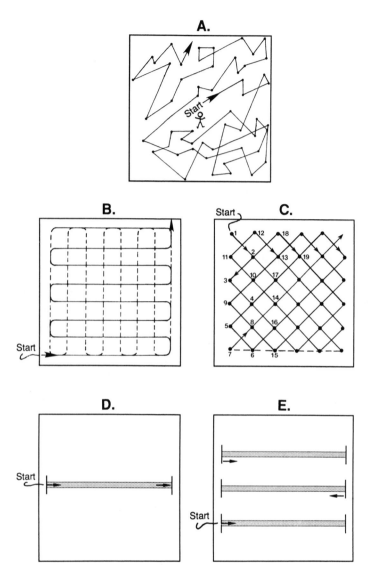

Figure 9. Experimental designs for visual encounter surveys. A. Randomized walk design. The observer chooses a series of compass directions at random and walks each in sequence for a given number of meters, also determined at random. B–C. Quadrat design. An area of given dimensions is systematically sampled either (B) by walking two sets, at right angles, of parallel adjacent paths across the plot or (C) by walking a zigzag pattern between numbered stakes (i.e., in this example, 1 to 13 in numerical order, then 10–14–8–15–6–16–4–17–2–18–19 and so forth). D–E. Transect design. A single transect (D) or multiple parallel transects (E) are set up, and areas on either side of the path are systematically sampled.

densities). The quadrat is then systematically sampled by walking parallel paths across the plot (Fig. 9B) or by walking a zigzag pattern between numbered stakes (Fig. 9C) (Hairston 1980a,b; Aichinger 1987; Donnelly 1989; Nishikawa 1990). If area grids have been established, the exact location of each individual encountered can be noted relative to the distance markers (this information could be used to examine spatial distribution patterns within the habitats). Multiple (at least 10) randomly placed plots can be used to test for changes in species richness or relative abundances over time or to determine differences in species richness or relative abundances among sites at one time. Breeding ponds can be surveyed using this design by constructing a checkerboard of boardwalks or paths at the site (Fig. 9B). Again, time spent per unit area must be standardized among fieldworkers and among sites to be compared.

A *transect design* is appropriate for sampling across microhabitats known to be different or potentially so. In the simplest case, a single transect of preestablished length (Fig. 9D) is laid out and walked (Jaeger 1978; Pough et al. 1987; Crump and Pounds 1989); all animals observed within 1 m of the transect path are recorded. If desired, the exact location of each individual can be noted according to its position relative to previously established distance markers. For large areas, 10 or more transects 100 m long and spaced 20 m apart in the area of interest are appropriate (Fig. 9E). As with the other designs, time spent per unit area must be standardized among workers and areas.

If only one inventory is to be done, it must be scheduled for the time of year, time of day, and weather conditions in which the maximum number of species are expected to be active. Because at any one time of year some species will be inactive, a one-time inventory should be interpreted as a minimal estimate of species richness for the area.

For long-term monitoring programs, sampling periodicity is crucial. One must sample often enough to ensure that within-year variation does not obscure year-to-year differences. Because activity patterns of amphibians are greatly influenced by weather, VESs should be done during each season of the year. Time of day likewise greatly affects behavior patterns, and time of the survey can bias both species composition and abundance data if not taken into consideration.

An important decision to be made during the design of the fieldwork is whether to capture each amphibian encountered to obtain additional information. If individuals are captured, measured, and weighed, less time will be available for additional survey work. If animals are captured, investigators must also decide whether to mark each one individually. Mark-recapture studies yield valuable information on population dynamics, but, again, less area can be surveyed. Marked animals are likely to be recaptured frequently in studies that involve area searches, so marking may be worth the effort. In contrast, the chance of recapturing individuals along a transect is fairly slim and, thus, probably does not warrant the additional time.

FIELD METHODS

Procedures for a VES are straightforward. Habitats are searched, either along a transect or in a plot, and the number of animals encountered per unit of time is recorded. The length of time and intensity of the search, the boundaries of the area to be searched, and the search pattern should be specified in advance. For example, instructions for a survey of salamanders should specify the type(s) of substrate to be examined (e.g., every possible cover item or just logs), whether or not the cover items will be turned over or torn apart, and the maximum amount of time to be spent tearing apart substrates (e.g., a single log). Search methods must be standardized among fieldworkers to reduce bias in the results.

For a complete inventory, all possible microhabitats are searched: ground, water, tree trunks, stems, and upper and lower surfaces of leaves as high as the observer can see accurately enough to identify the animals. Time spent per unit area is standardized as much as possible within a given habitat type, but habitats with differing heterogeneities will require different survey times. When animals are encountered, they are identified and, if need be, captured and measured or collected as vouchers. The VES can be performed at several levels of intensity, as follows.

Among the least intensive surveys are counts of animals active on the surface (e.g., Hairston

1980b; Pough et al. 1987; Nishikawa 1990) or of animal-associated items (e.g., burrows of salamanders—Dodd 1990, 1991a). This type of VES is particularly useful for species that are active on the surface of leaf litter or that climb plants on rainy or foggy nights. Under such wet conditions, a large proportion of the population may leave underground retreats and move to the surface. This method is especially suited for inventory of habitats containing endangered species where habitat disturbance must be avoided.

The intermediate-intensity search is one in which the field crew, in addition to counting already exposed animals, turns over surface objects such as rocks and logs and counts the animals uncovered. The cover objects must be returned to their original positions to minimize habitat disturbance. This type of search generally yields higher return per unit time than a low-intensity search because many amphibians hide under cover objects when conditions are not suitable for surface activity.

At the most intense level of VES, surface objects are turned, decayed logs and bromeliads are torn apart, and litter is raked. These activities obviously change the habitat; long-term effects of this type of search have not been measured for any habitat or target species. Habitat disturbance increases with increasing search intensity, but more animals are encountered. Intense surveys are probably the most reliable in terms of sampling the most species, especially rare ones.

For some studies, it is useful to set up a transect or grid system with permanent distance markers before the survey begins, so that the exact location of every animal can be recorded at the time of encounter. This allows the investigator to calculate interindividual distances, record detailed microhabitat data for specific sites where amphibians have been found repeatedly, evaluate the homogeneity of the area searched, and if a mark-recapture study is done, obtain valuable information on individual animal movements through time.

Depending on the goals of the study, the animals encountered can be observed only (assuming that positive identification can be made without holding the animal), or they can be captured temporarily for positive identification and measurement (see Appendix 1) and then released at the site of capture. Voucher specimens should be preserved and deposited in an established research museum collection (see Chapter 5). Many groups of amphibians are undergoing significant taxonomic revision, and sibling species are often difficult to distinguish in the field. Museum collections provide a basis for verifying field identifications, which greatly enhances the reliability and usefulness of surveys.

PERSONNEL AND MATERIALS

The number of persons needed to execute a VES depends on habitat complexity, size of the area to be sampled, and level of survey intensity. If reasonably short forest transects are to be surveyed, only one person may be needed; surveying a large breeding pond may require several persons, each doing a transect from the shore into the center of the pond. All persons involved must be well trained in the same search techniques, and interobserver differences must be considered. If animals are common and data are taken for each individual, designating a person as data recorder can speed the operation and keep the pace of the survey more uniform.

A VES requires minimal equipment: data paper, pencils or pens with permanent ink, and a millimeter ruler and spring balance if body length and weight are to be taken. Plastic bags and a marking pen are needed if amphibians are to be collected. Potato rakes are useful for searching in leaf litter. If microhabitat measurements are to be taken, appropriate instruments are needed (see Chapter 5). If the transect is to be marked at regular intervals, numbered flagging tape or permanent stakes should be set in place prior to the survey. For nighttime surveys, headlamps are required.

DATA TREATMENT AND INTERPRETATION

The kinds of data to be collected depend on the goals of the study and the time and personnel available. Minimum data to be collected during an inventory of an area that does not contain grids with distance markers include (1) the number of individuals of each species encountered, (2) the total time searched, and (3) the size of the area searched. For inventories and monitoring surveys in areas with distance markers, location within the transect or grid system should be recorded in addition to microhabitat data and the minimum elements previously listed (Chapter 5) for each amphibian encountered. If desired, wet mass and reproductive condition can be recorded. If animals are taken temporarily to a laboratory facility, much of this information can be recorded after the survey is completed to avoid taking up valuable field time. Another option is for a second person to follow the primary VES searcher and record additional data while the first person continues the survey.

Well-organized data sheets that incorporate the minimum data elements (see Chapter 5) and include extra space for notes that do not fit preestablished categories are recommended for use in the field. Data sheets can be simple or complex, depending on the goals of the study (Fig. 10).

A main application of VES generally is determination of the composition of an amphibian assemblage. The list of species compiled for the area surveyed can be compared with species lists from other areas. Mean numbers of individuals can be compared statistically, and coefficients of association calculated (see Chapter 9). Before any data are interpreted or compared, however, effects of the biases noted previously must be estimated (see "Assumptions" and "Limitations," under "Background," above).

As discussed previously, if relative abundances are to be compared among sites, then habitat structure, weather, and search techniques must be similar for all samples. For example, if the project is designed to determine the effects of disturbance (e.g., logging) on amphibians, then separate VESs would be conducted in logged and unlogged parts of a forest. If, however, the researcher wishes to compare two forests, then all VES transects must be located in forest habitats; it would be inappropriate for some transects to include forest edge ecotones while others did not. Until VESs have been validated and we have some idea of their variability and their relationships to actual population levels, data gathered during VESs should not be used to report individual species densities. Dodd (1990) used a Fourier series to estimate salamander burrow densities along transects; this technique may have limited usefulness in the analysis of other transect data.

If long-term monitoring is done, phenology of presence and activity of various species can be presented graphically with histograms or frequency curves. If activity patterns are to be interpreted in light of climatic factors, then correlations, multiple regressions, and analyses of variance may be appropriate types of analysis. Tests of differences in species' activity levels under different weather conditions or among seasonal components of the year are also possible.

SPECIAL CONSIDERATIONS

Campbell and Christman (1982a) surveyed amphibian assemblages in four habitat types in Florida and compared results from intensive VESs with those from road cruising, litter removal–quadrat sampling, and drift fence–pitfall arrays. Fifteen of the 22 species known to be present were recorded with road cruising, and 12 were recorded with VESs. Quadrats and drift fence–pitfall arrays yielded 6 and 7 species, respectively. Bury and Raphael (1983) compared techniques and recommended that VESs be combined with a drift fence–pitfall array to

Visual Encounter Survey

Date _____ Name of obvserver(s) _____

Place _____ Area searched _____

Weather conditions _____ Air temperature _____

Time begin survey _____ Time end survey _____

Habitat description _____

_____

No.	Species	Sex	SVL	Substrate	Location	Activity	Time
1							
2							
3							
4							
5							
6							
7							
8							
9							
10							
11							
12							
13							
14							
15							
16							

Figure 10. Sample data sheet for a visual encounter survey in which specific data are recorded for each individual encountered. If the survey requires only abundance data, the lower part of the data sheet can be redesigned so that individuals of each species seen on the survey can be recorded with tick marks; marks for each species are totaled later.

sample the herpetofauna more effectively. The VES can be validated by repeated sampling of the same areas or by comparison of results of VESs with those from surveys done in the same areas using different methods that estimate true population sizes. The need for validation is urgent. The VES done in conjunction with mark-recapture techniques is useful for studying population trends through repeated sampling of the same areas.

Acknowledgment. We thank Frank Hensley for helpful comments on a draft of the manuscript.

CONTRIBUTORS: *ROBERT G. JAEGER,*
A. STANLEY RAND, LILY O. RODRIGUEZ, AND
BARBARA L. ZIMMERMAN

3. Audio Strip Transects

BARBARA L. ZIMMERMAN

In the vast majority of frog species, males in reproductive condition use distinctive species-specific calls to advertise their position to potential mates and rivals (Wells 1977). The audio strip transect (AST) technique exploits this species-specific behavior. All calling frogs along a transect are counted. The width of the transect varies according to the detection distance of each species' advertisement call. The counts are then used to estimate or determine (1) relative abundances of calling males, (2) relative abundances of all adults, (3) species composition, (4) breeding habitat or microhabitat use, and (5) breeding phenology of species.

TARGET ORGANISMS AND HABITATS

Counting calling male frogs or aggregations of calling males (i.e., choruses) along strip transects can be the most effective way to inventory species composition, to provide a first approximation of relative abundances of breeding frogs, to determine breeding habitat use, and to map distributions of most frog species throughout a large area of several to hundreds of hectares. Audio transects are particularly efficient in tropical forests where species richness is high and frogs dwell at all strata and in many microhabitats. Most frogs are difficult to see in forest without time-consuming searching, which drastically limits the size of area that can be surveyed. The AST technique is generally inappropriate for sampling frogs in linear habitats such as streams and shorelines (see "Data Treatment and Interpretation," below).

Calling males of many species in tropical forest are widely dispersed or occur in groups small enough to be counted accurately by sound. It is usually impossible to count numbers of individuals in a large chorus by sound because calls overlap. Abundances of males in choruses have to be determined visually (see "Visual Encounter Surveys," above and "Surveys at Breeding Sites," below), although the choruses themselves can be counted aurally. Males of most temperate species aggregate at ponds to call. Therefore, the AST technique will probably be most useful in the temperate zone for acquiring species inventories and for mapping distributions of breeding populations (or choruses) and breeding habitats.

The AST technique should generate accurate estimates of the relative abundance of calling males and precise delineations of spatial distribution for species that call over a prolonged period of weeks or months. The method probably does not provide accurate density and distribution estimates for explosively breeding species (sensu Wells 1977) that call on only one day or very few days each year, because these species are encountered so infrequently.

The call count method for mapping distributions and estimating relative abundances of calling males is comprehensive and powerful. No time is spent searching, because within a certain strip width defined by the detection threshold of the species call, the probability of detecting a caller approaches 1. Therefore, hundreds of hectares can be surveyed quickly (Zimmerman 1991). More important, all habitats or microhabitats and forest strata are sampled practically equally; arboreal and fossorial species are counted as easily as ground dwellers, and concealed species are included as easily as unconcealed species. The only species not sampled are those with a short aural detection distance that call from high in forest canopy. We do not know how many, if any, such species exist.

Each person taking data must learn the advertisement calls and determine the detection distance for each species in each major habitat type at the study site.

BACKGROUND

Two transect methods are widely used for estimating terrestrial animal abundance. In *line transect sampling,* the perpendicular distance between each visually or aurally observed individual and the transect midline is estimated by the observer (Burnham et al. 1981). Line transect sampling compensates for the decrease in probability of detecting organisms with increasing distance by basing density estimates on perpendicular distances, so distant observations can be used. To estimate abundance, sample sizes are adjusted according to the detectability of a species (Burnham et al. 1981). An important assumption in line transect sampling is that all individuals on or near the center line are detected, although animals may go undetected away from the center line.

In *strip transect sampling,* all animals of interest within a fixed distance perpendicular to either side of the transect, the strip width, are recorded. The critical assumption of this method is that all individuals within the strip are detected. Because all individuals are counted, strip transects are treated as quadrats (Burnham et al. 1981; Seber 1982). Strip transect sampling has been used most widely to count birds, large mammals, and animal signs (Seber 1982, 1986).

Calling frogs satisfy the main criteria for strip transect analysis; they are readily detectable and identifiable (Eberhardt 1978). Members of a frog assemblage can be identified accurately by sound because species vocalizations are almost always species-specific and distinctive, vocal repertoires usually consist of only one or two call types, and normally fewer than 70 species of frog inhabit any site. If an animal calls within the observer's hearing range, it will be detected with high probability because the sound reaches the listener directly. In contrast, many variables affect whether a frog will be seen or not (e.g., size, movement, coloration, weather, position, observer search-pattern bias), even when it is well within the observer's visual range. In audio surveys, the animals advertise their presence; in visual surveys, the observer must find them.

Line transects have been widely used to sample singing birds (Ralph and Scott 1981) because distant observations can be used without worrying about changes in detectability. However, unlike the situation with many bird calls, the transmission distance of most frog calls is not great (Zimmerman 1991), and distance estimation is too inaccurate to be useful (Bart et al. 1984). Therefore, the main advantage of line transect sampling for birds, which is to extend the range of the survey, is not realized with frogs.

Emlen (1984) proposed a variable width strip technique for censusing calling birds that is essentially the same as the one outlined here for use on frogs. The strip width is twice the maximum distance the animal can be heard by the observer(s) and is determined separately for each species. All calls detected are recorded by the observer walking transects, and transects are surveyed repeatedly. Emlen (1984) concluded that densities calculated from average detection distances derived by the same experienced people working extensively and continuously in one area are more accurate than densities based on subjective observer-to-bird distances for all detections. Bart et al. (1984) compared line and strip transect methods for surveying calling yellow rails in Michigan. Their study is particularly relevant because the behavior of yellow rails resembles that of many rain forest frogs; that is, they are secretive and uncommon and call primarily at night (Bart et al. 1984:1382). The authors concluded that the strip transect method was superior to the line transect method for the following reasons: Estimating distances to calling individuals was not feasible; the length and width of the transects could be adjusted to the terrain, weather, and yellow rail density; and all calling birds could be found if they were calling when the transect was sampled.

ASSUMPTIONS AND INTERPRETATION. Several additional assumptions are specific to the AST technique when used with frogs. The first is that the observer is fully knowledgeable of the species-specific calls. If information about frogs at a site (e.g., species list, tapes of calls) is not available, it could take an entire season to learn the calls. The time required will depend on the complexity of the fauna. If a site is relatively well known or if the fauna includes few species, the time required for learning calls will be reduced. A second assumption is that calling generally equates with breeding and that only males call (Littlejohn 1977; Wells 1977). This assumption was validated at a site in the central Amazon by the concordant distributions of calling males and their conspecific tadpoles (Zimmerman and Rodrigues 1990; Gascon 1991). Therefore, call counts can be used to locate breeding sites and to estimate abundances of breeding males; they cannot be used to determine distributions and abundances of females, juveniles, or silent males.

Because most frogs call obligatorily and practically exclusively while attempting to breed at a site, often an investigator can identify breeding habitats or microhabitats and, consequently, critical subsets of areas for conservation without ever seeing a female, juvenile, or larva (Zimmerman and Bierregaard 1986). Exceptions to this general rule include members of the Neotropical family Dendrobatidae, which lay eggs near call sites but later transport tadpoles some distance to aquatic sites where development is completed.

Use of AST data to estimate total adult abundance requires that maximum abundance of calling males correlate in a constant way with the abundance of noncalling adult males and the abundance of adult females. The violations of these assumptions are usually too severe to allow investigators to extrapolate male calling data to total population size.

The AST technique has several other assumptions. (1) Each calling frog is counted only once per sample (i.e., it does not move a significant distance). (2) Every male calling singly within the strip is detected. (3) The detection distance of a given call remains constant (i.e., an individual always calls at the same decibel level). (4) Mean detection distance of a species is appropriate for all microhabitats in which the species is usually found and for solitary individuals and choruses. (5) All habitats within the study area are sampled.

Several factors may affect the accuracy of assessments of abundance and habitat occupancy based on AST counts. For example, if counts of a species are not made during its peak breeding period, when the maximum number of males is calling, differences between samples in numbers of calling males may simply reflect differences in stage of the breeding cycle. Length of the breeding period also may affect accuracy. Males and breeding sites are most likely to be recorded for species in which the breeding period is prolonged and males call continuously (i.e., nightly for weeks or months). Relative abundance and distribution of species that appear sporadically over months (i.e., call anytime during weeks or months but not on most nights or even every week) can also be determined if transects are sampled frequently over several years. Even so, values for these species may be underestimated compared with those for continuously calling species. Long-term sampling also increases chances of encountering choruses of explosively breeding species, but accuracy of the count is probably lower than for species with longer breeding periods.

To determine relative abundance accurately, the distribution of a species throughout its available breeding habitat must be considered. The most reliable estimates of densities of calling males are obtained for widespread, continuously calling, prolonged-breeding species, because sample sizes are greatest. Species with patchy or sparse distributions are encountered less frequently along randomly located transects, and mean densities are calculated from much smaller samples.

The error arising from differential phenology and spatial distribution of species reflects scale inequality. If calling males of a species nearly saturate their habitat spatially and/or temporally (by calling continuously), the number of individuals in the area and, therefore, the estimate of density vary little between transects, months, or years (Wiens 1981). If the species is rare, patchily distributed, and/or calls infrequently, then intertransect and intermonth density estimates will vary substantially even if the population is constant. A particular temporal and spatial scale may be too small to estimate densities of widely dispersed and infrequently calling species accurately, but adequate to measure densities of densely packed or continuously calling species. The implication is that only abundances of species that are sampled at roughly the same scale should be compared. Overall frog densities of continuously calling species cannot be compared with those of sporadically calling or clumped species, because populations of the former would be more evident and therefore better sampled.

OBSERVER EFFECT. Observers must have full hearing ability and be experienced (Emlen and DeJong 1981; Faanes and Bystrak 1981; Kepler and Scott 1981; Ramsey and Scott 1981). Even so, observer bias can profoundly affect the results of an acoustic survey, as has been shown with bird call counts. Methods proposed to reduce this bias in bird surveys (Ralph and Scott 1981; Bart and Schoultz 1984) apply equally well to frog surveys.

Observer effect is most likely to bias abundance estimates of species with high-frequency calls (4 kHz or more) and/or high call rates in large choruses. High frequencies attenuate more quickly than low frequencies, and high-frequency frog calls may be masked by insect noise in the same frequency band. Rapid call rates are a problem when more than a very few individuals are calling, and detection rates of such callers may vary among observers. It is nearly impossible to count individuals by call in large choruses because it is difficult to discern individual callers in the cacophony. Species with highly overlapping calls can be counted visually or, if callers are abundant and widespread, can be sampled aurally in small quadrats. Kepler and Scott (1981) recommended that observers perform simultaneous but independent trial surveys to identify species whose detection is inconsistent and to allow procedures to be corrected, where necessary, before the real survey.

To minimize potential observer bias from variable sound transmission, call surveys must be performed in similar habitats and under similar meteorological conditions (Emlen and DeJong 1981). Wind and rain are particularly disruptive because they reduce distances at which calls can be detected.

There is evidence that as the number of singing birds audible from a listening station increases, correct identification of the number of singers declines (Duke 1966; Bart and Schoultz 1984). Therefore, the number of animals recorded in a call survey may differ among populations, and the densities of abundant species and changes in their densities may be underestimated (Bart and Schoultz 1984). The importance of density-dependent bias in frog call samples is not known. It is likely that observer efficiency with frogs will decrease at caller densities somewhat higher than those measured for birds (Bart and Schoultz 1984). Densities of species in which aggregations of four or more callers occur regularly may be somewhat underestimated with this technique. Discerning number of callers in species with ventriloquial calls may be difficult with more than two individuals.

LIMITATIONS. The AST method has several limitations. (1) Numbers of calling males cannot be determined aurally for chorusing species or in situations of high call overlap (high densities of males calling at high rates). (2) Some reproductively active males of certain species do not call (e.g., Fellers 1979), so that even maximum counts probably underestimate the actual number of adult males present. (3) Explosively breeding species are acoustically evident for extremely short periods and are probably not sampled adequately. (4) Absolute population size cannot be estimated, because male and female survivorships may not be related and because maximum counts of calling males may not be constant proportions of the adult population.

RESEARCH DESIGN AND FIELD METHODS

Transects should approach a length of 1 km if they are to provide accurate estimates of relative abundances of rare as well as common species (Engel-Wilson et al. 1981; Hanowski et al. 1990). Transects should be spaced far enough apart so that frogs on one transect cannot be heard from another, ensuring independence of observations. Ideally, transects should be located at random with respect to frog breeding sites. In practice, observers usually use trails laid out for other purposes (e.g., hunting, travel between villages). Because such trails have been situated irrespective of frog breeding sites, the violation of criteria for random placement is minor enough to allow their use for this technique.[1] However, sampling order and starting points of the transects within each major habitat type must be determined randomly. It appears that 6 to 9 surveys during the breeding season of each of two to five 1-km transects are enough to provide

accurate and consistent estimates of relative abundance for moderately abundant species (1–5 individuals/ha). At least 15 censuses are required for rare species or for 0.5-km transects (Engel-Wilson et al. 1981).

Observer calibrations for transect strip widths are determined separately for each frog species. The observer measures the minimum distance at which the frog can no longer be heard clearly (Zimmerman 1991). Measurements are made for at least six different frogs of each species to derive the mean detection distance and standard deviation. Detection distances should be measured in all the microhabitats in which calling frogs normally occur, and for frogs calling both alone and in groups. Sound transmission distances, and therefore detection distances, vary greatly with gross vegetation structure (Marten and Marler 1977; Marten et al. 1977), so mean detection distances must be estimated in each habitat (e.g., primary forest, dense secondary growth, grassland, swamps). Accurate detection distances are imperative because they strongly influence resultant density estimates.

Calling activity of nocturnal tropical frogs is generally greater before midnight (between 1800 and 2400 hrs) than after midnight (between 0000 and 0600 hrs—Zimmerman 1991). Diurnal species, in contrast, have pronounced calling peaks at dawn and dusk and after rain (L. O. Rodriguez, pers. comm.; pers. obs.). In general, the most productive time to walk transects is from dusk through the first two or three hours of darkness because this period encompasses peak calling activity of most species in both tropical and temperate zones. Observers simply walk transects and record the species, number of individuals, habitat or microhabitat, location, and time of each frog or chorus heard. Transects are sampled at a walking speed that depends on observer preference and terrain. It is most efficient to record observations verbally on a small tape recorder while walking and to transcribe the data later.

---

1. Some trails made by local people follow streambanks, and in some places streams are important breeding sites. In these situations the trails are not independent of breeding sites, and the results must be interpreted accordingly.

PERSONNEL AND MATERIALS

One of the strengths of this technique is that data can be taken by a single person. During the observer calibration phase, a second person can be helpful.

A good-quality tape recorder, a microphone, and a sound-level measuring instrument (Appendices 3 and 6) facilitate the calibration phase of frog detection distance and can be used to record frog calls unknown to the observer. It is imperative that the calling individuals, as well as tape recordings of calls, be preserved as vouchers for the study (Appendix 4). Other materials needed are data forms (or paper), pencils or pens with indelible ink, headlamps (Appendix 6) for night work, and, if affordable, a hand-size tape recorder for taking data in the field.

DATA TREATMENT AND INTERPRETATION

Counts used to calculate calling male or chorus density must be made during the species' breeding period when males are likely to call. For purposes of this technique, a species' breeding period is defined as that interval when most calling is observed throughout the study area. This interval is determined by plotting the mean number of callers or choruses against week or month of the study and identifying activity peaks. If males appear equally likely to call in any month, as is the case with some tropical species, the breeding period is considered to be all year, and counts from all months are included in the analysis.

To estimate density of calling males (or choruses) of a species along a transect, the maximum count of individuals (or choruses) during the breeding period is divided by the strip area for that species. The strip area is the strip width (i.e., twice the mean detection distance of the species call) multiplied by the length of the transect. The mean density of calling males of the species in the study area during peak breeding activity is the mean of the maximum densities recorded on each transect. This meticulous tran-

sect-by-transect analysis is facilitated by use of a computer if there are many transects, many species, and many months (Zimmerman 1991).

If breeding individuals of a species are found only in certain subhabitats within the study area (e.g., stream valleys or temporary pools within a tract of primary forest), then caller densities must be standardized with respect to the subhabitat (e.g., callers per hectare of stream valley or per pool rather than callers per hectare of primary forest). Subhabitat-specific densities can be converted to values representing the entire study area if the proportion of different subhabitats within a study area is known (e.g., from aerial photography, topographic maps, or habitat surveys).

SPECIAL CONSIDERATIONS

One can sample species in linear habitats (e.g., shorelines of ponds or lakes, along streams) by counting calling individuals. This procedure does not require determination of a detection distance and thereby differs from AST. With linear habitats, calling-male density is calculated as numbers of calling males per kilometer of linear habitat.

CONTRIBUTOR: LILY O. RODRIGUEZ

4. Quadrat Sampling

ROBERT G. JAEGER AND ROBERT F. INGER

Quadrat sampling consists of laying out a series of small squares (quadrats) at randomly selected sites within a habitat and thoroughly searching those squares for amphibians. This technique can be used to determine the species present in an area, their relative abundances, and their densities. Because quadrats are placed at random in the area of interest, and because each quadrat constitutes an independent sample, statistical inferences can be drawn from the data, given that the number of quadrats used is sufficiently large. Statistical inferences can be used either for monitoring (changes in population abundance in a given area through time) or for inventory (differences among areas of interest at a given point in time).

The strength of quadrat sampling, with a large number of randomly placed quadrats, is that for any area, effects of habitat heterogeneity do not compromise the results. This is true even if the area of interest contains many different kinds of habitat "patches."

Quadrat sampling has been used most effectively for sampling amphibians in the forest litter, where species often occur in high densities but are difficult to detect because of their secretive habits. It also can be used to sample aquatic amphibians (e.g., salamander larvae). A pond is divided into quadrats, and the quadrats are randomly sampled by a standardized dipnetting method (see "Quantitative Sampling of Amphibian Larvae," below). Open-area habitats can also be divided into quadrats, and at a later time the number of amphibians (e.g., frogs) visible in each randomly selected quadrat can be counted. The method loses effectiveness in habitats with dense ground cover and on irregular or steep terrain where it is difficult to place quadrats on the ground at random. Quadrat sampling should be used only when (1) animals do not leave the quadrat due to sampling disturbance before being counted, (2) quadrats can be randomly (not haphazardly) placed, and (3) quadrats yield independent data (not repeated measures).

TARGET ORGANISMS AND HABITATS

Quadrat sampling is particularly useful for studying forest-floor or streamside species of amphibians. Although the method has been used in relatively open vegetation, it is most effective in closed-canopy forests. In species assemblages having a significant proportion of riparian species, riparian and nonriparian components of the assemblage can be sampled by separate sets of quadrats. Quadrat sampling has been effectively employed in tropical forests to determine density, species diversity, and relative abundances (Lloyd et al. 1968a; Scott 1976; Inger 1980; Lieberman 1986), and in temperate forests to follow densities of salamanders over long periods (Jaeger 1980a,b; Mathis 1990).

BACKGROUND

When attempting to test for temporal or spatial differences in number, relative abundances, and densities of species, statistical testing of the null hypothesis that any differences detected are due to chance alone can be used. Thus, it is important to satisfy the statistical conditions of random sampling and independence of data sets. Correctly employed quadrat sampling techniques meet these requirements.

MONITORING. For measuring changes through time in a given area of interest, multiple quadrats should be placed at random in the area at each period to be measured. If animals are not removed from the area during sampling, it may be possible to reuse previously established quadrats in subsequent sampling. If animals are removed during sampling, then subsequent quadrats should be placed randomly with the restriction that previously sampled quadrat localities are not resampled. This technique is superior when sampling a given area before and after some type of treatment (e.g., perturbation of the habitat, such as biocide treatment). Quadrats, in addition to being placed randomly in an area, should be sampled in random sequence to minimize the effects of uncontrolled short-term temporal changes (e.g., weather).

INVENTORY. For measuring differences at a given time among different areas (or habitat types), multiple, randomly placed quadrats should be established in each area of study and sampled in random sequence. Ideally, all quadrats in all areas or habitats would be randomly sampled sequentially, but this would require the observer to move back and forth among the different areas for sampling, expending valuable time.

ASSUMPTIONS. Effective use of quadrat sampling requires first that all animals be equally "available" to the researcher. If the study is concerned with a single species, it is best to lay out quadrats at a season or under weather conditions considered most favorable for that species, such as immediately after warm spring rains for terrestrial temperate salamanders. Repeated sampling in different years should be carried out at the same season and under similar weather conditions. If the study is concerned with many species in an assemblage, it is important to recognize that fossorial or semiarboreal species are not sampled as efficiently by this method as species remaining within or on the floor litter. Again, repeated sampling of an area (or of other areas) should be conducted at comparable times of the year.

Second, bias must not be introduced by changing observers during the study. Different observers have different visual quirks. If small quadrats (1 × 1 m) are used, it is best that a single person search all of the quadrats. If that is not practical, several observers should be assigned quadrats on a random basis. If large plots (8 × 8 m) are used, four or five persons are necessary to minimize escape of animals. The same team should be used for all quadrats.

STRENGTHS OF THE TECHNIQUE. Although quadrat sampling is labor-intensive, it has the advantage of bringing the eyes and hands close to the targets. Fossorial species, arboreal species that rest in the litter, and species that merely pass through the litter for short periods in the life cycle (e.g., juveniles) are all likely to be seen in quadrats, if sample sizes are large and plots are well distributed over the seasons. This technique is excellent for dealing with habitat heterogene-ity when sampling for multiple species with different microhabitat preferences. It also allows for powerful statistical analyses.

RESEARCH DESIGN AND FIELD METHODS

Ideally, the area of interest should be visualized as though covered by a rectangular grid, and sampling quadrats should be located within the grid by use of a table of random numbers (Appendix 7). Local topography may make such a scheme impractical, but any necessary modification should depart as little as possible from the ideal. Quadrats should be separated by enough distance to avoid presampling disturbances.

On a map of the sampling area of interest, relatively large squares (e.g., 100 × 100 m, although this particular size is not critical) are identified or located. Each square is assigned a number for use in randomized sampling. Two methods for quadrat sampling are now possible: point sampling and broad sampling. *Point sampling* (small quadrats) should be used when studying single species with small, densely distributed individuals (e.g., the salamander *Plethodon cinereus,* in which density can reach 3 individuals/m² and adult total length can range to about 9 cm). *Broad sampling* (large quadrats) should be used to sample species in which individuals are widely dispersed, large-bodied, or both and to sample multispecies populations. In either case, all quadrats in the study are the same size. Comparability among samples is limited to quadrats of the same size. We recommend that small quadrats measure 1 × 1 m. We recommend that large quadrats measure 8 × 8 m rather than 10 × 10 m, because in most of the previous studies of amphibians, large quadrats have measured 25 × 25 feet, which approximates 8 × 8 m.

POINT SAMPLING. A priori, one chooses the exact number of large squares (or units) to be sampled; 25 to 30 will provide sufficient data for statistical analysis. Using a random numbers table, the investigator identifies these squares and the randomized sequence of sampling. A sequential series of compass directions and distances (up to 20 m, although this may vary with the dimensions of the grid) are also determined. It is easiest to complete this phase of the study design prior to going to the field. Once in the field, the investigator goes to the center of the first square to begin a randomized walk. He or she walks in the compass direction and for the distance previously determined, to arrive at the first point-sampling spot. He or she drops a 1 × 1 m quadrat-frame on the ground, quickly removes every stone, piece of wood, and leaf in the quadrat, and counts the number of individuals of each amphibian species present. The debris and the amphibians (if resampling is to be done at a later time) are replaced, and the investigator walks for the next number of meters in the next compass direction in the sequence, again dropping the quadrat frame and sampling as before. This procedure is repeated for a total of 10 sample points. A restriction is that a given spot can be sampled only once in a particular sampling period. The investigator moves to the second randomly chosen large square and repeats the point-sampling procedures. The process is repeated until all of the large squares have been sampled.

The 10 point samples in each large square can be averaged to yield a mean density of each species in that sample unit. If the research design includes 25 to 30 large squares, then the procedure yields 25 to 30 independent data points. Two-sample statistical tests can be used to compare two areas (or habitats) or the same area (or habitat) at different times. Multiple sample statistical tests are used for comparisons among several areas or several samples through time.

BROAD SAMPLING. A priori, the investigator chooses the exact number of large quadrats to be sampled; 50 to 100 are sufficient. Using a table of random numbers, he or she determines the position of each quadrat. If, for example, the area to be sampled is 1,000 × 1,000 m, the first 3-digit number determines the position on the x-axis and the second 3-digit number determines the position on the y-axis for the corner of the first quadrat. An 8 × 8 m quadrat is laid out using stakes and twine. One person on each side of the quadrat removes all litter from a 30-cm swath along the outer perimeter in order to make an escaping animal more easily visible and to minimize possible bias due to edge effect. Each person removes the litter and ground cover from strips inside the quadrat and parallel to the boundary twine, working successive strips from the outside toward the center, until the entire area is covered. Appropriate information for all amphibians encountered is recorded. If the area is to be resampled later, all litter, ground cover, and amphibians should be replaced. This process is repeated, in a randomized sequence, for all quadrats.

Although statistical variances for average densities may differ from area to area, they usually approach an asymptote for means based on between 50 and 100 quadrats even where densities of species are low (Lloyd et al. 1968a). A sample from a single season or a single site should include at least 50 quadrats.

For valid estimates of species densities, investigators must take extraordinary care to follow completely randomized procedures, not an easy task under field conditions. The temptation to look for amphibians of interest in areas deemed "good" for such animals always exists. Acting on such temptation leads to sampling bias (see Chapter 4) and may invalidate any generalizations possible from statistical analysis (or the analysis itself), or it may undermine the goal of the study, which is to obtain accurate estimates of species number, relative abundances, and densities. Sampling biases usually result in incorrect estimates of species densities.

To illustrate, say that an investigator wishes to compare the densities of two species of salamanders in two forested valleys. In valley 1, species

Table 5. Sample Data from Broad Sampling of an Area Using the Quadrat Sampling Technique[a]

Quadrat number	Number of individuals of each species					
	Species A	Species B	Species C	Species D	Species E	Species F
02	1	0	0	0	4	8
05	1	0	0	0	10	2
11	0	0	0	0	8	2
15	1	0	0	0	16	4
19	2	0	0	1	11	10
21	1	1	1	0	7	4
22	0	0	7	0	8	21
24	10	1	1	1	9	15
32	0	1	0	1	0	11
35	1	4	1	0	7	20
37	0	0	0	0	9	9
40	1	0	1	0	4	32
49	13	5	1	0	8	14
52	1	0	0	0	5	19
56	1	2	1	0	7	27
60	0	0	0	0	4	1
61	1	1	3	2	9	18
62	1	1	1	0	7	45
68	1	2	2	0	15	17
73	0	0	0	0	0	0
77	9	3	2	1	9	9
78	1	0	0	0	7	23
82	1	1	1	0	9	23
85	1	1	0	0	9	23
91	0	1	1	0	1	10
96	0	0	0	0	8	16
97	1	1	0	0	10	14
Total Abundance	49	25	23	6	201	397
Average	1.81	0.93	0.85	0.22	7.44	14.70
Relative (%)	7.0	3.6	3.3	0.9	28.7	56.6

Species richness = 6 species

n = 27 quadrats

[a] Data are provided for 27 quadrats measuring 8 × 8 m. An actual data set should include samples from a minimum of 50 quadrats.

A is patchily distributed under logs; in valley 2, species B is evenly distributed in the forest leaf litter. The two methods of quadrat sampling described above will allow an unbiased sampling of individuals and species in both valleys, because a reasonably large number of randomly placed quadrats will include both patchy and more homogeneous areas of habitat. The need for biodiversity studies based on randomization cannot be overemphasized.

We recommend that the following information be recorded for each quadrat sampled: (1) location of the quadrat within the grid; (2) date, time at which sampling begins and is completed, and general weather conditions during sampling; (3) temperature and relative humidity; (4) vegetation type in the quadrat; (5) slope of area on which the quadrat is located (using a clinometer); (6) canopy cover (as a percentage of area directly above the quadrat); (7) leaf litter cover (percentage of the quadrat covered by leaves, and depth of the leaves—the latter can be estimated by pushing a sharp stick into the litter at the four corners of the quadrat and counting the number of leaves pinned to the stick); (8) herb cover (estimated percentage of quadrat covered by herbs and seedlings < 1 m tall); (9) shrub cover (estimated number of multi-stem plants > 1 m); (10) tree numbers and sizes (measured as diameter at breast height); (11) rock cover (estimated percentage of area covered, and size range of the rocks); and (12) logs (number and size).

PERSONNEL AND MATERIALS

Point sampling is minimally biased if a single person samples all quadrats. Broad sampling usually requires a minimum of four persons.

Quadrat sampling requires few materials: random numbers table, map of the sampling area(s), meter measuring tape, bags in which to place amphibians, watch, compass, and either string and stakes or a 1 × 1 m quadrat frame.

DATA TREATMENT AND INTERPRETATION

For comparisons of species numbers, relative abundances, and densities, only the number of individuals of each species in each quadrat needs to be recorded. Data from broad sampling may be recorded easily, as shown in Table 5; for point sampling only two columns would be used, one with the heading "Quadrat number" and another with the heading "Number of individuals in quadrat."

Species richness can be obtained from a simple tally of the number of species found in the target area, just as with other sampling methods. However, this total is the accumulation over all quadrats sampled. Species densities and relative abundances can also be determined (e.g., see Table 5).

Quadrat sampling can provide suitable data for investigation of spatial patterns. A variety of statistical distributions have been used to describe the scatter of different taxa in target geographical areas. The approach to fit and estimation is well described by Krebs (1989).

When data from more than one study are evaluated, locality or time comparisons can be made by descriptive and inferential statistical methods. Regardless of the procedure selected, the problems of zero entries and the so-called ties in ranking will need to be evaluated as possible sources of bias and reduced precision (see Chapter 9).

Quadrat sampling methods have been applied in several studies (e.g., Heatwole and Sexton 1966; Barbault 1967; Lloyd et al. 1968a; Toft 1980; Scott 1982; Lieberman 1986; Fauth et al. 1989), although not always precisely as we have defined them here.

CONTRIBUTORS: LEE-ANN C. HAYEK, A. STANLEY RAND, AND NORMAN J. SCOTT, Jr.

5. Transect Sampling

ROBERT G. JAEGER

Amphibians frequently respond differentially to environmental gradients, especially gradients that reflect moisture. Transect methodology can be used to sample either across these habitat gradients or within habitat types. Randomly located narrow strip transects (e.g., 2 m) are laid out, within which portions of the habitat are searched thoroughly for amphibians.

The strength of transect sampling, using a randomized design, is that it effectively tracks species numbers, relative abundances, and densities across habitat gradients. That is, the method is very useful in determining intraspecific and interspecific changes in amphibian populations across some continuously changing environmental feature. Thus, transect sampling is the best technique for studying elevational gradients (on mountains) or habitat gradients from lowland (e.g., streambed) to upland (e.g., forest floor), and is preferred over visual encounter survey techniques for such studies (see "Visual Encounter Surveys," above, for further discussion of differences between the two techniques).

Because transects are randomly placed and because transects constitute independent samples, statistical inferences can be drawn from the data, given that the number of transects used is sufficiently large. Statistical inferences can be used either to monitor changes in a given area through time or to evaluate faunal differences between areas at a given time.

TARGET ORGANISMS AND HABITATS

Transect sampling has been effectively employed in open temperate forests to determine the patchy distribution of the salamander *Plethodon cinereus* on the forest-floor (Jaeger 1970) and to determine the distributions of genotypes (i.e., relatedness of individuals) of this species in the forest (J. Neigel and R. G. Jaeger, unpubl. data). Transects also have been used for precise mapping of distributional and habitat discontinuities between parapatric species (Jaeger 1970) and for tracking changes in numbers and densities of salamander species with elevation on a mountainside (Hairston 1951) and along gradients from streams to upland areas (Hairston 1949, 1980b). Transect sampling also can be used with anuran species that exhibit low mobility during the sampling period (i.e., do not move out of the transect due to sampling disturbances).

BACKGROUND

To measure changes through time in a given area of interest, multiple transects should be placed at random in the area at the first sampling period. In subsequent sampling periods, transects are placed at random with the stipulation that previous transects are not resampled. Depending on the length of each transect, either the entire transect (for shorter transects) or randomly chosen subsections of it (for longer transects) can be sampled. To measure differences among two or more areas at a given time, the same procedure is used, except that each area is sampled (with replicates) only once.

The configuration of the multiple transects depends on the question being asked. If an investigator wishes to sample continuously—crossing a known gradient of habitats (e.g., up the side of a mountain; from a stream onto the forest floor)—then parallel transects should follow the gradient, and each should start at a randomly chosen point along a predetermined starting line (e.g., at a given elevation on the mountain; in the center of the stream). However, if the investigator wishes to compare differences at specific places on the gradient (e.g., within different habitats or ecotones), then parallel transects should be oriented perpendicular to the gradient, and each should start at some randomly determined point.

Whatever the configuration of the transects, they should be sampled in a randomized sequence to dampen the effects of short-term temporal changes in the sampling areas. For example, weather conditions may change over a short time, and this may influence the number of amphibian species or the density of each species observed in different transects. A thoroughly randomized design will allow for reasonably unbiased estimates. Each of the multiple transects should be sampled in random sequential order. Within a particular transect, at the very least, the end at which sampling begins should be determined randomly. If each transect is partitioned into subsections, those to be sampled should be selected randomly and sampled in a random sequence.

Multiple transects in each area to be sampled are preferred. It is difficult to obtain the replicated samples needed for statistical testing from a single transect. A single, very long transect certainly provides the easiest route to sampling in the field, but this method should be avoided whenever possible. However, a single transect will be necessary in certain circumstances, such as when sampling the species in a single stream or on the floor of a very narrow canyon.

Randomized placement of transects is important for preventing biased sampling of an area. Thus, establishing transects in areas that "look like good places" to find the species of interest must be avoided. Unbiased sampling procedures will estimate populational changes along the gradient, rather than in a particular location suspected to be favorable.

Interobserver differences also can lead to sampling errors. Such differences are reduced by a randomized sampling design. This point is discussed extensively in the section "Quadrat Sampling," above. Randomization can be implemented if each person samples the same number of transects in each area and if those transects are randomly assigned to each person.

RESEARCH DESIGN AND FIELD METHODS

Different approaches are used for comparing transect samples taken across an obvious habitat gradient and for comparing samples taken from among discrete subsets of the habitat gradient.

CROSSING THE GRADIENT. This approach is most commonly used to compare differences across habitats, such as sampling from a stream to uplands or sampling along an elevational gradient. In this technique, multiple transects are placed in parallel.

To sample from a stream to uplands, the stream itself becomes the starting line, where all transects begin. The portion of the stream of interest is marked at uniform intervals (e.g., every 5 m) to provide known points of origin for the transects.

To sample along an elevational gradient (e.g., a mountainside), the investigator chooses an elevational starting line. This line can be at the bottom of the mountain (if the entire mountain is to be sampled) or at any contour line on the mountain. Again, the starting line is marked at uniform intervals.

Transects used in gradient studies can be placed in various ways. With an arithmetical progression, transects begin at equal intervals along the starting line. This is a poor design, because it lacks randomization. Yet it is the technique easiest and fastest to use in the field. With a geometric progression, each transect is separated from the next by a geometrically increasing distance. For example, transects 1 and 2 might be separated by 2 m, transects 2 and 3 by 4 m, transects 3 and 4 by 8 m, and so forth. This design does not satisfy statistical randomness and is inappropriate for the kinds of studies of interest here. The preferred design is a randomized one. Here, randomly chosen points along the starting line, selected from a table of random numbers, define the origins of the transects.

The length of each transect and the number of sampling points on each will depend on the question being asked (or the hypothesis being tested) and the area to be sampled. The length of the transect is determined by the minimum distance that traverses the entire range of habitats in the gradient. Clearly, transects running from the bottom to the top of a mountain will be quite different from those running from a stream into the surrounding forest. Whether one area is to be sampled at several different times or several areas are to be sampled at one time, the shortest transects possible should be sampled. Sampling short transects allows for more replicated transects to be included in the survey. In general, the greater the number of replicates, the less the chance of committing a type 2 statistical error (see Chapter 4).

An excellent design for small-area sampling involves random location of the origins of 25 to 30 parallel transects on the starting line; using this many transects will provide sample sizes adequate for statistical testing. Transects should be 100 m long and 2 m wide and partitioned into 100 subsections measuring 1 × 2 m. Ten subsections are randomly chosen from each transect for sampling. Within each subsection, every rock, piece of wood, and leaf is turned, and the number of individuals of each species is recorded. This sampling procedure provides 250 to 300 blocks of data over all transects in the area. If shorter transects are established, it is possible to sample each along its entire length, but the risk that the observer will drive animals just ahead, out of the transect, increases.

SUBSETS OF THE GRADIENT. The technique described above is not designed to reveal changes in species parameters along transects. Rather, it is designed to estimate parameters for the entire given area of interest. Thus, a transect running from a stream to uplands will treat all species and individuals encountered as in the area of interest, despite the habitat gradient. In contrast,

certain types of studies may focus on just such parameter changes, as from a streambed to uplands. It is tempting to treat each transect described above (see "Crossing the Gradient") as a measure of change in species parameters along that transect. I do not recommend this treatment, because there is no information on distributions of individuals within the habitat types encountered along the gradient. An alternative method is to rotate the direction of the transects by 90° such that the first transect to be randomly subsampled lies in the center of the stream, the second at a given distance toward the edge of the stream, and each succeeding one at the same distance from the previous one and parallel to it, until the uplands is broached. Subsections of each transect provide independent data points to test for clinal changes in species and population parameters. Thus, each transect essentially surveys a different "habitat" along the cline, and the randomly chosen subsections of a transect become replicated data points for that habitat. The same approach can be used on elevational gradients (such as mountainsides), where transects can be placed, in arithmetical progression, along contour lines.

TRANSECTS IN HOMOGENEOUS AREAS. Relatively short transects are sometimes used within a relatively homogeneous area. Because habitat gradients are neither severe nor predictable (i.e., they do not occur in a straight line, such as up a mountainside), parallel transects are replaced by randomly positioned transects. I discourage use of this technique because the quadrat sampling method is far superior for determining species numbers, relative abundances, and densities in relatively homogeneous areas. Quadrat sampling also is more likely than transect sampling to uncover patchiness within an otherwise relatively homogeneous area. Finally, randomly placed transects tend to run into each other, causing problems of replicated samples (i.e., sampling the same place twice). Transects should be reserved for studies of known habitat gradients.

Ideally, every aspect of a sampling design should be randomized, including the placement of transects, the selection of subsections to be sampled, and the order of sampling. For a study in which 10 subsections are sampled from each of 30 transects, a total of 300 subsections must be visited in random order. If two or more areas are sampled in the same time frame, the order of visits to all subsections among all areas should be randomized, but travel and time restrictions often make this approach impossible. However, such thorough randomization would ameliorate the effects of short-term changes in the observed number and densities of species that are due to short-term changes in the environment (e.g., weather).

Each transect should follow a straight line. This can be accomplished by following a given compass direction and running a string (anchored at one end) the length of the transect. The observer also must be careful not to disturb sections of the transect yet to be sampled, either while establishing the transect or while sampling other subsections. All transects should be laid-out using a tape measure, before the first sampling begins, so that the transects can be explored in random order.

PERSONNEL AND MATERIALS

The best results are obtained when a single person samples all transects or subsections of transects. When several individuals are involved, procedures should be used to minimize inter-observer bias.

Transect sampling requires only a random numbers table, a map of the sampling area(s), a compass, a 100-m measuring tape, and string, stakes, and flagging to mark the transects.

DATA TREATMENT AND INTERPRETATION

For comparisons of species numbers, relative abundances, and densities through time or space, only the number of individuals of each species in each transect or subsection of each transect need be recorded. Data sheets used for quadrat sampling (Table 5) can be adapted easily for use with transects, merely by replacing "quadrat" with "transect" or "transect subsection."

If each transect is sampled entirely, then the data are analyzed by transect and can be presented as units (e.g., mean density of a given species, number of species) per square meter. When subsections of transects are sampled, each subsection can be used as an independent data point. However, it is preferable to collapse the data for the sampled subsections into a mean for the entire transect (i.e., mean density per square meter, as above) to provide area-wide data sets. Final data analysis, then, is conducted on a set of data points, including one for each transect.

A transect can be envisioned as a long, rectangular quadrat; therefore, if all amphibians are seen and counted along the entire transect, the analytical methods appropriate to quadrat sampling apply. The probability of observing an animal may vary with its perpendicular distance from the path walked by the observer. Krebs (1989) provided a lucid examination of the use of detectability functions as an aid in minimizing this possible source of bias.

When transects are subsampled, the subsection results can be used as the sampling units in any of the inferential or descriptive statistical procedures suitable to answering the research question. Alternatively, a mean per transect may be used as the focus of analysis.

Eberhardt (1978), among others, provided details of statistical analysis appropriate for line transect methods. Models for population density estimation have been and continue to be developed under a varied set of conditions and assumptions. Seber (1973) and Burnham and Anderson (1976) provided methods for density estimation under general conditions of transect sampling. Burnham and Anderson (1984) and

Burnham et al. (1985) discussed the problems of incomplete counts, the need for distance data, and the bias and efficiency of strip transect methods. Skellam (1958) provided a general method for estimating density that allows for individual specimen mobility, assuming that the observer's presence does not affect it. Smith (1979) derived a model to eliminate this latter constraint. Rao et al. (1981) described a sequential program in which sampling is continued until a prescribed number of target organisms has been included in the sample. With a combination transect method (Rao 1984), sampling stops when either a defined number of animals has been sighted or when observations have been completed along a defined length of transect. Seber (1986) provided a readable review of estimation methods and important methodological improvements developed after 1979.

CONTRIBUTOR: LEE-ANN C. HAYEK

6. Patch Sampling

ROBERT G. JAEGER

Amphibian density commonly varies within habitats. High densities are often associated with specific microhabitats or patches (i.e., logs, tree buttresses, bromeliads) that can be identified and randomly sampled. Patch sampling can be used to determine the number, relative abundances, and densities of species present in discrete subunits of an area of interest. Because patches are sampled at random in an area, and because each patch constitutes an independent sample, statistical inferences can be drawn from the data, given that the number of patches sampled is sufficiently large. Statistical inferences can be used either for monitoring (changes in a given area through time) or for inventory (differences between areas of interest at a given time).

TARGET ORGANISMS AND HABITATS

Patch sampling can be applied to any organism that is known or suspected to be confined to discrete microhabitats that can be considered as patches within a broader environment. For example, *Plethodon cinereus* in the eastern forests of the United States defend territories under rocks (Mathis 1990). Each rock on a section of forest floor can be considered as a patch. The technique also can be used to study the amphibian fauna of a particular patch type or habitat subunit.

BACKGROUND

Patch sampling is merely a modified form of quadrat sampling (technique 4). In quadrat sampling, the researcher studies all of the amphibians in a given area independent of whether individual species occupy patches, live in homogeneous areas between patches, or are found in both. Patches in the environment are randomly sampled along with the rest of the environment, and the area of interest is considered to be homogeneous.

In patch sampling, the researcher focuses on species of amphibians that inhabit patches and disregards species or individuals that occur between patches. Thus, the patches themselves can be treated as quadrats in a statistical sense. In quadrat sampling, the quadrats are placed at random in the environment; in patch sampling, the patches are fixed in space (but not necessarily in time), are treated as independent units, and are assigned numbers that can be used for purposes of randomization. Because patches can be treated as quadrats, the reader should consult the section on quadrat sampling for particulars about monitoring versus inventory and the necessity for a completely randomized design.

Several assumptions, in addition to those discussed for quadrat sampling, are basic to patch sampling. First, it is assumed that each patch has an unambiguous border and can be defined precisely. A bromeliad, for example, is a definable patch, whereas a particular elevation on a mountainside may not be so definable in a biological sense.

A second assumption is that patches are operationally definable. A log "ranging from 1 to 5 m long and 10 to 80 cm in diameter" is operationally defined, whereas "a log" is not. Operational definition is important if one wishes to compare attributes of a species within patches between areas, rather than of species within the areas as a whole. For example, if one forest has many logs that are 5 × 0.8 m, whereas another forest has few such logs but many that are 10 × 1.5 m, samples from the second forest should not include large logs, because they were not included in samples from the first.

A third assumption is that in areas to be compared statistically, observers can locate all patches, or at least can locate the same proportion of patches, in an unbiased way. This means that patches need to be visible to the observer; for example, logs must be visible in a forest containing many shrubs or brambles.

Finally, it is assumed that observers can count all individuals of interest in a patch once it has been located. If individuals escape from a patch before being counted, then estimates, particularly of relative abundances of species, may be biased.

RESEARCH DESIGN

The procedure is quite simple. First one identifies all of the patches in the area of interest and assigns a number to each, in sequential order of discovery. If the number of patches is small, all patches are sampled. If patches are too numerous for all to be sampled, or if some patches must be left undisturbed as habitat for patch-inhabiting species, patches are selected randomly for inclusion in the study.

The number of patches required for statistical treatments will depend on the variance in the data, which is not known a priori. I recommend a minimum of 30 patches per area (or per sample

period for monitoring). The 30 patches and the sequence of sampling are selected randomly. It is tempting to sample the patches in some sort of linear sequence, such as in a minimum-distance walk through the study area, but this is a poor option. Randomizing the sequence of sampling provides a degree of control for extraneous environmental variables.

FIELD METHODS

How a patch is actually sampled will depend entirely on the type of patch, and most patch sampling requires individualized techniques. It is important to detect every individual of every species that occurs in each patch. Wake and Lynch (1976) and Wake (1987) described procedures for sampling bromeliads and logs for salamanders. Heyer and Berven (1973) provided an example of sampling tree buttresses for amphibians and reptiles.

PERSONNEL AND MATERIALS

The basic tool for patch sampling is a table of random numbers (Appendix 7). Specific types of patches (e.g., logs, potholes) will require specific sampling materials. It is possible and desirable for a single person to sample all of the patches, to reduce interobserver sampling error.

DATA TREATMENT AND INTERPRETATION

To estimate species numbers, relative abundances, and densities in patches, only the number of individuals of each species in each patch need be counted. By substituting "patch" for "quadrat," data can be listed as shown for quadrat sampling (Table 5).

When one size or type of patch is sampled in only one target area, the results can be examined only in descriptive ways. For example, an estimate of richness or evenness may be obtained, as with quadrat sampling. If each patch's location is recorded (e.g., latitude and longitude), nearest neighbor and clustering techniques can be used to determine spatial distribution patterns. Data on environmental and microhabitat conditions in each patch can help to explain microhabitat sharing or avoidance patterns among species.

When patches are sampled across time or space, species or specimen data may be compared with inferential techniques in which the sampling unit is the individual specimen.

RECOMMENDATION

Randomized patch sampling is a particularly good approach for inventorying or monitoring species that are restricted to particular microhabitats.

CONTRIBUTORS: LEE-ANN C. HAYEK AND JAMES F. LYNCH

7. Straight-Line Drift Fences and Pitfall Traps

PAUL STEPHEN CORN

Straight-line drift fences typically are short barriers (5–15 m) that direct animals traveling on the substrate surface into traps placed at the ends of or beside the barriers. Traps (described below) can be pitfalls, funnel traps, or a combination of the two.

Drift fences with pitfall or funnel traps and pitfall traps without fences are used commonly to inventory and monitor populations of amphibians and reptiles. For example, 9 of 17 field studies reported for management of terrestrial vertebrates (Szaro et al. 1988) used these techniques to sample amphibians. Drift fences with pitfall traps can be used to determine species richness at a site and to detect the presence of rare species. They also can yield data on relative abundances and habitat use of selected species.

Pitfall traps arrayed in a grid without fences can also be used to study the population ecology and habitat use of selected species. Population density can be estimated with this latter technique if it used in conjunction with mark-recapture techniques (see Chapter 8). Drift fence arrays or pitfall grids can be left in place for long-term monitoring.

In this section, I discuss the use of this technique to obtain data on amphibians away from breeding ponds. Use of drift fences and traps to monitor amphibian activity at breeding ponds is discussed in the section "Drift Fences Encircling Breeding Sites," below (technique 9). Some materials and procedures are common to both techniques. Investigators contemplating the use of drift fences and traps in any context should read both accounts.

TARGET SPECIES AND HABITATS

Both arrays of drift fences and grids of individual pitfall traps have been used to sample amphibian assemblages in a variety of temperate habitats, including deciduous forests (Pais et al. 1988), coniferous forests (Jones 1988a), riparian woodlands (Friend 1984; Jones 1988b), wetlands (Beauregard and Leclair 1988), and sandhills (Campbell and Christman 1982a,b). Aquatic salamanders are difficult to trap with pitfalls, but drift fences with funnel traps at the ends have been used successfully to trap *Siren* and *Amphiuma* in seasonally flooded stream bottoms (D. E. Runde and K. M. Enge, unpubl. data).

Drift fences and pitfall traps capture some species more easily than others (Karns 1986; Corn and Bury 1990; Dodd 1991b). Anurans that are strong jumpers or climbers (e.g., *Acris, Gastrophryne*, most *Rana*, most *Hyla*) are more difficult to trap than terrestrial species (e.g., *Bufo, Scaphiopus*) that lack these abilities (Franz and Ashton 1989; Dodd 1991b). Accordingly, numbers of the former either should be omitted from an analysis or should be reported with caution. For example, several studies report the capture of large numbers of the eastern narrow-mouthed toad (*Gastrophryne carolinensis*) using drift fences (Campbell and Christman 1982a; Enge and Marion 1986; Mengak and Guynn 1987). Because of the climbing ability of this toad, however, the numbers of individuals captured probably do not accurately reflect its relative abundance.

Drift fences and pitfall traps usually sample terrestrial salamanders very well but undersample species closely associated with specific microhabitats. For example, in forests of the Pacific Northwest, the primary habitats of the plethodontids *Aneides ferreus* and *Batrachoseps wrighti* are large pieces of fallen trees, whereas *Ensatina eschscholtzii* and *Plethodon vehiculum* commonly are abroad on the forest floor. *Aneides* and *Batrachoseps* are seldom caught in pitfall traps (with or without fences), but *E. eschscholtzii* and *P. vehiculum* are captured in large numbers (Bury and Corn 1987; Corn and Bury 1990).

Some groups—for example, caecilians or tropical arboreal salamanders—normally cannot be sampled with conventional drift fences. However, Vogt (1987) captured the arboreal salamander *Bolitoglossa platydactyla* with funnel traps suspended between branches of trees on a plastic walkway.

Drift fences and pitfall traps are also effective at capturing ground-dwelling organisms other than amphibians, including insects (Greenslade 1964; Luff 1975), reptiles (Jones 1981, 1986; Campbell and Christman 1982a; Vogt and Hine 1982), and small mammals (Spencer and Pettus 1966; Beacham and Krebs 1980; Williams and Braun 1983).

BACKGROUND

Drift fences intercept amphibians moving on the surface of the ground and redirect them into a pitfall or funnel trap. Pitfall traps without fences act in a similar manner, but individual traps intercept only a few centimeters of ground versus several meters for a·fence. Therefore, large numbers of traps are needed if fences are omitted (Corn and Bury 1990).

If pitfall traps are used as live traps and population estimates are derived from mark-recapture data, biases from trap avoidance or trap attractiveness must be considered. Franz and Ashton (1989) observed only one recapture in drift fence arrays of *Gastrophryne carolinensis* tagged with radioactive (^{60}Co) wires. Conversely, Shields (1985) observed preferential use of pitfall traps by southern leopard frogs (*Rana sphenocephala*), possibly in response to warm or moist conditions inside the traps.

Pitfall trapping alone is insufficient if comparison of relative abundance among species within an assemblage is the objective. Drift fences with pitfall traps, however, effectively capture some individuals of most species, at least in temperate areas. Therefore, unequal capture rates are less of a problem for determining some indices of species richness. If one accepts the untested assumption that capture rates do not vary among habitats, trap data can be used to compare relative abundance of individual species among study areas.

If animals are released from traps, they must be marked to eliminate recaptures from calculations of relative abundance. If animals are not released, the researcher must consider the consequences for subsequent samples, especially if an area is to be sampled repeatedly. Drift fence arrays can decimate populations of small mammals (Bury and Corn 1987), but this effect has not been observed for amphibians. Corn and Bury (1991) operated the same grids of pitfall traps for 50 days in 1984 and 30 days in 1985 and removed all animals captured; captures of amphibians did not differ between the two years, except that one species was more abundant in the second year.

RESEARCH DESIGN

The objectives of a study determine the sampling design. Installation of arrays or grids of fences and traps is labor-intensive, and running the system can require significant funds and personnel time. Inventories of species present in different habitats may require less effort than comparisons of species' abundances and densities among habitat types. The objective of many inventories is to sample as many habitats as possible. Therefore, each habitat type may have only one array or grid. This methodology, however, reduces the probability of detecting rare species. Operating traps for a longer time may compensate for fewer arrays or grids.

Quantitative comparisons of species' abundances or densities among habitat types require replication—that is, multiple arrays or grids in each habitat type. This methodology makes detection of all species present in each habitat most likely.

Selection of the locations for arrays or grids should have a sound statistical basis. If a researcher is surveying different habitat types and more than one unit of each habitat type exists, habitats sampled must be selected at random from the larger pool, and arrays or grids must be placed randomly within them. To determine whether stratification is appropriate, a researcher must have fairly detailed knowledge of the habitat(s) in the study area. Decisions regarding stratification must be made before trap systems are installed.

The timing of trapping may also vary, depending on the study objectives. Vogt and Hine (1982) recommended operating arrays of drift fences opportunistically, after rainfall, to maximize captures. In other studies traps have been operated continuously for from 30 days (Corn and Bury 1991) to nearly two years (Campbell and Christman 1982a; Raphael 1988). Both sampling strategies have drawbacks. Opportunistic trapping may be logistically difficult, so that different sampling efforts are applied in different study areas, and short periods of trapping may not be adequate to verify presence of all species (Jones 1986; Bury and Corn 1987). Continuous trapping requires more personnel and may have a greater effect on resident animals, but continu-

ous trapping can be scheduled to accommodate known seasonal variations in amphibian activity. Bury and Corn (1987) trapped in forests of the northwestern United States continuously for 180 days, beginning at the end of May, but captured few amphibians until the onset of rainy weather in October. Subsequent trapping was conducted for a shorter time (30 or 50 days) and was begun on 1 October (Corn and Bury 1991).

Investigators have seldom used the same design for arrays of drift fences or grids of pitfall traps. Shields (1985) operated one hundred 3-liter pitfall traps spaced 10 m apart in a 10 × 10 grid; Raphael (1988) used ten 8-liter pitfall traps placed 20 m apart in a 2 × 5 grid; and Corn and Bury (1990, 1991) deployed thirty-six 8-liter pitfall traps 15 m apart in a 6 × 6 grid. D. B. Wake (pers. comm.), who uses 1-liter traps to live-trap *Ensatina eschscholtzii,* has 176 traps spaced 10 m apart in an 11 × 16 grid.

Several array designs for straight-line drift fences with pitfall and funnel traps are possible (see Vogt and Hine 1982). In most studies, three or four fences with pitfall and funnel traps are used (Fig. 11). An array is preferable to a single straight fence. Arrays intercept animals from any direction, whereas animals moving parallel to a single fence probably are not captured. Because arrays with three fences (Jones 1986; Bury and Corn 1987) use less material than those with four (Campbell and Christman 1982a), they are less expensive and less time-consuming to install. D. E. Runde and K. M. Enge (unpubl. data) found that arrays of different design, when tested side-by-side, yielded comparable results.

The length of the drift fence influences the number of animals captured, and the optimum length probably varies by habitat type. Vogt and Hine (1982) observed that single drift fences less than 15 m long captured fewer amphibians and reptiles than 15-m and 30-m fences, but the component fences of most arrays are either 5 or 7.6 m long (Fig. 11). Bury and Corn (1987) compared arrays of 2.5-m fences with those of 5-m

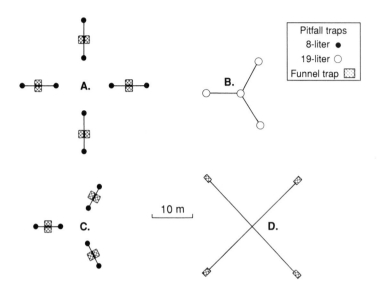

Figure 11. Designs for arrays of drift fences. A. Array used by Campbell and Christman (1982b). B. Array used by Jones (1981). C. Array used by Bury and Corn (1987). D. Array used by Dalrymple (1988). Fences and spacing are drawn to scale; trap sizes are not.

fences and found both adequate for sampling amphibians in coniferous forests in northwestern North America.

The pitfall traps that are used most often are 19-liter plastic buckets and 8-liter cans. Sometimes both are used in the same array. Funnel traps also may be effective for capturing amphibians (Campbell and Christman 1982a; Beauregard and Leclair 1988; D. E. Runde and K. M. Enge, unpubl. data), particularly in areas with saturated soils, where pitfall traps tend to fill with water. Some investigators have caught a variety of amphibians using a standard Campbell and Christman (1982a) four-fence array (Fig. 11A), in which the terminal pitfalls of each fence have been replaced with funnel traps (Vickers et al. 1985; Enge and Marion 1986). Indeed, K. M. Enge (pers. comm.) suggested that pitfall traps are not necessary if amphibians are the primary target animals.

Too little experimentation on the efficacy of different array designs has been done, and too much variation exists among amphibian assem-

blages for me to recommend a single design for all situations. However, a three-fence array with funnel traps (e.g., Fig. 11C) is probably suitable for most studies. Individual fences should be at least 5 m long. This length is convenient because fences for one array can be cut from a single roll of aluminum (see below).

FIELD METHODS

CONSTRUCTION. Large pitfall traps are made from 19-liter plastic buckets. Smaller pitfall traps (8-liter) are constructed by removing both ends and one end, respectively, of two number-10 tin cans (i.e., 3-lb coffee cans) and fastening the open ends of the two cans together with duct tape (Fig. 12). Single number-10 cans or 4-liter plastic jars may be used if the ground is particularly difficult to dig and the target organisms are small. Traps are buried in the ground, with the opening flush with the surface. For 8-liter cans a plastic collar is constructed by cutting the bottom out of a 1-lb plastic margarine tub, which is then inserted at the top (Fig. 12). This collar

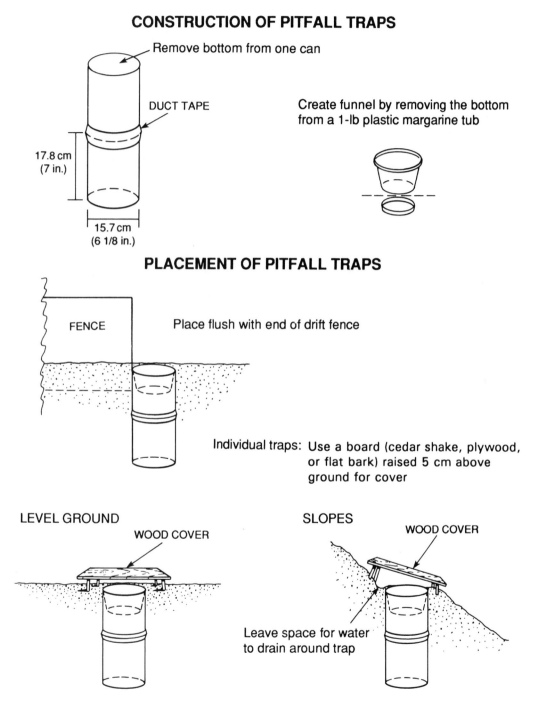

Figure 12. Construction of pitfall traps from two number-10 tin cans (reprinted with permission from Corn and Bury 1990).

keeps animals from crawling out of the trap (Vogt and Hine 1982). Pitfall traps should be closed when not in use. Plastic buckets come with lids, and although the shape of the buckets is often distorted after buckets are placed in the ground, lids will cover them effectively. The plastic lids from the margarine tubs can be used to cover 8-liter traps.

The hole for the trap is dug most easily with a posthole digger, which creates a hole with the correct diameter for 8-liter traps. A tile spade can also be used. Traps also may have a wood cover (Fig. 12). When the trap is open, the cover is raised above the opening. In hot, dry weather the cover protects trapped animals from desiccation and may inhibit predation by birds. The cover may also attract target animals.

Funnel traps consist of rounded tubes (or rectangles) with an inwardly directed funnel-shaped opening at one or (usually) both ends. They are constructed from window screen (Karns 1986) or rigid hardware cloth (Vogt and Hine 1982). Window screen can be purchased in rolls 76 cm wide. The body of the trap is constructed from a piece 90 cm long, and the cut ends are stapled together along the length of the tube. If the cut edges are folded before stapling, the tube is about 25 cm in diameter by 76 cm long. The funnel part of a trap is made from a square piece of screen rolled into a cone and stapled. The diameter of the large opening of a funnel matches that of the tube. A funnel is placed in one end of the tube, and the distal margins of both are attached to each other with staples. If only a single funnel is used, a piece of screen is stapled to the other end of the tube to close the trap. If two funnels are used, the funnel at the other end is attached to the tube with paper clips, so that it and animals can be removed easily from the trap. Funnel traps are placed parallel to the drift fence, midway along each side. Traps should be shaded with loose bark, palm fronds, litter, or plywood.

Drift fences can be constructed from a variety of materials, including hardware cloth, tar paper, window screen, or plastic. The preferred material is 50-cm-wide aluminum valley flashing (weatherproofing material), which comes in 15.2-m rolls. Desired lengths can be cut with tin snips. A mattock or hoe is used to dig a trench 20 cm deep for the length of the fence; the fence is placed in the trench, which is backfilled with soil. Occasionally an ax is needed to cut large roots. Loose dirt is tamped down and smoothed alongside the fence to create a runway, and small obstacles (twigs, rocks) are removed. In forests, aluminum fences 5 to 7 m long usually are self-supporting for a few months. Fences in open areas, fences left in place for several years, longer fences, or fences made from other materials need supporting stakes. Pitfall traps are placed at the ends of the fence so that no gaps occur between the fence and the rim of the trap. If desired, the edge of the trap can be slit and the fence run a short distance into its mouth (Jones 1986). An individual number is affixed to each trap for data recording purposes. Trap numbers can be written on the drift fence with a permanent marker.

For safety, fieldworkers should always wear gloves when handling the aluminum, because of sharp edges. In wet weather, tools quickly become coated with slick mud, so fieldworkers should exercise extreme caution when handling a mattock or an ax.

OPERATION. Ideally, traps should be checked daily, before noon, but with a large number of study areas, this schedule may not be possible. Traps should always be checked at least every three days. If the number of study sites is such that all traps cannot be opened on the same day, traps must be closed in the same order in which they were opened. This procedure ensures the same trapping effort for each area. Because traps can contain dangerous snakes and invertebrates, either long forceps or a small, stout aquarium net should always be used to check them.

If captured animals are to be released, they must be marked. Stockwell and Hunter (1989) released all animals but apparently did not mark them. They then reported total captures for each species. Because numbers of recaptures were unknown, their numbers of captures are difficult to interpret. Animals should be marked and processed in the field. If that is not possible, marking and processing can be done in the laboratory. Dead mammals, live amphibians, and dead amphibians should be placed in separate small plastic bags; all specimens from a single array or grid should be placed together in a larger bag. A cooler with reusable ice containers is best for transporting specimens from the field. Each day's catch should be processed on returning to the lab to reduce the likelihood of specimen and information loss. Processing of individuals to be marked and returned to the site should begin immediately. Live amphibians can be kept for a day or two in a cool place or refrigerator if processing must be delayed, but they must be checked frequently. Dead amphibians should not be frozen (Scott and Aquino-Shuster 1989; Appendix 4). Specimens should be processed by the person(s) who checked the traps, to minimize the introduction of inaccuracies into the data. See Appendices 1 and 4 for information on handling and preserving amphibians.

PERSONNEL AND MATERIALS

Installation of drift fences and pitfall traps is simple but labor-intensive. A large crew (4–6 people) can install three to six arrays or two grids per day. Fewer people are needed to check the traps once they are open. One person can check an array or a grid of 36 traps in an hour or less, depending on the number of animals captured. Several sites can be checked in one day, depending on the travel time between study areas.

Construction materials are expensive. Required items include posthole diggers, 15-m tape or measured nylon rope, plastic flagging (1–2 rolls), waterproof ink markers, aluminum flashing (in rolls 15 m long × 50 cm high, 1 roll per array) or suitable alternative for the fence, 19-liter plastic buckets, number-10 tin cans, 1-lb margarine tubs, and wood covers. Most items can be obtained from building supply stores.

Materials required for operation include a waterproof notebook and paper, large and small plastic bags, large forceps, a plastic cup or long-handled spoon, a small dipnet, and a small cooler with reusable refrigerant.

DATA TREATMENT AND INTERPRETATION

The species and the array and trap numbers of all individuals caught are recorded in the field. This record is important for quality control and should become a permanent part of the data set. It provides critical information during the initial processing of specimens and is a valuable reference for the questions that inevitably arise even after the data have been processed. The study area, date, and array and trap numbers are written in pencil on a small piece of waterproof paper and placed in each bag of specimens.

If animals are released, information must be recorded on formal data sheets at the time the animals are handled. If animals are retained, formal data sheets are completed when the animals are processed. Formal data sheets can be drawn by hand as needed, but preprinted forms are more convenient (Fig. 13). Several software packages can be used to design forms, and many word processing programs have table generation capabilities.

Proper identification of animals is essential, especially if animals are released. Identifications of preserved animals can be verified later. Discarding badly decomposed specimens from traps after field identification is risky. For example, a field crew in southern Washington captured more specimens than it was prepared to handle (Corn et al. 1988). Many small mammals were discarded in the field; the rest were preserved as skulls and deposited in the U.S. National Museum of Natural History. When the skulls were

Locality:	Oregon, Lane County, H.J. Andrews Experimental Forest								
Technique	Province	Stand Number	Habitat	Day	Month	Year	Trap Night	Collector's Name	
P I T	COAST RANGE	7 3 7	OLD GROWTH DOUGLAS FIR	2 2	1 0	8 5	2 2	P.S. CORN	

Catalog Number	Species	Trap Column	Trap Row	Snout-Vent Length (mm)	Total Length (mm)	Mass (g)*	Sex	Age
1 5 5 2 4 4	P L V E	A	1	8 0	3 8		M	S
1 5 5 2 4 5	P L V E	A	1	6 8	3 5			S
1 5 5 2 4 6	P L V E	F	2	9 5	4 8	1 9	F	A
1 5 5 2 4 7	P L V E	B	1	9 4	4 7	1 6	M	A
1 5 5 2 4 8	E N E S	A	4	1 0 3	5 0	3 2	M	A
1 5 5 2 4 9	E N E S	C	6	9 8	5 4	3 1	M	A
1 5 5 2 5 0	E N E S	E	5		1 9	2		J

* Right column is tenths
Trap Night: Number of nights since traps were opened
Sex: Male, Female (if unknown, leave blank)
Age: Adult, Subadult, Juvenile
PLVE: Plethodon vehiculum
ENES: Ensatina eschscholtzii

Figure 13. A sample data sheet used to record amphibians collected from a pitfall grid. Note that species are identified by a four-letter abbreviation using the first two letters of the genus followed by the first two letters of the species. Data are from an inventory of forest vertebrates in Oregon (Corn and Bury 1991).

cleaned and identified, up to 10% of the field identifications were shown to be wrong, even though they had been made by experienced biologists familiar with the vertebrate fauna of the Pacific Northwest. This finding threw into question the identifications of most of the discarded specimens and severely limited the data analyses.

Species richness of ground-dwelling forms is the minimum information obtained by pitfall trapping. Numbers of animals trapped most often are converted to rate values by dividing by the trapping effort, either trap-nights (i.e., 1 trap-night is 1 trap open for 1 night; a grid of 36 pitfall traps open for 30 nights is 1,080 trap-nights) or array-nights (the array is treated as the trapping unit, and individual traps are ignored). These values can then be used as a measure of relative abundance. Grids of pitfall traps can provide data for estimates of density of selected species if used with mark-recapture. A computer program for estimating density from trapping grid data, CAPTURE (Rexstad and Burnham 1991), is available, but to my knowledge, it has not been used for amphibians.

Data can be used to generate simple species lists, or they can be analyzed with complex multivariate ordinations. Various measures of species diversity and association are reviewed in Chapter 9. Gauch (1982) and Pielou (1984) described classification and ordination techniques and the use of multivariate statistics. Relative abundance can be compared among habitat types with analysis of variance (e.g., Corn and Bury 1991), but proper application of parametric statistics requires rigor (e.g., randomization) in selection of study sites and placement of arrays.

Diversity measures that include abundance (or anything but species richness) should be used with caution, because of species-specific capture rates. The numbers of each species trapped may bear little relation to real population sizes. The diversity index or abundance curves, therefore, are peculiar to the sampling scheme employed and may have quite limited biological meaning. Comparisons among habitat types (e.g., Stockwell and Hunter 1989) are probably not appropriate if the amphibian species assemblages differ. Determination of species richness can be enhanced by combining results from pitfall trapping with those from other techniques (Corn and Bury 1990; Bury et al. 1991), but abundance values are not comparable among different sampling methods.

SPECIAL CONSIDERATIONS

After collecting the required voucher specimens (see Chapter 5 and Appendix 4), the investigator must decide whether to collect or release the remaining animals captured. Release requires that all animals trapped be positively identified. Identification in the field may be impractical, particularly in areas where the fauna is poorly known. Collection of all animals trapped requires that arrangements be made for verification of identifications and deposition of specimens in a museum. Also, permits may be required for collecting.

In some habitats, large numbers of small mammals, especially shrews, die in pitfall traps (Bury and Corn 1987). These specimens are an important resource and should be saved. If project personnel are unable to process mammals, arrangements for outside help should be made. All applicable data should be recorded for mammals as well as amphibians. Pitfall traps also capture invertebrates, another important scientific resource. Generally, the collection of mammals, but not of invertebrates, is regulated by law.

Each time a trap is checked, debris and excess water must be removed. A small amount of water should be placed in traps when they are opened, but in wet weather, most traps accumulate more water than is desired. Previous workers (Raphael and Barrett 1981; Williams and Braun 1983) have recommended that water be placed in pitfall traps, as the quickest and most humane way to kill small mammals. Current guidelines for trapping small mammals with pitfall traps (American Society of Mammalogists 1987) specify drowning as the only acceptable method of kill-trapping. However, drowning is a slow and inhumane way to kill amphibians, and it is prohibited in the current guidelines for field methods for amphibians and reptiles (Committee 1987). A compromise between these apparently incompatible recommendations is to keep a small amount of water (2–5 cm) in the traps and to check the traps frequently. Small mammals, particularly shrews, will become hypothermic and drown in this amount of water, but most amphibians should survive. Daoust (1991) placed a $10 \times 5 \times 7$ cm piece of saturated sponge in funnel traps and improved survival of trapped *Rana sylvatica*. Dodd and Scott (technique 9, below) recommend using synthetic foam rather than sponge, which disintegrates rapidly.

CONTRIBUTORS: *RAY E. ASHTON, Jr., C. KENNETH DODD, Jr., KEVIN M. ENGE, DOUGLAS E. RUNDE, NORMAN J. SCOTT, Jr., RICHARD C. VOGT, DAVID B. WAKE, AND BRUCE D. WOODWARD*

8. Surveys at Breeding Sites

NORMAN J. SCOTT, Jr., AND BRUCE D. WOODWARD

Many amphibians are most conspicuous at breeding ponds. Therefore, surveys conducted at breeding sites are especially effective. Sampling at the breeding site involves counting the animals in some predetermined fashion. Generally, adults are counted along visual or aural transects. Techniques for counting larvae, which can also be used to document breeding populations, are treated separately (see "Quantitative Sampling of Amphibian Larvae," technique 10).

Data from surveys at breeding sites can be used to estimate species richness or abundances of breeding adults or larvae at one or several sites. Across-site comparisons are useful for identifying areas most suitable for development or preservation, studying the effects of acid precipitation or pollution from point sources (e.g., factories), and determining the presence of predators. The techniques can also be used to monitor changes in population levels of species, to detect changes in species assemblages through time, or to carry out detailed autecological studies.

TARGET ORGANISMS AND HABITATS

The techniques described here can be adapted for the study of any amphibian that breeds in communal aggregations in temporary or permanent ponds, lakes, or streams. This criterion excludes viviparous species, species with terrestrial nests, and those that breed in very small groups or that use small, ephemeral, widely scattered breeding pools (e.g., bromeliads and tree holes).

Breeding-site surveys can focus on adults or larvae. Adults are usually more conspicuous and easier to sample and identify than larvae. However, larvae are typically present at the breeding site for longer periods than adults. Sampling both adults and larvae is the best approach.

Monitoring adults at a breeding site is easiest when breeding is concentrated in a narrow, well-defined period, but it can be done also when the breeding period is extended. At some temperate zone sites, where water availability is predictable and freezing temperatures constrain activity, most amphibians breed in a relatively few weeks in spring and early summer. In arid areas most breeding is rain-dependent, and developmental times of larvae are often short; investigators must be ready to take advantage of the proper weather conditions whenever they occur (Low 1976; Wells 1977). At the other extreme, some tropical amphibians may breed at any time of year.

For short, infrequent surveys, larval sampling yields more complete species lists than adult surveys do (Wright 1914; Wiest 1982). However, if there is any doubt as to larval identification, larvae should be reared through metamorphosis. Larval densities can be strongly influenced by local factors (e.g., climate and co-occurring predators—Woodward and Mitchell 1991) and can vary greatly over short periods. Larval densities are not good predictors of adult population size.

Breeding-site studies are most thorough in small, shallow bodies of water that are free of emergent vegetation and that can be surveyed by investigators in a relatively short period.

BACKGROUND

The sites used by amphibians that congregate for breeding encompass nearly the entire spectrum of aquatic habitats (Crump 1974). Each type of habitat presents its own sampling problems, but the general objectives remain the same. A basic assumption in breeding-site studies of single species is that all individuals or all members of some population subset, such as breeding males, are equally available for sampling. For studies of whole amphibian faunas, this assumption implies that all species can be sampled equally well. This latter assumption is usually false.

Some species are more secretive than others, and some are present at breeding areas for a longer time than others and are thus more susceptible to observation. Breeding aggregations also may vary in structure (e.g., the percentage of satellite [noncalling but reproductively capable] males—Perrill et al. 1978). Violations of these assumptions typically pose problems for estimates of relative abundance; rarely should they interfere with compilation of species lists.

Many factors contribute to the configuration of an amphibian population at any single breeding site (Alford and Wilbur 1985; Wilbur and Alford 1985; Morin 1987; Woodward and Mitchell 1991), and many different sites must be surveyed if the investigator wants to understand the "typical" condition. Savage (1962) surveyed *Rana temporaria* breeding sites in England over a 10-year period and found that frogs did not breed in any specific pond every year. The number of ponds used also varied among years; in 1937, spawn was found in 11 of 78 ponds, but 22 of 86 ponds were used for breeding the following year. Large year-to-year differences in densities and number of breeding areas used are common in amphibians, probably because of the strong influences of environmental parameters and because of the boom-and-bust cycles typical of these fecund organisms. Investigators need to describe conditions under which they collect their samples and attempt to interpret the effects that these conditions may have on their results.

RESEARCH DESIGN

The sampling design must conform to the special rhythm of each species' breeding cycle. Different species may be active at different times. Surveys may need to run in 4-hour blocks of the 24-hour day, or nocturnal surveys may suffice. If the species of interest are erratic or explosive breeders (Low 1976; Wells 1977), sampling protocols must take into account the conditions (usually weather) that induce breeding, or the species must be studied by observations of eggs

or larvae. Most individuals of species with prolonged breeding periods spend only a fraction of the breeding season in the breeding area (Fellers 1979; Woodward 1982; Godwin and Roble 1983; Ryan 1985). Density estimates for these species require some sort of mark-recapture procedure (see Chapter 8), preferably over several samples. Unless a mark-recapture study can be done, investigators may have to rely on counts of larvae or recently transformed individuals. Larval densities drop rapidly throughout the larval period; thus for comparative purposes, samples must be collected when the larvae are at approximately the same ages. Even then, larval numbers are poor predictors of adult population size. If the habitat is extensive, populations can be subsampled either aurally (adult males only) or visually (adults and larvae under certain conditions) along randomly located transects (see "Visual Encounter Surveys" and "Audio Strip Transects," techniques 2 and 3).

The basic data obtained at a breeding site, for either larvae or adults, are species richness and abundances. These data also may be recorded for microhabitats within each breeding site to allow tests for differences across microhabitats. If the study area is large enough, the proportion of the total breeding habitat occupied by each species should be determined.

FIELD METHODS

Breeding-site monitoring involves counting animals in some preestablished manner. If the surveys are visual or aural, precise survey conditions, such as time of day and year, weather conditions, walking speed, the exact locations to be searched, and the time spent on each major habitat subdivision, should be specified. Characteristics of aquatic habitats vary with time, so descriptions should be detailed enough to allow interpretation of the effects of year-to-year variations, as well as within-year changes (see "Data Treatment and Interpretations," below).

With practice, investigators can recognize all possible anuran calls in an area. Aural surveys of calling anurans along predetermined routes are performed annually throughout Illinois and Wisconsin, and regular surveys are planned for Iowa and the Upper Peninsula of Michigan. Such surveys are especially efficient if species composition rather than abundance data are required.

In many breeding aggregations, total counts are possible; in larger aggregations, subsamples of the population should be counted by visual or aural transects. Sometimes adults migrate a few meters from the surrounding habitat to the breeding site (e.g., pond, lake) each night, migrating back late in the evening. Surveys must be restricted to those times of the day or night when most adults are present at the site.

Habitats differ in complexity. Therefore, spending equal amounts of time in different habitat types is usually not appropriate, because the effectiveness of the searches per unit of time in each area are not equal. In visual surveys the investigator must search until all frogs or salamanders have been counted and, if necessary, captured. This approach works only if sizable numbers of amphibians are not moving into or out of the breeding area. If they are, then numbers will be biased according to search time. For aural surveys, equivalent time spent per unit area in each habitat type is the appropriate approach.

Differences in the effectiveness of sampling amphibians in different habitats have seldom been examined. One way to address this problem would be to mark, release, and resample individuals in several habitat types to see what proportion of marked individuals in each habitat is resighted.

Three examples—the regional survey, the single-area survey, and the survey along a stream or river—will demonstrate the range of approaches that can be used for breeding-site surveys.

REGIONAL SURVEY. The regional breeding-site survey, an annual inventory of a series of breeding ponds, is one common approach. The question raised is usually whether amphibian populations are stable, increasing, or declining. The approach is exemplified by the frog and toad survey program of the state of Wisconsin, which was started in 1981 as a survey and was expanded in 1984 into a monitoring program (see "Group Activities and Field Trips," in Chapter 7). Survey routes consisting of up to 57 km of road with 10 preselected anuran breeding sites are assigned to volunteers. Each year, each route is surveyed one night in early spring, one night in late spring, and one night in summer, when the weather is calm and water temperatures are above stipulated minima for each season. Observers spend 5 to 10 minutes at each site recording data for all calling frogs. Call intensity is ranked according to number of individuals calling, and observations are entered on a data sheet (Fig. 14). The survey data are filed with the sponsoring state agency.

SINGLE-AREA SURVEY. A more detailed approach focuses on a single breeding area, such as a large pond, in order to determine the density of each amphibian species breeding in each habitat. A diagram of a hypothetical breeding area is given in Figure 15. If the resources are available to survey the entire area repeatedly, a mark-recapture program is appropriate. If the area must be subsampled, mark-recapture methods probably cannot be used, and the data will yield relative instead of absolute abundance.

Sites for subsamples should be stratified by major habitat type and located randomly within each, in and around the pond. However, if the area is too small for random placement of sampling sites (e.g., transects), then they should be placed wherever possible within each habitat. The order in which the selected sites are sampled is chosen randomly. If the data are to be analyzed statistically, at least three subsamples should be taken within each habitat type or stratum. Data analysis is facilitated if there are the same number of replicates in each habitat type.

A.

WISCONSIN FROG AND TOAD SURVEY -- Field Data Sheet
Bureau of Endangered Resources
Department of Natural Resources
Box 7921, Madison, WI 53707

Observer name(s), RUN 1 _____	Route No. _____
(Add address and RUN 2 _____	Year _____
phone on back.) RUN 3 _____	County _____

INSTRUCTIONS: Use this form for new or established survey routes. Each route consists of 10 listening sites, and is repeated 3 times during the breeding season, according to the minimum water temperatures and approximate range of dates given below for each survey period. Run surveys after dark, when wind velocity is less than 8 mph. Listen 5-10 minutes at each site and record a call index value of 1,2, or 3 (see below) for each species calling. See back of sheet for wind and sky codes and additional comments. Return to above address by 15 August.

	FIRST RUN — Water 50°F; 15-30 April	SECOND RUN — Water 60°F; 20 May - 5 June	THIRD RUN — Water 70°F; 1-15 July
	BEGIN: Date/Time/Wind/Sky/Air temp.(F) — END: Time/Wind/Sky/Air temp.(F)	BEGIN: Date/Time/Wind/Sky/Air temp.(F) — END: Time/Wind/Sky/Air temp.(F)	BEGIN: Date/Time/Wind/Sky/Air temp.(F) — END: Time/Wind/Sky/Air temp.(F)

CALL INDEX* columns: Site Number, Water Temp (F), Wood frog, Chorus frog, Spring peeper, Leopard frog, Pickerel frog, Am. toad, E. gray tree frog, C. gray tree frog, Cricket frog, Mink frog, Green frog, Bullfrog

SITE NAME: (rows 1–10 for each run)

For office use only: Mean / Freq.

*The call index is a rough estimate of the numbers of calling males of a particular species, according to the following index values:
1 Individuals can be counted; there is space between calls.
2 Calls of individuals can be distinguished but there is some overlapping of calls (intermediate between "1" and "3").
3 Full chorus. Calls are constant, continuous and overlapping.

Form 1700-8
4-86

B.

Please provide names, addresses, and phone numbers of all observers.
Place asterisk by name of cooperator who should receive materials next spring.

Route No. _____
Year _____
County _____

Name _____ _____ _____ _____
Address _____ _____ _____ _____
Phone _____ _____ _____ _____

Enter sky and wind codes on front of data sheet.

Sky code no.	Sky condition	Wind code no.	Wind speed (miles per hr)	Indicators of wind speed
0	Clear or a few clouds	0	less than 1	Smoke rises vertically.
1	Partly cloudy or variable	1	1-3	Wind direction shown by smoke drift.
2	Cloudy (broken) or overcast	2	4-7	Wind felt on face; leaves rustle.
4	Fog	3	8-12	Leaves and small twigs in constant motion; wind extends light flag.
5	Drizzle	4	13-18	Raises dust and loose paper; small branches are moved.
6	Showers			

Comments (difficulties, background noise levels, uncertain calls, habitat changes since previous run or previous year, etc):

Site	Run 1	Run 2	Run 3
1			
2			
3			
4			
5			
6			
7			
8			
9			
10			

Misc. comments:

***IMPORTANT: Documentation required for records of cricket frog and species outside known range--see instructional materials

Figure 14. Field data sheet used in the Wisconsin frog and toad survey. A. Front. B. Back.

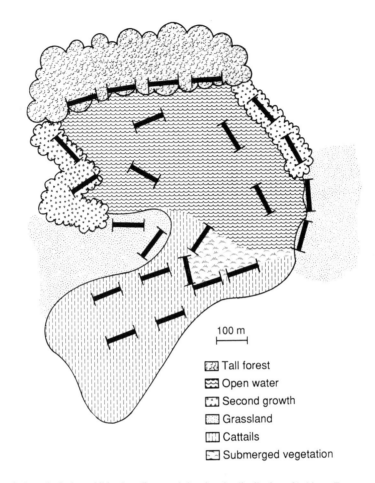

Figure 15. Diagram of a hypothetical amphibian breeding pond showing the distribution of habitats. Four survey transects are shown in each habitat except submerged vegetation. Four transects are located along an ecotone between the cattails and the submerged vegetation.

The sampling protocol should recognize that amphibian breeding choruses may be distributed in different ways. Transects should always be located within the chorus, regardless of its shape. If the interface between two habitats appears to be especially important to breeding amphibians, the ecotone should also be subsampled as if it were a separate habitat (Fig. 15).

SURVEY ALONG A STREAM OR RIVER. A detailed survey of breeding amphibians along a stream or river may pose special sampling problems, depending on the complexity and accessibility of the shoreline. Figure 16 illustrates the placement of transects in habitats, including a swampy backwater, along a deep, wide river with a relatively simple shoreline.

Inger and Greenberg (1966) used mark-recapture methods to estimate sizes of both breeding and nonbreeding *Rana* populations along a stream in Borneo. Their data provide actual density estimates. Where mark-recapture is not possible, visual and audio transects can provide data on relative abundances. In some rivers, it may be possible to carry out audio transects from canoes, although to our knowledge this has not

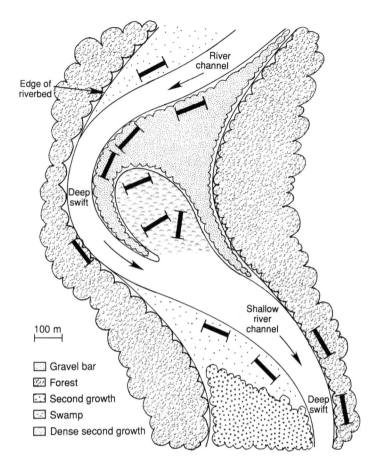

Figure 16. Diagram of a hypothetical section of river showing the distribution of habitats and three survey transects in each habitat except second growth.

been tried. Centrolenids and hylids breeding along larger streams might be especially amenable to canoe-based surveys.

Equal numbers of transects should be randomly placed (if possible) within each habitat type and should be sampled in random order.

PERSONNEL AND MATERIAL

The number of people required to survey a breeding site depends on the desired intensity of the survey and the sizes and numbers of the areas to be sampled. One person can survey a number of small sites if presence or absence of calling males is the only information needed. However, two or more people usually provide more reli-

able and more consistent data, because each person can check the other's results and maintain continuity if one person is unable to survey on a particular occasion. Sampling periods should be as short as possible to reduce temporal variation, and more people should be used if breeding sites are large or numerous. For nighttime surveys, good-quality headlamps and extra batteries are required (see Appendix 6). Some investigators prefer red light because it may be less disturbing to the animals.

Other materials needed for breeding-site surveys are thermometers, watches, hip boots or waders, wet suits, long-handled dipnets, waterproof data sheets, writing materials, plastic bags for captured amphibians, and colored flagging for marking the habitat.

DATA TREATMENT AND INTERPRETATION

The data recorded in a breeding-site survey depend on the goals of the study. In addition to the minimum data required with any technique (Chapter 5), the following information should be recorded: surface-water and deep-water temperatures, the presence or absence of calling sites (bushes, trees, floating and emergent vegetation), reproductive activity of adult amphibians, and, if possible, developmental stages of larvae. (Additional information that may be of interest can be found in the section "Sampling with Artificial Pools," in Chapter 7.) Data should be recorded by breeding site or, preferably, by transect and microhabitat within each breeding site. The data from breeding-site surveys can be used to produce a list of amphibian species encountered, or they can be combined with other information to form a basis for detailed ecological and population analyses.

Species lists can be compared across sites, although we caution against attributing too much to species absences if only a few breeding sites are examined per area. Not all species of amphibians in an area breed at any one site every year (Savage 1962; Bragg 1965; Heyer 1976). If several breeding sites are examined in each of two or more study areas, then frequency of occurrence can be compared across study areas. In a similar manner, species richness or abundance can be compared across study areas or across time in the same study area. Any estimates of abundance are referable to the breeding population present during the period of study and not to the entire adult population. In numerous species that live in cold (and possibly arid) environments and have short activity seasons, individual females breed only as often as they can store enough energy to produce a clutch, which may be every second or third year (Bragg 1940; Blair 1943; Turner 1960; Metter 1964).

Data can be pooled across many breeding sites to yield area-wide species lists and relative abundances. Data from several sites can be used as replicate samples under one treatment type (e.g., an area near a source of airborne pollution or an area subject to agricultural runoff) for comparison with sites from a control area.

Breeding-site surveys can be used to estimate effective population size and operational sex ratio, two parameters that are important for conservation work (Gilpin and Soulé 1986; Falconer 1989). For these purposes, surveys must be made over an extended period because breeding populations vary widely from night to night at a single pond (Fellers 1979; Woodward 1984; Ryan 1985).

Data derived from the Wisconsin survey routes (see "Regional Survey" under "Field Methods," above) have been analyzed in two ways and the results disseminated by M. J. Mossman in an unpublished newsletter (dated 3 April 1990).[2] In the first analysis, a regression of percentages of total sites occupied by a particular species against year was calculated. The slopes of the regression lines that were significantly different from zero were interpreted as indicating an increase (positive slope) or decrease (negative slope) for that species over time. In the second analysis, a trend for each route for the period 1984–1989 was computed using the call index values for each species (Fig. 14), summed over each year. The yearly sums were used in a regression against years. The resulting line was compared with the regression resulting from the averages of all routes compared among years. Trends that were significantly different from the average were interpreted as showing increases or decreases.

---

2. Available from Michael J. Mossman, State of Wisconsin, Department of Natural Resources, Southern District Headquarters, 3911 Fish Hatchery Road, Fitchburg, WI 53711-5397, USA.

The data from the second and third examples in the section "Field Methods" ("Single-Area Survey" and "Survey Along a Stream or River," above) are either absolute densities from mark-recapture studies or relative abundances resulting from visual or audio surveys. Unless all species are equally susceptible to the sampling methods, relative abundances cannot be determined across species except at a very coarse, qualitative level. If repeated samples are taken within habitat types, a one-way analysis of variance (ANOVA) may distinguish differences in relative abundances among habitats; a two-way ANOVA can be used to analyze patterns among habitats and sampling periods (such as years).

SPECIAL CONSIDERATIONS

Survey results can be affected by the experience of those conducting them. Observers must be well trained, but they still may differ subtly in walking speed, ability to find animals, disturbance caused, and concentration. With effort, such differences can be minimized for a group of observers working at the same time at one site. They can cause major problems when comparing data from different geographical areas or different years. It is important to design the sampling protocol to minimize differences among observers when making comparisons among sites or across time. Ideally, each person should sample each habitat an equal number of times.

One last caveat: Calling in frogs does not necessarily mean breeding. Many species, such as American bullfrogs (*Rana catesbeiana*) and some hylids, call well outside of the breeding season (Salthe and Mecham 1974). If precise information on the breeding season is desired, observations of more-explicit indicators, such as amplexus, egg masses, or larvae, are needed.

CONTRIBUTOR: MARTHA L. CRUMP

9. Drift Fences Encircling Breeding Sites

C. KENNETH DODD, Jr., AND DAVID E. SCOTT

Drift fences are typically used to sample species that move to aquatic breeding sites. A barrier fence with traps on either side is installed around a pond, and amphibians are monitored as they enter and leave the area. Straight-line drift fences and pitfall traps (technique 7), in contrast, are used to sample individuals away from breeding sites. Although procedures differ in many respects between the two techniques, investigators intending to use drift fences and traps can benefit from reading both accounts.

Drift fences at the breeding site are best employed for long-term population studies and assemblage monitoring, but they can be used in conjunction with short-term species inventories (e.g., during well-defined breeding seasons) and field experiments (e.g., Cortwright and Nelson 1990; Scott 1990). However, the efficiencies with which species are captured when this technique is used differ. Generally, only a subset of the amphibian assemblage using the pond is censused. Therefore, the technique should not be used alone if species richness information is needed. In addition, estimates of amphibian species richness, diversity, or evenness based on data gathered with this technique must be interpreted with caution, especially for among-site comparisons (see Chapter 9; Magurran 1988; Noss 1990). Investigators should be especially careful to distinguish replication from subsampling (Eberhardt and Thomas 1991).

This technique can also be applied to questions not involved with biological diversity per se (e.g., activity patterns—Gittens 1983a, Pechmann and Semlitsch 1986; homing—Gill 1978a; migration—Hardy and Raymond 1980, Gittens 1983b, Semlitsch 1985; orientation—Shoop 1965, Phillips and Sexton 1989).

TARGET ORGANISMS AND HABITATS

Small temporary or permanent ponds often are the foci of amphibian breeding activities and are particularly amenable to the drift-fence technique. Larger aquatic sites may be fenced, but the benefits of sampling larger areas often are offset by increased costs of materials and labor. Doubling the area to be sampled increases the cost of construction materials and the time for construction, maintenance, and daily operation by an exponential factor of two.

One of the major problems of the drift-fence technique is trespass (Gill 1985, 1987; Dodd 1991b), when an individual amphibian enters or exits a pond without being captured. Surface-dwelling species that breed in aquatic sites and that have limited climbing, jumping, or burrowing abilities, such as mole salamanders (*Ambystoma* spp.) and some anurans (*Pseudacris ornata, Bufo* spp.), are best sampled by the drift-fence technique. Sampling of species with good climbing abilities (*Notophthalmus* spp., *Eurycea quadridigitata, Gastrophryne carolinensis, Hyla* spp.) and jumping abilities (many *Rana* spp., *Acris* spp.) is far less efficient. The extent to which fossorial species (e.g., *Scaphiopus holbrooki*) trespass by digging under a fence is unknown but may depend on depth of the fence and soil structure and may be site-specific.

BACKGROUND

The principal assumption made when using an encircling drift fence is that an animal has a reason to enter or leave the encircled area. For many amphibians, reproduction and metamorphosis provide the appropriate motivations. A related assumption is that the behavior of the target species is not altered by encountering a drift fence. In theory, the animal walks along the fence until it falls into a pitfall trap, enters a funnel trap, or is otherwise captured; it does not leave and go elsewhere. Many amphibian species apparently prefer specific sites for breeding,

but the potential for non-site-specific reproductive behavior should be kept in mind.

Additional considerations may be important, depending on the type of question being asked. For example, the assumption of equal catchability among species or individuals probably is not valid. Trespass rates may vary spatially and annually (both intraspecifically and interspecifically) with size (juveniles versus adults; large females versus small males) and, perhaps, with reproductive condition (gravid versus nongravid females). In addition, some animals avoid traps after an initial encounter, whereas others deliberately seek out traps as cover from harsh environmental conditions (Shields 1985). Laboratory and field experiments and observations may assist in determining the likelihood of trespass as a threat to the validity of results and their interpretation.

Comparisons of species richness, reproductive output, relative abundance of breeding and transitory individuals, and population structure among sites should be made cautiously, particularly where the species assemblages among sites differ.

RESEARCH DESIGN AND FIELD METHODS

The basic methodology is to capture and process (e.g., measure, weigh, determine sex, mark) animals at the fence and release them on the opposite side of the fence. If possible, the fence should completely encircle the breeding site; interpretation of data from partially fenced ponds is hampered by ignorance of movement corridors used by different species, individuals, and age classes. The shape of the fence may conform to the shape of the water body. However, if orientation studies are included, a circular or near circular fence is necessary, because all statistical tests are based on circles, not ellipses or other shapes. The fence should be placed above the anticipated high-water mark. Drift fences may be constructed of a variety of materials: aluminum flashing, plastic sheeting, hardware cloth, highway filter fabric, or tar paper. Aluminum

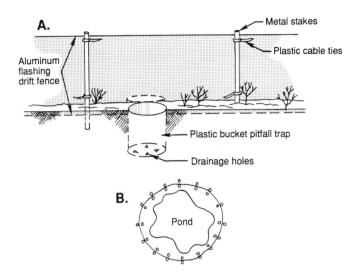

Figure 17. A drift fence with pitfall traps around a breeding site. A. Placement of stakes and pitfalls in relation to drift fence. B. Continuous fence around breeding pond. Reprinted with permission from Gibbons and Semlitsch (1982).

flashing is highly recommended for long-term studies despite its high cost. If possible, the lower edge of the fence should be sunk into the ground 20 cm below the surface (a mechanical trencher greatly facilitates installation). The fence should extend at least 35 to 40 cm above the ground surface.

When the substrate is too hard or rocky for the fence to be buried, plastic sheeting can be curved outward flush with the ground and covered with soil to close gaps under the fence. Wooden, metal, or plastic stakes placed on both sides of the fence as required keep the fence stable and upright, which minimizes trespass. Stakes are anchored to the fence by bolts or plastic electrical ties (Gibbons and Semlitsch 1982) and should extend as little as possible above the top of the fence. Each pitfall should be identified with an individual number painted or otherwise affixed to the adjacent fence for unambiguous future reference.

Amphibians are captured in open containers (pitfalls) placed along the fence (Fig. 17). Hard plastic buckets (19-liter capacity) are most effective because they resist collapse and do not dis-

integrate after prolonged exposure to water. However, availability of cans or buckets, nature of the substrate, or other requirements of the study may dictate alternate choices. Buckets should be the same color. We recommend using dark buckets, although the effect of bucket color on capture rate is unknown. A hole (slit) that will allow excess rainwater, but not captured animals, to escape should be cut in the bottom of the bucket. If shrews are common in the area and frequently captured, however, then the bottom of the bucket should be left intact. Numerous small holes (3–5 cm) should also be drilled in the bucket wall 4 to 5 cm from the bottom for drainage. In arid regions, an absorbent material (preferably a small square, 5 to 8 cm thick, of synthetic foam used for seat cushions; natural and synthetic sponges disintegrate rapidly) should be placed in the bottom of the bucket and saturated with water to provide moisture and cover. Buckets should be buried straight up, flush with the substrate surface; no gaps should exist between the bucket and the fence.

Buckets are paired on opposite sides of the fence at 10 m intervals. In areas with direct sun, buckets should be partially shaded. Shades made of pegboard are particularly effective. They can be slanted over the pitfall opening to allow room for transit beneath, while preventing an animal from climbing up the outside (a trespass). Vegetation should be removed outward from the base of the fence for at least 30 to 40 cm, and no vegetation should overhang the fence. Maintenance involves keeping the fence in place, repairing soil erosion, covering the results of digging activities of large or burrowing animals, and removing vegetation and other debris that fall on or across the fence. On downhill slopes, the sheet flow of surface water from heavy downpours can cause a fence to collapse or buckle. Although holes in the bottom or sides of pitfalls allow for some water drainage, heavy rains or compact soils may result in occasional flooding; water should be removed from pitfalls as soon as possible after a rain (see discussion of this problem in "Straight-line Drift Fences and Pitfall Traps," technique 7).

In order to minimize trespass, baffles can be installed at the top of the fence to form a "T" shape or down-slanted eave. However, the eaves of the T should not be so large as to provide shelter to climbing species, or the overhang will have to be checked in addition to checking the pitfall. Painting the top of the fence with teflon paint has been suggested as a way to prevent or minimize trespass. Teflon paint is expensive, however, and its effectiveness has not been determined. A lip on the bucket may keep animals from climbing out of pitfalls; the lip should be removable for easy checking. Plastic lids, which fit securely on buckets, often are available. A lip can be created by cutting a circle 50 mm from the edge and removing the center. However, buckets may change shape during the course of a study, making lid positioning difficult. Research is needed on bucket lip technology and effectiveness.

In addition to (or in place of) pitfalls, various types of screen-mesh funnel traps (with single or double openings) can be placed parallel to the drift fence (see technique 7, above, for additional information). The use of various diameters of open-ended or partially closed PVC pipe placed on or near the fence can supplement funnel trapping. PVC pipes are effective in capturing certain climbing species, particularly hylids, that use the pipes as diurnal hiding places (e.g., Lohoefener and Wolfe 1984).

Traps should be checked daily, preferably in the morning, to reduce mortality from desiccation and predation. Depending on capture rate, checking traps can be time-consuming. For example, checking and processing animals from 46 pitfalls at a north Florida drift fence enclosure (230 m perimeter) took from 30 minutes to more than 8 hours per day. Some sampling regimes may require checking pitfalls two or more times daily, depending on the question being asked, researcher time, and the capture rate of organisms. If traps are not checked for two or three days, the number of animals captured will be significantly underestimated and mortality will increase (some animals may escape as numbers in the trap increase, and other animals may be removed by predators).

Pitfall traps can capture poisonous snakes and invertebrates. One should never reach under a cover or into a trap without checking it first. Long forceps can be used to stir the bottom contents so that small secretive species hiding in debris, soil, or sand will be exposed. A small reinforced aquarium net can be used to check flooded pitfalls.

Animals can be processed at the site of capture. If it is necessary to process them elsewhere, they should be placed in small plastic bags with a plastic tag or a tag of high-rag-content or waterproof paper, on which the pitfall number is written in pencil or permanent ink. As animals are processed and released, the numbers can be crossed out and the tags reused. The species, number of specimens, and pitfall location should be written in a weatherproof field data book when the trap is emptied.

Vertebrate predators—birds, small mammals (particularly raccoons in North America), and even snakes—that learn the location of pitfalls and "run" the traps (routinely visit and remove animals) can be a nuisance. Amphibian mortality from invertebrates, particularly ants, is likely to be a more serious problem. Predators should always be removed from the pitfall. Commercial mammal or ant traps (or baits) can be used to effect long-term eradication of these pests. Boards (Fig. 12) or galvanized wire mesh (see Reading 1989:fig. 2) can be positioned over pitfalls to discourage avian predators.

PERSONNEL AND MATERIALS

Installing an encircling drift fence is labor-intensive. At one study site in Florida sandhills, it took CKD and a 4-person crew two days to install a 230-m fence. Much longer periods will be required for longer fences or areas with compact substrates or complex topography. Backhoes or mechanical diggers facilitate installation. Fence maintenance (repair, vegetation trimming) for most short drift fences can be handled easily by one person as long as problems are corrected routinely. Data collection will take varying amounts of time depending on distance to study site, types and amount of data collected, numbers of animals processed, and number of pitfalls to be checked.

The materials needed to install a drift fence include fence materials, pitfall buckets, cover boards (if required), pieces of foam (for moisture and cover in the bucket, if needed), stakes, bolts or electrical ties for stakes, paint (to number pitfalls), equipment to trim weeds (weed whacker, shears, machete), and shovels or posthole diggers. Data-recording materials include rain gauge, air and water maximum-minimum thermometers, water-depth marker, marking tools, ruler (preferably clear flexible plastic), scales for weighing animals, field notebook, long forceps, sturdy aquarium net, paper tags, plastic bags, field data sheets, clipboard, and pencils. Data

analysis equipment includes computer hardware and appropriate software.

DATA TREATMENT AND INTERPRETATION

The researcher should know in advance which data are to be taken and should prepare a data sheet accordingly (80-column computer data coding sheets make good data sheets). In addition to minimum data listed in Chapter 5 or emphasized for this technique, identification number (cohort or individually marked), pitfall number, method of capture (pitfall, funnel trap, by hand), capture status (first-time capture/recapture), weight, notes (e.g., reproductive condition, coloration, tail regeneration), maximum and minimum air and water temperature since last check, pond water depth (measured at same location), rainfall since last check, and weather conditions should be recorded. If available, data on barometric pressure and moon phase might be noted. The occurrence of unusual or cyclic events (weather fronts, hurricanes) also should be noted.

Data should be entered directly onto data sheets and into a computer database, if available, as soon as a sheet is completed. Computerized databases can be set up in the same format as the data sheets for easy transfer. Codes should not be used for recording original data, but can be used for convenience and to save space in the computerized database. For example, a 2-letter or 3-letter code, using the first letters of the scientific name, can be used to identify species (e.g., HC for *Hyla cinerea*), and numbers can be used to identify weather conditions described in the field (e.g., 01 for clear, 02 for partly cloudy, and so forth). Letters should be kept either in uppercase or lowercase to minimize errors (i.e., HC or hc but not Hc). Computer codes should be sufficient to allow one to distinguish among species at the site without reference to a key (e.g., codes for *Leptodactylus pentadactylus* and *Leptodactylus poecilochilus* could be LPD and LPC, but not LP and LPS). This practice keeps data current, facilitates data proofing, and allows rapid analysis for reports and periodic project assessments. Computer databases should be matched with statistical packages to ensure compatibility. For instance, databases compiled using dBASE III+ and IV software are easily loaded into SAS programs for analysis.

The type of data analysis will depend on the question asked. Indices of species richness and diversity are reviewed in Chapter 9 in this volume and in Magurran (1988). Krebs (1989) discussed a variety of ecological tests, including those used to estimate abundance, determine sample size, and measure survival rates; a software program (Krebs 1988) for these tests also is available (see Appendix 6). Problems may occur in the analysis and interpretation of results because of uncertainties involving the magnitude and significance of trespass (Gill 1985, 1987; Dodd 1991b). Trespass undoubtedly results in the underrepresentation of some species or size classes in a sample. Also, assumptions concerning equal catchability may not be valid.

Drift fences encircling breeding sites have been used in various studies of biological diversity. Examples include studies of species assemblage structure (Cortwright and Nelson 1990), population size and dynamics (Gill 1978a,b, 1985; Semlitsch 1983; Dodd and Charest 1988), and trespass (Gill 1985; Dodd 1991b).

SPECIAL CONSIDERATIONS

The costs of installing and maintaining drift fences encircling breeding sites are high. Initial capital outlay to purchase supplies may be considerable (fencing material for a 230-m fence is approximately U.S. $575 for galvanized metal and U.S. $625 for aluminum). Personnel costs are high for installation and may be high for day-to-day operation (data collection and analysis) and maintenance (minor equipment replacement; vehicle gas and repairs). If costs can be minimized, encircling a breeding site with a drift fence is an efficient, effective technique for amphibian sampling. Drift fences typically are used with mark-recapture studies (see Appendix 2).

If a study is suspended, the fence can be opened temporarily and the pits covered. At the termination of a drift fence–pitfall trap study, the fences and traps should be removed.

CONTRIBUTORS: ROSS A. ALFORD, PAUL STEPHEN CORN, RICHARD FRANZ, AND RICHARD C. VOGT

10. Quantitative Sampling of Amphibian Larvae

H. BRADLEY SHAFFER, ROSS A. ALFORD,
BRUCE D. WOODWARD, STEPHEN J. RICHARDS,
RONALD G. ALTIG, AND CLAUDE GASCON

There are various methods of removing amphibian larvae from water for counting and identification. These methods include seining, dipnetting, trapping, and enclosure sampling, in which larvae are captured with known quantities of water in boxes, stovepipes, or collapsible netting. These techniques provide a fast, relatively thorough, qualitative or quantitative sample with minimum personnel, material, and time. In addition, the techniques generally do not harm the animals, and so can be used to monitor rare or endangered species. The two primary goals of these procedures are to assess the species richness of larvae in a body of water and to determine larval population size.

TARGET ORGANISMS AND HABITATS

Although in this chapter we concentrate on larvae, the techniques described could be used for aquatic adult amphibians. The quantitative methods, however, depend on equal catchability of individuals and species. Because aquatic adults are often powerful swimmers, their capture with these techniques is somewhat haphazard. Thus, we recommend against using the techniques to estimate total population size and density of aquatic adults.

Each technique is most efficient in a particular type of habitat. Seining is extremely effective in shallow ponds and lakes with little vegetation. Dipnetting is frequently the simplest method for sampling vegetation-choked bodies of water, stream habitats with limited access or great structural complexity, and specialized habitats such as tree holes. Enclosure sampling is effective in shallow water habitats with relatively uniform substrates. Trapping may be the only way to sample deep-water habitats or those with complex bottoms of stones, wood, or rocks.

For large bodies of water, including large vernal pools and shallow lake habitats, seining may be the only effective way to generate sample sizes sufficient to estimate species richness and abundance of amphibian larvae, especially when samples are removed rather than marked and released for recapture. Dipnetting is most effective for estimates of abundance in small bodies of water and shallow streams (generally < 1 m deep) and with removal sampling. Its effectiveness increases as the size of the body of water decreases; in very small pools, it often is possible to count all individuals present. Enclosure sampling, which is generally used to estimate population size, is most appropriate in relatively small bodies of water as well. Traps may be effective in any habitat, except fast-moving, shallow streams, but they are generally used only in special situations where other, easier sampling efforts fail.

BACKGROUND

The primary assumptions for using any of these techniques to estimate species abundance are that all animals are equally catchable, and that sampling efforts are equal for each unit of field collecting time. The first assumption may be generally true for the same species in similar habitats but often will not hold for a diverse array of species or habitat types. When these assumptions do hold, then one may use either removal estimation procedures (see "Removal

Sampling," Chapter 8) or quadrat analysis methods (see "Quadrat Sampling," technique 4, above) to estimate the total population size of each species (see "Data Treatment and Interpretation," below). Which of these approaches is most appropriate depends on the scale of the area sampled relative to the size of the habitat. In general, if a sufficiently large fraction of the habitat is sampled so that sequential samples are not independent of each other, but rather deplete the population, then removal sampling analysis is most appropriate. However, if a smaller fraction of the habitat is being sampled, and sequential samples are independent, then treating the samples as quadrat samples for analysis is most appropriate.

Some of the quantitative sampling procedures described may be applicable only in certain situations. When unequal efforts are required for different microhabitats, quantitative comparisons may become impossible. However, species richness can still be estimated qualitatively.

RESEARCH DESIGN

Sampling designs fall into two general categories. In designs used for removal estimates of population size, sampling is random without regard to the independence of the samples. In designs used for quadrat sampling, the samples must be independent. Assessing independence in aquatic habitats is not always easy, because larvae may swim many meters to escape a net or a human intruder. Our experience suggests that samples more than 5 m apart can be considered independent. Thus, if one is sampling a small pond or stream, the samples are, by definition, dependent, and quadrat sampling estimates for abundance will be inappropriate. Amphibian larvae occur in three basic habitat types: small bodies of water; ponds; and streams. We discuss sampling schemes for each.

SMALL BODIES OF WATER. Here we include tree holes, small sinkholes, puddles, and other bodies of water less than 1 m in diameter. Such habitats are repeatedly sampled with a dipnet or small seine. The number of larvae caught is recorded for each sweep, but larvae are not returned to the water. After at least 10 sweeps fail to uncover any new larvae, it is safe to conclude that the total population, or at least most it, has been obtained. The larvae can be returned to the pool after data have been recorded.

PONDS. For temporary ponds, we suggest stratifying sampling effort by microhabitat type. The theoretical basis and techniques of stratified sampling are discussed in many statistical texts (e.g., Cochran 1963; Yates 1981) and in Chapter 4 (see "Sampling Methods"). At the simplest, we recommend using a random sampling scheme stratified by depth and shoreline location. To do this, a sampling transect is established along the pond perimeter. This transect could be a fixed length at a fixed location—for example, a 100-m transect centered on the northern shore of a pond. It could also be the entire pond perimeter. In either case the precise location of the transect can change as the pond grows and shrinks. The number of depth zones is determined separately. If enclosure sampling is used (see "Quantitative Enclosure Sampling" under "Field Methods," below), the maximum depth is equal to the height of the sampler. If that maximum depth is 50 cm, four equivalent depth zones could be used (0 to 12.5 cm, 12.5 to 25 cm, 25 to 37.5 cm, and 37.5 to 50 cm) or the zones might be divided less evenly by depth (e.g., 0 to 5 cm, 5 to 15 cm, 15 to 30 cm, 30 to 50 cm). Depth zones do not have to be of uniform or constant width.

An equal number of samples is taken each trip from each of the depth zones, which run parallel to the shoreline sampling transect, in the water. For example, 20 samples might be taken on each sampling trip. If there are 4 depth zones, 5 samples are taken in each depth along a 100-m shoreline transect, as follows. The transect is divided into five 20-m sections that extend from the shore into the water, perpendicular to the depth zones. Four random integers between 1 and 20 inclusive are used to select which 1-m segment of each section will be sampled. A sample is taken in the shallow depth zone, opposite the point indicated by the first number; in the second depth zone, opposite the point indicated by the second number; in the third depth zone, opposite the third point; and in the fourth depth zone, opposite the fourth point. This procedure is repeated for each of the transect sections. Figure 18 illustrates a sampling plan generated using this procedure. This scheme assures reasonably even coverage by depth and by shoreline location, while also eliminating bias in the selection of sampling sites. Because the sampling transect can move when the water body changes in size, problems associated with fixed sampling coordinates are eliminated.

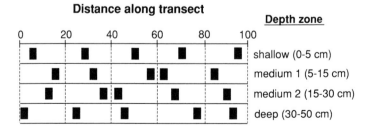

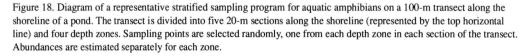

Figure 18. Diagram of a representative stratified sampling program for aquatic amphibians on a 100-m transect along the shoreline of a pond. The transect is divided into five 20-m sections along the shoreline (represented by the top horizontal line) and four depth zones. Sampling points are selected randomly, one from each depth zone in each section of the transect. Abundances are estimated separately for each zone.

A similar scheme can be used if the transect is the entire shoreline of a small pond. In this case, the total length of the transect changes as the pond expands and contracts. The sampling plan is set up in advance, and employs proportions of the length of the transect rather than absolute lengths. These proportions are converted into lengths after arrival at the sampling site.

If estimates of density within microhabitats are obtained with a stratified sampling scheme and then are used to estimate total abundances at the site, it is necessary to know the area occupied by each microhabitat. A site map that includes depth or elevation contours is constructed using simple plane-table surveying methods by establishing a benchmark for measurements of water depth on each sampling date. The area in each depth zone on each sampling date can then be reconstructed (see Harris et al. 1988 for an example of this procedure). When the surface areas occupied by each depth zone differ markedly, it may also be advisable to sample each zone in proportion to its relative area. For more details on sample allocation, consult Cochran (1963) and Yates (1981). Similarly, it is advisable to include in the site map and the stratification scheme other habitat features (e.g., substrate, areas of rooted vegetation) in the zones.

Regardless of the sampling technique used, it is useful to collect environmental data at the location of each sample. Minimum data should include water depth, water temperature, hour, substrate type, and weather conditions. Such factors as degree of illumination, dissolved oxygen concentration, water conductivity, water turbidity, and other parameters of the physical environment, as well as numbers of animals of other taxa (e.g., fish and invertebrates), may also be included.

STREAMS. Stream habitats tend to be more heterogeneous than ponds, making quantitative estimates of abundance more difficult. We therefore recommend quantification based on sampling of each habitat for a given amount of time, with larval samples averaged over all habitat types. As an example, we briefly describe a study of rain forest streams in Queensland, Australia (S. J. Richards, M. P. Trenerry, and R. A. Alford, unpubl. data). Larvae were sampled from a rain forest stream for more than 4 years. In a 500-m stretch of stream, three habitats were selected for sampling: pools (calm areas with clear water and relatively slow flow rates), runs (intermediate between pools and riffles), and riffles (rapidly flowing shallow water constantly boiling over a rocky substrate).

Riffles were sampled with five 1-minute samples. The investigator slowly moved up a riffle, turning and brushing undersides of rocks, then replacing the rocks. A dipnet placed immediately downstream caught dislodged tadpoles. The species, sizes, stages, and numbers of tadpoles collected in each period were recorded. Tadpoles were released at the upstream end of the riffle after all samples were taken. Runs were also sampled with five 1-minute periods. The substrate was a complex mixture of leaf packs, rocks, and sand, so microhabitats could not be delineated. The area was sampled with rapid sweeps of a dipnet near the substrate, with an occasional manual lifting of loose rocks. Tadpoles were released in the center of the run. Each microhabitat in pools (e.g., water over rocky substrate, sandy substrate, leaf pack) in pools was sampled with three 30-second sweeps.

Samples taken every 14 days over 3 of the 4 years of the study produced repeatable seasonal estimates of species richness and abundance with low variances. Tadpole populations at each sampling location were estimated at intervals with mark-recapture techniques to calibrate the dipnet counts. The mark-recapture and dipnetting data suggest that dipnets capture a rather constant fraction of tadpoles present, at least in the pools. The proportion captured is species-specific (*Litoria serrata,* about 0.10; *Mixophyes schevilli,* about 0.33), so the technique should be calibrated at each site.

FIELD METHODS

Several points must be kept in mind when sampling larval amphibians. First, most larvae are medium to strong swimmers that can outswim a slow-moving net. Second, larvae commonly escape by hiding on the bottom, making it essential to keep a seine or dipnet on the bottom when sampling. Third, vegetation and/or irregular bottom surfaces make any sampling difficult. Seines and rigid-frame samplers may become nearly useless in bodies of water with abundant vegetation. Sometimes an investigator can circumvent these difficulties—for example, by driving larvae from vegetation or removing bottom objects—but often will so disrupt the habitat that only species richness can be estimated. Fourth, many amphibian larvae are microhabitat specialists, so all important parts of the habitat should be identified as "strata" in a stratified sampling design.

SEINING. The seine most commonly used for amphibian larvae has a mesh size of 1.5 to 7 mm and is 1 to 1.5 m wide. For most applications, 3 to 4 m is an ideal length. A much larger seine (13–15 m long, 2 m wide, with a mesh size of 7–13 mm) is appropriate for sampling large bodies of water for large larvae; a small seine (0.5–1.0 m long, 10–30 cm wide, with a mesh size of 1.5–2.0 mm) is appropriate for small streams and pools. It is best to purchase seines pre-hung with lead weights along the lower edge and floats on the upper edge. Depending on the habitat to be sampled, some researchers attach a chain to the bottom of the seine for additional weight to ensure that no animals escape into a leaf-covered substrate. Seine poles made of 2.5-cm wood dowels are used to drag the seine. We fit the top and bottom of each pole with a 5-cm threaded eyebolt and then tie the rope of the seine to the eyes. The seine can be wrapped around the poles for storage.

For small ponds, the most effective sampling strategy is to seine directly across the entire body of water from shore to shore. It is important that the person sampling move slowly, so that the seine will remain on the bottom of the pond. However, that person must also move quickly enough to ensure that larvae do not escape. For larger ponds and lakes, it is often most productive to walk out to the depth of the seine before deploying it and then to work in toward shore in one continuous sweep. Alternatively, one can sample the mid-water without going to shore, although often many animals are lost as the seine is drawn up to the surface. For areas with dense vegetation, planting the seine in the bottom and driving larvae into the seine by walking through the vegetation is effective; the seine is then drawn through the water column as quickly as possible to collect the disturbed larvae.

A simple way to quantify seine sampling is to convert seining effort into square meters of bottom sampled; this conversion ensures that each seine haul represents about the same sampling effort. To accomplish this, one need only measure the distance traveled and multiply it by the length of the seine (measured pole to pole, which is generally about 10% less than the stretched length of the net). If the bottom is sufficiently clear of vegetation, distance traveled can be easily measured as strides; if not, short distances (up to 5 m or so) can usually be estimated fairly accurately. For large bodies of water, each seine haul should be completely independent of previous ones. This ensures that each haul gives an independent estimate of the density of animals. For smaller bodies of water, where areas seined will overlap, it may be advisable to wait a few minutes between hauls to let larvae come out of hiding.

DIPNETTING. At one extreme, a small aquarium net (about 10 cm wide) with a bendable frame is useful in capturing tadpoles from tree holes and other small catchments. A slightly larger net serves well for general collecting situations in both stream and pond habitats. Wire-mesh sieves (kitchen strainers) with a handle work very well. The mesh is small enough to capture all but the smallest hatchlings; the net stands open out of the water for easy sample processing but is deep enough to inhibit escape of all but the largest larvae; and the frame is strong enough, if gripped close to the net, for the net to be passed through most vegetation and to be used in areas with rocky substrates. Delta nets, D-shaped nets, and flat-bottomed nets (named for the shape of the metal frame) with fine, nylon mesh and long, strong handles are appropriate in larger, deeper bodies of water that also may have deep layers of soft substrate. Net size and mesh size determine passage rates through the water; some experimentation will be needed to find the equipment optimal for the body of water and larvae to be sampled.

All microhabitats must be sampled so that species with restricted distributions will not be missed. This is especially important because we do not know the microhabitat distribution of most larvae (e.g., Alford 1986). Also, sampling should be scheduled to accommodate diel variation in larval activity and catchability (see Anderson and Graham 1967; Gascon 1991).

There are no definitive rules about the number of sweeps needed to sample a habitat adequately. It is not uncommon to cover almost all of the surface area in small aquatic sites (< 0.01 ha), whereas only a fraction of larger bodies of water are covered. Twenty to 50 sweeps can be made in an hour, depending on how much vegetation and detritus must be removed from the net and how many larvae need to be identified. A reasonable procedure is to survey each aquatic habitat for an equal period or with an equal number of sweeps. Making more sweeps in the larger habitat increases the chance of encountering rare species. Increasing the number of sweeps also increases the chance of capturing highly habitat-specific species. Because of individual differences in sampling ability, each person should collect samples from every sampled habitat. No additional species should be captured in at least the last 10% of the sampling period or sampling sweeps.

To estimate densities of larvae, some measure of water volume sampled per sweep must be obtained. This can be achieved by standardizing the length of the sweep (1 m is a comfortable sweep length) and recording the depth of water on the net frame during the sweep (i.e., $\frac{1}{4}$, $\frac{1}{2}$, $\frac{3}{4}$, or full). Variation in sweep length or discrepancies between recorded and actual sweep depth will contribute to residual or unexplained variation in densities. Variations in sampling because of differences in sweep length or water depth make it more difficult to detect differences in densities between samples but should not cause densities in the areas being compared to be consistently overestimated or underestimated. Analysis of sweep sample data yields estimates of relative density. Absolute densities are best estimated with box or stovepipe sampling techniques (see "Quantitative Enclosure Sampling," below).

A growing body of literature (e.g., Wilbur and Fauth 1990; Woodward and Mitchell 1991) suggests that the nonamphibian species that coexist with amphibian larvae can strongly influence larval amphibian densities (Morin et al. 1988). Thus, recording the densities of all taxa obtained in the samples may be desirable for some studies. Other examples of studies using quantitative dipnetting include Heyer (1974, 1976, 1979), Berger (1984), and Vickery and Nudds (1991).

QUANTITATIVE ENCLOSURE SAMPLING. Enclosure sampling includes the techniques known as box sampling, quadrat sampling, and stovepipe sampling. It involves trapping animals inside an enclosure that can then be sampled, either exhaustively or until a fixed proportion of the trapped animals have been removed. Enclosure

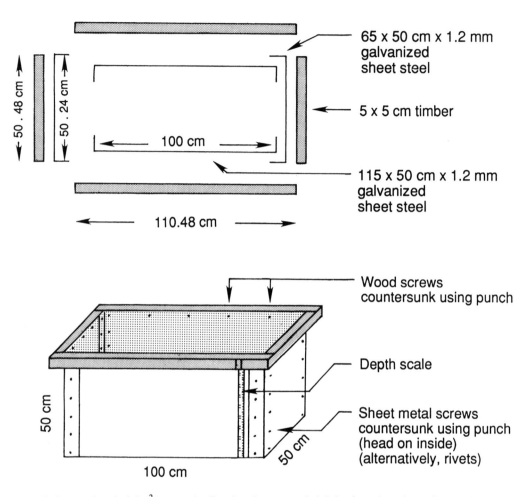

Figure 19. Construction of a 0.5 m^2 box sampler. Top view shows an exploded plan from above; lower diagram shows the assembled sampler (labels indicate inside dimensions). Depth scales should be attached to opposite corners, allowing two depth readings to be taken and averaged on uneven surfaces.

sampling is effective for habitats with shallow water and relatively uniform substrates. It has been used with some success by a number of investigators (Calef 1973; Turnipseed and Altig 1975; Morin 1983; Alford 1986; Harris et al. 1988).

The simplest enclosures are preexisting objects, such as a length of PVC (polyvinyl chloride) sewer pipe (Alford 1986). A more complex but generally more successful enclosure is the metal box sampler, 0.5 m^2 in area and 0.5 m deep (Fig. 19; also Harris et al. 1988). Depth scales should be attached to opposite corners of the box

so that two readings can be taken and averaged. The sampler illustrated is relatively heavy. If a sampler is to be used by persons of limited strength or carried to a remote site, one with dimensions of 0.5×0.5 m (0.25 m^2) can be used.

To use a sampler like that in Figure 19, the operator moves through the water to the sampling site with a slow, shuffling gait to minimize the likelihood of scaring away animals. He or she drops the enclosure, oriented so that the sharp edge faces down, and presses it into contact with the substrate. The number of animals trapped inside can be determined in two ways.

The investigator can try to remove every larva by repeatedly dipnetting in the sampler until no new animals have been caught for some fixed period of time or number of net sweeps. Alford (1986) used a period of 5 minutes with no new captures. With the second, more efficient scheme, a dipnet is constructed that has the same cross-sectional profile as the narrower axis of the rectangular sampler and fits closely inside it. The investigator slides it into the sampler at one end, presses it against the substrate, sweeps it through the sampler, and lifts it out at the other end. Sweeps are made in alternating directions. A few net sweeps reliably remove a high and constant proportion of the animals initially captured in the enclosure.

For example, Harris et al. (1988) sampled larvae with a $1.0 \times 0.5 \times 0.5$ m sheet steel box and a 0.5×0.5 m dipnet. They swept the box from one end to the other five times for each sample and recorded the numbers of tadpoles and newts captured in each sweep. They analyzed the results and efficiency of this technique extensively. On average, 52% of the *Notophthalmus viridescens* in the sampler were removed with each sweep of the net, so that with three sweeps they captured about 90% of the total; with four sweeps, 95% of the total; and with five sweeps, 97.5% (Harris et al. 1988). Had they analyzed their data after several sampling trips, found this result, and switched to three net sweeps per sample, they could have taken more samples on each trip for a better estimate of total numbers of animals in the habitat. Investigators using this approach should conduct initial validation trials with at least five sweeps per sample. They should analyze the results of the sweeps following Harris et al. (1988) to determine the effort needed to remove 90% or 95% of animals from the sampler. This will optimize the ratio of number of samples taken to accuracy of within-sample estimates.

A few problems should be considered in planning sampling programs with fixed enclosures.

First, the maximum depth that can be sampled is limited by the height of the enclosure. In addition, enclosures must be constructed of sturdy materials, such as galvanized sheet steel, to stand up to repeated use. This limits the size of sampler that can be handled by a single person, because of weight. The result is that simple box samplers (e.g., Fig. 19) are usable only in relatively shallow water. Alternatively, a two-handled sampler can be constructed for use by two people. Enclosure sampling is also limited by substrate type. To entrap animals effectively, the enclosure must make good contact with the substrate. Enclosures work well on soil or mud substrates and on fine gravel or coarse gravel interspersed with finer particles. Leaf packs and small submerged or emergent plants usually do not interfere with enclosure sampling, but rocks and large amounts of woody detritus may. If larval abundance estimates are needed for sites with deep water or unsuitable substrates, enclosure sampling must be supplemented with other devices or techniques, such as traps or mark-recapture.

If wariness or escape responses of species vary, mark-recapture or trapping may be used to calibrate the proportion of individuals caught with a rigid sampling device. Species that escape threats by flight tend to be underrepresented in enclosure samples compared with species that hide in the substrate. Disturbance by the operator when placing a box sampler may cause some tadpoles to evade capture. The degree to which this happens can be highly dependent on the skill and experience of the operator. Thus, if data collected by different researchers are to be compared, procedures for using the sampler should be as consistent as possible and should be reported in sufficient detail to allow others to employ them.

Another category of enclosure sampler is the bottom net (C. Gascon, unpubl. data). This method was designed for measuring absolute density. Bottom nets are box-shaped nets with frames at the open end. The entire (collapsed) net is placed on the bottom of water bodies some time prior to sampling. Gascon used nets of nylon mesh screening attached to 2.5 × 1 m wooden frames. The collapsed nets may be hidden in the substrate (for example, if the substrate is mulch or leaf mold) or may simply be placed on the bottom. At sampling times the frames are lifted vertically to the surface, trapping animals in the water column above the net.

The bottom-net technique should provide results comparable to those from enclosure sampling. Bottom-net sampling has proven especially useful for sampling salamander larvae from deep (5 m) vertical-sided canals that could not otherwise be sampled (H. B. Shaffer, pers. comm.). Bottom-net sampling has two advantages over enclosure sampling: It assures that all animals in the trapped space are removed, and it allows sampling in deeper water. It also has disadvantages. First, it cannot be carried out in as wide a range of microhabitats. If the substrate has a significant amount of rooted vegetation, a bottom net cannot be seated adequately. A bottom net that is not concealed in the substrate provides a novel substrate itself, which could affect the density of larvae in the water column above it. Second, concealing a bottom net may alter the substrate in ways that change larval density. Third, because of water resistance, a bottom net is likely to rise through the water column more slowly than an enclosure sampler descends through it. Mid-water larvae thus may escape from the sample.

TRAPPING. Relative abundance can be estimated using a variety of traps designed on the funnel-trap principle. Commercially available minnow traps are cylinders, about 0.5 m long × 0.3 m diameter, with funnels extending inward at one or both ends. Animals enter through the funnels but are discouraged from leaving by the small diameters and central locations of the exit holes at the bottom of the funnels. Calef (1973) used similar traps constructed from 3.5-liter plastic jugs and funnels made of window screen to capture larval *Rana aurora*. Calef calibrated his traps in enclosures, which allowed him to use his sampling results to estimate density. He constructed enclosures in the lake, cleared them of tadpoles, placed known numbers of tadpoles in each enclosure, and trapped for fixed time intervals. This enabled him to determine the relationship between density and catch per unit effort in his traps. Calef pointed out the possibility that tadpole aggregation along the walls of enclosures may have reduced capture rates below those that would be found in an unrestrained population at the same density. He double-checked his calibration using enclosure samples and visual counts.

Eggers et al. (1982) proposed a technique for calibrating traps directly. They suggested that each trap samples animals (fishes) from a circular area with a radius that is constant for each species and habitat type, and that if the radius can be determined, trapping data can be used to estimate absolute animal densities. They placed pairs of traps at increasing distances apart, set the traps for a constant time, and examined the relationship between number of animals captured and distance between the traps. Theoretically, the number of animals trapped should increase with increasing distance between traps, rising to an asymptote at the distance equal to the sum of the capture radii of the traps. Absolute density can then be estimated as number captured per area of the circle defined by the capture radius. This technique has not been validated with amphibians and should be considered experimental at present. In general, funnel-type traps should be regarded primarily as tools for estimating species richness and relative abundance only.

PERSONNEL AND MATERIALS

Materials for each technique are detailed above. Personnel needed depends on the technique used. In general, seining requires at least two workers, whereas the other techniques can be accomplished by one field researcher. In addition, we recommend strongly that one person be designated as the data recorder for a field trip. This practice is especially useful if several workers are dipnetting or seining; the recorder can wait on the shore and keep a running tally of each sampling team's results.

DATA TREATMENT AND INTERPRETATION

For all methods, the primary data will consist of the number of individuals of each species captured per sampling unit. This may be the number per seine haul, box sample, trap-hour, or the like. One advantage of recording data in this way is that it allows each investigator to estimate the repeatability of the sampling procedure. This is very important, because it allows for a quick estimation of the relative productivity of different microhabitats, as well as determination of the number of samples needed to estimate the mean number of individuals per sample, with a low standard deviation. If repeatability among samples is low, a stratified sampling program, different-sized samples, or use of other techniques may be warranted.

As was stressed earlier, data collected from all of these techniques can be analyzed either with techniques developed for removal sampling methods (see "Removal Sampling," Chapter 8) or with techniques developed for independent quadrat sampling methods (see "Quadrat Sampling," technique 4). For depletion methods, the critical assumption is that each sampling unit removes a constant fraction of the individuals in the habitat. Thus, if the fraction of animals removed is 50%, then 50% would be removed in the first sample, 50% of those remaining (25% of the original total) in the second sample, 50% of those remaining (12.5% of the original total) in the third, and so forth. To confirm that this assumption is being (roughly) met, the fraction of animals caught, F, should be determined for each sample.

F is calculated as follows:

$$F = \frac{\text{number caught in sample } (n+1)}{\text{number caught in sample } n}$$

If F is constant over samples, then depletion methods can be employed to estimate total population size for each species. If the sampling scheme is stratified according to depth or habitat, separate estimates can be calculated for each stratum.

When samples are independent, then quadrat sampling methods should be used. In general, the larger the number of independent samples, the greater the precision in estimates of relative or absolute density (for additional information, see Alford 1986 and Harris et al. 1988).

When independent samples are collected from a stratified sampling scheme and the area of each stratum is known, the total abundance of each species on each sampling date can be estimated as follows:

L = the number of strata sampled

n_h = the number of samples taken in stratum h (replicates)

N_h = the number of sampling units in stratum h (i.e., the maximum number of samples that could be taken without replacement in each stratum—if samples are 0.5 m^2 and the area of a stratum is 247 m^2, then N_h for that stratum is 494)

y_h = the mean count per sample in stratum h

s_h^2 = the sample variance of the count per sample in stratum h

$\hat{Y}_h = N_h y_h$ = the estimated size of the population in stratum h

$s\hat{Y}_h = \sqrt{\dfrac{N_h(N_h - n_h)}{n_h} \cdot s_h^2}$ = the standard error of $\hat{Y}_h$

$f_h = \dfrac{n_h}{N_h}$ = the sampling fraction for stratum h

$\hat{Y} = \displaystyle\sum_{h=1}^{L} N_h y_h$ = the estimated total population size

$s\hat{Y} = \sqrt{\displaystyle\sum_{h=1}^{L} \dfrac{N_h(N_h - n_h)}{n_h} \cdot s_h^2}$ = standard error of $\hat{Y}$

To apply these equations to samples taken according to the scheme illustrated in Figure 18, the four depth zones would be regarded as the strata, and the five samples taken in each stratum along the transect would be regarded as replicates. Thus, $L = 4$, $n_h = 5$, and $N_h = 20$ (assuming each sample occupies 1/20 of the transect area). Suppose the following data set was collected from the pond shown in Figure 18:

| Depth | Stratum | Number of tadpoles collected Sampling station | | | | |
		1	2	3	4	5
Shallow	1	1	2	4	3	2
Medium 1	2	2	4	4	6	5
Medium 2	3	5	2	7	4	3
Deep	4	0	0	1	0	2

Then:

$y_1 = 2.4$ $y_2 = 4.2$ $y_3 = 4.2$ $y_4 = 0.6$

$s_1^2 = 1.3$ $s_2^2 = 2.2$ $s_3^2 = 3.7$ $s_4^2 = 0.8$

$\hat{Y}_1 = 48$ $\hat{Y}_2 = 84$ $\hat{Y}_3 = 84$ $\hat{Y}_4 = 12$

$s_{\hat{Y}_1} = 8.8$ $s_{\hat{Y}_2} = 11.5$ $s_{\hat{Y}_3} = 14.9$ $s_{\hat{Y}_1} = 6.9$

$f_1 = f_2 = f_3 = f_4 = 0.25$

$\hat{Y}_h = 228$

$s_{\hat{Y}} = 21.9$

These data suggest that strata 2 and 3 are not significantly different, whereas strata 1 and 4 are different from each other and from 2 and 3. In addition, the confidence interval for the total population would be about 228 ± 44 (the mean ± 2 standard errors).

SPECIAL CONSIDERATIONS

The methods we describe are based on the assumption that all individuals are equally catchable. However, catchability often depends on size of the larva, details of the habitat, and even the presence of aquatic predators, a potentially serious problem that can be difficult to detect. Mark-recapture methods can be used to estimate true population size, but such techniques are exceedingly difficult to implement for most larvae (see Appendix 2). Quantitative estimates obtained using the techniques described in this chapter can be calibrated against a known population size determined with mark-recapture techniques. Alternatively and preferably, by using several different techniques, an investigator may be able to understand how a particular collection method misses certain individuals and to compensate accordingly (see Griffiths 1985).

Use of nets requires a compromise among mesh sizes. Very small mesh nets capture all larvae, but become clogged with filamentous algae and debris. They also are cumbersome and move through the water relatively slowly. Large mesh nets are much easier to use, but miss small individuals. In general, we advocate using nets of several mesh sizes to ensure that all size classes of animals are captured.

One disadvantage to seining is that it requires at least two persons to be effective. Single-person seining is far less efficient (Routman 1984). In general, the simpler the habitat is structurally, the more reliable seining is for quantifying abundances of larvae. Thus, this technique is especially suitable for surveying vernal pools, stock ponds, and other vegetation-free habitats.

Some jurisdictions require a special permit for use of seines (e.g., state of California). The legality of both seines and traps should be cleared with the local fish and game department or its equivalent.

We have purposely not recommended use of electric shocking devices for sampling aquatic amphibians. Commercially available devices are expensive, and constructing them may be dangerous because of the high voltages involved. All such devices, if not used with extreme care, can electrocute the user. Finally, in our experience, the techniques outlined in this section work as well as, or better than, electroshocking for sampling aquatic larval amphibians.

Often, the results obtained from the sampling approaches we describe will be used to make comparisons of species density or richness across study areas. Although making such comparisons is a goal of comparative quantitative sampling, caution should be exercised to ensure that results are comparable. Of special concern are differences in how individual investigators sample. The speed with which a net is passed through the water, how well it is pressed against the substrate, how quickly it is raised, and how it is passed through vegetation can all differ among investigators, often with major impacts on sampling effectiveness. To minimize these effects, a single person or team should do all of the actual sampling, or each should contribute equally to all aspects of a survey.

In a similar manner, extrinsic factors, especially weather and human disturbance, can influence the distribution and catchability of individual animals. Again, samples taken under similar conditions of wind, time of day, and human activity levels should be comparable. To facilitate standardization, brief mention of survey conditions should be made in all published reports.

Finally, amphibian larvae are fragile creatures. Tadpoles often have delicate tail fins, and salamander larvae can have delicate fins and gills, all of which can be damaged in nets. Trauma can be minimized by keeping animals cool, uncrowded, and in the net for as little time as possible while assembling a sample for analysis. A glass tube fitted with a rubber bulb is often a useful device for drawing up individual larvae and moving them among containers. We often use commercial turkey basters (i.e., large plastic or glass syringes with rubber bulbs). In addition, larvae can be measured and staged in such devices without trauma to the larva.

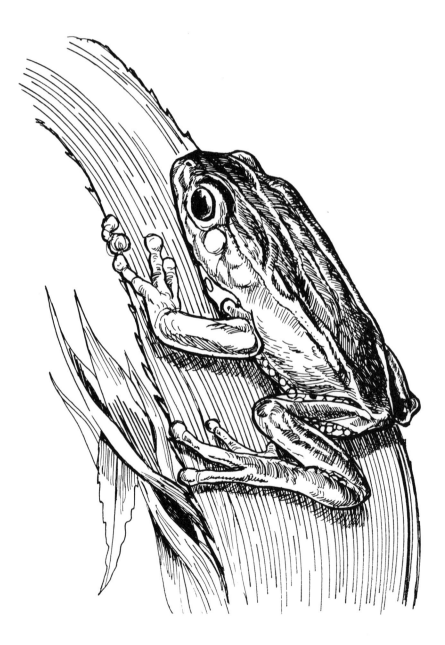

## Chapter 7

Supplemental Approaches to Studying Amphibian Biodiversity

Introduction

For the most part, the procedures described in Chapter 6 have been widely used and adequately tested, and we recommend them as standard techniques for field use. A number of other techniques appear promising, but they lack sufficient field testing, are more appropriate for research on single species than for studying general biodiversity, or provide data whose interpretation may be ambiguous. Nevertheless, workshop participants thought it important to bring these techniques to the attention of the potential user, and we describe them in this section. We encourage users to provide feedback about them to the editors for inclusion in future editions of this book.

Artificial habitats

Most of the traditional methods for surveying amphibians focus on concentrations of animals at their breeding sites. For many species, counts of adults, egg masses, or larvae provide reliable, quantitative estimates of population size. Although these techniques work well in many situations, they may be difficult to use in some bodies of water that are ephemeral, peculiar in form or topography, or support quantities of interfering vegetation.

A few herpetologists have experimented with artificial ponds, artificial cover, or other artificial "habitats" for increasing the efficiency and precision (i.e., repeatability) of surveys. Stewart and Pough (1983) and Townsend (1989) used "frog houses" made from sections of bamboo stalk to sample *Eleutherodactylus coqui* in Puerto Rico. These houses were designed to provide hiding and brooding sites. The bamboo sections were placed in arboreal situations, within easy reach of the researchers. This technique may be applicable to other anurans that use arboreal retreats. Fellers et al. (1988) described a more generic approach to providing artificial shelters, and Gascon (1992) described an artificial pond technique. Both of these approaches are recounted in detail here. The shelter technique has been used by J. W. Gibbons and B. W. Grant (pers. comm.).

The use of artificial cover and artificial ponds has been limited; hence we do not yet know the species and habitats for which these techniques may be useful. Likewise, interpreting the data collected may be difficult. The relationship of the sampled population to the overall population of the species in the area and the extent to which artificial habitats may lead to local population increases are not known. These techniques have potential advantages for sampling because they use standardized sampling units that can be replicated easily and applied consistently over time. Clearly, the techniques warrant further consideration and testing.

Sampling with Artificial Pools

CLAUDE GASCON

In this technique, artificial pools are randomly placed in the area to be sampled, during the breeding season. Pools are left in place for a period adequate to allow amphibians to locate them. The pools are checked frequently; all adults are counted visually, and larvae are sampled quantitatively.

Artificial pools can be used for two purposes. First, they can serve as "passive" devices to sample frog biodiversity. For example, artificial

pools can be used to obtain data on presence-absence of certain species based on the presence of tadpoles or eggs; to survey adults of some species that call around the basins, especially those that use small isolated ponds for reproduction; and to compare relative abundances or species composition of amphibians in different areas or habitats. Because artificial pools do not sample all frog species in an area, they must be used in conjunction with other survey techniques to obtain complete species lists.

Second, artificial pools can be used for quantitative sampling of tadpole populations. Overall tadpole abundance can be estimated if one knows the abundance of tadpoles in the pools and the abundance and size of all tadpole habitats. Juvenile production also can be estimated if drift fences are used with the pools.

In both instances, the technique relies on the frogs to use the pools for reproduction. The presence of tadpoles and/or eggs in the pool indicates a reproductive population.

TARGET ORGANISMS AND HABITATS

Artificial pools have been used successfully in the Neotropics to monitor populations of tadpoles of species in the families Dendrobatidae, Hylidae, Leptodactylidae, and Microhylidae (Gascon 1992 and unpubl. data). In some cases, adult frogs are also encountered in or around the pools. For example, adult *Pipa arrabali* (an aquatic frog) used the pools in Amazonia, but in this case the adults remained in the pools, and no free-living tadpoles were found. Frogs of other families also were encountered around pools where they oviposited or deposited larvae that had hatched in terrestrial nests. Other species used them for cover to avoid predators.

Pools can be deployed in virtually any habitat in which amphibians that breed in pools or ponds are found. Pools are not very effective for monitoring frog species that occur in stream habitats and are obviously ineffective for species that have completely dissociated their reproductive cycle from bodies of water. The effectiveness of artificial pools depends on the number of pools deployed and the abundance of frogs in the area.

BACKGROUND AND RESEARCH DESIGN

For passive species inventory, the more pools that are set out, the better the chance of attracting adult frogs and later finding breeding individuals or tadpoles. Pools can be set out singly in different areas, or they can be grouped in threes or fours (grouped pools may be more attractive to frogs, but this assumption is untested). Pools are best placed in areas removed from existing water, but of similar general habitat, where they are likely to attract frogs.

When making comparisons across areas or habitats, more than one pool should be placed at each site, and equal numbers should be placed in each habitat area. This methodology will provide data appropriate for statistical analysis. It also may require some advance planning, if the total number of pools is limited or if many areas are sampled simultaneously.

For tadpoles, the sampling interval for the pools must be shorter than the developmental period of the tadpole of the most rapidly developing species. In other words, if a tadpole completes aquatic development in 3 weeks, then the basins should be visited and sampled at least every 2 weeks. Otherwise, entire cohorts may be missed.

Because the objective is to mimic natural habitats, the size of the pools is an important consideration. Pools can be smaller than natural sites but should be large enough to allow a "natural" type of assemblage to develop (i.e., accumulation of organic matter, presence of aquatic insects, and so forth).

FIELD METHODS

Pools should always be buried flush with the substrate. Although many species will use artificial basins that are above ground, other species (especially small ones) are less likely to deposit eggs or tadpoles in them. Leaf litter from the surrounding area should be placed in the pool. It is also important to place a stick or branch diagonally in the pool to provide an exit ramp for juveniles that cannot otherwise get out. The stick should be longer than the diameter of the pool, with one end resting on its upper lip.

For qualitative sampling, any type of dipnet can be used to catch the tadpoles. Repeated dipnetting will ensure that all species are caught. For quantitative monitoring of tadpole populations, the pools can be emptied completely, and all organisms identified and counted. This is best accomplished by emptying the contents into a bucket through a fine-mesh net. The contained organisms can be counted and returned to the pool. The bucket should have a volume larger than that of the pool so that no water is lost. This will ensure that the water level in the bucket is close to the top and that the contents of the net remain submerged at all times. As tadpoles are sorted they can be staged to provide additional information on the number of cohorts of each species.

Care always should be taken when checking pools. Tadpoles of some species are fragile and easily damaged by extensive manipulation. It is advisable to return some of the water to the pool and release the tadpoles there as they are counted. Other organisms, such as insect larvae, should be returned as well. These procedures should minimize tadpole mortality from handling, disruption of the associated nonamphibian assemblage, and the influence of these factors on population fluctuations of tadpoles.

Samples of all larval species should be collected and preserved as vouchers.

PERSONNEL AND MATERIALS

The most strenuous activity associated with this technique is digging the hole for each pool. This can be carried out by as many individuals as the investigator can recruit. Sampling for the presence of tadpoles and night surveys of the pools for associated adults can be done by a single person. In most cases, two persons will be needed to empty the pools (large pools will be heavy to lift) and to process the material for quantitative sampling of tadpole populations. In a study in the tropical forest near Manaus, Brazil, it took a technician and a researcher an average of 15 to 20 minutes to empty one artificial basin (53 liters of water) and identify and count all individuals present.

Any plastic washbasin approximating the size of a small naturally occurring pool will suffice for nonquantitative sampling. Pools that are to be emptied at each sampling period must be rigid enough to hold their shape when lifted, even if full of water and debris. Additional basic materials include shovel, notebook, pencils or permanent-ink pens, strainers or small dipnets, large buckets and fine-mesh netting for emptying basins, collecting bags, and vials of 10% buffered formalin.

DATA TREATMENT AND INTERPRETATION

All pools should be identified with a number or an alphanumeric code. Each time the pools are surveyed, the pool identifier, date, time, weather, pH, and oxygen tension should be noted. The pH and oxygen tension readings should be compared with readings from natural pools to make certain that both have the same characteristics. For passive sampling (yielding species richness data), the investigator needs to record the species present at each visit. Individuals of unidentified tadpoles can be collected and reared for future identification or compared with a reference collection. For quantitative sampling of tadpole populations, data should include the name and number of tadpoles at each developmental stage for each species. The investigator can also record the presence of predators (i.e., dragonfly naiads, aquatic insects) and their abundance. For easy field notation of developmental stages, a modified version of Gosner's (1960) staging system can be used (Gascon 1991).

Data collected in the field should be transferred to computer files constructed so that each record in the file represents the number of tadpoles of a given species in one pool on a particular date. Constructing data files in this way greatly facilitates indexing and retrieval of information. The essential fields are species, date, and pond identifier. For quantitative sampling, the number of tadpoles of each species present in the pond on each sampling date and their corresponding developmental stages should also be included.

Statistical treatment will vary with the objective of the study. If an investigator wishes to compare relative abundances between two or more areas or habitats, methods using either counts or proportions may be used (see Chapter 9). If data were collected over a sufficiently long period, then breeding phenology of species can also be determined. Histograms of the number of species present in the different areas or habitats as a function of time (per month or week) can be constructed easily. The investigator can also build a detailed phenological histogram consisting of the presence and absence of tadpoles of each species through time.

With more quantitative data, the investigator can construct time-series graphs to show variations in species abundances over time. For each species in each pool, the abundance of each developmental stage encountered can be represented on the same graph, using different symbols. It is also possible to count the total number of cohorts of each species present in each basin.

Sampling with Artificial Cover

GARY M. FELLERS AND CHARLES A. DROST

Amphibians frequently take cover beneath surface objects. Thus, artificial wooden cover objects can be added to the environment in standard arrays for sampling amphibians. The cover objects are checked, and data on amphibians present are recorded.

This technique allows for the development of a reliable index of population size for amphibians using a standardized set of artificial cover boards, and for evaluation of the condition of each species' population. The first objective can be met without addressing the second, but a monitoring program will be much more efficient in providing an "early warning system" for population declines if it addresses both objectives simultaneously.

TARGET ORGANISMS AND HABITATS

This technique is relatively new and has not been extensively tested. However, it worked well for salamanders on the Channel Islands in southern California, for a variety of salamanders in coastal Georgia (J. W. Gibbons and B. W. Grant, pers. comm.), and for forest amphibians in British Columbia (T. M. Davis, pers. comm). It has good potential for a wide variety of terrestrial amphibians that normally are found under surface cover.

In California, artificial cover was used most extensively in grassland habitats, but it was also tested on the ground among low-growing shrubs and over ice plant (*Mesembryanthemum* sp.). In Georgia it was used in bottomland hardwood forest, upland pine stands, and old-field habitat, and along the borders of wetlands.

BACKGROUND

Many species of amphibians can be found under surface objects during wetter periods of the year. By setting out a standardized set of cover objects, it is possible to determine the numbers of different amphibian species under a consistent, uniform amount of cover. Advantages of this technique, compared with other survey techniques, include (1) standard number of cover items of standard size; (2) little between-observer variability, especially when compared with techniques such as time-constrained or area-constrained searches; (3) limited disturbance to cover items (e.g., logs fall apart with repeated disturbance, natural cover decays and changes character with time); (4) modest investment of time and money to establish transects or plots; (5) limited training required; and (6) easy maintenance of cover items.

There are also several disadvantages: (1) the method provides only an index of population size; (2) use of artificial cover may vary among species, depending on their habits and on the availability of natural cover objects; (3) counts may vary with local weather conditions (e.g., recent rains or drought); (4) cover boards may be difficult to locate in habitats with fast-growing vegetation.

RESEARCH DESIGN

Cover boards of different materials and sizes can be used, and they can be arranged in different ways. When surveying for the salamander *Batrachoseps pacificus* on the Channel Islands of California, we used $30 \times 30 \times 5$ cm ($12'' \times 12'' \times 2''$) pieces of untreated pine or fir, arranged in parallel lines or small grids. Larger boards may be more appropriate for other species. We tried plywood sheets as large as $122 \times 122 \times 1.25$ cm ($48'' \times 48'' \times 0.5''$); cover boards that size generally attract a greater number of species and individuals. From a practical standpoint, however, their size may limit the number that can be deployed. The number of boards needed for adequate statistical analysis depends on the heterogeneity of the habitat, the site fidelity of the organisms, the size of the area to be sampled, and whether species presence or individual abundance data are needed.

We also have tested 0.5-cm-thick ($\frac{1}{4}''$) plywood and 10-cm-thick ($4''$) thick boards, but have found them less suitable than boards 5 cm ($2''$) thick. Plywood works fairly well during the cooler times of the year, but 5-cm wood is much superior in its ability to retain moisture and provide a more stable thermal environment through-

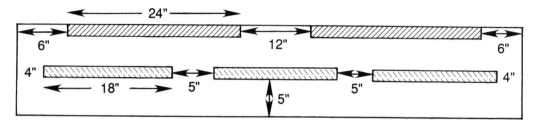

Figure 20. Diagram of the baseboard portion (viewed from above) of an artificial cover board designed to provide complex microhabitats for use in studying salamanders. Strips of cedar lathe (6 × 38 mm, or 0.25″ × 1.5″) in lengths of 46 cm (18″) or 61 cm (24″) are attached along the middle and edge of the baseboard (5 × 30.5 × 180 cm, or 2″ × 12″ × 72″), respectively. The strips along the edge are doubled, so that the lathe there rises above the baseboard about 12 mm (0.5″). The baseboard is placed on the ground with the lathe strips facing up. Two cover boards about 2.5 × 15 × 180 cm (1″ × 6″ × 72″) are placed on top the lathe strips, creating wedge-shaped spaces.

out the rest of the year. The 10-cm wood is also superior to plywood, but it is not appreciably better than 5-cm wood, so the extra expense and labor involved in deploying it does not seem warranted. Other types of cover material (e.g., corrugated metal) may work in some areas and habitats.

We set out cover boards in parallel lines, small grids, and "webs" consisting of several spokes radiating from a single central board. Our initial design consisted of two rows, 5 m apart of 30 boards each, spaced 5 m apart. This appears to be a reasonable density of cover material for small amphibians with relatively small home ranges. We marked the end board in each row with a metal tag showing the board number. Other boards were numbered with indelible ink.

A design to provide greater microhabitat complexity is currently being field-tested for amphibians in moist temperate forests of British Columbia, with promising early results (T. M. Davis, pers. comm.). The basic unit is a cover object consisting of three boards of untreated lumber. A recently cut (< 1-yr-old) 5 × 30.5 × 180 cm board is placed flat on the ground. Two other boards (2.5 × 15.3 cm) are placed on top of the base board but are separated from it with small strips of wood (Fig. 20). This design creates wedge-shaped spaces; water drips through the crack between the cover boards.

Grids potentially provide better information on movement and home range than do parallel transects. So far we have used only relatively small grids (9–25 boards, with spacings of 2–3 m). Larger grids (100 boards or more) will be necessary for reliable data on movements. For reasonably sedentary species, mark-recapture techniques may be used with such grids to estimate population size.

Cover boards arranged in the form of a web can be used to estimate density (Wilson and Anderson 1985), but a large array is required (e.g., a web with 12 rays of 12 boards each). Regardless of the arrangement used, it is important to place cover boards in areas that are representative of the habitat being sampled.

FIELD METHODS

Boards are checked by quickly lifting them and capturing all amphibians underneath. It is useful to have plastic bags or jars for temporarily holding specimens. Body length (SVL, or snout–vent length) can be measured either with a ruler fitted with a right-angle "stop" at one end or, in the case of salamanders, with a measuring tube (Fellers et al. 1988). Frogs and salamanders can be weighed in plastic bags of appropriate size. After being checked, the board is replaced directly on the ground; it should not be held up by vegetation or small rocks. Once the board is in place, the animals are released at the edge of the board. This is particularly important for species that must have both protection and the moisture available under the cover object.

A number of factors influence the number and diversity of amphibians found under artificial cover. These include time of day (or night), season or time of year, density of artificial or natural cover, and habitat type. Amphibians are encountered most frequently when the ground under the cover boards is moist. Data collected under poor conditions, or under different conditions from one year to the next, obviously are not suitable indicators of trends in amphibian population levels. For this reason, it is not possible to specify a sampling protocol that will work everywhere, because the schedule will need to reflect local weather patterns and the behavior of local amphibians. In California, sampling is most consistent if boards are checked just after a winter storm or two.

Cover boards should be checked several times, to accommodate seasonal differences in activity, both among species and for single species among years. Depending on the species or assemblages being sampled, it may be necessary to sample at weekly or monthly intervals throughout the peak season. The number of boards per transect, grid, or array should be evaluated after an initial sampling period. If a species of interest is rare or populations levels are highly variable, it may be necessary to increase the number of boards.

PERSONNEL AND MATERIALS

Transects can be checked by one person with experience in identifying local amphibians. Materials needed include cover boards (e.g., measuring $30 \times 30 \times 5$ cm, 60 boards per transect); walking stick or pole used for locating boards in dense vegetation; spring scales and a ruler with an end stop, both of sizes appropriate for the anticipated species; plastic bag for weighing amphibians; plastic 1-gallon jar for shielding amphibians being weighed on windy days; water container and water for wetting amphibians that begin to dry; data forms; and waterproof pens.

DATA TREATMENT AND INTERPRETATION

The board number, species identification, body length, sex (if possible), weight, and any comments about the individual should be recorded for each animal located under a board on the transect. Use of a data form will ensure that all required information is recorded in a systematic manner.

If only a summary count is recorded for a transect, it will not be possible to determine within-sample variability. Data relating to microhabitat and successional changes along a transect will also be lost.

POPULATION INDEX. Data analysis will involve calculating a population index for each species along a transect. The procedure for doing this will depend on how the data are collected and the behavior of the amphibians sampled. For counts made primarily during periods of peak activity, it is appropriate to calculate the index by combining counts for a year and calculating the mean capture rate (animals per board) for each species. If transects are checked over a longer period, it is more appropriate to use either the peak count or the average of the three to four highest counts, because the pattern of use of cover boards may change with weather or behavior (e.g., migration, courtship). The best analytical procedure can be determined only after reviewing the patterns of abundance exhibited over several years. To help visualize changes in abundance, the data for each species should be graphed as capture rate (± standard error) by year.

Changes in population indices must be interpreted in light of recent weather patterns. As was noted earlier, data collected when conditions are not suitable for amphibians should not be used in analyses for trends in population size or composition.

Short-term changes in population indices can be examined by comparing indices between years using a chi-square or G test. Long-term trends can be examined using autoregressive time series analysis (Edwards and Coull 1987), which is appropriate for detecting trends in auto-correlated time series data.

Data should be examined for year-to-year fluctuations in numbers. Normal year-to-year changes may be relatively greater for some species than for others; it may be necessary to collect data for several years before the magnitude of these natural fluctuations can be determined. Until then, the observed changes will be difficult to evaluate. Data also may reveal local changes in distribution, particularly as habitats in the area change. Such changes would be expected when fires, hurricanes, or other disturbances initiate a successional process. Transect data will provide a baseline for documenting changes in both the abundance and microdistribution of amphibians.

WEIGHT–LENGTH REGRESSION. The relative mass of an animal can provide an indication of its health because healthier animals are likely to weigh more than less healthy individuals. Differences in relative mass between years may be evaluated by calculating a regression of weight on length for each year. Because weight has a curvilinear relationship with body length, it is appropriate to calculate the regressions as length versus cube root of weight; this approach provides a more linear relationship. Results for different years may then be compared to determine whether the regression lines or their slopes differ significantly (Zar 1974). If the weights of small individuals are reasonably constant, a shallower slope indicates that the animals are in poorer condition.

SPECIAL CONSIDERATIONS

In some habitats, vegetation can grow over boards and obscure them. It is useful to carry a walking stick or pole to tap the ground at sta-tions where you cannot visually locate the boards. Tapping the ground is much more efficient than searching through the vegetation by hand. Also, boards occasionally crack and break apart with age. Such boards do not provide nearly as good shelter as intact boards, and data are not comparable to those obtained from entire boards. Extra replacement boards should be carried when checking transects. In some areas, the ground cracks and forms a depression under a board after a few years. When this happens, the board should be moved permanently to one side, and its distance from the other boards in the study noted.

CONTRIBUTOR: TED M. DAVIS

Acoustic monitoring at fixed sites

A. STANLEY RAND AND GEORGE E. DREWRY

Automatic acoustic monitoring of frog calls at fixed sites can provide continuous estimates of population size and breeding activity for target frog species. Fixed acoustic recording stations are placed where frogs of target species are known to call, and data on calling activity are recorded automatically through manipulation of the equipment. The technique can be used to quantify vocal activity of selected species using call rate (calls per unit time). It also can be used to average call intensity (sound energy) over time and record it automatically. The resultant data can be used to estimate number of calling males during the breeding season, to assess long-term changes in the number of calling males, and to compare populations of calling males at different sites.

The data also provide detailed records of daily and seasonal frog activity that reflect the influence of day-to-day climatic conditions. Although the equipment is expensive and installation requires substantial effort, once the system is operating, it collects data automatically with little additional investment of either time or money. The technique differs from the data logger-based technique earlier (see "Recording Frog Calls," under "Automated Data Acquisition," in Chapter 5) in being usable in more-complex sound environments and in providing preliminary analyses of the data automatically as they are gathered.

Target Organisms and Habitats

Acoustic monitoring is, as the title indicates, a technique for monitoring, not inventory. It does not generate species lists. Because only one or a very few recording stations are installed, relative abundances of calling males of at most a few species are obtained. Density data can be obtained for the area immediately surrounding the recording station if sampling methods that yield estimates of absolute numbers are used simultaneously. This technique is most valuable for comparing activity at single sites through time, rather than data from different sites.

This technique yields data on behavior and advertisement calls and estimates relative abundances of calling males. It can be used for any species with a locally unique call. Call rates can be counted for species with short calls given persistently, regularly, and antiphonally. Data can be interpreted for calls that overlap, if the calls overlap in a regular fashion. Target species must occur in densities sufficient to ensure that a number of calling males are audible from a particular recording site. The technique is more useful for species with prolonged calling seasons than for explosive breeders with short reproductive seasons. A system, particularly one in which a computer controls the data acquisition, can easily process data for several species at a time.

This technique is appropriate for almost any habitat, but the recording equipment must be safe from theft or vandalism and must be accessible for frequent inspection. The technique is probably best suited for permanent field stations where meteorological data also are being recorded. It is certainly appropriate for use in tropical forests (Drewry 1970).

Background

In many species of anurans, males call regularly and repetitively either from sites in their home ranges or from a restricted breeding area, so that a number of individuals are audible from any one spot. Calling males often space themselves relative to other calling males within the area. For these species the call rate and/or call intensity can be used to estimate numbers of calling males and their activity. Calling males are assumed to represent a fraction of the entire population, but that fraction likely changes over time.

The number and repeat rate of calls heard from a spot depends on call intensity, noise interference, number of males calling, and the level of calling activity. The maximum distance from which a male can be detected by a microphone of a given sensitivity is the radius of the area being sampled by that microphone. It should be kept in mind that the frequency spectrum and the intensity of calls reaching the microphone are influenced by differential transmission through the environment.

Although call intensity differs greatly among species, relatively little difference typically exists among males of the same species or among successive advertisement calls of individual males. Diel and seasonal patterns of calling generally are modulated by weather conditions. These influences must be considered when comparing years or sites. Although calls that overlap greatly in time cannot be counted easily, numbers of calling males can be estimated under certain conditions by analyzing several minutes of sound in the primary frequency band of the species under study and dividing intensity by the average intensity value characteristic of the male of that species. Corrections must be made for the effects of climatic variables (Drewry 1970).

Narins and Capranica (1977) described a technique for the automated analysis of animal vocalizations using a system that recognizes calls. Their technique was designed to make fine scale measurements of temporal features of calls, but it also could be used to count calls.

Research Design

Research design will depend on how calls are distributed in space and time and on whether the calls are being counted or their intensity is being measured. The placement of a microphone is critical to success of the technique. Local call rate variation throughout the habitat may be sampled by recording from several nearby but nonoverlapping areas. For averaging the sound energy over time in order to compare magnitude of calling effort, the location of the microphone relative to the calling animals should be adjusted to minimize the relative contribution of any single individual. Suspending the microphone well above the chorus is usually the easiest way to accomplish this.

Diel sampling should include at least all the activity maxima expected throughout the breeding season. The best time-sampling unit for counting calls is probably the call repetition interval (usually species-specific); use of this interval maximizes the likelihood that each call included is contributed by a different animal. For example, if a species characteristically calls every 3 seconds, a sampling unit of 3 seconds should indicate how many different individual males are calling. Data may be treated statistically and stored in a computer file. Data should be recorded, as well, for the following relevant physical variables: time of sunset, light intensity, rainfall, leaf wetness, relative humidity, and temperature.

Special Considerations

The only published study of frogs based on automatic call recording of which we are aware is that of Drewry (1970). The equipment now available is far superior to that which he used, but it has not yet been configured for this technique. Someone familiar with computer and recording equipment and computer programming would have to design a custom system in order to use the technique. One of the authors (A. S. Rand) is presently setting up a prototype system in Panama; operational details for the system may be available at a later time.

Tracking

A major difficulty in the study of amphibians is the relocation of known individuals. Relocation is a problem particularly away from breeding sites, where amphibians are less conspicuous (i.e., do not call) and more widely dispersed. The problem has restricted many investigations of amphibian ecology to breeding sites, although adults may spend only a fraction of their lives in such places. Most nonbreeding activities occur in other habitats. Any assessment of the status of amphibian populations or assemblages should identify which habitats are used and which are of greatest significance. This identification can be done with tracking, which involves the tagging and release of individuals and their subsequent relocation through the location of the tags that they carry.

Tracking of individuals is not essential to, nor sufficient by itself for inventory or monitoring studies. It can, however, provide information on habitat use and a means of testing assumptions implicit to the estimation of population size not available with other techniques. Tracking also can be used with other techniques to monitor populations (Chapter 8). Amphibians have been tracked successfully with thread bobbins, radio telemetry, and radioactive tags. These techniques have similar advantages, assumptions, and limitations.

The major assumption associated with all three techniques is that tracking devices do not alter the behavior of the individual in any significant way. Radio telemetry and radioactive tracking are advantageous in allowing individual amphibians in aquatic, terrestrial, or fossorial habitats to be relocated without handling. However, all three methods are intrusive and likely have some effect on behavior, at least immediately after installation of the device. Radio transmitters, radioactive tags, and receivers are expensive; tracking is time-consuming; and designing experiments to test the effects of the devices on individual behavior is nearly impossible. Therefore, the effects of these techniques on individuals are not yet well known. Nevertheless, because in certain situations tracking is the only method that can provide individual data on habitat use, these techniques are important tools for consideration.

Generally, only a few individuals can be monitored at a time using any of the tracking techniques. If different portions of the population exhibit different behaviors, it is unlikely that enough individuals can be tracked at one time to distinguish differential habitat use. Studies have shown that subadult frogs are more vagile than adults (e.g., Daugherty and Sheldon 1982; Breden 1987). Differences may exist within age classes (van Gelder and Rijsdijk 1987), and some frog species have three classes with different activity patterns: adult males, adult females, and subadults (Sinsch 1989a; M. P. Cohen and R. A. Alford, unpubl. data). Tracking studies should be planned with these differences in mind and ideally should include equal-sized samples from each class that behaves (or is expected to behave) differently. If equal sampling is not possible, studies should concentrate on classes that can be tracked, and data should be interpreted accordingly.

Thread Bobbins

W. RONALD HEYER

In this technique, a bobbin loaded with thread is fastened to an amphibian; as the animal moves through the environment, thread is paid out. The researcher follows the thread to determine the movements of the individual. This technique is an inexpensive way to follow individual frogs for short distances (up to 50 m) during the observation period.

Because of the physical dimensions of the apparatus and its tether, this technique is probably limited to use with large ($\geq$ 60 mm SVL) terrestrial frogs. Frogs with a trailing device often become entangled and drown when they enter water or die when they attempt to enter crevices (Dole 1965:241). The technique has been used successfully to track species of *Rana* and *Bufo* in the United States (Dole 1965, 1972; Tracy and Dole 1969).

It is assumed that the movements and pattern of activity of a frog fitted with the trailing device will be normal, and that the track of the thread actually reflects the path moved by the frog.

RESEARCH DESIGN AND FIELD METHODS

Trailing devices are made of sewing machine bobbins wound with white nylon sewing thread and mounted in a holder carried on the frog's back. The holder for the bobbin is made from a section of rigid plastic tubing with a flat plastic bottom glued on one end and mounted on an elastic band 6.3 mm wide (Fig. 21). A short wire, run through the holes in the top of the holder, keeps the bobbin in place. The elastic band is placed around the waist of a frog. The loose end of the thread is tied to a small stake placed at the site where the frog is released. As the frog moves, the thread unwinds through a wide slot cut in the back of the holder, and the frog leaves a trail of thread marking its route.

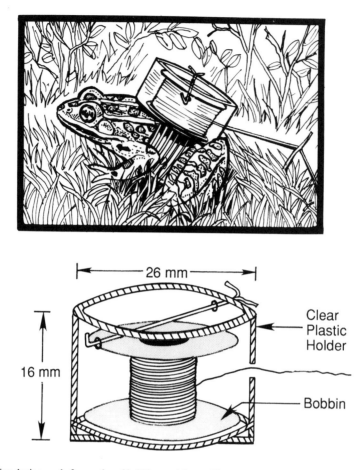

Figure 21. A trailing device, made from a thread bobbin, used for tracking amphibians. The device is attached to a frog with an elastic band, and the thread trails behind (above); details of the device are shown in the lower diagram. Redrawn with permission from Dole (1965).

When full, the bobbin device weighs about 8.5 g and holds about 50 m of thread, usually enough to trail moderately active frogs for 2 to 3 days. When frogs are very active, the thread lasts only 1 to 2 hours. The end of the thread is tied to the bobbin so that the frog cannot readily escape when the thread runs out. However, the frog can escape from the elastic band through vigorous movements and, thereby, avoid predators.

Frogs must be recaptured each time the thread is changed. If frogs are released slowly and gently, they usually will remain at the release point, so that no investigator-instigated movement results. The device apparently does not seriously hinder a large frog's ability to jump. However, it or the belt can irritate the skin on the hip and thighs. As soon as any irritation is noticed, the device should be removed. Frogs with trailing devices should be individually recognizable, either by dorsal patterns or by marking (Appendix 2).

PERSONNEL AND EQUIPMENT

Sewing bobbins and thread are available commercially, but the device must be assembled by the researcher. Materials are easily obtained. A single researcher can effectively use the technique.

DATA TREATMENT AND INTERPRETATION

The study site should be mapped before tracking is initiated. Travel routes are plotted in the field on graph paper, usually each morning and evening. After the trail has been mapped, the thread is removed from the field. Bobbins should be resupplied with thread as necessary.

Because activity varies with climate and among individuals, many frogs should be trailed for many days. Dole (1965), for example, followed 136 frogs for up to 35 days each. Maps derived from movement records of individuals can be compared and used to evaluate habitat use, to determine distances moved daily or weekly, and to estimate home range size. Because of the nature of the data, statistical analyses usually are inappropriate.

Radio Tracking

STEPHEN J. RICHARDS, ULRICH SINSCH, AND ROSS A. ALFORD

Devices that emit radio waves can be attached to individual amphibians for tracking movements. The radio waves are detected by a remote, transportable receiver. The closer the transmitter is to the receiver, the stronger is the signal that is received. The investigator follows the signal and locates the amphibian.

For studies of biological diversity, radio tracking can be used to investigate microhabitat use at a fine scale and to determine home range sizes, movement patterns, and daily and seasonal activities. These data may reveal habitats occupied away from breeding sites and may point to areas where conventional monitoring techniques can most profitably be used. Radio transmitters can also be used to monitor physiological parameters such as temperature, locomotory activity, and heart rate.

TARGET ORGANISMS AND HABITATS

This technique is restricted to medium and large amphibians (≥ 10 g), although some successful trials have been completed with smaller frogs (about 5 g; S. J. Richards, unpubl. data). The major constraint on radio tracking of amphibians is the size and mass of the transmitter-battery package. As a general rule, transmitter packages should not exceed 10% of body mass. As technology has improved, however, smaller transmitters have appeared on the market; transmitters with a total mass of less than 1 g are now available.

Animals can be tracked in both terrestrial and aquatic habitats. Successful projects have been carried out in the semiarid Chaco of South America (McClanahan and Shoemaker 1987), the Andes (Sinsch 1989b), the Rhineland of Germany (Sinsch 1988, 1989a), and tropical rain forest (S. J. Richards, unpubl. data). Implantable transmitters also work successfully for amphibians in aquatic environments such as streams (Stouffer et al. 1983) and are particularly useful for locating amphibians that burrow when they are away from breeding sites. Battery lives ranging from 5 to 95 days and detection distances from 10 to 100 m have been reported for 1.3-g to 11.6-g transmitters attached to free-ranging amphibians (van Nuland and Claus 1981; Stouffer et al. 1983; Bradford 1984; McClanahan and Shoemaker 1987; Fukuyama et al. 1988; Sinsch 1988, 1989b). Other investigators have used implanted transmitters to monitor amphibians in outdoor enclosures (Smits 1984; Smits and Crawford 1984; Shoemaker et al. 1987).

BACKGROUND

White and Garrott (1990) provided a detailed overview of radio tracking techniques, research design, and data analysis. Anyone contemplating radio tracking of amphibians should first read this book. Kenward (1987) also provided worthwhile information on designing a radio tracking study. We restrict our discussion to the particular problems and possibilities associated with radio tracking amphibians.

PROBLEMS AND PRACTICALITIES

One of the major assumptions of radio tracking is that the presence of a transmitter has little or no effect on an animal's normal behavior. However, given that the aim of the technique is to locate and observe animals in situations where they cannot normally be observed, it is difficult, if not impossible, to test whether the tracked animal's behavior is the same as that of an animal without a radio. A controlled study in which the behavior of marked and unmarked individuals can be compared (e.g., under seminatural conditions such as in an outdoor enclosure) may be necessary to determine whether transmitters affect behavior.

The use of radio tracking invariably involves compromises. Choosing the smallest possible transmitter clearly will reduce potential effects of the package on an animal's normal behavior. However, small packages have limited battery life, on the order of only a few days to several months. Battery life can be extended, however, by increasing pulse interval or reducing pulse length. Small transmitters also have limited transmission range, and implanted transmitters require the use of loop antennae, which further reduce transmission range.

Transmitter function can also be influenced by the habitat being investigated. Very high frequencies transmit over long distances in the open, whereas slightly lower frequencies travel shorter distances but have less attenuation and are more stable (van Nuland and Claus 1981). Thus, lower frequencies may be preferable when working in dense vegetation such as rain forest. Optimum frequency range needs to be determined for each project.

The most sensible approach is to develop a transmitter in collaboration with the manufacturer, rather than purchasing ready-made packages. That way, transmitter characteristics can be tailored to the needs of the project.

RESEARCH DESIGN

Transmitters can be attached to amphibians externally, or they can be implanted. Each method has advantages and disadvantages.

EXTERNAL ATTACHMENT. The moist nature of amphibian skin precludes direct attachment of transmitters with glue. Several investigators have used harnesses or waistbands to attach transmitters to frogs. Van Nuland and Claus (1981) developed a harness for larger amphibians, such as toads, that consists of a flexible latex cover with four holes cut to the diameter of a toad's legs. The legs pass through the holes, and the cover rides on the animal's back. The transmitter is glued to the dorsal surface of the harness. Some toads were able to remove the latex harness in brambles and in water (van Gelder et al. 1986).

Fukuyama et al. (1988) glued transmitters to a rubber waistband, which was slipped on to frogs as they arrived at a breeding stream in Japan. S. J. Richards (unpubl. data) did the same with *Litoria serrata* in Australian rain forest, using small elastic bands. Richards found that bands caused no apparent damage to skin, and no bands were removed by the frogs over a period of 4 days.

The major advantage of external attachment is that a surgical operation is not required. An external transmitter also can have a relatively long antenna, thereby increasing transmission range. However, carrying an external package may hinder the activity of frogs that shelter in confined spaces, may induce stress, and may increase the visibility of frogs to predators. External attachment probably should be used only for short-term studies of arboreal or terrestrial frogs. When attaching external transmitters to amphibians, care must be taken to ensure that the animals' normal movements are not hindered. Transmitters should not be brightly colored.

IMPLANTED TRANSMITTERS. For larger species or long-term studies, implantation is preferable to external attachment and has been used more commonly with amphibians. In this technique the body wall is opened and the transmitter package inserted into the peritoneal cavity. Implantation in the lymph space under the skin is also possible with very small transmitters. Stouffer et al. (1983) described the surgical technique used to implant transmitters in hellbenders (*Cryptobranchus alleganiensis*); this procedure has been used by most researchers.

The transmitter needs to be embedded in beeswax or a synthetic, nontoxic, waterproof substance such as heat-shrink plastic. The animals are anesthetized by immersion in an anesthetic solution (Appendix 1). The animal is ready when it is completely flaccid when handled. Animals should be continuously dampened with the anesthetic solution during the operation. The skin in the region of the incision is cleaned with antiseptic, and all instruments and gloves should be sterilized with ethanol. A single incision just large enough to insert the transmitter is made in the ventral surface, parallel or perpendicular to, and to the left of, the midline. The transmitter is inserted carefully into the peritoneal cavity to avoid disturbing the intestine and gonads. The wound is closed with an absorbable gut suture. Separate closure of the skin and the body wall with a few stitches each may be required. Animals revive after 15 to 30 minutes in fresh water and can be released after as little as 4 hours (Sinsch 1989b). Transmitters should be removed at the conclusion of the study, using the same procedure. Tracked amphibians should be identified with a unique mark so that individuals can be recognized and transmitters reclaimed if batteries fail.

In at least some species of toads (e.g., *Bufo spinulosus* and *B. calamita*), a sterile environment is not required for implantation operations. One of the authors (U. Sinsch, unpubl. data) did not use sterile techniques during several years of fieldwork on these species; mortality rate was less than 5%, and infection of the wound was never observed. Olders et al. (1985) reported similar results with *Bufo bufo*.

FIELD METHODS

Following the animal on foot with a portable receiver and hand-held antenna is probably the only way to track the signals of moving amphibians. Automatic tracking stations using triangulation systems (White and Garrott 1990) are of little use because of the limited range of the transmitters and because habitat features mask or reflect signals. A detailed map or grid system for the study area is essential. Locations of animals should be marked directly onto a map in the field or marked with flags and transferred to a map the next day.

Radio tracking is a time-consuming task. Depending on the type of habitat and the vagility of the species under investigation, it may take 1 to 2 hours after each interval between observations to locate each individual. If continuous tracking is done, the time between sightings should not exceed 1 hour. Given these constraints, we recommend a ratio of no more than 1:4 between investigators and animals with transmitters.

PERSONNEL AND EQUIPMENT

Radio tracking is extremely time-consuming and requires some expensive equipment. In addition to radio transmitters (discussed above), essential equipment includes a portable receiver, an antenna, and headphones to damp extraneous noise.

Technological advances in recent years have led to great improvements in transmitter performance and versatility. These improvements have particular advantages for amphibian studies, because miniature transmitters can now be fitted with a range of additional functions. Temperature-sensitive and movement-sensitive transmitters weighing only 2 g to 3 g are now available. Transmitters cost anywhere between U.S. $30 and $150, depending on size and functions.

Receivers must cover the frequency band of the transmitters and be capable of monitoring as many frequencies as are likely to be in use at one time (i.e., the maximum number of amphibians to be tracked simultaneously). For work with nocturnal amphibians an illuminated dial is a great advantage; durability also is important. Most receivers available today are of good quality, and price may be the major consideration when making a selection. Receivers cost between U.S. $600 and $1,000.

A frequently used antenna is the 3-element yagi, which is both highly directional and excellent at distinguishing between reverse and true bearings (Kenward 1987). However, this antenna is cumbersome in dense vegetation such as rain forest, and one of the many types of smaller antennae now available may be more suitable in such environments. A loop antenna can be useful for final location of concealed animals. Suitable antennae now cost between U.S. $75 and $300.

Radio tracking equipment is manufactured by dozens of specialist companies in Europe, North America, Australia, and New Zealand (see Appendix 6 for vendors). These companies usually employ biologists experienced in wildlife radio tracking, who normally are pleased to help design transmitters and to provide advice on the equipment most appropriate for a given project.

DATA TREATMENT AND INTERPRETATION

The type of data recorded and the analysis required will depend on the objectives of the study. Pertinent data for each sighting usually will include date, time, position, habitat, microhabitat, activity, and temperature (if temperature data are being transmitted). Environmental parameters should be recorded and include, where relevant: rainfall (past and current), air and water temperatures, wet bulb temperature, soil temperature, humidity, cloud cover, and moon phase. The establishment of a long-term weather station to record environmental variables, including maximum and minimum temperatures and rainfall,

on a continuing basis would be advantageous (see Chapter 5).

If statistical procedures are to be used, they must be planned prior to the study to determine the amount and the type of data to be collected. A major problem with radio tracking is the low number of individuals that can be tracked at a given time. Statistical comparisons among individuals are difficult, and most studies to date have been descriptive, reporting patterns of movement and habitat use. White and Garrott (1990) provided a summary of statistical design and examples of statistical analyses suitable for radio tracking data that included tests for habitat preference and techniques to estimate survivorship and population size.

Tracking with Radioactive Tags

RAY E. ASHTON, Jr.

The use of a radioactive tag on an amphibian allows a high level of dependability in the relocation of study animals even if the animal is underground or underwater. Small amounts of radioactive material emitting alpha and gamma radiation can be inserted into the amphibian and detected by a portable scintillation counter. The closer the counter is to the emitting material, the greater the number of rays intercepted and read by the scintillation counter. An investigator can track and locate the emitting source by always maximizing the reading on the counter.

TARGET ORGANISMS AND HABITATS

This technique seemingly has wide applicability to most amphibians in a wide variety of habitats. At present, it is the only tracking technique that can be used with small individuals. A summary of the detectability of cobalt-60 tags is presented in Table 6. The technique has been used successfully on frogs and salamanders that inhabit burrows or use rocky retreats. Animals have been

Table 6. Maximum Detection of Cobalt-60 Tags through Natural Barriers[a]

Barrier type	$\bar{x}$ thickness (m)
Air (specimen on surface of soil)	5.00
Water	0.70
Sand	0.80
Soil	0.50
Limestone	0.40
Granite	0.35
Wood (pine)	1.00

[a]Figures are for detection of cobalt-60 tags (30–45 microcuries) using a Thyac III survey meter, a Thyac model 491 scintillation probe, and earphones for audible detection. Data taken from Karlstrom 1957, Harvey 1965, and Ashton 1975.

tracked from 1 to 69 weeks, moving distances of up to 1,822 m in a day (Barbour et al. 1969; Ashton 1975; R. E. Ashton, Jr., unpubl. data).

BACKGROUND, PROBLEMS, AND RESEARCH DESIGN

The technique is rooted in the physics of radioactive decay, which will not be described here. Drawbacks associated with the technique include bureaucratic problems involved in obtaining permits to use radioactive materials and procedures for handling the tagging material safely. Initial costs are high, and research areas where the tagged animals will not come into contact with people not involved in the study may not be available. The loss of animals and tags is low, apparently no greater than with radio transmitters. The method has not been used much by researchers probably because of concerns stemming from an ignorance of radioactive materials and inexperience with their use. The concerns are misplaced. As long as approved safety procedures are followed, no known deleterious effects to either the researchers or the tagged animals will result.

Regulations governing radioactive material are rather stringent in most countries, and permission to use these materials may not be given if radiation sources are lost because tagged animals disappear after release. Therefore, it is advisable to evaluate the suitability of radioactive tagging for a particular species carefully before selecting it as a technique for the study. Tree dwellers or species that burrow deep in the ground, beyond detection range of the equipment, are not good candidates. They are simply too difficult to find often enough to obtain information on movement and microhabitat use. Amphibians that move 15 m or more several times during a week also are extremely difficult to follow on a regular basis.

Amphibians caught at breeding sites can move long distances, and relocating tagged individuals may be difficult and time-consuming. The best results are obtained when an amphibian is located and tagged within its home range. Finally, at least 50% to 75% of the attempts made to locate each tagged animal should be successful if the study is to succeed.

A major problem in determining suitability of radioactive tagging for a particular species is the lack of adequate information on movements and microhabitat use of most species. Therefore, a pilot project is often required to address the issue. Two individuals of the same species are tagged and followed at 24-hour intervals for 3 to 4 weeks. If the animals disappear or other problems are encountered, then the project should be stopped and another species or technique selected.

Selecting a study site is almost as important as selecting a species. Generally, home ranges of suitable species are less than 100 m^2. However, animals often are first captured outside their core activity areas. Because a researcher will traverse a study site for weeks or months under all conditions, the site should be rather easy to work without causing considerable alteration. Another concern is security. For safety reasons, the research area should be secure from use by humans, or the tagged animals should not be so mobile that they will move into areas used by people.

To some degree, the size of the study area can be determined during the pilot project. Each tagged animal must occupy an area free of other tagged animals; otherwise individual identification will be impossible unless the animal is recaptured. To ensure that crossover (movement of one tagged animal into the area occupied by another tagged animal) does not occur, the area around the tagged animal should be at least twice the diameter of the expected home range or twice the longest distance traveled by tagged animals during the preliminary study. It usually is not necessary to have tagged animals separated by such great distances that they use different breeding areas. Animals are often conspicuous during the reproductive period and usually do not require recapture for identification. However, handling animals at the breeding site appears to be less disruptive than handling them at other times.

Time and money available for these personnel-intensive studies will determine the length of time an animal can be studied. The longer an animal can be studied, the more valuable are the data collected. The duration of the study influences the selection of type of isotope used to make the radioactive tags. The longer the half-life, the longer the tag can be detected. Tantalum has been used successfully for studies lasting less than 100 days. Cobalt-60 is the usual tag of choice because it has a half-life of 5.2 years, making a 40- to 50-microcurie tag effective for at least 3 years.

Cobalt-60 is relatively easy to obtain; however, it (as well as other isotopes) must be modified for use as a subcutaneous or in-muscle tag. It is important to put the cobalt-60 into an aluminum alloy wire or otherwise suspend it in another solid metal. The wire should be sealed in a gold or platinum tube, or it should be plated.

Plating is cheaper and just as effective. The outer metal layer prevents rejection of the tag by the animal's tissues. It is important that the ends of the tube or plated wire be melted to a smooth rounded surface to reduce tissue damage during insertion. Isotope for tags usually can be obtained from the radiation control or nuclear physics departments within universities or research centers.

Radioactive tags are expensive and cost about U.S. $100 each.

FIELD METHODS

Field behavioral studies are extremely labor intensive. For the first 7 days, animals are tracked at frequent intervals throughout the day. After the first week, the tagged animal are followed an average of 2 hours per day and thereafter are monitored at intervals of 24 to 48 hours. If animals are monitored at longer intervals, then the time required to relocate each one increases greatly. Actual time spent depends on a number of factors, including changes in distances moved and microhabitats used.

I highly recommended that the number of tagged animals in the field at any one time be low. The maximum number that I was able to track at one time was 15, under ideal habitat conditions and with animals that were easy to follow. Loss of tagged animals to predation, injury, or other causes will occur. Replacements of lost animals can be made during a long-term study.

During the breeding season, animals usually move more frequently, and during peak breeding periods, they should be monitored closely. Close monitoring provides interesting data and helps to prevent animal loss. Animals should be monitored at different times during the day and night to provide a better picture of behavior and microhabitat use. Once located, a tagged animal should not be disturbed. Animals observed without harassment yield valuable behavioral data. At night, red filters should be placed over lights.

Walking over the same piece of study area every other day for long periods can cause considerable habitat change. Such changes can alter the behavior of the tagged animals, because microhabitats, food availability, and other factors may be affected. Once movement patterns of animals become obvious, the investigator should modify his/her approach to the home range to reduce impact on the area.

Many researchers have a desire to see the tagged animal, especially if it has not been seen after weeks of detecting radiation and hearing the roar over the earphones. As long as the animal has been moving, however, it should not be disturbed. Moving even a few leaves can affect relative humidity enough to cause an animal to abandon its burrow and never return. There is no way to determine if the researcher's interference caused this change.

If an animal has not moved after 10 weeks, then the researcher should attempt to find it, being careful to cause as little disturbance as possible. With experience, the researcher will learn to interpret behavior and how to respond to it. If a "reliable" animal suddenly disappears from its home range, it is likely to have been eaten. A wide area should be surveyed immediately; the missing tag may be recovered if the predator or the uneaten portion of the animal that contained the tag is located.

PERSONNEL AND MATERIALS

MONITORING EQUIPMENT. Monitoring equipment should be as sensitive as possible and should include earphones. Normally, such equipment is designed for light field use, not the grueling day-after-day field monitoring required in this type of study. A few simple modifications will help ensure equipment serviceability. Connections where probe wires enter the aluminum housing and the connection to the survey meter are prone to loosening; these should be strengthened. Rubber sleeves help to stiffen the wires, keeping them from bending and pulling at these

sites. Also, a 3-m wire provides some flexibility in using the probe.

The most delicate part of the equipment is the scintillation probe. It should be encased in water-resistant rubber or foam. Factory repairs of a probe can cost U.S. $500 or more. Many universities have electronics shops that can handle simple repairs more cheaply. Encasing the probe in a plastic or aluminum pipe 1 to 2 m long can increase efficiency by extending the search radius and allowing the probe to be held closer to the ground or extended into trees. A counterweight at the opposite end of the probe increases maneuverability and ease of handling.

ADDITIONAL EQUIPMENT. Additional equipment needed will depend on the data required for the project. Data on temperature, moisture, and incident light taken wherever a tagged animal is found can be extremely valuable in developing a picture of microhabitat use. If a species is fossorial, probes will be required for monitoring. Specialized equipment for measuring oxygen levels, water quality and chemistry, and stream flow will be required when working with aquatic species. Automated weather stations near the study area can provide useful data (see "Automated Data Acquisition," Chapter 5).

Standard safety equipment is required and includes a lead storage bottle and a secure facility in which to store radioactive tags. Radiation monitoring badges for individuals may be required by permit regulations.

DATA TREATMENT AND INTERPRETATION

One of the greatest frustrations in doing field behavioral studies on animals that are secretive and only infrequently seen is the long period of time required to collect a small amount of data that gives only a glimpse of a species' behavior. Because major shifts in behavior take place seasonally in most temperate species, animals should be observed throughout a year if possible.

Data collected in such a study should include the following:

1. Date and time of sampling, including hours since last check and sighting.
2. Distance moved from previous site, and compass heading.
3. Weather conditions, including precipitation since last check, maximum and minimum temperatures, range of barometric pressure since last check, and phase of the moon.
4. Microhabitat data, including temperature, relative humidity, and moisture on the surface and at the site of the animal; percentage of sun or shade and percentage of vegetative cover over the site; depth below the surface and type of cover (e.g., rock, leaves, soil, log); presence in and description of retreats (e.g., burrows, cracks, hollows under logs); and pH of soil.
5. Activity at time of observation (active or not; if active, whether moving on the surface, moving underground, feeding, breeding, and so on).
6. For aquatic sites, water level fluctuations between checks; levels of dissolved oxygen, carbon dioxide, and nitrogen (various forms); pH of the water; and turbidity.

Because of the type of data collected and the relative paucity of those data, even over a long period, it is important to determine—before the study begins—how data will be collected and managed. Results of tracking studies usually are descriptive and are not treated statistically. Frequently, microhabitat data have to be grouped to provide adequate sample sizes with which to work.

SPECIAL CONSIDERATIONS

PERMITS. Use of radioactive materials often is controlled by governmental agencies, and regulations are not uniform from country to country. The requirements for use of radioactive materi-

als in the United States are given here as an example.

All states in the United States require that individuals have permits for the use of radioactive materials. Generally, states issue permits to universities, allowing those institutions to authorize the use of radioactive materials by individuals. Typically, a professional radiation safety officer and a radiation safety committee oversee the use of radioactive materials on campus. Before applicants can be issued permits, they must do the following:

1. Complete a radiation safety course (usually provided at the university).
2. Receive some training or be experienced in the proposed technique.
3. Provide a plan for safe handling and storage of radioactive materials before, during, and after the study. (Most committees also require routine dosage monitoring on the researcher.)
4. Be authorized to use radioactive materials in the research area and show that the area is secure.
5. Agree to submit routine reports for review.

Authorization from an animal care committee may also be required by some institutions. The requirements that such a committee may impose on the researcher are difficult to determine. However, it can be shown that this method is as humane as any other similar technique and is often the only method available for tracking small amphibians. The effects of radiation on tagged animals are discussed in Griffin (1952).

TAGGING. Experience has shown that the greater the stress on the study animal from capture and handling, the greater the deviation in its behavior. Erratic movements, usually longer and more frequent than normal, are observed immediately after the initial release or after the animal has been recaptured. In fact, most animal losses occur within 72 hours after tagging and release; most animal deaths occur within the first 7 days. Animals held in captivity for 24 hours or longer are less likely to survive once released. For these reasons, it is important to handle study animals with great care and to capture, tag, and release them as quickly as possible. The entire operation should take less than 5 minutes.

To facilitate successful use of the technique, and investigator should do the following:

1. Flag the exact capture locality so that the animal can be returned to it after tagging.
2. Practice the tagging technique on a preserved specimen before working on living individuals.
3. Have everything ready for tagging before an animal is captured. Tags usually are 2.0 × 0.3 mm and fit easily into the barrel of an 18-gauge hypodermic needle. The needle should already be loaded with the radioactive tag and plunger (a thin stiff wire that will easily slide through the needle barrel).
4. Sterilize the hypodermic needle, plunger, and tag with an agent such as ethyl alcohol.
5. Make sure that the hypodermic needle is sharp. Even new needles may require sharpening.
6. Wear surgical gloves for safety of the animal and the researcher. Salts and oils from the researcher's fingers add to the stress of the animal being handled.
7. Place the animal in a wet zip-lock plastic bag and tag it directly through the plastic. Salamanders or frogs can be restrained in the proper position at the corners or bottom of the bag so the needle can be inserted rather easily. In salamanders, the tag should be injected into the musculature of the tail, dorsally and near the base. In frogs, the tag should be inserted between the musculature and skin at the juncture of the body and legs.
8. Weigh and measure animals while they are in the plastic bag (also see Appendix 1).

9. Mark the animal, preferably with a "finger printing" method (Appendix 2).

Night driving

H. BRADLEY SHAFFER AND J. ERIC JUTERBOCK

Night driving is a kind of line transect in which the transect is a road. The investigator drives back and forth over a certain section of the road and counts the amphibians (and other organisms) that cross it per unit time.

The technique was first used by Klauber (1939) who noted its effectiveness in sampling nocturnally active desert snakes (see also Dodd et al. 1989). For amphibians, it is one of a cluster of techniques that provide estimates of species richness and relative abundance for actively moving individuals. Depending on the proximity of the road to breeding, overwintering, or other habitat, the technique can also provide information on movements and habitat use for many species.

We recommend using night driving in conjunction with other techniques to provide species richness data for inventories and to monitor particular species that must cross a road to reach a breeding pond. Night driving by itself cannot provide reliable quantitative estimates of absolute abundance for most species.

Target Organisms and Habitats

Night driving is most effective for surveying highly mobile amphibians as they cross a road. In general, these are animals migrating to and from a breeding site or animals that are mobile when foraging. This technique is not particularly effective for animals with small home ranges (e.g., some plethodontid salamanders—Jaeger et al. 1982), especially if the road is heavily traveled. Individuals whose home ranges include the road are killed by vehicles fairly quickly, so that sedentary species soon disappear from night driving samples. Mobile species continue to cross the road and continue to be killed by vehicles.

Night driving requires a road and a car. Thus, in general, habitats in primary forest, in wilderness areas, or between roads cannot be surveyed with this technique. The best roads for night driving are those recently put through a previously undisturbed habitat and those with relatively low vehicle use (especially after dark) that are located near a breeding site. Warm, rainy nights provide optimal conditions for night driving.

Background

Because the road is a relatively neutral part of an amphibian's habitat, night driving provides a reasonable estimate of the general composition of assemblages of actively foraging species or those migrating to breeding sites. (This is not true for desert snakes for which the road is a heated corridor of habitat that attracts individuals.) J. E. Juterbock (unpubl. data) encountered all but one species of anuran (*Pseudacris ocularis*) known to occur in the Everglades National Park in his night driving survey of the main park road. If a road is situated near a breeding site, it can provide a reasonable estimate of the number of animals moving to the site. Relative abundances of visible, mobile species can be estimated even when a road is far removed from a breeding site.

The effects of road traffic on amphibian populations are virtually unknown. A road may be a barren corridor, with all but the commonest, most mobile species eliminated by vehicles, or it may constitute a perfectly reasonable transect through a habitat. To determine the magnitude of the effect requires comparison of independent estimates of population size based on night driving and on transects away from a road, and this has not been attempted. Campbell and Christman (1982a) provided comparative data on spe-

cies richness in Florida using night driving, quadrat sampling, time-constrained general collecting, and trapping; their results indicated that night driving was by far the most productive technique. Campbell and Christman (1982a) did miss several small species (*Acris gryllus, Hyla femoralis,* and *Limnaoedus* [= *Pseudacris*] *ocularis*) and one large ranid (*Rana grylio*), although all other native anurans were recorded. Night driving provides quantitative data that can be compared with data from other night driving surveys or from surveys of the same section of road over time. This technique is of equivocal value in providing comparative density estimates among different species with different movement patterns.

An investigator using night driving for amphibian sampling makes the following implicit assumptions:

1. Species do not treat a road as a barrier to dispersal.
2. Individuals do not learn to avoid roads, or are not attracted to them.
3. Features associated with the road itself (e.g., runoff, burrow pits and ditches) do not affect species richness or abundance in the immediate vicinity of the road.
4. Individuals are sampled only once during an evening (important for relative density estimates).

The following limitations apply to night driving:

1. Sedentary species with restricted home ranges may not be sampled in their usual proportions in the assemblage, because they are quickly eliminated from roads.
2. Small immobile species are harder to see from a moving vehicle than are large active species.
3. Habitat specialists, especially arboreal species, may be missed.

Research Design

For night driving, the experimental unit is the stretch of road to be surveyed. Thus, the research design consists of choosing a section of road to survey and determining the number of times to drive it. To maximize the number and types of species recorded, it is useful to plan a route passing near a series of breeding sites. Because most amphibians are active during rains, night driving on rainy nights is often much more productive than driving on dry nights. For many species, especially in the western United States, species move to their breeding ponds during the first rains of the season (Stebbins 1962), and those nights provide the best time for estimating relative abundance of migrating individuals. In contrast, some species have special migrations that can be sampled only during specific periods (e.g., the autumn premigration of *Ambystoma* in the midwestern United States—Johnson 1977).

Because individuals being sampled with night driving almost always are moving, the most informative data are obtained by sampling one stretch of road several times in an evening. Cruising speeds of 20 to 35 kph permit most investigators to see all individuals, yet allow for a reasonably long transect to be covered. We often wait at the end of the road for about 15 minutes between passes. In this way, 30 km of road can be surveyed twice in less than 3 hours, and two to three round-trips are feasible on a given evening.

One of the most important potential uses of night driving is repeated monitoring of set routes during a season and over many years for quantification of changes in species richness and relative abundance. For data to be maximally informative, sampling procedures must be consistent from year to year and from survey to survey. Thus, the same section of road should be surveyed at the same speed at the same hour after sunset. Although some researchers believe that surveying on the same date each year is the best strategy for consis-

tent, interpretable results, we think that comparable weather conditions are more important. Thus, night driving on the night of the first heavy rain of the year or on the first night on which a critical temperature is reached provides more appropriate comparative data than do surveys based on the same date. Of course, if activities of many groups of night drivers are being coordinated on a regional basis (see "Group Activities and Field Trips," below), the only feasible strategy may be to use a common date, given that weather patterns vary across large areas.

Field Methods

Field methods for night driving are simple: one picks a stretch of road and drives along it slowly, stopping briefly, as necessary, to note all amphibians seen. A strong flashlight is essential for locating and identifying each animal after it is spotted in the vehicle headlights. We have found that a detailed map of the area through which the road passes can greatly enhance the interpretation of night driving results. All ecologically relevant features of the area, including breeding ponds and streams, habitat transitions, changes in elevational or exposure, and proximity to human activity, are noted on the map, along with distances from each end of the survey section. As animals are discovered, the exact distance along the section can be noted.

It is assumed that individuals are seen only once during a night and that they are accurately identified. To confirm this assumption, each animal can be given a date-specific mark (e.g., one toe clipped for each evening). An animal should be released off the road in the direction it was moving, after time, mileage, species, sex, approximate age (adult, subadult, newly metamorphosed), direction of movement, and weather conditions are recorded. Obviously, it is crucial to record the mileage at the end of each section of the route so that position of each capture on the road can be plotted later.

Personnel and Materials

A single person can conduct a night driving survey, although teams of two persons are optimal (one person to drive and one to capture the animal, record data, and process road kills). Besides a car, an investigator needs a flashlight, note pad, ice chest, dry ice (if tissue samples are collected), plastic bags, and a marking pen.

Data Treatment and Interpretation

There are so many problems in determining the effects of the road on the animals that it is pointless to use the road as a sampling transect for estimating total population sizes. However, by simply counting the number of individuals encountered per drive through or per night, it is possible to develop a reliable estimate of the number of animals crossing that particular stretch of road. These data apparently provide good estimates of species richness at a site (Campbell and Christman 1982a; J. E. Juterbock, unpubl. data). Assuming that migration patterns remain constant, these numbers can be compared over time to follow trends in abundance and habitat use by each species. For example, a 7-month survey of *Bufo terrestris* and *Rana sphenocephala* based on extensive night driving revealed differential use of habitats along the road (Fig. 22).

Special Considerations

One unique aspect of night driving is that recently killed animals are routinely encountered on the road. These animals, even if badly mutilated, can (and should) be collected as voucher specimens to document the species that were present on each survey. Each specimen should be assigned a number, placed in a separate plastic bag, and stored on ice until it can be preserved (Appendix 4). Tissue samples for molecular genetics research almost always can

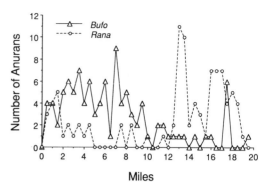

Figure 22. Distribution of *Rana sphenocephala* and *Bufo terrestris* along a road transect through the Everglades National Park. The total numbers of each species observed along each 0.5-mile segment of road between October 1988 and April 1989 are plotted. Differences in abundances of the two species in different parts of the transect correspond to different habitat types along the road.

be taken from these specimens (see Appendix 5), which should be numbered, placed in a zip-lock bag, and immediately placed in a separate container with dry ice to prevent tissue degradation. Later, tissue samples can be removed and transferred to an ultracold freezer or to liquid nitrogen for long-term storage.

Stopping for amphibians at night on a road can be dangerous. Drivers should use common sense and follow accepted safety practices.

Geographic information systems

GIS and Remote Sensing Techniques

LEE-ANN C. HAYEK AND ROY W. McDIARMID

INTRODUCTION

A geographic information system (GIS) is a computerized tool that integrates geographic or spatial information with data on the physical or biological attributes of the space. The technology combines cartography with relational databases and analytical tools. Spatial data recorded on commercially available or manually produced maps are digitized and linked to multiple databases from other sources through identifiable attributes (e.g., latitude and longitude, boundary values). These databases can include positional and geographic material at a wide range of scales (e.g., soil and contour maps, satellite images), site-specific information (e.g., water temperature of ponds, drainage patterns, kinds of biological associates, soil topography), or data from a particular study (e.g., abundance of calling males, dates of site use for frog reproduction).

In a computer-based GIS application, large volumes of data can be maintained and manipulated efficiently and integrated with other measurement tools. Spatial data and records of associated amphibian biodiversity can be treated separately or overlaid and integrated with, for example, global positioning systems (Slonecker and Carter 1990), satellite image processing (Roughgarden et al. 1991), or remote sensing procedures (Ehlers et al. 1991). The quality of visual and automated analyses of relationships among many kinds of geographic features and types of data is unequaled by the quality of analyses carried out with manual methods. The capability of the GIS to process spatial data distinguishes it from related computer graphics systems. Not only can data from multiple sources be combined in a GIS but also, as data such as, for example, changes in water level or reductions in habitat area are entered, the accuracy of the changes can be checked and the relevant maps and associated amphibian microhabitat or diversity data updated in the GIS. These spatial capabilities enable geo-referenced information to be created and used in a context completely different from that in which it was collected. Complex evaluations can be done rapidly, and spatial as well as some temporal changes in habitat features can be detected and analyzed. Because each computer analysis can be carried out quickly and at relatively low cost, successive analyses are now practical and can enhance planning and decision making.

A computer-based GIS provides a useful method for integrating quantitative data obtained from amphibian inventory or monitoring projects (Chapter 6) with ancillary data associated with their microhabitats (Chapter 5). However, to our knowledge no one has used computerized GIS technology to analyze amphibian populations or habitats. Several investigators have used a GIS in wildlife habitat studies of mammals and birds (e.g., Davis and DeLain 1986; Lancia et al. 1986; Ormsby and Lunetta 1987; Johnston and Naiman 1990; Pereira and Itami 1991). Hodgson et al. (1988) evaluated the seasonal availability of wetland foraging habitat for the wood stork (*Mycteria americana*) using GIS, and Palmeirim (1988) used remote sensing data to map habitats of bird species. These authors used land cover types and spatial habitat characteristics (such as minimum patch size and distance to quadrat edge) together with bird counts to estimate population sizes. Generally, the results obtained have been more informative and reliable for species that are relatively abundant and restricted to specific habitats than for species that are rare, wide-ranging, or generalists with regard to habitat use.

APPLICATION

A researcher interested in learning how species use certain habitats or in managing geographically defined sites and their contained biota could use GIS profitably. The GIS provides computer methods for delineation and management of specific habitats of different sizes and distributions (bogs, wet meadows, patches of emergent vegetation along lake shoreline) or of areas associated with certain map features (ponds, talus slopes, caves). This technique also can provide for random selection of study sites within well-defined areas (i.e., strata), so that many of the more consequential threats to internal and external validity of the study are minimized or avoided. Decisions about the use of space in managing for biodiversity can be facilitated. For example, the locations of a series of breeding sites within a protected area or the locations of optimal sites for detailed study and possible animal reintroductions can be determined.

In addition, the GIS provides a unique approach to integrating quantitative data from an amphibian inventory or monitoring project with geographic and climatic data from the study site, including data obtained through remote sensing (e.g., Rango 1989). A GIS also may be useful for discovering changes in the distribution of habitats important to amphibians, for identifying patterns and trends in the climatic or hydrologic data that may be related to demographic changes in amphibian populations through time, and for modeling the consequences of such changes.

BACKGROUND

Terms and applications used in other spatial information technologies are sometimes confused with those used in a GIS. To avoid confusion, we place any integrated information system that has a geographic component in the GIS category. For biodiversity purposes we view *spatial data* simply as data that represent real objects of any scale on earth; these objects can be converted conveniently to (*x,y*) coordinates, such as latitude and longitude or locations on a sampling plot or transect. The element that distinguishes the GIS from other information technologies (database management systems or spreadsheets) and graphics systems is the processing of this spatial data. Links between spatial data sets allow for analyses of factors important in the spatial variability of habitats and can be used to develop predictive models of habitat suitability.

Spatial data occur in three basic forms within the context of most GIS applications: *points, lines,* and *polygons* (or *areas*). These three are sufficient to describe all relevant features on a two-dimensional landscape. For example, a forest or breeding pond would appear as a polygon or area; a stream, cliff face, or road would be a

line; and a log, cave mouth, or spring would appear as a point. Spatial data are structured topologically and rely on mathematical relationships between contiguous data elements (lines, points, and polygons). Topological relationships are built from simple to complex: points are the simplest elements, lines are sets of connected points, and areas or polygons are sets of connected lines.

Raster and *vector* are two major types of GIS and are distinguished by how the computer handles data. A raster GIS uses points in a network of *grid cells* and is efficient for handling complex mathematical manipulations and modeling. A vector GIS is used when accurate calculations of distance and area are needed. The same general operating principles apply to both approaches, and many software packages now incorporate both capabilities.

Computerization of data allows for the association of three kinds of information with each item of spatial data: the coordinate location of the feature (where it is); the name and associated attributes of the feature (what it is); and the relationship of the selected feature to other nearby components of the environment (map topology). The use of map topology is an essential element and distinguishes a GIS from other types of computer graphics systems. The expression of map topology allows for complex *spatial analyses* (the quantitative study of the patterns of points, lines, and polygons defined by coordinates in two-dimensional or three-dimensional space) within a GIS, including site suitability studies and delineation of buffer zones (e.g., individuals' ranges) and patterns of habitat use. It also provides for information retrieval based on specific map locations (e.g., breeding ponds).

The quantitative results of any monitoring or inventory effort may be analyzed with a GIS, provided that supplementary locality or geographical data are available. Spatial data usually are recorded on maps and then digitized for computer entry. Digital maps are produced with digitizers (manual), interactive computer data terminals, or scanners. These processes are expensive. Spatial data available from other sources (e.g., satellite images, remote sensing, aerial photographs) must be entered into databases (e.g., Ehlers et al. 1991) and linked with the amphibian database.

Database management systems currently available have capabilities for data storage, retrieval, updating, and logical query. A GIS is able to perform these functions graphically, using the locations of geographic features and the information obtained from an inventory or monitoring project. Maps and information are stored in a hierarchical and spatial format to allow for complex queries not available with other systems.

A key aspect of GIS output is the derivation of new data. By generating solutions to complex, spatially oriented research questions, a GIS introduces unique combinations or views of the data that were not in the original database. For example, the boundaries of a species' distribution across habitats may be generated from a logical overlay of specific values for rainfall, vegetation, elevation, slope, aspect, and other factors relevant to an amphibian's existence.

DATA ANALYSIS AND INTERPRETATION

GIS are predicated on the idea that visual presentations of geographical data usually are more effective than tabular ones. The ability to detect patterns in the data is enhanced by visual inspection of the output, the nature of which will vary with the intended audience and the questions asked. Printed thematic maps are common products.

The mathematical theory and statistical methods underlying geographical science applications have been adapted for use with GIS and are appropriate for assessing sites and for monitoring change with data collected from a network of sampling locales (e.g., Lyon et al. 1987). These analytical methods would be especially suitable for producing contour maps of amphibian abundances within microhabitats or between habitats that could be characterized by available satellite imagery (e.g., Palmeirim 1988). Geographical-statistical methodology has been used most frequently in GIS applications involving meteorological, hydrological, and soil data (Cliff and Ord 1981). These methods also have been applied to analyses of wildlife habitats to select sampling sites for vegetation (Davis and DeLain 1986; Pereira 1989) and to monitor foraging habitat of the wood stork (Hodgson et al. 1988).

Surprisingly, usually only simple univariate measures (e.g., range, mean, variance) can be calculated within GIS. However, spatial data layers can be exported from a GIS for more-complex statistical treatment with a computerized statistical package (e.g., SYSTAT, SAS, SPSS, BMDP). These analyses then can be included with the visual presentations in the GIS. Linear models can be used to identify habitat suitability based upon topography, vegetation, and hydrology. For example, densities of beaver colonies in boreal landscapes were predicted using multiple regression techniques that modeled vegetation and hydrologic patches on a landscape (Broschart et al. 1989). Likewise, critical habitat features for endangered red squirrels were identified using logistic regression to rank active and inactive sites with respect to elevation, slope, aspect, distance to open area, estimates of canopy closure, and other habitat descriptors (Pereira and Itami 1991). Bayesian methodology also has been suggested for statistical analysis of data in a GIS framework (Strahler et al. 1978; Strahler 1980). However, a Bayesian statistical approach requires a priori knowledge of species distributions or geographic patterns, and such knowledge usually is unavailable in spatial work.

Frequently, the quality of data used in GIS applications is poor; data often come from several sources and contain errors of unknown magnitude and direction. Working with such problems is not equivalent to working with sampling errors; there may be no way of estimating the size or direction of these errors and no way of correcting the problem.

An important statistical consideration in GIS applications is that spatial data are characterized by nonindependence of neighboring observations. In a geographical sense, *nearness* implies similarity and *distance* denotes dissimilarity in both two-dimensional and three-dimensional plots. Most computerized packages are not designed to deal with this type of data, and variance probably will be underestimated. It is possible to overcome such problems, but only with difficulty. For example, most GIS programs do not allow for export of data about common or overlapping boundaries; such capability could be used to adjust for these spatial effects. We believe that in most cases emphasis should be on exploratory rather than confirmatory statistical analyses, and we warn investigators to seek expert advice from mathematical statisticians before attempting such analyses.

SPECIAL CONSIDERATIONS

Three points need to be considered before attempting to use a GIS application with amphibian data. First, the volume of data to be incorporated into a GIS application often determines the kind of computer hardware needed. Small to moderate volumes of information from associated databases can be handled on a personal computer with MS-DOS or Macintosh OS, although a UNIX system may be required for some applications. Hundreds of gigabytes of data require a mainframe. The availability of hardware, in turn, often limits the choice of operating system and the range of GIS products that can be created.

The second consideration is that no proven criteria for selecting an appropriate GIS system exist. Many articles have been written on the "best" approach to selecting a specific GIS (e.g., Braden and Webster 1989). Frequently, they

suggest that a potential user compare a list of features across different GIS products. The major drawback to this method is that technical terms (e.g., overlay, transfer properties) have not been standardized across products and companies, possibly because of rapid development within the field. A second approach is for the potential user to identify systems used for applications similar to his or her own. For amphibian work this could prove difficult, if not impossible, because the GIS has been so little used with amphibians. Although an amphibian expert would know his or her particular needs, this knowledge would not be of use in choosing between general-purpose or specifically designed GIS applications, because the user would not know if the properties of the system were relevant for the amphibian study questions. A third possibility is to base the choice on the system architecture (the set of rules used to design the system). The key to the system architecture is the *data model,* or the set of rules used by the system to represent geographic information in discrete, digital form in the database. Braden and Webster (1989) argued that this is the only objective and reliable basis upon which to classify GIS software, because it allows the user to choose a system based on specific research needs. GIS data modeling is one of the most active research and development fields at present. Users are being provided with increasing numbers of choices for customizing their systems with fewer restrictions to analyses.

The third major consideration regarding use of a GIS involves computer graphic systems. Although these systems are related to the GIS, they cannot be used in place of it for complex data sets, because they are more severely affected than GIS by small errors in the data. A cursory review of this field will show the interested user that the simple act of creating a map for interpretive purposes may be risky. A slight change in class interval, scale, or other variable, or a subtle change of color shading in a small area can lead to significant errors and, often, to incorrect interpretations. If the data themselves are incorrect, mapping will invariably amplify, not diminish, the error. For example, the most extreme effect in percentage can occur in the area with the smallest population. Data must be examined from several perspectives, and an overemphasis on either the visual (easily done with computer graphics) or the inferential can lead the user to incorrect decisions. Openshaw (1990) discussed some methods for exploratory visual analysis of spatial data (e.g., fuzzy pattern analysis, visualization enhancers, automatic spatial response modelers) that are less likely than simple graphic presentations to mislead the user.

REMOTE SENSING AND MANUAL OVERLAY

One can use a GIS to identify and quantify change. Change is detected by comparing remotely sensed imagery (data obtained from aircraft or satellites) with mapped data or by comparing previously obtained images with recent images. In either case, highly accurate images are required. Remote sensing systems often provide immense amounts of data that can overwhelm computer processing and storage capabilities. Regardless, such data, once collected, can be interpreted by either manual or computer-assisted image analysis procedures. Image processing and interpretation of remotely sensed data usually require that ancillary data and information verified by on the ground investigation (ground-truthed) be integrated with aerial photographs or satellite images. The GIS permits this integration. Manual overlay systems (manual GIS), albeit limited in scope, have been part of remote sensing methodology for many years. The overlaying of contour, elevation, area, and volume measures (photogrammetry) and environmental variables or ground cover information (photo interpretation) has served as an excellent manual GIS tool. Several examples of the use of manual GIS for studies of amphibians with specific habitat requirements are described in the

next section. We know of no specific examples of the use of a computer-based GIS combination with inventories of amphibian populations or habitats or with data from programs for monitoring species or sites to ascertain changes in biodiversity. We think that such applications will be forthcoming. The GIS is particularly appropriate for such work.

CONTRIBUTOR: DANIEL G. COLE

Manual GIS Application for Habitat Specialists

J. ERIC JUTERBOCK, SAMUEL S. SWEET, AND ROY W. McDIARMID

A number of amphibian species, because of the uncommon and often spatially isolated habitats they occupy, are difficult to inventory and monitor with standard inventory techniques. Many of these species are restricted to specific habitats that can be located on maps or detected with some form of remote sensing. Therefore, such species are amenable to study with a GIS. Although a computer-based GIS would be most efficient (see the previous section) and especially useful for long-term study of certain species or entire amphibian faunas on dedicated research sites, considerable information on ecological and geographic distributions of populations of amphibians can be obtained with a manual GIS application.

The approach we describe in this section is used to determine the distribution and status of populations of selected species by locating their habitats by remote sensing. Whether relative abundance, density, or population size is estimated depends primarily upon characteristics of the population and the effort expended. In situations in which the assumptions of mark-recapture estimation techniques (Chapter 8) are not obviously violated, absolute population estimates are possible and often preferable (see "Special Considerations," below).

TARGET ORGANISMS AND HABITATS

Any species of amphibian may be studied with remote sensing techniques, but for some species the method is much better than the available alternatives. The manual overlay approach may be the only efficient method for locating and studying amphibians restricted to uncommon and often spatially isolated habitats. Examples of salamanders in this category include *Aneides aeneus,* which is restricted to rock outcrops with abundant crevices in the Appalachian Mountains of eastern North America; *Typhlotriton spelaeus, Eurycea lucifuga,* and other *Eurycea* and *Typhlomolge* species, which are confined to caves or limestone ravines with permanent water in the Ozark and in the Appalachian mountains, and on the Edwards Plateau, respectively; and *Plethodon shenandoah,* which is found on north-facing talus slopes in Shenandoah National Park, Virginia.

Frogs in this category include habitat specialists with moderate to limited distributions, such as *Bufo microscaphus californicus,* which is restricted to the subset of stream terraces adjacent to suitable breeding pools in southern California and adjacent Mexico, and *Ascaphus truei,* which is found only along clear, cold, rocky streams in humid forests in the northwestern United States and adjacent Canada.

Frequently, species within restricted habitats have irregular patterns of activity, so that individuals are unevenly accessible to investigators and therefore are difficult to sample by most standard procedures. Their patchy distribution, irregular activity, and certain other ecological and behavioral characteristics also preclude accurate estimation of population size by standard techniques. Ohio populations of *Aneides aeneus* illustrate the point well. Individuals, already restricted to crevices in sandstone or dolomite outcrops, are territorial (Cupp 1980), and females

are observed at the surface of the outcrops only irregularly when they are brooding eggs (Juterbock 1989).

Troglodytic salamanders pose other problems. Observed population densities of such species often vary, despite the seeming constancy of their environment. In repeated visits to a site, individuals may not be seen at all or may vary in number by an order of magnitude.

Salamanders, especially those in marginal (e.g., seasonally dry) environments, may be highly responsive to rather subtle environmental cues, such that the animals only rarely are in sites that can be sampled by standard techniques. Some species of *Batrachoseps* are notorious in this respect, as are *Plethodon* species in the Allegheny Mountains and the Cumberland Plateau, much of the Ozarks, central Texas, and northern New Mexico. Some benefits accrue from persistent sampling efforts if environmental variables are monitored regularly on-site, because the responses of the animals can then be used to refine otherwise crude interpretations of limiting conditions.

Many other species of amphibians fall into one of the above categories and may be good prospects for study with an analysis of remote sensing data and manual overlay techniques (e.g., *Plethodon larselli, P. petraeus,* and *P. punctatus*—Buhlmann et al. 1988; several species of *Batrachoseps* and *Eurycea tynerensis*—Tumlison et al. 1990; species of frogs with highly restricted distributions, such as *Hyla andersoni, Rana okaloosae,* and *Eleutherodactylus cooki,* as well as *Rheobatrachus silus,* which is now possibly extinct—Tyler 1989).

BACKGROUND

The manual GIS has not been used often with amphibians, and the theoretical foundation is undeveloped. The technique is useful for habitat specialists and for restricted populations for which standard sampling techniques are not suitable. Dodd (1990, 1991a) employed a manual

GIS application in conjunction with a standard technique for which theory is well established to study the fossorial salamander *Phaeognathus hubrichti*. He used geological maps to locate a formation to which the species was restricted and then overlaid contour maps on the formation map to identify sites with steep slopes where the salamanders burrow. He then surveyed several sites, estimated burrow density with line transect techniques, and argued that burrows provide an index of density for this species. Presumably, other species that use specific microhabitats (e.g., burrows, crevices in rock ledges, holes in bamboo stems, bromeliads of certain shapes and sizes) within habitats that are easily detectable with remote sensing could be inventoried effectively with a similar approach. Sweet (1982) used geologic and topographic criteria to determine the location and temporal reliability of springs on the Edwards Plateau, Texas, and demonstrated that the distribution of the salamander *Eurycea neotenes* could be delimited using these characters. Having established limiting values, he then estimated the total distribution of the species and the number of extant populations, using manual GIS techniques.

Any overlay application, whether manual or computer aided, requires good maps or aerial photographs, and their availability should be established before attempting a study. Actual on-site verification (i.e., ground-truthing) of identified habitat also is essential and should be incorporated into any study using remote sensing for amphibian studies. Finally, to make effective use of the technique, investigators must be aware of seasonal variation in activity and other peculiarities of the life history of the target species.

RESEARCH DESIGN

Habitat-restricted species that can be studied effectively with some form of remote-sensing manual GIS fall into two categories: species that are inaccessible much of the year but periodically occupy a site or behave in a way (e.g., spring migration to a specific breeding site) that allows them to be sampled by standard inventory techniques, and species that are continuously inaccessible and not easily sampled.

Many amphibians in the former group select highly specific habitats for breeding and do so under relatively specific weather conditions. If these habitats or breeding sites can be detected with remote sensing, and if the periodicity of utilization of the habitat or site can be determined, then the species usually can be inventoried or monitored readily during the breeding season (see "Surveys at Breeding Sites," Chapter 6). Using the same information, larval and metamorphosing individuals may be more easily located and sampled than juveniles or adults (see "Quantitative Sampling of Amphibian Larvae," Chapter 6). Sampling design generally would follow that outlined for the standard technique.

Some form of manual GIS also may be useful for identifying the presence of specific habitats that contain continuously inaccessible species. However, detecting abundances or determining densities within these habitats may be very difficult. Considerable effort with repeated samples, especially if variance is high, has to be put into one or two sites before data obtained from those sites can be extrapolated to others. Even then, projecting estimates of population size and density obtained at one site to similar sites identified with remote sensing is fraught with problems. Variations in species densities between sites are common, and we do not advise projecting densities without some ground sampling. Amphibian activity often is closely tied to local weather conditions. When weather varies between sites, ground-truthing may give very different results, even when actual densities are nearly the same. Workers should make such projections with extreme caution.

METHODOLOGY

Conceptually, the approach is relatively simple. To utilize remote-sensing data for amphibian studies, the investigator (1) establishes the general distribution, habitat requirements, and life history parameters of the target species; (2) estimates the amount (ha) of suitable habitat available; (3) determines the population densities and proportion of the habitat(s) occupied at one site; and (4) multiplies the density by the area of occupied habitat and extrapolates for all areas, if an estimate of minimum population size for the total area is desired.

Obtaining data on distribution and habitat requirements may be a simple matter for well-known species such as *Aneides aeneus* (Juterbock 1989) or *Eurycea lucifuga* (Guttman 1989), or it may require detailed habitat analyses, as for *E. tynerensis* (Tumlison et al. 1990) and *E. neotenes* (Sweet 1982). Ways of estimating habitat availability include consulting geologic, topographic, and soil maps, aerial photographs, and previous surveys; driving roads to look for appropriate habitat; and using other forms of remote sensing. Ideally, the ecobehavioral characteristics of the target species will allow estimation of relative abundance or density with one of the recommended standard techniques. Unfortunately, there often is no efficient substitute for iterative sampling in arriving at a realistic picture of a species' true ecological or distributional range, by a process of successive approximation. We cannot emphasize too strongly that accurate and realistic assessments of occurrence or abundance are labor-intensive and require continuing efforts to "think like the target species." In practice, an index such as minimum population size may be the best available estimate. Once data for a few sites are obtained and predictions of density estimates for other sites seem reliable, projections for all available habitat units are possible. It is always necessary to ground-truth a significant sample of the habitat units to get some idea of the accuracy of the density estimates within the total habitat. If habitat units are sufficiently large, it may be useful to apply the same principles within a unit and to index population size only for a portion of any single unit.

PERSONNEL AND EQUIPMENT

There are no fixed personnel requirements. Good maps, aerial photographs, or other kinds of geographical information are needed. Specific field expenses and personnel needs will vary with the project, be defined by the selected techniques, and especially depend on the project length. If mark-recapture techniques are used, other field equipment may be required. Typically, we have worked alone, often over several field seasons, using a flashlight, a camera, some anesthetic, and scissors for marking.

DATA TREATMENT AND INTERPRETATION

The data to be recorded will vary with the species and the goal of the project. If it is necessary to identify habitat characteristics first, a wide variety of physical and, perhaps, biotic factors must be evaluated (Tumlison et al. 1990), with the provision that much useless effort can be avoided by thinking through the candidate factors and eliminating those that are not likely to make a significant contribution. The tendency is often to adopt habitat parameters and measures from a standard menu developed for bird or mammal studies, the great majority of which are simply irrelevant to amphibians. Once the specific type of habitat is known, its extent must be determined (e.g., number of ponds, linear meters of rock outcrop or spring flow). To index or estimate population size, the techniques discussed earlier in this chapter should be applied.

Analysis and interpretation of relative abundance and density data are described with the standard sampling technique selected.

SPECIAL CONSIDERATIONS

Assumptions critical to population estimates, especially assumptions relating to equal likelihood of capture for all members of the population, often are violated when sampling species with restricted habitat requirements or behavioral peculiarities. In such cases only relative abundance estimates are possible. In populations in which individuals of a certain age, size, or sex are more likely to be caught than others, as with brooding females of plethodontid salamanders or calling or territorial males of many anurans, marking new individuals over an extended period may allow an estimation of minimum population size. Any standard estimator that allows for mark-recapture data that are biased by unequal catchability can be used.

As with any indirect estimator, caution must be used in interpreting projections derived from this approach. To provide for acceptable extrapolations, the original data delineating the habitat and determining the degree of habitat use must be extensive, and the abundance and density estimates accurate. Sites for intensive investigation should be representative of those available and should include both prime and marginal areas. If the variance of the population estimators obtained from the intensive surveys is great, it may be preferable to rank habitats (e.g., marginal, good, excellent) and to project estimates accordingly, rather than to assign an average number of individuals to all habitats in the range of the target species.

Group activities and field trips

ROY W. McDIARMID AND MAUREEN A. DONNELLY

Organized field trips and similar group activities can be valuable components of survey and monitoring programs when projects are labor-intensive and require considerable field effort. Volunteers, students, and nonspecialists can monitor populations at specific sites or survey species and habitats simultaneously across broad geographic areas (e.g., states, provinces, or regions). These activities can provide worthwhile data and a positive educational experience for the participants if the specific goals of the project are clearly specified before the fieldwork begins, and the field trip leader is knowledgeable of the biology of target species and the habitats to be surveyed. We support such programs, provided that they use the techniques recommended in this book or follow some other rigorously defined set of standards (see "Regional Surveys" under "Examples of Group Activities," below). In that way, data obtained will be comparable with data from other projects.

Target Organisms and Habitats

Organized group activities can focus on a variety of species and habitats. Wetland sites with small permanent or temporary ponds in which amphibians breed are particularly suitable. Because participants in group activities often are nonspecialists, such programs work only where the amphibian fauna is well known and identification guides are readily available. Even so, eggs and larvae, which indicate reproductive activity at a site and should be noted, are difficult to identify. Volunteers probably should not attempt identifications unless these can be confirmed with voucher specimens.

Background

Organized group trips can be an integral part of a college or high school course curriculum, an annual meeting sponsored by a regional herpetological society, an educational program sponsored by a wildlife or conservation group, or a regional monitoring effort (e.g., state and province monitoring and survey projects). If the trips are conducted on a regular basis (e.g., first week-end of April, day after first summer rains, week after spring thaw) and if quantitative sampling methods are used, data gathered can provide valuable information on amphibian species richness, relative abundance, and density.

Data taken on field trips must be collected in a standardized way if they are to provide reliable information. Quantitative data are more informative than qualitative data, and preferable, especially if comparisons among samples or sites are a goal of the project. Nevertheless, the use of standardized field techniques and data collection methods can be tedious, and the field trip sponsors should consider the enjoyment factor in the project design. For example, members of a regional herpetological society may be more interested in capturing all amphibians observed in 3 hours at a given site than in searching carefully along a transect line or in plots of known size. The results from such a time-constrained search can be used to generate a species list for the site (= species richness). In contrast, however, careful searching along a transect or in a plot can generate data on density and relative abundance, as well as a species list. If an organized group visits the same site year after year and uses the same sampling methods, changes in the local fauna over time can be assessed (= monitoring). Likewise, observations that changes in amphibian density or species composition at a site are correlated with successional changes in aquatic habitats may be useful in making decisions regarding management of wetlands for select amphibian species.

Research Design

Sampling methods must be standardized among sites or within sites between sampling periods. Breeding activity of many species is associated with warming temperatures or the first heavy rains after a dry period. Specific dates of these phenomena vary from year to year at a site, but with some flexibility, groups can schedule their activities to coincide with such events. The lack of experience of the participants may require that sampling procedures be simplified, but the project goals and data quality must not be compromised. The research design discussed for each field survey technique used should be reviewed (see Chapter 6).

Personnel and Materials

Personnel and materials are those outlined for the specific techniques used. A data coordinator or center is recommended, and probably required, for larger projects.

Data Treatment and Interpretation

Data sheets designed to facilitate recording pertinent information and to minimize decision making are essential to the success of group activities, especially if different groups are sampling species or sites at the same time in different geographic areas. Standardized data sheets also are essential for monitoring the same site through time. Scoring by choosing from specific alternatives often is easier for the volunteer than filling in blanks and makes data handling easier. Several practice trips may be required to perfect the procedures and develop useful data sheets. Data sheets should be field-tested as part of the development process.

Data gathered during group activities should be analyzed according to the recommendations given in Chapter 9 and those made for each technique in Chapter 6.

Special Considerations

Organizers of group activities must provide participants with training, pertinent background information, sampling protocols, and data sheets. They should follow techniques outlined in this book to maximize the information obtained during organized events. Because these projects often are staffed by volunteers, sponsors should appoint a data coordinator (or establish a data center) to receive completed data sheets from participants. An efficient and effective means for disseminating project results and their interpretation to the participants (e.g., a newsletter) is also essential to a successful ongoing project.

Examples of Group Activities

STATE AND PROVINCE SURVEYS

We briefly describe three successful ongoing programs that effectively use interested volunteers to inventory or monitor amphibians over large geographic areas. Two programs were designed to monitor frogs in Wisconsin or in Illinois; the third was designed to inventory amphibians and reptiles throughout the province of Ontario. Additional information on these programs is available from the Wisconsin Bureau of Endangered Resources (P.O. Box 7921, Madison, WI 53707, USA), the Illinois Department of Conservation (Carl N. Becker, Chief, Division of Natural Heritage, 600 North Grand Ave. W., Springfield, IL 62706, USA), and the Ontario Herpetofaunal Summary (Ontario Field Herpetologists, RR #22, Cambridge, Ontario N3C 2V4, Canada). For a brief description of the Wisconsin program, see also "Field Methods" under "Surveys at Breeding Sites," Chapter 6.

The Wisconsin Bureau of Endangered Resources (WBER) and the Illinois Department of Conservation (IDC) initiated their monitoring programs in 1984. Prospective volunteers contact the agency (WBER or IDC) and receive a packet consisting of an introduction to the project, a detailed set of instructions, route assignments, species accounts, and data sheets (Fig. 14). The accounts include a brief description of each species of frog, to aid in identification; information on its breeding biology, habitat use, and other aspects of its natural history traits; and a tape recording of its call. Volunteers are required to learn the calls and to record data

three or four times a year. They drive a predetermined route on one or more prescribed dates and estimate the number of calling frogs of each species that they hear along the route, either by listening at preselected sites on the route or by listening for calling frogs at predetermined intervals along the route. An index of calling activity is generated for each species at all sampled sites. These efforts provide the agencies with information on state species richness, statewide distribution patterns, calling phenology, relative abundance of calling males, and habitat use. Agency personnel analyze the data.

The Ontario Herpetofaunal Summary was started in 1984 to compile information on distributions and life histories of species of amphibians and reptiles in Ontario, Canada. The project is staffed entirely by volunteers and coordinated by individuals in the Ontario Field Herpetologists club. Sources of data include records from an ongoing field observation program begun in 1984, pre-1984 field notes and files of local naturalists, literature reports, and museum and university collections. Observations are submitted annually on preprinted data cards (Fig. 23A) to compilers who verify the information and enter it into a computer that plots records on a map of Ontario marked with a 10×10-km grid. In the first 7 years of its operation, the field observation program involved an extensive network of nearly 2,500 volunteers who contributed more than 50,000 observational records to the project (Fig. 23B). Data are stored in a dBASE file and used to produce annual species accounts that include maps; information on habits, habitats, breeding biology, and behavior; and other relevant aspects of the distributions and life histories of Ontario amphibians and reptiles (summary data for the western chorus frog, *Pseudacris triseriata,* are presented in Fig. 24). A newsletter and these annual summaries provide background data and baseline information for future research, contribute to a global examination of issues related to declining amphibians, aid na-

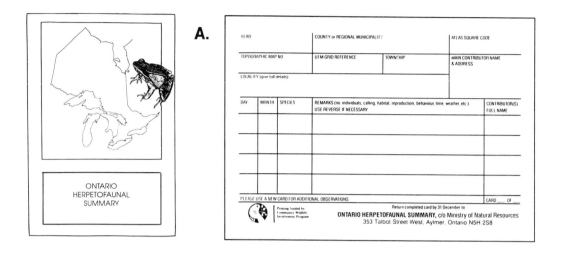

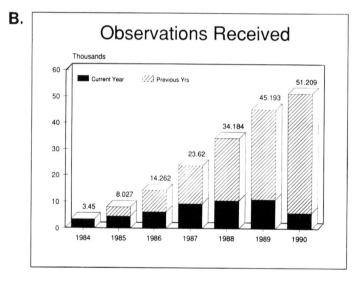

Figure 23. Ontario Herpetofaunal Summary. A. Observation data card. B. Cumulative summary of all observations received from 1984 through 1990.

tional and local agencies in making appropriate decisions on management and land use practices that may affect amphibian populations, supply data to organizations charged with the conservation of amphibian species, and generally contribute to an increasing public awareness about the importance of amphibians in a healthy environment. This impressive effort should serve as a model for other groups interested in similar issues.

HERPETOLOGICAL SOCIETY FIELD TRIPS

Members of regional herpetological societies are enthusiastic and generally knowledgeable about local species of amphibians and reptiles, and enjoy the interaction of organized events. Annual field trips often are popular aspects of regional society programs and can provide useful quantitative data on amphibian populations if the goal of the excursion is clearly identified,

A.

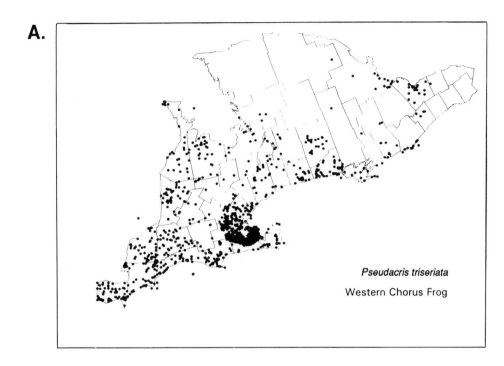

Pseudacris triseriata

Western Chorus Frog

B.

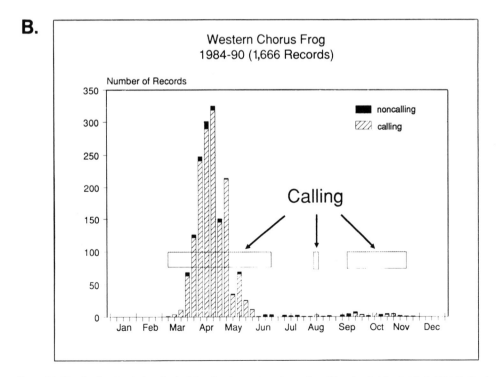

Figure 24. Distributional and phenological data for the western chorus frog (*Pseudacris triseriata*). A. Distribution in southern Ontario. B. Monthly plot of activity. Data are from the Ontario Herpetofaunal Summary.

Amphibian Population Survey

Country —————————— Date —————————
State —————————— Surveyor name —————————
County —————————— Society name —————————
Site name —————————— Time (24 hr system) —————————

Site latitude/longitude Weather, previous 48 hr:

Site elevation —————————

temperature	moisture
—— unseasonably warm	—— unseasonably warm
—— unseasonably cold	—— unseasonably cold.
—— normal	—— normal

Species

Codes A = adult J = juvenile L = larvae E = eggs	Ambystoma tigrinum	Ambystoma texanum	Eurycea longicauda	Necturus maculosus	Typhlotriton spelaeus	Acris crepitans	Bufo americanus	Bufo cognatus	Bufo debilis	Gastrophryne olivacea	Hyla chrysoscelis	Pseudacris crucifer
Total number seen (add letter E if # is estimate)												
Calling?												
Amplexing or copulating pairs present?												
HABITAT DATA												
Aquatic												
stream												
permanent												
intermittent												
river												
natural lake												
reservoir												
pond												
floodplain												
upland												
marsh												
floodplain												
upland												
bog												
ditch												
seasonally flooded												
spring or rock seep												
Terrestrial												
upland												
mountaintop												
slope												
lowland												
floodplain												
streamside												

Air temp. —— (°F or °C) **Water temp.** —— (°F or °C) **pH** —— water —— soil

Nearby land characteristics

—— crops   —— active livestock pasture   —— unused pasture   —— prairie   —— woodland

—— town   —— industrial   —— other (what is it?)

Figure 25. Sample population survey sheet modified from one used in the survey of Kansas amphibians.

AMPHIBIAN SURVEY DATA SHEET – US FISH & WILDLIFE SERVICE, 4612 McMURRY AVE, FT. COLLINS, CO 80525-3400

(circle choice for shaded variables; supply value for others)   (ver. 2/7/92)

DATE	BEGIN TIME	END TIME	OBSERVERS

LOCALITY

STATE	COUNTY	MAP NAME	OWNER	ELEVATION (circle scale)	M FT

T	R	S	SECTION DESCRIPTION	UTM ZONE	NORTHING (or LAT)	EASTING (or LON)

AMPHIBIAN AND/OR GARTER SNAKE SPECIES PRESENT
(INDICATE NUMBERS IN CATEGORIES IF POSSIBLE)

CIRCLE METHOD AND INDICATE IF
VOUCHER SPECIMEN WAS COLLECTED

SPECIES	ADULTS/JUVENILES	CALLING?	TADPOLES/LARVAE	EGG MASSES	METHOD:
		Y N			VISUAL/AURAL ID DIP NET/SEINE HAND COLLECTED TRAPPED VOUCHER COLLECTED? YES NO
		Y N			VISUAL/AURAL ID DIP NET/SEINE HAND COLLECTED TRAPPED VOUCHER COLLECTED? YES NO
		Y N			VISUAL/AURAL ID DIP NET/SEINE HAND COLLECTED TRAPPED VOUCHER COLLECTED? YES NO
		Y N			VISUAL/AURAL ID DIP NET/SEINE HAND COLLECTED TRAPPED VOUCHER COLLECTED? YES NO
		Y N			VISUAL/AURAL ID DIP NET/SEINE HAND COLLECTED TRAPPED VOUCHER COLLECTED? YES NO

FISH PRESENT? YES ??? NO	FISH SPECIES:	
ENTIRE SITE SEARCHED? YES NO	IF NO, INDICATE AREA	METERS OF SHORELINE M² OF HABITAT

PHYSICAL AND CHEMICAL ENVIRONMENT (CHEMISTRY VARIABLES OPTIONAL - USE EXTRA SPACES FOR ADDITIONAL MEASUREMENTS)

WEATHER: CLEAR OVERCAST RAIN SNOW	WIND: CALM LIGHT STRONG

AIR TEMP (circle scale) °C °F	WATER TEMP (circle scale) °C °F	COLOR: CLEAR STAINED	TURBIDITY: CLEAR CLOUDY
pH	ANC		

SITE DESCRIPTIONS - (SKETCH SITE AND PUT ADDITIONAL COMMENTS ON BACK OF SHEET)
OMIT THIS SECTION IF DATA HAVE BEEN COLLECTED ON A PREVIOUS VISIT

ORIGIN: NATURAL MAN-MADE	DRAINAGE: PERMANENT OCCASIONAL NONE

DESCRIPTION:	PERMANENT LAKE/POND	TEMPORARY LAKE/POND	MARSH/BOG	STREAM	SPRING/SEEP	ACTIVE BEAVER POND	INACTIVE BEAVER POND

SITE LENGTH (M)	SITE WIDTH (M)	MAXIMUM DEPTH:	< 1 M	1 – 2 M	> 2 M

STREAM ORDER	1	2	3	4	5 +

PRIMARY SUBSTRATE:	SILT/MUD	SAND/GRAVEL	COBBLE	BOULDER/BEDROCK	OTHER

% OF POND LAKE MARGIN WITH EMERGENT VEGETATION:	0	1 – 25	25 – 50	> 50

EMERGENT VEGETATION SPECIES (LIST IN ORDER OF ABUNDANCE)			

NORTH SHORELINE CHARACTERS:	SHALLOWS PRESENT	SHALLOWS ABSENT	EMERGENT VEG PRESENT	EMERGENT VEG ABSENT

DISTANCE (M) TO FOREST EDGE	FOREST TREE SPECIES:			

Figure 26. Sample amphibian survey data sheet developed by the U.S. Fish and Wildlife Service and recommended by the Declining Amphibian Populations (DAP) program. The back of the sheet is marked with a grid to facilitate mapping of the survey site. Some data categories are also explained on the back of the survey sheet.

data collection is carefully organized, and field methods are standardized. We include two sample data sheets developed for different amphibian survey programs (Figs. 25 and 26). Either could be customized easily for other areas or needs. Regional societies may wish to use one form for the group leader and another for the other field volunteers. The group leader would be responsible for providing information on the locality, elevation, vegetation, habitats, date, weather conditions, number of volunteers, and so forth. The volunteers would record only time and species-associated data such as microhabitat, number of individuals, size, life history stage, and so on. Well-organized field trips can enhance camaraderie among society members and involve the group in an effort of potential importance to the conservation of local amphibian species and habitats. Officers of regional societies should consult a local herpetologist (if knowledgeable persons are not members) or state or federal agency personnel when selecting areas or habitats to be sampled and species to be studied.

Regional societies have contributed successfully to a survey of *Hyla andersoni* populations and habitats in North Carolina (R. E. Ashton, Jr., pers. comm.), efforts to monitor amphibians and reptiles in Ontario, Canada, and annual HERP-COUNTs in Kansas (a program for monitoring amphibians and reptiles that is sponsored by the Kansas Herpetological Society—E. Rundquist, pers. comm.). Additional information about field trip organization, methods, and data handling is available from G. R. Pisani.

CONTRIBUTORS: GEORGE R. PISANI,
STEVE HAMMACK, AND MICHAEL J. OLDHAM

## Chapter 8

Estimating Population Size

Introduction

All monitoring programs are designed to detect change in population size. Some require, in addition, estimates of population size itself. Two approaches to making such estimates, using various mark-recapture methods or removal sampling, are described in this chapter. Whatever the method, estimation of population size requires extensive data collection and analysis and is labor-intensive and time-consuming (Southwood 1978). Therefore, such estimates should be included in a project design only when the research question requires detailed knowledge of the target population.

Mark-recapture

MAUREEN A. DONNELLY AND CRAIG GUYER

The mark-recapture (M-RC) method of population estimation consists of the capture and marking of animals, their release, and their subsequent recapture or resighting one or more times.

Objectives

Mark-recapture methods are valuable in monitoring studies because they extend beyond estimation of population size to include estimation of demographic parameters (birth, death, immigration, emigration, and survival rates), space use patterns (home range size and utilization), and individual growth rate.

Several mathematical estimators of population size based on M-RC data are available (Caughley 1977; Southwood 1978; Begon 1979). Describing all of them is beyond the scope of this book, so we limit our treatment to four commonly used methods. For readable descriptions of M-RC techniques and models, we recommend Begon (1979) and Schemintz (1980).

Target Organisms and Habitat

Mark-recapture techniques have been used by herpetologists since the 1920s to study many species of salamanders and frogs in a variety of habitats (Woodbury 1956). Marking methods are detailed in Appendix 2. Marking amphibian larvae is difficult, and some marking methods may have adverse effects on individuals (e.g., Travis 1981). To our knowledge, no M-RC study has ever been performed on caecilians. Although these amphibians could be captured, marked, and released, their aquatic or fossorial habits would make recapture difficult.

Background

The mathematical estimation of animal population size was formalized by Petersen (1896) and popularized in North America by Lincoln (1930). The Petersen estimate (also referred to as the Lincoln Index and the Lincoln-Petersen Index) is relatively simple mathematically and is the basis for more-complicated estimators.

Assumptions inherent to all M-RC models are that (1) the initial sample taken is representative of the entire population (i.e., not biased by age or sex); (2) all animals taken in the initial sample are marked, and the marks are permanent and recorded correctly; (3) the marked animals are released and become distributed randomly in the population; and (4) marking does not affect the probability of recapture or survival (i.e., marked and unmarked animals have equal catchability). These assumptions should be tested in the field or the laboratory prior to initiation of a long-term study. Activity patterns and behaviors can be influenced by age and sex, and some marking methods can affect survival, growth, and/or behavior. In some cases, marked animals are more conspicuous (to investigators and predators) than unmarked ones, thus violating assumption 4. Although few investigators have tested assumption 4, Clarke (1972) demonstrated that toe clipping adversely affected young toads, and Travis (1981) showed that staining tadpoles with neutral red dye reduced growth rate. If species exhibit age- and sex-related behavioral differences (violation of assumption 1) or if recapture rates vary with age or sex (violation of assumption 4; van Gelder and Rijsdijk 1987), then each subgroup (i.e., age class or sex) can be analyzed separately.

The Petersen estimate of population size assumes, in addition to the above assumptions, that the population is closed (no immigration, emigration, birth, or death). If two samples are closely matched in time, the population can act as if it were closed, and the Petersen estimate is appropriate. If detailed data on population processes (immigration, emigration, birth, death, survival) are necessary, then other models must be used.

Caughley (1977), Southwood (1978), and Begon (1979) described how to test the assumptions of equal catchability, the effects of marking, and the permanence of marks. Additionally, Begon (1979) described tests of constancy of survival rate (Fisher-Ford estimator), differences between subgroups, and random sampling. Nichols (1992) recently reviewed mark-recapture models and advances in computer software for analyses of M-RC data. Table 7 summarizes some of the effects of violating the basic assumptions of M-RC models.

Table 7. Assumptions of Mark-Recapture Models and Effects of Their Violation

Assumption	Effects of violation
Marks permanent and noted correctly	Population size overestimated
	Survival rate underestimated
Probability of recapture not affected by marking	If recapture rates increase with mark:
	Population size underestimated
	Survival rate underestimated (with Manly-Parr method)
Survival not affected by marking	If marking decreases survival:
	Survival rate underestimated
	Population size overestimated in closed populations
	Gains overestimated[a] (with Jackson's Positive method)
Equal catchability	Population size underestimated

[a] Gains result from immigration and recruitment.

Research Design and Field Methods

Before a M-RC study is conducted, the investigator must clearly state the goals of the research, establish a sampling protocol that will satisfy the goals, select an estimator of population size (taking underlying assumptions into account), and decide how the data will be analyzed statistically. The first step in any M-RC study is to define the target population (e.g., the reproductive amphibians at a breeding site or the number of amphibians in a 1-ha plot or along a 100-m transect). The results of the study must be interpreted specifically and only in terms of this target population (Begon 1979). The sampling protocol is dictated by the information needed (e.g., estimate of population size only, specific information on population gains and losses, annual or seasonal variation in population parameters or space use patterns). Detailed knowledge of the biology of the target organisms facilitates designing the appropriate sampling protocol and improves the accuracy of the results. The estimator and the statistical tests selected are dictated by the sampling protocol. The availability of

resources (funds, field time, personnel, and computers) must also be considered.

All M-RC techniques require that the population under study be sampled at least twice (see "Data Analysis and Interpretation," below). Animals can be sampled in plots of known size or along permanent transects. If animals are sampled within a site of known area, then density can be calculated. In the field, the study area is sampled, and individuals are captured and marked, or if they are recaptured, the mark is recorded, and they are released. In some cases, an investigator can capture all active animals in the study area; in others cases, time-constrained searches must be used to ensure equal sampling effort in all areas.

Data sheets designed for the study are a convenient way to record data in the field; data also can be recorded in a waterproof field notebook, dictated into a microcassette recorder, or entered directly into small, hand-held computers. Field notebooks are relatively small and easy to transport. For every animal captured, Donnelly (1989) recorded capture date, plot number, time (24-hr clock), location on the plot, major habitat feature at capture point, number of individuals at each location, age (adult or juvenile, based on body size), sex, body size, mass (measured with a Pesola scale), clip code (= marking code), and variation in color pattern. R. A. Alford (pers. comm.) recorded relative humidity, air temperature, substrate temperature, water temperature, percentage of cloud cover, and rainfall, prior to each of his samples.

Many amphibians can be captured by hand or in pitfall traps, and some can be attracted with artificial habitats (see "Artificial Habitats" in Chapter 7, and Stewart and Pough 1983) or bait (Parmenter et al. 1989). If individuals are marked (e.g., with radios or fluorescent dye) such that they can be resighted without being recaptured, the effects of handling on study organisms are reduced. Analysis of capture-resight data is described briefly in a later section.

Recapture periods must be designed carefully to meet the assumption that marked animals are redistributed randomly in the population. The number of times the population is sampled with M-RC techniques depends on the question being addressed.

Data Analysis and Interpretation

Microcomputers and database management programs allow one to store and manipulate data gathered on marked populations. The management of data is dictated by the mathematical estimator used. All M-RC studies with four or more sampling periods use an individual capture history matrix, and several software programs use these matrices to estimate abundance or survival (Nichols 1992).

If M-RC data are gathered over a long period, and if the population is sampled at least three times per interval (where intervals are weeks or months), then the data obtained may be extensive enough to allow calculation of the minimum number of individuals known to be alive (Donnelly 1989). Birth rate (or recruitment), im-

migration, loss rates, and survival rate (persistence) can be determined directly from these data. Partitioning emigration and death can be problematic. If the length of the study is short relative to the lifetime of the target organism, losses can be assumed to be the result of emigration rather than death.

Standard analytical tools (t-tests, ANOVAs, and nonparametric counterparts) can be used to analyze M-RC data—for example, to determine whether two populations differ in size or whether the size of one population has changed during some period. If individuals at a study site are sampled repeatedly, then observations are not independent, and the data must be analyzed with repeated-measures models (Winer 1971; Fowler 1990).

Personnel and Materials

Mark-recapture studies can be conducted by single individuals or by teams. The materials required depend on the marking system used. Microcomputers or mainframe computers are essential for managing and analyzing large data sets.

Population Estimators

Mark-recapture models for population estimation can be grouped according to the number of samples taken, that is, those that require two samples (Petersen, Bailey's modification of the Petersen estimate, and Chapman's modification of Petersen), those that require three (Triple Catch), and those that require several (Table 8). The models in the first group do not allow for gains or losses to the population under study and are best used when the population can be sampled only twice. The Triple Catch method estimates population size, gains (resulting from immigration and birth), and survival rates. Models in the last group (e.g., Fisher-Ford, Jolly's, Manly-Parr) estimate population size, gains, and survival rates.

Table 8. Population Estimators and Their Characteristics[a]

Estimator	Samples required	Mark type[b]	Standard error	Gains	Losses	Survival rate	Assumption
Petersen[c]	2	D/I	+	−	−	−	Closed population
Bailey's and Chapman's modifications of Petersen	2	D/I	+	−	−	−	Closed population
Triple Catch[d]	3	D/I	+	+	−	+	Variable gain, variable survival
Weighted Mean	Several	D/I	+	−	−	−	Closed population
Schumacher	Several	D/I	+	−	−	−	Closed population
Jackson's Positive method[e]	Several	D/I	+	+	−	−	Constant gain, variable loss
Jackson's Negative method[f]	Several	D/I	+	+	−	+	Constant survival, variable gain
Fisher-Ford	Several	I	−	+	+	−	Constant survival
Jolly-Seber Stochastic	Several	I	+	+	+	+	Age-independent survival
Manly-Parr	Several	I	+	+	+	+	Variable survival

[a] In columns 4 through 7, + indicates that the method estimates the value; − indicates that the value is not estimated.

[b] D = date; I = individual.

[c] If losses (death and emigration) occur, the estimate measures population size on day 2; if gains (recruitment and immigration) occur, the method estimates population size on day 1.

[d] The method estimates population size on day 2, survival rate on day 1, and gains on day 2 with variable gain and survival rates. Population sizes on days 1 and 3, survival rate on day 2, and gains on day 1 assume a constant survival rate.

[e] This method generates little information per unit effort.

[f] This method is best used when capturing and marking are relatively easy but recapturing (or mark screening) is difficult.

The Petersen estimate assumes that the population under study is closed, but it is robust when assumptions are violated (Menkens and Anderson 1988). The Triple Catch model provides considerable demographic information per unit effort. The three models that provide the most detailed information about a population are Fisher-Ford, Jolly-Seber Stochastic, and Manly-Parr. Of these, the Fisher-Ford model is best used when the sampling intensity is low, survival rates are low and constant, and the population is small (Begon 1979). Both the Fisher-Ford and Jolly-Seber methods assume age-independent survival. The Jolly-Seber method fails when age-dependent survival is pronounced, but if separate age-classes are used, this problem can be avoided. The Manly-Parr method has the least restrictive assumptions, but it requires the most extensive data, and data management is tedious, especially if more than five samples are taken and the study population is large. Begon (1979) described how gains and losses can be partitioned if they are estimated using these estimators.

If the design of the monitoring project is such that animals are sampled on only two occasions with M-RC methods, then the Petersen method (or the modifications of Petersen's estimate) must be used. If the animals are sampled on only three occasions, then it is best to use the Triple Catch method because it does not assume that the population is closed. If sampling is extensive (more than three samples), we recommend the Fisher-Ford or Jolly-Seber method. We describe these four methods in detail below. We follow the notation and format of Begon (1979). We use *day* to refer to sampling session, although the actual interval between "days" may be weeks, months, or some other time interval designated by the investigator.

Although we provide examples with hand calculation of some population estimators, in most cases, calculation by hand is time-consuming and tedious. Therefore, we recommend that extensive M-RC data be analyzed with a computer. A number of programs appropriate for this type of analysis are available. CAPTURE (Otis et al. 1978; White et al. 1978, 1982; Appendix 6) is a comprehensive program that has been in use for many years (Nichols 1992) and that has recently been revised (Rexstad and Burnham 1991). This program is for closed populations (no gains due to immigration or recruitment and no losses due to emigration or death). Menkens and Anderson (1988) critiqued the model selection algorithm in CAPTURE. They noted that not all goodness-of-fit tests used are independent and that the tests often have low power, especially for small populations. Recently, Pollock et al. (1990) developed two FORTRAN computer programs, JOLLY and JOLLYAGE, for open populations (Appendix 6). Pollock et al. (1990) and Nichols (1992) reviewed approaches to the estimation of population size and available computer programs.

PETERSEN ESTIMATE

The Petersen estimate of population size N is given by:

$$\hat{N} = \frac{rn}{m} \tag{1}$$

where

r = number of animals caught, marked, and released on day 1
n = total number of animals caught on day 2
m = total number of marked animals caught on day 2.

For example, if on the first day 900 animals are captured, marked, and released, and 1,000 animals are caught on day 2, of which 600 had been previously marked, then using equation 1,

$$\hat{N} = \frac{900 \cdot 1,000}{600} = 1,500$$

BAILEY'S MODIFICATION. This estimator ($\hat{N}_B$) derived by Bailey (1951), gives a more accurate estimate of population size when numbers of recaptures are small. It should be used when recaptures are 10 or fewer. It is calculated as follows:

$$\hat{N}_B = \frac{r(n+1)}{m+1} \tag{2}$$

For example, if 16 animals are caught, marked, and released on day 1, and 17 animals are caught on day 2, of which 9 are marked, then using equation 2,

$$\hat{N}_B = \frac{16(17+1)}{9+1} = 28.8$$

Bailey (1951) also provided a formula for calculating the standard error of N_B:

$$SE_{\hat{N}_B} = \left[\frac{r^2(n+1)(n-m)}{(m+1)^2(m+2)} \right]^{1/2} \quad (3)$$

Using equation 3 and the above example,

$$SE_{\hat{N}_B} = \left[\frac{16^2(17+1)(17-9)}{(9+1)^2(9+2)} \right]^{1/2} = 5.79$$

Given these data, the estimated population size is 28.8 individuals, and the standard error of the estimate is 5.79.

CHAPMAN'S MODIFICATION. Chapman (1951) also modified the Petersen estimate to correct for low number of recaptures (i.e., $m \leq 10$), as follows:

$$\hat{N}_C = \frac{(r+1)(n+1)}{(m+1)} - 1 \quad (4)$$

Seber (1970, 1982) provided a formula for calculating the standard error of $\hat{N}_C$:

$$SE_{\hat{N}_C} = \left[\frac{(r+1)(n+1)(r-m)(n-m)}{(m+1)^2(m+2)} \right]^{1/2} \quad (5)$$

Using the data from the previous example ($r = 16$, $n = 17$, $m = 9$) and equations 4 and 5,

$$\hat{N}_C = \frac{(16+1)(17+1)}{(9+1)} - 1 = 29.6$$

and

$$SE_{\hat{N}_C} = \left[\frac{(16+1)(17+1)(16-9)(17-9)}{(9+1)^2(9+2)} \right]^{1/2} = 3.95$$

TRIPLE CATCH METHOD

This estimator requires three samples (Begon 1979) and estimates population size (N), sur-

vival (ϕ), and gains (g). Gains are defined as the proportion of the day ($i + 1$) population added between days i and ($i + 1$). Survival is defined as the proportion of the day i population that survives until day ($i + 1$). The Triple Catch method allows both gain and loss rates to vary. It makes few assumptions and provides considerably more information regarding the population under study than does Petersen's estimate (and both modifications).

The following equations are corrected for bias from small sample sizes. On day 1, r_1 animals are captured, marked, and released. Marks can be date- or individual-specific. On day 2, n_2 animals are caught, of which m_{21} are already marked. All unmarked individuals captured on day 2 are marked (given a date-specific mark for day 2 or individual-specific marks), and all are released. On day 3, n_3 animals are caught. Some are unmarked, some were marked on day 1 and were not captured on day 2 (m_{31}); some were marked on day 2 (m_{32}). Animals captured on both day 1 and day 2 are included in m_{32}. The number of day j marks available for capture on day i is indicated by M_{ij}; this variable is referred to as the number of marks-at-risk. For example, on day 2 there are M_{21} marks-at-risk. This method allows the gain and survival rates to vary initially, and if the marked proportion in the sample is the same as in the population, that is

$$\frac{M_{21}}{N_2} = \frac{m_{21}}{n_2}$$

then population size on day 2 (N_2) can be estimated with equation 6:

$$\hat{N}_2 = \frac{\hat{M}_{21}(n_2+1)}{(m_{21}+1)} \quad (6)$$

The M_{21} animals are "survivors" (number of the animals marked on day 1 that survive until day 2) of r_1 animals released, so the survival rate (ϕ) can be calculated as follows:

$$\hat{\phi}_1 = \frac{M_{21}}{r_1} \qquad (7)$$

$$\hat{\phi}_1 = \frac{59.44}{67} = 0.89$$

To calculate $\hat{N}_2$ (estimated population size on day 2), an estimate of M_{21} ($\hat{M}_{21}$ = number of day 1 marks at risk on day 2) is required:

$$\hat{M}_{21} = \frac{m_{31}(r_2 + 1)}{(m_{32} + 1)} + m_{21} \qquad (8)$$

$$\hat{g}_2 = 1 - \left[\frac{18 \cdot 57}{69 \cdot 20}\right] = 0.26$$

If we assume that gain rates and survival rates are constant, and if the interval between sample periods is the same, then $\hat{\phi}_2 = \hat{\phi}_1$ and $\hat{g}_1 = \hat{g}_2$. If these assumptions are made, then population sizes on day 1 and day 3 can be estimated using the equations:

Gains between day 2 and 3 (g_2) are estimated as follows:

$$\hat{g}_2 = 1 - \frac{(m_{31} + 1)n_2}{(n_3 + 1)m_{21}} \qquad (9)$$

$$\hat{N}_1 = \frac{(1 - \hat{g}_1)\hat{N}_2}{\hat{\phi}_1} \qquad (10)$$

For example, 67 animals are captured, marked, and released on day 1. Fifty-seven animals are captured on day 2; 20 animals have a day-1 mark and are given a day-2 mark, and 37 unmarked animals are given a day-2 mark. Of the 68 animals captured on day 3, 17 have a day-1 mark, 16 have a day-2 mark, and 8 have day-1 and day-2 marks.

$$\hat{N}_3 = \frac{\hat{N}_2 \hat{\phi}_2}{1 - \hat{g}_2} \qquad (11)$$

Continuing with our example, $\phi_2 = \phi_1 = 0.89$, $\hat{g}_1 = \hat{g}_2 = 0.26$, and using equations 10 and 11, estimated population sizes on days 1 and 3 are as follows:

$r_1 = 67$	$m_{21} = 20$	$n_1 = 67$
$r_2 = 57$	$m_{31} = 17$	$n_2 = 57$
$r_3 = 68$	$m_{32} = 24$	$n_3 = 68$

$$\hat{N}_1 = \frac{(1 - 0.26)164.17}{0.89} = 136.50$$

Using equations 6 through 9,

$$\hat{N}_3 = \frac{164.17 \cdot 0.89}{(1 - 0.26)} = 197.45$$

$$\hat{M}_{21} = \frac{17 \cdot 58}{25} + 20 = 59.44$$

$$\hat{N}_2 = \frac{59.44 \cdot 58}{20 + 1} = 164.17$$

The Triple Catch method includes standard error estimates for population size on day 2 (N_2) and survival rate (ϕ_1) on day 1 as follows:

$$SE_{\hat{N}_2} = \left\{ \hat{N}_2 (\hat{N}_2 - n_2)\left[\frac{\hat{M}_{21} - m_{21} + r_2}{\hat{M}_{21}}\left(\frac{1}{m_{32}} - \frac{1}{r_2}\right) + \frac{1}{m_{21}} - \frac{1}{n_2}\right] \right\}^{1/2} \qquad (12)$$

$$SE_{\hat{\phi}_1} = \left\{ (\hat{\phi}_1)^2 \frac{(\hat{M}_{21} - m_{21})(\hat{M}_{21} - m_{21} + r_2)}{(\hat{M}_{21})^2}\left(\frac{1}{m_{32}} - \frac{1}{r_2}\right) + \frac{1}{\hat{M}_{21}} - \frac{1}{r_1} \right\}^{1/2} \qquad (13)$$

Applying equations 12 and 13 to our sample data yields

$$SE_{\hat{N}_2} = \left\{ 164.17(164.17 - 57)\left[\frac{59.44 - 20 + 57}{59.44}\left(\frac{1}{24} - \frac{1}{57} \right) + \frac{1}{20} - \frac{1}{57} \right] \right\}^{1/2} = 35.54$$

and

$$SE_{\hat{\phi}_1} = \left\{ 0.89^2 \frac{(59.44 - 20)(59.44 - 20 + 57)}{59.44^2}\left(\frac{1}{24} - \frac{1}{57} \right) + \frac{1}{59.44} - \frac{1}{67} \right\}^{1/2} = 0.15$$

FISHER-FORD ESTIMATOR

The Fisher-Ford estimator of population size is a modification of the Petersen estimate that assumes that the ratio of marks to the total number of animals captured in the day i sample is the same as the ratio of total marks to the total population. It requires that animals be marked and recaptured on several occasions and assumes a constant survival rate that is obtained by "trial and error." The estimate of population size on day i is given by the equation:

$$\hat{N}_i = \frac{(n_i + 1)}{(m_i + 1)}(M_i) \tag{14}$$

where

$\hat{N}_i$ = estimated population size on day i
n_i = total number captured on day i
m_i = number of marked animals captured on day i
M_i = number of marks at risk (number of marks available for recapture) on day i.

The number of marks-at-risk (M_i) has to be estimated by a complicated and indirect process. The total number of marks caught on day i is given by the equation

$$m_i = \sum_j m_{ij}$$

where

m_i = number of marked animals captured on day i
m_{ij} = individuals caught on day i with a day-j mark
j = day mark was given (or last seen), ranging from 1 to $(i - 1)$
$\sum_j$ = summation for all j values.

Each mark is $(i - j)$ days old, and the total age of all marks (the number of days survived by marks caught on day i) is

$$\sum_j m_{ij}(i - j) \tag{15}$$

The total days survived by marks (TDS) during the study is given by the equation

$$TDS = \sum_i \sum_j m_{ij}(i - j) \tag{16}$$

To calculate TDS, the M-RC data are arranged in a table in which the rows indicate the day of the study and the columns indicate the day of the marks. To construct the table, the capture history for every individual must be tabulated. In Table 9 we illustrate this procedure with data from Dowdeswell et al. (1940). Examination of these data shows that on some days (3, 7, 10, 11),

Table 9. Mark-Recapture Data for Sample Calculations of Population Estimates[a,b]

i	n_i	r_i	1	2	4	5	6	8	9	12	13
						Date of mark					
1	43	40	—								
2	43	40	5								
3	0	0									
4	13	12	0	3							
5	52	50	3	8	5						
6	56	51	6	12	6	15					
7	0	0									
8	52	52	4	10	3	16	14				
9	50	50	4	5	1	11	5	14			
10	0	0									
11	0	0									
12	15	15	1	1	1	3	1	5	5		
13	20	20	1	1	2	3	2	7	8	6	
14	20	—	0	0	0	2	2	4	1	0	4

[a] Data are from Dowdeswell et al. 1940.

[b] i = day; n_i = total number of animals captured each day; r_i = total number released.

no animals were captured. On some days (1, 2, 4, 5, 6) not all animals were marked and released (i.e., some died during handling or were collected as vouchers). On day 8 of the study, 52 animals were caught; 47 were already marked, and the remaining 5 were marked at that time; all 52 were released. Of the 47 marked animals captured on day 8, 14 had day-6 marks, 16 had day-5 marks, 3 had day-4 marks, 10 had day-2 marks, and 4 had day-1 marks.

Once the data are arranged in the table, another table is constructed to calculate the observed TDS (see Table 10). It has three columns: i (day); m_i (the number of marked animals caught on day i); and $\sum_j m_{ij} (i - j)$ [the total age of all marks on day i]. The value m_i (Table 10) is

obtained by summing row values for day i (Table 9). For example, on day 6,

$$m_6 = (15 + 6 + 12 + 6) = 39$$

and

$$\sum_j m_{6j}(6 - j) = m_{65}(6 - 5) + m_{64}(6 - 4) + m_{63}(6 - 3)$$
$$+ m_{62}(6 - 2) + m_{61}(6 - 1)$$
$$= 15(1) + 6(2) + 0(3) + 12(4) + 6(5)$$
$$= 105$$

Total days survived by marks (TDS) is the sum of column 3 in Table 10. In this example, TDS = $(0 + 5 + 0 + 6 + \ldots + 67) = 788$.

The next step is to estimate TDS based on the average age of marks with a survival rate se-

Table 10. Calculation of Observed TDS Using the Fisher-Ford Method of Population Estimation[a,b]

i	m_i	$\sum\limits_{j} m_{ij}\,(i-j)$
1	0	0
2	5	5
3	0	0
4	3	6
5	16	41
6	39	105
7	0	0
8	47	176
9	40	145
10	0	0
11	0	0
12	17	91
13	30	152
14	13	$\dfrac{67}{788}$

Observed TDS $= \sum\limits_{i}\sum\limits_{j} m_{ij}\,(i-j)$

[a] Based on data from Table 9. See text for explanation. TDS = total days survived by marks.

[b] i = day; m_i = total number of marked animals caught on day i; $\sum\limits_{j} m_{ij}\,(i-j)$ = total age of all marks on day i.

lected by the investigator. The goal of this step is to find a survival rate that results in an estimated TDS that equals the observed TDS (calculated in Table 10). The average age of marks on day i is denoted as A_i, and before day i there are M_i marks-at-risk. On day i, some marked animals are captured, and unmarked animals are marked and released (r_i). After the day i sample, there are ($M_i + r_i$) marks-at-risk, the M_i marks are $A_i M_i$ days old, and the r_i marks are zero days old. On day ($i + 1$), the marks are 1 day older:

$$A_{i+1} = \frac{A_i\,M_i}{M_i + r_i} + 1 \qquad (17)$$

All values of r_i are known, and M_i values are calculated using an arbitrarily selected survival rate (ϕ). This survival rate has to be adjusted iteratively so that the estimated TDS ($\sum\limits_{i} A_i m_i$) equals the observed TDS. If the M_i values are known, then the mean age of marks on day 2 = 1, and A_3 can be calculated with equation 17.

On day ($i + 1$), there are ($M_i + r_i$) marks-at-risk, but only some survive (ϕ = daily survival rate, which is assumed to be constant). The number that survive to day ($i + 1$) is expressed as

$$M_{i+1} = \phi\,(M_i + r_i) \qquad (18)$$

All r_i values are known, and ϕ is selected by the investigator; the number of marks-at-risk on day 1 (M_1) = zero. The number of marks-at-risk on day 2 (M_2) is equal to the survival rate (ϕ) multiplied by the number of marked animals released on day 1 (ϕr_1), because M_1 = zero (equation 18). Because r_2, ϕ, and M_2 are known, M_3 and all other values can be calculated.

To obtain a reasonably accurate estimated TDS (i.e., one that equals the observed TDS), an iterative procedure is used wherein the value of ϕ is varied. Equations 17 and 18 are used with the selected value ϕ (given that $M_1 = 0$, $M_2 = (\phi r_1)$, and $A_2 = 1$). In Table 11, the daily survival rate is 0.8, $M_2 = 0.8 \cdot 40 = 32$, $M_3 = 0.8(32 + 40) = 57.6$, and no animals were captured on day 3, so $M_4 = \phi M_3 = 0.8 \cdot 57.6 = 46.1$. Similarly, $A_2 = 1$, so

$$A_3 = \frac{1 \cdot 32}{32 + 40} + 1 = 1.44 \approx 1.4$$

and because there were no captures on day 3, $A_4 = A_3 + 1 = 1.4 + 1 = 2.4$. Examination of Table 11 shows that by using $\phi = 0.8$, the estimated TDS of 755.67 is less than the observed TDS of 788. The

Table 11. TDS Estimated Using the Fisher-Ford Method and a Survivorship Value (ϕ) of 0.8[a,b]

i	r_i	M_i	A_i	m_i	A_im_i
1	40	0	—	0	0
2	40	32.0	1.00	5	5
3	0	57.6	1.44	0	0
4	12	46.1	2.44	3	7.33
5	50	46.5	2.94	16	47.04
6	51	77.2	2.42	39	94.38
7	0	102.6	2.46	0	0
8	52	82.0	3.46	47	162.62
9	50	107.2	3.12	40	124.80
10	0	125.8	3.12	0	0
11	0	100.6	4.12	0	0
12	15	80.5	5.12	17	87.04
13	20	76.4	5.32	30	159.60
14	—	77.1	5.22	13	67.86
				Estimated TDS =	755.67

Table 12. TDS Estimated Using the Fisher-Ford Method and a Survivorship Value (ϕ) of 0.9[a,b]

i	r_i	M_i	A_i	m_i	A_im_i
1	40	0	—	0	0
2	40	36.0	1.00	5	5
3	0	68.4	1.47	0	0
4	12	61.6	2.47	3	7.41
5	50	66.2	3.07	16	49.12
6	51	104.6	2.75	39	107.25
7	0	140.0	2.85	0	0
8	52	126.0	3.85	47	180.95
9	50	160.2	3.73	40	149.20
10	0	189.2	3.84	0	0
11	0	170.3	4.84	0	0
12	15	153.3	5.84	17	99.28
13	20	151.5	6.32	30	189.60
14	—	154.4	6.58	13	85.54
				Estimated TDS =	873.35

[a] Values for r_i are from Table 9; values for m_i are from Table 10. TDS = total days survived by marks.

[b] i = day; r_i = total number of animals released on day i; M_i = number of marks at risk on day i; A_i = average age of marks on day i; m_i = total number of marked animals caught on day i; A_im_i = estimated days survived by marks caught on day i.

[a] Values for r_i are from Table 9; values for m_i are from Table 10. TDS = total days survived by marks.

[b] i = day; r_i = total number of animals released on day i; Mi = number of marks at risk on day i; A_i = average age of marks on day i; m_i = total number of marked animals caught on day i; A_im_i = estimated days survived by marks caught on day i.

estimated TDS is recalculated in Table 12 using a daily survival rate of 0.9, yielding a TDS of 873.35.

At least one additional table (similar to Tables 11 and 12) with ϕ varying must be constructed so that a survival rate can be obtained graphically; the goal is to get an estimated TDS equal to the observed TDS. In our example, ϕ = 0.8 gives an estimated TDS that is too low, and ϕ = 0.9 gives one that is too high. By varying ϕ two or three times, the obtained TDS values can be plotted against these selected survival rates, and ϕ can be determined by interpolation (Fig. 27). With ϕ = 0.75, the estimated TDS = 698.04, and if

ϕ = 0.85, the estimated TDS = 813.62. From Figure 27, the ϕ that gives an estimated TDS of 788 is 0.828. Table 13 estimates TDS with ϕ = 0.828.

Now that we have a sequence of M_i values, we can estimate population size (N) using equation 14 (n_i values are from Table 9, M_i and m_i values are from Table 13). For example, on day 12:

$$\hat{N}_{12} = \frac{(15+1)}{(17+1)}(96.4) = 85.7 \approx 86$$

The estimated number of losses (L_i) between day i and ($i + 1$) is given by the equation:

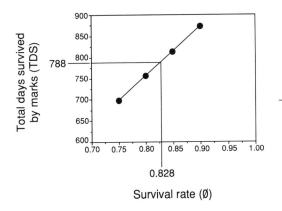

Figure 27. Graphical estimation of the total days survived by marks (TDS). The investigator selects three (or four) survival rates, calculates an estimated TDS, and plots the result. The survival rate that yields a TDS equal to the observed TDS is determined by interpolation. In this example, a survival rate of 0.828 gives a TDS equal to the observed TDS of 788.

Table 13. TDS Estimated Using the Fisher-Ford Method and a Survivorship Value (ϕ) of 0.828[a,b]

i	r_i	M_i	A_i	m_i	$A_i m_i$
1	40	0	—	0	0
2	40	33.1	1.00	5	5
3	0	60.5	1.45	0	0
4	12	50.1	2.45	3	7.35
5	50	51.4	2.98	16	47.68
6	51	84.0	2.51	39	97.89
7	0	112.0	2.56	0	0
8	52	92.7	3.56	47	167.32
9	50	119.8	3.28	40	131.20
10	0	140.6	3.31	0	0
11	0	116.4	4.31	0	0
12	15	96.4	5.31	17	90.27
13	20	92.2	5.60	30	168.00
14	—	93.0	5.60	13	72.80
				Estimated TDS =	787.51
					≈788

[a] Values for r_i are from Table 9; values for m_i are from Table 10. TDS = total days survived by marks.

[b] i = day; r_i = total number of animals released on day i; M_i = number of marks at risk on day i; A_i = average age of marks on day i; m_i = total number of marked animals caught on day i; $A_i m_i$ = estimated days survived by marks caught on day i.

$$\hat{L}_i = (1 - \phi)\hat{N}_i \qquad (19)$$

The estimated number of gains (g_i) between day i and day ($i + 1$) is given by:

$$\hat{g}_i = \hat{N}_{i+1} - \phi\hat{N}_i \qquad (20)$$

For day 12,

$$\hat{L}_{12} = (1 - 0.828)86 = 14.8 \approx 15$$
$$\hat{g}_{12} = 63 - 0.828 \cdot 86 = -8.2 \approx -8$$

The estimates in Table 14 are rounded up to reflect biological reality—tenths of organisms do not exist. Although losses can be estimated for each day of the study, gains can be calculated only for days on which animals were captured. Negative gains are a mathematical artifact; gains on days 5 and 12 (Table 14) are, in reality, equal to zero. Negative losses would also be interpreted as zeros.

Based on the values in Table 14, the size of the population is estimated to have decreased from 237 at the beginning of the study to 53 on the last day of the study.

JOLLY-SEBER STOCHASTIC METHOD

The advantage of the Jolly-Seber Stochastic method over the Fisher-Ford estimator is that the Jolly-Seber model allows survival rates to vary and is, therefore, more realistic biologically. This method estimates population size (N_i), survival rates (ϕ_i), and gains (g_i). Each estimate has an associated formula for the calculation of the standard error (not available with Fisher-Ford). The Jolly-Seber estimator of population size re-

Table 14. Population Size ($\hat{N}_i$), Losses ($\hat{L}_i$), and Gains ($\hat{g}_i$) Estimated Using the Fisher-Ford Method and Assuming a Constant Survivorship (ϕ) of 0.828[a]

i	n_i	m_i	M_i	$\hat{N}_i$	$\hat{L}_i$	$\hat{g}_i$
1	43	0	0	—	—	—
2	43	5	33.1	237.0	41	—
3	0	0	60.5	60.5	10	—
4	13	3	50.1	175.0	30	15
5	52	16	51.4	160.0	28	–12
6	56	39	84.0	120.0	21	—
7	0	0	112.0	112.0	19	—
8	52	47	92.7	85.0	15	79
9	50	40	119.8	149.0	26	—
10	0	0	140.6	140.6	24	—
11	0	0	116.4	116.4	20	—
12	15	17	96.4	86.0	15	–8
13	20	30	92.2	63.0	11	1
14	20	13	93.0	53.0	9	—

[a] i = day; n_i = the total number of animals captured on day i; m_i = the total number of marked animals caught on day i; M_i = the number of marks at risk on day i; $\hat{N}_i$ = estimated population size on day i; $\hat{L}_i$ = estimated number of losses (from death and emigration) on day i; $\hat{g}_i$ = estimated number of gains (from birth and immigration) on day i.

quires several sampling periods, but only the most recent mark (= most recent recapture) is considered in calculations. Detailed capture histories are required for all individuals, and these data are arranged in a table (see Table 15). For this example, we use M-RC data from Jolly (1965) as modified by Begon (1979). To construct the table, the animals recaptured on any day (m_{ij}) are tallied according to the most recent date of recapture. On day 7 of the sample data set, 250 animals were captured, 112 of which were already marked. Of those, 56 were last captured on day 6, 34 on day 5, 10 on day 4, 5 on day 3, 6 on day 2, and 1 on day 1.

The number of marked individuals at risk on day i (M_i) has to be estimated so that population size (N_i) can be estimated. The estimation of the number of marked individuals at risk is given by the equation

$$\hat{M}_i = m_i + \frac{z_i\,r_i}{y_i} \tag{21}$$

The number of marked animals released on day i (r_i) is known; m_i, y_i, and z_i are obtained from the table (Table 15). The number of marked animals (m_i) caught on day i is the sum of m_{ij} values in row i of the table. For example, on day 7,

$$m_7 = 1 + 6 + 5 + 10 + 34 + 56 = 112$$

The number of animals marked and released on day i and caught after day i is y_i, or the sum of m_{ij} values for column j of the table. For animals released on day 7,

$$y_7 = 46 + 28 + 17 + 8 + 7 + 2 = 108$$

The calculation of z_i—the number of animals marked before day i that are not caught on day i but are caught after day i—is more complicated. The sum of m_{ij} in columns to the left of column j (i.e., j values less than j_i values) and in rows below row i (i.e., row numbers greater than i) equals z_i (see Table 15; for day 7, these values are enclosed by dashed lines). For example, on day 7,

$$
\begin{aligned}
z_7 = {}& 0 + 4 + 0 + 3 + 14 + 19 \\
& + 0 + 2 + 4 + 2 + 11 + 12 \\
& + \ldots \\
& + 0 + 1 + 0 + 2 + 3 + 3 \\
= {}& 110
\end{aligned}
$$

The estimated M_i values (using equation 21) based on data in Table 15 are presented in Table 16. Given that there are no marked indi-

Table 15. Mark-Recapture Data for Sample Calculations of Population Size Using the Jolly-Seber Method[a,b]

i	n_i	r_i	\multicolumn{12}{c}{Day of mark (j)}
			1	**2**	**3**	**4**	**5**	**6**	**7**	**8**	**9**	**10**	**11**	**12**
			\multicolumn{12}{c}{Recaptured marks (m_{ij})}
1	54	54												
2	146	143	10											
3	169	164	3	34										
4	209	202	5	18	33									
5	220	214	2	8	13	30								
6	209	207	2	4	8	20	43							
7	250	243	1	6	5	10	34	56						
8	176	175	0	4	0	3	14	19	46					
9	172	169	0	2	4	2	11	12	28	51				
10	127	126	0	0	1	2	3	5	17	22	34			
11	123	120	1	2	3	1	0	4	8	12	16	30		
12	120	120	0	1	3	1	1	2	7	4	11	16	26	
13	142	—	0	1	0	2	3	3	2	10	9	12	18	35

[a] Mark-recapture data are from Jolly (1965) as modified by Begon (1979).

[b] Dashed lines enclose m_{ij} values that are included in the calculation of z_7 (see text for explanation); i = day; n_i = total number of animals captured on day i; r_i = total number of animals released on day i; j = day the animal was captured (or last seen); m_{ij} = number of animals captured on day i with a day-j mark.

viduals at risk on day 1, M_1 = zero. For example, on day 7:

$$\hat{M}_7 = 112 + \frac{110 \cdot 243}{108} = 359.50$$

Once Table 16 is constructed, population size can be estimated as follows:

$$\hat{N}_i = \frac{\hat{M}_i (n_i + 1)}{(m_i + 1)} \qquad (22)$$

On day ($i + 1$), there are ($M_i - m_i + r_i$) marked individuals in the population. Of these marked individuals, M_{i+1} survive until day ($i + 1$). The survival rate (ϕ) is estimated as follows:

$$\hat{\phi}_i = \frac{\hat{M}_{i+1}}{(\hat{M}_i - m_i + r_i)} \qquad (23)$$

Gains (g_i) between day i and day ($i + 1$) are estimated as follows:

$$\hat{g}_i = \hat{N}_{i+1} - \hat{\phi}_i \hat{N}_i \qquad (24)$$

For example, on day 6,

$$\hat{N}_6 = \frac{\hat{M}_6(n_6 + 1)}{(m_6 + 1)} = \frac{324.99(209 + 1)}{(77 + 1)} = 874.97 \approx 875$$

$$\hat{\phi}_6 = \frac{M_7}{\hat{M}_6 - m_6 + r_6} = \frac{359.50}{324.99 - 77 + 207} = 0.79$$

$$\hat{g}_6 = \hat{N}_7 - (\hat{\phi}_6 \hat{N}_6) = 799 - 0.79 \cdot 875 = 107.8 \approx 108$$

Table 16. Calculated Values Required for Estimating Population Size Using the Jolly-Seber Method[a,b]

i	r_i	m_i	y_i	z_i	$\hat{M}_i$
1	54	—	24	—	0
2	143	10	80	14	35.03
3	164	37	70	57	170.54
4	202	56	71	71	258.00
5	214	53	109	89	227.73
6	207	77	101	121	324.99
7	243	112	108	110	359.50
8	175	86	99	132	319.33
9	169	110	70	121	402.13
10	126	84	58	107	316.45
11	120	77	44	88	317.00
12	120	72	35	60	277.71
13	—	95	—	—	—

[a] Calculations based on data from Table 15.

[b] i = day; r_i = total number of animals released on day i; m_i = number of marked animals caught on day i; y_i = number of individuals marked and released on day i and caught after day i; z_i = number of animals caught before and after, but not on, day i; $\hat{M}_i$ = estimated number of marks at risk on day i, calculated with equation 21.

Table 17. Estimates of Population Size ($\hat{N}_i$), Population Gain ($\hat{g}_i$), and Survival Rate ($\hat{\phi}_i$) and Their Standard Errors, Calculated Using the Jolly-Seber Method[a]

i	$\hat{N}_i$	$\hat{g}_i$	$\hat{\phi}_i$	$SE_{\hat{N}_i}$	$SE_{\hat{g}_i}$	$SE_{\hat{\phi}_i}$
1	—	—	—	—	—	—
2	468	288	1.015	136	168	0.11
3	763	289	0.867	126	136	0.10
4	951	396	0.564	138	120	0.06
5	932	96	0.836	118	110	0.07
6	875	108	0.790	94	75	0.07
7	799	130	0.651	72	55	0.06
8	650	−13	0.985	59	53	0.09
9	627	47	0.686	59	35	0.08
10	477	82	0.884	49	40	0.12
11	504	71	0.771	65	40	0.13
12	460	—	—	69	—	—

[a] Survival rate = chance of an individual in the day-i population surviving until day (i + 1); population gain = number of births plus number of immigrants; i = day.

All population parameters estimated with the Jolly-Seber method have standard errors (equations 25–27) associated with them as follows:

$$SE_{\hat{N}_i} = \left\{ \hat{N}_i (\hat{N}_i - n_i) \left[\frac{\hat{M}_i - m_i + r_i}{\hat{M}_i} \left(\frac{1}{y_i} - \frac{1}{r_i} \right) + \frac{1}{m_i} - \frac{1}{n_i} \right] \right\}^{1/2} \quad (25)$$

$$SE_{\hat{\phi}_i} = \hat{\phi}_i \left\{ \frac{(\hat{M}_{i+1} - m_{i+1})(\hat{M}_{i+1} - m_{i+1} + r_{i+1})}{(\hat{M}_{i+1})^2} \left(\frac{1}{y_{i+1}} - \frac{1}{r_{i+1}} \right) + \left(\frac{\hat{M}_i - m_i}{\hat{M}_i - m_i + r_i} \right)\left(\frac{1}{y_i} - \frac{1}{r_i} \right) \right\}^{1/2} \quad (26)$$

The following equation (27) for the standard error of gains is from Jolly (1965). Equations in Southwood (1978), Begon (1979), and Davis and Winstead (1980) are different.

$$SE_{\hat{g}_i} = \left[\frac{(\hat{g}_i)^2 (\hat{M}_{i+1} - m_{i+1})(\hat{M}_{i+1} - m_{i+1} + r_{i+1})}{(\hat{M}_{i+1})^2} \left(\frac{1}{y_{i+1}} - \frac{1}{r_{i+1}} \right) \right. $$

$$+ \frac{\hat{M}_i - m_i}{\hat{M}_i - m_i + r_i} \left(\frac{\hat{\phi}_i \, r_i \left(1 - \frac{m_i}{n_i} \right)}{\frac{m_i}{n_i}} \right)^2 \left(\frac{1}{y_i} - \frac{1}{r_i} \right)$$

$$+ \frac{(\hat{N}_i - n_i)(\hat{N}_{i+1} - \hat{g}_i)\left(1 - \frac{m_i}{n_i}\right)(1 - \hat{\phi}_i)}{\hat{M}_i - m_i + r_i} + \hat{N}_{i+1}(\hat{N}_{i+1} - n_i)\left(\frac{1 - \frac{m_{i+1}}{n_{i+1}}}{m_{i+1}} \right) + (\hat{\phi}_i)^2 \, \hat{N}_i \, (\hat{N}_i - n_i)\left(\frac{1 - \frac{m_i}{n_i}}{m_i} \right) \left. \right]^{\frac{1}{2}} \quad (27)$$

Estimates of population size ($\hat{N}$), survival rate (ϕ), and gains (g) for the data in Table 15 are presented in Table 17. Values needed to calculate standard errors of these estimates are given in Tables 15, 17, and 18. If values are calculated and summarized as in Table 18, then hand calculation of the standard errors is relatively easy. The following are calculations of the standard errors given in Table 17 for day 9 of our example:

$$SE_{\hat{N}_9} = \left[627 \cdot 455 \cdot \frac{461.13}{402.13} \cdot \left(\frac{1}{70} - \frac{1}{169} \right) + \frac{1}{110} - \frac{1}{172} \right]^{\frac{1}{2}} = \left\{ 285,285[1.147(0.008) + 0.009 - 0.006] \right\}^{\frac{1}{2}} = 58.9 \approx 59$$

$$SE_{\hat{\phi}_9} = 0.686 \left[\frac{232.45 \cdot 358.45}{316.45^2} \cdot \left(\frac{1}{58} - \frac{1}{126} \right) + \frac{292.13}{461.13} \cdot \left(\frac{1}{70} - \frac{1}{169} \right) \right]^{\frac{1}{2}} = 0.686[0.832(0.009) + 0.634(0.008)]^{\frac{1}{2}} = 0.078 \approx 0.08$$

$$SE_{\hat{g}_9} = \left[\frac{47^2 \cdot 232.45 \cdot 358.45}{316.45^2} \cdot 0.009 + 0.6335 \left(\frac{115.93 \cdot 0.360}{0.640} \right)^2 \cdot 0.008 + \frac{455(477 - 47) \cdot 0.360 \cdot 0.314}{461.13} \right.$$

$$\left. + 477 \cdot 350 \cdot \left(\frac{0.339}{84} \right) + 0.471 \cdot 627 \cdot 455 \left(\frac{0.360}{110} \right) \right]^{\frac{1}{2}} = 34.63 \approx 35$$

Table 18. Sample Calculated Values Required for Determining Standard Error for Population Estimators Derived Using the Jolly-Seber Method[a]

i	$\hat{M}_i - m_i$	$\hat{M}_i - m_i + r_i$	$\hat{M}_i$	m_i	$\frac{1}{y_i} - \frac{1}{r_i}$	$\frac{\hat{M}_i - m_i}{\hat{M}_i - m_i + r_i}$	$\hat{\phi}_i r_i$	$1 - \frac{m_i}{n_i}$	$\frac{m_i}{n_i}$	$\hat{N}_i - n_i$	$1 - \hat{\phi}_i$	$(\hat{\phi}_i)^2$
1	—	—	0	—	—	—	—	—	—	—	—	—
2	25.03	168.03	35.03	10	0.006	0.1490	145.15	0.931	0.069	322	−0.015	1.030
3	133.54	297.54	170.54	37	0.008	0.4488	142.19	0.781	0.219	594	0.133	0.752
4	202.00	404.00	258.00	56	0.009	0.5000	113.93	0.732	0.268	742	0.436	0.318
5	174.73	388.73	227.73	53	0.005	0.4495	178.90	0.759	0.241	712	0.164	0.699
6	247.99	454.99	324.99	77	0.005	0.5450	163.53	0.632	0.368	666	0.210	0.624
7	247.50	490.50	359.50	112	0.005	0.5046	158.19	0.552	0.448	549	0.349	0.424
8	233.33	408.33	319.33	86	0.004	0.5714	172.38	0.511	0.489	474	0.015	0.970
9	292.13	461.13	402.13	110	0.008	0.6335	115.93	0.360	0.640	455	0.314	0.471
10	232.45	358.45	316.45	84	0.009	0.6485	113.38	0.339	0.661	350	0.116	0.782
11	240.00	360.00	317.00	77	0.014	0.6667	92.52	0.374	0.626	381	0.229	0.594
12	205.71	325.71	277.71	72	0.020	0.6316	—	0.400	0.600	340	—	—

[a] i = day; $\hat{M}_i$ = estimated number of marks at risk on day i; m_i = number of marked animals caught on day i; r_i = number of animals released on day i; y_i = number of animals marked and released on day i and caught after day i; $\hat{\phi}_i$ = estimated survival rate on day i; n_i = total number of animals captured on day i; $\hat{N}_i$ = estimated population size on day i.

Capture-Resight

Minta and Mangel (1989) developed an estimator of population size using capture-resight data. It is important to note that this method works only in conjunction with a technique (such as radio telemetry) that allows an investigator to estimate the number of marked animals never seen that are still alive. Minta and Mangel's method employs a Monte Carlo simulation that gives a full probability distribution for the population. From this distribution, the maximum likelihood estimate and likelihood interval on the population can be computed. The likelihood interval allows asymmetric interval estimates, rather than the symmetric interval estimates of Petersen's variance equations. A paper describing this method and the BASIC program (for IBM compatible computers) used to calculate the estimator are available from S. Minta (see "Computer Programs" in Appendix 6).

Bayesian Approach to Mark-Recapture Data

Gazey and Staley (1986) provided a sequential Bayes algorithm (= equation) for estimating population size. This approach can be used when populations are small and recapture frequencies are low. The Bayesian approach is an attractive alternative to Petersen's estimate (and all methods based upon it), which underestimates population size at low densities. The advantages of the Bayesian approach include estimation of the population distribution from Bayes's theory rather than from an assumed normal distribution (Kempthorne and Folks 1971); estimation of population size free from effects of sample size or sampling procedure; assessment of the degree of population closure; and description of the magnitude of difference between two or more populations, not just the presence of a difference.

CONTRIBUTORS: J. ERIC JUTERBOCK AND ROSS A. ALFORD

Removal sampling

LEE-ANN C. HAYEK

Removal sampling is a means of estimating the size of a population, usually from a certain area; it may or may not provide information on the entire population. Animals are physically removed from a designated area (locality, plot, or quadrat) for a short interval. At the end of the study, they are released as near to their original capture point as possible. Removal sampling is an important means of investigating long-term population stability. Age, size, breeding condition, and sex can also be obtained from the animals held in captivity.

Target Organisms and Habitats

This technique is most useful for species with low mobility or limited home ranges and for aquatic larvae (see Chapter 6), because a high proportion of the population is available for capture at any given time. It is inappropriate for secretive species, fossorial species, and highly mobile species, including frogs and salamanders that disperse widely from breeding ponds. Hairston (1981, 1986, 1987) used removal methods as a tool for estimating population density in species of *Plethodon* and *Desmognathus*. Harris et al. (1988) used this technique to evaluate the effectiveness of enclosure sampling methods for the broken-striped newt, *Notophathalmus viridescens dorsalis*.

Background

The most widely used removal sampling methods are based on analytical models that assume a closed population and a constant sampling effort. Open-population models are much less common, and more general models relax the second assumption (below) to varied degrees. Several important conditions should be met in

most applications of removal-sampling methods:

1. There should be a reasonable chance that the target population is closed, or at least stationary, during the sampling period. This assumption usually requires that time intervals between successive sampling periods be short. Some models, such as certain catch-per-unit-effort (CE) models (e.g., Dupont 1983), are applicable if the population does not remain closed during sampling.

2. It should be possible, at least in theory, to remove all animals in the study area (White et al. 1982). At least two samples are needed for estimation of population size (Seber 1982), but three to five are usual. White et al. (1982) recommended three or more samples unless the capture probability is 0.8 or more on each pass.

3. Each individual within any single sample should be equally catchable, and any individual's probability of being caught should be independent of that for any other individual. This condition is relaxed with the heterogeneity and trap response model (model M_{bh} in the 1991 version of CAPTURE). Harris et al. (1988) pointed out that taxa differ in their catchability and described the assumptions and calculations that can be used to determine whether this condition is met. In some situations, stratified sampling may be required. Hayne (1949) suggested a plot of number of individuals caught in each sample versus the total of all previously collected specimens from the same stratum or group to detect problems with this assumption. Zippin (1958) used regression estimates to evaluate equal catchability.

4. Catchability of individuals should be equal over sampling periods. Meeting this condition may be a problem for comparative studies, especially over seasons or when

individuals of more than one species are re-moved. Some models (e.g., M_{tb} in the 1991 version of CAPTURE) can handle temporal variation, but comparison of results across studies is problematic. Changes in the structure of vegetation or the size of a study plot (e.g., drying of pond), and fluctuations in temperature or rainfall between samples can affect catchability. Some models can deal with such change.

5. The sampling proficiency of the investigator should remain constant. This condition is a special case of condition 4 because learning and/or fatigue can produce variation over sampling periods. This problem can be minimized by providing equivalent training for all personnel.

6. Time and intensity of effort devoted to collection and removal should remain constant over samples. This condition is another special case of condition 4 and is a potential source of temporal variation. For example, in successive larval removal samples, the decrease of both larvae and vegetative growth may contribute to a change in sampling effort. Temporal variation can be handled by some models (e.g., some CE models in the 1991 version of CAPTURE).

If the number of traps remains constant and the amount of observer time is equal over the course of the study, a generalized removal model (M_{bh}) can be used (Rexstad and Burnham 1991). The catch-per-unit-effort is then equal to the number of animals caught, and this model allows for unequal catchability due to behavioral or other changes.

Research Design and Field Methods

Animals can be removed physically or by marking (from the unmarked population). Thus, mark-recapture methods (see previous section in this chapter) and removal methods (described

here) can be equivalent for use in population estimation when the assumption of a closed population is met. In general, models based on removal are special kinds of capture-recapture models; the latter were developed for the many situations to which removal models do not apply (see, e.g., Pollock et al. 1990).

In designing removal studies, the investigator must consider plot size and location, sampling interval, number of samples, and capture method. Removal methods are suitable for short-term studies with temporary plots and for long-term monitoring at sites where permanent plots can be established. For long-term studies the location of the plot must be recorded with precision. Plots should be large enough to ensure that a representative target population is available for sampling. However, they must be small enough to allow the investigator to capture a major proportion of the target population over the duration of the study. Study plots should be located so as to minimize short-term migration in and out of the plot and movement of animals into areas vacated by previous samples. In some cases, temporary fencing of plots may be desirable. The time between samples must be such that the population can reasonably be considered to be closed. For pond larvae or populations of explosively breeding species in which most of the adults are available and relatively easily captured, the time interval should be quite short. Zippin (1956) provided methods useful for ascertaining if assumptions hold during the removal period. He demonstrated how a suspected violation of a design assumption often can be verified by increasing the number of removal samples. In addition, the 1991 version of CAPTURE includes formal statistical goodness-of-fit and between-model tests specifically designed for testing assumptions.

Removal sampling requires hand capture, netting, or trapping of animals. The animals are placed in plastic bags that are labeled with a waterproof felt-tip pen. The animals are immediately brought to the laboratory and held in suitable containers until the end of the study. For short-term studies a container such as a Styrofoam ice chest may be used as a holding area at the site. When sampling is complete, all animals are returned to the original study plot.

Removal methods have appeal for practical reasons as well as scientific ones. In particular, they allow in certain cases for collection of data by persons other than the primary investigator (e.g., volunteers or students; see "Group Activities and Field Trips," Chapter 7) with minimal threat to the animals, minimal disruption of the study plot, and reduced individual effort and cost.

Data Analysis and Interpretation

Data include simple counts of captures (removals) for each sample; from these, abundance and density may be estimated. Hairston (1981) provided a clear example of the calculations; Harris et al. (1988) discussed use of the counts and of their associated environmental and morphological data.

Estimation of population size by removal methods is based on the assumption that the size of the available population is reduced by a large proportion on each sampling occasion. Zippin (1958:87) reported the proportion of the total population that would have to be trapped to obtain a specified level of precision for the sampling. For example, for a true population composed of 200 individuals, 55% would have to be captured over the entire sampling period to have a two-thirds chance that an estimate of size would be correct to within 30%.

Three types of population estimation methods are described below. The 1991 version of the program CAPTURE (see Appendix 6) performs the calculations required in most of the standard removal models.

CATCH-PER-UNIT-EFFORT ESTIMATORS

Catch-per-unit-effort is a general regression estimation method based on the relationship between the expected decrease in catch per unit of effort expended over repeated samples and the total catch. Effort expended can be constant (standard removal models—M_b, M_{bh}, and M_{tb} in CAPTURE) or variable (regression estimators—Pollock et al. 1984). An expected catch of zero is the logical presumed end of the study and the point at which all of the specimens have been removed. In practice, tactical problems are involved in any attempt to remove 100% of the individuals, so that this zero point is predicted from a linear regression equation. It is not the usual least-squares equation, because both the catch-per-unit-effort (the y-variable) and the summed removals (the x-variable) in most cases depend upon the same removals. This procedure has been used under varied conditions with a variety of taxa, and its properties have been widely discussed (Leslie and Davis 1939; Chapman 1954; Overton 1969; Seber 1982).

Assumptions of this method include the following: a closed population, except for removals (for standard models); equal probability of capture per unit effort over the duration of the study; all removals known; linear decline in catch per unit effort with time or with decrease in number of remaining animals, when removal is intense; and actual capture of a large proportion of the population.

The method also has several limitations. Equal probability of capture per unit effort may be difficult to obtain, but it can be evaluated by an examination of the regression line (over time) itself. If the regression trend is nonlinear, the assumption is violated, and the procedure should not be used (Caughley 1977). Another limitation is that a negative population estimate (which is the x-intercept) can be obtained when the regression slope is positive (Overton 1969). Also, estimates of population size are unrealistic if the slope is negative (as it should be) and close to zero. This situation can occur if the removal proportions are not sufficiently large (i. e., under approximately 75%).

CHANGE-IN-RATIO ESTIMATORS

In the change-in-ratio type of estimation procedure, simultaneous algebraic equations are used to relate population sizes before and after sample removal. The desired estimates are the solutions to these equations. The Petersen-type estimators discussed previously in this chapter are a special case. Krebs (1989) pointed out that large samples are usually required for this class of estimator, and the sampling program must be carefully planned with the model assumptions in mind.

This method requires that the population, in addition to being closed, include only two classes (called x-type and y-type) of animals. This requirement is minor because the amphibians in the target population can be designated as adult and larva or male and female. The method estimates population size based on changes in the proportions of the two classes between the first and second removals. The first sample provides the initial estimate of the proportion of the two types, and an additional proportion estimate is obtained from the second sample. Under an assumption of preremoval and postremoval estimate independence, Seber (1982) derived variance estimates for total population size as well as for the number of animals of each type in the preremoval population. He also derived a solution for the special case of the removal of only one of the two types.

This method assumes that observed proportions of both classes of animals are unbiased estimates of the true proportions in the population; this assumption can be evaluated when equal catchability of the two classes can be reasonably assumed. The method further assumes a closed study population, except for removals, and a known number of removals of both classes. The latter should be true for amphibian studies. The methods of Paulik and Robson (1969) provide for estimation of removals when the number is unknown.

Several limitations apply to this method. The method cannot be used if the proportion of x-types (and therefore y-types) is the same before and after removal. The reason for this limitation is not biological but algebraic. The difference between the two proportions (the change in ratio, or ΔP) forms the denominator in the equation for the total population size estimate. If ΔP is zero, no mathematical calculations can be made. A second limitation is that the interrelationships of the preremoval estimate, ΔP, and the total sample size (number of animals removed) directly affect both the accuracy and the precision of these estimates (Paulik and Robson 1969; Seber 1982), as is shown by a review of the algebraic equations for the method. Also, negative population estimates can occur if ΔP is near zero.

TWO-STAGE-CHANGE-IN-RATIO ESTIMATORS

The two-stage-change-in-ratio method is similar to the change-in-ratio procedure described above, but the former requires that the proportions of the animal classes be estimated in at least three removal periods (t_1, t_2, t_3), and it does not assume equal catchability. Between each pair of removal periods, two additional samples are taken, in which only one type or class of animal is removed and counted. These interim values are used to estimate relative observability. Variances for both the type proportions and the relative observability estimates are available with this procedure (Pollock et al. 1985). Pollock et al. (1985) provided a detailed description of the method, with illustrative examples.

This method assumes a closed population; two classes of animals (x-types and y-types), as in the single stage procedure; and constant observability or catchability only within the study period from t_1 to t_3.

The procedure has several limitations. The assumption of equal catchability is difficult to meet because it requires constant conditions during the period of study. An estimate of catchability can be obtained, however, from formulas in Pollock et al. (1985). Another limitation is that, generally, as the proportions of animals decrease, the accuracy and precision of the estimates decrease (Pollock et al. 1985).

Additional refinements of change-in-ratio methods are described by Udevitz and Pollock (1991).

OTHER METHODS

Eberhardt (1982) described a catch-per-unit-effort method in which the number of points upon which the regression is based is reduced. This decrease appears to make predictions based on the regression less reliable, and I do not recommend this method for amphibian studies. Dupont (1983) provided an estimation method useful for open populations.

Special Considerations

When the target population consists of easily observable individuals, a counting method that uses quadrat, patch, or transect sampling is preferable to either mark-recapture or removal sampling. However, many amphibians are not readily observable, and capture methods must be employed for population estimation. Removal methods are less expensive than M-RC methods and require less time and personnel. However, the M-RC methods may yield more-precise estimates per unit of effort expended. Other advantages of removal methods include elimination of changes in capture probability after first capture, easier handling of animals (no tagging required), and reduced field time because numbers of animals caught usually decline after the first sample. However, removal methods are inappropriate for endangered, rare, or highly mobile species, and temporary removal methods require good temporary holding facilities.

The degree to which the assumptions of the removal method are met determines its reliability as a method of population estimation (Carle and Strub 1978), although, under certain limited conditions, unequal probability of capture across individuals may have negligible effect on certain estimation procedures (Seber and Whale 1970; Carle and Strub 1978). Other threats to validity are not easily detectable, but they can affect the final results and must be considered. If a violation of assumptions is not correctable, I advise use of alternative methods of estimation.

I recommend that the investigator record morphological and environmental data while the animals are being held (e.g., see Harris et al. 1988). Other parameters relevant to population studies (e.g., age structure) can be estimated from these data.

## Chapter 9

Analysis of Amphibian Biodiversity Data

Lee-Ann C. Hayek

Introduction

In this chapter I discuss problems of use, misuse, and problematical interpretation of data, specifically for amphibian biologists. I focus on statistical procedures that are appropriate for amphibian sampling and monitoring and consider limiting factors and assumptions of statistical models in terms suitable for observational and other studies. The number of formulas I present is negligible, and they involve only simple algebraic statements. This chapter is not all-encompassing.

No technique is universally appropriate, and *standardization,* as used here, does not imply that only a single method of analysis exists. Indeed, in some cases a good amount of work will have to be done before any choice can be made. Only a mathematical and probabilistic evalua-

tion of a situation and its definition in operational terms can lead to a correct choice for data analysis. When in doubt about correct statistical procedures, or when irregularities arise, investigators should always seek the advice of a mathematical statistician with experience in biological applications. Theory is always well behaved; data never are.

Species richness

Presence-Absence Data

Amphibian data may be recorded on a nominal, ordinal, interval, or ratio scale (see "Measurement Scales and Statistical Analysis," Chapter 4). Data measured against the first two scale types are called *nonmetric;* those measured against the latter two are called *interval, metric, or continuous.* Single inventories can lead directly to nonmetric data by providing a total species count with a designation of species as abundant, common, or rare; a list of species by name; or a record of presence or absence of each species within a selected habitat or sample. In some instances, the results of a monitoring effort also may be presented as nonmetric data because of the nontrivial reduction in effort relative to a study design calling for interval data. Results can be obtained quickly or inexpensively with a preliminary analysis of the research effort, and problems with sampling techniques can be detected.

Nonmetric data also may be the only possible or reasonable choice when the precision with which the data will be collected is in question—for example, if collector reliability is low. In addition, with some sampling methods (e.g., audio strip transects and night driving, discussed in Chapters 6 and 7, respectively), measurement or observation error can be high, and the recording of precise continuous variables may be problematic, unnecessary, or even deleterious to the study. Alternatively, for certain studies a continuous variable may be categorized after it has been recorded, as when age data for juveniles or adults are grouped.

Presence-absence data can be coded using the numbers *1* and *0* for computer input. Whether a species is rare or abundant, its simple presence is indicated by a *1*. Such data are termed *two-state, binary, categorical,* or nonmetric, as well as nominal.

A list of presence-absence data for species in a particular area provides information on geographic or habitat distribution of those species, but little else. These data can, however, provide information on species interactions that may be particularly useful in explaining observed distributions. Such interactions are generally examined by means of pairwise comparisons of presence-absence among species or localities in

Table 19. Generalized 2 × 2 Frequency Table Using Counts

State, habitat, or species B	State, habitat, or species A		
	Present	**Absent**	**Total**
Present	a	b	$a + b$
Absent	c	d	$c + d$
Total	$a + c$	$b + d$	n

a given area. *Fourfold* (or *2 × 2*) *contingency tables* are especially convenient for summarizing data regarding the relationship between two species, populations, habitats, or localities (e.g., Table 19), because the number of categories (four) is less than the sample size (number of observations). Pairwise comparisons for all combinations of species over an entire data set are a realistic means by which to summarize a large set of observations and to examine interspecific relationships. When associations among species are not obvious and a priori assumptions are neither desirable nor possible, methods such as *R*-mode and *Q*-mode cluster analyses (e.g., Gower 1967; Hazel 1970; Anderberg 1973; Sneath and Sokal 1973) can be used to identify relationships.

The amount of information in data sets that merely record presence and absence is considered to be minimal, and information is presumed to be lost when a continuous variable has its scale categorized. Presumably, the smaller the number of categories, the greater the loss of information. Several authors have addressed this question (Bonham-Carter 1965; Buzas 1967, 1972a; Erez and Gill 1977). Gill and Tipper (1978) tested the hypothesis that the results obtained from a study with metric variables can be obtained from binary nonmetric data. They dichotomized and reanalyzed the data from six large multivariate studies and showed agreement between the pairs of analyses that ranged from

75% to 97%. They concluded that for those studies, nonmetric binary data were entirely adequate.

Measures of Association

Measures, or coefficients, of association have been in existence since at least the late 1800s. They are appropriate for use with binary data and thus are especially important for faunal comparisons because the data from such studies are often in binary form. Ancillary data on presence or absence of taxonomic characters, environmental states, observer concordance, and chemical properties also can be recorded in binary form and analyzed with measures of association.

Measures of association have several important applications in amphibian studies: expression of faunal resemblance as similarity or dissimilarity among species observed at two or more sample sites; assessment of the degree of coexistence in different localities or habitats of particular species of amphibians, based on their frequency of co-occurrence in a series of samples or observations; and measurement of the similarity or dissimilarity of habitat or microhabitat choices or conditions for selected species. Additionally, these measures are useful for condensing data on the resemblance of species, habitats, or samples and for summarizing large amounts of species data.

CLASSES OF COEFFICIENTS

Resemblance, similarity, matching, and *association* are the adjectives most commonly applied to the class of coefficients used to describe two-state presence-absence data. Distinct disciplines have spawned a vast array of such coefficients, many of which are redundant. The 46 most popular measures are presented in Table 20. I have grouped them into three categories, that are not mutually exclusive but that facilitate consideration.

1. *Similarity-dissimilarity coefficients.* These coefficients reflect the proportion of the sample that represents mutual occurrence (Hohn 1976). Formulas for their calculation do not include specific consideration of joint absences of variables (species).
2. *Matching coefficients.* Formulas for these indices include joint absences or non-occurrences and do not discriminate between positive and negative association (Hohn 1976).
3. *Traditional association coefficients.* Usually, these coefficients are based upon the chi-square statistic (Table 20: section C) or a statistic computationally related to chi-square, or they have an underlying assumption of normality. These coefficients are calculated with formulas that include joint absences, and they can be evaluated against a probability distribution.

Coefficients in the first two categories treat a sample as if it were devoid of sampling or measurement error. They can be based loosely or strictly upon a probabilistic model. They are not test statistics, however, and have no related probability or sampling distributions. Alternatively, the traditional coefficients assess the probability that an observed number of co-occurrences between two species has arisen by chance.

Some argue that before a measure of association is calculated, a significance test should be applied. The test would be used to indicate the existence (at a stated probability level) of an underlying relationship between the species, habitats, or localities being considered. It would describe how likely the observed result is under the null hypothesis of no association and would help to determine if an association were "real." Both the test statistic and its significance level are influenced by sample size. For any given alternative hypothesis, chi-square (or an equivalent) increases and the significance level decreases as sample size increases. The binary

Table 20. Measures of Association

#	Coefficient	Reference	Alternative names	Formula	Relationship to others
A. Similarity coefficients					
1	Simpson	Simpson (1943)	Simpson coefficient Degree of Faunal Resemblance	$\dfrac{a}{a + \min(b, c)}$	Equals Mountford's (#8) if population follows a log distribution
2	Kulczynski	Kulczynski (1927)	Second Kulczynski coefficient Driver and Kroeber coefficient	$\dfrac{1}{2}\left(\dfrac{a}{a+b} + \dfrac{a}{a+c}\right)$	Can be written as the arithmetic mean of Simpson's (#1) and Braun-Blanquet's (#10)
3	Ochiai/ Otsuka	Ochiai (1957)	Ochiai coefficient Otsuka coefficient	$\dfrac{a}{[(a+b)(a+c)]^{\frac{1}{2}}}$	Same as the cosine coefficient for binary data Actually attributed to Otsuka in the Ochiai reference
4	Dice	Dice (1945)	Dice coefficient Coincidence index Sørensen (1948) coefficient Quotient of similarity Czekanowski (1912) coefficient Burt coefficient (Peters 1968) Pirlot coefficient (Peters 1968) Whittaker (1952) index Bray (1956) index of amplitudinal correspondence	$\dfrac{2a}{2a + b + c} = \dfrac{a}{a + \frac{1}{2}(b + c)}$	Equivalent to the additive inverse of the Bray-Curtis Coefficient on binary data Equivalent to 1–Nonmetric (#13) Goodman & Kruskal's (1954) $\lambda_r = 2(\text{Dice})-1$
4a	Dice's asymmetric indices	Dice (1945)		(a) Index B | A $= \dfrac{a}{a+c}$ (b) Index A | B $= \dfrac{a}{a+b}$	The asymmetric versions of Dice (#4)
5	Jaccard	Jaccard (1901)	Jaccard coefficient Coefficient of floral communities Coefficient of community Similarity index (Sneath 1957)	$\dfrac{a}{a + b + c}$	

Description	Range	Nonlinearity-linearity[a]	Invariance[a]	Max/Min[a,b] condition		Max E-Coefficient[c]	Known large sample theory
				Min	Max		
The proportion of joint occurrences or matches compared with the minimum number of occurrences for one species	(0, 1)	Linear	Yes	Yes	Yes	No	
The proportion of all localities in which both of a pair of species have been found relative to the smallest number of localities in which one species was found							
The arithmetic mean of the proportions of species jointly present over their separate marginals	(0, 1)	Linear	Yes	Yes	Yes	No	
Devised to avoid the selection of a minimum mismatch in Simpson's (#1) formula							
The geometric mean of the proportions of species present jointly relative to their separate marginals	(0, 1)	Linear	Yes	Yes	Yes	Yes	Yes
The harmonic mean of the proportions of species present jointly relative to the weighted total	(0, 1)	Linear	Yes	Yes	Yes	Yes	Yes
Weights mismatches less than matches so that weight of a frequency is twice the combined weight of *b* and *c*							
May be interpreted as a conditional probability							
Index (a): the proportion of time or samples that A occurs when it was associated with B	(0, 1)	Linear	Yes	Yes	Yes	No	
Index (b): the proportio of time or samples that B occurs when it was associated with A							
Devised to differ depending on the species used; to be used for a one-sided or nonreciprocal species dependency							
The proportion of localities in which both species occur relative to the total number of localities in which any species was found	(0, 1)	Convex	Yes	Yes	Yes	Yes	Yes

Table 20. (*Continued*)

#	Coefficient	Reference	Alternative names	Formula	Relationship to others
6	Sokal and Sneath UN_2	Sokal and Sneath (1963)		$\dfrac{a}{a+2b+2c} = \dfrac{a}{a+2(b+c)}$	
7	Kulczynski	Kulczynski (1927)	First Kulczynski coefficient	$\dfrac{a}{b+c}$	
8	Mountford	Mountford (1962)	I	$\dfrac{2a}{2bc+ab+ac} = \dfrac{a}{\frac{1}{2}(ab+ac)+bc}$	An estimate of the multiplicative inverse of Fisher's α When the population follows a log distribution, Simpson's Index (#1) = Mountford's I = 1/Fisher's α
9	Correlation ratio	Sorgenfrei (1958)		$\dfrac{a^2}{(a+c)(a+b)}$	The square of Ochiai/ Otsuka's (#3)
10	Braun-Blanquet	Braun-Blanquet (1932)	Incorrectly called Jaccard (#5) by Peters (1968)	$\dfrac{a}{a+\max(b,c)}$	
11	Fager	Fager and McGowan (1963)	Fager and McGowan coefficient	$\dfrac{a}{[(a+c)(a+b)]^{\frac{1}{2}}} - \dfrac{1}{2}\max(b,c)$	Ochiai/Otsuka's (#3) plus a correction factor
12	Savage	Savage (1960)	Coefficient of difference	$1 - \dfrac{a}{a+\max(b,c)}$	The additive inverse of Braun-Blanquet's (#10)
13	Nonmetric	Sneath and Sokal (1973)		$\dfrac{b+c}{2a+b+c}$	Equals 1 – Dice (#4)
14	McConnaughey	McConnaughey (1965)		$\dfrac{a^2-bc}{(a+b)(a+c)}$	A scale-transformed Kulczynski (#2) coefficient Equals 2(Kulczynski)–1
15	Johnson	Johnson (1967)		$\dfrac{a}{a+b} + \dfrac{a}{a+c}$	Twice the Kulczynski (#2) coefficient

Description	Range	Nonlinearity-linearity[a]	Invariance[a]	Max/Min[a,b] condition		Max E-Coefficient[c]	Known large sample theory
				Min	Max		
Devised as an alternative to Jaccard's (#5) by differentially weighting the mismatches	(0, 1)	Convex	Yes	Yes	Yes	Yes	
The rate of joint occurrences per number of mismatches	(0, ∞)	Convex	Yes	Yes	Yes	No	
Derived from Fisher's α diversity index, the parameter estimate from the log series distribution The actual similarity index was $I = 1/\alpha$, for which the formula in this table was suggested as an approximation	(0,∞)	Convex	No	Yes	No	No	
Not defined if $a = c$ or if $a = b$	(0, 1)	Convex	Yes	Yes	Yes	Yes	
The proportion of joint occurrences compared with the maximum number of occurrences for one species The proportion of all localities in which both of a pair of species have been found relative to the largest number of localities in which one species was found	(0, 1)	Linear	Yes	Yes	Yes	No	
Derived from Ochiai/Otsuka (#3) The geometric mean of the proportions of co-occurrence for each of the two species with a correctino factor for the pairs of rare species (sample size) Authors said ≥ .5 meant association or affinity.	(−∞, 1)	Linear	No	No	Yes		
	(0, 1)	Linear	Yes	Yes	Yes		
A scaled Euclidean distance for binary data	(0, 1)	Linear	Yes	Yes	Yes		
The proportion of mismatches over a weighted sum of all occurrences	(−1, 1)	Linear	Yes	Yes	Yes		
The unweighted sum of the two basic proportions involving joint occurrences	(0,2)	N/A	Yes	Yes	Yes		

(Continued)

Table 20. (*Continued*)

#	Coefficient	Reference	Alternative names	Formula	Relationship to others
16	Forbes[d]	Forbes (1907)		For a' = the expected value of a, $$\frac{a}{a'} = \frac{na}{(a+b)(a+c)}$$	
17	Gilbert and Wells	Gilbert and Wells (1966)		$\log a - \log n - \log\left(\frac{a+b}{n}\right) - \log\left(\frac{a+c}{n}\right)$	log of Forbes's (#16)
18	Forbes	Forbes (1925)		$\dfrac{a-a'}{a_{max}-a} = \dfrac{na-(a+b)(a+c)}{n \cdot min(b,c)-(a+b)(a+c)}$	When $ad > bc$, equals Cole's (#45)
19	Tarwid	Tarwid (1960)		$\dfrac{a-a'}{a+a'} = \dfrac{na-(a+b)(a+c)}{na+(a+b)(a+c)}$	
20	Resemblance equation coefficient	Preston (1962a) Hagmeier and Stults (1964)		$\left(\dfrac{a+c}{n}\right)^{1/2} + \left(\dfrac{a+b}{n}\right)^{1/2} = 1$ where $1-z$ is the coefficient	

B. Matching coefficients

#	Coefficient	Reference	Alternative names	Formula	Relationship to others
21	Simple matching coefficient	Sokal and Michener (1958)	Sokal and Michener coefficient	$\dfrac{a+d}{a+b+c+d} = \dfrac{a+d}{n}$	If $d = 0$, equals Jaccard's (#5) Numerator is "index of crude agreement" (Rogot and Goldberg 1966)
22	Sokal and Sneath UN$_5$	Sokal and Sneath (1963)		$\dfrac{ad}{[(a+b)(a+c)(b+d)(c+d)]^{1/2}}$	
23	Sokal and Sneath UN$_4$	Sokal and Sneath (1963)	Rogot and Goldberg (1966) index	$\dfrac{1}{4}\left(\dfrac{a}{a+b} + \dfrac{a}{a+c} + \dfrac{d}{b+d} + \dfrac{d}{c+d}\right)$	
24	Sokal and Sneath UN$_3$	Sokal and Sneath (1963)		$\dfrac{a+d}{b+c}$	If $d = 0$, equals the first Kulczynski coefficient (#7) Numerator is index of crude agreement (see #21)
25	Sokal and Sneath UN$_1$	Sokal and Sneath (1963)		$\dfrac{2(a+d)}{2(a+d)+(b+c)}$	If $d = 0$, equals Dice's (#4)
26	Russell and Rao	Russell and Rao (1948)		$\dfrac{a}{a+b+c+d} = \dfrac{a}{n}$	If $d = 0$, equals Jaccard's (#5)

Description	Range	Nonlinearity-linearity[a]	Invariance[a]	Max/Min[a,b] condition		Max E-Coefficient[c]	Known large sample theory
				Min	Max		
Compares the number of associated occurrences of the two species in a series of random samples with the number of such co-occurrences expected by chance	$(0,\infty)$	Linear	Yes	Yes	No		
When this equals 1, shows that the two species occur together in exactly the number of samples expected by chance							
Is the ratio of actual to calculated joint occurrences							
Min not defined for $a = 0$	$(-\infty,\infty)$	Concave	Yes	No	No		
For max, log n – log a							
	$(-\infty,\infty)$	Convex	Yes	No	No		
	$(-1,1)$	Concave	Yes	No	No		
Equation is transcendental with no general solution, only a set of approximate solutions			Yes				
Assumes individuals are distributed according to log normal distribution							
An alternative to Jaccard's (#5) by including negative matches or joint absences in both numerator and denominator	$(0,1)$	Linear	Yes	Yes	Yes	Yes	
The proportion of (1,1) and (0,0) agreements in the totals of n species comparisons							
Square of the geometric mean of the four basic proportions in the table	$(0,1)$	Convex	Yes	Yes	Yes	Yes	
The arithmetic mean of the four basic proportions in the table	$(0,1)$	Linear	Yes	Yes	Yes	No	
Equals ½ when degree of agreement is exactly that predicted by chance							
A comparison of the joint events with the single species events or of matches with mismatches	$(0,\infty)$	Convex	Yes	Yes	No	No	
Max not defined for $b = c$							
The weighted proportion of joint events compared with the (weighted) sum of all events	$(0,1)$	Convex	Yes	Yes	Yes	No	
Mismatches are given half the weight of matches.							
An alternative to Jaccard's (#5) by inclusion of d, the joint absences, in denominator	$(0,1)$	Linear	No	Yes	No	No	
The proportion of joint occurrences in the total n comparisons							

(Continued)

Table 20. (*Continued*)

#	Coefficient	Reference	Alternative names	Formula	Relationship to others
27	Rogers and Tanimoto	Rogers and Tanimoto (1960)		$\dfrac{a+d}{a+d+2(b+c)}$	If $d = 0$, equals UN_2 (#6) Reflects a completely different situation from UN_5 (#25) Index of crude agreement in numerator (see #21)
28	Hamann	Hamann (1961)	G-Index G-Index of agreement Holley and Guilford (1964)	$\dfrac{a+d-(b+c)}{a+d+(b+c)}$	Is a scale-transformed SMC (#21) to change the range 2(#21)-1 Mathematically related to Yule's Q (#43) Equals the ϕ coefficient (#42) only when the marginal proportions all equal .5
29	Baroni-Urbani and Buser	Baroni-Urbani and Buser (1976)	S*	$\dfrac{\sqrt{ad}+a-b-c}{\sqrt{ad}+a+b+c}$	Is (#30) scale transformed to change the range 2(#30)-1
30	Baroni-Urbani and Buser	Baroni-Urbani and Buser (1976)	S**	$\dfrac{\sqrt{ad}+a}{\sqrt{ad}+a+b+c}$	
31	Total difference	Sneath (1968)	Binary distance coefficient Sokal binary distance coefficient	$\dfrac{b+c}{a+b+c+d}$	For binary data, the square root is equivalent to average Euclidean distance coefficient. Related to Nonmetric (#13) without weighting the joint occurrences and by including the joint absences
32	Pattern difference	Sneath (1968)		$\dfrac{2\sqrt{bc}}{a+b+c+d}$	
33	Angular transformation of simple matching coefficient	Goodall (1967) Austin and Colwell (1977)		$\dfrac{1}{50\,\pi}\arcsin[SMC\,(\#\,21)]^{\frac{1}{2}}$	

Description	Range	Nonlinearity-linearity[a]	Invariance[a]	Max/Min[a,b] condition		Max E-Coefficient[c]	Known large sample theory
				Min	Max		
The proportion of joint events compared with the weighted sum of all events	(0,1)	Convex	Yes	Yes	Yes	Yes	
Mismatches are given twice the weight of matches.							
Requires no assumptions about the data	(−1,1)	Linear	Yes	Yes	Yes	Yes	
Based on the probability of agreement of responses							
Not a correlation coefficient even though it can equal ϕ in one case							
Max not defined if $a + d = b + c$.							
Devised as an adjustment to Hamann's (#28) to correct the problem that Hamann's does not approach 1 as $a + d$ approaches n when $a \neq 0$.	(−1,1)	Concave	No	Yes	Yes	No	
Distribution varies with n	(0,1)	Concave	Yes	Yes	Yes	No	
Devised to express similarity as the difference of positive weighted matches and equal but negative weighted mismatches							
The proportion of mismatches to the total	(1,0)	Linear	No	No	No		
Equals 1 if $a = d = 0$ and $b = c$	(0,1)	Linear	Yes	No	No		
	(0,.57)	Concave (in Absolute Value)	Yes	Yes	Yes		

(Continued)

Table 20. (*Continued*)

#	Coefficient	Reference	Alternative names	Formula	Relationship to others
34	Michael	Michael (1921)	Called McEven and Michael by Cole (1949) with no reference	$\dfrac{4(ad-bc)}{(a+d)^2+(b+c)^2}$	
35	Faith	Faith (1983)	C-coefficient	$\dfrac{2a+d}{2n}=\dfrac{a+\frac{d}{2}}{n}$	
36	Omega	Yule (1912)	Coefficient of colligatum ω	$\dfrac{\sqrt{ad}-\sqrt{bc}}{\sqrt{ad}+\sqrt{bd}}$	$\dfrac{2\omega}{1+\omega^2}=$ Yule's Q
37	Eyraud	Eyraud (1936)		$\dfrac{a-[(a+b)(a+c)]}{(a+b)(c+d)(a+c)(b+d)}$	

C. Traditional association measures

#	Coefficient	Reference	Alternative names	Formula	Relationship to others
38	χ^2 statistic		Binomial index of dispersion	$\dfrac{n(ad-bc)^2}{(a+b)(c+d)(a+c)(b+d)}$	
39	Coefficient of mean square contingency	Pearson (1901) Doolittle (1885)	$\hat{\phi}^2$ Pearson's mean square contingency Discriminate association ratio	$\dfrac{(ad-bc)^2}{(a+b)(c+d)(a+c)(b+d)}$	The χ^2 statistic scaled by the total$=\chi^2/n$ For the 2×2 table, is Pearson's ρ^2 Doolittle derived it as asymmetric version of Pearce's (#44). Tschouproff's $t=\left(\dfrac{\phi^2}{\sqrt{(r-1)(c-1)}}\right)^{1/2}$ Sakoda's ρ^* $\rho/\rho_{max}=$ $\left(\dfrac{\min(r,c)\phi^2}{[\min(r,c)-1](1+\phi^2)}\right)^{1/2}$
40	Cramér's υ	Cramér (1946)		$\left\{\dfrac{(ad-bc)^2}{(a+b)(c+d)(a+c)(b+d)[\min(r,c)-1]}\right\}^{1/2}$ $\left[\phi^2/\min(r,c)-1\right]^{1/2}$	
41	Pearson's contingency coefficient	Pearson (1904)	P	$\dfrac{ad-bc}{[(a+b)(c+d)(a+c)(b+d)+(ad-bc)^2]^{1/2}}$	An estimate of Pearson's ρ Equals $\left(\dfrac{\phi^2}{1-\phi^2}\right)^{1/2}$ Equals $\left(\dfrac{\chi^2/n}{1+\chi^2/n}\right)^{1/2}$ Equals $\left(\dfrac{\chi^2}{n+\chi^2}\right)^{1/2}$

Description	Range	Nonlinearity-linearity[a]	Invariance[a]	Max/Min[a,b] condition		Max E-Coefficient[c]	Known large sample theory
				Min	Max		
The factor (*ad-bc*) in numerator relates this to traditional statistical association measures.	(–1,1)	Convex	Yes	Yes	Yes		
Is author's "asymmetric" measure to count shared presence as 1, a mismatch as –1, and a shared absence as 0	(0,∞)	Linear	Yes	Yes	No		
Author recommends it when one-state homogeneity is to be maximized. That is, groups with large number of matches and few mismatches are desirable							
	(–1,1)	Concave	Yes	Yes	Yes		
	(–1,0)	N/A	No	No	Yes		
Range depends on table's dimensions. Can attain its maximum only when each row and column contains all nonzero entries	(0, *n*[min(r, c) – 1]), so for 2 × 2 table it is (0,*n*)						
Even though this is a χ^2 dividing out the factor of total size, its range still depends on the table's dimensions. When there are no missing data, it is of little consequence to scale χ^2.	[0, min(r, c) – 1], so for 2 × 2 table it is (0,1)						
Developed this nonparametric statistic as a scaled version of an estimate of $\hat{\phi}^2$ (#39) Range is independent of table dimensions.	(0,1)						
Can be seen as the maximum likelihood estimator of ρ (correlation coefficient) under multinominal sampling Proposed by Pearson to transform the scale on his first index (#39)	(0,1)						

(*Continued*)

Table 20. (*Continued*)

#	Coefficient	Reference	Alternative names	Formula	Relationship to others
42	Phi coefficient	Pearson (1901) Yule (1911) Boas (1909) Tschouproff (1919)	ϕ Yule's Q' Pearson's correlation coefficient ρ Product sum correlation (Yule 1912) Fourfold point (tetrachoric) coefficient (Pearson and Heron 1913) McEwen's coefficient Kendall and Stuart's υ	$\dfrac{ad-bc}{[(a+c)(b+d)(a+b)(c+d)]^{1/2}}$	Equals $(\chi^2/n)^{1/2}$ Equals $\sqrt{\phi^2}$ $t = \dfrac{\phi}{[(r-1)(c-1)]^{1/2}}$
43	Yule's Q	Yule (1900)		$\dfrac{ad-bc}{ad+bc} = \dfrac{n[a - \frac{(a+b)(a+c)}{n}]}{ad+bc}$	
44	Pearce	Pearce (1884) Youden (1950)	J ϕ θ Youden coefficient	$\dfrac{ad-bc}{(a+c)(b+d)} = \dfrac{a}{a+c} - \dfrac{b}{b+d}$	A special case of the phi coefficient (#42) if row totals and column totals, respectively, are equal
45	C_7	Cole (1949)	Index of interspecific association	For $ad \geq bc$: $\dfrac{ad-bc}{(a+b)(b+d)}$ For $bc > ad, d \geq a$: $\dfrac{ad-bc}{(a+b)(a+c)}$ For $a > d$: $\dfrac{ad-bc}{(b+d)(c+d)}$	Is $\dfrac{\chi^2}{\sqrt{\chi^2_{max}}}$ with the sign of $ad-bc$

| | | | | Max/Min[a,b] condition | | Known large |
| | | Nonlinearity- | | | | Max E- | sample |
Description	Range	linearity[a]	Invariance[a]	Min	Max	Coefficient[c]	theory
Range still depends on the table's dimensions.							
$0 \leq \rho \leq \sqrt{\dfrac{\min(r,c) - 1}{\min(r,c)}} \leq 1$							
Not defined for $a = d = 0$ or for $b = c = 0$							
Pearson derived this as the correlation between errors in the position of means of two variables when each is measured in terms of its own standard deviation.	(-1,1)						
Yule separately (apparently differing notation caused the problem) derived it as "a theoretical value" of the correlation coefficient. This use is correctly severely criticized.							
The probability interpretation of Yule's Q is the probability that two individuals selected have their A and B states in the same order, minus the probability that they have different A and B states in opposite orders.							
When $ad = bc$ then Q = 0, a value midway between the two extremes.	(−1,1)						
Yule wrote: "For moderate association, this coefficient gives much the larger values."							
Heron (1911) said it should be used only when $a + b = c + d$ and $a + c = b + d$.							
When equals 0, is equivalent to randomized prediction using just the row marginal frequencies, i.e., corresponds to independence.	(−1,1)						
Equals $\dfrac{a}{a + b} + \dfrac{d}{b + d} - 1$							
Is the difference between the conditional column-wise probabilities							
Basic assumption is that false positives (c cell) are as undesirable as false negatives (d cell).							
Not independent of the frequencies	(−1,1)						

(Continued)

Table 20. (*Continued*)

#	Coefficient	Reference	Alternative names	Formula	Relationship to others
46	C_8	Hurlbert (1969)		$\dfrac{ad-bc}{\mid ad-bc \mid}$ with the sign of $ad-bc$	Is $\pm\left[\dfrac{\chi^2-\chi^2_{min}}{\chi^2_{max}-\chi^2_{min}}\right]^{1/2}$ with the sign of $ad-bc$ When table yields a statistically significant result, $\chi^2_{min}=\chi^2$ (observed value) and $C_7=C_8$.

[a]See the section on "Properties of Association Measures" for explanations, and see Appendix in this chapter for examples.

[b]These columns indicate whether the coefficient attains its maximum and minimum values at the respective end points of its range.

[c]Jansen and Vegelius (1981).

[d]Dice (1945) showed that Forbes' coefficient measures the degree to which the association of two species conforms to expectation on the basis of chance, not the degree of association itself.

Description	Range	Nonlinearity-linearity[a]	Invariance[a]	Max/Min[a,b] condition		Max E-Coefficient[c]	Known large sample theory
				Min	Max		
Measures the degree to which two species' joint occurrences are more or less frequent than based on chance alone	(−1,1)						

measure, in contrast, describes the size of the association (or effect) and cannot be influenced by sample size.

A measure of association should be selected in keeping with the questions being asked; no single coefficient is sufficient for all amphibian data. The most common approach to selection appears to be familiarity with a similar study. I outline here a rationale for selection of a coefficient in keeping with the inventory and monitoring objectives.

I have not considered the distance metric, a measure of spatial relationship in coordinate space, because it generally is not appropriate for the unordered nominal data of our discussion. Besides, similarity coefficients (under certain circumstances) can be transformed quite simply into distance metrics. These coefficients are treated by Legrendre and Legrendre (1983).

NOTATION AND EVALUATION

I have restricted discussion specifically to pairwise comparisons, that is, to contingency tables with 2 rows (R) and 2 columns (C) (2×2 tables), because they are the basis for most of the coefficients. Nevertheless, much of the discussion is applicable to measures based upon generalized tables (R × C, for any number of rows and columns). The most acceptable and easily generalized presentation of two-state data is in terms of the four cells of a 2×2 frequency table, in which a = frequency of positive matches, joint presence, or co-occurrence (1, 1); d = frequency of negative matches, joint absences, or non-co-occurrences (0, 0); and b and c = frequency of mismatches [(0, 1) and (1, 0)] (Table 19), with n equaling the number of amphibians, individual elements, samples, or characters in the study (i.e., $n = a + b + c + d$). Every possible associative relationship between states, habitats, or species A and B (usually called factors or variables) is expressible in terms of these four quantities. Much of the redundancy among the coefficients is due to the lack of a common notational system.

Table 21. Generalized 2×2 Frequency Table Using Proportions

State or species B	State or species A		Total
	Present	Absent	
Present	A	B	$(a + b)/n$ $= A + B$
Absent	C	D	$(c + d)/n$ $= C + D$
Total	$(a + c)/n$ $= A + C$	$(b + d)/n$ $= B + D$	1.00

A 2×2 table can be rewritten in terms of the related proportions. In this case, $A = a/n, B = b/n, C = c/n, D = d/n,$ and $A + B + C + D = 1$ (Table 21). Alternatively, we could write these with symbols for the proportion in the ith row and jth column, $p_{ij}, j = 1,2$.

Binary measures must be evaluated from the standpoint of operationalization, that is, the meaning in the study of *association*. Is this word synonymous just with joint presence events? Are two species "highly" associated when they occur in a large number of localities together and never alone? Would specimens of *Rana ingeri* and *R. blythi* be associated if they co-occurred in 40% of the samples and also were absent from 40% of the samples in which one might have expected them? Answers to such questions form the basis for selection of the appropriate measure of association for a specific sampling situation. All aspects of the study must be considered and the related hypotheses and research questions operationalized in order to arrive at the proper choice.

CLASSIFYING DATA

Confusion exists in the ecological literature about four aspects of the classification of data for use with binary measures. Each of these factors influences the choice of an index for a particular amphibian study and its interpretation.

UNDERLYING CONTINUA. For data arranged in a contingency table, the factors (species, habitats) describing the columns and rows could be assumed to arise from an underlying continuum. For example, species occurrences could be based upon population distributions defined on a continuum of depth or vegetation height, or, in other words, a specific nonrandom abundance distribution of amphibian species could exist within the breeding habitats being sampled. The value of such an assumption is disputed. Pearson and Heron (1913) argued that it is most often justified, whereas Yule (1912) believed that it is most often misleading. When all factors from a study originate from a multivariate normal distribution on an underlying continuum (unlike our fourfold tables), most investigators agree that the measure of association should be based on a correlation coefficient (e.g., tetrachoric correlation coefficient).

ORDER. A fundamental ordering may exist between (or among) the classifications of a factor. For example, aquatic or montane habitats occupied by frog species can be ordered by depth, elevation, ambient temperature, time, or abundance. The latter three classifications normally use interval or continuous variables. Depth and elevation can be categorized on ordinal or interval scales. In ordinal classifications, categories are intrinsically ordered (e.g., shallow, deep; at sea level, above sea level), but not quantitatively comparable. Shallow is less than deep, but by an unknown amount. An interval scale results if *shallow* and *deep* are defined by number of meters from a precisely determined shoreline.

Only the existence of intrinsic ordering is relevant, not its direction. Ordering may be ignored if it is not relevant to the nature of the investigation. Finally, confirmation of an underlying unidimensional continuum is a sufficient condition for recognizing an underlying order among categories.

Presence or absence of inherent ordering of the data is an important consideration in the selection of association measures. Some measures assume an ordered structure in the data, and some traditional association measures can statistically test for its existence. However, in a 2×2 table, the two possible orderings of the categories can alter only the measure's sign; they do not provide important statistical information to the analysis.

ASYMMETRY. Asymmetry in binary data occurs when one of the two states is interpreted as "more informative" than the other. This would be the case with presence-absence data in which the state of "presence" provides more information on species similarity than does the frequency of absences. When an investigator is reasonably assured, a priori, that a causal relationship exists and runs in one direction only, or if the coding of the character can be reversed with no sacrifice of information, then the data must be viewed in an asymmetric manner.

Many authors (e.g., Sneath and Sokal 1973; Baroni-Urbani and Buser 1976) have argued not only that absences contribute less information than presences, but also that shared absences have no part in a measure of similarity. Some authors (e.g., Green 1974; Ludwig and Reynolds 1988) have stated that any index of bioassociation should be independent of the number of joint absences (= d in the frequency table). An inspection of the formulas given in Table 20 shows that the inclusion or exclusion of shared absences (d) in a formula may not be relevant because d [= n − (a + b + c)] is part of n. A measure may implicitly incorporate d through n; thus, d may be of major consequence to the size of a measure even though it is not explicit in the formula.

The rule in amphibian projects with large samples is to select a coefficient that makes explicit use of the d frequency only when at least three species or habitats have been examined.

Table 22. Frequency Distribution of *Eleutherodactylus guentheri* Frogs among Four Microhabitats, by Age and Sex

	Microhabitat			
Age and sex	**In leaf litter**	**Exposed on ground**	**On vegetation <0.5 m**	**On vegetation >0.5 m**
Juvenile males	0.25	0.00	0.00	0.00
Juvenile females	0.00	0.25	0.00	0.00
Adult males	0.00	0.00	0.00	0.25
Adult females	0.00	0.00	0.25	0.00

The *d* cell then represents the number of joint absences of a pair of species that had been expected in similar samples, or the absence of a species from a pair of habitats in which it had been expected. Use of the *d* cell frequency speaks to the chance that an occurrence could reasonably have occurred but did not.

CATEGORY DEFINITIONS. Because the operational definitions of the categories used in a study can affect the degree of association, the definitions should be carefully formulated in keeping with the expected uses of the final conclusions (Goodman and Kruskal 1954). This is particularly important because the same data set, combined in different ways, yields quite different tables and coefficients and can provide distinctly different impressions of the degree of association between factors.

For example, consider a study that calls for collecting *Eleutherodactylus guentheri* from four microhabitats, in which the number of frogs collected in each varies by sex and age (Table 22). Because the tabled array of data includes a number of empty cells, the researcher may wish to collapse the table to reduce the number of categories with zero values. He or she could combine the data over categories, for example, contrasting juveniles and adults collected

in the leaf litter with those collected from exposed ground or vegetation (Table 23). An alternative would be to combine terrestrial and arboreal microhabitats and compare adults and juveniles between them (Table 24). It could be argued, equally, that habitat preferences of the age groups were associated with higher and lower humidity rather than cover or height above ground. The change from a more subtle to a coarser description of habitat can affect the magnitude of the measure. Clearly, without precise definitions, inventory data cannot be summarized in a useful way with any binary coefficient.

Table 23. Alternate 1 of Collapsed Microhabitat Frequency of Occurrence Data for *Eleutherodactylus guentheri*, Contrasting Specimens from Leaf Litter with Those from Exposed Sites, for Juveniles and Adults

	Microhabitat	
Age	**In leaf litter**	**Exposed on ground or on vegetation above ground**
Juveniles	0.25	0.25
Adults	0.00	0.50

Table 24. Alternate 2 of Collapsed Microhabitat Frequency of Occurrence Data for *Eleutherodactylus guentheri*, Contrasting Specimens from Terrestrial Microhabitats with Those from Arboreal Microhabitats, for Juveniles and Adults

	Microhabitat	
Age	Terrestrial microhabitats	Arboreal microhabitats
Juveniles	0.50	0.00
Adults	0.00	0.50

In addition, it is important to remember that a test of significance in tables (e.g., with a chi-square approximation) assumes that the sample is random and that the category designations are chosen a priori. Pooling of tabled values affects randomness with undeterminable consequences and may result in meaningless calculations without statistical interpretation.

CONCEPTUAL RELATIONSHIPS

Another problem that interferes with the formulation of an operational definition of association (and its measures) is the confusion of terms used in the literature to describe association. I briefly discuss the relationships of some of these terms below.

ASSOCIATION AND INDEPENDENCE. In the frequency notation for 2×2 tables, if no association exists between species A and species B, an equal proportion of species B should be found among the samples with species A and the samples without species A. This relationship can be written as $a/(a + c) = b/(b + d) = (a + b)/n$. By rearranging this set of equations, we can alternatively say that $a = (a + b)(a + c)/n$. This algebraic statement shows that when two species are not associated, the proportion of joint occurrences (a) is equivalent to the product of the proportions of each separate species in the entire sample. If

the species are associated, then $a \neq (a + b)(a + c)/n$, and the difference could be written as $D = a-(a + b)(a + c)/n = (ad-bc)/n$, which is the term found in the formula for calculating the usual chi-square statistic (χ^2) and all of its monotonically related statistics (see Table 20: section C).

The χ^2 test is used to determine whether two species (or attributes) are independent. However, the term *independent* in this context does not imply the usual stochastic independence of the variables used to generate the 2×2 table (Kendall and Stuart 1973). Rather, in the context of association measures, independence of the variables indicates species independence (or lack of association), which may or may not coincide with stochastic independence. Likewise, although results of tests of association correspond to intuitive notions of association and independence in many situations, this is not always the case.

Consider an example of two species of *Crossodactylodes* captured in an arboreal bromeliad sampling session (Table 25). If the species are independent (lack association), the frequency in cell *a*, which indicates joint occurrences, should be $(a + b)(a + c)/n$ or $50 \cdot 49/100 = 24.5$. In fact, the observed frequency of *a* is 48, greater than expected under independence, so the two species may be said to be positively associated in this microhabitat. Alternatively, consider tadpoles of *Pseudacris crucifer* and *Rana clamitans* (Table 26) dipnetted from a series of ponds. If these two species are independent, then $50 \cdot 60/75$, or 40,

Table 25. The Occurrence of Two Species of Frogs (*Crossodactylodes* spp.) in Bromeliads

C. izecksohni	*C. bokermanni*		
	Present	Absent	Total
Present	48	2	50
Absent	1	49	50
Total	49	51	100

Table 26. Data from 75 Dipnet Samples of Tadpoles of Two Species of Frogs; Arranged in a 2 × 2 Frequency Table Using Counts

Rana clamitans	*Hyla crucifer*		Total
	Present	Absent	
Present	40	10	50
Absent	20	5	25
Total	60	15	75

joint occurrences are expected. In this instance, the observed frequency of joint occurrences (*a*) is 40, and we conclude that the tadpoles are not associated.

If the data in Table 25 are considered as a sample from an infinite population and are subjected to a chi-square test of independence, then highly significant association is indicated, in agreement with our previous statement. The cross-classified dipnet tadpole data (Table 26) yield a nonsignificant test result, which corresponds to a decision in favor of independence.

Note, however, that in the *Crossodactylodes* example, for which we indicated association, 48% of the frogs sampled co-occurred, whereas in the tadpole example, for which we indicated independence, co-occurrence was approximately 53%. Investigators should always provide operational definitions of terms before selecting or applying a measure. Otherwise, logical inconsistencies may result.

ASSOCIATION AND CORRELATION. A relationship exists between the intuitive notion of association and the statistical measure of correlation in a 2 × 2 table. However, association analyses group species based upon mutual presence, whereas correlation and covariance coefficients give a picture of the linear correlation between fluctuations in abundances of two species. Thus, even if two species co-occur 100% of the time, a correlation coefficient (e.g., Pearson's or a variant of it) will not show the relationship unless the relative numbers of individuals of the two species are constant or nearly so (Cole 1949). The assumption that the abundances (frequencies) of two positively associated species increase or decrease together is unrealistic if their association is merely the result of similar habitat requirements (Hurlbert 1969).

The correlation coefficient also is not a reasonable indicator of association when the table is asymmetric. Low correlation values do not have significance, but that does not imply, necessarily, lack of species relationship (e.g., Legrendre and Legrendre 1983). With site-by-site classifications, many of the estimated correlations are small, because a few species are abundant and others are rare (e.g., Clifford and Stephenson 1975).

TRADITIONAL ASSOCIATION MEASURES For continuous data, the strength of an association can be assessed by the reduction in variance in a dependent variable that results from knowing the value of the independent variable. For categorical variables, the variance quantity, strictly speaking, is not defined. Historically, three approaches have been used to find a substitute quantity for the desired variance (Hays 1973): statistical independence between the two attributes (measures based upon the χ^2 statistic), predictive association, and information theory. Each approach, in turn, leads to a measure by which to assess association strength.

None of these measures depends upon the order of the categories. The first approach (χ^2) is the only method commonly used in ecological studies of amphibians. Association is measured by the difference between the probability of a joint occurrence and the product of the two marginal probabilities. If two events are statistically independent, the difference should be zero. Pearson and Yule used this fact in the development of what is commonly known as the ϕ^2 statistic (Table 20: # 42).

Meaningful interpretation of measures of association based on the χ^2 statistic is difficult. None of the measures has a straightforward probabilistic interpretation, and none is widely accepted in the statistical literature. In addition, the range of many of these measures (Table 20: section C) depends on the table dimensions, so the measures are not really comparable across tables of different size.

The two other approaches to the study of association are not widely encountered in the amphibian literature and will be mentioned only briefly. The first deals with predictive association and assesses the relative utility of one factor for improving the ability to predict the second factor's categories. Two factors (e.g., species) are associated if one factor is of value for reducing the error when predicting the other (Goodman and Kruskal 1954). Goodman and Kruskal (1979) developed an asymmetric measure of predictive association, lambda (λ). This measure is intuitively appealing for amphibian studies. However, lambda depends on the marginal frequencies and may not be suitable for comparative studies across species or habitats unless sample sizes and, therefore, marginal frequencies are equal.

The final approach to studying association uses an information theory strategy to derive a variance analogue for binary data (see, e.g., Lambert and Williams 1966; Wallace and Boulton 1968; Field 1969). The derived measure is related to diversity indices and other indices for numerical data. One diversity index that can be used is Shannon's index H, which is a measure of the information given by the sample. When used with qualitative data, H can be written as an analogue of the variance of the distribution, becoming larger as the distribution spreads out along the axis and smaller as it nears the average. In general, the greater the variance, the less the information. Because of this tendency, an investigator can define an asymmetric measure of the relative gain in information about one species, given information of the other.

Association then would be defined operationally as an increase in information or a decrease in uncertainty. Sampling theory exists for this type of measure, and tests of no association are possible.

PROPERTIES OF ASSOCIATION MEASURES

Empirical and theoretical aspects of association measures related to the goals of the study should be thoroughly investigated prior to selection of a measure. Some important mathematical arguments for selection of a particular measure of association do exist, but most have been advanced to support informed opinion. Likewise, certain measures are appropriate for a unique problem but not for general use. Below and in Table 20, I consider some aspects of association indices that appear to contribute most often to the problem of selecting an appropriate measure.

RANGE OF THE MEASURE Many authors argue that a particular range of a measure (i.e., values the measure may assume, such as all values between 1 and –1) is "best" when, in fact, it is merely acceptable convention. Most of the measures in Table 20 range between limits of 0 and 1 or of 1 and –1, although some measures can assume any real-valued positive number or are undefined (e.g., cannot equal 0 in the range –1 to 1) about particular points. The importance of ranges per se is minimal, because it is quite simple to transform either of the two most popular ranges to the other with a simple linear transformation. When a coefficient C1 is defined on (0,1) and coefficient C2 is defined on (1,–1), we use:

$$C1 = (1/2)(C2 + 1)$$
$$C2 = 2C1 - 1$$

It seems reasonable to require that the limits of the range be known and achievable and that the coefficient assume the central or minimum value of its range when factors are not associated. Beyond this, the scale should be easily interpretable to the user. The popularity of the (0,1) interval coincides with the natural preference to avoid negative numbers and may be preferable when values that are symmetric about zero are not a consideration.

INVARIANCE OR HOMOGENEITY. Homogeneity means, simply, that the value of a descriptive measure is constant as long as the factors occur in the same proportions (Jansen and Vegelius 1981). Seemingly, no cogent biological reason argues for the use of a measure that is not invariant in this sense. Each coefficient is examined for this condition empirically in the Appendix at the end of this chapter (see "Examples for Invariance").

LINEARITY. The value of a coefficient should increase as the relationship from nonassociation to association strengthens. The form of this change is important for interpretation of a measure in a given study. As a minimum condition, it appears sensible to expect that a coefficient increase or decrease in a systematic way relative to association. In a mathematical sense, however, *systematic* may be defined in a variety of ways. Linearity in measures of association means equal amounts of change in the value of the coefficient when values of joint occurrence change by a factor of one. When an amphibian worker selects a coefficient as a measure of ecological resemblance, the change in values probably should be linear for ease of interpretation, because such a relationship appears to correspond best to intuition. Examples of linearity, and an evaluation of this attribute in each coefficient are given in the Appendix at the end of this chapter (see "Examples for Linearity Conditions").

CONDITIONS ON MAXIMA AND MINIMA. The set of conditions under which the value of an association measure will equal the largest and smallest values in its range must be defined. Maximum values of association indices should occur when $b = c = 0$ (e.g., Jansen and Vegelius 1981). Minima can occur when $a = d = 0$ (Jansen and Vegelius 1981), but a stronger condition would be that only $a = 0$ (Kendall and Stuart 1973; Hubalek 1982). These conditions are inherent attributes of the coefficients.

In the "Range Conditions" section of the Appendix at the end of this chapter, I show how each of the measures varies as some conditions for attaining the limits of the range (maximum and minimum) are varied. The values in the cross-classified tables are purposefully extreme to highlight the dangers of uninformed selection or of selection not based upon the operational meaning of the study. These values should be examined carefully prior to selection of a coefficient and in light of the study to be done. Questions such as the following should be asked: (1) Should the two species of the study be regarded as similar or associated largely on the basis of their shared presence only in the selected locality? (2) Should association be defined as a combination of joint occurrences and joint absences of the two species? (3) Which of the coefficients—Simpson, Dice, or Simple Matching (Table 20), for example—best adheres to my preconceptions concerning the nature of the relationship being studied?

To illustrate what Table 20 tells us, consider the latter question, focusing on the maximum. The Simpson coefficient attains its maximum under a wider set of conditions than do the other two coefficients. The Dice coefficient and the simple matching coefficient become 1 when $b = c = 0$, whereas Simpson's demands only that $b = 0$ or $c = 0$. Conditions on a and d do not affect the ability of any of the three coefficients to attain its maximum. Thus, although the three indices vary between the same limits of 0 and 1, the range does not depend solely on the proportion of species found together.

Mathematically, it is acceptable that conditions under which maximum and minimum values are attained differ, but empirically, the researcher most definitely should be aware of the specific conditions under which the measure used fluctuates.

If only one of the possible *b* and *c* cell frequencies must equal zero to achieve maximum values of association, then the association could be called *undistributed* because all *A*'s are *B*'s but not all *B*'s are *A*'s. Put in more concrete terms, if all frogs are amphibians, undistributed association exists between frogs and amphibians. The problem of what to do with the many amphibians that are not frogs is unresolved. If alternatively, we require that two cell frequencies equal zero ($b = 0$ and $c = 0$) before a coefficient can assume its upper limit, then the coefficient will equal 1 (the maximum) only if all *A*'s are *B*'s and all *B*'s are *A*'s. This kind of association is termed *proper* association and is also the absolute statistical association of Kendall and Stuart (1973).

MONOTONIC RELATIONSHIP AMONG MEASURES. A monotonic relationship exists between binary coefficients when they are related by an inequality—that is, one coefficient is always less than or equal to the other, regardless of the values in the observed table. Almost all of the traditional association measures are monotonically related to χ^2, as well as to each other (see, e.g., Hubalek 1982). When comparative analyses are run with different coefficients, it is possible to confuse predetermined monotonicities with differences caused by the data, unless the relationships of coefficients are known.

WARNINGS ABOUT INTERPRETATION

Significance tests of the chi-square type are given wide attention in ecological and bioassociational studies, but they are not a panacea. They produce approximate results dependent upon sample size that indicate a vaguely defined concept of independence between factors. Although simple and intuitively appealing, they are not applicable in all cases, as I show in the section on Species Abundance, below. If a test indicates a dependence, the investigator must ask what that dependence means for the study. The selection of an operational definition of association in keeping with the character of the study is most important at this stage.

Dice (1945) warned that the abundance of a species and the social behavior of its individuals can affect the frequency with which the species appears in a sample and, therefore, can affect measures of association. Interaction or correlation among the specimens that form the cell counts, for reasons extraneous to the association analysis, can also affect these measures. However, if the samples are drawn at random and are representative of the species, the cell frequencies may be subjected to association analysis. It is, therefore, important to emphasize that measures of association should be applied only across comparable samples. For example, coefficients cannot be used to compare samples taken from breeding habitats with samples from nonbreeding habitats, because the a priori expectation is one of marked difference (i.e., nonassociation). The fundamental feature of the approach is the assumption of an association of the two species, observable when their presence-absence is recorded in the same sample.

Association analysis cannot usually be applied to samples from a very large and heterogeneous area unless the species and habitats sampled have been judiciously selected. Alternatively, if a sample plot is relatively small, species are likely to occur in only a small proportion of the space, and all will appear to be rare. Hohn (1976) showed that when two taxa occur in a majority of samples, a similarity coefficient will be high even if the taxa can be described by an effectively random distribution; such a coefficient lacks meaning because the total number of samples is not considered. The most efficient measure of association is obtainable when the more abundant of the species occurs in about half of the samples in the group (Dice 1945).

Generally, an association analysis is applicable only to the particular habitat and time of the sample. The dimensions or conditions of the sample (time, place, size), therefore, must be clearly delineated and described. If the same sampling considerations described above apply, samples taken over time can also be compared.

Despite the most scrupulous presentation, it is still possible that the association of two species is only accidental—that is, that it reflects a chance selection by the two species of the same habitat at the moment of sampling for specific but independent reasons. Because the primary causes of variation in associative frequencies cannot be distinguished merely from inspection of a list of coefficients, Forbes (1907) and others suggested an accompanying study of species distributions to differentiate between local population effects (e.g., abundance, rarity) and general ecological factors (e.g., climate, topography, hydrography).

SUMMARY AND RECOMMENDATIONS

Significance tests and binary measures of association are distinct. If investigation of independence is the aim, the observed frequencies of co-occurrence of the two factors in the 2×2 table should be examined to determine if, indeed, a statistically significant dependence relationship exists. If the relationship cannot be distinguished from random occurrence, there is no basis for continued study, although extended sampling to increase frequencies could be beneficial. When the test shows the relationship to be significant, the size of this relationship can be examined with a judiciously selected binary coefficient whose form describes the sampling situation operationally and is in keeping with the study purposes.

Alternatively, binary coefficients may be used simply to describe an associative relationship

between two factors without concern for independence testing. In this case the intended meaning of association (see "Conceptual Relationships," above), as well as the operational descriptors of the study situation, must be reflected in the choice of a measure.

Standardization in this section on presence-absence data cannot be extended to a delineation of conditions for the selection of a single coefficient. In fact, Hubalek (1982) recommended that "three or so" alternative coefficients be used and compared for each data set. I prefer the development of an underlying rationale for selection in keeping with the study objectives. To make a final selection of a coefficient, the definition of association must be a meaningful reflection of the study design and purposes.

Species abundance

Individual Counts and Proportions

A monitoring project can produce abundance data, or counts of individuals, n_i, for $i = 1, \ldots, s$ species. These numbers also can be presented in the form of proportions (when divided by the related total number for all species). In this section I describe several methods for the examination of this type of data. I begin with the R × C table organization for R rows and C columns and detail the specific 2×2 case, which is common for analysis of amphibian data.

OBSERVED SITUATIONS

It is often important in biology to test whether the frequencies of observations in a series of categories are the same. The observed distribution of abundances among categories defined by species and their occurrences is of interest for amphibian sampling studies. The hypothesis of homogeneity—for example, across **k** classes when a set of abundances (n_i) or occurrences has been observed—may be tested in different ways.

The selection of an appropriate test depends substantially on the relevant aspects of a particular data set.

It is usual to summarize individual counts or abundance data across some factor (e.g., sex, height above ground) by using the numbers obtained directly or after adjustment for sampling, in a cross tabulation for analysis by a test such as chi-square. Factors such as height are ordered, whereas factors such as sex are unordered. In some situations, the same factors or variables may be observed at two different times or in two related samples (e.g., juvenile and adult); this is called identical categorization.

For a general table with R rows and C columns, each cell shows the frequency of one possible joint event that occurred in the data (say, a shared presence at a given height on a gradient). The general assumption is that a *joint frequency distribution* represents the spread of frequencies in the table cells. However, if one factor is fixed rather than random, it is not meaningful to talk of a joint distribution. The *joint probability distribution* in the population, which corresponds to the joint frequency distribution for a sample, is described in Table 27. For a table with this type of organization, the marginal distributions give information on only a single variable. For a fixed value of factor *A*, one can look at the *B* probability distribution (called the *conditional distribution* of *B* at level *i* of *A* in a selected column). For example, an investigator interested in eleva-

tional gradients could compare conditional distributions of *B* at various elevations.

Given these probabilities, we could ask if the joint probability distribution is of some exact form. Distributions of some exact form are unusual in amphibian biodiversity work. Instead, frequencies or proportions are used as unbiased estimates of these probabilities, and a test is applied to ask questions about the independence of the tabled factors.

SIZE OF THE SAMPLE

From a purely statistical point of view, the size of a sample affects only the magnitude of the difference in proportions expected to result in a statistically significant test outcome for the stated type 1 error risk. A small sample may suffice if, in the long run, the average proportions are greatly different for the two groups. If they are not very different, a statistically significant result is not expected unless a large sample is obtained. This is the problem of substantive significance, which is discussed in Chapter 4 (see "Statistical versus Substantive Significance"). Computations are less complicated for small samples, but a strong biological association effect must exist to be termed statistically significant when samples are not large, and small samples may not well represent the true population heterogeneity. Thus, a small sample contains a penalty for the investigator in terms of the inferences to be drawn from the statistics, only if it is, in reality, a rather close call. If a significant result can be observed despite a small sample size, then the statistical conclusion is that the finding has substantial merit. With any statistic whose sampling distribution involves the number of individuals, a significance test can almost always be set to any level of false rejection risk; that is, the usual type 1 error risk (e.g., 0.05) can be used with any small number of observations, if power is sacrificed.

Table 27. Generalized Joint Probability Distribution

		A		**Total**
B	$p(A_1B_1)$	$p(A_2B_1)$	$p(A \mid B_1)$
	$p(A_1B_2)$	$p(A_2B_2)$	$p(A \mid B_2)$
Total	$p(B \mid A_1)$	$p(B \mid A_2)$	1.00

TERMINOLOGY

RATES, PROPORTIONS, AND PERCENTAGES. The terms rate and proportion are often used interchangeably, but the terms differ. *Rate* means a given amount of something per unit of something else. The latter item may be a count or a period of time or it may be an entity such as area of habitat. The division of the two quantities yields the rate—for example, the number of species per quadrat. With rate, the units of measure in the numerator differ from those in the denominator. Conceptually, a rate is a dynamic measure relating to change. Alternatively, a *proportion* is the size of a subset, or portion, of the whole relative to that whole. It is essentially a static measure or a measure of what prevails at a given time or in a given place. A proportion is expressed as a fraction; the subset is the numerator and the whole is the denominator, and the units of measure in both the numerator and the denominator are the same. Proportions occupy a scale of zero to one. For example, a 50-ha lake might include 40 ha of open water; the proportion of open water in the lake would be 0.8. *Percentages* are rescaled proportions, that is, proportions on a scale from zero to 100. Percentages are obtained by multiplying proportions by 100. Thus, in our example, 80% of the lake is open water. There is no substantive difference between the two quantities. However, in statistics it is usual to perform calculations on proportions.

The term *ratio* is defined in a much more general sense. It is the result of the division of any two numbers. Alternative terms are *quotient* and *fraction*. In biodiversity work, the denominator of a percentage is often a known quantity with no variance. For example, when density is expressed as number of individuals per area, area is effectively invariant and the variance of the percentage is merely a transformation of the numerator's variance. Alternatively, both the numerators and the denominators of the ratios used in biodiversity studies often have associated variances.

COMPARISONS. Different types of descriptive comparison should be used carefully to avoid confusion. For example, let us say that a particular sample includes 60 specimens of *Hyla microps* and 30 of *Hyla minuta* and that a comparison is desired.

The type of comparison in which we say that there are 30 more *H. microps* specimens than *H. minuta* specimens (or 30 fewer *H. minuta* than *H. microps*) is called an *absolute comparison*. The *absolute difference* in number of specimens is 30. Absolute comparisons can be made only when the items compared are expressed in equal units.

A statement that breeding males of *H. microps* are twice as common as breeding males of *H. minuta* (or that *H. minuta* are half as common as the *H. microps*) is a relative comparison. This type of comparison demands not only equal units but also a definite zero point or ratio scale. For example, it is incorrect to say that a temperature of 100° Fahrenheit is twice as warm as one of 50°, because the zero point on the Fahrenheit scale is arbitrary and does not correspond to absolute lack of warmth.

Relative comparisons may be expressed as percentages. If we use the specimens of *H. minuta* as the base of comparison, 30 specimens is equivalent to 100%, and the number of *H. microps* specimens is equivalent to (60/30) · 100, or 200%. The number of specimens of *H. microps* is 100% greater than the number of *H. minuta* specimens, which is equivalent to the earlier statement of the relative comparison the species (i.e., that *H. microps* is twice as common as *H. minuta*). Alternatively, the specimens of *H. microps* can be used as the base, and we find that the specimens of *H. minuta* represent only 50% of those of *H. microps,* or number 50%

fewer (i.e., *H. minuta* is half as common as *H. microps*).

USE OF PERCENTAGE COMPARISONS. The seemingly trivial distinctions between relative and absolute comparisons and between proportion and percentage are important, because the terms are frequently confused and because their misuse leads to misunderstandings. Some guidelines for use of these expressions follow.

Consider, for example, that any zero value is 100% smaller than any nonzero quantity, and that no positive non-zero quantity can be more than 100% less than another. Given these conditions, a report that the average number of breeding males of *Hyalinobatrachium valerioi* fell 150% from one year to the next is impossible, and there is no way to understand the correct meaning of the statement. Confusion can be alleviated by avoiding expression of relative comparisons as percentages or by always stating clearly the base that is being used.

Suppose that some quantity is observed to rise from 60% to 70%. This is an absolute rise of 10% (70% – 60%) or a relative rise of 16.7% [(70% – 60%)/60%]. Quotation of the increase in absolute terms clarifies the situation; for example, "There was a rise of 10%, from 60% to 70%."

Percentages should not be used to describe change unless all figures are changing in the same direction, that is, unless changes are all positive or all negative.

When relative comparisons are made between or among figures that differ in orders of magnitude, percentages should be avoided. For example, one could say that the breeding population of males observed within an enclosure was about 2,000% larger than the sample of nonbreeding males. This expression might be correct, but it is not as clear as the statement that one population was about 20 times larger than the other.

Because an incorrect preposition or description can affect interpretation, absolute counts or numbers should always be given when percentages or proportions are used. Consider the following statements.

1. The average number of *Ololygon hayii* in the sample was 200% *of* the average number of *Hyla polytaenia*.
2. The average number of *O. hayii* was 100% *larger than* that of *H. polytaenia*.
3. The average number *O. hayii* in the sample was 200% *more than* that of *H. polytaenia*.

Is the average number of *O. hayii* per sample two or three times that of *H. polytaenia*?

Even when the hypothesis of interest legitimately involves a proportion, actual counts or frequencies also should be presented. For example, if an investigator reports that 60% of a sample was found to be tagged on recapture, whereas only 50% of the sample was tagged the last time the area was sampled, then it is difficult to know whether a change has occurred. In contrast, reports of the figures of 3 out of 5 (60%) and 500 out of 1,000 (50%), provide better information for evaluation. The sampling situation is made clear (i.e., a sample of 5 versus as sample of 1,000), and the biological significance of the figures can be readily assessed.

Interrelationships of Standard Tests

The same tabular arrangement of data can be used to examine proportional and absolute abundances. In this section I discuss the equivalence of many of the common test statistics for both types of abundance data.

COUNTS AND PROPORTIONS

The number of counts or observations in a sample of size *n*, as well as the proportion of observations, can be seen as random variables. The distribution of sample proportions can be described by the *binomial distribution* (assuming sampling with replacement or a sufficiently large sample). The probability (p) of any proportion (P) of observations being found in a sample of size $\boldsymbol{n}$ is exactly the same as the probability of that number of observations (r) being found. Thus,

$$p(X = r) = p(P = X/n)$$

and the only difference between the equations is the random variable that is being considered: X, the count, or X/n, the proportion. The basic test of significance of association performed on the frequencies in the contingency table is therefore related to the test of the equality of the proportions formed from the tabled frequencies.

TESTS ON R × C TABLES

In general, observed data are tested for significance by calculating a particular statistic that is then compared with the tail area of some appropriate theoretical distribution for determining significance. When the observed data are counts that can be arranged in tabular or cross-classified form, the underlying or comparative distribution usually is the multinomial. That is, if the identical probability distribution applies across all observations, and if all n observations are independent, then the counts per species are multinomially distributed, and the marginal distribution is binomial.

The traditional chi-square tests of goodness of fit and independence for R × C tables and the likelihood ratio (G test) are each approximations for this multinomial distribution. They test the goodness of fit of the observed frequencies to a theoretical distribution assumed to fit the observed sample or the sampled population. Although treated as distinct in most texts, these interrelated tests are equivalent under some circumstances.

TESTS ON 2 × 2 TABLES

When the table is 2 × 2, the usual Pearson chi-square statistic yields the same value as z^2, the square of the standardized normal variable, ap-

plied to the problem of testing for a single proportion. That is,

$$z^2 = \chi^2$$

or

$$z = |\sqrt{\chi^2}|$$

In addition, if the two proportions of interest are $p_1 = a/(a + b)$ and $p_2 = c/(c + d)$, we can form

$$p = \frac{a + c}{n} = 1 - q$$

to test the difference of these proportions. We use

$$t = \frac{p_1 - p_2}{\left[pq\left(\dfrac{1}{n_1} + \dfrac{1}{n_2} \right) \right]^{1/2}}$$

to calculate t, which can be compared with a Student t table. For a Yates correction, we form

$$t_c = |p_1 - p_2| - \frac{1}{2} \frac{\left(\dfrac{1}{n_1} + \dfrac{1}{n_2} \right)}{\left[pq\left(\dfrac{1}{n_1} + \dfrac{1}{n_2} \right) \right]^{1/2}}$$

which is a Studentized version of the χ^2 statistic.

Each of these statistics can be formed from the values in the single 2 × 2 table and can be used interchangeably to test the hypothesis of interest.

Model-Based Methods

Usually categorical data are analyzed by the classical analytical methods described above. However, in the early 1960s, model-based methods were developed with broad analogues to general linear models (especially regression models) for continuous variables. These models do not assume a normal distribution but instead have been based primarily upon binomial, multinomial, and Poisson distributions. *Dependence models* usually correspond to conditional probabilities of a dependent or response variable, given a set of independent or explanatory variables. *Association models* correspond to joint probability distributions when the underlying variables are considered as equivalent, not causative. The theory behind these models is well developed, and sampling theory has been examined, at least in part, empirically as well as theoretically. These models provide a promising new approach for some of the more advanced analysis of amphibian data. At present, these model-based methods are being incorporated into computer packages, which should spur their use.

Advice about Tests for R × C Tables

The apparent simplicity and clearness of tests on categorical data hide a basic problem inherent in their application. Starting with different premises about the data, it is possible to reach quite distinct numerical probability figures for the same table. It is these figures that are used to judge the significance of the data in the table. With tests for independence, an investigator must also be concerned about operationalization of the study design because more than one test may be appropriate, and each test could lead to a different observed probability level. For example, at least seven test procedures are available for comparing binomial proportions and can lead to varied answers (Storer and Kim 1990). In practice, probability figures derived from an analysis of observed data help shape conclusions of a study; however, the form of these probabilities likely is a matter of opinion.

ASSUMPTIONS FOR PEARSON'S CHI-SQUARE TEST

The computational simplicity of the chi-square test is deceptive in that it is based on a fairly elaborate mathematical rationale and therefore requires some important assumptions (Hays 1973). Three assumptions are of concern.

The first assumption is that each observation is independent of every other. Repeated observation of some or all of the same individuals in the samples may negate use of the chi-square and related tests. The novice user should consider these tests only when each animal contributes to one and only one cell.

The second assumption is that cells are well defined, so that each observation can be placed in one and only one cell. Because a joint frequency distribution is assumed, rather than just that the cells contain observed numbers, each amphibian or observation must be classifiable into only one unique row and one unique column.

The third assumption is that the sample size is large enough for the asymptotic theory to hold. However, there are no generalized rules for knowing when this assumption is true, that is, for knowing how well the approximation fits the multinomial.

PROBLEMS IN THE APPLICATION OF CHI-SQUARE

No rules can explicitly cover all practical situations involving problems with fit for the chi-square statistic; therefore, no rule will tell how close the observed level of significance (from the computer program or the hand calculations) is to the correct one.

An index, *h,* to the amount of bias can be used to identify situations in which bias is large enough to be of consequence to the test. The index is calculated as follows:

$$h = \frac{\sum\limits_{i=1}^{k} \frac{1}{e_i} - \frac{k}{n}}{[32(k-1)]^{1/2}}$$

or

$$h = \frac{\sum\limits_{i=1}^{k} e_i \left(\frac{1}{e_i} - \frac{k}{n}\right)^2}{[32(k-1)]^{1/2}}$$

for the total k cells in the table and for the e_i expected values in the k cells.

The χ^2 statistic is biased whenever **h** is not zero. Values of h that exceed 0.1 warn that bias may exist; values of h that exceed 1 indicate serious problems with bias, in which the statistic is systematically distorted and not representative of the true value for the distribution. This bias can be as large as the size of the test α even though the chi-square approximation is valid. Although it may not be possible to correct this bias in some cases, calculation of h will help prevent misinterpretation of p levels.

In practice, we know that chi-square is an approximation and, in addition, that the estimator χ^2 is *inconsistent,* or does not converge in probability to the parameter it estimates, as sample size increases. It is wise, therefore, when noting the observed probability, not to consider as correct any obtained value near to the desired level of the test.

SAMPLE SIZE, CELL SIZE, AND BIAS. When sample sizes are small or expected cell sizes are small or highly variable, the Pearson and the likelihood ratio chi-square statistics may be substantially biased (Chapman 1976; Haberman 1988). Zelterman (1986) devised a test statistic that corrects bias when h > 1. Baglivo et al. (1988) provided methods to calculate corrected tail probabilities when exact methods are not feasible.

Tate and Hyer (1973) noted that chi-square yields many identical outcome values when expectations are small or variable, but that the multinomial probabilities become distinct as the number of categories increases. The authors used these observations to explain why, when the expected values per cell remain small, the chi-square approximation is inconsistent (varies) as sample size increases. Identical outcome values are less likely to occur with the log likelihood ratio (Cochran 1936).

Conahan (1970) compared the χ^2 statistic, the log likelihood function, and the exact multinomial probability when expected frequencies are small and found that the likelihood ratio test is best when the number of categories is at least five and the expected value for each cell is at least 3. He concluded that (1) the likelihood function is an adequate (but not perfect) approximation to the exact multinomial when expected values per cell are greater than 10; (2) the multinomial should be used directly when there are five or more categories and the expected value for each cell is less than 3; and (3) the log likelihood function should be used with five or more categories when the expected value for each cell is greater than or equal to 3.

Agresti (1990) recommended that the log likelihood ratio be used when n/RC < 5. He also claimed that when the R or C value is large, the χ^2 approximation can be "decent" with n/RC as small as 1, if the table does not contain both very large and very small expected cell values.

MINIMUM CELL SIZE. An issue of constant concern is the minimum expected frequency for a cell in a table. The value of 5 appears to have become a convention, but there seems to be no theoretical or widespread empirical basis for this choice. Total sample size has been suggested as a more appropriate criterion for goodness-of-fit tests, but the distribution of the frequencies within the cells is also important. Expected cell frequencies as low as 3 or even 1 have been investigated and have proven adequate (Conahan 1970; Agresti 1990).

Cohen and Sackrowitz (1975) showed that the chi-square test is unbiased if each expected cell frequency equals *n/k,* but that is a highly unlikely event in amphibian observational studies.

For these reasons, and because most studies for independence are compared with a uniform case in amphibian work, I suggest that an average expected frequency (i.e., $\overline{E} = n$/RC) of 5, which appears adequate from both biological and statistical standpoints, be used. This average is considerably less restrictive and easier to obtain, given the vagaries of amphibian sampling, than a minimum expected frequency of 5.

FISHER'S EXACT TEST

An alternative to the chi-square and likelihood ratio tests is Fisher's Exact Test. It is rarely used for large tables, because the computations seemingly would be impractically large, but its underlying theory is applicable to R × C tables. Pagano and Halvorsen (1981) developed a computational algorithm that is easily programmed on a desk microcomputer. Mehta and Patel (1983) provided what they asserted is a more efficient algorithm for the same calculation. For 2 × 2 tables, a form of Fisher's procedure is uniformly the most powerful and unbiased test (see "Fisher's Exact Test" under "Advice about Test for 2 × 2 Tables," below). The same is not true when Fisher's test is used for data in R × C tables. Therefore, even though Fisher's procedure could yield a correct significance level for an R × C table by use of Mehta and Patel's method, other methods may be superior. As the cell expectations become large, the exact values approach those from the chi-square distribution, and the χ^2 and Fisher's tests are equivalent.

TESTS FOR TREND IN PROPORTIONS

The usual tests (χ^2 and G^2) treat factors as having nominal scales. If data follow an ordinal scale or have another intrinsic order, then information is being ignored with these tests, and a more powerful test of independence should be used.

A tabled array with two rows and any number of columns (C) greater than two is often of interest in ecological studies because of the possible existence of a trend. This occurs, for example, with the presence or absence of some attribute across C samples. To reveal the presence of a trend in the data, a modified form of the general χ^2 formula is used, and both exact and approximate methods are available for parametric estimation. The C samples are binomially distributed with expected probability of success constant. The test is one of homogeneity of the samples. Many procedures are available for testing for trend.

Yates (1948) dealt specifically with groupings based on direct quantitative characters and discussed many tests for trend over categories. Armitage (1955) discussed tests for linear trend. Wood (1978) provided a comparison of methods for trend detection with one quantitative and one qualitative factor. Lee (1980) provided a test in the general table array for multinomial data. These tests are becoming more widely available in statistical packages, but, to my knowledge, have not been evaluated empirically. Nam (1987) determined minimal but approximate sample sizes for detecting linear trend in proportions.

Advice about Tests for 2 × 2 Tables

CHI-SQUARE TEST STATISTIC

For tests of independence with 2 × 2 tables, the Pearson chi-square, with its inherent bias problems, is usually used even though it is only applicable for a large *n*. The statistic (Table 20: # 38) used for testing is

$$\chi^2 = \frac{n(ad - bc)^2}{(a + c)(b + d)(a + b)(c + d)}$$

Its actual distribution function is discrete and not easily specifiable, so the continuous chi-square distribution found in most statistics texts is still used as an approximation for the probability statements.

Berkson (1978) used a normal variate, $z = |\sqrt{\chi^2}|$, and found it superior for a range of sizes when the random (nonfixed) margins were of equal sizes (see note 3 at the end of this chapter). D'Agostino et al. (1988) showed that for $n \leq 15$, the two-independent-sample t-test with pooled variance and the uncorrected χ^2 were both robust in the actual levels of significance and close to or smaller than the nominal level (see note 3). However, this pooled t is only slightly more robust than the usual uncorrected χ^2 (Heeren and d'Agostino 1987) under limited conditions, so that either this uncorrected statistic or the z is probably just as appropriate.

FIXED AND RANDOM CLASSIFICATION FACTORS

In tests for independence in 2×2 tables (as well as general R $\times$ C tables), each expected cell frequency is the product of the frequency in the column (the column marginal) and the frequency in the row (the row marginal) divided by the total sample size (Barnard 1947; Pearson 1947). Forming these expected values depends (or is conditional) on only the four marginals and the total sample size. Therefore, different methods of obtaining the samples could lead to the approximation of different underlying distributions and, in turn, require different test statistics. There are three possibilities: (1) Both marginal totals (sample sizes) are fixed; (2) one marginal is fixed and the other is random or free to vary during the sampling; (3) both marginals are random. (This problem is discussed, and each of the three sampling situations is examined in note 1 at the end of this chapter.)

FISHER'S EXACT TEST

Fisher (1935) developed a test based upon the hypergeometric distribution only for the case in which marginals are fixed, which appeared to solve the problem of testing small samples in 2×2 tables. Fisher's Exact Test is thus actually based only on one possible case but is used for tables described by all three cases. The power of the test when applied in each of these three cases is quite distinct (e.g., Bennett and Hsu 1960). The power differs because it is related to the alternative, not the null, hypothesis, and the former is distinct in the three cases, as might be expected.

The exact test devised by Fisher is the subject of some commonly held misconceptions. When Fisher's Exact Test is used, the probability level usually is reported and interpreted in the literature as being exact. However, the term *exact* has at least two senses in statistics. *Exact* can refer to the underlying distribution, meaning that it is an exact representation of the sampling situation you intended to encounter or have encountered. *Exact* also can refer to the test level; for example, an investigator may wish to perform a test with α at exactly the 0.05 level.

For Fisher's Exact Test, the term *exact* means that the method provides the exact probability of observing a result identical to a more extreme case, according to the underlying distribution. This assumes that the given 2×2 table was generated by sampling from a four-variable hypergeometric distribution, which is strictly applicable only for the fixed marginals case. This distribution is discrete, not continuous, and therefore cannot give a test with a predetermined significance level of α.

Because of this discreteness, the observed level of significance will always be less than or equal to the true level; the observed value will depend upon the fixed marginal frequencies. That is, the test is *conservative*. It results in an unnecessary loss of power, but whether the test is considered conservative or destructive depends upon whose interests are being served (Berkson 1978).

Tocher (1950) showed that if Fisher's test is turned into a randomized test, it is exact in both senses, as well as being the uniformly most powerful, unbiased test available under any of the three described conditions of the marginals. In other words, the test, when randomized, is robust under variations in the basic model and therefore could be important for amphibian work. However, this randomized version is not the Fisher's Exact Test that is available in texts and computer packages, and I agree with most statisticians and developers of computer packages that randomizing is not worth the effort.

YATES'S CONTINUITY CORRECTION
TO CHI-SQUARE

In 1934, Yates proposed a so-called correction for continuity for use when the χ^2 is applied. This correction of χ^2 is the one most widely used in biological applications and is used (as are other corrections, e.g., Kendall and Stuart 1973) to bring the obtained probabilities more in line with those that would be obtained with Fisher's Exact Test. This test has become the standard against which all other tests are compared, although the randomized version of Fisher's test is actually the correct standard, as is discussed in the previous section.

The χ^2 statistic involves only cell frequencies that are non-negative integers. Therefore, Yates subtracted the amount $1/2$ from the cell frequency sums to adjust mathematically for the problem of a discrete distribution by correcting for the noncontinuity in the possible outcomes. Nevertheless, it is disconcerting to a researcher to obtain a chi-square value that indicates hypothesis rejection and then to calculate a "corrected" value that indicates a nonsignificant result.

Plackett (1964) and Grizzle (1967) showed that Yates's approach corrected too much, resulting in an excessively conservative test. In contrast, Mantel and Greenhouse (1968) argued that because the hypergeometric model can describe the 2×2 tabled data (both marginals and total size fixed), the continuity correction is indeed appropriate in this one situation, a point also made in general terms by Pearson (1947). (See note 2 for a discussion of the use of the continuity correction for each of the three sampling situations that can describe data for a 2×2 table.)

CORRELATED PROPORTIONS

Observations that are not independent are also of interest in amphibian work. For example, two observers may judge the same aspect of some characteristic (e.g., duration of call, distance from call, species presence or absence) of a sample of frogs. The observers' ratings are independent, but the same frogs are observed. The question is whether the two observers rated the characteristics in the same way—for example, whether they rated the same proportion of calls as strong or weak or as near or far from the base point. In this case, each sample or observed proportion is, at least partially, based upon the same frogs, so the proportions are dependent.

McNemar (1947) devised an "exact" test of the hypothesis that the two proportions are equal, using the binomial distribution. Cochran (1950) generalized this test to situations involving repeated measurements in more general tables ($2 \times C$) but in which the dependent variable remained binary. Schork and Williams (1980) gave the exact power function and constructed sample size tables for pairs of correlated proportions, and Patil (1975) provided an exact distribution for the statistic.

Summary and Recommendations

CAVEATS

For any single 2×2 contingency table, there are many choices of statistics that can lead to quite distinct values for the final observed probabilities. The investigator must choose how many margins are fixed; this decision, in turn, determines the number of random variables in the study, the number of possible outcomes in the probability space, and the form of the descriptive underlying distribution.

Nevertheless, Fisher (1935) developed an "exact" test. Some argued that this test would suffice for any table, but they did not prove that the test is uniformly the most powerful and unbiased. Rather, Fisher's Exact Test with randomization was the subject of the proof. However, the randomized version is never available in practice and cannot be considered a practical choice.

Mathematical statisticians disagree on which test method is most appropriate. Philosophical arguments are strong, convincing, and correct on many sides. As for practical advice, three points are most vital to remember when testing categorized data.

1. There is no single correct method. The standard for correctness of the approach is determined by the problem to be solved, the study design, and the hypothesis being tested.
2. Unless there is a clear winner on power and feasibility of use, several tests may be appropriate.
3. There may be no "exact" answer even after an appropriate test has been selected. It may not be possible to perform a test at exactly the desired level of significance or to obtain an answer that the investigator considers to be correct. The most one can hope to obtain is the closest approximation; even then, the meaning of *closest* is different under different circumstances. If the observed value is close to a decision level of the test, it indicates caution, not decision.

D'Agostino et al. (1988) pointed out that major statistical packages (e.g., SAS, SPSS, BMDP) have incorporated the traditional approach of χ^2 for large samples, χ^2 with Yates's correction for intermediate-sized samples, and the Fisher's Exact Test for small samples. All of these packages issue warnings about small expected values. This practice does not mean that sample size is the best determinant for test selection; it means that this is what someone has decided is feasible for computer packages.

The statistical approach used by an investigator who keeps these cautions in mind will always be defensible and, with wise and cautious application, these suggestions will not lead anyone astray.

2 × 2 TABLES

When no margins are fixed, the uncorrected χ^2 should be used regardless of sample size. When one margin is fixed, neither Fisher's Exact Test nor Yates's corrected chi-square is appropriate. If the t with pooled variance (d'Agostino et al. 1988) is not readily available or programmable, a program for the usual t-test may be employed with fixed sample means of $\overline{X}_1 = a/(a + c)$ and $\overline{X}_2 = b/(b + d)$ equated to the sample proportion of successes $(a + c)/n$ in the null hypothesis. Yates's correction should not be used, especially for sample sizes greater than 30. For amphibian samples, I am unconvinced of the need to consider ancillary statistics.

In situations when both margins and the total sample size are fixed, if the margins are equal, Fisher's Exact Test or Yates's correction to Pearson's chi-square is the test of choice. Recall, however, that the hypergeometric probability calculations are the exact values sought. These calculation are available in many statistical computer packages. If the margins are unequal, I recommend use of the uncorrected χ^2 regardless of sample size.

R × C TABLES

Under conditions in which both n and expected values are large, the chi-square distribution should fit reasonably well, and the usual χ^2 or the G^2 may be used with confidence.

Under conditions of large n and small or variable expected values, the χ^2 or G^2 test statistic, available in large statistical packages for computers, can be used with the simultaneous calculation of h for identification of bias problems. The method of Mehta and Patel (1983) is of value for the calculation of exact probabilities. This calculation is easily programmed and should avoid some of the difficulties of the approximations for the case of a hypergeometric distribution.

When both n and expected values are small, Conahan's (1970) recommendations could be applicable. However, if conditions of sampling prevent an investigator from obtaining a sample of sufficient size, then the methods of analysis and the questions asked should be reevaluated, and expert guidance may be necessary.

Species density and continuously distributed data

Species density can refer to the number of species or to the number of individuals of a species found per unit of area, time, or effort. Density values are derived from actual counts of individuals or species. Because these counts and the standard methods for obtaining them, rather than measures derived from them, are the focus of this book, I discuss only a few approaches to the analysis of such measures.

Species density, as well as number of individuals caught from each species, may be treated as continuously distributed data for the purpose of statistical tests under certain circumstances. Many peripheral variables (e.g., environmental factors such as temperature, water depth) also may be considered to be continuously distributed. The common justification for calling a variable "continuous" is that between any two of its values, it is theoretically possible to obtain another. In fact, regardless of whether a variable under study is termed discrete or continuous, most often the measurements themselves are discrete because of limits to the precision of measuring instruments and constraints imposed by numbering systems. Thus, a continuous variable could be defined as a variable for which a value intermediate between any two obtained values is meaningful. Theoretically, an investigator could measure an amphibian's age to the nearest year, month, day, or even minute, but there is a limit to the fineness of the recording. Hence, the "continuous" variable of age actually is recorded as discrete measurements, yet between ages 1 and 2, the value of 1.75 has meaning. The obtained values as well as the intermediate value can be evaluated for both *accuracy* (closeness of the value to the quantity intended to be observed or used) and *precision* (reproducibility).

Continuously distributed variables can be subjected to a wide variety of both univariate and multivariate statistical treatments, depending upon the questions asked. Many texts discuss these techniques, both descriptive and inferential, for the study of density and its relationship to ancillary data collected in the field. However, because of the vagaries of the data, expert advice should be sought when dealing with questions about such relationships and associated threats to validity.

Graphical Representation

Hypotheses of interest with density studies usually specify a relationship—for example, "Density of *Eleutherodactylus brandsfordii* increases as depth of forest litter increases." It is often of interest to characterize the form of that relationship, as well as to test it. When two or three variables or characteristics are involved, there is no substitute for a plot for obtaining information on both the general shape and the scatter of the field results. Such a pictorial representation is indispensable for the development of the appropriate statistical strategy and will often save computing time. Fienberg (1979) provided a simple taxonomy of visual methods for data display to characterize the state of graphics, including computer generated plots. These same graphical displays, or innovative adaptations of them, are described by Chambers et al. (1983) and can be found in many good computer packages.

Hypothesized relationships must always be examined graphically before the application of any model or analytical technique. The plotted data will show whether the relationship effectively represents the situation. They also can show whether nonlinearity rather than lack of substantive relatedness, is the cause of a small correlation coefficient. Atkinson (1985) provided some illuminating examples of such problems.

Descriptive Statistics

Once preliminary graphs have been obtained and examined for the existence of hypothesized relationships between density and ancillary variables, simple descriptive measures should be obtained. Mallows (1979) provided a readable account of robust descriptive methods, as do most ecology texts.

Lately, it has become fashionable to deemphasize or even eliminate elementary descriptive statistics in favor of multivariate statistical treatment, which is deemed more sophisticated and difficult and, therefore, "better." No knowledgeable statistician would begin an analysis at the multivariate stage, and logic precludes this tactic. The existence of an overall multivariate effect does not indicate the nature or even necessarily the existence of univariate effects. A great portion of the most useful work done with field sampling data consists in simply arranging the masses of data into a comprehensible form. Summarization into descriptive measures, tables, and plots allows attention to be focused on patterns and possible substantive interactions.

Manipulation of field data or compilation into standard tabled summaries is fruitless, in general, unless carried out under the discerning eye of an expert. Successful statistical description demands subject matter expertise. Amphibian experts, among others, have increasingly tended to abnegate this responsibility. Statisticians, as well as those who apply statistical methodology and terminology to their studies, have intimidated others into using only significant results of hypothesis tests to define scientific merit. This is a critical defect in the process. One must rely on the opinions and knowledge of experts to define substance and to ensure that substantive effects are under consideration.

Species diversity

The concept of species diversity is variously and chaotically defined in the literature. It probably originated with Jaccard (1908, 1912) and Gleason (1922), who proposed the first species diversity indices. Despite considerable interest in the concept, no generally accepted definition of diversity has emerged (Peet 1974). By 1967, complaints concerning the lack of an operational definition were rampant (McIntosh 1967), and Hurlbert (1971) was of the opinion that diversity per se does not exist.

Basically, *diversity* includes two concepts: *richness* (number of species) and *evenness* (distribution of individuals among species). Thus, a statement that the tropics are more diverse than temperate zones implies that there are more species in the tropics and that each such species has, on average, proportionally fewer individuals than comparable species outside the tropics. Diversity measures should be clear in their incorporation of these two concepts. The basic mathematical theme underlying diversity is the pattern of allocation of a given quantity (abundance) among a number of well-defined divisions or categories (species), and the fundamental problem is the determination of the evenness of this apportionment.

In the following sections, I describe diversity measures that can be used with each type of data (e.g., species lists, species abundances) normally obtained from inventory or monitoring studies, and I discuss their limitations and advantages.

Inventories and Richness

SPECIES LISTS

When an investigator performs an inventory, he or she obtains a list of species. This basic species count for a taxonomic group is the simplest and most common measure of species diversity (Caughley 1977; Kempton 1979). The count, first identified as *species number* (Lloyd and Ghelardi 1964) and then redefined as *species richness* (McIntosh 1967; Hurlbert 1969), is observed independent of area sampled or time. Nevertheless, diversity measured as the number of frog species in a single pond in the midwestern United States during a breeding season has an intrinsic meaning different from diversity measured as the number of frog species in the Serra da Mantiqueira of Brazil. Likewise, direct counts cannot be used to compare two populations of frogs if one is fossorial and the other is arboreal, because an extraneous (environmental) factor impinges too greatly upon the species' populations to allow for comparison.

A species count is a simple quantitative aspect of diversity; it cannot be related to the fundamental nature of the diversity concept, although it is a basic component of any study of biological diversity. In addition, this seemingly unambiguous and direct measure in fact depends on the sample size (number of individuals) obtained, which in turn depends on the nature of the target populations and the time spent searching. This dependence is clearly illustrated when different-size samples from the same assemblage are compared; as sample size increases, "diversity" also increases, sometimes without apparent limit (Taylor et al. 1976). The same is true for full censuses (not samples) from similar macro-

habitats (Connell and Orais 1964; Diamond and May 1976). Even when a species count is thought to include all species in a habitat, it still reflects the size of that habitat and the "density" of individuals (Kempton 1979).

A measure of species richness is the best indicator of diversity that can be obtained with an inventory that merely identifies presence or absence of species and provides a total species count. Because species richness represents but one facet of the diversity picture, its value as a comparative index is severely limited (Yapp 1979).

NUMBER OF SPECIES AND AREA

The total count of species observed without regard to the area sampled, although clearly an important aspect of species diversity, is not sufficient for understanding that diversity. By adding information on collection area to the basic species list, *species-area curves* can be obtained. In the species-area curve, which likely was first suggested by Jaccard (1908, 1912) and later discussed by Arrhenius (1921) and Gleason (1922), total species number is plotted against size of the area sampled.

The shape of a species-area relationship curve is roughly exponential regardless of taxonomic group (Preston 1962a; Williams 1964). For example, if the numbers of species of frogs inventoried from increasingly larger bodies of water in a region are plotted against the log of the area of each, the species-area curve will have an exponential shape. If the logarithmic transforms of both the species counts and the areas are taken, the resultant curve approximates linearity, and its regression line can be used to predict values for areas in which observations were not obtained (Gleason 1922). The parameters of the fitted curve depend upon the unit of measure of the area. Thus, a curve based on quadrats measured in square meters yields estimates of the number of species in one square meter.

Connor and McCoy (1979) examined conditions of the species-area relationship and the fit of alternative models (especially semilog and log-log) to the observed curves. They asserted that these fitted curves have little biological meaning and provided evidence to support their claim. Martin (1981), in contrast, provided data for which evidence of biological pattern was obtained. He cautioned, however, that interpretation of species-area curves can be compromised by threats from correlated environmental and other factors. Preston (1962b) showed that the species-area curve for single sites can be understood comparatively easily, but that, because of the vagaries of sampling, interpretation of curves based on data from multiple sites (especially if number of sites is limited) present greater difficulties.

The common qualitative perception of species diversity is often positively correlated with species richness as, for example, over habitats along latitudinal gradients (Hurlbert 1971). Such positive correlation is neither a biological nor a mathematical necessity. Gradients can exist along which apparent increases in the diversity of species are accompanied by decreases in species richness.

TOTAL COUNTS OF SPECIES AND INDIVIDUALS

Another way to eliminate the sample-size dependence of direct species counts is to measure species richness in terms of the number of individuals observed. Hurlbert (1971) used the term *numerical species richness* to denote the number of species in a collection containing a specified number of individuals or amount of biomass, and the term *areal species richness* (or density, sensu Simpson 1964), to denote the number of species present in a given area or volume of the environment. In the same publication, however, he appears to have used the terms *species richness* and *numerical species richness* synonymously, with the former being the preferred term. Another well-known index that is frequently applied to biological richness deals with the problem of sample size effect by taking the total species count (s), reducing it by 1, and then dividing it by the log of the total number of individuals sampled: $(s - 1)/\log n$. This index usually is attributed to Margalef (1958), but he only cited it. It is correctly attributed to Gleason (1922). A second popular richness index (Menhinick 1964) is calculated by dividing total species count by the square root of the total number of individuals. Such indices simply and arithmetically delete the sample size effect, but in so doing, they assume that the two counts used are functionally related in a specific manner in the population. For example, in Menhinick's index, the expected number of species, $E(s)$, in the population is equal to a constant times the square root of the total number of individuals. Gleason's index is based on the presumed linear relation of $E(s)$ and the log of the number of individuals. There are two fundamental conditions for the use of this type of index: (1) The functional relationship between $E(s)$ and n must remain constant over any studied assemblages; and (2) the relationship must be of the exact form stated.

Peet (1974) noted that if these conditions do not hold, the richness indices will vary with sample size in an unpredictable manner. Unless an investigator can demonstrate these relationships for the particular taxonomic group and sample situation, no conclusion can be reached concerning the merits of these indices, and I cannot generally recommend them.

If an inventory provides a species count and a total individual count, an investigator can calculate indices of species richness but not of overall species diversity.

Monitoring, Richness, and Evenness

SPECIES' ABUNDANCES AND TOTAL COUNTS OF SPECIES AND INDIVIDUALS

A monitoring study can provide (1) a species list with a total species count, s, as an estimate of the possible species in the target population S;

(2) the total number of individuals sampled, n, as an estimate of N; and (3) the numbers of individuals sampled or located from each species, n_i (where $i = 1, \ldots, s$), as an estimate of the abundance of each species. The values can be used to calculate various measures of diversity.

SLOPE INDICES. Whittaker (1965) devised what he called dominance diversity curves, graphical presentations of the three quantities s, n, and n_i. He also proposed two slope indices to measure in a distinct manner what he called richness or species per logarithmic cycle. Peet (1974) pointed out that both of these indices are influenced by their assumed population distribution (e.g., log normal) and therefore are subject to limitations similar to those of simpler richness indices. Whittaker's indices have not achieved any popularity in ecological studies, although Krebs (1989) included them on his list of recommended diversity measures. At present, the limitations of these indices appear to outweigh their advantages for amphibian work.

RAREFACTION. Sanders (1968), in an attempt to obtain a richness measure that is independent of sample size, developed a method called *rarefaction,* which reduces the observed samples to a common size. In this procedure, the species in a sample are ranked according to their relative representation (number of individuals) in that sample, and cumulative percentages are calculated. Based on these figures, a simple scaling algorithm, the rarefaction methodology (see note 4), is used to estimate the species richness that would be expected in a sample of individuals of some designated (rarefied) size. The numbers of species that would be expected at alternative sample sizes are obtained by interpolation from the curve (number of species plotted against number of specimens or sample size), assuming that the relative representation of the species present is fixed. As the sample size (i.e., number of specimens) decreases, the number of species represented would also be expected to decrease. The curve may be used alone as a representation of the parent assemblage, or it can be compared with curves generated from samples taken at other times or from other assemblages.

Sanders (1968) suggested that the curve that is generated represents the cardinal features of the diversity of the parent assemblage sampled, but it actually is a preliminary solution with little probabilistic basis. In addition, the rarefaction methodology of Sanders generally overestimates the expected number of species present in samples of differing sizes or of highly disparate species abundances, especially for small samples and clumped populations (Hurlbert 1971; Fager 1972; Peet 1974). Only for samples in which the numbers of individuals within species are approximately equal do his rarefaction estimates and their correct values coincide (Peet 1974). Hurlbert (1971) refined Sanders's method for calculating the expected number to have a probabilistic basis (see note 5).

The rarefaction procedure is based on certain problematic assumptions concerning the relationship between the collections or assemblages to be rarefied and their parent populations. One assumption is that individuals are randomly sampled. In fact, because most naturally occurring amphibian assemblages are spatially heterogeneous (Crump 1971; Heyer et al. 1990), individuals (of distinct species) are not located randomly but are sampled from discrete habitats, microhabitats, or patches. The statistical term for this is *cluster sampling.* The clusters can be defined at random, but the individuals within each cluster are not randomly sampled with respect to the population as a whole. Observed variation can be partitioned into components for spatial variability and sampling error (Smith and Grassle 1977). Nevertheless, results of the rarefaction procedure will be biased in an unpredictable way if the individuals are not sampled randomly.

A second assumption is that replicate samples from a homogeneous assemblage, or samples from habitats or microhabitats within a heterogeneous assemblage, belong to the same target population in the statistical sense.

Buzas (1979) and James and Rathbun (1981) suggested that rarefaction methods are particularly useful for comparison of richness when assemblage sizes differ. Rarefaction, as refined by Hurlbert (1971), is a reasonable approach to measurement of richness and is appropriate for across-study comparisons. It should be used, however, only when sampling and analytical methods have been consistently applied across the samples to be compared. In addition, samples should be compared only if they are taxonomically similar. Raup (1975) noted that the degree of similarity between collections, determined at the discretion of the investigator, could be biased. Potential bias can be avoided if *similarity* is operationally defined. Samples to be compared should also come from similar habitats. Intrahabitat comparisons minimize the threat to generalizability from habitat heterogeneity, which has been shown to be correlated with diversity. As far as can be ascertained, Sanders used *habitat* to mean some limited aspects of the substrate and did not control for any other variables. Arbitrarily allowing certain ecological factors to vary and others to be restricted is not reasonable.

When comparing diversity among several assemblages, the entire curve of rarefied values for each assemblage should be used. The specific species values at each rarefied point (sample size) form the richness measure (Raup 1975). One does not measure diversity of a single entity by rarefaction, or state that the rarefaction curve exemplifies high or low diversity. Finally, rarefaction should be constrained to expected values calculated within the range of the sample.

EVENNESS

Species *equitability, evenness,* and *dominance* are terms that have been used synonymously to designate the distribution of species' abundances (i.e., the number of individuals per species or the related proportions). Peterson (1975) stated that evenness can be indicative of relative numerical dominance without regard to diversity; the species with the largest number of observed individuals is numerically dominant in the distribution. However, dominance in this sense has been confused with the concept of dominance defined as the degree of influence or control that one species exerts over another species of the assemblage as a result of competition or behavior (Grieg-Smith 1957). Use of the term *dominance* for evenness, therefore, is best avoided.

PARAMETERS OF PROBABILITY DISTRIBUTIONS. Many probabilistic models have been used to explain distributions of species abundance, and organization patterns of species assemblages (May 1975). The most commonly cited models are the log series (Fisher 1943), the log normal (Preston 1948), the negative binomial (Brian 1953), and the broken stick (MacArthur 1957). Many reviews discuss the uses and abuses of these models, especially for comparing abundance relationships across assemblages. Gilbert (1989) noted that it is difficult to establish that a sample belongs to one particular statistical distribution, especially with small samples from heterogeneous biological populations. Statistically, it is not reasonable to discuss best-fit alternatives from among these abundance distributions based upon single amphibian samples. However, the application of these models is a credible approach to the definition of such patterns, and selection of one or more should be considered. Buzas et al. (1982) fitted both the log series and the log normal models to data on species abundance and on species occurrence (i.e., number of localities per species). This has not, apparently, been tried for amphibians but certainly could provide insight into patterns of occurrence and abundance.

INDICES. Because of the need to compare abundance distributions, researchers developed evenness indices, with the impossible task of summarizing an underlying observed abundance pattern with one number. Most of the popular indices use equal abundance of all species as a base against which to compare some manner of divergence. Evenness is actually defined as a balance point in the observed sample, because there is only one balance point and an infinite number of ways to be unbalanced.

It is most common to describe evenness with a single index that is based on various methods for normalization or scaling by minimum and maximum values. Hurlbert (1971) showed that normalized indices decrease non-monotonically to zero from the maximum value of the fully balanced case (i.e., a uniform distribution of observed abundances over species). Alatalo (1981) discussed the most common measures, and Heip and Engels (1974) compared the statistical behavior of seven evenness indices in low richness environments. (see note 6 for a discussion of the most useful and popular indices.)

DIVERSITY

Richness and evenness are both facets of an operational definition of diversity. Simpson (1949) was the first to imply, based on Yule's (1944) semantic work, that a diversity index should encompass both. Diversity indices that incorporate richness and evenness into one numerical quantity are termed *dominance diversity indices* (Sanders 1968), *equitability indices* (Auclair and Goff 1971), and *heterogeneity indices* (Good 1953). These indices can be influenced by the heterogeneity and magnitude of the area sampled, which can lead to great confusion regarding their interpretation and use. Fisher's alpha (Fisher 1943) is probably the most widely cited

of these measures. However, it requires sample sizes in the thousands, and so I shall not discuss it further.

I also omit some popular measures that assume that all individuals of a finite assemblage or population have been identified and counted (e.g., Brillouin's *H*—Brillouin 1956). This assumption is usually tentative for amphibian inventory and monitoring, and in general such measures are formally related (Pielou 1975) to a family of measures proposed by Hill (1973). Two of the most commonly used diversity indices—Simpson's and Shannon's—are included in this family. Smith and Grassle (1977) derived unbiased estimators for these indices that have minimum variance and allow for calculation of confidence limits.

REPEAT RATE (SIMPSON'S INDEX). The first diversity measure of import, developed as a single index, is attributed to Simpson (1949), but actually it has a rather involved history (see note 7). As a diversity measure, it is the straightforward probability that two organisms selected at random from a population will "repeat" their classification, that is, that they will belong to the same species.

Whittaker (1965) stated that the Repeat Rate and the total species count together are sufficient to characterize the pattern of species' abundances in a sample. Hill (1973) showed the sense in which this is true, on average.

INFORMATION INDICES. The most routinely used measures of diversity are based upon information theory; they equate diversity in a natural faunal system with the amount of information in a transmitted message. If the actual message to be interpreted is selected (sampled) from a finite number of messages, then this message information or sample, or any monotonic function of it, can be taken as a measure of information. For a sample, the associated entropy is not an indicator of the amount of knowledge available about that sample, but rather it is a measure of the degree of randomness in that sample. The tendency for a biological system to become less organized (i.e., less perfectly balanced or more shuffled) implies a high degree of entropy.

A common information index is Shannon's index, or the H function (see note 8). The formula for H is as follows:

$$H = -\sum_{i=1}^{s} p_i \ln p_i$$

Because P_i (the proportion in the population belonging to the ith of s species), is usually estimated by $p_i = n_i/n$ (the proportion in the sample), the formula for H can be rewritten directly in terms of the observed sample results (e.g., see Pielou 1966a; Lloyd et al. 1968b).

The maximum diversity possible for n individuals occurs when each belongs to a separate species; the largest value for the index occurs when $p_i = 1/n$. The entropy (information) calculated for a given sample can be compared with the maximal value possible in the population, subject only to the assumption that the two situations (sample and population) are similar. This comparison is called *relative entropy* of the source (it reflects the relative species abundances).

Peet (1975) illustrated the limitations of such a relativized statistic and stated that it and all similar diversity ratios are not appropriate for ecological application because they do not approach a constant limit with increasing sample size. When the number of species is fixed, the information is greater and the probabilities (relative abundances) of the various species are more balanced. Alternatively, the information index decreases when sample size increases if samples of all species are not equally likely to be obtained. Thus, Shannon's measure of the average density per individual is reasonable when random samples are taken from a very large population, and all or many of the species in the population are

represented in the sample. There can be a sizable error increase with the use of any information based index when the proportion of total species represented in the sample declines (Peet 1974).

Pielou (1966a) discussed the use and misuse of this and other information theoretic measures. The most frequently cited disadvantage of these measures is difficulty of computation, but with the current availability of desk microcomputers, this complaint is no longer valid. Routledge (1979) discussed a set of basic properties, both mathematical and ecological, that should be characteristic of diversity indices. He showed that these properties hold only for the indices in Hill's family of measures and recommended that only Shannon's index and the Repeat Rate be used.

The logarithmic base used in Shannon's index varies across studies and investigators. This variation is not of biological consequence as long as the base used is clearly indicated, because a base change is effected only by a multiplicative factor. A scale factor can be used to convert logarithms from base 10 to any other base. For example, the index in base 10 would be multiplied by 3.321928 to obtain base 2, or by 2.302585 to work in the natural log base e. Gibson and Buzas (1973) clearly stated that the low-information example in their publication, with $H = 0.45$, was calculated with a natural log base. If base 10 had been used, their value would have decreased to 0.20. Their example with the complete balance of species abundances yielded more uncertainty and an H value of 1.6. Log_{10} would have reduced H to 0.69. Large and small values of H reflect both biological reality and the log base used.

Good (1953) generalized the Repeat Rate and Shannon's index and determined the sampling distribution for the Shannon equation that allows for variance, standard error, and confidence interval calculations. Basharin (1959) showed that the use of an estimate in an information index formula produces a bias whose magnitude is a function of both the species and the individual counts. Calculation of variance using formulas of Good and Basharin appropriate to Shannon's index allows for comparison across random samples. Pielou (1966b) discussed the use of alternative estimation procedures to reduce bias for these indices based upon properties of the assemblage sampled and the sampling method selected. Most authors have ignored Pielou's procedures. Buzas (1979) determined that when the sample contains at least several hundred individuals, the correction is negligible. May (1975) indicated that because the statistical distribution of this index is skewed for small numbers of species, characterizing the spread by the standard deviation is not exact, but it is good enough for practical purposes.

If the sample individuals are not randomly obtained in a field study, alternative methods of estimation specific to the study design may be needed. Pielou (1966a) devised a sequentially cumulative method for estimating the Shannon measure when using random quadrat sampling. Liebelt (in Heyer and Berven 1973) improved upon Pielou's methodology and developed a standard error formula for this case. Hutcheson (1970) defined an approximate t-test. Because Shannon's indices are normally distributed (Taylor 1978), parametric statistical techniques can be used to compare them. MacArthur et al. (1966) used Shannon's formula to compare bird samples across forest canopy heights and to measure the difference in profile between habitats; the authors provided useful formulas for their calculations. A major advantage of information-based indices is that they are additive; this permits the partitioning of numbers obtained for larger groups into specific values for smaller groups or subgroups.

Summary and Recommendations

When amphibian populations are compared, species counts and abundance distributions can be used separately or combined to describe diversity. However, no single index will provide all the diversity information because each gives different weight to specific properties of the species' abundance distributions. When any index is used, sources of variability known to be peripheral are controlled by transformation of the raw data and weighted aggregates. In general, indices cannot be used uncritically because incomplete knowledge of the ecological influences on such relative measures precludes the development of any effective, all-encompassing measure. Selection of an index tacitly involves a decision concerning the ordering of species assemblages that are not intrinsically comparable (Patil and Taillie 1982). Peet (1975) cited the need for a theory, or set of rules, of index response upon which to base a choice. I recommend that an investigation of the species monitored include an examination of all three types of measures when possible: richness, evenness, and diversity (the last measured by the Repeat Rate or Shannon's index), so that the relative effects of each component can be evaluated. The evaluation should be accompanied by dimensions of the area from which the specimens were selected.

Across samples, the use of a single number, such as an index, to represent a multifaceted situation can be highly misleading without the use of standard errors. Peet (1975) provided a similar warning for evenness indices. For presentation of results across samples, I recommend that samples (equivalent areas) be randomly selected from similar habitats. This procedure obviates the need for rarefaction; increases the interpretability of the selected measures of richness, evenness, and diversity; and allows for maximal comparability among studies. However, when such random selection is not feasible, rarefaction is an alternative. When the investigator clearly understands what is being measured with a particular index, and indicates what has been accomplished in space and time, the inherent misunderstanding surrounding species diversity studies will be alleviated (Buzas 1979).

Notes

1. Obtaining and Describing Values for a 2×2 Table. The simplest way to investigate the problem of the correct reference distribution for the 2×2 table is to use a predetermined sample size. That is, the sample size will always be n and possible distributions are examined. Three conditions are possible.

(a) The first condition is that both sets of marginal frequencies are random variables. This condition occurs when a sample of size n is taken from a bivariate distribution and subsequently classified into a double dichotomy. For example, each amphibian is randomly sampled from a selected region, and both sex and site characteristics are merely observed and recorded. The only constant in this case is the total sample size; no marginal totals are fixed. That is, the number of males or females is not decided in advance, and the samples at each of the sites are not stipulated before going into the field. This test is a test of independence and the exact probability depends on two unknown parameters and cannot be evaluated (Kendall and Stuart 1973). It is assumed that an individual selected at random will possess characteristic A with probability $p(A)$, and not possess it with $1 - p(A)$. Corresponding probabilities are assumed for factor or characteristic B.

(b) Alternatively, one set of marginal frequencies may be fixed. A fixed classification is merely a labeling of the two samples (e.g., males and females) that are to be compared with respect to the other classification (e.g., numbers in breeding condition). Predetermining the sample sizes before observing some characteristic (e.g., deciding to examine gonad development in 50 males and 50 females) results in one fixed set of marginal frequencies and one variable or random set. Comparison of these two (or more) samples (i.e., male and female in this example) with respect to a characteristic is a test of homogeneity (2×2 comparative trial of Barnard 1947). The comparison tests whether the proportions of individuals with characteristic A are the same in two different populations where $a + c$ has been drawn at random from the first population and $b + d$ from the second. For large samples, the test is equivalent to the first condition, in which both sets of marginal frequencies are random variables. For small samples, evaluation is not possible (Kendall and Stuart 1973).

(c) Finally, both sets of marginal frequencies may be fixed in advance. This practice is rare, or perhaps nonexistent in amphibian literature. It is similar to, but does not exactly fit, having the total sample size and all four marginals of breeding, nonbreeding, males, and females fixed, predetermined, or obtained in advance. The null hypothesis of interest is

$$H_0 = \frac{p(11)}{p(1\cdot)} = \frac{p(21)}{p(2\cdot)} = \frac{a}{a+c} = \frac{b}{b+d}$$

The distribution of the one cell free to vary is hypergeometric, a small sample description of the binomial distribution. Kendall and Stuart (1973) gave the mean and variance formulas and the asymptotic normality condition. The mean and variance can be used in a t^2 test (compared with a standardized normal distribution), and t^2 is proportional to the Pearson χ^2 statistic. This procedure (2×2 independence trial of Barnard 1947) tests the significance of the difference between two characteristics that have been observed to occur randomly in a group of $n = (a + c) + (b + d)$ individuals. The random process is applied within the set of n, with no assumption about selection from a larger universe or target population.

2. Correcting for Continuity of Distribution. In this note, I examine the application of the continuity correction to each of the three cases that can describe data for a 2×2 table.

(a) In the first case, both the marginals and the total sample size are fixed in advance. Conover (1974) and Starmer et al. (1974) considered two conditions in this situation: marginals equal and marginals unequal.

Marginals equal ($a + b = c + d$, or $a + c = b + d$). Under this condition, Yates's correction improves the probability estimates (Mantel and Greenhouse 1968; Starmer et al. 1974), as does an alternative to Yates's correction developed by Kendall and Stuart (1973). The Kendall and Stuart correction is defined as the arithmetic average of the χ^2 observed with its next smaller possible value. The exception for both corrections is when the distribution is extremely asymmetric.

Marginals unequal ($a + b \neq c + d$, and $a + c \neq b + d$). Conover (1974) showed that Yates's corrected χ^2

and the uncorrected χ^2 statistic each improve the exact probability estimates about half the time, but Conover was unable to provide general rules for their application. The Kendall and Stuart correction improved the estimate consistently.

(b) In the second case, only one marginal is fixed. In this case Fisher's Exact Test and Yates's corrected chi-square test are each too conservative and should not be used. However, any correction should depend on the degree of discreteness. Liddell (1978) substituted a Yates correction of $\frac{1}{4}$ and found it to be too liberal for asymmetric distributions. Berkson (1978) compared Fisher's Exact Test with both Yates's $\frac{1}{2}$-corrected test and an uncorrected normal z-test and found the latter to be more powerful with an effective level closer to the nominal level desired. Finally, d'Agostino et al. (1988) showed that the two-independent-sample t-test with pooled variance is best for sample sizes less than or equal to 15. Berkson and d'Angostino et al. found no need to condition on the marginal.

(c) In the third case, both marginals are random. Many agree that the best test of independence when both marginals are random is the uncorrected χ^2 (Conover 1974; Liddell 1978; but see Pirie and Hamden 1972 for a contrary view). However, the Yates correction should not be used in this case (Conover 1974), because the correction does not provide reasonable estimates of the probabilities from the randomized version of Fisher's Exact Test. Actually Yates's correction results in the performance of a different test. Under certain conditions, the correction leads to values that indicate significance but are called nonsignificant, and vice versa.

3. Comparison of Tests for One-Fixed-Marginal 2×2 Table Data.
The two-independent-sample t-test is very close in computation to the χ^2. For a comparison of the statistics of Berkson (1978) with that of d'Agostino, et al. (1988), we have the following:

$$\pm\sqrt{(\chi^2)} = z = \frac{\dfrac{a}{(a+c)} - \dfrac{b}{(b+d)}}{\left[n\left(\dfrac{1-(a+b)}{n}\right)\left(\dfrac{1}{a+b} + \dfrac{1}{b+d}\right)\right]^{1/2}}$$

The t statistic can be written as a Studentized Pearson statistic:

$$t = \left[\frac{(n-2)}{n}\right]^{1/2} \frac{ad - bc}{[(b+d)ac + (a+c)bd]^{1/2}}$$

The values of z and t differ only in their variance estimate formulas.

4. Rarefaction.
This procedure uses the expected value of a function of samples drawn randomly from the data. Therefore, it is related to the Bootstrap method (nonparametric technique for inferring a statistic's distribution, derived from using samples from the data) of Efron (1979). Rarefaction is not a sampling plan, although it may be useful as an indicator of excessive sampling (Heck et al. 1975).

5. Hurlbert's Refinement of Sanders's Rarefaction Method.
Hurlbert (1971) refined Sanders's method for calculating the expected species richness of a sample of individuals. Hurlbert's refinement is a special case of the hypergeometric distribution. Plots of rarefaction values are monotonically increasing, downwardly concave curves that conveniently pass through the points (0,0), (1,1), and (N,S). Smith and Grassle (1977) provided a solution to the minimum-variance unbiased estimator problem of the expected number that allows for the calculation of confidence bounds. Heck et al. (1975) argued that biological reasons account for a multinomial approximation for large numbers. I am unable to devise a situation in which that statement could be said to hold for either amphibians or general faunal representations, and I recommend that only the hypergeometric family described by Hurlbert's equations be used.

6. Evenness Indices.
The indices discussed below can be written as a ratio of Hill's (1973) ordered set. They are of the normalized form specified by Hurlbert (1971).

Pielou's J' (Pielou 1975) is probably the index most widely known among ecologists, although many problems with it have been identified (see Sheldon 1969; Heip and Engels 1974). This index is the log ratio of Hill's first two numbers (i.e., $\log(N_1/N_0)$). Buzas and Gibson (1969) first proposed an index that is the simple untransformed ratio of Hill's first two ordered numbers N_1/N_0 and related by exponentiation to Pielou's J'. Buzas and Gibson's index is commonly attributed to Sheldon (1969) who first called this value e. Heip's index (Heip 1974) is the same fraction used by Buzas and Gibson but with the lower bound of 1 subtracted from both numerator and denominator to effect a limit change. Hill (1973) suggested that the ratio of second- and first-order numbers was an evenness index (Hill's index). When this ratio is restrained to approach a limit of zero, as is preferable, it is called Hill's modified ratio. Because each of these indices is a scaled diversity index (the ratio of two indices is itself an index but on a new scale), each can incorporate the problems as well as the advantages of the original indices. Sheldon (1969) showed, for example, that Pielou's J' and the Buzas and Gibson index are affected to varying degrees by species count, especially for low-richness assemblages. The same is true for numbers less than approximately 10 (Buzas 1972b). Hill (1973) stated that because of this sample dependence, evenness measures cannot be regarded as measuring a property of the target population.

7. Repeat Rate (Simpson's Index).

The Repeat Rate measure probably was first used for cryptography in 1879 in a German publication by Lexis (see Keynes 1921:399; Friedman 1922). In 1941, A. W. Turing (see Good 1979) gave this quantity, defined by the formula $\sum_{i=1}^{s} p_i^2$, its most "natural name" (Good 1982), the Repeat Rate. Turing also derived its unbiased estimate and used it, as did Sacco (1951), in cryptoanalysis. Peet (1974) and Bhargava and Uppuluri (1975) attributed the additive inverse $(1 - \sum_{i=1}^{s} p_i^2)$ form of this measure, which is also used as a diversity index, to Gini (1912). Weaver (1948) used a function of the repeat rate $(1 / \sum_{i=1}^{s} p_i^2)$ as a "surprise" index, deriving the name from the notion that it is less surprising to locate a specimen of a rare species in a highly heterogeneous assemblage than in a more

balanced one. The ultimate reference on this index appears to be that of Good (1982).

8. Information Indices.

Shannon's information index was formed when he used Boltzmann's H function from statistical mechanics theory as an index of "entropy," for the evaluation of missing information (Shannon 1948). This information index has incorrectly been termed the Shannon-Weiner index because Weiner applied Shannon's entropy formulas to his research. Weiner always attributed the entropic ideas to Shannon. The index has also been called the Shannon-Weaver Index, because Shannon's (1949) second and most widely referenced presentation of it appeared in an article in his book with Weaver (Shannon and Weaver 1949—the article and book have the same title). Hartley (1928) showed that the log function was the best form for amount of information.

The additive inverse (a number that when added to a second number results in zero) of Shannon's index is called the *redundancy* of the population and represents the fraction of the information message determined by the governing stochastic process (i.e., unnecessary noise). Many of the objections to the use of Shannon's index for sparse or small samples may be overcome by jackknifing the index, a procedure that reduces bias in estimation and provides approximate confidence intervals in cases where ordinary statistical distribution theory proves intractable (Quenouille 1949, 1956; Zahl 1977). Adams and McCune (1979) devised a computer program for applying this procedure to Shannon's index. Hypothesis tests and confidence intervals can be obtained for the unknown parameter using the Student's t-distribution (Miller 1974). In theory, jackknifing is valid and extremely useful. However, the appropriateness of the resultant confidence intervals is dependent upon the approximate normality of the estimate, which needs investigation under conditions of amphibian sampling.

Several other indices are interconvertible with Shannon's index. Hill (1973) showed that his N_1 equals e^H and interpreted the multiplicative inverse of this $(1/e^H)$ as the weighted geometric mean of the proportional abundances. Buzas and Gibson's evenness index, defined as N_1/N_0, is equal to e^H/s, for s species.

Appendix: properties of association measures

Coefficients are listed in the appendix by names and numbers corresponding to those in Table 20. The Resemblance Equation Coefficient (Table 20: # 20) is not included because it has no general solution.

Examples for Invariance

In the table below, the frequency values in the first row are multiplied by 10 to produce those in the second row. This process in turn multiplies the total by 10 but leaves the proportions the same. Coefficients that change when proportions remain the same but sample sizes differ are not invariant (NI) and are indicated as such. The values for each coefficient as calculated using the values from each row of the table are listed.

a	b	c	d	n
2	4	3	6	15
20	40	30	60	150

A. Similarity Coefficients

1. Simpson	.400	.400
2. Kulczynski	.367	.367
3. Ochiai/Otsuka	.365	.365
4. Dice	.364	.364
4a. Dice's Asymmetric B|A	NA	NA
4b. Dice's Asymmetric A|B	NA	NA
5. Jaccard	.222	.222

B. Matching Coefficients

21. Simple matching	.533	.533
22. UN$_5$	.231	.231
23. UN$_4$	.500	.500
24. UN$_3$	1.430	1.430
25. UN$_1$	.696	.696
26. Russell and Rao	.133	.133
27. Rogers and Tanimoto	.364	.364

6. UN$_2$	.125	.125
7. Kulczynski	.286	.286
8. Mountford	.105	.011 NI
9. Correlation ratio	.133	.133
10. Braun-Blanquet	.333	.333
11. Fager	.161	.301 NI
12. Savage	.667	.667
13. Nonmetric	.636	.636
14. McConnaughey	-.267	-.267
15. Johnson	.833	.833
16. Forbes 1907	1.000	1.000
17. Gilbert and Wells	-1.1E-19	-1.1E-19
18. Forbes 1925	.000	.000
19. Tarwid	.000	.000

28. Hamann/G-Index	.067	.067
29. Baroni-Urbani and Buser 1	-.123	-.123
30. Baroni-Urbani and Buser 2	.438	.438
31. Total difference	.467	.467
32. Pattern difference	.462	.462
33. Angular transform	.051	.051
34. Michael	.000	.000
35. Faith	.333	.333
36. Omega	.000	.000
37. Eyraud	-.010	-.010 NI

Examples for Linearity Conditions

Two sets of four tables of frequency values are provided below. The marginal frequencies and total frequencies in the tables are fixed for the purposes of examining linearity conditions and providing insight into values and ranges of the measures under this set of conditions. In the tables in set 1, the *d* cells have the largest values.

Each table in set 2 has the same total frequency as in set 1, but the marginals are fixed at different values. In both sets the values of *a* increase linearly from 0.

	Set 1						Set 2			
a	*b*	*c*	*d*	*n*		*a*	*b*	*c*	*d*	*n*
0	30	30	40	100		0	40	40	20	100
1	29	29	41	100		1	39	39	21	100
2	28	28	42	100		2	38	38	22	100
3	27	27	43	100		3	37	37	23	100

Each coefficient is listed below with two sets of four values of that coefficient, calculated using the sample data. The differences between each pair of successive values, in order, are also provided. Each set of differences is categorized according to pattern of change, as follows:

Linear—Differences are constant.

Convex—When the *a* cell value increases, differences increase.

Concave—When the *a* cell value increases, differences decrease.

ND—Coefficient is not defined for the chosen values.

*—Coefficient does not detect the change in marginals when the total remains constant (the values are equal for both sets).

+—Coefficient does not detect this slight unit change in the *a* cell value.

	Set 1		Set 2	
	Value	Difference	Value	Difference
A. Similarity Coefficients				
1. Simpson	.000		.000	
	.033	.033	.025	.025
	.067	.033	.050	.025
	.100	.033 Linear	.075	.025 Linear
2. Kulczynski	.000		.000	
	.033	.033	.025	.025
	.067	.033	.050	.025
	.100	.033 Linear	.075	.025 Linear
3. Ochiai/Otsuka	.000		.000	
	.033	.033	.025	.025
	.067	.033	.050	.025
	.100	.033 Linear	.075	.025 Linear
4. Dice	.000		.000	
	.033	.033	.025	.025
	.067	.033	.050	.025
	.100	.033 Linear	.075	.025 Linear
4a. Dice's asymmetric B|A	.000		.000	
	.033	.033	.025	.025
	.067	.033	.050	.025
	.100	.033 Linear	.075	.025 Linear

	Set 1		Set 2	
	Value	Difference	Value	Difference
4b. Dice's asymmetric A│B	.000		.000	
	.033	.033	.025	.025
	.067	.033	.050	.025
	.100	.033 Linear	.075	.025 Linear
5. Jaccard	.000		.000	
	.017	.017	.013	.0127
	.034	.018	.026	.0130
	.053	.018 Convex	.039	.0133 Convex
6. UN_2	.000		.000	
	.009	.0085	.006	.006
	.018	.0090	.013	.007
	.027	.0095 Convex	.020	.007 Convex
7. Kulczynski	.000		.000	
	.017	.017	.013	.013
	.036	.018	.026	.013
	.056	.020 Convex	.041	.014 Convex
8. Mountford	.000		.000	
	.001	.001	.0006	.0006
	.002	.001	.001	.0007
	.004	.0010 Convex	.002	.0001 Convex
9. Correlation ratio	.000		.000	
	.001	.001	.0006	.0006
	.004	.003	.003	.002
	.010	.006 Convex	.006	.003 Convex
10. Braun-Blanquet	.000		.000	
	.033	.033	.025	.025
	.067	.033	.050	.025
	.100	.033 Linear	.075	.025 Linear
11. Fager	−.091		−.079	
	−.058	.033	−.054	.025
	−.025	.033	−.029	.025
	.009	.033 Linear	−.004	.025 Linear
12. Savage	1.000		1.000	
	.967	−.033	.975	−.025
	.933	−.033	.950	−.025
	.900	−.033 Linear	.925	−.025 Linear

(Continued)

	Set 1		Set 2	
	Value	Difference	Value	Difference
13. Nonmetric	1.000		1.000	
	.967	−.033	.975	−.025
	.933	−.033	.950	−.025
	.900	−.033 Linear	.925	−.025 Linear
14. McConnaughey	−1.000		−1.000	
	−.933	.067	−.950	.050
	−.867	.067	−.900	.050
	−.800	.067 Linear	−.850	.050 Linear
15. Johnson*,+	ND		ND	
	1.000	ND	1.000	ND
	1.000	.000	1.000	.000
	1.000	.000	1.000	.000
16. Forbes 1907	.000		.000	
	.111	.111	.063	.063
	.222	.111	.125	.063
	.333	.111 Linear	.188	.063 Linear
17. Gilbert and Wells	ND		ND	
	−.954	ND	−.200	ND
	−.635	.301	−.903	.301
	−.477	.176 Concave	−.727	.176 Concave
18. Forbes 1925	−.429		−.667	
	−.400	.029	−.652	.014
	−.368	.032	−.636	.016
	−.333	.035 Convex	−.619	.017 Convex
19. Tarwid	−1.000	−1.000		
	−.800	.200	−.882	.118
	−.636	.163	−.778	.105
	−.500	.136 Concave	−.684	.094 Concave
B. Matching Coefficients				
21. Simple matching	.400		.200	
	.420	.020	.220	.020
	.440	.020	.240	.020
	.460	.020 Linear	.260	.020 Linear
22. UN_5	.000		.000	
	.020	.020	.009	.009
	.040	.021	.018	.010
	.061	.022 Convex	.029	.011 Convex

	Set 1		Set 2	
	Value	Difference	Value	Difference
23. UN$_4$	.286	.167		
	.310	.024	.188	.021
	.333	.024	.208	.021
	.357	.024 Linear	.229	.021 Linear
24. UN$_3$	.667		.250	
	.724	.057	.282	.032
	.786	.062	.316	.034
	.852	.066 Convex	.351	.036 Convex
25. UN$_1$	.571		.333	
	.592	.020	.361	.027
	.611	.020	.387	.026
	.630	.020 Concave	.413	.026 Concave
26. Russell and Rao*	.000		.000	
	.010	.010	.010	.010
	.020	.010	.020	.010
	.030	.010 Linear	.030	.010 Linear
27. Rogers and Tanimoto	.250		.111	
	.266	.015	.124	.012
	.282	.016	.136	.013
	.299	.017 Convex	.149	.014 Convex
28. Hamann/G-Index	−.200		−.600	
	−.160	.040	−.560	.040
	−.120	.040	−.520	.040
	−.080	.040 Linear	−.480	.040 Linear
29. Baroni-Urbani and Buser 1	−1.000		−1.000	
	−.774	.226	−.866	.134
	−.668	.106	−.796	.070
	−.580	.087 Concave	−.735	.061 Concave
30. Baroni-Urbani and Buser 2	.000		.000	
	.003	.113	.067	.067
	.166	.053	.102	.035
	.210	.044 Concave	.133	.031 Concave
31. Total difference	.600		.800	
	.580	−.020	.780	−.020
	.560	−.020	.760	−.020
	.540	−.020 Linear	.740	−.020 Linear
32. Pattern difference	.600		.800	

(Continued)

	Set 1		Set 2	
	Value	Difference	Value	Difference
	.580	−.020	.780	−.020
	.560	−.020	.760	−.020
	.540	−.020 Linear	.740	−.020 Linear
33. Angular transform	.043		.029	
	.044	.001	.031	.002
	.046	.001	.032	.001
	.047	.001 Concave	.034	.001 Concave
34. Michael	−.692		−.941	
	−.624	.068	−.914	.028
	−.559	.070	−.896	.030
	−.477	.075 Convex	−.845	.037 Convex
35. Faith	.200	.	100	
	.215	.015	.115	.015
	.230	.015	.130	.015
	.245	.015 Linear	.145	.015 Linear
36. Omega	−1.000		−1.000	
	−.638	.362	−.790	.211
	−.507	.131	−.703	.087
	−.408	.099 Concave	−.633	.069 Concave
37. Eyraud+	−.0002		−.0003	
	−.0002	.000	−.0003	.000
	−.0002	.000	−.0003	.000
	−.0002	.000	−.0003	.000

Range Conditions

For this section, the matrices were selected to show possible conditions under which a maximum or a minimum value of the index is attained. The total sample size was held constant, and extreme cell values were selected. Although mention is never made of conditions on the two cells not affected, I also compared restrictions on these quantities. For example, restrictions versus no restrictions were compared on a and d while examining conditions for the maximum when b and/or $c = 0$.

a	b	c	d	n	Conditions
500	0	0	500	1,000	$b = c = 0$; $a = d$
900	0	0	100	1,000	$b = c = 0$; no restrictions on a or d
100	0	0	900	1,000	$b = c = 0$; no restrictions on a or d

a	b	c	d	n	Conditions
499	0	2	499	1,000	b or $c = 0$; $a = d$
1	0	1	998	1,000	b or $c = 0$; no restrictions on a or d
1	1	0	998	1,000	b or $c = 0$; no restrictions on a or d
998	1	0	1	1,000	b or $c = 0$; no restrictions on a or d
0	500	500	0	1,000	$a = d = 0$; $b = c$
0	900	100	0	1,000	$a = d = 0$; no restrictions on b or c
0	100	900	0	1,000	$a = d = 0$; no restrictions on b or c
0	1	99	900	1,000	a or $d = 0$; no restrictions on b or c
900	1	99	0	1,000	a or $d = 0$; no restrictions on b or c
998	1	1	0	1,000	a or $d = 0$; $b = c$
0	1	1	998	1,000	a or $d = 0$; $b = c$
1	1	1	997	1,000	incremental change from $a = d = 0$ and $b = c$, but d still largest

A. Similarity Coefficients		B. Matching Coefficients		C. Traditional Association Measures	
1. Simpson	1.000	21. Simple matching	1.000	38. χ^2	1,000.000
	1.000		1.000		1,000.000
	1.000		1.000		1,000.000
	1.000		.998		992.030
	1.000		.999		499.500
	1.000		.999		499.500
	1.000		.999		499.500
	.000		.000		1,000.000
	.000		.000		1,000.000
	.000		.000		1,000.000
	.000		.900		.110
	.9989		.900		.110
	.9990		.998		.001
	.000		.998		.001
	.500		.998		248.990
2. Kulczynski	1.000	22. UN$_5$	1.000	39. Coefficient of mean square contingency	1.000
	1.000		1.000		1.000
	1.000		1.000		1.000
	.998		.996		.992
	.750		.707		.499
	.750		.707		.499
	.999		.707		.499
	.000		.000		1.000

(Continued)

A. Similarity Coefficients		B. Matching Coefficients		C. Traditional Association Measures	
	.000		.000		1.000
	.000		.000		1.000
	.000		.000		.0001
	.950		.000		.0001
	.999		.000		.000001
	.000		.000		.000001
	.500		.499		.249
3.Ochiai/Otsuka	1.000	23. UN$_4$	1.000	40. Cramérs υ	1.000
	1.000		1.000		1.000
	1.000		1.000		1.000
	.998		.998		.996
	.707		.875		.707
	.707		.875		.707
	.999		.875		.707
	.000		.000		1.000
	.000		.000		1.000
	.000		.000		1.000
	.948		.475		.011
	.999		.475		.011
	.000		.499		.001
	.000		.499		.001
	.500		.749		.499
4. Dice	1.000	24. UN$_3$	ND	41. Pearson's contingency coefficient	.707
	1.000		ND		.707
	1.000		ND		.707
	.998		499.000		.706
	.667		999.000		.577
	.667		999.000		.577
	.999		999.000		.577
	.000		.000		−.707
	.000		.000		−.707
	.000		.000		−.707
	.000		9.000		−.010
	.947		9.000		−.010
	.999		499.000		−.001
	.000		499.000		−.001
	.500		499.000		.446

A. Similarity Coefficients		B. Matching Coefficients		C. Traditional Association Measures	
4a. Dice's asymmetric B|A	1.000	25. UN$_1$	1.000	42. Phi coefficient	1.000
	1.000		1.000		1.000
	1.000		1.000		1.000
	1.000		.999		.996
	1.000		.999		.707
	.500		.999		.707
	.999		.999		.707
	.000		.000		−1.000
	.000		.000		−1.000
	.000		.000		−1.000
	.000		.947		−.010
	.999		.947		−.010
	.999		.999		−.001
	.000		.999		−.001
	.500		.999		.499
4b. Dice's asymmetric A|B	1.000	26. Russell and Rao	.500	43. Yule's Q	1.000
	1.000		.900		1.000
	1.000		.100		1.000
	.996		.499		1.000
	.500		.001		1.000
	1.000		.001		1.000
	1.000		.998		1.000
	.000		.000		1.000
	.000		.000		1.000
	.000		.000		1.000
	.000		.000		1.000
	.901		.900		1.000
	.999		.998		1.000
	.000		.000		1.000
	.500		.001		1.000
5. Jaccard	1.000	27. Rogers and Tanimoto	1.000	44. Pearce	1.000
	1.000		1.000		1.000
	1.000		1.000		1.000
	.996		.996		.997
	.500		.998		.500
	.500		.998		.999
	.999		.998		.500
	.000		.000		−1.000
	.000		.000		−1.000

(Continued)

A. Similarity Coefficients		B. Matching Coefficients		C. Traditional Association Measures	
	.000		.000		−1.000
	.000		.818		−.000
	.900		.818		−.099
	.999		.996		−.001
	.000		.996		−.001
	.333		.996		.499
6. UN$_2$	1.000	28. Hamann G-index	1.000	45. C$_7$	1.000
	1.000		1.000		1.000
	1.000		1.000		1.000
	.992		.996		1.000
	.333		.998		1.000
	.333		.998		.499
	.998		.998		.499
	.000		−1.000		−1.000
	.000		−1.000		−1.000
	.000		−1.000		−1.000
	.000		.800		−1.000
	.818		.800		−1.000
	.996		.996		−1.000
	.000		.996		−1.000
	.200		.996		.499
7. Kulczynski	ND	29. Baroni-Urbani and Buser 1	1.000	46. C$_8$	1.000
	ND		1.000		1.000
	ND		1.000		1.000
	249.500		.996		1.000
	1.000		.940		1.000
	1.000		.940		1.000
	998.000		.998		1.000
	.000		−1.000		−1.000
	.000		−1.000		−1.000
	.000		−1.000		−1.000
	.000		−1.000		−1.000
	9.000		.800		−1.000
	499.000		.996		−1.000
	.000		−1.000		−1.000
	.500		.884		.499

A. Similarity Coefficients		B. Matching Coefficients		C. Traditional Association Measures
8. Mountford	ND	30. Baroni-Urbani and Buser 2	1.000	
	ND		1.000	
	ND		1.000	
	1.000		.998	
	2.000		.970	
	2.000		.970	
	2.000		.999	
	.000		.000	
	.000		.000	
	.000		.000	
	.000		.000	
	.020		.900	
	.999		.998	
	.000		.000	
	.500		.942	
9. Correlation ratio	1.000	31. Total difference	.000	
	1.000		.000	
	1.000		.000	
	.996		.002	
	.500		.001	
	.500		.001	
	.999		.001	
	.000		1.000	
	.000		1.000	
	.000		1.000	
	.000		.100	
	.900		.100	
	.998		.002	
	.000		.002	
	.250		.002	
10. Braun-Blanquet	1.000	32. Pattern difference	.000	
	1.000		.000	
	1.000		.000	
	.996		.000	
	.500		.000	
	.500		.000	
	.999		.000	
	.000		1.000	
	.000		.600	

(Continued)

A. Similarity Coefficients		B. Matching Coefficients		C. Traditional Association Measures
	.000		.600	
	.000		.020	
	.901		.020	
	.999		.002	
	.000		.002	
	.500		.002	
11. Fager	.978	33. Angular	.099	
	.983	transform	.099	
	.950		.099	
	.976		.096	
	.354		.097	
	.354		.097	
	.984		.097	
	−.022		.000	
	−.017		.000	
	−.017		.000	
	−.050		.078	
	.933		.078	
	.983		.096	
	−.500		.096	
	.146		.096	
12. Savage	.000	34. Michael	1.000	
	.000		.360	
	.000		.360	
	.004		.999	
	.500		.004	
	.500		.004	
	.001		.004	
	1.000		−1.000	
	1.000		−.360	
	1.000		−.360	
	1.000		−.0005	
	.099		−.0005	
	.001		−.000	
	1.000		−.000	
	.500		.003	

A. Similarity Coefficients		B. Matching Coefficients		C. Traditional Association Measures
13. Nonmetric	.000	35. Faith	.750	
	.000		.950	
	.000		.550	
	.002		.749	
	.333		.500	
	.333		.500	
	.001		.999	
	1.000		.000	
	1.000		.000	
	1.000		.000	
	1.000		.450	
	.053		.900	
	.001		.998	
	1.000		.499	
	.500		.4995	
14. McConnaughey	1.000	36. Omega	1.000	
	1.000		1.000	
	1.000		1.000	
	.996		1.000	
	.500		1.000	
	.500		1.000	
	.999		1.000	
	−1.000		−1.000	
	−1.000		−1.000	
	−1.000		−1.000	
	−1.000		−1.000	
	.900		−1.000	
	.998		−1.000	
	−1.000		−1.000	
	.000		.939	
15. Johnson	1.000	37. Eyraud	−.00000	
	1.000		−.00009	
	1.000		−.00000	
	1.040		−.00000	
	2.000		−.00000	
	.500		−.00000	
	.999		−.49950	
	ND		−.00000	

(*Continued*)

A. Similarity Coefficients	B. Matching Coefficients	C. Traditional Association Measures
ND	−.00001	
ND	−.00001	
ND	−.00000	
1.110	−.01009	
1.000	−.99900	
ND	−.00000	
1.000	−.00000	
16. Forbes 1907 2.000		
1.110		
10.000		
1.996		
500.000		
500.000		
1.001		
.000		
.000		
.000		
.000		
.999		
.999		
.000		
250.000		
17. Gilbert and .301		
Wells .046		
1.000		
.300		
2.700		
2.700		
.0004		
ND		
ND		
ND		
ND		
.000		
−.000		
ND		
2.400		

A. Similarity Coefficients	B. Matching Coefficients	C. Traditional Association Measures
18. Forbes 1925	−1.000		
	−.111		
	−9.000		
	−.996		
	−499.000		
	−499.000		
	−.001		
	−1.000		
	−9.000		
	−9.000		
	−.110		
	−.0001		
	−.000001		
	−.001		
	1.000		
19. Tarwid	.333		
	.053		
	.818		
	.332		
	.996		
	.996		
	.0005		
	−1.000		
	−1.000		
	−1.000		
	−1.000		
	−.00005		
	−.0000		
	−1.000		
	.992		

## Chapter 10

Conclusions and Recommendations

During the course of preparing this book, several important philosophical issues regarding the conduct of inventory and monitoring projects and the use of the resultant data came to the attention of the editors. Some were discussed at length by the workshop participants or grew out of conversations with colleagues about declining amphibian populations and the need for long-term studies; other issues arose as we worked with the material in the book itself. Each of these matters bears on the activities of and should be considered by people who study amphibian biodiversity. We present these issues here, along with our conclusions and recommendations.

The importance of inventory data

The field data gathered during amphibian inventory and monitoring studies have special importance. These data, rather than the summary statistics or analyses of them, form the bases for evaluating the statuses of amphibian species over broad areas and for determining whether their populations are changing. These data are used to compare species richness among assemblages, for evaluating the importance of specific habitats and sites for maintaining species, and for making conservation and management-related decisions about amphibians. It is essential, therefore, that the data be available for use by scientists, conservationists, managers, and others. Unfortunately, most scientific journals discourage publication of basic data, including raw data on presence and abundance.

We urge scientific societies and editors to adopt a policy of including original inventory and monitoring data in articles published in their journals. We also recommend that archives be established to house the data derived from inventory and monitoring studies and to make them available to qualified users. Such data should have been gathered in standard ways and not be otherwise available.

The Society for the Study of Amphibians and Reptiles (SSAR) has made a commitment to archive data taken on field trips organized by regional herpetological societies in the United States. We commend the SSAR for this effort and encourage other persons, organizations, and agencies to develop similar data repositories. The IUCN/SSC Declining Amphibian Populations Task Force will serve as an interim repository for data provided by its collaborating working groups, but a more permanent solution is needed. Clearly, organizations and agencies whose responsibilities include the management of areas for the maintenance of biodiversity or the protection of species need to address this issue. The Center for Environmental Data Management, a centralized data repository that is an integral part of the proposed U.S. National Institutes for the Environment, may provide such a solution.

Flexibility and insight

Some of the very features that make amphibians a key group for understanding biological diversity and allow them to serve as indicator species of the quality of their environments also constrain aspects of their study. For example, most amphibians are active primarily during specific periods of the year and only under certain weather conditions; studies done at these times will be most informative and most comparable among sites. Studies must be scheduled, therefore, with an appreciation of these activity patterns and with sufficient flexibility to accommodate the variable weather conditions that influence them. We are especially concerned that personnel from government agencies may wish that amphibian studies be accomplished during specific periods for reasons unrelated to science, not realizing, for example, that variations in seasonal weather patterns could invalidate the results. The vagaries of amphibian activity patterns can also be accommodated with long-term studies. Such studies provide additional, important information on population dynamics, and we encourage government agencies and other institutions to make commitments to support long-term investigations. Only with an appreciation of amphibian activity patterns and the factors that control them, and an understanding of population processes derived from long-term studies, can we hope to make progress in comprehending the role of amphibians in the natural world.

Modification of techniques

In this book, we have assembled current information on techniques known to be successful for the inventory and monitoring of amphibians. Data derived from similar studies using the same techniques, as described, should be comparable. We urge, therefore, that all users follow to the letter the procedures indicated. On the other hand, we realize that some techniques will require modification in some situations, so investigators should not hesitate to modify a technique *if the change is truly an improvement*. In such situations, however, it is critical that the investigator clearly explain any change and the reasons for it, so that it may become part of the standard procedure for the future. We urge investigators to send us information on changes that have been clearly demonstrated to improve techniques, so that we can include the changes in subsequent editions of this book. Other suggestions and comments are also welcome and should be sent to Amphibian Techniques Book, National Museum of Natural History, Smithsonian Institution, Washington, DC 20560-0162 USA.

Comparisons with previous studies

Some users of this book may wish to sample amphibian populations at specific sites for comparison with previously published data. Such efforts were recommended by participants at the Declining Amphibian Populations Workshop (Anonymous 1991a) as a source of information on the status of certain amphibian populations. If the sampling technique used in the original study does not correspond exactly to a procedure outlined in this book, we nevertheless recommend that the investigator use one of the techniques discussed in Chapter 6, selecting the one most similar to the original and most appropriate for the target population or habitat. The information obtained will serve as a baseline against which data from future monitoring or inventory efforts can be compared. When the original sampling methodology is unknown, the investigator should use common sense in selecting an appropriate sampling technique.

Epilogue

When we began this project more than three years ago, we were largely motivated by our perception of the need for standardized sampling techniques. We were concerned about a possible global decline of amphibians and concluded that only through the use of standardized techniques could the size and consequences of such a loss of amphibian diversity be rigorously assessed. This volume is the culmination of our efforts to present in a useful format the best approaches available for measuring amphibian diversity. Some people may believe that we are trying to legislate research techniques. If recommending standardized protocols for sampling in order to facilitate rigorous, quantitative cross-sample comparisons is viewed as legislating techniques, then perhaps we are guilty. It was never our intent to bypass or slight any promising sampling technique, and from our perspective, we have not.

We experienced great excitement in assembling this book, because we realized that we were potentially making a significant contribution to amphibian inventory and monitoring studies and, thereby, to the understanding and conservation of these animals and their habitats. We hope that our enthusiasm for this project will carry over to our readers and that they will be stimulated to use these techniques in the field. Only through the continued study of amphibian diversity and habitats will we come to understand the place of these organisms in the natural environment. Nonprimate life-forms have complex and important roles to play in the maintenance of nature, a fact of which we have grown increasingly aware over the past decade as our understanding of the nature and interdependence of ecosystems has increased. Amphibians are among the significant players, and we encourage everyone to accord them the respect and attention they deserve.

Handling Live Amphibians

Gary M. Fellers, Charles A. Drost, and W. Ronald Heyer

Philosophy

In order to gather data on amphibians, it is often necessary to handle live individuals and sometimes to preserve them. Here, we provide guidelines for proper handling of live specimens; our aim is to describe an attitude of treatment, rather than to provide exhaustive coverage of methods of amphibian care. In all instances, live amphibians should be treated with care and respect.

Specific guidelines for the use of live amphibians in field research have been promulgated jointly by three herpetological societies (see Committee 1987). The Scientists' Center for Animal Welfare has also published guidelines for field research, with a discussion of their impact on institutional committees on animal care and use (Orlans 1988). Humane treatment of amphibians to be prepared as voucher specimens is reviewed in Appendix 4.

Handling

Amphibians should be captured carefully. In particular, contact with the tails of salamanders should be avoided because the tails break off easily when handled. Tail loss may have a significant effect on survivorship, reproduction, and dominance interactions with conspecifics.

Amphibians dry rapidly during handling, especially if they struggle. When an animal begins to dry, 5 to 10 ml of water should be poured over it. If the animal is held in cupped hands with water for a minute or so, it can absorb moisture more easily. Amphibians should be maintained in captivity as briefly as possible and under conditions that match their natural habitat as closely as possible.

If surgical procedures (e.g., toe clipping) are used, all equipment must be sterilized before moving from one collecting site to the next. This practice will prevent the inadvertent introduction of disease from one amphibian population to another.

Anesthesia

Some techniques (e.g., those involving surgery) require that amphibians be anesthetized. Amphibians are species-specific in their response to anesthetic chemicals; no single anesthetic is effective for all amphibians. A solution of 30% ethyl alcohol in water should be the first anesthetic agent tried, because of its wide availability and its effectiveness for many species. The amphibian is carefully placed in the solution. It is anesthetized as soon as it is completely flaccid when held or does not respond when nudged with a blunt probe.

Other anesthetic agents that have been used successfully include a solution of equal parts of saturated benzocaine solution and water; MS 222, or tricane methanosulfonate (ethyl M-aminobenzoate methanosulfonate) in aqueous solution ranging from 0.03% to 0.05%; and an aqueous solution of chlorobutanol (often referred to as Chloretone; for information on solution preparation, see "Procedures for Killing" in Appendix 4). All anesthetic solutions should be at pH 7.0 to avoid damage to the skin of sensitive species; this is particularly critical with MS 222.

Measurement

Body length, or snout-vent length (SVL), can be measured with a ruler fitted with a right-angle stop at one end, or, in the case of salamanders, a measuring tube can be used (Fellers et al. 1988). SVL is measured from the tip of the snout to the opening of the vent. When a ruler is used, it is best viewed from the side, as the frog or salamander is held against the ruler with its snout touching the stop. (Metal rulers with stops can be purchased from some bird-banding suppliers; see Appendix 6.) The animal's head, neck, and body should follow a straight line and be relaxed. The amphibian vertebral column is somewhat flexible. Therefore, it is important that one not try to straighten the animal by pulling hard on its body. Doing so stretches the animal and may harm it, and may result in inaccurate measurement.

Frogs, caecilians, and salamanders may be weighed in plastic bags of an appropriate size. After the animal is in a bag, the top should be folded over two or three times to reduce the space in which the animal can move and to decrease the surface area against which the wind can blow. The bag and animal are weighed with a spring balance, and the weight of the bag subtracted. On windy days the bag can be suspended in, but should not touch the sides of a jar.

Techniques for Marking Amphibians

Maureen A. Donnelly, Craig Guyer, J. Eric Juterbock, and Ross A. Alford

Marking adult amphibians

Several methods are available for marking adult salamanders and anurans (see Ferner 1979). The type of
system used depends on the size and natural history
of the target organism as well as time and resources.
Some marking methods require special equipment,
training, or permits from state or national wildlife
agencies. Marks can be permanent, temporary, date-
specific, or individual-specific. Long-term studies of
populations require that marks be permanent. Temporary marks can be used if information on behavior
over the course of a day or night is required (Jacobson 1985). Date-specific marks (all animals are
given identical marks during a sample period) can be
applied more rapidly in the field than individual-
specific marks, and it is simpler to take data from recaptured animals marked by date. Most population
estimators accommodate the use of date-specific

marks. If a project requires detailed information on
space-use patterns or growth rates in addition to an
estimate of population size, individual-specific
marks must be used.

Pattern Mapping

Color patterns of some amphibians vary among individuals and are analogous to fingerprints. These patterns can be recorded or "mapped" with photographs
or sketches (Forester 1977; Tilley 1977; Andreone
1986). Photographs should be sharp and shadow-
free, with good color rendition. Best results are obtained when animals are anesthetized (see
Appendix 1) and then photographed underwater. Several animals can be photographed together (3 to
4 adults or 8 to 12 juveniles per photograph), each
being assigned a two-part number (#A-#B) to denote

photograph (A) and position (B). Photoidentification requires a camera body, a macro lens, lighting (flash/strobe), film, and film processing. Color film provides the most realistic record of animal pattern, but if an animal's colors are contrasting, black and white film is a less expensive alternative. In field situations, Polaroid cameras allow for immediate results, but resolution is poor. Sketching animals requires more time but is less expensive than photography.

Loafman (1991) described a technique analogous to pattern mapping for spotted salamanders, which may be suitable for any spotted amphibian. He described each animal's pattern as the number of spots found on defined parts of the body (for example, head, neck, body, limbs). Loafman grouped all animals with the same head-spot pattern together. Within each head-spot group, animals were further classified by snout-vent spot counts, neck spot counts, and sex.

Marking and Tagging

Both tags and marks are permanent. They vary, however, in ease of application, cost, and potential negative effects on study organisms. Ideally, animals should be marked in the field and released at their capture point. If animals must be transported to a laboratory or field camp for marking, they should be returned to their capture point as soon as possible. Most tagging methods presently available probably work best for medium-sized to large frogs. We discuss several methods here. Radioactive and radiotelemetric marking are described in Chapter 7.

TAGS

Raney (1940), adapting a jaw tag used for fish (Shetter 1936), attached Monel metal strap or clip tags to the lower jaw of frogs with pliers. He recommended number 3 tags for adults and number 2 (fingerling) tags for juveniles. Raney (1940) asserted that the tags did not cause infection, but he did note that frogs pulled at the tags with their forelimbs, although the flesh did not tear. Stille (1950) reported tag loss, and Stebbins (in Woodbury 1956) observed irritation at the site of tag attachment. Kaplan (1958) tagged frogs with small, numbered, aluminum bird bands (butt-end) placed around the outer toe. The cylinder was closed with pliers only tightly enough to secure the band, but the toe webbing was pierced. Both Monel metal strap and butt-end bird bands are

available from National Band and Tag Company (Appendix 6).

Breder et al. (1927) attached tags to cords that were tied around the waist of the frog just in front of the hind limbs. The string was tied tightly enough to prevent tag loss; when it was too tight, it wore through the skin (Breder et al. 1927). Cardboard tags, which lasted approximately three months in the field, were attached with soft monofilament line. Aluminum tags were stamped with letter punches and attached with enameled trout line. For small species, tags consisting of three different-color beads were attached with a silk thread. Savage (1934) attached a small, waterproof, numbered paper tag to the waist of each frog in a field study of breeding behavior. He observed some tag loss and associated it, in part, with a decrease in female size after oviposition. The tags did not adversely affect breeding behavior.

Waistbands made from preshrunk nylon elastic banding that was painted and numbered were used to tag amphibians for behavioral studies (Woodbury 1956; Emlen 1968). The colored bands were visible from a distance of more than 5 m. The bands were tight enough not to catch on vegetation but loose enough to permit normal activity. Bands of this type are probably best used in short-term studies and must be removed at the end of the study.

Elmberg (1989) followed 637 *Rana temporaria* that had Floy-T tags (FT F-69 Fingerling tag) tied to their knees with elastic thread. These tags (6 × 3 mm), designed originally for small fish, come with thread and needle (tags available from Floy-Tag and Manufacturing; see Appendix 6). Tag loss ranged from 3% to 15% and resulted largely from imperfect application (Elmberg 1989). This method can be used for any frog or toad whose knee is narrower than the upper and lower legs. The size of the tag relative to the size of the frog must be considered, and this method may not be useful for small species or for juveniles of large species.

Nace and Manders (1982) used glass beads to identify individual *Xenopus* in laboratory populations. They anesthetized the animals (see Appendix 1) and inserted a 21-gauge hypodermic needle through the upper arm (lateral to the humerus) or leg (medial to the femur). A surgical wire (Ethicon Sutupak 0000 [32-gauge] or 00 [28-gauge] surgical steel monofilament Type B noncapillary) was passed through the needle, and the needle was withdrawn. A sequence of beads was strung on the wire, which was secured by tying a square knot on the medial side of the upper arm or the lateral side of the leg. The humerus or femur anchored the bracelet. This type of marking device should be tested before it is used in the field to ensure that the bracelet does not snag surrounding vegetation. In the laboratory, some frogs maintained their marks for more than 3 years.

POLYMERS AND PIGMENTS

Woolley (1973) tagged salamanders (*Eurycea lucifuga* and *E. longicauda*) with acrylic polymers. He filled a 2-cc syringe fitted with a 22-gauge hypodermic needle with a mixture of two parts acrylic polymer (Liquitex) and one part distilled water. He injected the mixture into the tail of each salamander until a mark 7 to 10 mm wide was obtained. The marks were distinct for 19 months and visible from a distance of 3 to 5 m.

Fluorescent pigments have been used to mark fishes (Phiney et al. 1967; Phiney and Mathews 1969), and some researchers have adapted these techniques to mark amphibians. Taylor and Deegan (1982) sprayed fluorescent pigments into the skin of aquatic amphibians (adults and larvae) with pressurized air (using a spray gun) to mass-mark individuals. Nishikawa and Service (1988) modified this technique to mark individuals of terrestrial species. They reduced the inner diameter of the spray gun nozzle to increase mark density, reduce mark size, and improve control over mark location. With the Nishikawa and Service technique, marks can be applied in the field without anesthesia, recapture rate is high, and marks are visible in light or dark. A portable ultraviolet light source is required for nighttime identification of individuals marked with fluorescent pigments. All supplies used in fluorescent marking (including four inert, nontoxic pigments) can be obtained from Scientific Marking Materials (Appendix 6). Fluorescent pigments (nine colors) are also available from Radiant Color Company (Appendix 6).

For salamanders, 10 mark locations (five on each side: anterior and posterior to arm, midbody, anterior and posterior to leg) coupled with five colors can be used to mark millions of salamanders (Nishikawa and Service 1988). It may be possible to mark small individuals in only three or four locations. Marks can last up to 2 years, but the survival rates of marked animals relative to those of animals marked with other techniques are not known.

Ireland (1991) described another fluorescent marking method, less expensive than those that use pressurized air. A probe dipped in glycerol and fluorescent powder is pressed on an area of skin that has been roughened with a pencil eraser. Several animals can be marked by varying color and position. The marks last approximately 6 months.

TRANSPONDERS

A passive integrated transponder (PIT) is a radio-frequency identification tag that consists of an electromagnetic coil, tuning capacitor, and microchip encased in glass. It is small (10×2.1 mm, 0.05 g) and carries a 10-digit hexadecimal number that is read with a portable scanner.

Camper and Dixon (1988) implanted PITs intraabdominally (with a modified metal syringe and a no. 12 cannula) into frogs with snout-vent lengths (SVL) of 80 mm or greater. The PIT and implanter were cleaned with 70% ethanol before implantation; after implantation the site was cleaned with ethanol and sealed with Krazy Glue (a brand of superglue). The PIT was detected most easily when it was oriented parallel to the main body axis. To implant large numbers of tags, a spring-loaded syringe with a trigger can be used (available from Destron/IDI vendors; see Appendix 6). Sam S. Sweet (pers. comm.) inserts PITs into the dorsal lymph sacs of toads (SVL > 40 mm) to avoid potential damage to internal organs. He uses scissors to make a posteriorly directed nick in the skin anterolateral to the sacrum; the PIT is inserted into the opening. The PIT tag method is appealing because up to 34 billion unique codes are possible, but the method is expensive. PIT tag vendors are listed in Appendix 6.

TOE CLIPPING

The least expensive option for marking anurans and salamanders is to remove toes in unique combinations. Alford et al. (unpubl. data) marked more than 12,000 *Bufo marinus* and hundreds of native frogs in Australia by clipping toes. The technique requires good scissors and alcohol to clean them. Antibiotic or antifungal creams or powders can be applied to digits to reduce the probability of infection. Martin and Hong (1991) successfully used Bactine® to treat wounds in captive amphibians; this antiseptic could be applied to clipped digits to prevent infection. For several salamander species, toes regenerate quickly and should be cut at an angle so that regenerating digits grow back at an angle. Salamanders should be anesthetized (Appendix 1) prior to toe clipping; anurans do not need to be anesthetized, but a local anesthetic can be used.

A variety of coding schemes for use with toe clipping have been developed (Figs. 28 and 29). In

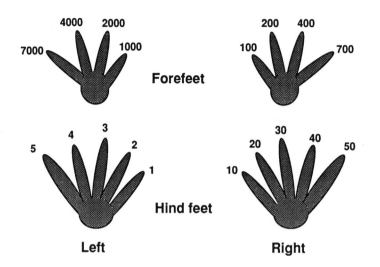

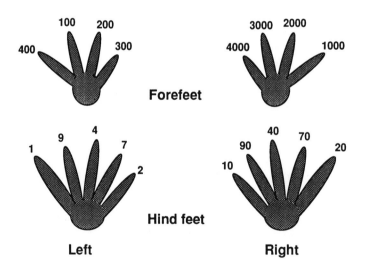

Figure 28. Clip-code schemes for marking salamanders. A. Twitty (1966) scheme. B. Scheme used by David B. Wake (pers. comm.). Using the Twitty scheme, code 4967 would require clipping one toe on the left forefoot (4000), two toes on the right forefoot (200 and 700), two toes on the right hind foot (20 and 40), and two toes on the left hind foot (5 and 2). Using the Wake scheme, code 4967 would require clipping one toe on the right forefoot (4000), three toes on the left forefoot (400, 200, and 300), two toes on the right hind foot (40 and 20), and one digit on the left hind foot (7).

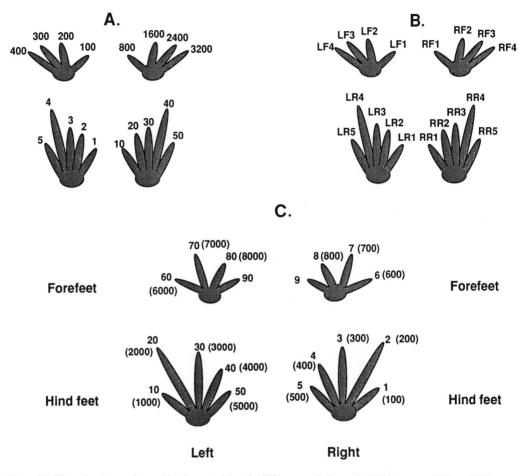

Figure 29. Clip-code schemes for marking frogs. A. Martof (1953) system. B. Donnelly (1989) system. C. Hero (1989) system. Using the Martof system, code 4967 would require clipping two toes on the right forefoot (3200 and 1600), one toe on the left forefoot (100), two toes on the right hind foot (40 and 20), and two toes on the left hind foot (2 and 5). See text for explanation of the Donnelly scheme. See text and Table 28 for explanation of the Hero scheme.

most, toes represent numbers. In the Martof (1953) scheme, for example, to mark animal number 577, two toes from the right forefoot and two toes each from the right and left hind feet must be cut (Fig. 29A). Hero (1989) devised a system (Fig. 29C) that requires clipping fewer toes than does the Martof scheme. Eighteen unique marks result when one toe is clipped, 124 marks when two toes are clipped, and 736 marks are obtained by clipping three toes (Table 28). Not all consecutive numbers are available after 99 in the Hero scheme. When two toes are cut on the same side of the body, the lower number is used; for example, if the third and fifth digits are clipped from the right hind foot, the code

is 103 rather than 301 (Fig. 29C)—clip code 301 does not exist in the Hero scheme (Table 28).

In the Donnelly (1989) scheme (Fig. 29B), toes are clipped in sequence, but they do not correspond to numbers. The code associated with each toe refers to foot location (left, right, front, rear) and toe position (innermost = 1, outermost = 4 or 5). The first 18 animals have one toe excised (LF1, LF2, LF3, LF4, RF1, RF2, . . ., RR3, RR4, RR5). After all unique one-toe codes are used, two toes are excised in unique combinations. For example, the first toe on the left front foot is cut (LF1) and one sequential digit on a remaining foot is cut (LF1-RF1, LF1-RF2, LF1-RF3, . . ., LF1-RR5). After code LF1-RR5 is

Table 28. Clip-Code Numbers Available for Marking Individuals, Using the Hero (1989) Toe-Clipping System[a]

Number of toes clipped	Clip-code number
1	1–10, 20, 30, 40, 50, 60, 70, 80, 90
2	11–19, 21–29, 31–39, 41–49, 51–59, 61–69, 71–79, 81–89, 91–99, 102–109, 203–209, 304–309, 405–409, 506–509, 607–609, 708, 709, 809, 1020, 1030, 1040, 1050, 1060, 1070, 1080, 1090
3	112–119, 122–129, 132–139, . . . , 192–199
	213–219, 223–229, 233–239, . . . , 293–299
	314–319, 324–329, 333–339, . . . , 349–399
	415–419, 425–429, 435–439, . . . , 495–499
	516–519, 526–529, 536–539, . . . , 596–599
	617–619, 627–629, 637–639, . . . , 697–699
	718, 719, 728, 729, 738, 739, . . . , 798, 799
	819, 829, 839, 849, 859, 869, 879, 889, 899
	1021–1029, 1031–1039, 1041–1049, . . . , 1091–1099
	2031–2039, 2041–2049, 2051–2059, . . . , 2091–2099
	3041–3049, 3051–3059, 3061–3069, . . . , 3091–3099
	4051–4059, 4061–4069, 4071–4079, 4081–4089, 4091–4099
	5061–5069, 5071–5079, 5081–5089, 5091–5099
	6071–6079, 6081–6089, 6091–6099
	7081–7089, 7091–7099
	8091–8099

[a] Not all sequential numbers after 99 are available (see text and Fig. 29C).

used, the same two-clip sequence is followed but the second toe on the left front foot is cut (LF2-RF1, LF2-RF2, . . ., LF2-RR5); this pattern is continued until all unique two-toe combinations are used (LR5-RR5). After all two-toe combinations are used, three digits are clipped in unique combinations. With this system, thousands of individuals can be marked by removing no more than two toes per foot. Waichman (1992) proposed an alphanumeric code that is equivalent to the code used by Donnelly (1989).

BRANDING

Four types of brands (tattoo, heat, silver nitrate, and freeze) have been used to mark amphibians. Kaplan (1958) tattooed frogs by scarifying a numeral into the ventral skin with a 27-gauge hypodermic needle. The needle did not penetrate the entire dermal layer. India ink mixed with a drop of glycerin was applied to the grooves to make the mark. Kaplan (1958) did not observe infection, redness (erythema) disappeared rapidly, and the numbers stood out vividly against the light ventral skin. Kaplan (1959) similarly marked frogs using a small electric tattoo maker with a narrow needle. He recommended tattooing the upper abdomen, after the skin was wiped dry with cotton. Most tattoo machines (Appendix 6) require electricity to power the needle. Two vendors (S & W Tattoo Supply Company and Tatoo-A-Pet) sell battery-operated machines for field use. These machines are portable and less expensive than those that require electricity.

Clark (1971) used a small-diameter chromium (20%) and nickel (80%) wire that was shaped into numerals or letters to brand *Bufo valliceps*. He heated the brands with a small propane torch and applied them to the ventral skin until the dermal layer was penetrated. A scab formed over each mark but disappeared after 2 weeks. Brands were legible for more than 20 months.

Thomas (1975) branded *Hyla cinerea* with silver nitrate. He made brands with commercial silver nitrate applicators (used in veterinary cauterization) and applied them to the dorsal skin. A brown mark formed on the skin immediately upon contact. One frog smeared silver nitrate over its dorsal surface; it was found dead 5 days later. Thomas noted that frogs had a brief reaction to the chemical, but he reported no other adverse effects. The dark mark faded 2 weeks after application.

Daugherty (1976) described freeze branding of *Ascaphus truei*. He fashioned branding irons from 12-cm lengths of insulated copper electrical wire. He removed the insulation from the terminal 3 cm of the wire and shaped it into numerals with pliers. He placed the branding irons in chips of dry ice (liquid nitrogen could also be used) for 30 minutes and then applied one to the ventral skin for approximately 10 seconds; the skin was not penetrated. The branding iron was returned to the dry ice and could be used again after 1 minute. Brands were legible within 24 hours and were visible for up to 2 years.

Marking larval amphibians

Marking larvae is difficult, and most methods generate date-specific rather than unique individual marks. Methods include fin clipping (Turner 1960; Guttman and Creasey 1973) and staining by immersion in a solution of neutral red dye (Herreid and Kinney 1966; Guttman and Creasey 1973). Travis (1981) found that the mark generated by the latter procedure was short-lived and resulted in decreased tadpole growth even at low tadpole densities. Seale and Boraas (1974) injected organic dyes into the tail; Cecil and Just (1976) injected acrylic polymers into the tail fins.

Ireland (1973) marked salamander larvae on the middorsal surface of the body with a paste made of fluorescent pigments and acetone. He applied the mark with a heated probe that had been dipped in the pigment paste. The probe burned through the outer epidermal layers, and the pigment was incorporated into the regenerated epithelium. Ireland (1983a,b; 1989) used two additional marking methods for salamander larvae. Small larvae (total length < 15 mm) were marked with a spray-paint gun that contained fluorescent pigment. Large larvae (total length > 15 mm) were tagged by applying a paste made of Congo red stain and dimethyl sulfoxide (DMSO) to a small lesion on the tail. He created the lesion by reflecting the skin on the lateral tail and teasing the superficial muscle with a sharp probe. After the paste was applied, the wound was sealed with super glue. The red stain was incorporated into the muscle after 15 days and was visible with a 10× hand lens.

Recommendations

Marking methods should be tested in the laboratory and in the field prior to the initiation of any long-term study. We do not recommend jaw-tagging amphibians, because tag loss violates mark-recapture assumptions 2 and 4 (see "Background" under "Mark-Recapture" in Chapter 8). Tags should not snag vegetation or interfere with movement or reproductive activities. Fluorescent marks and tags may make animals more conspicuous to investigators and predators. Because PIT tag implantation could damage internal organs, we recommend inserting PITs into the dorsal lymph sac rather than intraabdominally. Silver nitrate brands should be avoided because Thomas (1975) observed a reaction by the frogs to the chemical. Brands should never be applied to the ventral "pelvic patch," because that site is important in water-balance physiology of anurans. Branding methods should be practiced before adoption, so that damage to underlying muscles and organs can be avoided.

Pattern mapping does not affect animals adversely, but the methodology is relatively expensive if animals are photographed. Sketching is time-consuming but inexpensive and does not harm the study organisms; we recommend this method for species in which the variation in color pattern allows for individual recognition.

Although Clarke (1972) demonstrated that toe clipping can have adverse effects, it is the least expensive marking method that enables one to mark large numbers of animals quickly. This marking method may not be suitable for salamanders, because they regenerate toes quickly. Handling time in the field (especially for anurans) and equipment costs for toe clipping are minimal relative to time and costs required for other marking and tagging methods.

Recording Frog Calls

W. Ronald Heyer

Frog calls are used in conjunction with several inventory techniques described in this book, for example, audio strip transects and acoustic monitoring at fixed sites. To utilize such techniques successfully, an investigator must have tape recordings of frog calls from which to learn the calls and verify species identifications. In addition, tape recordings of frog calls may be important for systematic and behavioral studies and as voucher material (see "Voucher Specimens" in Chapter 5).

Equipment

Analyses of vocalizations are based on tape-recorded calls. To obtain suitable quality recordings for signal analysis, recording machines must accurately capture the dominant frequencies of frog calls, have good recording speed control, include an electronic record-level meter, and be portable and relatively easy to use. A variety of portable tape recorders meeting these requirements are available. Because frogs do not emit sounds of extremely high frequency, the recording equipment requirements for frogs are less demanding than those for bats, some birds, and many insects. Most species of frogs have dominant frequencies of about 4,000 Hz or less; only a few have calls with dominant frequencies in the 8,000–10,000 Hz range. Thus, a tape recorder with a flat frequency response from around 20 to 15,000 Hz is suitable.

Reliable recording speeds can be obtained with all but the least expensive recorders. However, speeds vary with all recorders when batteries begin to lose their charge. Some recorders have a safeguard against this problem and will not record when the battery charge is below a certain level; nevertheless, recording speed (or battery level) needs to be checked frequently. A peak-level light indicator (or other electronic recording-level meter) is important to ensure that calls are recorded at optimal levels. If levels are too high (calls too loud), signals can be distorted. Regular view meters (also known as VU meters) cannot track click-like calls of some frogs, which often results in defective recordings (distorted signals with clipped waveforms when analyzed on an oscilloscope). Recorders with both a VU meter and a peak-level light indicator are recommended. Click-like calls also cannot be recorded properly with machines in which gain (intensity level of signal being recorded) is controlled automatically. Recorders that do not have the option of manually adjusted gain should be avoided.

The best recorders available for fieldwork at present are reel-to-reel Uher or Nagra recorders (Nagra recorders do not have peak lights). Both brands are expensive (U.S. $2,000–$6,000), and neither the machines nor their manufacturers' authorized repair services are readily available. Because the popular market for recording and playback equipment has shifted from reel-to-reel format to cassette tape format, at this time the most accessible and least expensive machines are cassette recorders. Many workers use Marantz and Sony equipment in the U.S. $250–$500 range with good results. Currently, most frog workers use analogue tape recorders. Digital (DAT) recorders probably will be preferred when they are more widely known and used. Currently, a portable SONY DAT recorder is about U.S. $800 but does not work consistently under conditions of high humidity.

Microphone quality is as important as tape recorder quality. An acceptable microphone should have no noticeable distortion in the 20 to 10,000 Hz range (this information is documented in the specifications that come with microphones and recorders). If documentation accompanying a microphone does not include distortion information, the microphone is probably of low quality and should be avoided. Because most frogs are (or should be) recorded from short distances, either omnidirectional or directional microphones can be used. Some workers use "shotgun" microphones, which are directionally intermediate. Generally, parabolic reflectors are cumbersome and not necessary for recording frog vocalizations.

None of the portable recording equipment currently available is built to withstand the kind of field use required for tape recording frog vocalizations.

Most recorders do not function well when exposed to high humidity for extended periods. Yet many species of frogs call only when it is raining or very humid. Even the best-maintained machines rarely last more than 10 years in tropical humid conditions. It is important to store recording equipment in plastic bags with drying agents in the field and in a dry place otherwise. When several individuals share equipment, availability of multiple recorders and microphones will ensure that at least one set is working properly at all times. This practice probably dictates the use of cassette rather than reel-to-reel equipment, considering unit costs.

Recordings made with the equipment recommended above will be suitable for all research applications. In the absence of good equipment, whatever is available should be used—any recording is better than none.

Making the recording

Investigators may record either frog choruses or calling individuals. Chorus recordings are not particularly useful for research and are little used. If chorus recordings are desired, one tapes the chorus from a distance at which no individual call is distinguishable to the human ear. Chorus recordings should be complemented by recordings of individuals at the site. Individual calling males are recorded at distances from 0.5 to 1.5 m. It is critical that the frog being recorded be observed calling. Using an appropriate gain level is important; this level can be determined by monitoring several calls before recording. One begins recording with the gain meter purposely high and then adjusts it to the point just below that at which the peak light comes on. Background noise from other calling males should be minimized to the degree possible.

Recordings should be made only on one side of a tape. This will minimize problems with tape "bleeding" (migration of the magnetic signal from one piece of tape to an adjacent section of the reel under certain long-term storage conditions) and also will accommodate some variation in head alignment when the tape is replayed. Thin tape should not be used. For reel-to-reel recording, 1.0-mil tape is acceptable; 1.5-mil tape is recommended. For cassette tapes, tape thickness rarely is stated, but usually it is inversely correlated with recording time. Sixty-minute tapes (30 minutes per side) are sufficiently thick to be used; 90-minute tapes are too thin.

The duration of a recording depends on various factors, including how often the frog calls and how much tape is available. Most species call regularly enough so that a minimum of 5 to 10 calls and often 40 or more can be recorded in a few minutes. Some species may have very long calls or low call rates. In such instances, care should be taken to record the entire call, as well as the complete interval between calls (within reason), to provide call rate information.

At the end of each recording segment (recording of chorus or of individual), the person making the recording should add a voice label giving, at a minimum, the place, time, species field identification, temporary voucher information, and temperature (see below). Voice labels aid immeasurably in later location of the recording on a tape. Stating "the end" on tape when each recording unit is finished is also useful.

Calling rate, pulse rate, call length, and sometimes broadcast frequencies vary greatly with ambient temperature (Duellman and Trueb 1986:104). Thus, temperature data are critical for comparing different recordings, audiospectrograms, and other call data. If a frog is calling in water, water temperature should be taken. If a frog is calling from land, air temperature should be taken at or near the site. For large frogs, cloacal or mouth temperatures should also be taken with a quick-reading thermometer.

Voucher specimens

It is essential to capture and identify frogs that are recorded. At least one voucher specimen per species per calling site must be preserved (see Appendix 4), but we recommend that a voucher be made of each individual recorded. Call vouchers are important for species identification and for documenting the size of the individual recorded. Broadcast frequencies and other call variables vary with body size (Duellman and Trueb 1986:89).

Associated data

The following data in order of priority should be written in a field book (unless indicated otherwise) for each recording:

Mandatory. Tape identification—name of person making the recordings, field site, and tape number, to be written on the tape and the tape box (for example, "R. F. Inger, Borneo 1991, Tape 2"); field number of voucher specimen; specific locality at which recording was made; date of recording; temperature of air, water, and animal.

Strongly Recommended. Time of recording (24-hr clock); name of person recording the call if different from above (e.g., field assistant or student).

Highly Desirable. Weather conditions; calling site habitat; list of other species calling in background; tape recorder and microphone (equipment) used (microphone and tape recorder information can be noted on the tape box unless the equipment differs for different recordings on the same tape).

CONTRIBUTOR: REGINALD B. COCROFT

Preparing Amphibians as Scientific Specimens

Roy W. McDiarmid

Introduction

Documentation of the species recorded in biodiversity and inventory projects frequently involves preparation of voucher specimens, which are extremely important for the credibility of such studies (see Chapter 5). In addition, these specimens and their accompanying field notes are valuable sources of scientific information used in systematic, biogeographic, evolutionary, and ecological studies.

Most vouchers are preserved specimens from the study site, although photographs of individuals or tape-recorded calls of frogs are sometimes substituted. To be useful as vouchers and to facilitate identifications of species, preserved specimens must be well prepared and well documented. Poorly prepared or improperly documented specimens are of little scientific value and usually not worth the effort of preparation. In this section I review the steps involved in the proper preparation of amphibians as scientific study specimens (for additional discussion, see Pisani 1973; Karns 1986; Simmons 1987).

Documentation

Field notes should be written on 100% cotton rag paper with permanent ink. Most field biologists record field notes on loose-leaf paper stored in a three-ring binder. Although some people argue that loose-leaf binders are inferior to bound volumes because pages may be lost, this is not a problem if a person is careful. A loose-leaf format provides flexibility and allows for easy insertion of extra pages, maps, lists, and other important documents. Because bound books have a fixed size, they may contain too many pages for short trips and too few pages for

Roy W. McDiarmid
Field Catalogue

Venezuela
1984

8 January 1984	Venezuela: Territorio Federal Amazonas; Neblina Basecamp, on Rio Baria; 140m; 0°50'N, 66°10'W
17081	Pseudogonatodes sp. in leaf litter in camp, 11:40 photographed
17082	Hyla sarayacuensis under log in heliport clearing; afternoon photographed
9 January 84	Venezuela: Territorio Federal Amazonas; Neblina Massif, Camp II, 2.8 km NE Pico Phelps (= Neblina); 2085-2100 m; 0°49'40"N, 65°59'W
17083	Hyla photograph 9(26-28)
17084	Hyla photograph 9(29-32) both collected from the central axils of a bromeliad (Brocchinia sp.?), near camp both in axil with head up — colo notes — both bright green dorsally with bright yellow sides; yellow line on upper eyelid; blue green on chin & pectoral area; opalescent white peritoneum; iris bright coppery tissue taken from 17084
17185	leptodactylid?
17186	eggs from mass with 17185, under moss on rock — adult gave defense posture

Figure 30. Sample page from a field notebook.

long ones. Nevertheless, I recommend against taking a bound volume with original notes into the field on a subsequent trip because of the possibility of loss. This is not a problem with a loose-leaf notebook, because original pages can be left behind. Loose-leaf pages can easily be bound into annual or trip-related volumes for permanent archives.

Preserved specimens should be accompanied by the minimum data discussed in Chapter 5: locality, date and time of collection, collector, sampling method, habitat, and other locality-related information. Other specimen-related information—such as color notes and references to photographs, tape recordings, and tissue samples—should be recorded in the field notes (Fig. 30). Each reference to a voucher specimen in the notes should include the field number and temporary field identification (e.g., frog; *Rana* sp.; small brown salamander).

The number used in the field notes is written on a field tag and attached to the specimen (see below). Most field biologists use field numbers that include their initials followed by a number (e.g., RWM 19503), but any distinct numbering scheme will suffice (simpler is better). Field tags should be relatively small and of sturdy paper stock (Karns [1986] suggested Resistall Index Bristol, 100% rag, 110 lb. wt. paper, available from University Products; see Appendix 6). Field numbers should be written on the tag in permanent ink. Printed tags with consecutive numbers and other identifiers are available commercially. Although printed tags are relatively expensive (U.S. $20–$100 per 1,000 tags, National Tag Company), I recommend them because they save valuable field time and prevent double numbering. Tags of cloth or plastic can be used if paper tags are not available, but metal tags should be avoided because they sometimes corrode, and sharp edges can damage fragile specimens. Field tags should be strung with a fine white linen thread as shown in Figure 31. Colored thread should not be used because the dye may dissolve in preservative and discolor the specimens.

Specimen processing

Immature and adult amphibians collected as vouchers should be maintained in plastic bags until processed. Eggs and larvae require immediate attention, and I discuss them separately. When I capture a specimen, I usually place a numbered plastic tag in the bag with it and use that number to reference associated data in a small pocket notebook. I do not write data on paper tags and place them in the bag with the specimen because these quickly become wet and illegible. As soon as possible, I transfer pertinent data for each specimen from the pocket notebook to permanent field notes and assign a field number to the specimen. The plastic field tags can be washed and reused. I try to process all specimens as quickly as possible to avoid loss of individuals and confusion of associated data. Dead amphibians generally do not preserve well and make poor voucher specimens.

In some situations specimens may be frozen for later processing. However, Scott and Aquino-Shuster (1989) showed that amphibians frozen before preservation are softer and grayer than specimens that were not frozen, often have twisted toes, and lose their epidermis. Because some of the traits affected are important for species identification (e.g., coloration, toe and webbing characters, skin texture), I strongly recommend that specimens not be frozen.

Procedures for Killing

Amphibians should be killed as quickly and humanely as possible in a way that leaves them in a relaxed condition. The most efficient method for killing adult amphibians is to immerse them in a solution of Chloretone. A Chloretone solution is made by dissolving a small amount (1 teaspoon) of hydrous chlorobutanol crystals in a liter of water. Note that chlorobutanol crystals (and hypodermic syringes) are controlled substances in some countries, and investigators may need permits to obtain them. Be-

Figure 31. Numbered field tag and attached thread. Letters are the initials of the collector, and the numbers are consecutively printed ones. Note the location of the loop hitch, which holds the tag, and the knot, which holds the tag away from the animal.

cause chlorobutanol dissolves slowly, I often carry a small container of stock solution (95% ethyl alcohol saturated with chlorobutanol) and prepare a Chloretone solution in the field by adding a few milliliters of stock solution to 750 ml of water in a wide-mouthed liter bottle. I prepare a Chloretone solution as soon as I arrive at a field site so that it is ready when needed. Such a solution is effective for about 1 to 2 weeks (with heavy use) and then gradually loses its strength.

Species have noticeably different responses to Chloretone solutions. Some amphibians die rather quickly (5 min); others may take longer (10–15 min). The solution often increases in effectiveness, probably from the addition of various skin secretions from amphibians killed in the solution. If amphibians do not die after 20 to 30 minutes in the solution, additional chlorobutanol should be added or, preferably, a new solution prepared. Amphibians should not be left in the solution very long after they die, as they become rigid and difficult to position for fixation.

If Chloretone is not available, amphibians may be killed by drowning in warm water (43°–47°C) or in weak alcohol (15%–25%) solutions (Pisani 1973). Pithing may be effective, but it often damages the specimen, especially the skull. Benzocaine-containing gels, sold in most pharmacies as toothache medication, can be used as an alternative to Chloretone (Altig 1980). A small amount smeared on the head of an amphibian kills it within a few minutes, and the specimen is completely relaxed. Freezing is not recommended as a method for killing (Scott and Aquino-Shuster 1989).

Preservatives

Preserving amphibians for scientific study is usually a two-step process. Initially, specimens are fixed in an appropriate preservative, and then they are transferred to an alcohol solution for storage. The most common general fixative for amphibians is formaldehyde. At room temperatures, formaldehyde is a gas; under pressure, it polymerizes to a solid called paraformaldehyde. An aqueous solution of formaldehyde is easier to handle than the gas and has been used as a histological fixative for about 100 years (Fox and Benton 1987). Formaldehyde is commercially available as a liquid that is made by dissolving formaldehyde gas in water as a 37% to 40% solution. A formaldehyde solution of this strength is equivalent to 100% formalin (formaldehyde diluted with water). One part of this full strength formalin is diluted with nine parts water to make a 10% solution of formalin.

A 10% solution is the standard for specimen fixation in the field. A fixed specimen retains whatever position it had when placed in the formalin. This stabilization (fixation) is effected by cross-linkage of the formalin with protein end groups in the tissue. This process stops autolysis and prevents further tissue deterioration. Although the rate of fixation varies with the size of the specimen and probably with the nature of the tissues, most small amphibians set in a few hours; larger specimens require much longer. Fixation generally is considered to be irreversible, but Pearse (cited in Taylor 1977) found that many of the cross-linking bonds are reversible with the simple process of washing; others are not. Because washing under certain situations may reverse fixation, I recommend that amphibians not be soaked in water prior to transfer to ethyl alcohol.

Because formaldehyde is a gas, a formalin solution exposed to air decreases in strength and becomes more acidic. It is especially important, therefore, to use freshly prepared 10% solutions to fix specimens. I recommend replacing formalin in trays after preserving 50 to 100 specimens of various sizes. Old formalin can be used in the field as a storage solution for specimens after fixation, or it should be properly discarded in keeping with regulations of the country where the investigator is working.

Formaldehyde oxidizes to form formic acid, which, after a time, will decalcify bone and discolor specimens. Specimens fixed in formalin that is alkaline, in contrast, tend to become transparent, or "cleared" (Taylor 1977). Because decalcification, excessive discoloration, and clearing are undesirable, most field herpetologists buffer formalin to maintain the pH as close to neutral as possible. Fox and Benton (1987) indicated that an optimum pH for formalin fixation is 7.2. Although borax has been suggested as a suitable buffer (Pisani 1973), Taylor (1977) argued against its use because specimens tend to clear in borax-buffered formalin; instead he recommended calcium carbonate. In the field I have used powdered magnesium carbonate with good results (about 1/2 teaspoon per liter of 10% formalin). To buffer formalin used in the museum, I add 4.0 g of sodium phosphate monobasic and 6.5 g of sodium phosphate dibasic (anhydrous) to each liter of 10% formalin.

In the museum, I prepare formalin with distilled water, but in the field I use whatever water is available. Field researchers should be aware, however, that stream or pond water may be quite naturally acidic or basic, and, therefore, formalin made with such water may require additional treatment. The use of rainwater often alleviates the pH problem, but even rainwater can be acidic. If the pH of water at a field site is potentially a problem, then it may be desirable to check the pH of the solution with indicator paper. I use a pH meter in the museum.

Occasionally in remote areas, one purchases bad formalin (i.e., it does not fix animals as well as expected). I suspect that such formalin has been oxidized extensively and probably contains considerable formic acid. Workers need to be aware of this problem and to test the pH of all formalin solutions. I repeatedly examine fixed materials in the field to avoid problems of poor fixation. Formaldehyde fixation is a complicated process and can be influenced by many extraneous factors. If an investigator is obtaining the desired results, I recommend that he or she continue the process. In the absence of desired results, I recommend starting over with fresh solutions. If the problem persists, help from a chemist or a museum curator should be sought.

As most herpetologists know, formaldehyde is irritating to the eyes, upper respiratory passages, and skin. Some people develop an allergic reaction to formalin and must wear rubber gloves to prevent skin rashes. Formaldehyde also has been reported to be a potential carcinogen (Simmons 1987); thus, it should be used only in well-ventilated areas. Fortunately, most field situations fall into this category.

If formaldehyde is not available as a fixative, 70% ethyl alcohol can be used. I do not recommend other kinds of alcohol (e.g., methyl, isopropyl, rubbing). Fixatives such as formalin-acetic-alcohol (FAA), glutaraldehyde (Taylor 1977), and Bouin's solution (especially good for histological work) are more difficult to prepare but also can be used. Formalin solutions also can be prepared from paraformaldehyde (see recommendations in Huheey 1963; Pisani 1973; Saul 1981).

Fixation

Once an amphibian is dead and relaxed, it can be fixed in a preserving tray in 10% formalin. Typically, I use a plastic refrigerator tray ($33 \times 21 \times 6$ cm) with a tightly fitted lid. I line the bottom with a white paper towel soaked with 10% formalin (dye from colored towels will discolor specimens). Each specimen is positioned in the tray in a way that will facilitate measurement and examination of key features on preserved specimens and that also will allow for more-effective storage and hence long-term maintenance of the specimens. I position frogs so that their limbs are drawn in next to the body and flexed in a natural way; fingers and toes are straightened and spread to display webbing (Fig. 32). I do not recommend the positioning illustrated by Pisani (1973: plate 1) or Karns (1986: fig. 24), in which one or both hind limbs of a frog are extended posteriorly. In my experience extended limbs easily become tangled with other specimens and tags as animals are removed from a storage jar. Often the epidermis is scraped excessively and the hind feet damaged. From a practical perspective, frogs with extended limbs require more storage space (fewer frogs per container). They also require closer monitoring; the toes and webbing on the hind feet are particularly subject to desiccation and may be the first structures exposed to air as the alcohol level in the jar drops.

Most salamanders are laid out straight with the limbs pointing forward parallel to the body. The hands and feet are arranged with palmar surfaces down and toes spread, and the tail is straight (Fig. 32). Caecilians are preserved with the body straight or in a flat loop of a size appropriate for the containers used in the collection (Fig. 32). I preserve caecilians with their mouths held open by a small stick or piece of paper towel; this practice facilitates later examination of tooth arrangement.

Formalin penetrates the body cavity of small amphibians rather quickly, so injection is not necessary. Large frogs (adults of many species of *Bufo, Rana,* and *Leptodactylus*), salamanders (sirenids, cryptobranchids, and adults of larger species of *Ambystoma*), and caecilians may require injections of formalin into the body cavity and larger muscle masses. Care should be taken not to distend the body by injecting too much formalin and not to introduce air into the body cavity. Frogs distended with air float in the hardening solution, so some areas of the body are not covered with fixative. It also is important to keep track of individuals in the tray so that the correct field tag can be associated with the appropriate individual after it has hardened. I sometimes lay the tag across the specimen in the tray. Once the floor of the tray is covered with specimens, I blanket them with a second paper towel wet with formalin and carefully fill the tray with formalin to about one third its depth.

After a few hours, most specimens will have hardened enough to maintain their shape. This is the

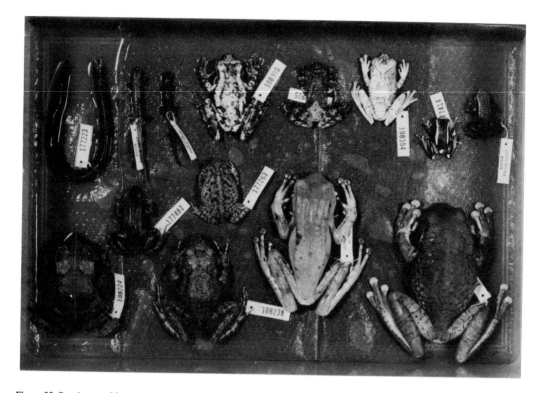

Figure 32. Specimens of frogs, salamanders, and a caecilian preserved in the recommended postures (see text for explanation).

time to attach the field tag. Some herpetologists prefer to attach tags to specimens prior to positioning them in the hardening tray to ensure that tags and specimens do not get mixed. I have found, however, that specimens are more difficult to position for hardening with the tag attached. The tag is tied with a square knot above the knee on the right rear leg of frogs and large salamanders, and around the neck of small salamanders and caecilians; ends of the thread are trimmed. The specimens are transferred to a hardening jar, where they remain immersed in 10% formalin for at least 4 days or, preferably, for the remainder of the field season.

Eggs and Larvae

Amphibian eggs and larvae usually require special treatment. They are easily damaged, especially during collecting, if not handled carefully. As a result, when collecting eggs or tadpoles I usually preserve some in the field and take others back to camp alive.

I place single, short strings or small clumps of aquatic eggs directly into small bottles or vials of freshly prepared 10% buffered formalin that I carry with me in the field for that purpose. I usually place terrestrial eggs, eggs adhering to leaves, and larger egg masses (e.g., those of some species of *Ambystoma*), into plastic bags and carefully transport them back to the work area for examination, rearing (see below), and preservation in suitably sized containers. I put some larvae directly into formalin as they are collected, and carry others back to camp in plastic bags. Because eggs and larvae, especially of anurans, contain much more water than adults contain, they seemingly require a larger volume or slightly stronger concentration of fixative initially than do adults. I sometimes carry a small amount of pure formalin into the field to meet such needs.

On returning to camp or the lab, I routinely sort and transfer all preserved eggs and larvae to larger containers of fresh 10% formalin. During the sorting process, I identify larval morphotypes, write color notes, and take photographs. At this time I also decide whether to maintain some of the live eggs until hatching or to rear some of the live tadpoles through metamorphosis. I often preserve a few eggs from a clutch and place the remainder in an appropriate container to continue their development. With larvae, I often return to the site and collect additional specimens for rearing (see below). After sorting the specimens, I write field notes and assign tags to the larval samples. Tadpoles that have been in an adequate volume of fresh formalin for 24 hours are well fixed and can be transferred with their field tags to smaller vials for storage and eventual transport. A tag should never be tied to a tadpole or to a small salamander or caecilian larva; tags may be attached to larger salamander and caecilian larvae if tagging does not damage the specimen. I prefer to sort samples into morphotypes in the field and tag them accordingly. However, if storage space or tags are limited, all specimens collected at a single site on a single day can be maintained as a single sample. Samples collected at different localities or sites or on different days must not be mixed.

Because the eggs and larvae of many species are unknown, efforts should be made to associate each with its respective adult form. If time permits, an investigator can obtain and rear eggs from known adults or can rear unknown larvae through metamorphosis in the field. Aliquot samples representative of the eggs and larvae from a single known sample can be preserved at appropriate intervals during development. Such developmental series are very useful in understanding the ecology of species and may contribute significantly to investigations of the evolution of morphological traits in amphibians.

Containers suitable for rearing tadpoles can be set up in camp, and tadpoles of specific morphotypes can be reared. I usually maintain each sample (species) separately in water taken from its habitat and, if possible, feed the tadpoles natural-occurring food. I use artificial food (e.g., tropical fish food, trout chow, rabbit pellets) if natural foods are not easily obtainable. Periodic sampling of tadpoles from the same aquatic habitat sometimes is more efficient than rearing them. Tadpoles sampled from populations maintained artificially in the field or laboratory should be given separate numbers and cross-referenced in field notes to the field number of the original sample. Date, time of sampling, and rearing conditions (e.g., container size, temperature, food) for each sample should be recorded.

Special preparations

Sometimes it is desirable to prepare specimens for osteological study. Because of distortion from drying, cleared and stained preparations (see below) are preferable for most species of amphibians. However, dry preparations of larger species are suitable and sometimes preferred. Simmons (1986) described a method for making osteological preparations from alcoholic specimens. I recommend his approach, although it is time-consuming. If a specimen is prepared as a dry skeleton in the field, the selected individual should be weighed and measured before it is put into Chloretone. Skinning should follow the steps outlined by Simmons (1986), except that no parts of the skeleton should be disassociated. The sex of the specimen should be determined when the animal is eviscerated, and stomach contents should be recorded. If the latter seem interesting, they should be preserved and referenced with the same field number as the specimen.

To make an osteological specimen, the preparator removes most of the muscle mass, being careful not to cut the pectoral girdle or hyoid apparatus, and attaches a field tag to the leg once it is mostly free of tissue. The specimen is then wrapped into a compact but loose ball with string and hung in a dry place, preferably within a screened enclosure or cage to discourage flies and animals that may carry off a carcass. If the specimen does not dry quickly, it can be immersed in alcohol for a few hours and dried again. It should not be put in formalin, because dermestid beetles, which are used to clean skeletal material, will not eat formalin-treated carcasses. Putting the carcass in a small cheesecloth bag will help to exclude flies and to maintain all skeletal elements in a single package. Once a carcass is thoroughly dry, it can be packed in its cheesecloth bag for shipment back to the museum. Simmons (1987) provided many references to techniques for preparing skeletons and cleared and stained specimens.

Packing and shipping

At the end of a field season or work at a site, all prepared specimens should be checked to see that field tags are attached and that no problems with associated data remain. If live material is to be taken to the next site or back to the museum for continued rearing (a job that is sometimes difficult but potentially worth the effort), then a sample should be preserved at the last possible moment to ensure that representative material at that stage of development is available for study.

Preserved specimens are sorted by shape, size, and method of preparation. Dry skeletal preparations should be packed in dry containers (small cans or durable cardboard boxes) with lots of padding. Vials containing eggs and larvae are grouped by size and wrapped with packing material or strips of paper towel. Vials of similar size are packed tightly in plastic jars, cans, or other appropriate containers with paper or cardboard dividers, as necessary. I pack vials in sealable containers (cans or plastic jars) rather than in cardboard boxes because of the possibility of leaks or breakage during transport. If cardboard boxes are used, they should be sealed in plastic bags. Wet specimens should be loosely wrapped in paper towels or cheesecloth for protection and easier packing. Many small packages, each containing a few specimens, seem to be better than fewer, larger packages. If the collecting site is near the laboratory, so that collections can be returned from the field by car, then transporting wrapped specimens in trays with formalin works well if the trays are kept flat. Small specimens can be left in formalin in sealed containers.

If collections have to be shipped from the field site to the laboratory or taken as baggage on an airplane, then different packing is required. Weight and leakage are primary considerations, and plastic containers are much better than glass ones. Wet specimens should be wrapped in cheesecloth or paper towels and placed in a plastic bag. When the bag is about one third full of one or more equal-sized bundles, just enough formalin to soak the packages should be added, and the bag tied securely or closed with a rubber band. After the bag is checked for leaks, it is placed in a second bag that also is tied. Bags of comparable size can be packed snugly in plastic jars, preserving trays, or other sealable containers, which are then taped shut. These containers can be packed into shipping boxes or fiberboard drums designed for shipping wet materials. An address label should be placed on the inside as well as on the outside of each shipping container. Sometimes I hand-carry small containers of fragile specimens or vials of eggs and larvae. I have carried half-liter plastic jars filled with small frogs and salamanders packed between layers of cheesecloth wet with formalin, with good success. The formalin in these containers can be replaced with 70% ethyl alcohol for transport on an airplane. If I know that a trip is going to be short (< 12 hr), and I am hand-carrying specimens, I sometimes replace the formalin in vials with water. This ensures that formalin will not be spilled during transport. I refill the vials with fresh 10% formalin *immediately* on reaching my destination. Larvae need to be shipped in vials or similar containers with some liquid and should never be wrapped in cheesecloth. With careful packing and common sense, important materials will arrive unharmed.

Field equipment and supplies

One or more good-quality headlamps, along with batteries and replacement bulbs, are essential for nighttime survey work. I rely on a plastic headlamp with four D-size batteries. I prefer D-cells over a single 6-volt battery because D-cells generally are more readily available and easier to pack. Some people use rechargeable D-cells, but in my experience, they do not last very long and do not provide the service that an alkaline cell gives. Another option is the more powerful, rechargeable miner's lamp with a wet-cell (motorcycle type) battery. A miner's lamp gives a brighter beam and, though initially more expensive, may be less expensive in the end, because the batteries can be recharged hundreds of times. However, like nickel-cadmium dry cells, the batteries require electricity or solar panels for recharging; also they are hard to pack and burdensome to maintain during long periods of disuse.

The following list of equipment and supplies is provided as an aid to preparing for fieldwork. Sources for these supplies can be found in Appendix 6.

Collecting Equipment. Headlamp and batteries; replacement bulbs; small flashlight and batteries; assorted plastic bags; cloth bags; temporary plastic field tags; thermometers; compass; altimeter; machete and file; pocket knife; insect repellent.

Equipment for Observing, Studying, and Measuring. Measuring tape; marking flag; calipers; plastic rulers (10- and 30-cm); spring scales (10-, 100-, and 500-g); small scissors; hand lens; camera and film; tape recorder, microphone, batteries, and tape; binoculars.

Equipment for Recording Data. Notebook and waterproof paper; small pocket notebook; pens and ink; pencils; Sharpie indelible-ink marking pen; field tags; waterproof paper for duplicate tags; thread; scissors (for paper); cigarette lighter; candles for light when writing.

Equipment for Larval Sampling. Dipnets (large and small); spare net bags; small-mesh strainers; assorted vials and small jars; large-gauge pipette; rearing containers (plastic food containers with lids); plastic bags; artificial food (trout chow, tropical fish flakes); plastic spoon.

Preserving Equipment. Forceps (long and needle-nosed); dissecting scissors; scalpel and blades; single-edged razor blades; needle and thread; preserving trays; wide-mouth jar for Chloretone; syringes (1-, 10-, and 30-cc); syringe needles (various sizes); hardening and storage jars; paper towels.

Chemicals. Formalin (full strength); buffer (magnesium carbonate); chlorobutanol or Chloretone (saturated solution); alcohol (full-strength ethanol).

Containers. Assorted plastic jars (0.5- to 3.2-liter); shipping containers; bucket or Liquipak (a watertight fiber drum for shipping wet materials).

Packing Supplies. Fiber tape; string; rubber bands; cheesecloth; heavy plastic bags; scissors (for cheesecloth); paper towels; mailing labels; Sharpie indelible-ink pen.

Collecting Tissue for Biochemical Analysis

Jeremy F. Jacobs and W. Ronald Heyer

Biochemical techniques have opened up new sources of data with relevance to many questions in ecological and evolutionary biology. Currently, molecular analytical techniques range from protein assays to determination of DNA sequences. Not all current molecular techniques require frozen tissues, but frozen tissues, if properly sampled and stored, are suitable for most analyses. For this reason, we recommend collection and storage of frozen tissues. If it is impossible to freeze tissues in the field, certain tissue-specific preservatives can be used to provide material for microcomplement fixation and DNA analysis (Dessauer et al. 1990:29–30).

Freezing tissues in the field

Two materials can be used to freeze tissues in the field: dry ice (solid CO_2) and liquid nitrogen. Tissues frozen in ice (solid water) are not suitable for most standard biochemical assays of proteins or DNA.

Dry ice can be stored in a sealed plastic bag in a Styrofoam chest or box, but even so, it evaporates quickly (about 2–3 kg/day). Maximum field time for dry ice, using a very large portable ice chest, is about a week. Dry ice generally is available from industrial chemical supply firms or frozen food (ice cream) distributors.

Liquid nitrogen tanks or refrigerators (essentially large stainless steel vacuum flasks, about U.S. $500; see Appendix 6) are used in the field for freezing and storing tissues. The common term among users for this type of container is *tank* or, rarely, *Dewar flask;* however, the vendor's term is *refrigerator*. Tanks come in a variety of sizes with capacities of 3 to 34 liters. The largest hold enough liquid nitrogen to keep tissues frozen for at least several months in the field. A tank containing liquid nitrogen must be kept upright at all times and under shade as much as possible. Liquid nitrogen is not generally available, but it often can be found in larger industrial cities, because it has various industrial and agricultural applications. Liquid nitrogen generally is less readily available than dry ice; some vendors require 48 hours to fill a tank to capacity.

Both dry ice and liquid nitrogen (in its refrigerator) are legally transportable, including by air. However, many airline personnel are reluctant to allow shipment of liquid nitrogen. Patience on the part of the shipper is required. Copies of the appropriate pages from the most recent International Air Transport Association regulations (Anonymous 1991b), to which all airlines adhere, are often helpful in demonstrating that liquid nitrogen can be shipped safely and legally. A useful strategy, if there is a good mass of tissues and if it is certain that the tank will be in transit for no more than 24 hours, is to empty the tank of liquid nitrogen just prior to return by air. An alternative is to add dry ice pellets after pouring off the liquid nitrogen (before going to the airport, as the addition of dry ice results in hissing sounds and fog). Tissues in a tank with dry ice will remain frozen for 3 to 4 days. In the laboratory, tissues should be maintained either in liquid nitrogen or in an ultracold freezer (constant temperature of at least −70° C).

Protocol for preparing tissue samples

First, the amphibian to be sampled is killed by anesthesia (see Appendices 1 and 4) or by pithing before tissues are removed. Next, tissues are collected separately for each individual. Tissues are removed as quickly as possible under as cool conditions as possible (shade) to avoid degradation, especially when small animals are processed in hot, dry weather.

Liver, heart, kidney, muscle (abdominal or thigh), and, for large amphibians, blood are sampled (the tissues analyzed will depend on the research question). The abdominal cavity is opened, and the organs are pulled from the body and cut into small chunks that will fit in cryotubes (e.g., Nunc tubes). Two tubes (up to 2 cc total) of tissue are prepared if the animal is large enough and time permits. Muscle and all viscera are sampled from small individuals (the stomach and intestine should be opened and cleaned, and the gall bladder either removed or not broken). We do not recommend freezing the entire specimen. Whole frozen amphibians make poor voucher specimens when preserved, and if the entire specimen is consumed in analysis, there is no voucher. If, because of time constraints, it is necessary to freeze entire specimens, other specimens of the species from the same population should be preserved as vouchers.

Tissues are placed either in commercially available screw-top plastic tubes designed for ultracold temperatures or in aluminum foil. We recommend plastic tubes. Mixing of different tissues from the same individual within tubes is acceptable for most analytical procedures. An air space should always be left in the tube for expansion of the tissue when it freezes.

Each tissue sample is labeled with a field number that is the same as the number of the voucher specimen from which the tissues were taken. A label with the specimen field number is also placed inside the tube (written in India ink, preferably, or in pencil); the label must be dry before the tissue is added. In addition, the field number (and, if space is available, brief locality information) should be written on the outside of the dry tube before the tissue is added. Ink that neither decays at cold temperatures nor smears when moist must be used on the outside of the tube (not India ink); a pen such as the Sharpie by Sanford works well.

After each specimen is sampled, scissors, forceps, all other equipment, and all working surfaces should be cleaned thoroughly. Material from one individual must not be contaminated with tissues from another individual or with blood or skin from the investigator. This precaution is especially critical for DNA analysis, because current replication techniques (e.g., polymerase chain reaction) can amplify tiny amounts of DNA.

Finally, the carcass is prepared as a voucher specimen (see Appendix 4) with the same number as the tissue sample and is deposited in a museum. For more detailed guidelines on collection and storage of tissues, see Dessauer et al. (1990). Tissue depositories are listed in Dessauer and Haffner (1984).

Sample size

The number of specimens to be sampled from each locality depends on the research question. For example, a single individual may be adequate for a phylogenetic question using DNA sequencing techniques, but 30 individuals per population may be needed to study interpopulational variation using electrophoretic or mitochondrial restriction site techniques (for more explicit guidelines, see Baverstock and Moritz 1990). However, most researchers using molecular techniques subscribe to the idea that one specimen is better than none.

We strongly encourage persons who are taking tissues to collect samples from amphibians other than those in which they have a direct research interest. Such sampling is particularly important if rarely encountered species are collected or remote areas are visited.

CONTRIBUTOR: JOHN E. CADLE

Vendors

The list of vendors is provided to aid investigators (particularly those outside of the United States) in locating equipment necessary for amphibian biodiversity studies. This list is not exhaustive, and inclusion on the list is not intended as an endorsement of any vendor. The list is organized alphabetically by vendor, and the products offered are indicated in brackets.

Equipment and supplies

ALLFLEX S.A. (sales in Europe excluding the UK)
26 rue Berthollet
75005 Paris
France
Telephone: 33-1-43-36-6060
Fax: 33-1-43-37-8130
[PIT tags and scanners—AVID]

Animal Electronic ID Systems Ltd. (AEIDS) (sales in Australia and New Zealand)
33 Bong Bong Street
Kiama NSW 2533
Australia
Telephone: 61-4232-3333
FAX: 61-4232-3350
[PIT tags and scanners—Destron/IDI]

Animal Identification and Marking Systems, Inc.
221 Second Avenue
Piscataway, NJ 08854
USA
Telephone: 908-356-9366
Fax: 908-271-8857
[tattooing equipment]

AVID
Douglas E. Hull
3179 Hammer, Suite 5

Norco, CA 91760
USA
Telephone: 714-371-7505
Fax: 714-737-8967
[PIT tags and scanners—AVID]

AVID (UK) Ltd. (sales in the UK)
Panorama House
89a Church Road
Hove, East Sussex, BN3 2GH
England
Telephone: 02-73-74-9017
Fax: 02-73-20-5036
[PIT tags and scanners—AVID]

AVM Instrument Co., Ltd.
2356 Research Drive
Livermore, CA 94550
USA
Telephone: 510-449-2286
Fax: 510-449-3980
Telex: 262229 AVM UR
[radio transmitters]

Belfort Instrument Co.
727 S. Wolfe Street
Baltimore, MD 21231
USA
Telephone: 301-342-2626
telex: 87-528 (Belfort Bal)
[data loggers]

Ben Meadows Co.
P.O. Box 80549
3589 Broad Street
Atlanta, GA 30366
USA
Telephone: 800-241-6401, 404-455-0907
Fax: 404-457-1841
[air meters, altimeters, altimeter-barometers,
anemometers, barometers, clinometers, flagging,
hand lenses, hygrothermographs, rain gauges, scales,
soil moisture meters, tensiometers, thermographs,
thermometers, waterproof field books]

BioMedic Data Systems, Inc.
255 W. Spring Valley Avenue
Maywood, NJ 07607
USA
Telephone: 800-526-2637, 201-587-8300
Fax: 201-843-8816
[PIT tags and scanners—BioMedic Data Systems]

BioQuip
17803 LaSalle Avenue
Gardena, CA 90248-3602
USA
Telephone: 310-324-0620
Fax: 310-324-7931
[fluorescent pigments, headlamps, hand lenses, nets,
Pesola scales, pH meters, thermometers, ultraviolet
lights, waterproof field books]

BioSonics, Inc. (sales in North, Central, and South
America)
3670 Stone Way N.
Seattle, WA 98103
USA
Telephone: 206-634-0123
Fax: 206-634-0511
[PIT tags and scanners—Destron/IDI]

Campbell Scientific, Inc.
P.O. Box 551
Logan, UT 84321
USA
Telephone: 801-753-2342 (USA), 05-09-672516
(UK)
Fax: 801-752-3268 (USA), 05-09-674928 (UK)
Telex: 453058
[data loggers, leaf wetness sensors
(= wetness-sensing grids), pyranometers, relative
humidity probes, tipping bucket rain gauges]

Carolina Biological Supply Co.
2700 York Road
Burlington, NC 27215
USA
Telephone: 800-334-5551, 919-584-0381
Fax: 919-584-3399
[anemometers, barometers, hand lenses, headlamps,
minnow traps, nets, pH meters, psychrometers, rain
gauges, seines, seine poles, thermometers, weather
stations]

Climatronics
140 Wilbur Place
Bohemia, NY 11716
USA
Telephone: 516-587-7300
Fax: 516-567-7585
[data loggers]

Cole-Parmer Instrument Co.
7425 N. Oak Park Avenue

Chicago, IL 60648
USA
Telephone: 800-323-4349 (Canada and USA, exclusive of Alaska and Chicago, Illinois), 312-647-7600 (Alaska; Chicago, Illinois; other countries)
Fax: 708-647-9660 (USA and Canada), 708-647-9600 (all other countries)
[anemometers, barometers, cryotubes, data loggers, hand lenses, humidity sensors, hygrometers, hygrothermographs, liquid nitrogen tanks, pH meters, psychrometers, temperature-humidity meters, thermistors, thermocouples, thermometers, ultraviolet lamps (battery-operated), weather stations]

Commercial Fishing Supplies
2200 Highway 111
Granite City, IL 62040
USA
Telephone: 800-878-6387, 618-797-0211
Fax: 618-797-0212
[nets, seines, custom-made nets]

Corning Glass Works
Corning, NY 14831
USA
Telephone: 800-222-7740 (USA), 607-974-4401 (Canada)
[cryotubes. Corning sells only to companies; write or call Corning for vendor information.]

Custom Electronics of Urbana, Inc.
2009 Silver Court W.
Urbana, IL 61801
USA
Telephone: 217-344-3460
[radiotelemetry equipment]

Custom Telemetry and Consulting, Inc.
185 Longview Drive
Athens, GA 30605
USA
Telephone: 404-548-1024
[custom radiotelemetry equipment]

Delta-T Devices
128 Low Road
Burwell, Cambridge, CB5 0EJ
England
Telephone: 06-38-742922
Fax: 06-38-743155
[data loggers, thermocouple wire]

Didcot Instrument Co., Ltd.
Station Road
Abingdon, Oxon, OX14 3LD
England
[data loggers, thermocouple wire]

Electronic Controls Design, Inc.
13625 S. Freeman Road
Mulino, OR 97042-9639
USA
Telephone: 800-323-4548
[data loggers]

Eppley Laboratories
P.O. Box 419
Newport, RI 02840
USA
Telephone: 401-847-1020
Fax: 401-847-1031
[thermopile pyranometers]

Euro I.D. (sales in Europe)
Grossbuellesheimer Strasse 56
5350 Euskirchen 16
Germany
Telephone: 02-251-71125
Fax: 02-251-73488
[PIT tags and scanners—Trovan Electronic Identification Systems]

Fish Eagle Trading Co. (sales in Europe)
Little Faringdon Mill
Lechlade, Gloucestershire
England
Telephone: 44-3675-2754
Fax: 44-3675-3406
[PIT tags and scanners—Destron/IDI]

Fisher Scientific (USA orders)
52 Fadem Road
Springfield, NJ 07081
USA
Telephone: 800-766-7000, 201-467-6400
Fax: 201-379-7415
Telex: 4754246 or 138287
[see next entry for products]

Fisher Scientific (international orders)
50 Fadem Road
Springfield, NJ 07081
USA
Telephone: 800-955-5090, 201-467-6400

Fax: 201-379-7415
Telex: 6859651/Fishersci
[anemometers, barometers, buckets, hand lenses, hygrometers, hygrometers-thermometers, hygrothermographs, pH meters, psychrometers, relative humidity-dew point probe, telethermometers, thermo-anemometers, thermometers, ultraviolet lamps (battery-operated)]

Floy-Tag and Manufacturing, Inc.
4616 Union Bay Place N.E.
Seattle, WA 98105
USA
Telephone: 800-843-1172, 206-524-2700
Fax: 206-524-8260
[knee tags]

Forestry Suppliers, Inc.
205 W. Rankin Street
P.O. Box 8397
Jackson, MS 39284-8397
USA
Telephone: 800-647-5368, 601-354-3565
Fax: 800-543-4203 (USA), 601-355-5126
   (international)
[altimeters, anemometers, barometers, clinometers, flagging, hand lenses, headlamps (battery-operated and rechargeable), humidity-dew point sensors, Pesola scales, psychrometers, rain gauges, thermographs, thermometers, waterproof field books, weather stations, wind recorders]

Holohil Systems Ltd.
3387 Stonecrest Road
Woodlawn, Ontario, K0A 3M0
Canada
Telephone: 613-832-3649
Fax: 613-832-2728
[radio transmitters]

Identity Devices (sales in Africa south of equator, Mauritius, Madagascar, Comoros, Seychelles)
P.O. Box 4561
Johannesburg 2000
South Africa
Telephone: 27-11-8837-376
Fax: 27-11-8837-376
[PIT tags and scanners—Destron/IDI]

InfoPet Identification Systems, Inc. (sales in USA)
5655 Lindero Canyon Road, Suite 702
Westlake Village, CA 91361

USA
Telephone: 800-858-0248, 818-707-9942
Fax: 818-707-9947
[PIT tags and scanners—Trovan Electronic Identification Systems]

Johnston Telemetry
Route 4, Box 313
El Dorado Springs, MO 64744
USA
Telephone: 417-876-5083
[custom radiotelemetry equipment]

Joe Kaplan Tattoo Supply Corp.
Dept. AM-EC1
P.O. Box 1374
Mt. Vernon, NY 10550
USA
Telephone: 914-668-5200
Fax: 914-668-2300
[tattooing equipment]

Kawamura (sales in Asia)
Joe Nishi
27-9, 3 Chome
Asakusabashi Taito-Ku, Tokyo 111
Japan
Telephone: 81-3861-4171
Fax: 81-3861-4175
[PIT tags and scanners—Destron/IDI]

Kipp and Zonen Delft bv
Meruriusweg 1
2624 BC Delft
Holland
Telephone: 015-561000 (Holland), 516-589-2885
   (USA)
Fax: 015-620351 (Holland), 516-589-2068 (USA)
[thermopile pyranometers]

Labelmaster
5724 N. Pulaski Road
Chicago, IL 60604-6797
USA
Telephone: 800-621-5808, 313-478-0900
[*Dangerous Goods Regulations,* 33d ed. Regulations effective 1 January 1992]

LI-COR Instruments
Box 4425
Lincoln, NB 68504
USA

Telephone: 402-467-3576
Fax: 402-467-2819
[data loggers, silicon cell pyranometers]

Markson Science, Inc.
10201 S. Fifty-first Street
Phoenix, AZ 85044-9972
USA
Telephone: 800-528-5114, 602-894-5317
Fax: 602-496-8246
[altimeters, anemometers, barometers, data loggers, dew point meters, humidity sensors, hygrometers, pH meters, thermometers]

Miller and Weber, Inc.
Dept. H
1637 George Street
Ridgewood, Queens, NY 11385
USA
Telephone: 718-821-1673
[quick-reading thermometers]

Mineroff Electronics, Inc.
574 Meacham Avenue
Elmont, NY 11033
USA
Telephone: 516-775-1370
Fax: 516-775-1371
[tape-recording equipment and supplies]

MiniMitter
P.O. Box 3386
Sunriver, OR 97702
USA
Telephone: 503-593-8639
[data loggers, radio transmitters]

National Band and Tag Co.
P.O. Box 430
721 York Street
Newport, KY 41072
USA
Telephone: 601-261-2035
Fax: 601-261-8247
[catalogue available: bands and tags]

National Tag Co.
815 S. Brownschool Road
Vandalia, OH 45377
USA
Telephone: 513-898-1334
[numbered field tags]

Newark Electronics
Administrative Offices
4801 N. Ravenswood Avenue
Chicago, IL 60640-4496
USA
Telephone: 312-784-5100
Fax: 312-784-3850
[relay switches]

Nite Lite Co.
P.O. Box 8210
Little Rock, AR 72221
USA
Telephone: 800-732-6895 (Arkansas), 800-648-5483 (outside Arkansas)
[flashlights, headlamps (battery-operated and rechargeable)]

Omega Engineering, Inc.
Box 4047
Stamford, CT 06907
USA
Telephone: 800-826-6343 (USA), 203-359-1660 (other countries)
Fax: 203-359-7700 (USA), 203-359-7807 (other countries)
[data loggers, pH and conductivity probes, thermistors, thermocouple wire]

Omnidata International
750 W. 200 N.
Logan, UT 84321
USA
Telephone: 801-753-7760
Fax: 801-753-6756
[data loggers]

Onset Computer Corp.
P.O. Box 1030
199 Main Street
North Falmouth, MA 02556-1030
USA
Telephone: 508-563-9000
Fax: 508-563-9477
[data loggers]

Panther Products Canada
P.O. Box 298
West Lorne, Ontario NOL 2PO
Canada
Telephone: 519-768-2841

Fax: 519-768-2841
[tattooing equipment]

Pelican Wire Co.
6266 Taylor Road
Naples, FL 33942
USA
Telephone: 813-597-8555
Fax: 813-598-5783
[thermocouple wire]

PGC Scientifics
9161 Industrial Court
Gaithersburg, MD 20877
USA
Telephone: 301-840-1111
[cryotubes]

Physical Chemical Scientific Corp.
36 W. 20th Street
New York, NY 10011
USA
Telephone: 212-924-2070
[humidity probes]

Radiant Color Co.
2800 Radiant Avenue
Richmond, CA 94804
USA
Telephone: 800-777-2968, 510-233-9119
Fax: 510-233-9138
[fluorescent pigments]

S & W Tattoo Supply Co.
P.O. Box 263
East Northport, NY 11731
USA
Telephone: 516-842-9777
[tattooing equipment]

Scientific Marking Materials, Inc.
P.O. Box 24122
Seattle, WA 98124
USA
Telephone: 206-524-2695
[fluorescent marking materials: pigments and
ultraviolet lights, air gun]

Scientific Sales, Inc.
P.O. Box 6725
Lawrenceville, NJ 08648
USA

Telephone: 800-788-5666
Fax: 609-844-0460
[anemometers, pyranometers, relative humidity
probes, thermistor probes, tipping-bucket rain
gauges]

Skye Instruments Ltd.
Ddole Industrial Estate
Llandrindod Wells, Powys, LD1 6DF
England
Telephone: 05-97-4811, 215-453-9484 (USA)
Fax: 05-97-4812
[hygrometers, pyranometers]

Solar Light Co.
721 Oak Lane
Philadelphia, PA 19126
USA
Telephone: 215-927-4206
Fax: 215-927-6347
[UV radiation sensors]

Solomat Instrumentation
Glenbrook Industrial Park
652 Glenbrook Road
Stamford, CT 06906
USA
Telephone: 800-932-4500, 203-348-9700
Fax: 203-356-0125
[conductivity probes, data loggers, pH electrodes]

Sonoco Semibulk Packaging, Inc.
1850 Parkway Place, Suite 820
Marietta, GA 30067
USA
Telephone: 404-423-2500
Fax: 404-423-2509
[Liquipak. Sonoco manufactures the containers;
contact the company for vendor information.]

Spaulding and Rogers Manufacturing, Inc.
Route 85, New Scotland Road
Voorheesville, NY 12186
USA
Telephone: 518-768-2070
Fax: 518-768-2240
[tattooing equipment]

SSAC
P.O. Box 1000
Baldwinsville, NY 13027
USA

Telephone: 315-638-1300
[timers]

Sterling Marine Products
18 Label Street
Montclair, NJ 07042
USA
Telephone: 800-342-0316, 201-783-9800
Fax: 201-783-9808
Telex: 220-883-TA-UR
[minnow traps, nets, seines, custom-made nets]

Superior Tattoo Equipment
P.O. Box 36452
Phoenix, AZ 85067
USA
Telephone: 602-277-1725
[tattooing equipment]

Tandy Corporation
1 Tandy Center
Fort Worth, TX 76012
USA
[electronic equipment and supplies, tape recorders. Tandy manufactures equipment distributed through Radio Shack stores in the USA. Contact Tandy for additional vendor information.]

Tatoo-A-Pet
1625 Emmons Avenue
Brooklyn, NY 11235
USA
Telephone: 718-646-8200
Fax: 718-934-0686
[tattooing equipment]

Taylor-Wharton Co.
Cryogenic Customer Service
1505 N. Main Street
Indianapolis, IN 46224
USA
Telephone: 800-428-3304
[cryogenic refrigerators (= liquid nitrogen tanks). Taylor-Wharton manufactures the tanks; contact for vendor information.]

Telonics, Inc.
932 E. Impala Avenue
Mesa, AZ 85204-6699
USA
Telephone: 602-892-4444

Fax: 602-892-9139
Telex 160231
[radiotelemetry equipment]

Texas Electronics
P.O. Box 7225
Dallas, TX 75209
USA
Telephone: 214-631-2490
[tipping-bucket rain gauges]

Thermo Electric Co., Inc.
109 Fifth Street
Saddlebrook, NJ 07662
USA
Telephone: 800-833-2781, 201-843-5800
Fax: 201-843-7144
[thermocouples, thermocouple wire]

Thomas Scientific
P.O. Box 99
99 High Hill Road
Swedesboro, NJ 08085-0099
USA
Telephone: 609-476-2000, 800-345-2100 (USA domestic orders), 800-524-0027 (orders from Europe, Asia, and Africa), 800-524-0018 (orders from Central and South America)
Fax: 609-467-3087
TWX: 710-991-8749
Telex: 685-1166(WUI)
Cable: BALANCESWEDESBORO
[anemometers, barometers, cryotubes, hand lenses, hygrometers, hygrothermographs, pH meters, psychrometers, tensiometers, thermographs, thermometers]

Trimble Navigation Ltd.
645 North Mary Avenue
Sunnyvale, CA 94088-3642
USA
Telephone: 800-TRIMBLE
Fax: 408-730-2997
[global positioning devices]

Unidata
17408 S.W. Boones Ferry Road
Lake Oswego, OR 97035
USA
Telephone: 503-697-3570
[data loggers]

University Products, Inc.
P.O. Box 101
517 Main Street
Holyoke, MA 01041
USA
Telephone: 800-628-1912
Fax: 413-532-9281
[Resistall paper]

UNO bv (sales in Europe)
P.O. Box 15
6900 AA Zevenaar
Marconistraat 31
6942 PX Zevenaar
Holland
Telephone: 08-360-24451
Fax: 08-360-23785
[PIT tags and scanners—BioMedic Data Systems]

Vaisalia, Inc.
100 Commerce Way
Woburn, MA 01801
USA
Telephone: 617-933-4500
Fax: 617-933-8029
[relative humidity probes]

VWR Scientific (USA orders)
CN 1380
Piscataway, NJ 08854
USA
Telephone: 800-777-8977, 908-756-8030
[see next entry for products]

VWR Scientific International (international orders)
P.O. Box 1002
600C Corporate Court
South Plainfield, NJ 07081
USA
Telephone: 908-757-4045
Fax: 908-7570313
[anemometers, barometers, cryotubes, hand lenses,
humidity monitors, hygrometers,
hygrometer-thermometers, hygrothermographs, pH
meters, psychrometers, telethermometers,
thermo-anemometers, thermometers]

Ward's Natural Science Establishment, Inc.
5100 W. Henrietta Road
P.O. Box 92912
Rochester, NY 14692-9012
USA

Telephone: 800-962-2660, 716-358-2502
Fax: 800-635-8439, 716-334-6174
[anemometers, barometers, clinometers, hand
lenses, humidity sensors, hygrometers,
hygrothermographs, minnow traps, nets, pH
meters, psychrometers, rain gauges, seines,
thermographs, thermometers, waterproof field
books, weather stations]

Weathermeasure/Weathertronics
Qualimetrics, Inc.
1165 National Drive
Sacramento, CA 95834
USA
Telephone: 916-923-0055
Fax: 916-923-5737
[anemometers, pyranometers, relative humidity
probes, thermistor probes, tipping-bucket rain
gauges. Contact for vendor information.]

Wildlife Materials, Inc.
RR 1, Box 427A
Giant City Road
Carbondale, IL 62901
USA
Telephone: 618-549-6330, 618-549-2242
[radiotelemetry equipment]

The Wildlife Society
5410 Grosvenor Lane
Bethesda, MD 20814-2917
USA
Telephone: 301-897-9770
Fax: 301-530-2471
[*Wildlife Techniques Manual*]

Yankee Environmental Systems (YES)
12 N. Taylor Hill Road
Montague, MA 01351
USA
Telephone: 413-367-2238
[UVB radiation sensors]

Yuasa Shoji Co., Ltd. (sales in Japan)
13-10 Nihombashi-Odemmacho
Chuo-Ku, Tokyo 103
Japan
Telephone: 03-665-6742
Fax: 03-665-6994
[PIT tags and scanners—BioMedic Data
Systems]

Computer programs

To obtain a copy of any of the following programs, send a written request and a formatted blank floppy disk to the address listed below for the program.

CAPTURE Program
Colorado Cooperative Fish and Wildlife Research
  Unit
Room 201 Wagar Building
Colorado State University
Fort Collins, CO 80523
USA
Telephone: 303-491-6942

The program CAPTURE, the user's guide to the program, and the publications by Otis et al. (1978) and White et al. (1978, 1982) are available from the Colorado Cooperative Fish and Wildlife Research Unit.

CAPTURE-RESIGHT Program
Dr. Steven Minta

Division of Biological Sciences
University of Montana
Missoula, MT 58912
USA

ECOLOGICAL METHODOLOGY Programs
Dr. C. J. Krebs
Department of Zoology
University of British Columbia
Vancouver
British Columbia V6T 2A9
Canada

JOLLY and JOLLYAGE Programs
Dr. James E. Hines
Patuxent Wildlife Research Center
Laurel, MD 20708
USA

The publication that describes this program (Pollock et al. 1990) can be purchased from The Wildlife Society (see entry under "Equipment and Supplies" in this appendix).

Table of Random Numbers

Lee-Ann C. Hayek

Instructions for use

This table of random numbers consists of a sequence of 32,768 random digits (integers 0 through 9), generated using SAS-PC Release 6.04. It is presented as an *octal* table with eight pages of eight columns and eight rows, divided into blocks that themselves consist of eight columns and eight rows of digits. Random number tables are commonly organized in groups of 10 with instructions for use that include a nonrandom component. Use of this table of random numbers to select a sample of size k includes the selection of a random starting point and a rule for proceeding from that point to selecting the k sample elements.

The first step is to list or number all K elements in the available population from which the sample of size k is to be taken. The lowest integer power of 10 that produces a number at least as large as k is then identified. This integer will be the length (in digits)

of the random number to be selected, as shown in the following table:

k	Length of integer (number of digits)
$1 \leq k \leq 10$, or 10^1	1
$11 \leq k \leq 100$, or 10^2	2
$101 \leq k \leq 1{,}000$, or 10^3	3
$1{,}001 \leq k \leq 10{,}000$, or 10^4	4
.	.
.	.
.	.
$10^i \leq k \leq 10^{i+1}$	$i + 1$ ($i = 0, 1, 2, \ldots$)

The k elements corresponding to the set of k random numbers identified are the random sample.

For simplicity, the value 0 is taken to correspond to the largest value of k for which the indicated length is appropriate. Thus, 0 corresponds to the 10th element of the group for which selection is being made; 00 corresponds to the 100th such element; 000 corresponds to the 1,000th such element; 0000 corresponds to the 10,000th such element; and so on. In general, the number consisting of i zeros corresponds to selection of element $10^i + 1$.

Numbers larger than K may be ignored, and selection is continued until k numbers less than or equal to K are selected. Similarly, duplicates should be ignored and additional numbers selected.

The method of random table entry may be based on any dichotomous experiments—assumed here to be flips of a coin. Each decision to be made in our octal layout will require three coin flips—referred to as a *tripflip*. Alternatively, three coins may be flipped once, but their order must be determined prior to flipping. The result of a tripflip is an ordered set of results of three individual flips, which we denote with H for heads and T for tails. The set of possible tripflips is HHH, HHT, HTH, THH, TTH, THT, HTT, and TTT.

One tripflip is used to identify the page of entry, as designated in the upper left-hand corner of each page. Two additional tripflips identify the row and column of the block, and a final two tripflips identify the row and column of the digit within the selected block (the arrangements of heads and tails shown at the top of the page and along the left side identify, in connection with these two pairs of tripflips, both the row and column of the block to be selected and the row and column within the block). The process identifies a specific digit that serves as the first digit of the first number to be selected and that may be referred to as the *entry point*. For convenience, the investigator may want to omit the final two tripflips and begin with the first digit of the selected block; however, this procedure reduces the number of entry points from 32,768 to 512, and I do not recommend it. Aisles between blocks of numbers and between pages may be ignored for the purpose of selecting the number to be used.

The entry process could be repeated $k-1$ times. This would, however, be a tedious procedure and is not generally considered to be worth the effort. Other approaches are limited only by one's imagination; many researchers select numbers simply by continuing down the page (and onto the next page or back to the first if necessary). A slightly more complex but recommended procedure is to follow one of the eight possible straight paths away from the initial digit, selecting numbers contiguously. The path is chosen by use of an additional tripflip. For convenience, the following diagram could be used when selecting a path. Here O_1 denotes the number of the first observation.

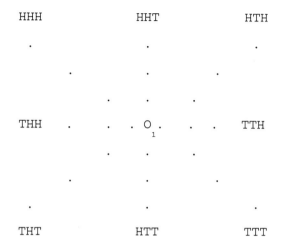

Example

Assume that a random sample of size 30 is to be taken from a collection of 100 elements. Thus, 30 unique two-digit numbers are needed. A list of the 100 elements is compiled, and each is assigned a unique integer from 1 to 100. A coin is flipped 18 times, yielding, for example,

$$T\,H\,H\,H\,H\,T\,T\,H\,T\,H\,T\,H\,T\,H\,T\,T\,H\,H$$

These flips can be considered as six tripflips. The tripflips and their corresponding uses are as follows:

THH	HHT	THT	HTH	THT	THH
Page	Block row	Block column	Row	Column	Path

This sample set of tripflips thus identifies the starting digit as 4—corresponding to the fifth page (THH), second row of blocks (HHT), sixth column of blocks (THT), third row (HTH), and sixth column (THT)—and the first two-digit number obtained is 43, which is ignored because it is larger than 30. Because the path selected (THH) is to the left (see diagram, above), the next two-digit number is 31, which is also ignored (because it is larger than 30), and the third is 09, which selects element 9 as the first observation in our sample. The second element would be 7 (ignoring 79 and 50), the third 25 (ignoring 77, 84, and 79), and so forth.

An alternative, *modulo system* could be used to reduce the number of steps required to select the sample. A modulo system is one in which all multiples of a given number (in our example, the sample size) are subtracted from any number identified in the table. For example, if an investigator wished to select one item from 25 items, the numbers 4, 29, 54, and 79 in the table would all identify the fourth item for selection (by subtraction of multiples of 25).

Note that if 30 items were to be sampled, as in our first example, the numbers 91–99 would be ignored to avoid giving the numbers 1 to 9 a greater chance of being selected than those from 10 to 30.

If a modulo system had been used in our example above, it would not have been necessary to ignore as many numbers. The numbers from 31 through 60 and those from 61 through 90 would have been used to identify sample elements by subtracting 30 in the first case and 60 in the latter. For example, the first value of 43 would have designated element 13 as part of the sample. The numbers 91 through 100 (00) would still have been ignored and replaced if obtained.

Table of random numbers

This table was designed and prepared by Charles R. Mann Associates, Inc., a Washington, D.C., statistical consulting firm.

HHH	HHH	HHT	HTH	HTT	THH	THT	TTH	TTT
HHH	18690397	11918532	66601968	77040187	00201468	70870951	12737739	86205251
	64523500	33711091	76092869	96283931	92186107	35644871	51983555	60242068
	57243033	95196310	39966207	14969833	71395689	17927888	64891645	40958903
	51391391	55243302	74000551	78307991	73248209	67038085	70604928	25323583
	83790183	14817791	57159452	00531460	10411732	30234717	60416789	55547259
	67240122	17766145	10400875	35438031	56967025	51938632	58123846	92861914
	24352731	04526465	98603628	79320580	25689996	70729599	21209421	89471768
	56603342	89568542	99818849	90561616	66899505	28322136	20554683	10280424
HHT	03893607	22146827	58172988	62780377	26692825	63196686	56447502	42567921
	02964028	48830405	12102002	52645552	57926882	16958796	03690513	98974571
	89657939	70063123	93979399	77604203	57704768	71607186	49620181	42404821
	23033568	95818740	49596983	39507849	68619050	48098746	76378230	46290172
	32802477	69098720	87360118	31977607	86751205	04846084	15397880	67685301
	53465825	82867460	49476748	75107052	63936299	52863835	64186622	27236440
	25553512	00462346	76776282	45111008	76801591	64239665	65594816	55082358
	67309539	68952203	57473647	84289966	87469779	44387800	52772492	09949150
HTH	91871904	29477762	47523801	28864948	66388733	79473688	00752299	24187281
	33543542	37755356	03718422	68190433	31608699	40287823	03293426	24102150
	72468782	70901965	63798056	22880533	22887385	06049915	19624923	94043056
	08267875	80444780	53634671	52338408	40408108	29215395	49215374	69027430
	57169577	49205816	64311776	10209865	35463887	99596507	80017106	42438347
	17684277	82052858	80215206	85959428	12936885	18665638	85013718	95750486
	38369168	41144361	20690462	80750652	60931407	72666292	74966858	52364045
	02659718	39526540	96246568	68967550	24376044	89118294	17072857	23363067
HTT	85411990	74348133	19375142	53094239	24183746	82676023	94314849	37410897
	73073380	46440119	55925855	48390049	52234227	86015837	64208763	16528798
	21752062	06673699	07927457	51521828	94661191	12177070	24616401	31564081
	33765125	36754911	38706141	64945825	39416528	40554986	53063534	91728617
	52005521	59096943	91111113	87415865	15046314	75292149	31754987	68589941
	67332967	09824980	08793541	05059043	37078129	38721263	83949456	09341968
	15123639	86853897	37361460	73878164	01872046	88610435	83684736	77273035
	80757533	45908014	39422294	99124467	15469754	96427171	18513656	04934016
THH	07833863	21154462	96604886	85089435	05543667	15675984	13033379	55466515
	34475768	08844848	54987067	99804055	40695910	30456498	50012261	81230259
	49343172	44058395	99603373	31154048	36444164	47288397	03800561	04302745
	17348702	89269966	75088544	38177324	39673979	07510058	83338795	95730819
	36714017	29283194	41034932	08662498	36856531	28438189	21078478	18296628
	76859836	34502954	86077485	59428569	42354316	82109604	92958752	84884159
	62806656	41350678	43793484	21302209	97600827	07163827	40641782	07355352
	49669489	43960710	47045149	91766235	12757256	14875488	77906943	69764367
THT	81215857	85931312	98384939	93218670	13007947	02159537	94403555	04104237
	87067798	57417777	12155227	37383701	04108061	55179947	16977319	89304125
	96879127	80958269	51559316	24840974	01239435	20360555	45449981	41456475
	06724434	31338454	60260577	12475807	87448267	76519786	40446530	46340186
	60170362	92470154	17219186	54386302	29223022	84680177	79021236	19637138
	06159657	63492321	31571839	02659646	99802016	11557743	76077121	99165063
	85840530	57577791	41676650	45379159	91129889	48156230	32238799	90962283
	03933858	27734649	68629669	16044711	82441066	99783803	33571778	02124116
TTH	91116129	74744189	31629207	02840329	92383931	26436908	44450351	01392724
	19847546	51453538	45375387	64840532	50497355	75482461	80355682	77931340
	02707513	57241737	40905668	15972963	64119250	79627096	84190852	99822201
	32642938	68465890	23694936	46064239	13475645	65329387	31937239	22024670
	75201619	66074592	36335851	24073983	89478010	90829348	10855075	84536560
	85042075	02417343	72761972	82158255	56839852	22691341	86710967	15202731
	61442981	89466398	12759382	35473039	05973735	27563540	69490782	31141590
	21836172	81825353	64245169	56703800	30621510	30765640	27481773	70501702
TTT	70214420	12615149	62028975	73347647	66679176	99989425	07558056	00223205
	90096558	27064177	44655377	26748456	71488190	15128909	52767803	40329869
	65602885	38522179	88503369	04668675	09681815	76477163	49964402	53116795
	81592129	01000062	03824803	26213884	56823398	62767963	86987793	23259217
	40007925	23178796	82244569	37879390	44793771	80544493	73673242	19109496
	18895326	20548512	30816371	97207184	30495239	29504865	08937725	72470706
	40300358	18229182	57194404	43052249	93337532	22790339	15219833	07759809
	49690630	00119404	65762324	35209983	89076943	48391372	60368891	87119103

HHT	HHH	HHT	HTH	HTT	THH	THT	TTH	TTT
HHH	44939377	49659364	39797583	02118489	91843795	59890564	94345466	74346755
	82198413	14424939	24378277	55166792	13402303	01033751	20337519	13587196
	25773059	58144069	13810459	10175872	34333189	96433820	65514459	74784643
	58942388	07870574	89256553	68716160	93838324	20308673	66748226	19166720
	21731767	27504373	40406619	88842244	45680153	30545169	19098953	07366957
	53901969	48772479	48717756	57888747	33318189	00286779	27497662	33835372
	58307766	37710516	81027461	51387781	69913270	55250209	20339895	37129657
	27373696	41806445	87879577	50047370	96588419	13281477	97176767	08968148
HHT	61518690	25422093	19495932	30471839	49393764	68923027	61195132	02731001
	35729875	88802954	13813985	65250822	43096970	06061959	57997114	41664501
	23962446	00467579	12150914	14062009	42423701	82456948	66723842	06227931
	50065723	07856559	22822562	32570235	61838508	91759860	56680135	03349353
	43174149	76369298	49764616	82085472	59206606	80364100	27809757	99411466
	41240483	64278275	33612787	93842983	59842201	22295086	21454560	49539571
	08334374	78724479	69682100	02351928	89900964	77507789	98074449	64146953
	46815979	90097854	07369791	80613135	17669317	59497324	80224914	30126308
HTH	31454165	35851697	50152934	89813061	41773593	08052428	70220285	71670829
	20429216	80430134	70437287	60938419	46561388	85802774	06852986	97762475
	70342755	89940459	77867248	72492398	62667921	42923587	12739548	65789010
	59183805	51140248	39830157	22298940	34689894	09732557	74326708	10033886
	68296003	47843006	76942114	51867498	83476541	55614692	63442369	37759427
	28007549	86733783	55710102	77305840	60868872	49765947	42102538	66773680
	58195764	41017972	23899523	29761545	07350970	14894949	15128690	20359987
	98633513	48179023	21158852	35291772	44314291	09470435	81367438	46772085
HTT	66837543	01863957	81854972	08498702	49462789	55610323	81604813	59446931
	56332680	60522590	64645080	11065936	38862219	24360799	84507459	52699871
	75230314	92559654	49153960	17498960	00923673	00562083	25846025	38548540
	86047310	99941528	23491409	67250708	01339709	16235873	21265374	47951421
	88463062	18609904	18490541	44471792	06980070	02617757	21908532	40963916
	80974241	75222928	82743449	75026147	64197646	53069491	69914295	20873873
	91585300	70462498	11912440	04759812	73470911	38611638	43732000	99974355
	96843530	65278277	95762339	75621419	79312544	48577661	13870066	32948405
THH	58326880	66840204	33476691	59802817	24530988	31142064	69221022	23164501
	05336059	02344387	98526551	45890892	43173791	92183049	75471308	97334644
	74129395	30699659	78105918	14043976	44952257	32836900	90681364	82407351
	84314774	79354592	02767343	32573985	28420771	22169255	61852211	88760841
	24413188	73011381	52450154	89190992	40540854	27490831	36394909	23946752
	54946922	88238297	55333325	37397493	48057197	87627029	13538614	69284918
	39626491	83587200	94240896	72749856	26016625	88636041	93895509	52755561
	59331816	03357133	57339396	57515066	94499159	77434184	96994238	06263202
THT	17961813	13517094	35098133	71685904	43175865	41484008	62575331	54864244
	31936444	79940442	51710773	26089514	87209006	95512020	51475574	99593278
	94069188	56257407	15998561	34026224	11459511	26033042	32456515	08752092
	98297784	03311720	37605207	65787338	28520713	02739776	70395602	40560684
	03037933	73324297	22074275	68440687	57535942	40489310	42592309	80565946
	51294889	30168571	04817418	08622091	24296589	29288381	46618895	41821778
	79889907	40249716	91392037	14056841	50379961	82757578	16838403	10963575
	22252701	13912986	25490190	20292801	73044612	36320366	30206003	02496308
TTH	93020835	61159151	63457106	77680385	04653861	06425607	26219384	79209365
	59650620	91744028	62238810	33176903	36450862	89344058	21001817	96893132
	44682037	18833340	20547932	56476830	84614253	09515268	63153539	39164157
	71326505	62463110	11327515	83961333	61189023	30807449	65798276	73871923
	55466375	23749737	18123694	27906073	68932068	53999457	84118753	04685308
	35683346	51382478	94213053	20849915	41352982	94077735	11293866	48214649
	89480743	06677835	82465130	73511984	14112738	42825034	83033521	46840048
	83376873	28975338	19205726	22370454	90824118	63300777	72011394	38576634
TTT	29313558	95325320	83543961	80383699	35907255	60373378	86441909	19803391
	56672841	05144431	64558805	48386006	07203032	75786554	89583295	17489639
	68171030	40723152	62746173	03984310	82925653	81376072	00786642	87696687
	64358298	40259168	57574397	26949072	23863852	71499263	80528049	53452601
	82275966	43209532	24304602	94663678	12299920	98357978	93358598	22531436
	94520715	79753817	73730443	73216384	40654936	18449083	52895504	20590165
	84716899	56751204	94815486	30814877	22245765	55984146	92955237	17482002
	93003490	67839703	84020892	21839322	53610199	14406548	68134495	62457482

HTH	HHH	HHT	HTH	HTT	THH	THT	TTH	TTT
HHH	72204903	88752845	24608058	64719294	69202447	84750555	63477608	50756914
	12502346	11220081	66619917	07264035	45817213	18608609	41042693	94851153
	35391572	00323474	58902323	46859340	53170803	25402663	60329994	26669351
	40503296	45406860	19069554	54468838	60963538	00961557	78400014	69378794
	64829884	70360832	14945869	57702365	72265619	06803063	49073247	96324102
	65715663	93833588	95484812	73483440	86026499	59688694	52806703	98976436
	27757562	81351563	10360425	17299207	91708606	33537473	72612809	61416368
	38149726	81544591	56608435	36172228	42155154	08891898	65523175	48677801
HHT	88495331	99284663	35281117	49287880	36487778	41577932	12908444	48811074
	94474666	86712883	91666319	67534500	86433247	16004700	06561730	73051169
	49754802	40437701	48497644	63165975	23538853	48602170	30311254	15310398
	71046850	69802441	49797248	37624581	93053445	08420048	73223026	13818253
	17729442	27113812	15950254	65002938	84168837	72378778	24504073	94606348
	41456387	78272536	63633297	73343740	67710883	49682855	61594827	97468226
	28788779	83955227	57988488	39532346	09567110	35074288	33824366	71428849
	58013689	73359776	49742818	06748246	51293904	04859598	88121715	00337698
HTH	14582566	94714390	46530025	60785146	79711938	91028467	56538815	81757068
	97517689	56414106	74429276	35588035	48982748	49150858	41370035	78873390
	51087624	34250933	45694024	69560057	09796255	33726469	24509902	15002979
	70123110	38690191	79034224	84657074	38563368	23143182	22949493	88799934
	02074890	60867723	02594967	24267641	20157849	99557214	23939150	07460889
	63035137	83378292	87970502	15415856	07241941	67218205	80432441	96963269
	44542213	55962922	57970344	31946826	60885966	40741545	28765374	17225914
	23068890	50048850	26131570	52228687	78803949	03803019	06671406	85767340
HTT	61606118	99936132	99788456	24080670	37544287	15635282	08189198	08106470
	31335846	77388288	30623803	71422014	14406355	05209192	08542899	05311139
	52976504	45775408	48414062	35568499	47824690	44183303	52414793	94045129
	28696097	69247171	51761630	28190062	56200126	07277262	15131724	03532321
	50545007	83673750	95814563	38804506	10826046	84400165	27588229	15017609
	94667981	06896417	79205925	89718461	03232954	00423547	62526081	07163269
	95934475	02189333	79922392	21601788	65240216	57561787	29580748	39390790
	89395780	09572066	02682447	70078270	41413141	93435618	42557549	50142638
THH	59875579	65314905	92556946	95870333	99475504	82864873	82401386	32291610
	39915973	93388769	61866577	91558567	76246667	52942084	70960696	67916866
	62142029	63492905	60198027	44758256	99780532	56481348	98985382	25190157
	58659065	95122277	98735671	06671729	23775824	91210266	37934280	26207805
	84910740	03735955	60373117	14921523	85078268	55149278	12203697	06313911
	68431470	67376482	62575914	80031605	06937467	40112221	11295869	35234940
	47029015	71053464	04159166	01878870	82138551	87652915	82795023	00987964
	72801998	54283680	81544460	00622572	38252002	31507574	43812412	87359052
THT	78670256	65645593	47079723	48139155	50743535	89901302	86348452	94446525
	76663452	66473064	04928354	15014771	66301172	13183395	90042741	80914756
	27681119	51904543	58763652	99281857	06324140	85713981	15166575	83160487
	12254997	74284673	64871019	71898690	47802598	57464519	18522515	29403485
	08462822	38946770	11096019	38767920	71640265	54188888	31507401	82247667
	23330215	24081099	91529920	34439984	86181843	99597371	41072897	48032494
	11719364	44359625	29477921	86226423	02196829	66318985	67870542	96673671
	20113161	78122842	23155388	28295982	27294425	56627980	51619113	78808307
TTH	94508956	78925698	81518308	69768738	09821347	78793845	48970506	27701465
	18008952	77919009	82881082	25998066	53385838	84204206	74895815	33839252
	69898351	83986908	56952534	46239568	76354884	40333427	20087666	77425084
	65973490	47537590	51460062	15489824	16720189	69078375	72684592	55990810
	62818161	78029584	98770920	40274634	93390926	71497479	48471720	82467611
	35587739	49780855	66745447	33076223	53214660	96168617	67711961	19535736
	19962688	50754392	10712961	01762729	38125429	82020269	22736264	03265557
	28734667	11987880	65883838	95849970	75319643	21276221	25601516	73890109
TTT	06224351	13317702	56837248	93504639	53604174	57700648	78278171	95690714
	16891834	41638870	32690556	74389582	22677575	19763060	85493065	15499631
	61373268	83589676	92254585	58380000	71992657	03714592	17519959	25002313
	45212114	82893985	72341523	38616687	55884066	77900417	11829595	72910365
	48193623	56069310	93891169	75589847	20537434	00754102	65723945	90130388
	17310410	28732100	42814250	45856554	44327513	92166734	71386251	78066477
	09793957	61940654	33707036	22034859	63748041	22128681	92240933	36735499
	93080427	94603248	23673998	33585988	53438493	45283094	53426936	07232736

HTT	HHH	HHT	HTH	HTT	THH	THT	TTH	TTT
HHH	97664164	87639349	90203481	70541358	71081865	04826301	39566587	06725065
	77575647	94576743	54199726	83891127	53935887	74388263	34694811	40484850
	23128498	94776467	14231720	02424238	58044556	94744287	35392825	60613838
	79600654	14137304	91166053	89298668	97967237	66432627	10252714	21213775
	23033292	13014835	86988602	43694338	45222341	37770071	94909827	59640494
	39610845	41241179	13395019	76065254	31531974	42019748	74943840	52537740
	17445083	24076543	21205607	53543640	44977801	28589517	95213892	04647605
	00766361	57404455	99498931	72308767	90552720	93394506	96666896	36677334
HHT	51416577	59290956	89284128	15709570	34321907	56224797	02271352	51180461
	15479768	79498680	82325990	46671607	23822956	00270952	12155834	43612179
	29704555	26250782	13412245	37463084	65265854	82820883	45874150	06457123
	37456171	92458018	48739455	14243517	48227999	33424916	03995864	25636961
	65757367	01135512	79743195	18565204	91488180	88479010	72189941	07850775
	47254031	69606518	24185280	23366045	54579690	18604878	35970708	73972641
	43226878	38978072	57445884	27455777	61056357	79627710	60797989	28891374
	40797253	70918329	70456688	04454972	28792533	85726820	40134223	63246163
HTH	47987354	65614723	75468452	80841523	78160509	67984441	49371927	15677534
	23954517	01738817	69713725	65356254	24846978	45607235	38277903	60017558
	79469689	34683952	87341627	42315000	51888186	41580998	98949437	97959278
	37618111	97093365	83840277	74243943	32798850	40153605	75327297	80510185
	52882774	65886313	23337457	40011888	47129267	22259118	42636364	56965248
	79283420	08558307	43362585	81302381	92608555	45453770	07902089	30568201
	41787381	83278547	24010871	09532259	80860033	03318422	00413830	85574118
	59951521	42104170	82535990	83250580	04999983	27429942	52720058	87594671
HTT	08471846	32647240	08174677	94276736	42951184	15981226	06424486	06877453
	26519977	02844542	78226910	98109505	34824556	62516497	03491303	82130889
	58040291	52041085	71908278	49671380	28986702	01248435	58413819	23137214
	05662139	37802406	73803188	55948849	59636522	71897749	90478932	32099216
	53740463	77222262	12370893	54001041	15803746	64442724	98078078	69934862
	33221406	20827361	30712532	90303733	80694610	67683264	19666708	99869560
	17874066	95131498	35062002	18374695	44772853	73486689	51379891	71648920
	87007858	97385364	56783075	32493048	21753572	77280146	99650056	61711337
THH	76347876	53657605	84917117	21618439	16360573	28740709	27346293	78933924
	56291757	68983945	46082999	11503608	11470053	93651244	70890141	31217648
	24230463	64072026	07526244	71288268	97433623	89699099	70557294	93680003
	07773469	67127701	13708359	31553053	31690342	98781990	59506903	60286154
	55007251	17430423	65987092	15179635	24897460	23365277	06790824	33339384
	45637259	03426008	97056751	91411536	47683112	27312365	65645347	31354086
	50270677	23562628	49596950	03706565	25222651	20766277	73735898	98744308
	47905560	20300336	52386903	41828317	87302835	31977145	44333282	37955488
THT	09457838	81447326	21791933	19797061	20009909	28117255	32994535	05381164
	65278750	28710820	67809750	40702115	53240550	15050725	00302163	50954304
	84645622	54083734	31359174	43789838	97914190	29877435	23005271	15789703
	29728342	35671316	28353694	22332922	59726403	36748325	13081148	00240372
	24255507	65513426	27804777	02171074	97559668	43061108	54198453	36676574
	92502628	74507013	76016591	77120316	78914830	95590001	60260772	30288820
	51628996	42886468	54418807	89980569	84307643	55041621	49220219	23062686
	27264798	61093106	33156784	77192817	63215792	52191045	85562214	54260444
TTH	49310339	73711581	05378143	39103286	75176905	47606426	17930099	48676903
	25171943	77214273	54071685	50880000	10236879	84064405	86168860	87661961
	76653929	26431431	99666674	88007952	86183629	63985265	77457107	93930098
	72441945	49130381	52813450	88717963	96998943	16038740	70415724	58165266
	06529933	81414724	96939639	37432849	01096077	13540271	73627060	30232420
	58556113	04921823	73920614	30188367	37044520	87199439	95003796	69839136
	29171964	26719522	07775926	03631111	89807621	64521703	22702807	42623841
	54515135	35595360	73213536	50630307	97739959	67685433	75316939	73107063
TTT	99491830	74021662	59869702	12269840	41761383	93531582	91953968	38646277
	72909611	86274366	67483029	78251763	38882305	06765158	25363529	53932203
	47077004	25678992	90768334	75707769	61417556	25635398	53929189	28272714
	69635500	87613353	10832996	39777217	19616092	52891409	63811038	72409518
	62084564	28090213	83181000	46388286	28368793	45238006	49145087	00242230
	69420326	28462259	06838782	24946533	15364580	68903414	78205567	27143107
	55728990	55077935	11317626	63339821	66196841	41896044	98345467	45047590
	90883836	55134984	53190383	87027312	41672307	59039088	12563681	67081737

THH	HHH	HHT	HTH	HTT	THH	THT	TTH	TTT
HHH	83855133	05635177	94032166	55113759	88731692	22430035	29677768	50361879
	12186359	83974184	73228403	69093273	17173423	98288379	21807739	70770844
	14365099	24380721	34673330	91123986	18710998	59466288	58479960	44148317
	81611434	82678572	08895854	82102472	91201927	76203962	53558897	51096736
	00313468	38690757	71564044	48428847	45130406	40617585	85761084	66924413
	13174432	59972604	92378004	89314526	28357388	97466695	27347975	23284781
	55617358	14605941	56771860	41931509	81196803	28551735	50193725	22508078
	76078328	77634812	46818112	22126466	80785060	15741761	48803652	13066786
HHT	36691863	72016423	64405573	47265159	98182473	70116736	45019495	92729878
	49485045	93664913	95698385	42297027	07069534	18449627	00154599	66263275
	19400995	90008191	79587980	28325798	47707507	90931433	82254263	07154203
	48685068	62931092	60612555	33735766	31690199	15273054	42271198	14224185
	19623120	85439018	97840718	20573478	95538554	36599231	70859483	02538217
	17387168	11372577	71391674	85087251	09136118	35493121	57248652	64541325
	12462483	34941691	31089989	27593964	46960163	53449628	62733964	99839944
	05952097	67771729	09282567	34829426	60019294	49403784	04478000	12231742
HTH	62044015	31420274	86035019	05392360	16886155	04603633	03794319	76994392
	30257344	84165728	51285104	30185156	27644312	40460667	06501157	86479943
	18596290	74754307	94887474	23356409	35099903	54865139	11499385	93443052
	74044647	64346063	15203406	49650508	03148450	57915365	93208158	90512929
	64359355	60781435	49985540	48071187	36608450	85831792	30895191	79069402
	81994282	90587232	50346702	93614461	55544811	59461908	22503298	53795361
	13977525	90298535	20971541	22483525	80674291	21889190	50701216	05992241
	73020895	41210446	68749332	90920996	27154383	90823544	26407271	16731455
HTT	34996394	02062183	65269905	27704536	38638214	98043086	24091895	89763647
	83188153	52964496	94032322	06597108	86398206	23677992	72584782	34263917
	38532116	56209685	70940514	20215637	77028279	78418380	04110118	45828393
	80887579	53158705	16334942	52506249	31179581	89636279	02594162	90450731
	09848333	63173861	57140075	86046079	54847031	61069172	71504298	66359166
	73584120	02796389	79784291	46254684	42875052	23034591	77080896	31514140
	93490758	93382806	01122575	75643370	25831499	12686684	71553702	40730640
	56809024	82673925	97486460	26631559	44802849	18324459	38229218	93868861
THH	25186264	23605296	77388462	47677319	26477465	88942803	57144459	97663412
	58051656	67016420	54111330	01668227	38265626	25924087	38339602	27135016
	27018443	15785442	03718214	26914236	95970546	98787862	03978622	52070359
	99348913	67807402	03936301	74909623	80952130	34512581	54275931	97464967
	90198963	82185202	67371489	49391053	79849009	10674868	45656088	64936764
	34274104	87228259	31908911	27548371	95282571	94220384	05082881	45012349
	68110930	50107893	29758249	19725624	82098644	58426649	85845980	77991245
	57013503	29040060	18815241	76887830	51268031	73502742	77026909	21996790
THT	70206260	02526615	15411392	12137459	68577056	05055934	78991941	50384604
	37022559	56466518	59031745	15845073	74018176	74583243	37117861	37058706
	57452700	98575291	37622828	67925663	82529823	94464628	41076514	74267386
	54880285	59534189	90034935	79371801	42505173	37131845	55511748	06628060
	22399307	08642807	54140264	65981552	30523892	09358643	13771426	81708134
	05867936	83729909	37223876	28938645	42087713	38852165	74959626	54180909
	45843555	88175958	53704819	35811489	68640250	42473862	72433265	87280239
	60269043	83424055	43467364	42070672	00676901	32250685	64015819	85498440
TTH	82954316	04391414	35607573	52998572	40455533	49657640	49416504	75568947
	82508624	02947277	31358598	52609683	13128571	47298649	17181618	32599594
	49008024	98944543	59846705	02225489	83618797	30017235	23310830	24780691
	83341722	48489637	50274141	45082104	09641394	96543870	51144252	43945599
	97218054	63792540	34323337	87855324	07530813	71993419	83982564	85649893
	97584644	95456085	32551116	13157982	98246042	50373427	35947891	08051359
	96159974	47979694	23822435	01140349	70918507	00143388	66379837	21607181
	79768812	60959999	14904708	83223167	84529529	16704074	35890856	85581898
TTT	96071851	87356397	07059700	89877666	48710708	16461864	94447122	39730366
	62082327	19934732	00920040	70562387	69757488	29171876	65334999	93911081
	97030523	78125135	67871650	63078619	22283026	79918627	69750978	18912076
	98170040	09953828	37426940	03528890	42871732	02919245	50520560	04246862
	29269495	82682107	59763373	25542980	57509451	71321015	38727477	35458704
	55216846	10558679	58016989	55122049	92399665	41746056	01974771	65046871
	81277527	59354470	88468809	45142905	50427979	16039977	31001171	13794035
	39886907	44216844	73386451	38073790	53779962	86756079	26560669	30993472

THT	HHH	HHT	HTH	HTT	THH	THT	TTH	TTT
HHH	68679569	05026845	89210240	72424338	92410325	34368222	51915557	22938883
	16646538	30688780	64053478	04460063	09530967	35743749	19097004	28034709
	50573740	44156912	09747668	98138831	26043067	06659645	78622629	15959275
	37349386	97901504	68572800	84160274	62148633	36191808	85283547	93225340
	57910481	94798322	18009951	67142507	32149539	29187336	85660577	45252955
	84027828	61271906	89136282	77234916	22235752	38777887	21462279	15111914
	10849521	06492493	57868403	18041601	43539514	83090245	07395215	30007767
	27348694	86996329	75585452	03352113	42340457	04151476	48497085	34097160
HHT	29044586	99505140	48177344	23575928	50516208	77602992	07053175	64875521
	86564903	98407926	19049054	99287505	69363456	15675140	64315688	21811342
	92639870	63837935	24878810	35451389	59711254	89915644	78010201	35861965
	45343712	66931067	87845849	66603928	61940423	58738717	31111740	10734097
	93859355	06804631	47519637	64091801	54031280	70651622	76486290	08814200
	76987915	37903633	44148764	75152263	46907698	20106714	86381086	74798483
	60953869	93650542	47334849	37434446	89176880	90914798	30838822	01044842
	84840513	98581088	81165772	11320189	75369038	70381326	95087593	17211244
HTH	39713071	30284051	60928990	46402714	93594730	44092456	05269266	67269221
	25295500	87144326	16518817	92978093	83266635	33504766	64114931	55250823
	78450775	69189959	95545581	18319019	42481071	11510368	57607389	80509737
	00394348	43532985	52372568	72575171	73289102	80520921	42373876	16358723
	72450806	64879011	76965831	65473676	41942084	07172434	55248686	00255292
	61985120	01980631	78536741	86648666	28475006	83202633	15501996	45814053
	03061138	80133614	06881629	93402286	03313428	02867460	96063273	84338990
	87873049	26247348	95963550	36176286	21026014	91871367	34702131	89074967
HTT	11756276	12833053	12816768	79268805	91838128	35942030	35613891	32664633
	19105129	65930507	40537650	18544142	52951385	72878982	58807951	33060260
	54817416	52004969	30481648	59912094	75753704	20132627	38955315	62673651
	03886421	87288048	64068702	74176653	57098052	31413771	83747454	16478292
	70451618	02520950	23794422	18805105	26104312	09256555	77709109	28292051
	43806188	88628352	54950093	53864987	80424808	61044947	71253159	56060491
	13796281	77368645	88074686	46049859	65860712	58692494	17558463	06516934
	73834286	15309165	42191906	98812424	95175278	42492707	52145194	86576024
THH	29989187	68782849	23312822	05631932	04920507	36765671	13318249	13871761
	59710043	87234107	47349508	92666133	08865733	00228615	66736494	20753740
	63461093	94270576	58077578	82450593	30503536	81596413	67619967	02062022
	49724489	80000049	59445876	20171921	57439695	22872898	58096326	34459228
	60319852	67913599	20240929	12090511	12813796	81681888	12574999	97378693
	20000318	35570373	18709397	84166211	05440066	88254259	65309172	44374838
	45656466	02513515	22382185	64424249	71127873	06123661	23912449	27692319
	64115188	17596851	73404071	92242059	31718099	58621486	89722664	27418112
THT	45100041	56853398	31817521	43520230	24126315	75555900	45738578	66285549
	34003295	43543930	75621152	43730092	63814565	34402122	05043520	17331825
	46340676	40793815	25799019	32389192	41761238	55134937	64452116	93111389
	59329545	89475228	91504606	54708087	14448231	70617034	89732532	65175323
	47215349	73442628	63549528	98311911	31288670	15980787	75743602	31165365
	52304751	34282765	54034436	88002279	79676772	58206845	17848173	69932799
	49037094	27817027	09036557	54304715	81274664	69023863	21929656	05537470
	30337965	05307906	53794341	71964587	07975773	45811483	35690692	02387734
TTH	16782293	09120350	88442577	04185889	33835819	33352338	04930770	52255890
	29726530	61349568	43072380	06133622	80198597	59515271	85635913	25298474
	80070293	67163424	50785947	14294384	93490111	32403268	71825563	99822767
	13594154	69423966	69893016	08275797	11652649	78936301	83293045	37682169
	69552112	70911236	65104387	22111559	85014888	47740851	13187397	39871535
	26328190	77785220	97923044	19157574	71897891	15040269	91210719	40048404
	49448290	54118689	65159125	50239060	49433217	15132487	12673031	16976574
	15658722	28013929	21910402	47185494	90158709	29829446	42364772	17216020
TTT	15829166	60151769	59012243	38909696	49633322	52591513	99669086	97578457
	12828289	93697544	47778667	09046279	95318745	78524386	00798549	76547149
	84959442	87484763	95974507	79429227	96540771	17723371	88587299	66373182
	95506882	29968928	31731399	52623090	29423917	29635163	18532265	42156732
	99070970	20109544	33391693	82985596	73138988	40797547	71322344	14383034
	53697530	53698578	63991907	72575507	57316916	26449420	55768844	39022582
	79268416	26137243	47758003	02529139	23517369	75029518	56210644	01353062
	17925521	15186670	09928533	44619233	72530208	46494681	72261852	67131917

TTH	HHH	HHT	HTH	HTT	THH	THT	TTH	TTT
HHH	46319271	17775686	00975244	68177364	57086643	50756914	34143029	01119658
	96120977	02081174	53303617	94679605	53541858	94851153	43941647	67858029
	96933781	45297001	79070929	03734528	90547953	26669351	43351703	35519438
	98385890	31297476	43138692	23445280	08617821	69378794	60632786	57995597
	67145708	01847010	13036465	57905497	03421002	96324102	67629571	36568345
	32475922	16330711	30566902	81180147	05850596	98976436	46710304	31270365
	88789964	31499916	97359174	84412426	87991755	61416368	08366203	88267013
	49645258	13181192	13628656	94192139	18906580	48677801	64807511	51212445
HHT	17558053	99004150	34649182	50148208	34165735	48811074	71046942	14947411
	72229873	03100727	64887261	03326598	36222252	73051169	95152976	11639962
	96277644	61102057	24726306	64360861	26273413	15310398	40070343	46489088
	34805775	07639204	76438277	88164985	69694560	13818253	68621283	76553668
	97929465	23521621	16224619	12344227	16951409	94606348	05607225	56830999
	21832599	75004650	55583207	44697760	20454723	97468226	43943535	17093630
	18640260	72928471	36818473	33546743	22490257	71428849	40611046	30378101
	99126011	40373742	28555040	96018065	15202898	00337698	63279830	89755546
HTH	55827271	92658157	10421161	81822273	95793393	81757068	52590757	71884578
	16672799	57821382	23154879	16237111	44257246	78873390	21380800	29908637
	98943797	68306107	17111888	05062872	99327206	15002979	39394123	85004254
	31518853	85223559	12123095	43223185	08355529	88799934	20972029	40700553
	88781367	37498431	89579539	27897711	29599460	07460889	79212431	49751501
	88750288	65663366	28519552	54060696	45209741	96963269	70335280	33777161
	19785873	12766191	43732609	94023169	78865858	17225914	37310763	47472752
	00230550	56740306	60305169	53575880	14063064	85767340	51344668	28882550
HTT	88520522	26943043	39487338	44862242	95307388	08106470	25059305	21651352
	55758167	69251645	09124995	34587781	48097894	05311139	57020375	14164209
	03036462	84084944	26777175	23545597	87515875	94045129	10805768	37868380
	71296641	05942767	87797635	71598350	55384008	03532321	76948508	24943669
	95560174	23302160	58723118	25474041	99875115	15017609	89402757	59244481
	32935662	57603699	89136411	41340556	15872089	07163269	56466100	44147787
	79169547	91808877	08659830	45842679	29070894	39390790	86239027	17607891
	84505670	52521587	06349296	07645937	35798966	50142638	49634985	57387174
THH	53570264	09982239	10729439	50265939	03399716	32291610	51321828	47765403
	83177523	64413111	02849182	97302561	86001280	67916866	03100113	14295096
	86221939	68138214	03013880	79750193	65538289	25190157	28027935	96611711
	96512748	25760250	40706029	59580017	62847717	26207805	11606526	28876709
	81052160	40076172	63426892	96374910	28250123	06313911	85715484	74341961
	29534609	45115054	13111948	97992370	99183690	35234940	58345780	53639114
	06232052	68808649	92990071	67931453	10581818	00987964	96305166	22362508
	75096305	20306090	90350965	19114233	36200473	87359052	63868744	88949579
THT	65994197	55573723	41511993	02645158	85382114	94446525	82512040	25352005
	96194358	43684016	13470783	08130389	29674869	80914756	45824972	97879610
	05382560	87122965	02538397	01360516	02803121	83160487	57701522	83096588
	12032560	87465752	14098951	37524054	69420367	29403485	41743347	49292205
	27783883	83693102	40817430	06587434	29461493	82247667	42397374	64624459
	43060304	79329141	84491259	15873303	70866041	48032494	25920499	16776553
	23492209	80915718	89824170	34253179	75657047	96673671	82371816	91212713
	90223723	30444038	21568962	47376866	50560833	78808307	57824838	07829383
TTH	99729031	40169194	15247286	16515010	91037172	27701465	50118735	13271417
	95292129	91417322	37086950	58666431	62525522	33839252	07422465	73127442
	45908753	45546803	50854104	56766503	80498331	77425084	69593928	35696230
	43734371	84868660	79610240	90592175	31484190	55990810	30360686	61421090
	47630180	99068064	35177597	82797159	39333168	82467611	48551406	83732157
	70044665	44177965	33995637	82053262	42763242	19535736	60610265	17291180
	14448728	59212721	01312288	17868045	92111185	03265557	10132098	68408405
	67834368	01392127	42344263	06693458	50667689	73890109	79511758	71136874
TTT	18161953	89635169	51827706	98952619	28702616	95690714	56594443	28844270
	92498242	08001971	62545818	71700150	18111862	15499631	87747217	78223602
	97998517	12624056	70575761	39274007	86058761	25002313	45186701	46586057
	32826808	66830750	89850476	91777512	51310637	72910365	23127509	26759450
	30844035	75510258	25021099	71670188	74940627	90130388	32227247	76522651
	37093729	66314046	58914897	83613531	43803888	78066477	31650418	21880752
	21417325	83509000	56506709	67455546	90839691	36735499	16026502	02651917
	83549395	64099724	92156803	30148426	87054401	07232736	44850303	92009664

TTT	HHH	HHT	HTH	HTT	THH	THT	TTH	TTT
	34779902	09816035	92263628	49982202	91859473	31721278	65153036	39224726
	08272033	92734465	78767849	43585049	84972810	26472902	29743575	75766564
	79393459	55086425	30394365	23794700	22963032	72058684	64384859	12760534
HHH	32870779	05456255	92896805	21739444	75919230	13999458	12299725	69567424
	47124639	16270170	24909250	83151887	68026752	84857413	89638869	19896283
	14913798	52586093	16259039	87158938	97448605	67901840	89939011	40816274
	29489136	69269247	27797956	14959549	47026196	96678220	05021384	25635221
	27100255	52684968	96153215	79286213	92097016	71372601	47701138	54405149
	11792716	70313082	68073743	90710785	88094911	10307511	99136303	27603179
	38321746	92883960	66243416	72715738	40480845	52546743	46777509	25287199
	44374678	15073621	24897744	43014153	45951729	26078252	08510261	41799796
HHT	40878774	80196744	45479893	26565365	04525100	25341424	73224034	20789404
	65781084	66771634	62137765	50263502	75775580	13692812	30745632	88714284
	44727293	39114124	38538173	01347875	08882731	14929803	27088420	47469197
	88453813	84529383	01464636	34016398	60784925	93017474	19826432	60116408
	85821463	91171398	71178829	79236609	09835490	61964481	83442262	91526010
	73666327	91413951	74547751	89444961	94391310	28368196	34201036	77464852
	65376407	75996140	86918982	74842810	51434059	05590959	62838231	79826346
	52326768	68042779	15608008	21000920	32968683	41851179	17149534	22516395
HTH	18552892	44149571	48819451	37572078	55787291	90774742	82623604	46251374
	87876354	90567945	85667241	89100908	32610897	26969059	65330671	55245982
	59604849	50831077	02200031	02482769	24799515	28760466	11739989	88005928
	01862669	64409302	61057981	95537563	03318024	75912889	56731107	50152245
	82202238	04492173	48044277	12104857	84176103	83807053	79849707	73025859
	75738436	41378329	58182033	83255316	44861274	50606013	86035972	90239098
	61566937	04800073	26280186	26913604	13341901	51214421	02764266	03371428
	49285336	22961354	40942073	52689139	05891111	63912300	18406658	05039239
HTT	41991082	71626878	76246615	33074376	73166488	27313473	24531580	18568308
	51978614	99857540	01014333	59220855	50038085	72419965	23353494	80390359
	81558392	51237849	13562182	94868753	69703025	91366995	78480692	22420803
	91242275	50547481	75370846	28010001	25641439	54851234	92171984	50375967
	40299957	68915392	77907816	34131442	36442373	36733632	33626781	99968817
	47978178	82236267	25184602	03171143	12815532	14623470	88351304	42303947
	87849604	30781946	69307947	82013299	18028598	45280976	58696816	73665239
	96895763	83201531	20076769	27877336	58823208	39179195	26541367	95481833
THH	97398087	07574580	63479655	61251282	52407633	39045343	23666347	50593756
	19769373	12074601	26164484	39596337	95385858	05441165	69844179	14855540
	29385821	45256846	27802435	55482299	81231228	26977173	19613564	54107331
	58156025	46286898	34959086	63374463	82593726	03861423	67667261	03510917
	46023136	55858847	71585166	80069775	48334441	51018812	89894415	04978213
	12253330	75352084	01109300	81199139	33734588	61351119	60911173	86601098
	95050028	86703698	83021495	03511823	72206468	66446274	89790233	14194490
	33989422	83175020	01577860	58055786	81551915	73921568	03456503	18911605
THT	27026922	62226818	55123762	47738956	34024478	75807706	81384837	51238403
	67591384	57271818	00961090	82897566	34503455	20840044	04797894	53483362
	35653384	15729958	58035142	65417792	09952709	72371658	80345180	65064199
	67974406	39525949	30775408	50316416	27472172	04718395	66119483	34984352
	10457925	32198497	90920663	26887016	53462826	71887862	54218927	26435282
	44178990	69544441	93476098	75744696	56211933	66768788	41437214	88971341
	69739748	87593219	50667912	87058454	75935582	67120046	62594172	99987904
	60256358	51593219	83684468	68306616	88719418	26984721	07381609	01161421
TTH	90210442	20508858	36265518	58430739	12096727	67180809	13893885	27342402
	54256636	39850702	37345803	21904265	17959094	76019501	45211648	57316677
	77643615	94275459	09118419	59643067	28335313	02333050	62809148	72001907
	40652878	20882983	54790070	77122111	94584064	57677552	82785052	71465391
	51169247	76347112	82110471	93263761	90072701	35664594	41628369	67793470
	15727448	24821232	17151716	57118581	54274433	20847905	90871686	67251957
	89448229	91180121	90036736	81058185	18737156	17389674	42930845	94841566
	59537763	40765805	16246680	14089548	69855380	70976353	16431937	78957394
TTT	36277102	13332605	50951778	36689365	10836813	44428362	09898128	72570299
	87965970	78182605	00870096	17053774	38755502	52835736	34302161	36947749
	87293038	41463173	41862442	14344536	73237490	69132122	89485970	89569004
	64191855	21558670	52628715	25838485	58151668	36483643	84935454	07166691
	48867584	90142910	08782981	90366931	38264437	82949644	74928389	35523446

Glossary

This glossary includes definitions of terms as we use them in the book. Most of these terms are used multiple times and in different chapters, but they are always used with the same meaning. The list is not exhaustive, and the reader should refer to the Index to locate definitions of other terms.

Assemblage—all amphibians that occur at a site at a particular time and from which samples are taken. We use *assemblage* in an ecological sense and imply no historical component to the unit. See also **community.**

Audio strip width—twice the maximum straight-line distance at which an observer can hear a calling male frog from a point on the transect perpendicular to the calling individual.

The width is determined separately for each species by each observer.

Bayesian statistics—an approach to the estimation of population parameters by the use of inverse probability and, in particular, Bayes's theorem.

Biodiversity—jargon for *biological diversity.*

Biological diversity—the variety of all living organisms on earth. The term encompasses several levels of diversity, including genetic (individual), species, and ecosystem. This book focuses on species diversity.

Biphasic complex life cycle—typical life cycle of an amphibian that involves at least two stages (adult and larva) often with different morphologies and habits. The different stages usually occupy different habitats (terrestrial and aquatic).

Call intensity—the loudness of a frog call, measured in decibels.

Call rate—the number of calls given by a frog in a specified period of time. For individual frogs, usually, the number of advertisement calls per second or minute.

Closed population—a population that remains unaltered demographically during the study period; immigration, emigration, mortality, and natality are nonexistent or negligible.

Community—a term used in the ecological literature to denote an association of interacting populations of various species, often implying some organization more than the sum of the individual species interactions. We avoid use of the term *community;* we use **assemblage** to denote amphibians that occur at a site, regardless of ecological organization.

Dominance—a term used in diversity indices that is equivalent in meaning to the preferred term, **species evenness.**

Drift fence—an upright, fencelike structure, usually made of metal or plastic, that intercepts an amphibian as it moves through the environment. Drift fences usually are placed in strategic locations (e.g., around a breeding pond) and direct amphibians toward a sampling device (e.g., a pitfall trap).

Equitability—a term equivalent to **species equitability.**

Evenness—a term equivalent to **species evenness.**

Explosive breeding—breeding periodicity in which most or all individuals in a population synchronize reproductive activity to a period of hours. Such breeding is characteristic of species in arid areas and usually is triggered by rainfall.

Funnel trap—a tubular or rectangular trap with one or two inwardly directed funnel-shaped openings. Such traps are used with drift fences to capture terrestrial or aquatic amphibians.

General collecting—specimen collecting with no specific target species or habitat. Any area may be searched, and all species potentially are of interest. Specimens are acquired as they are encountered.

Homogeneity of samples—constancy of the relative proportions of species, regardless of sample sizes.

Inventory—study of a specific area, site, or habitat to determine the number of species present (i.e., species richness).

Line transect—sampling approach in which a line (usually straight) is laid out in a habitat using a random procedure. The observer walks the line and counts all observed amphibians of interest. The procedure is used to estimate species' abundances within a habitat or across a gradient.

Mark-recapture techniques—methods for determining population size that involve capturing, marking, and releasing animals, and subsequently recapturing or resighting them one or more times.

Microhabitat—limited subset of a habitat at a site; usually defined by the presence of an amphibian (e.g., leaf litter between tree buttresses in lowland tropical evergreen rain forest).

Monitoring—study of the abundance of individuals in one or more populations of a species at a site through time.

Monte Carlo method for simulation—method for solving a mathematical problem through the use of sampling procedures. A stochastic model of a mathematical process is constructed and then tested with data drawn randomly from a computer-generated, simulated population.

Number-constrained sampling—sampling that continues until a prescribed number of amphibians has been included in the sample. The procedure may be used in systematic sampling surveys (SSS) and transect sampling.

Operative temperature—a single-number representation of the thermal environment of an amphibian; includes environmental factors of air and substrate temperatures, radiation, humidity, soil moisture, and wind speed, as well as amphibian properties of shape, size, integumentary reflectivity, and skin permeability.

Pattern mapping—an individual-specific recognition procedure that relies on recording with sketches or photographs the components of a color pattern that are unique for an individual amphibian. The unique pattern is used as a basis for recognizing individuals at a later time without reliance on other marking techniques.

PIT tag—a marking tag made of a passive integrated transponder (PIT) that relies on passive radio-frequency identification of a 10-digit hexadecimal number read with a scanner and portable reader.

Pitfall trap—a can or bucket buried flush with the substrate that traps amphibians that fall into it; an effective sampling device when used with a drift fence.

Prolonged breeding—a breeding periodicity in which individuals in a species population are reproductively active (calling males and amplexing pairs) over a prolonged period (usually weeks or months); often characterized by male territorial behavior.

Random sample—a sample that has been selected by a random process.

Relative abundance—proportional representation of species in a sample.

Richness—a term equivalent to **species richness.**

Sequential sampling—a sampling procedure in which single individuals (or elements) or groups of individuals are selected in order. The results of the selection determine whether sampling is to continue—that is, sample size is not predetermined but depends on the results obtained.

Short-term collecting—generally nonquantitative sampling that does not cover the full range of seasons and habitats at a site. When used with time-constrained sampling, comparisons between habitats are possible. Sometimes used as part of complete species inventories.

Species dominance—in diversity indices, a term equivalent to the preferred term, **species evenness.** The term is also used to refer to the most abundant species.

Species equitability—a term equivalent to **species evenness.**

Species evenness—a measure of the distribution of individuals among species in an assemblage.

Species richness—the number of species observed in an assemblage. The term used in diversity studies.

Strip transect—a sampling technique in which a line (usually straight) is laid out using a random procedure, and all amphibians observed or heard within a fixed distance perpendicular to the line are counted. The procedure is used to estimate species abundances and densities within habitats or across gradients.

Time-constrained sampling—a sampling procedure that provides data on the numbers of individuals or species collected per person-hour of effort. Effort should be standardized, and sampling should be stratified by habitat. The method is most effective with assemblages of comparable size and species densities and is used with complete species inventories, visual encounter surveys, and breeding site surveys.

Tracking—any of a number of techniques used to follow individual organisms under natural conditions.

Trespass—the undetected movement of an amphibian across a drift-fence-and-trap system around a breeding pond.

U.S. $—United States dollars.

Vernal pond—a pond that fills in the spring of the year (often from snowmelt or rain) and that is used by amphibians, especially in temperate forests, for breeding.

Voucher—one or more individuals or a part or parts thereof that are representative of the population of a particular species and serve to document the occurrence of that species at a site. To fulfill its function, the voucher must be deposited in a museum and available for study.

Literature Cited

Adams, J. E., and E. D. McCune. 1979. Application of the generalized jackknife to Shannon's Measure of Information used as an index of diversity. Pp. 117–131. *In* J. F. Grassle, G. P. Patil, W. Smith, and C. Taille (eds.), Ecological Diversity in Theory and Practice. International Cooperative Publishing House, Fairland, Maryland.

Agresti, A. 1990. Categorical Data Analysis. Wiley, New York.

Aichinger, M. 1987. Annual activity patterns of anurans in a seasonal Neotropical environment. Oecologia 71:583–592.

Alatalo, R. V. 1981. Problems in the measurement of evenness in ecology. Oikos 37:199–204.

Alford, R. A. 1986. Habitat use and positional behavior of anuran larvae in a northern Florida temporary pond. Copeia 1986:408–423.

Alford, R. A., and H. M. Wilbur. 1985. Priority effects in experimental pond communities: Competition between *Bufo* and *Rana*. Ecology 66:1097–1105.

Altig, R. 1980. A convenient killing agent for amphibians. Herpetological Review 11:35.

Altig, R., and G. F. Johnston. 1989. Guilds of anuran larvae: Relationships among developmental modes, morphologies, and habitats. Herpetological Monographs 3:81–109.

American Society of Mammalogists. 1987. Acceptable field methods in mammalogy: Preliminary guidelines approved by the American Society of Mammalogists. Journal of Mammalogy 68 (suppl.): 1–18.

Anderberg, M. R. 1973. Cluster Analysis for Applications. Academic Press, New York.

Anderson, J. D., and R. E. Graham. 1967. Vertical migration and stratification of larval *Ambystoma*. Copeia 1967:371–374.

Andreone, F. 1986. Considerations on marking methods in newts, with particular reference to a variation of the "belly pattern" marking technique. Bulletin of the British Herpetological Society 16:36–37.

Anonymous. 1991a. Declining amphibian populations—a global phenomenon? Findings and recommendations. Alytes 9(2):33–42.

Anonymous. 1991b. Dangerous Goods Regulations. 32d ed. International Air Transport Association, Montreal, Quebec.

Armitage, P. 1955. Tests for linear trends in proportions and frequencies. Biometrics 11:375–386.

Arnold, E. N., and J. A. Burton. 1978. A Field Guide to the Reptiles and Amphibians of Britain and Europe. Collins, London, England.

Arrhenius, O. 1921. Species and area. Journal of Ecology 9:95–99.

Ashton, R. E., Jr. 1975. A study of movement, home range, and winter behavior of *Desmognathus fuscus* (Rafinesque). Journal of Herpetology 9:85–91.

Atkinson, A. C. 1985. Plots, Transformations, and Regression: An Introduction to Graphical Methods of Diagnostic Regression Analysis. Clarendon Press, Oxford, England.

Auclair, A. N., and F. G. Goff. 1971. Diversity relations of upland forests in the western Great Lakes area. American Naturalist 105:499–528.

Austin, B., and R. R. Colwell. 1977. Evaluation of some coefficients for use in numerical taxonomy of micro-organisms. International Journal of Systematic Bacteriology 27:204–210.

Baglivo, J., D. Olivier, and M. Pagano. 1988. Methods for the analysis of contingency tables with large and small cell counts. Journal of the American Statistical Association 83:1006–1013.

Bailey, N. T. J. 1951. On estimating the size of mobile populations from recapture data. Biometrika 38:293–306.

Baker, B. O., C. F. Hardyck, and L. F. Petrinovich. 1971. Weak measurements vs. strong statistics: An empirical critique of S. S. Stevens' proscriptions on statistics. Pp. 370–381. *In* B. Lieberman (ed.), Contemporary Problems in Statistics. Oxford University Press, New York.

Bakken, G. S. 1992. Measurement and application of operative and standard operative temperatures in ecology. American Zoologist 32:194–216.

Bakken, G. S., and D. M. Gates. 1975. Heat-transfer analysis of animals: Some implications for field ecology, physiology, and evolution. Pp. 255–290. *In* D. M. Gates and R. B. Schmerl (eds.), Perspectives of Biophysical Ecology. Springer-Verlag, New York.

Barbault, R. 1967. Recherches ecologiques dans la savane de Lamto (Cote d'Ivoire): Le cycle annuel de la biomasse des amphibiens et des lezards. Terre et Vie 3:297–318.

Barbour, R. W., J. W. Hardin, J. P. Shafer, and M. H. Harvey. 1969. Home range, movements, and activity of the dusky salamander, *Desmognathus fuscus*. Copeia 1969:293–297.

Barinaga, M. 1990. Where have all the froggies gone? Science 247:1033–1034.

Barnard, G. A. 1947. Significance tests for 2×2 tables. Biometrika 34:123–138.

Baroni-Urbani, C., and M. W. Buser. 1976. Similarity of binary data. Systematic Zoology 25:251–259.

Bart, J., and J. D. Schoultz. 1984. Reliability of singing bird surveys: Changes in observer efficiency with avian density. Auk 101:307–318.

Bart, J., R. A. Stehn, J. A. Herrick, N. A. Heaslip, T. A. Bookhout, and J. R. Stenzel. 1984. Survey methods for breeding yellow rails. Journal of Wildlife Management 48:1382–1386.

Basharin, G. P. 1959. On a statistical estimate for the entropy of a sequence of independent random variables. Pp. 333–336. *In* N. Artin (ed.), Theory of Probability and Its Applications. Society of Industrial and Applied Mathematics, Philadelphia, Pennsylvania.

Baverstock, P. R., and C. Moritz. 1990. Sampling design. Pp. 13–24. *In* D. M. Hillis and C. Moritz (eds.), Molecular Systematics. Sinauer, Sunderland, Massachusetts.

Beacham, T. D., and C. J. Krebs. 1980. Pitfall versus live-trap enumeration of fluctuating populations of *Microtus townsendii*. Journal of Mammalogy 61:486–499.

Beauregard, N., and R. Leclair, Jr. 1988. Multivariate analysis of the summer habitat structure of *Rana pipiens* Schreber, in Lac Saint Pierre (Quebec, Canada). Pp. 129–143. *In* R. C. Szaro, K. E. Severson, and D. R. Patton (eds.), Management of Amphibians, Reptiles, and Small Mammals in North America. U.S. Department of Agriculture, Forest Service, General Technical Report RM-166.

Begon, M. 1979. Investigating Animal Abundance: Capture Recapture for Biologists. Edward Arnold, London, England.

Bennett, B. M., and P. Hsu. 1960. On the power function of the exact test for the 2×2 contingency table. Biometrika 47:393–398.

Berger, T. J. 1984. Community Ecology of Pond-Dwelling Anuran Larvae. Unpubl. Ph.D. dissert. University of Kansas, Lawrence, Kansas.

Berkson, J. 1978. In dispraise of the exact test. Journal of Statistical Planning and Inference 2:27–42.

Berry, P. Y. 1975. The Amphibian Fauna of Peninsular Malaysia. Tropical Press, Kuala Lumpur, Malaysia.

Bhargava, T. N., and V. R. R. Uppuluri. 1975. On an axiomatic derivation of Gini diversity with applications. Metronome 33:41–53.

Bingham, M. J., and S. P. Long. 1988. Equipment for Crop and Environment Physiology: Specifications, Sources and Costs. Department of Biology, University of Essex, Colchester, England.

Blair, A. P. 1943. Population structure in toads. American Naturalist 77:563–568.

Blaustein, A. R., and D. B. Wake. 1990. Declining amphibian populations: A global phenomenon? Trends in Ecology and Evolution 5:203–204.

Blommers-Schlösser, R. M. A., and C. P. Blanc. 1991. Amphibiens (première partie). Faune de Madagascar 75(1).

Boas, F. 1909. Determination of the coefficient of correlation. Science 26:823–824.

Bonham-Carter, G. F. 1965. A numerical method of classification using qualitative and semi-quantitative data, as applied to the facies analysis of limestones. Bulletin of Canadian Petroleum Geology 13:482–502.

Borchelt, R. 1990. Frogs, toads, and other amphibians in distress. National Research Council News Report 40(4):2–5.

Borenstein, M., and J. Cohen. 1988. Statistical Power Analysis: A Computer Program. Lawrence Erlbaum, Hillsdale, New Jersey.

Braden, I., and C. Webster. 1989. Towards a typology of geographical information systems. International Journal of Geographic Information Systems 3:137–152.

Bradford, D. F. 1984. Temperature modulation in a high-elevation amphibian, *Rana muscosa*. Copeia 1984:966–976.

Bragg, A. N. 1940. Observations on the ecology and natural history of Anura, I. Habits, habitat and breeding of *Bufo cognatus* Say. American Naturalist 74:424–438.

———. 1965. Gnomes of the Night: The Spadefoot Toads. University of Pennsylvania Press, Philadelphia, Pennsylvania.

Braithwaite, R. B. 1955. Scientific Explanation: A Study of the Function of Theory. Cambridge University Press, Cambridge, Massachusetts.

Braun-Blanquet, J. 1932. Plant Sociology: The Study of Plant Communities. (Authorized English translation of Pflanzensoziologie; trans. G. D. Fuller and H. S. Conard.) Stechert-Hafner, New York.

Bray, J. R. 1956. A study of mutual occurrence of plant species. Ecology 37:21–28.

Breden, F. 1987. The effect of post-metamorphic dispersal on the population genetic structure of Fowler's toad, *Bufo woodhousei fowleri*. Copeia 1987:386–395.

Breder, C. M., Jr., R. B. Breder, and A. C. Redmond. 1927. Frog tagging: A method for studying anuran life habits. Zoologica 9:201–229.

Brian, M. V. 1953. Species frequencies in random samples from animal populations. Journal of Animal Ecology 22:57–64.

Bridgeman, P. W. 1927. The Logic of Modern Physics. Macmillan, New York.

Brillouin, L. 1956. Science and Information Theory. Academic Press, New York.

Broschart, M. R., C. A. Johnston, and R. J. Naiman. 1989. Predicting beaver colony density in boreal landscapes. Journal of Wildlife Management 53:929–934.

Buhlman, K. A., C. A. Pague, J. C. Mitchell, and R. B. Glasgow. 1988. Forestry operations and terrestrial salamanders: Techniques in a study of the Cow Knob salamander, *Plethodon punctatus*. Pp. 38–44. *In* R. C. Szaro, K. E. Severson, and D. R. Patton (eds.), Management of Amphibians, Reptiles, and Small Mammals in North America. U.S. Department of Agriculture, Forest Service, General Technical Report RM-166.

Burnham, K. P., and D. R. Anderson. 1976. Mathematical models for nonparametric inferences from line transect data. Biometrics 32:325–336.

———. 1984. The need for distance data in transect counts. Journal of Wildlife Management 48:1248–1254.

Burnham, K. P., D. R. Anderson, and J. L. Laake. 1981. Line transect estimation of bird population density using a Fourier series. Pp. 466–482. *In* C. J. Ralph and J. M. Scott (eds.), Estimating Numbers of Terrestrial Birds. Studies in Avian Biology 6.

———. 1985. Efficiency and bias in strip and line transect sampling. Journal of Wildlife Management 49:1012–1018.

Burton, T. M., and G. E. Likens. 1975. Salamander populations and biomass in the Hubbard Brook Experimental Forest, New Hampshire. Copeia 1975:541–546.

Bury, R. B., and P. S. Corn. 1987. Evaluation of pitfall trapping in northwestern forests: Trap arrays with drift fences. Journal of Wildlife Management 51:112–119.

Bury, R. B., and M. G. Raphael. 1983. Inventory methods for amphibians and reptiles. Pp. 416–419. *In* J. F. Bell and T. Atterbury (eds.), Renewable

Resource Inventories for Monitoring Changes and Trends. Oregon State University, Corvallis, Oregon.

Bury, R. B., P. S. Corn, and K. B. Aubry. 1991. Regional patterns of terrestrial amphibian communities in Oregon and Washington. Pp. 340–350. *In* L. F. Ruggiero, K. B. Aubry, A. B. Carey, and M. H. Huff (eds.), Wildlife and Vegetation of Unmanaged Douglas-fir Forests. U.S. Department of Agriculture, Forest Service, General Technical Report PNW-GTR-285.

Buzas, M. A. 1967. An application of canonical analysis as a method for comparing faunal areas. Journal of Animal Ecology 36:563–577.

———. 1972a. Biofacies analysis of presence or absence data through canonical variate analysis. Journal of Paleontology 46:55–57.

———. 1972b. Patterns of species diversity and their explanation. Taxon 21:275–286.

———. 1979. The measurement of species diversity. Pp. 3–10. *In* J. H. Lipps, W. H. Berger, M. A. Buzas, R. G. Douglas, and C. A. Ross (eds.), Foraminiferal Ecology and Paleoecology. Society Economic Paleontologists and Mineralogists, Houston, Texas.

Buzas, M. A., and T. G. Gibson. 1969. Species diversity: Benthonic foraminifera in western north Atlantic. Science 163:72–75.

Buzas, M. A., C. F. Koch, S. J. Culver, and N. F. Sohl. 1982. On the distribution of species occurrence. Paleobiology 8:143–150.

Calef, G. W. 1973. Natural mortality of tadpoles in a population of *Rana aurora*. Ecology 54:741–758.

Campbell, D. T., and J. C. Stanley. 1963. Experimental and quasi-experimental designs for research on teaching. Pp. 171–246. *In* N. L. Gage (ed.), Handbook for Research on Teaching. Rand McNally, Chicago, Illinois.

Campbell, G. S. 1990. Biophysical Measurements and Instrumentation: A Laboratory Manual for Environmental Biophysics. Department of Agronomy and Soils, Washington State University, Pullman, Washington.

Campbell, H. W., and S. P. Christman. 1982a. Field techniques for herpetofaunal community analysis. Pp. 193–200. *In* N. J. Scott, Jr. (ed.), Herpetological Communities. U.S. Department of the Interior, Fish and Wildlife Service, Wildlife Research Report 13.

———. 1982b. The herpetological components of Florida sandhill and sand pine scrub associations. Pp. 163–171. *In* N. J. Scott, Jr. (ed.), Herpetological Communities. U.S. Department of the Interior, Fish and Wildlife Service, Wildlife Research Report 13.

Campbell Scientific, Inc. 1990. CR10 Measurement and Control Module Operator's Manual. Logan, Utah.

Camper, J. D., and J. R. Dixon. 1988. Evaluation of a microchip marking system for amphibians and reptiles. Texas Parks and Wildlife Department, Research Publication 7100–159. Austin, Texas.

Carle, F. L., and M. R. Strub. 1978. A new method for estimating population size from removal data. Biometrics 34:621–630.

Carnap, R. 1936. Testability and meaning. Philosophy of Science 3:419–471.

Caughley, G. 1977. Analysis of Vertebrate Populations. Wiley, New York.

Cecil, S. G., and J. J. Just. 1976. Use of acrylic polymers for marking of tadpoles (Amphibia, Anura). Journal of Herpetology 12:95–96.

Cei, J. M. 1980. Amphibians of Argentina. Monitore Zoologico Italiano, n.s., Monografia 2.

Chambers, J. M., W. S. Cleveland, B. Kleiner, and P. A. Tukey. 1983. Graphical Methods For Data Analysis. Wadsworth, Belmont, California.

Chapman, D. G. 1951. Some properties of the hypergeometric distribution with applications to zoological censuses. University of California Publications in Statistics 1:131–160.

———. 1954. The estimation of biological populations. Annals of Mathematical Statistics 25:1–15.

Chapman, J.-A. W. 1976. A comparison of the χ^2, -2 log R, and multinomial probability criteria for significance tests when expected frequencies are small. Journal of the American Statistical Association 71:854–863.

Chappell, M. A., and G. A. Bartholomew. 1981. Activity and thermoregulation of the antelope ground squirrel *Ammospermophilus leucurus* in winter and summer. Physiological Zoology 54:215–223.

Clark, D. R., Jr. 1971. Branding as a marking technique for amphibians and reptiles. Copeia 1971: 148–151.

Clarke, R. D. 1972. The effect of toe clipping on survival in Fowler's toad (*Bufo woodhousei fowleri*). Copeia 1972:182–185.

Cliff, A. D., and J. K. Ord. 1981. Spatial Processes Models & Applications. Pion, London, England.

Clifford, H. T., and W. Stephenson. 1975. An Introduction to Numerical Classification. Academic Press, New York.

Cochran, D. M. 1955. Frogs of southeastern Brazil. Bulletin of the U.S. National Museum 206.

Cochran, D. M., and C. J. Goin. 1970. Frogs of Colombia. Bulletin of the U.S. National Museum 288.

Cochran, W. G. 1936. The χ^2 distribution for the binomial and Poisson series, with small expectations. Annals of Eugenics 7:207–217.

———. 1950. The comparison of percentages in matched samples. Biometrika 37:256–266.

———. 1963. Sampling Techniques. 2d ed. Wiley, New York.

Cochran, W. G., F. Mosteller, and J. W. Tukey. 1954. Principles of sampling, I. Samples and their analysis. Journal of the American Statistical Association 49:13–35.

Cogger, H. G. 1983. Reptiles and Amphibians of Australia. Ralph Curtis Books, Sanibel, Florida.

Cohen, A., and H. B. Sackrowitz. 1975. Unbiasedness of the chi-square, likelihood ratio, and other goodness of fit tests for the equal cell case. Annals of Statistics 3:959–964.

Cohen, J. 1977. Statistical Power Analysis for the Behavioral Sciences. Academic Press, New York.

Cole, L. C. 1949. The measurement of interspecific association. Ecology 30:411–424.

Committee. 1987. Guidelines for the Use of Live Amphibians and Reptiles in Field Research. American Society of Ichthyologists and Herpetologists, Herpetologists' League, and Society for the Study of Amphibians and Reptiles.

Conahan, M. A. 1970. The Comparative Accuracy of the Likelihood Ratio and χ^2 as Approximations to the Exact Multinomial Test. Unpubl. Ed.D. dissert., Lehigh University, Bethlehem, Pennsylvania.

Conant, R., and J. T. Collins. 1991. A Field Guide to Reptiles and Amphibians of Eastern and Central North America. Houghton Mifflin, Boston, Massachusetts.

Connell, J. H., and E. Orais. 1964. The ecological regulation of species diversity. American Naturalist 98:399–414.

Connor, E. F., and E. D. McCoy. 1979. The statistics and biology of the species-area relationship. American Naturalist 113:791–833.

Connor, R. F. 1977. Selecting a control group: An analysis of randomization process in twelve social reform programs. Evaluation Quarterly 1:195–244.

Conover, W. J. 1974. Some reasons for not using the Yates continuity correction on 2 × 2 contingency tables. Journal of the American Statistical Association 69:374–376; Rejoinder: p. 382.

Cook, T. D., and D. T. Campbell. 1979. Quasi-experimentation, Design, and Analysis Issues for Field Settings. Rand McNally, Chicago, Illinois.

Corn, P. S., and R. B. Bury. 1990. Sampling methods for terrestrial amphibians and reptiles. U.S. Department of Agriculture, Forest Service, General Technical Report PNW-GTR-256.

———. 1991. Terrestrial amphibian communities in the Oregon Coast Range. Pp. 304–317. *In* L. F. Ruggiero, K. B. Aubry, A. B. Carey, and M. H. Huff (tech. coords.), Wildlife and Vegetation of Unmanaged Douglas-Fir Forests. U.S. Department of Agriculture, Forest Service, General Technical Report PNW-GTR-285.

Corn, P. S., R. B. Bury, and T. A. Spies. 1988. Douglas-fir forests in the Cascade Mountains of Oregon and Washington: Is the abundance of small mammals related to stand age and moisture? Pp. 340–352. *In* R. C. Szaro, K. E. Severson, and D. R. Patton (eds.), Management of Amphibians, Reptiles, and Small Mammals in North America. U.S. Department of Agriculture, Forest Service, General Technical Report RM-166.

Cortwright, S. A., and C. E. Nelson. 1990. An examination of multiple factors affecting community structure in an aquatic amphibian community. Oecologia 83:123–131.

Cramér, H. 1946. Mathematical Methods of Statistics. Princeton University Press, Princeton, New Jersey.

Crawford, K. M., J. R. Spotila, and E. A. Standora. 1983. Operative environmental temperature and basking behavior of the turtle *Pseudemys scripta*. Ecology 64:989–999.

Crump, M. L. 1971. Quantitative analysis of the ecological distribution of a tropical herpetofauna. University of Kansas, Museum of Natural History, Occasional Papers 3:1–62.

———. 1974. Reproductive strategies in a tropical anuran community. University of Kansas, Museum of Natural History, Miscellaneous Publications 61.

Crump, M. L., and J. A. Pounds. 1989. Temporal variation in the dispersion of a tropical anuran. Copeia 1989:209–211.

Cupp, P. V., Jr. 1980. Territoriality in the green salamander, *Aneides aeneus*. Copeia 1980:463–468.

Czekanowski, J. 1912. Obkective Kriterien in der Ethnologie. Mitteilungen der Anthropologischen Gesellschaft in Wien Sitzungberichte 1911–12, sect. 17–21.

d'Agostino, R. B., W. Chase, and A. Belanger. 1988. The appropriateness of some common procedures for testing the equality of two independent binomial populations. American Statistician 42:198–202.

Dalrymple, G. H. 1988. The herpetofauna of Long Pine Key, Everglades National Park, in relation to vegetation and hydrology. Pp. 72–86. *In* R. C. Szaro, K. E. Severson, and D. R. Patton, (eds.),

Management of Amphibians, Reptiles, and Small Mammals in North America. U.S. Department of Agriculture, Forest Service, General Technical Report RM-166.

Daoust, J.-L. 1991. Coping with dehydration of trapped terrestrial anurans. Herpetological Review 22:95.

Daugherty, C. H. 1976. Freeze branding as a technique for marking anurans. Copeia 1976:836–838.

Daugherty, C. H., and A. L. Sheldon. 1982. Age-specific movement patterns of the frog *Ascaphus truei*. Herpetologica 38:468–474.

Davis, D. E. (ed.) 1982. CRC Handbook of Census Methods for Terrestrial Vertebrates. CRC Press, Boca Raton, Florida.

Davis, D. E., and R. L. Winstead. 1980. Estimating the numbers of wildlife populations. Pp. 221–245. *In* S. D. Schemnitz (ed.), Wildlife Management Techniques Manual, 4th ed. Wildlife Society, Washington, D.C.

Davis, L. S., and L. I. DeLain. 1986. Linking wildlife-habitat analysis to forest planning with ECOSYM. Pp. 361–370. *In* J. Verner, M. L. Morrison, and C. J. Ralph (eds.), Wildlife 2000. University of Wisconsin Press, Madison, Wisconsin.

Dessauer, H. C., and M. S. Hafner (eds.). 1984. Collections of Frozen Tissues: Value, Management, Field and Laboratory Procedures, and Directory of Existing Collections. Association of Systematics Collections, Lawrence, Kansas.

Dessauer, H. C., C. J. Cole, and M. S. Hafner. 1990. Collection and storage of tissues. Pp. 25–41. *In* D.M. Hillis and C. Moritz (eds.), Molecular Systematics. Sinauer, Sunderland, Massachusetts.

Diamond, J. M., and R. M. May. 1976. Island biogeography and the design of nature reserves. Pp. 228–252. *In* R. M. May (ed.), Theoretical Ecology. Blackwell, Oxford, England.

Dice, L. R. 1945. Measures of the amount of ecologic association between species. Ecology 26:297–302.

Dodd, C. K., Jr. 1990. Line transect estimation of Red Hills salamander burrow density using a Fourier series. Copeia 1990:555–557.

———. 1991a. The status of the Red Hills salamander *Phaeognathus hubrichti*, Alabama, USA 1976–1988. Biological Conservation 55:57–75.

———. 1991b. Drift fence-associated sampling bias of amphibians at a Florida sandhills temporary pond. Journal of Herpetology 25:296–301.

Dodd, C. K., Jr., and B. G. Charest. 1988. The herpetofaunal community of temporary ponds in north Florida sandhills: Species composition, temporal use, and management implications. Pp. 87–97. *In* R. C. Szaro, K. E. Severson, and D. R. Patton (eds.), Management of Amphibians, Reptiles, and Small Mammals in North America. U.S. Department of Agriculture, Forest Service, General Technical Report RM-166.

Dodd, C. K., Jr., K. M. Enge, and J. N. Stuart. 1989. Reptiles on highways in north-central Alabama. Journal of Herpetology 23:197–200.

Dole, J. W. 1965. Summer movements of adult leopard frogs, *Rana pipiens* Schreber, in northern Michigan. Ecology 46:236–255.

———. 1972. Homing and orientation of displaced toads, *Bufo americanus,* to their home sites. Copeia 1972:151–158.

Donnelly, M. A. 1989. Demographic effects of reproductive resource supplementation in a territorial frog, *Dendrobates pumilio*. Ecological Monographs 59:207–221.

Doolittle, M. H. 1885. The verification of predictions. Bulletin of the Philosophical Society of Washington 7:122–127.

Dorcas, M. E., and K. D. Foltz. 1991. Environmental effects on anuran advertisement calling. American Zoologist 31:111A. (Abstr.)

Dowdeswell, W. H., R. A. Fisher, and E. B. Ford. 1940. The quantitative study of populations in the Lepidoptera, 1. *Polyommatus icarus* (Rott). Annals of Eugenics 10:123–136.

Drewry, G. 1970. Factors affecting activity of rain forest frog populations as measured by electrical recording of sound pressure levels. Pp. E55-E68. *In* H. T. Odum and R. F. Pigeon (eds.), A Tropical Rain Forest: A Study of Irradiation and Ecology at El Verde, Puerto Rico. Division of Technical Information, U.S. Atomic Energy Commission, Oak Ridge, Tennessee.

Duellman, W. E. 1970. The hylid frogs of Middle America. University of Kansas, Museum of Natural History, Monograph 1, vols. 1 and 2.

———. 1978. The biology of an equatorial herpetofauna in Amazonian Ecuador. University of Kansas Museum of Natural History, Miscellaneous Publications 65.

———. 1990. Herpetofaunas in Neotropical rainforests: Comparative composition, history, and resource use. Pp. 455–505. *In* A. H. Gentry (ed.), Four Neotropical Rainforests. Yale University Press, New Haven, Connecticut.

Duellman, W. E., and L. Trueb. 1986. Biology of Amphibians. McGraw-Hill, New York.

Duke, G. E. 1966. Reliability of censuses of singing male woodcocks. Journal of Wildlife Management 30:697–707.

Dupont, W. D. 1983. A stochastic catch-effort method for estimating animal abundance. Biometrics 39:1021–1033.

Eberhardt, L. L. 1978. Transect methods for population studies. Journal of Wildlife Management 42:1–31.

———. 1982. Calibrating an index by using removal data. Journal of Wildlife Management 46:734–740.

Eberhardt, L. L., and J. M. Thomas. 1991. Designing environmental field studies. Ecological Monographs 61:53–73.

Edwards, D., and B. C. Coull. 1987. Autoregressive trend analysis: An example using long-term ecological data. Oikos 50:95–102.

Efron, B. 1979. Bootstrap methods: Another look at the jackknife. Annals of Statistics 7:1–26.

Eggers, D. M, N. A. Rickard, D. G. Chapman, and R. R. Whitney. 1982. A methodology for estimating area fished for baited hooks and traps along a ground line. Canadian Journal of Fisheries and Aquatic Sciences 39:448–453.

Ehlers, M., D. Greenlee, T. Smith, and J. Star. 1991. Integration of remote sensing and GIS data: Data and data access. Photogrammetric Engineering and Remote Sensing 57:669–676.

Ehmann, H., and H. Cogger. 1985. Australia's endangered herpetofauna: A review of criteria and policies. Pp. 435–447. *In* G. Grigg, R. Shine, and H. Ehmann (eds.), The Biology of Australasian Frogs and Reptiles. Surrey Beatty and Sons and Royal Zoological Society, Chipping Norton, New South Wales, Australia.

Elmberg, J. 1989. Knee-tagging—a new marking technique for anurans. Amphibia-Reptilia 10:101–104.

Emlen, J. T. 1984. An observer-specific, full season, strip map method for censusing songbird communities. Auk 101:730–740.

Emlen, J. T., and M. J. DeJong. 1981. The application of song threshold distance to census operations. Pp. 346–352. *In* C. J. Ralph and J. M. Scott (eds.), Estimating Numbers of Terrestrial Birds. Studies in Avian Biology 6.

Emlen, S. T. 1968. A technique for marking anuran amphibians for behavioral studies. Herpetologica 24:172–173.

Enge, K. M., and W. R. Marion. 1986. Effects of clearcutting and site preparation on herpetofauna of a north Florida flatwoods. Forest Ecology and Management 14:177–192.

Engel-Wilson R. W., A. K. Webb, K. V. Rosenberg, R. O. Ohmart, and B. W. Anderson. 1981. Avian censusing with the strip method: A computer simulation. Pp. 445–449. *In* C. J. Ralph and J. M. Scott (eds.), Estimating Numbers of Terrestrial Birds. Studies in Avian Biology 6.

Engelmann, W.-E., J. Fritzche, R. Günther, and F. J. Obst. 1986. Lurche und Kriechtiere Europas. Ferdinand Enke, Stuttgart, Germany.

Erez, J., and D. Gill. 1977. Multivariate analysis of biogenic constituents in recent sediments off Ras Bunka, Gulf of Elat, Red Sea. Mathematical Geology 9:77–98.

Eyraud, H. 1936. Les principes de la mesure des corrélations. Annales de l'Université de Lyon, ser. 3, sec. A, Science Mathematiques et Astronomie 1:30–47.

Faanes, C. A., and D. Bystrak. 1981. The role of observer bias in the North American breeding bird survey. Pp. 353–359. *In* C. J. Ralph and J. M. Scott (eds.), Estimating Numbers of Terrestrial Birds. Studies in Avian Biology 6.

Fager, E. W. 1972. Diversity: A sampling study. American Naturalist 106:293–310.

Fager, E. W., and J. A. McGowan. 1963. Zooplankton species groups in the north Pacific. Science 140:453–460.

Faith, D. P. 1983. Asymmetric binary similarity measures. Oecologia 57:287–290.

Falconer, D.S. 1989. Introduction to Quantitative Genetics. 3d ed. Longman-Wiley, New York.

Fauth, J. E., B. I. Crother, and J. B. Slowinski. 1989. Elevational patterns of species richness, evenness, and abundance of the Costa Rican leaf-litter herpetofauna. Biotropica 21:178–185.

Fellers, G. M. 1979. Mate selection in the gray treefrog, *Hyla versicolor.* Copeia 1979:286–290.

Fellers, G. M., C. A. Drost, and B. W. Arnold. 1988. Terrestrial Vertebrates Monitoring Handbook. U.S. National Park Service, Channel Islands National Park, Ventura, California.

Ferner, J. W. 1979. A review of marking techniques for amphibians and reptiles. Society for the Study of Amphibians and Reptiles, Herpetological Circular 9.

Ferrari, F., and L. C. Hayek. 1990. Monthly differences in the distributions of sex and asymmetry in a looking-glass copepod: *Pleuromamma xithias* off Hawaii. Journal of Crustacean Biology 10:114–127.

Field, J. G. 1969. The use of the information statistic in the numerical classification of heterogeneous systems. Journal of Ecology 57:565–569.

Fienberg, S. E. 1979. Graphical methods in statistics. American Statistician 33(4):165–178.

Finklestein, P. L., J. C. Kaimal, J. E. Gaynor, M. E. Graves, and T. J. Lockhart. 1986. Comparison of wind monitoring systems, Part I: In situ sensors. Journal of Atmospheric Oceanic Technology 3:583–593.

Fisher, R. A. 1935. The Design of Experiments. Olivier Boyd, Edinburgh, Scotland.

———. 1943. The relation between the number of species and the number of individuals in a random sample of an animal population, Part 3. A theoretical distribution for the apparent abundance of different species. Journal of Animal Ecology 12: 54–58.

Flowers, E. C. 1978. Comparison of Solar Radiation Sensors from Various Manufacturers. U.S. National Oceanic and Atmospheric Administration, Environmental Research Laboratory, Solar Radiation Facility, Boulder, Colorado.

Forbes, S. A. 1907. On the local distribution of certain Illinois fishes: An essay in statistical ecology. Bulletin of the Illinois State Laboratory of Natural History 7:273–303.

———. 1925. Method of determining and measuring the associative relations of species. Science 61:524.

Forester, D. C. 1977. Comments on the female reproductive cycle and philopatry by *Desmognathus ochrophaeus* (Amphibia, Urodela, Plethodontidae). Journal of Herpetology 11:311–316.

Foster, M. S. 1982. The research natural history museum: Pertinent or passe? Biologist 64:1–12.

Fowler, N. 1990. The 10 most common statistical errors. Bulletin of the Ecological Society of America 71:161–164.

Fox, C. H., and C. Benton. 1987. Formaldehyde: The fixative. Journal of Histotechnology 10:199–201.

Franz, R., and R. E. Ashton, Jr. 1989. Behavior and Movements of Certain Small Sandhill Amphibians and Reptiles in Response to Drift Fences. Unpubl. Report. Florida Game Fresh Water Fish Commission, Nongame Program, Tallahassee, Florida.

Frazer, J. F. D. 1978. Newts in the New Forest. British Journal of Herpetology 5:695–699.

Friedman, W. F. 1922. The Index of Coincidence and Its Applications in Cryptography. L. Fournier, Paris, France.

Friend, G. R. 1984. Relative efficiency of two pitfall-drift fence systems for sampling small vertebrates. Australian Zoologist 22:423–433.

Frith, H. J. 1973. Wildlife Conservation. Angus Robertson, Sydney, Australia.

Fritschen, L. J., and L. W. Gay. 1979. Environmental Instrumentation. Springer-Verlag, New York.

Frost, D. R. (ed.). 1985. Amphibian Species of the World: A Taxonomic and Geographical Reference. Allen Press and Association of Systematics Collections, Lawrence, Kansas.

Fukuyama, K., T. Kusano, and M. Nakane. 1988. A radio-tracking study of the behaviour of females of the frog *Buergeria buergeri* (Rhacophoridae, Amphibia) in a breeding stream in Japan. Japanese Journal of Herpetology 12:102–107.

Gascon, C. 1991. Population- and community-level analyses of species occurrences of central Amazonian rainforest tadpoles. Ecology 72:1731–1746.

———. 1992. Spatial distribution of *Osteocephalus taurinus* and *Pipa arrabali* in a central Amazonian forest. Copeia 1992:894–897.

Gauch, H. G., Jr. 1982. Multivariate Analysis in Community Ecology. Cambridge University Press, New York.

Gazey, W. J., and M. J. Staley. 1986. Population estimation from mark-recapture experiments using a sequential Bayes algorithm. Ecology 67:941–951.

Gibbons, J. W., and R. D. Semlitsch. 1982. Terrestrial drift fences with pitfall traps: An effective technique for quantitative sampling of animal populations. Brimleyana 7:1–16.

Gibson, T. G., and M. A. Buzas. 1973. Species diversity: Patterns in modern and Miocene foraminifera of the eastern margin of North America. Bulletin of the Geological Society of America 84:217–238.

Gilbert, N. 1989. Biometrical Interpretation: Making Sense of Statistics in Biology. 2d ed. Oxford University Press, Oxford, England.

Gilbert, N., and T. C. E. Wells. 1966. Analysis of quadrat data. Journal of Ecology 54:675–685.

Gill, D. E. 1978a. The metapopulation ecology of the red-spotted newt, *Notophthalmus viridescens* (Rafinesque). Ecological Monographs 48:145–166.

———. 1978b. Effective population size and interdemic migration rates in a metapopulation of the red-spotted newt, *Notophthalmus viridescens* (Rafinesque). Evolution 32:839–849.

———. 1985. Interpreting breeding patterns from census data: A solution to the Husting dilemma. Ecology 66:344–354.

———. 1987. Reply to Nichols et al. Ecology 68: 217–220.

Gill, D., and J. C. Tipper. 1978. The adequacy of non-metric data in geology: Tests using a divisive-omnithetic clustering technique. Journal of Geology 86:241–259.

Gilpin, M. E., and M. E. Soulé. 1986. Minimum viable populations: Processes of species extinction. Pp. 19–34. *In* M.E. Soulé (ed.), Conservation Biology: The Science of Scarcity and Diversity. Sinauer, Sunderland, Massachusetts.

Gini, C. 1912. Variabilita e mutabilita. Studi Economico-Giuridici. Cura Facolta Giurisprudenza Universita Cagliari, A 3, pt. 2, Cagliari, Italy.

Gittens, S. P. 1983a. Diurnal activity of the common toad (*Bufo bufo*) during the breeding migration to a pond in mid-Wales. British Journal of Herpetology 6:292–294.

———. 1983b. The breeding migration of the common toad (*Bufo bufo*) to a pond in mid-Wales. Journal of Zoology (London) 199:555–562.

Gleason, H. A. 1922. On the relation between species and area. Ecology 3:158–162.

Godwin, G. J., and S. M. Roble. 1983. Mating success in male treefrogs, *Hyla chrysocelis* (Anura: Hylidae). Herpetologica 39:141–146.

Good, I. J. 1953. The population frequencies of species and the estimation of population parameters. Biometrika 40:237–264.

———. 1979. Studies in the history of probability and statistics, XXXVII: A. M. Turing's statistical work in World War II. Biometrika 66:393–396.

———. 1982. Comment on "Diversity as a concept and its measurement" by G. P. Patil and C. Taille. Journal of the American Statistical Association 77:561–563.

Goodall, D. W. 1967. The distribution of the matching coefficient. Biometrics 23:647–656.

Goodman, L. A., and W. H. Kruskal. 1954. Measures of association for cross classifications. Journal of the American Statistical Association 49:732–764.

———. 1979. Measures of Association for Cross Classifications. Springer-Verlag, New York.

Gosner, K. L. 1960. A simplified table for staging anuran embryos and larvae with notes on identification. Herpetologica 16:183–190.

Gower, J. C. 1967. A comparison of some methods of cluster analysis. Biometrics 23:623–637.

Grant, B. W., and A. E. Dunham. 1988. Thermally imposed time constraints on the activity of the desert lizard *Sceloporus merriami*. Ecology 69:167–176.

Green, R. H. 1974. A multivariate statistical approach to the Hutchinsonian niche: Bivalve molluscs of central Canada. Ecology 52:543–556.

Greenslade, P. J. M. 1964. Pitfall trapping as a method for studying populations of Carabidae (Coleoptera). Journal of Animal Ecology 33:301–310.

Grieg-Smith, P. 1957. Quantitative Plant Ecology. Butterworth, London, England.

Griffin, D. R. 1952. Radioactive tagging of animals under natural conditions. Ecology 33:329–335.

Griffiths, R. A. 1984. Seasonal behaviour and intrahabitat movements in an urban population of smooth newts, *Triturus vulgaris* (Amphibia: Salamandridae). Journal of Zoology (London) 203:241–251.

———. 1985. A simple funnel trap for studying newt populations and an evaluation of trap behavior in smooth and palmate newts, *Triturus vulgaris* and *T. helveticus*. Herpetological Journal 1:5–10.

Grizzle, J. E. 1967. Continuity correction in the χ^2-test for 2×2 tables. American Statistician 21:28–32.

Guttman, S. I. 1989. *Eurycea lucifuga* Rafinesque, cave salamander. Pp. 210–213. *In* R. A. Pfingsten and F. L. Downs (eds.), Salamanders of Ohio. Ohio Biological Survey Bulletin, n.s., 7(2).

Guttman, S. I., and W. Creasey. 1973. Staining as a technique for marking tadpoles. Journal of Herpetology 7:388.

Guyer, C. 1990. The herpetofauna of La Selva, Costa Rica. Pp. 371–385. *In* A. H. Gentry (ed.), Four Neotropical Rainforests. Yale University Press, New Haven, Connecticut.

Haberman, S. J. 1988. A warning on the use of chi-squared statistics with frequency tables with small expected cell counts. Journal of the American Statistical Association 83:555–560.

Hagmeier, E. M., and C. D. Stults. 1964. A numerical analysis of the distributional patterns of North American mammals. Systematic Zoology 13:125–155.

Hairston, N. G. 1949. The local distribution and ecology of the plethodontid salamanders of the southern Appalachians. Ecological Monographs 19:47–73.

———. 1951. Interspecies competition and its probable influence upon the vertical distribution of Appalachian salamanders of the genus *Plethodon*. Ecology 32:266–274.

———. 1980a. The experimental test of an analysis of field distributions: Competition in terrestrial salamanders. Ecology 61:817–826.

———. 1980b. Species packing in the salamander genus *Desmognathus:* What are the interspecific interactions involved? American Naturalist 115:354–366.

———. 1981. An experimental test of a guild: Salamander competition. Ecology 62:65–72.

———. 1986. Species packing in *Desmognathus* salamanders: Experimental demonstration of predation and competition. American Naturalist 127: 266–291.

———. 1987. Community Ecology and Salamander Guilds. Cambridge University Press, Cambridge, England.

Hamann, U. 1961. Merkmalbestand und Verwandtschaftsbeziehungen der Farinosae: Ein Beitrag zum System der Monokotyledonen. Willdenowia 2:639–768.

Hanowski, J. M., G. J. Niemi, and J. G. Blake. 1990. Statistical perspectives and experimental design when counting birds on line transects. Condor 92: 326–335.

Hardy, L. M., and L. R. Raymond. 1980. The breeding migration of the mole salamander, Ambystoma talpoideum in Louisiana. Journal of Herpetology 14:327–335.

Harris, R. N., R. A. Alford, and H. M. Wilbur. 1988. Density and phenology of Notophthalmus viridescens dorsalis in a natural pond. Herpetologica 44:234–242.

Hartley, R. V. 1928. Transmission of information. Bell System Technical Journal 7:535–563.

Harvey, M. J. 1965. Detecting animals tagged with Co-60 through air, soil, water, wood, and stone. Transactions of the Kentucky Academy of Sciences 26:63–66.

Hayne, D. W. 1949. An examination of the strip census method for estimating animal populations. Journal of Wildlife Management 13:145–157.

Hays, W. L. 1973. Statistics for the Social Sciences. 2d ed. Holt, Rinehart Winston, New York.

Hazel, J. E. 1970. Binary coefficients and clustering in biostratigraphy. Bulletin of the Geological Society of America 81:3237–3252.

Heatwole, H., and O. J. Sexton. 1966. Herpetofaunal comparisons between two climatic zones in Panama. American Midland Naturalist 75:45–60.

Heck, K. L., Jr., G. van Belle, and D. Simberloff. 1975. Explicit calculation of the rarefaction diversity measurement and the determination of sufficient sample size. Ecology 56:1459–1461.

Hedges, B. S., and R. Thomas. 1991. The importance of systematic research in the conservation of amphibian and reptile populations. Pp. 56–61. In J. A. Moreno (ed.), Status y Distribución de los Reptiles y Anfíbios de la Región de Puerto Rico. Departamento de Recursos Naturales de Puerto Rico, Publicación Cientifica Miscelanea 1.

Heeren, T., and R. d'Agostino. 1987. Robustness of the two independent samples t-test when applied to ordinal scaled data. Statistics Medicine 6:79–90.

Heip, C. 1974. A new index measuring evenness. Journal of the Marine Biological Association (United Kingdom) 54:555–557.

Heip, C., and P. Engels. 1974. Comparing species diversity and evenness indices. Journal of the Marine Biological Association (United Kingdom) 54:559–563.

Hero, J.-M. 1989. A simple code for toe clipping anurans. Herpetological Review 20:66–67.

Heron, D. 1911. The danger of certain formulae suggested as substitutes for the correlation coefficient. Biometrika 8:109–122.

Herreid, C. F., II, and S. Kinney. 1966. Survival of Alaskan woodfrog (Rana sylvatica) larvae. Ecology 47:1039–1041.

Heyer, W. R. 1974. Niche measurements of frog larvae from a seasonal tropical location in Thailand. Ecology 55:651–656.

———. 1976. Studies in larval amphibian habitat partitioning. Smithsonian Contributions to Zoology 242:1–27.

———. 1979. Annual variation in larval amphibian populations within a temperate pond. Journal of the Washington Academy of Sciences 69:65–74.

Heyer, W. R., and K. A. Berven. 1973. Species diversities of herpetofaunal samples from similar microhabitats at two tropical sites. Ecology 54: 642–645.

Heyer, W. R., A. S. Rand, C. A. G. da Cruz, O. L. Peixoto, and C. E. Nelson. 1990. Frogs of Boracéia. Arquivos de Zoologia 31:231–410.

Hill, M. O. 1973. Diversity and evenness: A unifying notation and its consequences. Ecology 54:427–432.

Hodgson, M. E., J. R. Jensen, H. E. Mackey, Jr., and M. C. Coulter. 1988. Monitoring wood stork foraging habitat using remote sensing and geographic information systems. Photogrammetric Engineering and Remote Sensing 54:1601–1607.

Hohn, M. E. 1976. Binary coefficients: A theoretical and empirical study. Journal of the International Association for Mathematical Geology 8:137–150.

Holley, J. W., and J. P. Guilford. 1964. A Note on the G Index of Agreement. Educational Psychological Measurement 24:749–753.

Hubalek, Z. 1982. Coefficients of association and similarity, based on binary (presence-absence) data: An evaluation. Journal of the Biological Reviews of the Cambridge Philosophical Society 57:669–689.

Huey, R. B., C. R. Peterson, S. J. Arnold, and W. P. Porter. 1989. Hot rocks and not-so-hot rocks: Retreat-site selection by garter snakes and its thermal consequences. Ecology 70:931–944.

Huheey, J. E. 1963. Concerning the use of paraformaldehyde as a field preservative. Copeia 1963:192–193.

Hurlbert, S. H. 1969. A coefficient of interspecific association. Ecology 50:1–9.

———. 1971. The nonconcept of species diversity: A critique and alternative parameters. Ecology 52:577–586.

Hutcheson, K. 1970. A test for comparing diversities based on the Shannon formula. Journal of Theoretical Biology 29:151–154.

Inger, R. F. 1980. Densities of floor-dwelling frogs and lizards in lowland forests of Southeast Asia and Central America. American Naturalist 115:761–770.

Inger, R. F., and R. K. Colwell. 1977. Organization of contiguous communities of amphibians and reptiles in Thailand. Ecological Monographs 47:229–253.

Inger, R. F., and B. Greenberg. 1966. Ecological and competitive relations among three species of frogs (genus *Rana*). Ecology 47:746–759.

Inger, R. F., and R. B. Stuebing. 1989. Frogs of Sabah. Sabah Parks Publ. 10. Kota Kinabalu, Sabah, Malaysia.

Ireland, P. H. 1973. Marking larval salamanders with fluorescent pigments. Southwestern Naturalist 18:252–253.

———. 1983a. Tagging larval salamanders. Association of Southeastern Biologists Bulletin 30:63–64. (Abstr.)

———. 1983b. Tagging larval salamanders. Catesbeiana, Bulletin of the Virginia Herpetological Society 3(2):7–10.

———. 1989. Larval survivorship in two populations of *Ambystoma maculatum*. Journal of Herpetology 23:209–215.

———. 1991. A simplified fluorescent marking technique for identification of terrestrial salamanders. Herpetological Review 22:21–22.

Jaccard, P. 1901. Distribution de la flore alpine dans le Bassin des Dranses et dans quelques régions voisines. Bulletin de la Société Vaudoise des Sciences Naturelles 37:241–272.

———. 1908. Nouvelles recherches sur la distribution florale. Bulletin de la Société Vaudoise des Sciences Naturelles 44:223–270.

———. 1912. The distribution of the flora in the alpine zone. New Phytologist 11:37–50.

Jacobson, S. K. 1985. Reproductive behavior and male mating success in two species of glass frogs (Centrolenidae). Herpetologica 41:396–404.

Jaeger, R. G. 1970. Potential extinction through competition between two species of terrestrial salamanders. Evolution 24:632–642.

———. 1978. Plant climbing by salamanders: Periodic availability of plant-dwelling prey. Copeia 1978:686–691.

———. 1980a. Density-dependent and density-independent causes of extinction of a salamander population. Evolution 34:617–621.

———. 1980b. Fluctuations in prey availability and food limitation for a terrestrial salamander. Oecologia 44:335–341.

Jaeger, R. G., D. Kalvarsky, and N. Shimuzu. 1982. Territorial behaviour of the red-backed salamander: Expulsion of intruders. Animal Behaviour 30:490–496.

James, F. C., and S. Rathbun. 1981. Rarefaction, relative abundance, and diversity of avian communities. Auk 98:785–800.

Jansen, S., and J. Vegelius. 1981. Measures of ecological association. Oecologia 49:371–376.

Johnson, S. C. 1967. Hierarchical clustering schemes. Psychometrika 32:241–254.

Johnson, T. R. 1977. The Amphibians of Missouri. University of Kansas, Museum of Natural History, Public Education Ser. 6.

Johnston, C., and R. J. Naiman. 1990. The use of a geographic information system to analyze long-term landscape alteration by beaver. Landscape Ecology 4:5–19.

Jolly, G. M. 1965. Explicit estimates from capture-recapture data with both death and immigration—stochastic model. Biometrika 52:225–247.

Jones, K. B. 1981. Effects of grazing on lizard abundance and diversity in western Arizona. Southwestern Naturalist 26:107–115.

———. 1986. Amphibians and reptiles. Pp. 267–290. *In* A. Y. Cooperrider, R. J. Boyd, and H. R. Stuart (eds.), Inventory and Monitoring of Wildlife Habitat. U.S. Department of the Interior, Bureau of Land Management, Denver, Colorado.

———. 1988a. Comparison of herpetofaunas of a natural and altered riparian ecosystem. Pp. 222–227. *In* R. C. Szaro, K. E. Severson, and D. R. Patton (eds.), Management of Amphibians, Reptiles, and Small Mammals in North America. U.S. Department of Agriculture, Forest Service, General Technical Report RM-166.

———. 1988b. Distribution and habitat associations of herpetofauna in Arizona: Comparisons by habitat type. Pp. 109–128. *In* R. C. Szaro, K. E. Severson, and D. R. Patton (eds.), Management of

Amphibians, Reptiles, and Small Mammals in North America. U.S. Department of Agriculture, Forest Service, General Technical Report RM-166.

Juterbock, J. E. 1989. *Aneides aeneus* (Cope and Packard) green salamander. Pp. 190–195. *In* R. A. Pfingsten and F. L. Downs (eds.), Salamanders of Ohio. Ohio Biological Survey Bulletin, n.s., 7(2).

Kaplan, H. M. 1958. Marking and banding frogs and turtles. Herpetologica 14:131–132.

———. 1959. Electric tattooing for permanent identification of frogs. Herpetologica 15:126.

Karlstrom, E. L. 1957. The use of CO^{60} as a tag for recovering amphibians in the field. Ecology 38:187–195.

Karns, D. R. 1986. Field herpetology: Methods for the study of amphibians and reptiles in Minnesota. James Ford Bell Museum of Natural History, Occasional Paper 18.

Kempthorne, O. 1955. The randomization theory of experimental inference. Journal of the American Statistical Association 50:946–967.

Kempthorne, O., and L. Folks. 1971. Probability, Statistics, and Data Analysis. Iowa State University Press, Ames, Iowa.

Kempton, R. A. 1979. The structure of species abundance and measurement of diversity. Biometrics 35:307–321.

Kendall, M. G., and A. Stuart. 1973. The Advanced Theory of Statistics. 3d ed. Vol. 2. Hafner, New York.

Kenward, R. 1987. Wildlife Radio Tagging Equipment, Field Techniques, and Data Analysis. Academic Press, London.

Kepler, C. B., and J. M. Scott. 1981. Reducing bird count variability by training observers. Pp. 366–371. *In* C. J. Ralph and J. M. Scott (eds.), Estimating Numbers of Terrestrial Birds. Studies in Avian Biology 6.

Kerlinger, F. N. 1973. Foundations of Behavioral Research. 2d ed. Holt, Rinehart Winston, New York.

Keynes, J. M. 1921. A Treatise on Probability. Macmillan, London, England.

Kish, L. 1959. Some statistical problems in research design. American Sociological Review 24:328–338.

Klauber, L. M. 1939. Studies of reptile life in the arid Southwest. Bulletin of the Zoological Society, San Diego 14.

Krebs, C. J. 1988. Fortran Programs for Ecological Methodology. C. J. Krebs, Department of Zoology, University of British Columbia, Vancouver, British Columbia, Canada.

———. 1989. Ecological Methodology. Harper Row, New York.

Kulczynski, S. 1927. Zespoly roslin w pieninach.— Die Pflanzenassoziationen der Pieninen. Bulletin International de L' Academie Polonaise des Sciences et des Lettres, ser. *B:* Sciences Naturelles 1(suppl. 2):57–203.

Lambert, J. M., and W. T. Williams. 1966. Multivariate methods in plant ecology, VI. Comparison of information-analysis and association-analysis. Journal of Ecology 54:635–664.

Lambiris, A. J. L. 1988. A review of the amphibians of Natal. Lammergeyer 39.

———. 1989. The frogs of Zimbabwe. Museo Regionale di Scienze Naturali Monografie 10. Torino, Italy.

Lancia, R. A., D. A. Adams, and E. M. Lunk. 1986. Temporal and spatial aspects of species-habitat models. Pp. 65–69. *In* J. Verner, M. L. Morrison, and C. J. Ralph (eds.), Wildlife 2000. University of Wisconsin Press, Madison, Wisconsin.

Laurent, R. F. 1964. Reptiles et amphibiens de l'Angola (3me contrib.). Museu do Dundo Publicações Culturais 67:1–165. Lisbon, Portugal.

Lee, W. L., B. M. Bell, and J. F. Sutton. 1982. Guidelines for acquisition and management of biological specimens. Association of Systematics Collections, Lawrence, Kansas.

Lee, Y. J. 1980. Test of trend in count data: Multinomial distribution case. Journal of the American Statistical Association 75:1010–1014.

Legrendre, L., and P. Legrendre. 1983. Numerical Ecology. Elsevier Scientific, Amsterdam, Netherlands.

Leslie, P. H., and D. H. S. Davis. 1939. An attempt to determine the absolute number of rats in a given area. Journal of Animal Ecology 8:94–113.

Liddell, D. 1978. Practical tests of 2×2 contingency tables. Statistician 25:295–304.

Lieberman, S. S. 1986. Ecology of the leaf litter herpetofauna of a Neotropical rain forest: La Selva, Costa Rica. Acta Zoológica Mexicana 15:1–72.

Lincoln, F. C. 1930. Calculating waterfowl abundance on the basis of banding returns. U.S. Department of Agriculture Circular 118:1–4.

Lipsey, M. W. 1990. Design Sensitivity. Sage, Newbury Park, California.

Littlejohn, M. J. 1977. Long-range acoustic communication in anurans: An integrated and evolutionary approach. Pp. 263–294. *In* D. H. Taylor and S. I. Guttman (eds.), The Reproductive Biology of Amphibians. Plenum, New York.

Lloyd, M., and R. J. Ghelardi. 1964. A table for calculating the "equitability" component of species diversity. Journal of Animal Ecology 33:217–225.

Lloyd, M., R. F. Inger, and F. W. King. 1968a. On the diversity of reptile and amphibian species in a Bornean rain forest. American Naturalist 102:497–515.

Lloyd, M., J. H. Zar, and J. R. Karr. 1968b. On the calculation of information-theoretical measures of diversity. American Midland Naturalist 79:257–272.

Loafman, P. 1991. Identifying individual spotted salamanders by spot pattern. Herpetological Review 22:91–92.

Lohoefener, R., and J. Wolfe. 1984. A "new" live trap and a comparison with a pit-fall trap. Herpetological Review 15:25–26.

Low, B. S. 1976. The evolution of amphibian life histories in the desert. Pp. 149–195. *In* D. W. Goodall (ed.), Evolution of Desert Biota. University of Texas Press, Austin, Texas.

Ludwig, J. A., and J. F. Reynolds. 1988. Statistical Ecology: A Primer on Methods and Computing. Wiley, New York.

Luff, M. L. 1975. Some features influencing the efficiency of pitfall traps. Oecologia 19:345–357.

Lyon, J. G., J. T. Heinen, R. A. Mead, and N. E. G. Roller. 1987. Spatial data for modeling wildlife habitat. Journal of Surveying Engineering 113:88–100.

MacArthur, R. H. 1957. On the relative abundance of bird species. Proceedings of the National Academy of Sciences (U.S.) 43:293–295.

MacArthur, R., H. Recher, and M. Cody. 1966. On the relation between habitat selection and species diversity. American Naturalist 100:319–325.

Maeda, N., and M. Matsui. 1989. Frogs and Toads of Japan. Bun-ichi Sogo Shuppan, Tokyo, Japan.

Magurran, A. E. 1988. Ecological Diversity and Its Measurement. Princeton University Press, Princeton, New Jersey.

Mallows, C. L. 1979. Robust methods—some examples of their use. American Statistician 33:179–184.

Mantel, N., and S. W. Greenhouse. 1968. What is the continuity correction? American Statistician 22:27–30.

Margalef, D. R. 1958. Information theory in ecology. Yearbook of the Society for General Systems Research 3:36–71.

Margenau, H. 1950. The Nature of Physical Reality. McGraw-Hill, New York.

Marriott, F. H. C. 1990. A Dictionary of Statistical Terms. Longman Group, Essex, England.

Marshall, B., and F. I. Woodward (eds.). 1985. Instrumentation for Environmental Physiology. Cambridge University Press, Cambridge, England.

Marten, K., and P. Marler. 1977. Sound transmission and its significance for animal vocalization, I. Temperate habitats. Behavioral Ecology and Sociobiology 2:271–290.

Marten, K., D. Quine, and P. Marler. 1977. Sound transmission and its significance for animal vocalization, II. Tropical forest habitats. Behavioral Ecology and Sociobiology 2:291–302.

Martin, D., and H. Hong. 1991. The use of Bactine® in the treatment of open wounds and other lesions in captive anurans. Herpetological Review 22:21.

Martin, T. E. 1981. Species-area slopes and coefficients: A caution on their interpretation. American Naturalist 118:823–837.

Martof, B. S. 1953. Territoriality in the green frog, *Rana clamitans*. Ecology 34:165–174.

Mathis, A. 1990. Territoriality in a terrestrial salamander: The influence of resource quality and body size. Behaviour 112:162–175.

May, R. M. 1975. Patterns of species abundance and diversity. Pp. 81–120. *In* M. L. Cody and J. M. Diamond (eds.), Ecology and Evolution of Communities. Belknap, Cambridge, Massachusetts.

McClanahan, L. L., and V. H. Shoemaker. 1987. Behavior and thermal relations of the arboreal frog *Phyllomedusa sauvagei*. National Geographic Research 3:11–21.

McConnaughey, B. H. 1964. The determination and analysis of plankton communities. Marine Research of Indonesia (Penelitian Laut Di Indonesia), special no., Jakarta, Indonesia.

McGinnis, R. 1958. Randomization and inference in sociological research. American Sociological Review 23:408–414.

McIntosh, R. P. 1967. An index of diversity and the relation of certain concepts to diversity. Ecology 48:392–404.

McNemar, Q. 1947. Note on the sampling error of the difference between correlated proportions or percentages. Psychometrika 12:153–157.

Mehta, C. R., and N. R. Patel. 1983. A network algorithm for performing Fisher's Exact Test in R × C contingency tables. Journal of the American Statistical Association 78:427–434.

Mengak, M. T., and D. C. Guynn, Jr. 1987. Pitfalls and snap traps for sampling small mammals and herpetofauna. American Midland Naturalist 118:284–288.

Menhinick, E. F. 1964. A comparison of some species-individuals diversity indices applied to samples of field insects. Ecology 45:859–861.

Menkens, G. E., Jr., and S. H. Anderson. 1988. Estimation of small-mammal population size. Ecology 69:1952–1959.

Merchant, H. 1972. Estimated population size and home range of the salamanders *Plethodon jordani* and *Plethodon glutinosus*. Journal of the Washington Academy of Sciences 62:248–257.

Metter, D. E. 1964. A morphological and ecological comparison of two populations of the tailed frog, *Ascaphus truei* Stejneger. Copeia 1964:181–195.

Michael, E. L. 1921. Marine ecology and the coefficient of association: A plea in behalf of quantitative biology. Journal of Ecology 8:54–59.

Miller, R. G. 1974. The jackknife—a review. Biometrika 61:1–15.

Minta, S., and M. Mangel. 1989. A simple population estimate based on simulation for capture-recapture and capture-resight data. Ecology 70:1738–1751.

Morin, P. J. 1983. Predation, competition, and the composition of larval anuran guilds. Ecological Monographs 53:119–138.

———. 1987. Predation, breeding asynchrony, and the outcome of competition among treefrog tadpoles. Ecology 68:675–683.

Morin, P. J., S. P. Lawler, and E. A. Johnson. 1988. Competition between aquatic insects and vertebrates: Interaction strength and higher order interactions. Ecology 69:1401–1409.

Mountford, M. D. 1962. An index of similarity and its application to classificatory problems. Pp. 43–50. *In* P. W. Murphy (ed.), Progress in Soil Zoology. Butterworth, London, England.

Myers, C. W., and J. W. Daly. 1983. Dart-poison frogs. Scientific American 248(2):120–133.

Myers, C. W., and A. S. Rand. 1969. Checklist of amphibians and reptiles of Barro Colorado Island, Panama, with comments on faunal change and sampling. Smithsonian Contributions to Zoology 10:1–11.

Nace, G. W., and E. K. Manders. 1982. Marking individual amphibians. Journal of Herpetology 16:309–311.

Nam, J. 1987. A simple approximation for calculating sample sizes for detecting linear trend in proportions. Biometrics 43:701–705.

Nams, V. O. 1989. A technique to determine the behavior of a radio-tagged animal. Canadian Journal of Zoology 67:254–258.

Narins, P. M., and R. R. Capranica. 1977. An automated technique for analysis of temporal features in animal vocalizations. Animal Behaviour 25:615–621.

Nichols, J. D. 1992. Capture-recapture models: Using marked animals to study population dynamics. BioScience 42:94–102.

Nishikawa, K. C. 1990. Intraspecific spatial relationships of two species of terrestrial salamanders. Copeia 1990:418–426.

Nishikawa, K. C., and P. M. Service. 1988. A fluorescent marking technique for individual recognition of terrestrial salamanders. Journal of Herpetology 22:351–353.

Noss, R. F. 1990. Indicators for monitoring biodiversity: A hierarchical approach. Conservation Biology 4:355–364.

Ochiai, A. 1957. Zoogeographical studies on the soleoid fishes found in Japan and its neighboring regions, II. Bulletin of the Japanese Society of Scientific Fisheries 22:526–530.

O'Connor, M. P. 1989. Thermoregulation in Anuran Amphibians: Physiology, Biophysics, and Ecology. Unpubl. Ph.D. dissert., Colorado State University, Fort Collins, Colorado.

Olders, J. H. J., J. J. van Gelder, and J. Krammer. 1985. A thermo-sensitive transmitter for radio tracking small animals. Netherlands Journal of Zoology 35:479–485.

Openshaw, S. 1990. Spatial analysis and GIS: A review of progress and possibilities. Pp. 153–164. *In* H. J. Scholten and J. C. H. Stillwell (eds.), GIS for Urban and Regional Planning. Kluwer, Dordrecht, Netherlands.

Orlans, F. B. (ed.). 1988. Field Research Guidelines. Scientists Center for Animal Welfare, Bethesda, Maryland.

Ormsby, J. P., and R. S. Lunetta. 1987. Whitetail deer food availability maps from thematic mapper data. Photogrammetric Engineering and Remote Sensing 53:1081–1085.

Otis, D. L., K. P. Burnham, G. C. White, and D. R. Anderson. 1978. Statistical inference from capture data on closed animal populations. Wildlife Monographs 62.

Overton, W. S. 1969. Estimating the numbers of animals in wildlife populations. Pp. 403–455. In R. H. Giles, Jr. (ed.), Wildlife Management Techniques Manual. 3d ed. Wildlife Society, Washington, D.C.

Pagano, M., and K. T. Halvorsen. 1981. An algorithm for finding the exact significance levels of R × C contingency tables. Journal of the American Statistical Association 76:931–935.

Pais, R. C., S. A. Bonney, and W. C. McComb. 1988. Herpetofaunal species richness and habitat associations in an eastern Kentucky forest. Southeastern Association of Fish and Wildlife Agencies Proceedings 42:448–455.

Palmeirim, J. M. 1988. Automatic mapping of avian species habitat using satellite imagery. Oikos 52:59–68.

Parmenter, R. R., J. A. MacMahon, and D. R. Anderson. 1989. Animal density estimation using a trapping web design: Field validation experiments. Ecology 70:169–179.

Passmore, N. I., and V. C. Carruthers. 1979. South African Frogs. Witwatersrand University Press, Johannesburg, South Africa.

Patil, G. P., and C. Taillie. 1982. Diversity as a concept and its measurement. Journal of the American Statistical Association 77:548–567.

Patil, K. D. 1975. Cochran's Q test: Exact distribution. Journal of the American Statistical Association 70:186–189.

Paulik, G. J., and D. S. Robson. 1969. Statistical calculations for change-in-ratio estimators of population parameters. Journal of Wildlife Management 33:1–27.

Pearce, C. S. 1884. The numerical measure of the success of predictions. Science 4:453–454.

Pearcy, R. W. 1989. Field data acquisition. Pp. 15–27. *In* R. W. Pearcy, J. R. Ehleringer, H. A. Mooney, and P. W. Rundel (eds.), Plant Physiological Ecology Field Methods and Instrumentation. Chapman Hall, London, England.

Pearcy, R. W., J. R. Ehleringer, H. A. Mooney, and P. W. Rundel (eds.). 1989. Plant Physiological Ecology Field Methods and Instrumentation. Chapman Hall, London, England.

Pearson, E. S. 1947. The choice of statistical tests illustrated on the interpretation of data classed in a 2 × 2 table. Biometrika 34:139–165.

Pearson, K. 1901. Mathematical contributions to the theory of evolution—VII: On the correlation of characters not quantitatively measurable. Philosophical Transactions of the Royal Society (London), ser. A, 195:1–47.

———. 1904. Mathematical contributions to the theory of evolution—XIII: On the theory of contingency and its relation to association and normal correlation. Draper's Company Research Memoirs, Biometric Ser. 1.

Pearson, K., and D. Heron. 1913. On theories of association. Biometrika 9:159–315.

Pechmann, J. H. K., and R. D. Semlitsch. 1986. Diel activity patterns in the breeding migrations of winter-breeding anurans. Canadian Journal of Zoology 64:1116–1120.

Pechmann, J. H. K., D. E. Scott, R. D. Semlitsch, J. P. Caldwell, L. J. Vitt, and J. W. Gibbons. 1991. Declining amphibian populations: The problem of separating human impacts from natural fluctuations. Science 253:892–895.

Peet, R. K. 1974. The measurement of species diversity. Annual Review of Ecology and Systematics 5:285–307.

———. 1975. Relative diversity indices. Ecology 56:496–498.

Pereira, J. M. C. 1989. A Spatial Approach to Statistical Habitat Suitability Modelling: The Mt. Graham Red Squirrel Case Study. Unpubl. Ph.D. dissert., University of Arizona, Tucson, Arizona.

Pereira, J. M. O. C., and R. M. Itami. 1991. GIS-based habitat modelling using logistic multiple regression: A study of the Mt. Graham red squirrel. Photogrammetric Engineering and Remote Sensing 57:1475–1486.

Perrill, S. A., H. C. Gerhardt, and R. Daniel. 1978. Sexual parasitism in the green tree frog (*Hyla cinerea*). Science 200:1179–1180.

Peters, J. R. 1968. A computer program for calculating degree of biogeographical resemblance between areas. Systematic Zoology 17:64–69.

Petersen, C. G. J. 1896. The yearly immigration of young plaice into Limfjord from the German sea. Report of the Danish Biological Station 6. Copenhagen, Denmark.

Peterson, C. H. 1975. The effects of clumping on sample evenness. American Naturalist 109:373–377.

Peterson, C. R. 1987. Daily variation in the body temperatures of free-ranging garter snakes. Ecology 68:160–169.

Peterson, C. R., and V. A. Cobb. 1991. Thermal ecology of hibernation in Great Basin rattlesnakes. American Zoologist 31:42A. (Abstr.)

Peterson, C. R., and M. E. Dorcas. 1992. The use of automated data acquisition techniques in monitoring amphibian and reptile populations. Pp. 369–378. *In* D. R. McCullough and R. H. Barrett (eds.). Wildlife 2001: Populations. Elsevier Applied Science, New York.

Petron, S. E., F. F. Gilbert, and W. H. Rickard. 1987. Portable automatic radiotelemetry recording system. Wildlife Society Bulletin 15:421–426.

Pfingsten, R. A., and F. L. Downs (eds.). 1989. Salamanders of Ohio. Ohio Biological Survey Bulletin, n.s., 7(2).

Phillips, C. A., and O. J. Sexton. 1989. Orientation and sexual differences during breeding migrations of the spotted salamander, *Ambystoma maculatum.* Copeia 1989:17–22.

Phillips, K. 1990. Where have all the frogs and toads gone? BioScience 40:422–424.

Phiney, D. E., and S. B. Mathews. 1969. Field test of fluorescent pigment marking and finclipping of coho salmon. Journal of the Fisheries Research Board of Canada 26:1619–1624.

Phiney, D. E., D. M. Miller, and M. L. Dahlberg. 1967. Mass-marking young salmonids with fluorescent pigment. Transactions of the American Fisheries Society 96:157–162.

Pielou, E. C. 1966a. Shannon's formula as a measure of species diversity: Its use and misuse. American Naturalist 100:463–465.

———. 1966b. The measurement of diversity in different types of biological collections. Journal of Theoretical Biology 13:131–144.

———. 1975. Ecological Diversity. Wiley, New York.

———. 1984. The Interpretation of Ecological Data. A Primer on Classification and Ordination. Wiley, New York.

Pierce, B. A. 1985. Acid tolerance in amphibians. BioScience 35:239–243.

Pisani, G. R. 1973. A guide to preservation techniques for amphibians and reptiles. Society for the Study of Amphibians and Reptiles, Herpetological Circular 1.

Plackett, R. L. 1964. The continuity correction in 2 × 2 tables. Biometrika 51:327–337.

Pollock, K. H., J. E. Hines, and J. D. Nichols. 1984. The use of auxiliary variables in capture-recapture and removal experiments. Biometrics 40:653–662.

Pollock K. H., R. A. Lancia, M. C. Connor, and D. L. Wood. 1985. A new change-of-ratio procedure robust to unequal catchability of types of animal. Biometrics 41:653–662.

Pollock, K. H., J. D. Nichols, C. Brownie, and J. E. Hines. 1990. Statistical inference for capture-recapture experiments. Wildlife Monographs 107.

Pough, F. H., E. M. Smith, D. H. Rhodes, and A. Collazo. 1987. The abundance of salamanders in forest stands with different histories of disturbance. Forest Ecology and Management 20:1–9.

Preston, F. W. 1948. The commonness, and rarity, of species. Ecology 29:254–283.

———. 1962a. The canonical distribution of commonness and rarity: Part I. Ecology 43:185–215.

———. 1962b. The canonical distribution of commonness and rarity: Part II. Ecology 43:410–432.

Quenouille, M. H. 1949. Approximate tests of correlation in time-series. Journal of the Royal Statistical Society, ser. B, 11:68–84.

———. 1956. Notes on bias in estimation. Biometrika 43:353–360.

Ralph, C. J., and J. M. Scott (eds.). 1981. Estimating Numbers of Terrestrial Birds. Studies in Avian Biology 6.

Ramsey, F. L., and J. M. Scott. 1981. Tests of hearing ability. Pp. 341–345. *In* C. J. Ralph and J. M. Scott (eds.), Estimating Numbers of Terrestrial Birds. Studies in Avian Biology 6.

Rand, A. S., and C. W. Myers. 1990. The herpetofauna of Barro Colorado Island, Panama: An ecological summary. Pp. 386–409. *In* A. H. Gentry (ed.), Four Neotropical Rainforests. Yale University Press, New Haven, Connecticut.

Raney, E. C. 1940. Summer movements of the bullfrog, *Rana catesbeiana* Shaw, as determined by the jaw-tag method. American Midland Naturalist 23:733–745.

Rango, A. (ed.). 1989. Remote Sensing and Large-Scale Global Processes. International Association of Hydrological Science, Washington, D.C.

Rao, P. V. 1984. Density estimation based on line transect samples. Statistics Probability Letters 2:51–57.

Rao, P. V., K. M. Portier, and J. A. Ondrasik. 1981. Density estimation using line transect sampling. Pp. 441–444. *In* C. J. Ralph and J. M. Scott (eds.), Estimating Numbers of Terrestrial Birds. Studies in Avian Biology no 6.

Raphael, M. G. 1988. Long-term trends in abundance of amphibians, reptiles, and mammals in Douglas-fir forests of northwestern California. Pp. 23–31. *In* R. C. Szaro, K. E. Severson, and D. R. Patton (eds.), Management of Amphibians, Reptiles, and Small Mammals in North America. U.S. Department of Agriculture, Forest Service, General Technical Report RM-166.

Raphael, M. G., and R. H. Barrett. 1981. Methodologies for a comprehensive wildlife survey and habitat analysis in old-growth Douglas-fir forests. California-Nevada Wildlife Transactions 1981:106–121.

Raup, D. M. 1975. Taxonomic diversity estimation using rarefaction. Paleobiology 1:333–342.

Reading, C. J. 1989. Opportunistic predation of common toads *Bufo bufo* at a drift fence in southern England. Pp. 105–111. *In* T.E.S. Langton (ed.), Amphibians and Roads: Proceedings of the Toad Tunnel Conference. ACO Polymer Products, Shefford, Bedfordshire, England.

Rexstad, E., and K. Burnham. 1991. Users' Guide for Interactive Program CAPTURE. Colorado Cooperative Fish and Wildlife Research Unit, Fort Collins, Colorado.

Rogers, D. J., and T. T. Tanimoto. 1960. A computer program for classifying plants. Science 132:1115–1118.

Rogot, E., and I. D. Goldberg. 1966. A proposed index for measuring agreement in test-retest studies. Journal of Chronic Diseases 19:991–1006.

Rotenberry, J. T., and J. A. Wiens. 1985. Statistical power analysis and community-wide patterns. American Naturalist 125:164–168.

Roughgarden, J., S. W. Running, and P. A. Matson. 1991. What does remote sensing do for ecology? Ecology 72:1918–1922.

Routledge, R. D. 1979. Diversity indices: Which ones are admissible? Journal of Theoretical Biology 76:503–515.

Routman, E. J. 1984. A modified seining technique for single person sampling of deep or cold water. Herpetological Review 15:72–73.

Russell, P. F., and T. R. Rao. 1940. On habitat and association of species of anopheline larvae in south-eastern Madras. Journal of the Malaria Institute of India 3:153–178.

Ryan, M. J. 1985. The Tungara Frog: A Study in Sexual Selection and Communication. University of Chicago Press, Chicago, Illinois.

Sacco, L. 1951. Manuel de Cryptographie. Payot, Paris, France.

Salthe, S. N., and J. S. Mecham. 1974. Reproductive and courtship patterns. Pp. 309–521. *In* B. Lofts (ed.), Physiology of the Amphibia, vol. 2. Academic Press, New York.

Sanders, H. L. 1968. Marine benthic diversity: A comparative study. American Naturalist 102:243–282.

Saul, W. G. 1981. Paraformaldehyde problems. Curation Newsletter 3:1.

Savage, I. R. 1957. Non-parametric statistics. Journal of the American Statistical Association 52:331–344.

Savage, J. M. 1960. Evolution of a peninsular herpetofauna. Systematic Zoology 9:184–212.

Savage, R. M. 1934. The breeding behaviour of the common frog, *Rana temporaria temporaria* Linn., and of the common toad *Bufo bufo bufo* Linn. Proceedings of the Zoological Society of London 1934:55–70.

———. 1962. The ecology and life history of the common frog (*Rana temporaria temporaria*). Harper, New York.

Schemintz, S. D. 1980. Wildlife Management Techniques Manual. 4th ed. Wildlife Society, Washington, D.C.

Scherba, S., Jr., and V. F. Gallucci. 1976. The application of systematic sampling to a study of in-fauna variation in a soft substrate environment. Fishery Bulletin 74:937–948.

Schiøtz, A. 1975. The Treefrogs of Eastern Africa. Steenstrupia, Copenhagen, Denmark.

Schork, M. A., and G. W. Williams. 1980. Number of observations required for the comparison of two correlated proportions. Communications in Statistics-Simulation and Computation B9:349–357.

Scott, D. E. 1990. Effects of larval density in *Ambystoma opacum:* An experiment in large-scale field enclosures. Ecology 71:296–306.

Scott, N. J., Jr. 1976. The abundance and diversity of the herpetofaunas of tropical forest litter. Biotropica 8:41–58.

———. 1982. The herpetofauna of forest litter plots from Cameroon, Africa. Pp. 145–150. *In* N. J. Scott, Jr. (ed.), Herpetological Communities. U.S. Department of the Interior, Fish and Wildlife Service, Wildlife Research Report 13.

Scott, N. J., Jr., and A. L. Aquino-Shuster. 1989. The effects of freezing on formalin preservation of specimens of frogs and snakes. Collection Forum 5:41–46.

Seale, D., and M. Boraas. 1974. A permanent mark for amphibian larvae. Herpetologica 30:160–162.

Seber, G. A. F. 1970. The effects of trap-response on tag-recapture estimates. Biometrics 26:13–22.

———. 1973. The Estimation of Animal Abundance. Griffin, London, England.

———. 1982. The Estimation of Animal Abundance and Related Parameters. 2d ed. Macmillan, New York.

———. 1986. A review of estimating animal abundance. Biometrics 42:267–292.

Seber, G. A. F., and J. F. Whale. 1970. The removal method for two and three samples. Biometrics 26:393–400.

Semlitsch, R. D. 1983. Structure and dynamics of two breeding populations of the eastern tiger salamander, *Ambystoma tigrinum.* Copeia 1983:608–616.

———. 1985. Analysis of climatic factors influencing migrations of the salamander *Ambystoma talpoideum.* Copeia 1985:477–489.

Shannon, C. E. 1948. A mathematical theory of communication. Bell System Technical Journal 27(1,2):379–423; 27(3):623–656.

———. 1949. The mathematical theory of communication. Pp. 29–125. *In* C. E. Shannon and W.

Weaver (eds.), The Mathematical Theory of Communication. University of Illinois Press, Urbana, Illinois.

Shannon, C. E., and W. Weaver (eds.). 1949. The Mathematical Theory of Communication. University of Illinois Press, Urbana, Illinois.

Sheldon, A. L. 1969. Equitability indices: Dependence on the species count. Ecology 50:466–467.

Shetter, D. S. 1936. The jaw-tag method of marking fish. Papers of the Michigan Academy of Sciences, Arts, and Letters 21:651–653.

Shields, M. A. 1985. Selective use of pitfall traps by southern leopard frogs. Herpetological Review 16: 14.

Shoemaker, V. H., L. L. McClanahan, P. C. Withers, S. S. Hillman, and R. C. Drewes. 1987. Thermoregulatory response to heat in the waterproof frogs *Phyllomedusa* and *Chiromantis*. Physiological Zoology 60:365–372.

Shoop, C. R. 1965. Orientation of *Ambystoma maculatum:* Movements to and from breeding ponds. Science 149:558–559.

Siegel, S. 1989. Nonparametric Statistics for the Behavioral Sciences. McGraw-Hill, New York.

Simberloff, D. 1972. Properties of the rarefaction diversity measurement. American Naturalist 106: 414–418.

Simmons, J. E. 1986. A method of preparation of anuran osteological material. Pp. 37–39. *In* J. Waddington and D. M. Rudkin (eds.), Proceedings of the 1985 Workshop on Care and Maintenance of Natural History Collections. Life Science Miscellaneous Publications, Royal Ontario Museum, Toronto, Ontario, Canada.

———. 1987. Herpetological collection and collection management. Society for the Study of Amphibians and Reptiles, Herpetological Circular 16.

Simpson, E. H. 1949. Measurement of diversity. Nature 163:688.

Simpson, G. G. 1943. Mammals and the nature of continents. American Journal of Science 241:1–31.

———. 1964. Species density of North American recent mammals. Systematic Zoology 13:57–73.

Sinsch, U. 1988. Temporal spacing of breeding activity in the natterjack toad, *Bufo calamita.* Oecologia 76:399–407.

———. 1989a. The migratory behaviour of the common toad *Bufo bufo* and the natterjack toad *Bufo calamita.* Pp. 113–124. *In* T. E. S. Langton (ed.), Amphibians and Roads: Proceedings of the Toad Tunnel Conference. ACO Polymer Products, Shefford, Bedfordshire, England.

———. 1989b. Behavioural thermoregulation of the Andean toad (*Bufo spinulosus*) at high altitudes. Oecologia 80:32–38.

Skaar, J., K. Hegg, T. Moe, and K. Smedstud. 1989. WMO International Hygrometer Intercomparison. Instruments and Observing Methods Rept. 38. World Meteorological Organization, Geneva, Switzerland.

Skellam, J. G. 1958. The mathematical foundations underlying the use of line transects in animal ecology. Biometrics 14:385–400.

Slonecker, E. T., and J. A. Carter. 1990. GIS applications of global positioning system technology. GPS World 1(3):50–55.

Smith, G. E. J. 1979. Some aspects of line transect sampling when the target populations [sic] moves. Biometrics 35:323–329.

Smith, W., and J. F. Grassle. 1977. Sampling properties of a family of diversity measures. Biometrics 33:283–292.

Smits, A. W. 1984. Activity patterns and thermal biology of the toad *Bufo boreas halophilus.* Copeia 1984:689–696.

Smits, A. W., and D. L. Crawford. 1984. Emergence of toads to activity: A statistical analysis of contributing cues. Copeia 1984:696–701.

Sneath, P. H. A. 1957. Some thoughts on bacterial classification. Journal of General Microbiology 17:184–200.

———. 1968. Vigour and pattern in taxonomy. Journal of General Microbiology 54:1–11.

Sneath, P. H. A., and R. R. Sokal. 1973. Numerical Taxonomy. W. H. Freeman, San Francisco, California.

Sokal, R. R., and C. D. Michener. 1958. A statistical method for evaluating systematic relationships. University of Kansas Science Bulletin 38:1409–1438.

Sokal, R. R., and P. H. A. Sneath. 1963. Principles of Numerical Taxonomy. W. H. Freeman, San Francisco, California.

Sørensen, T. 1948. A method of establishing groups of equal amplitude in plant sociology based on similarity of species content, and its application to analyses of the vegetation on Danish commons. Det Kongelige Danske Videnskkabernes Selskab, Biologiske Skrifter 5:1–34.

Sorgenfrei, T. 1958. Molluscan assemblages from the marine middle Miocene of South Jutland and their environments. Danmarks Geologiske Undersoegelse, ser. 2, 79. Copenhagen, Denmark.

Southwood, T. R. E. 1978. Ecological Methods with Particular Reference to the Study of Insect Populations. 2d ed. Chapman Hall, London, England.

Spencer, A. W., and D. Pettus. 1966. Habitat preferences of five sympatric species of long-tailed shrews. Ecology 47:677–683.

Spotila, J. R., and E. N. Berman. 1976. Determination of skin resistance and the role of the skin in controlling water loss in amphibians and reptiles. Comparative Biochemistry and Physiology 55A:407–411.

Stanner, M., and E. Farhi. 1989. Computerized radio-telemetric system for monitoring free ranging snakes. Israel Journal of Zoology 35:177–186.

Starmer, C. F., J. E. Grizzle, and P. K. Sen. 1974. Comment. Journal of the American Statistical Association 69:376–378.

Stebbins, R. C. 1962. Amphibians of Western North America. University of California Press, Berkeley, California.

———. 1985. A Field Guide to Western Reptiles and Amphibians. Houghton Mifflin, Boston, Massachusetts.

Stevens, S. S. 1946. On the theory of scales of measurement. Science 103:677–680.

Stewart, M. M., and F. H. Pough. 1983. Population density of tropical forest frogs: Relation to retreat sites. Science 221:570–572.

Stille, W. T. 1950. The loss of jaw-tags by toads. Natural History Miscellanea, Chicago Academy of Sciences 74:1–2.

Stockwell, S. S., and M. L. Hunter, Jr. 1989. Relative abundance of herpetofauna among eight types of Maine peatland vegetation. Journal of Herpetology 23:409–414.

Storer, B. E., and C. Kim. 1990. Exact properties of some exact test statistics for comparing two binomial proportions. Journal of the American Statistical Association 85:146–155.

Stouffer, R. H., Jr., J. E. Gates, C. H. Hocutt, and J. R. Stauffer, Jr. 1983. Surgical implantation of a transmitter package for radio-tracking endangered hellbenders. Wildlife Society Bulletin 11:384–386.

Strahler, A. H. 1980. The use of prior probabilities in maximum likelihood classification of remotely sensed data. Remote Sensing Environment 10:135–163.

Strahler, A. H., T. L. Logan, and N. A. Bryant. 1978. Improving forest cover classification accuracy from Landsat by incorporating topographic information. Pp. 927–942. *In* Proc. 12th International Symposium on Remote Sensing Environment. Environmental Research Institute, Ann Arbor, Michigan.

Sweet, S. S. 1982. A distributional analysis of epigean populations of *Eurycea neotenes* in central Texas, with comments on the origin of troglobitic populations. Herpetologica 38:430–444.

Szaro, R. C., K. E. Severson, and D. R. Patton (eds.). 1988. Management of Amphibians, Reptiles, and Small Mammals in North America. U.S. Department of Agriculture, Forest Service, General Technical Report RM-166.

Tanner, B. D. 1990. Automated weather stations. Pp. 73–98. *In* N. S. Goel and J. M. Norman (eds.), Instrumentation for Studying Vegetation Canopies for Remote Sensing in Optical and Thermal Infrared Regions. Remote Sensing Review 5(1).

Tarwid, K. 1960. Szacowanie zbieznosci nisz ekologicznych gatunkow droga oceny prawdopodobienstwa spotykania sie ich w polowach. Ekologia Polska, ser. B, 6:115–130.

Tate, M. W., and L. A. Hyer. 1973. Inaccuracy of the χ^2 test of goodness of fit when expected frequencies are small. Journal of the American Statistical Association 68:836–841.

Taylor, E. H. 1962. The amphibian fauna of Thailand. University of Kansas Science Bulletin 43:265–599.

Taylor, J., and L. Deegan. 1982. A rapid method for mass marking of amphibians. Journal of Herpetology 16:172–173.

Taylor, L. R. 1978. Bates, William, Hutchison—A variety of diversities. Pp. 1–18. *In* L. A. Mound and N. Warloff (eds.), Diversity of Insect Faunas. Blackwell, Oxford, England.

Taylor L. R., R. A. Kempton, and I. P. Woiwod. 1976. Diversity statistics and the log-series model. Journal of Animal Ecology 45:255–272.

Taylor, W. R. 1977. Observations on specimen fixation. Proceedings of the Biological Society of Washington 90:753–763.

Terborgh, J. 1989. Where Have All the Birds Gone? Essays on the Biology and Conservation of Birds That Migrate to the American Tropics. Princeton University Press, Princeton, New Jersey.

Thomas, A. E. 1975. Marking anurans with silver nitrate. Herpetological Review 6:12.

Tilley, S. G. 1977. Studies of life histories and reproduction in North American plethodontid salamanders. Pp. 1–39. *In* S. Guttman and D. Taylor (eds.), Reproductive Biology of Plethodontid Salamanders. Plenum, New York.

Tocher, K. D. 1950. Extension of the Neyman-Pearson theory of tests to discontinuous variates. Biometrika 37:130–144.

Toft, C. A. 1980. Feeding ecology of thirteen syntopic species of anurans in a seasonal tropical environment. Oecologia 45:131–141.

Toft, C. A., and P. J. Shea. 1983. Detecting community-wide patterns: Estimating power strengthens statistical inference. American Naturalist 122: 618–625.

Toft, C. A., A. S. Rand, and M. Clark. 1982. Population dynamics and seasonal recruitment in *Bufo typhonius* and *Colostethus nubicola* (Anura). Pp. 397–403. *In* E. G. Leigh, Jr., A. S. Rand, and D. M. Windsor (eds.), The Ecology of a Tropical Forest: Seasonal Rhythms and Long-Term Changes. Smithsonian Inst. Press, Washington, D.C.

Torgerson, W. S. 1958. Theory and Methods of Scaling. Wiley, New York.

Townsend, D.S. 1989. The consequences of microhabitat choice for male reproductive success in a tropical frog (*Eleutherodactylus coqui*). Herpetologica 45:451–458.

Tracy, C. R. 1976. A model of the dynamic exchanges of water and energy between a terrestrial amphibian and its environment. Ecological Monographs 46: 293–326.

Tracy, C. R., and J. W. Dole. 1969. Orientation of displaced California toads, *Bufo boreas,* to their breeding sites. Copeia 1969:693–700.

Travis, J. 1981. The effect of staining on the growth of *Hyla gratiosa* tadpoles. Copeia 1981:193–196.

Tschouproff, A. A. 1919. On the mathematical expectation of the moments of frequency distributions. Biometrika 12:185–210.

Tumlison, R., G. R. Cline, and P. Zwank. 1990. Surface habitat associations of the Oklahoma salamander (*Eurycea tynerensis*). Herpetologica 46: 169–175.

Turner, F. B. 1960. Population structure and dynamics of the western spotted frog, *Rana p. pretiosa* Baird and Girard, in Yellowstone Park, Wyoming. Ecological Monographs 30:251–278.

Turnipseed, G., and R. Altig. 1975. Population density and age-structure of three species of hylid tadpoles. Journal of Herpetology 9:287–291.

Tyler, M. J. 1989. Australian Frogs. Viking O'Neill, Penguin Books Australia, Victoria, Australia.

Tyler, M. J., and M. Davies. 1986. Frogs of the Northern Territory. Conservation Committee of the Northern Territory, Adelaide, Australia.

Twitty, V. C. 1966. Of Scientists and Salamanders. Freeman, San Francisco, California.

Udevitz, M. S., and K. H. Pollock. 1991. Change-in-ratio methods for estimating population size. Pp. 90–101. *In* D. R. McCullogh and R. H. Barrett (eds.), Wildlife 2001: Populations. Elsevier Applied Science, New York.

van Gelder, J. J., and G. Rijsdijk. 1987. Unequal catchability of male *Bufo bufo* within breeding populations. Holarctic Ecology 10:90–94.

van Gelder, J. J., H. M. J. Aarts, and H. W. M. Staal. 1986. Routes and speed of migrating toads (*Bufo bufo* L.): A telemetric study. Herpetological Journal 1:111–114.

van Nuland, G. J., and P. F. H. Claus. 1981. The development of a radio tracking system for anuran species. Amphibia-Reptilia 2:107–116.

Vickers, C. R., L. D. Harris, and B. F. Swindel. 1985. Changes in herpetofauna resulting from ditching of cypress ponds in coastal plains flatwoods. Forest and Ecology Management 11:17–29.

Vickery, W. L., and T. D. Nudds. 1991. Testing for density-dependent effects in sequential censuses. Oecologia 85:419–423.

Villa, J. 1972. Anfibios de Nicaragua. Instituto Geográfico Nacional y Banco Central de Nicaragua, Managua, Nicaragua.

Vogt, R. C. 1987. You *can* set drift fences in the canopy! Herpetological Review 18:13–14.

Vogt, R. C., and R. L. Hine. 1982. Evaluation of techniques for assessment of amphibian and reptile populations in Wisconsin. Pp. 201–217. *In* N. J. Scott, Jr. (ed.), Herpetological Communities. U.S. Department of the Interior, Fish and Wildlife Service, Wildlife Research Report 13.

Waichman, A. V. 1992. An alphanumeric code for toe clipping amphibians and reptiles. Herpetological Review 23:19–21.

Wake, D. B. 1987. Adaptive radiation of salamanders in Middle American cloud forests. Annals of the Missouri Botanical Garden 74:242–264.

Wake, D. B., and J. F. Lynch. 1976. The distribution, ecology, and evolutionary history of plethodontid salamanders in tropical America. Science Bulletin, Natural History Museum of Los Angeles County 25.

Wallace, C. S., and D. M. Boulton. 1968. An information measure for classification. Computer Journal 11:185–194.

Walter, H. 1973. Vegetation of the Earth in Relation to Climate and the Eco-physiological Conditions. Springer-Verlag, New York.

Weaver, W. 1948. Probability, rarity, interest and surprise. Scientific Monthly 67:390–392.

Wells, K. D. 1977. The social behaviour of anuran amphibians. Animal Behaviour 25:666–693.

White, G. C., and R. A. Garrott. 1990. Analysis of Wildlife Radio-Tracking Data. Academic Press, San Diego, California.

White, G. C., D. R. Anderson, K. P. Burnham, and D. L. Otis. 1982. Capture-recapture and removal methods for sampling closed populations. Publication of the Los Alamos National Laboratory, LA-8787-NERP, Los Alamos, New Mexico.

White, G. C., K. P. Burnham, D. L. Otis, and D. R. Anderson. 1978. Users' Manual for Program CAPTURE. Utah State University Press, Logan, Utah.

Whittaker, R. H. 1952. A study of summer foliage insect communities in the Great Smoky Mountains. Ecological Monographs 22:1–44.

———. 1965. Dominance and diversity in land plant communities. Science 147:250–260.

Wiens, J. A., Jr. 1981. Scale problems in avian censusing. Pp. 513–521. *In* C. J. Ralph and J. M. Scott (eds.), Estimating Numbers of Terrestrial Birds. Studies in Avian Biology 6.

Wiest, J. A., Jr. 1982. Anuran succession at temporary ponds in a post oak-savanna region of Texas. Pp. 39–47. *In* N. J. Scott, Jr. (ed.), Herpetological Communities. U.S. Department of the Interior, Fish and Wildlife Service, Wildlife Research Report 13.

Wilbur, H. M., and R. A. Alford. 1985. Priority effects in experimental pond communities: Responses of *Hyla* to *Bufo* and *Rana*. Ecology 66:1106–1114.

Wilbur, H. M., and J. E. Fauth. 1990. Experimental aquatic food webs: Interactions between two predators and two prey. American Naturalist 135:176–204.

Williams, C. B. 1964. Patterns in the Balance of Nature and Related Problems in Quantitative Ecology. Academic Press, London, England.

Williams, D. F., and S. E. Braun. 1983. Comparison of pitfall and conventional traps for sampling small mammal populations. Journal of Wildlife Management 47:841–845.

Wilson, K. R., and D. R. Anderson. 1985. Evaluation of two density estimators of small mammal populations size. Journal of Mammalogy 66:13–21.

Winer, B. J. 1971. Statistical Principles in Experimental Design. 2d ed. McGraw-Hill, New York.

Wood, C. L. 1978. Comparison of linear trends in binomial proportions. Biometrics 34:496–504.

Woodbury, A. M. 1956. Uses of marking animals in ecological studies: Marking amphibians and reptiles. Ecology 37:670–674.

Woodward, B. D. 1982. Male persistence and mating success in Woodhouse's toad (*Bufo woodhousei*). Ecology 63:583–585.

———. 1984. Arrival to and location of *Bufo woodhousei* in the breeding pond: Effect on the operational sex ratio. Oecologia 62:240–244.

Woodward, B. D., and S. L. Mitchell. 1991. The community ecology of desert anurans. Pp. 223–248. *In* G. Pollis (ed.), The Ecology of Desert Communities. University of Arizona Press, Tucson, Arizona.

Woolley, H. P. 1973. Subcutaneous acrylic polymer injections as a marking technique for amphibians. Copeia 1973:340–341.

World Meteorological Organization. 1983. Guide to Meteorological Instruments and Methods of Observation. 5th ed. World Meteorological Organization, Geneva, Switzerland.

Wright, A. H. 1914. North American Anura: Life-histories of the Anura of Ithaca, New York. Carnegie Institute, Washington, D.C.

Wright, D. H. 1991. Correlations between incidence and abundance are expected by chance. Journal of Biogeography 18:463–466.

Wygoda, M. L. 1984. Low cutaneous evaporative water loss in arboreal frogs. Physiological Zoology 57:329–337.

Wygoda, M. L., and A. A. Williams. 1991. Body temperature in free-ranging green tree frogs (*Hyla cinerea*): A comparison with "typical" frogs. Herpetologica 47:328–335.

Yapp, W. B. 1979. Specific diversity in woodland birds. Field Studies Council 5:45–58.

Yates, F. 1934. Contingency tables involving small numbers and the χ^2 test. Journal of the Royal Statistical Society 1 (suppl.):217–235.

———. 1948. The analysis of contingency tables with groupings based on quantitative characters. Biometrika 35:176–181.

———. 1981. Sampling Methods for Censuses and Surveys. 4th ed. Macmillan, New York.

Yoccoz, N. G. 1991. Use, overuse, and misuse of significance tests in evolutionary biology and ecology. Bulletin of the Ecological Society of America 72:106–111.

Youden, W. J. 1950. Index for rating diagnostic tests. Cancer 3:32–35.

Yule, G. U. 1900. On the association of attributes in statistics: with illustrations from the material of the Childhood Society, &c. Philosophical Transactions of the Royal Society London, ser. A, 194:257–319.

———. 1911. An Introduction to the Theory of Statistics. Charles Griffin, London, England.

———. 1912. On the methods of measuring association between two attributes. Journal of the Royal Statistical Society 75:579–642.

———. 1944. The Statistical Study of Literary Vocabulary. Cambridge University Press, Cambridge, England.

Zahl, S. 1977. Jackknifing: An index of diversity. Ecology 58:907–913.

Zar, J. H. 1974. Biostatistical Analysis. Prentice-Hall, Englewood Cliffs, New Jersey.

Zelterman, D. 1986. The log-likelihood ratio for sparse multinomial mixtures. Statistics Probability Letters 4:95–99.

Zimmerman, B. L. 1991. Distribution and Abundance of Frogs in a Central Amazonian Forest. Unpubl. Ph.D. dissert., Florida State University, Tallahassee, Florida.

Zimmerman, B. L., and R. O. Bierregaard. 1986. Relevance of the equilibrium theory of island biogeography and species-area relations to conservation with a case from Amazonia. Journal of Biogeography 13:133–143.

Zimmerman, B. L., and M. T. Rodrigues. 1990. Frogs, snakes, and lizards of the INPA-WWF reserves near Manaus, Brazil. Pp. 426–454. *In* A. H. Gentry (ed.), Four Neotropical Rainforests. Yale University Press, New Haven, Connecticut.

Zippin, C. 1956. An evaluation of the removal method of estimating animal populations. Biometrics 12:163–189.

———. 1958. The removal method of population estimation. Journal of Wildlife Management 22:82–90.

Index

Addresses of Authors
and Contributors

Ross A. Alford
Department of Zoology
James Cook University
Townsville, Queensland 4811
Australia

Ronald G. Altig
Department of Biological Sciences
P.O. Drawer GY
Mississippi State University
Mississippi State, Mississippi 39762
USA

Ray E. Ashton, Jr.
Water and Air Research, Inc.
6821 S.W. Archer Road
Gainesville, Florida 32608
USA

John E. Cadle
Museum of Comparative Zoology
Harvard University
Cambridge, Massachusetts 02138
USA

Reginald B. Cocroft
Neurobiology/Behavior, Seeley G. Mudd Hall
Cornell University
Ithaca, New York 14853
USA

Daniel G. Cole
ADP Programs
NHB Mail Stop 136
Smithsonian Institution
Washington, DC 20560-0136
USA

Paul Stephen Corn
National Biological Survey
National Ecology Research Center
4512 McMurry Avenue
Fort Collins, Colorado 80525–3400
USA

Ronald I. Crombie
Amphibians and Reptiles
NHB Mail Stop 162
Smithsonian Institution
Washington, DC 20560
USA

Martha L. Crump
Department of Biological Sciences
Box 5640
Northern Arizona University
Flagstaff, Arizona 86011
USA

Ted M. Davis
Department of Biology
University of Victoria
P.O. Box 1700
Victoria, British Columbia V8W 2Y2
Canada

C. Kenneth Dodd, Jr.
National Biological Survey
412 N.E. 16th Avenue, Room 250
Gainesville, Florida 32601
USA

Maureen A. Donnelly
Department of Biology
University of Miami
Coral Gables, Florida 33124
USA

Michael E. Dorcas
Department of Biological Sciences
Idaho State University
Pocatello, Idaho 83209
USA

George E. Drewry
Division of Endangered Species
U.S. Fish and Wildlife Service
4401 N. Fairfax Drive, Suite 452
Arlington, Virginia 22203
USA

Charles A. Drost
CPSU/UCD
2138 Wickson Hall
University of California
Davis, California 95616
USA

Kevin M. Enge
Little River Ranch
Route 7, Box 3055
Quincy, Florida 32351
USA

Gary M. Fellers
Point Reyes National Seashore
Point Reyes, California 94956
USA

Mercedes S. Foster
National Biological Survey
NHB Mail Stop 111
National Museum of Natural History
Washington, DC 20560-0111
USA

Richard Franz
Department of Natural Sciences
Florida Museum of Natural History
University of Florida
Gainesville, Florida 32611
USA

Claude Gascon
Biological Dynamics of Forest Fragments
    Project
Instituto Nacional de Pesquisas da Amazônia
C.P. 478
69011-970 Manaus, Amazonas
Brazil

Craig Guyer
Department of Zoology/Wildlife Sciences
Funchess Hall
Auburn University
Auburn, Alabama 36849
USA

Steve Hammack
Department of Herpetology
Fort Worth Zoological Park
1989 Colonial Parkway
Fort Worth, Texas 76110
USA

Lee-Ann C. Hayek
Statistics and Mathematics
NHB Mail Stop 136
Smithsonian Institution
Washington, DC 20560-0136
USA

W. Ronald Heyer
Amphibians and Reptiles
NHB Mail Stop 162
Smithsonian Institution
Washington, DC 20560-0162
USA

Robert F. Inger
Amphibians and Reptiles
Field Museum of Natural History
Roosevelt Road at Lake Shore Drive
Chicago, Illinois 60605
USA

Jeremy F. Jacobs
Department of Vertebrate Zoology
NHB Mail Stop 108
Smithsonian Institution
Washington, DC 20560-0108
USA

Robert G. Jaeger
Department of Biology

University of Southwestern Louisiana
Lafayette, Louisiana 70504
USA

J. Eric Juterbock
Department of Zoology
Ohio State University, Lima Campus
4240 Campus Drive
Lima, Ohio 45804
USA

James F. Lynch
Smithsonian Environmental Research Center
P.O. Box 28
Edgewater, Maryland 21037
USA

Roy W. McDiarmid
National Biological Survey
NHB Mail Stop 111
National Museum of Natural History
Washington, DC 20560-0111
USA

Michael J. Oldham
Ontario Ministry of Natural Resources
Aylmer District Office
353 Talbot Street W.
Aylmer, Ontario N5H 2S8
Canada

Charles R. Peterson
Department of Biological Sciences
Idaho State University
Pocatello, Idaho 83209
USA

George R. Pisani
Division of Biological Sciences
University of Kansas
Lawrence, Kansas 66045
USA

A. Stanley Rand
Smithsonian Tropical Research Institute
Unit 0948
APO AA 34002–0948
USA

Robert P. Reynolds
National Biological Survey
NHB Mail Stop 111
National Museum of Natural History
Washington, DC 20560-0111
USA

Stephen J. Richards
Department of Zoology
James Cook University
Townsville, Queensland 4811
Australia

Lily O. Rodriguez
Departamento de Herpetología
Museo de Historia Natural
Universidad Nacional de San Marcos
Apartado 14–0434
Avenida Arenales 1256, Lima 14
Perú

Douglas E. Runde
Florida Game and Fresh Water Fish
  Commission
620 S. Meridian
Tallahassee, Florida 32399–1600
USA

David E. Scott
Savannah River Ecology Laboratory
Drawer E
Aiken, South Carolina 29801
USA

Norman J. Scott, Jr.
National Biological Survey
Piedras Blancas Research Station
P.O. Box 70
San Simeon, California 93542-0700
USA

H. Bradley Shaffer
Department of Zoology
University of California

Davis, California 95616
USA

Ulrich Sinsch
Institut für Biologie
Universität Koblenz-Landau
Rheinaue 3–4
D-5400 Koblenz
Federal Republic of Germany

Samuel S. Sweet
Department of Biological Sciences
University of California
Santa Barbara, California 93106
USA

Richard C. Vogt
Estación de Biología Tropical "Los Tuxtlas"
Instituto de Biología, UNAM
Apartado Postal 94
San Andrés Tuxtla, Veracruz
México

David B. Wake
Museum of Vertebrate Zoology
Department of Integrative Biology
University of California
Berkeley, California 94720
USA

Bruce D. Woodward
Reynolds Electrical and Engineering
P.O. Box 98521
Mail Stop 740
Las Vegas, Nevada 89193-8521
USA

Barbara L. Zimmerman
348 Hillsdale Avenue
Toronto, Ontario M4S 1T8
Canada